ASPECTS OF THE SECULAR CANTATA
IN LATE BAROQUE ITALY

In memory of Nigel Fortune (1924–2009)

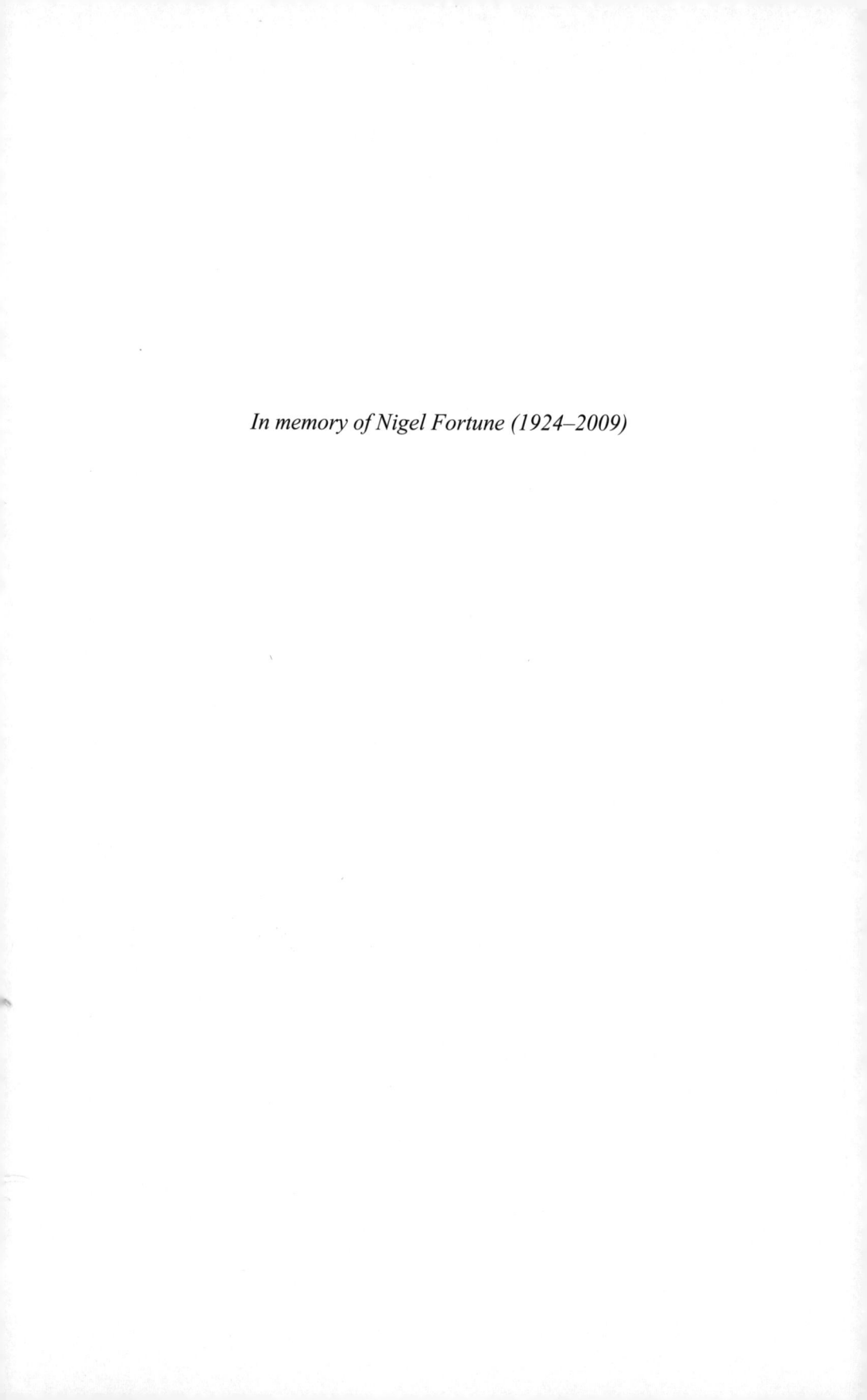

Aspects of the Secular Cantata in Late Baroque Italy

Edited by

MICHAEL TALBOT
University of Liverpool, UK

ASHGATE

5.1a	Scarlatti, cantata *Al fin m'ucciderete, o miei pensieri*, first recitative, bars 1–4 (first version of the refrain).	133
5.1b	Scarlatti, cantata *Al fin m'ucciderete, o miei pensieri*, first recitative, bars 27–32 (second version of the refrain).	133
7.1	B. Marcello, Opening aria of the cantata *Dove fuggisti, o dio* (source: Florence, Biblioteca del Conservatorio 'Luigi Cherubini', Ms. B. 2849, ff. 233r–234v).	185
7.2	B. Marcello, *Salmo XXI* (B621), bars 1–29.	192
9.1	Clérambault, cantata *La muse de l'Opéra* (1716), 'Tempeste' bars 9–11; continuo derived from a second, simplified bass line (here omitted) marked 'Contrebasse, et Basse Continüe'. Violins originally in G1 clef.	244
9.2	As 1, with added viola parts (*hautes-contre* and *tailles*). Violins originally in G1 clef.	245
9.3a	Campra, opéra-ballet *Les festes vénitiennes* (1710), air 'Suivez-moy, venez tous', bars 45–53: (a) from *partition réduite* (Paris: Christophe Ballard, 1710), 'Les Sérénades et les Joueurs', pp. 22–3. Violins originally in C1 clef.	247
9.3b	Campra, opéra-ballet *Les festes vénitiennes* (1710), air 'Suivez-moy, venez tous', bars 45–53: (b) from F-Po, A. 78a (ms full score, c. 1710), p. 122. Violins and *hautes-contres* originally in soprano clef, *tailles* in C2 clef, *quintes* in C3 clef.	248
9.4	Jacquet de La Guerre, cantata *Le temple rebasti* (1711), opening *Symphonie*, bars 1–3. Violins originally in G1 clef.	250
9.5	Campra, cantata *Le jaloux*, book 3 (1728), air 'Som[m]eil, vien soulage', opening *Symphonie* (with added editorial inner parts), bars 1–7. Violins originally in G1 clef.	250
10.1	Albinoni, cantata *Lontan da te, mia vita*, opening recitative.	260
10.2	Pistocchi, cantata *Su la riva del mar tutto dolente*, second recitative.	264
10.3	Vivaldi, cantata *Tremori al braccio e lagrime sul ciglio*, RV 799, opening recitative.	267
10.4	Brusa, cantata *Però che scende in petto*, opening recitative.	270
11.1	Gasparini, cantata *Ed ecco in fine, oh Dio*, aria 'Congiurati ecco a miei danni', bars 1–4.	278
11.2	Polani, cantata *Verrà un dì che la mia bella*, aria 'Quando sarai senz'onde', bars 21–24.	281
11.3	Gasparini, cantata *Andate, o miei sospiri*, aria 'Se vedrete il cor di lei', bars 67–91.	283
11.4	Scarlatti, cantata *Il Nerone*, aria 'Vuò che tremi', bars 1–3: realization anticipating the voice.	287
11.5	Scarlatti, cantata *Il Nerone*, aria 'Vuò che tremi', bars 1–3: realization amplifying the bass.	288
11.6	Vivaldi, cantata *Fonti del pianto*, RV 656, opening aria, bars 1–8, with simple realization.	288

Aspects of the Secular Cantata in Late Baroque Italy

Edited by

MICHAEL TALBOT
University of Liverpool, UK

ASHGATE

© Michael Talbot and the contributors 2009

All rights reserved. No part of this publication may be reproduced, stored in a retrieval system or transmitted in any form or by any means, electronic, mechanical, photocopying, recording or otherwise without the prior permission of the publisher.

Michael Talbot has asserted his right under the Copyright, Designs and Patents Act, 1988, to be identified as the editor of this work.

Published by
Ashgate Publishing Limited
Wey Court East
Union Road
Farnham
Surrey, GU9 7PT
England

Ashgate Publishing Company
Suite 420
101 Cherry Street
Burlington
VT 05401-4405
USA

www.ashgate.com

British Library Cataloguing in Publication Data
Aspects of the secular cantata in late Baroque Italy.
 1. Cantatas, Secular – History and criticism. 2. Music – Italy – 16th century – History and criticism. 3. Music – Italy – 17th century – History and criticism.
 I. Talbot, Michael.
 782.4'8'0945'09031–dc22

Library of Congress Cataloging-in-Publication Data
Aspects of the secular cantata in late baroque italy / Edited by Michael Talbot.
   p. cm.
  Includes bibliographical references and index.
  ISBN 978-0-7546-5794-1 (hardcover: alk. paper)
  1. Cantatas, Secular – History and criticism. 2. Music – Italy – 17th century – History and criticism. 3. Music – Italy – 18th century – History and criticism. I. Talbot, Michael.
 ML2400.A87 2009
 782.4'80945–dc22

2009007668

ISBN 9780754657941 (hbk)

Mixed Sources
Product group from well-managed forests and other controlled sources
www.fsc.org Cert no. SGS-COC-2482
© 1996 Forest Stewardship Council

Printed and bound in Great Britain by
TJ International Ltd, Padstow, Cornwall

Contents

List of Figures	*vii*
List of Music Examples	*ix*
List of Tables	*xiii*
List of RISM Sigla	*xv*
Notes on Contributors	*xvii*
Preface	*xxi*

1   The When and How of Arioso in Stradella's Cantatas   1
     Carolyn Gianturco

2   A Lost Volume of Cantatas and Serenatas from the 'Original Stradella Collection'   27
     Colin Timms

3   Narration, Mimesis and the Question of Genre: Dramatic Approaches in Giovanni Legrenzi's Solo Cantatas, Opp. 12 and 14   55
     Hendrik Schulze

4   A Tale of Two Cities: Cantata Publication in Bologna and Venice, c.1650–1700   79
     Reinmar Emans

5   'Al tavolino medesimo del Compositor della Musica': Notes on Text and Context in Alessandro Scarlatti's *cantate da camera*   111
     Norbert Dubowy

6   Bononcini's 'agreable and easie style, and those fine inventions in his basses (to which he was led by an instrument upon which he excells)'   135
     Lowell Lindgren

7   The 'Humble' and 'Sublime' Genres, the Pastoral and Heroic Styles: Rhetorical Metamorphoses in Benedetto Marcello's Cantatas   177
     Marco Bizzarini

8   Investigations into the Cantata in Naples During the First Half of the Eighteenth Century: The Cantatas by Leonardo Vinci Contained in a 'Neapolitan' Manuscript   203
     Giulia Veneziano

9	The Orchestral French Cantata (1706–30): Performance, Edition and Classification of a Neglected Repertory *Graham Sadler*	227
10	Patterns and Strategies of Modulation in Cantata Recitatives *Michael Talbot*	255
11	'Imitando l'Arietta, ò altro allegro, cantato di fresco': Keyboard Realization in Italian Continuo Arias *Giulia Nuti*	273
12	The Revival of the Italian Chamber Cantata on Disc: Models and Trends *Roger-Claude Travers*	295

Bibliography   *371*
Index of Vocal Works   *393*
General Index   *409*

List of Figures

2.1	Spines of (a) GB-Bu, Barber Music Library, MS 5019, and (b) I-Tn, MSS Foà 12, Foà 14, Giordano 13 and Foà 11 (by permission, respectively, of Special Collections, Library Services, University of Birmingham, and the Biblioteca Nazionale Universitaria di Torino).	33
2.2	Giovanni Battista Vulpio, cantata *Doppo lunga stagione*, beginning of first recitative, GB-Bu, Barber Music Library, MS 5019, f. 91r (by permission of Special Collections, Library Services, University of Birmingham).	35
2.3	Alessandro Stradella, cantata *Da cuspide ferrate* (extract), GB-Cfm, Mu MS 655, f. 32v (by permission of The Fitzwilliam Museum, Cambridge).	36
2.4	Alessandro Stradella, opera *Moro per amore*, beginning of Act III, I-Tn, MS Giordano 11, f. 124r (by permission of the Biblioteca Nazionale Universitaria di Torino).	36
6.1	Giovanni Bononcini, the 'A' section of 'Il vedermi tradita così', first aria of the cantata *Impara a non dar fede*, US-CAh, Ms Mus 63, ff. 10v–11r (by permission of the Houghton Library, Harvard University, Cambridge, MA).	152
6.2	Giovanni Bononcini, the 'A' section of 'Benché speranza, sia mensogniera', second aria of the cantata *Impara a non dar fede*, US-CAh, Ms Mus 63, ff. 14r–14v (by permission of the Houghton Library, Harvard University, Cambridge, MA).	153

List of Music Examples

1.1	Stradella, cantata *Sono in dubbio d'amar*, bars 1–11.	10
1.2	Stradella, cantata *Già languiva la notte*, bars 1–11.	11
1.3	Stradella, cantata *Io non vuò più star così*, bars 1–4.	12
1.4	Stradella, cantata *Noiosi pensieri, fuggite dal seno*, bars 1–10.	12
1.5	Stradella, cantata *Ferma, ferma il corso*, aria 'Vincerò di tua fierezza', bars 192–7.	13
1.6	Stradella, cantata *Apre l'uomo infelice all'or che nasce*, bars 1–8.	14
1.7	Stradella, cantata *Noiosi pensieri, fuggite dal seno*, bars 20–35.	16
1.8	Stradella, cantata *Se Nerone lo vuole*, bars 59–71.	18
1.9	Stradella, cantata *Se Nerone lo vuole*, bars 149–56.	19
1.10	Stradella, two-voice cantata *Misero amante*, recitative 'Ché ardendo per beltà fida e severa', bars 1–19 and concluding ritornello.	20
1.11	Stradella, three-voice cantata *Si apra al riso ogni labbro*, aria 'Le caligini oscure il ciel disgombra', bars 1–12.	22
1.12	Stradella, serenata *La forza delle stelle*, recitative 'Possente incantatrice è la preghiera', bars 1–17.	24
2.1	Giacomo Simonelli, cantata *Sotto quest'empie mura*, aria 'O miei fidi, e che s'aspetta, bars 1–5.	48
2.2	Simonelli, cantata *Sotto quest'empie mura*, aria 'Quel timore che nel core', bars 7–12.	48
2.3	Vulpio, cantata *Doppo lunga stagione*, aria 'Consigliatemi, pensieri', bars 71–80.	52
2.4	Vulpio, cantata *Doppo lunga stagione*, aria 'Son miserabile', bars 26–39.	54
3.1	Legrenzi, cantata *Ad altro amante in seno*, bars 1–14.	60
3.2	Legrenzi, cantata *A povero amator*, bars 86–127.	64
3.3	Legrenzi, opera *Totila*, I.11, bars 1–22.	65
3.4	Legrenzi, cantata *Non ho che lagnarmi*, bars 205–21.	67
3.5	Legrenzi, cantata *A piè d'un fonte*, bars 142–7.	69
4.1	Albergati, cantata *D'Acheronte errini horribili* (*Musico raffredato*), aria 'Non posso cantare', bars 1–16.	90
4.2	Brevi, cantata *Rendimi un sguardo solo*, first aria, bars 1–5.	93
4.3	G. B. Bassani, cantata *Ha più foco un sen ferito*, aria 'Non mi far più languir', bars 6–14.	97
4.4	Porfirii, cantata *O ch'io son pur sfortunato*, aria 'È gran pena amar chi teme', bars 1–33.	100
4.5	Albergati, cantata *D'Acheronte errini horribili*, first aria, bars 1–10	107

5.1a	Scarlatti, cantata *Al fin m'ucciderete, o miei pensieri*, first recitative, bars 1–4 (first version of the refrain).	133
5.1b	Scarlatti, cantata *Al fin m'ucciderete, o miei pensieri*, first recitative, bars 27–32 (second version of the refrain).	133
7.1	B. Marcello, Opening aria of the cantata *Dove fuggisti, o dio* (source: Florence, Biblioteca del Conservatorio 'Luigi Cherubini', Ms. B. 2849, ff. 233r–234v).	185
7.2	B. Marcello, *Salmo XXI* (B621), bars 1–29.	192
9.1	Clérambault, cantata *La muse de l'Opéra* (1716), 'Tempeste' bars 9–11; continuo derived from a second, simplified bass line (here omitted) marked 'Contrebasse, et Basse Continüe'. Violins originally in G1 clef.	244
9.2	As 1, with added viola parts (*hautes-contre* and *tailles*). Violins originally in G1 clef.	245
9.3a	Campra, opéra-ballet *Les festes vénitiennes* (1710), air 'Suivez-moy, venez tous', bars 45–53: (a) from *partition réduite* (Paris: Christophe Ballard, 1710), 'Les Sérénades et les Joueurs', pp. 22–3. Violins originally in C1 clef.	247
9.3b	Campra, opéra-ballet *Les festes vénitiennes* (1710), air 'Suivez-moy, venez tous', bars 45–53: (b) from F-Po, A. 78a (ms full score, c. 1710), p. 122. Violins and *hautes-contres* originally in soprano clef, *tailles* in C2 clef, *quintes* in C3 clef.	248
9.4	Jacquet de La Guerre, cantata *Le temple rebasti* (1711), opening *Symphonie*, bars 1–3. Violins originally in G1 clef.	250
9.5	Campra, cantata *Le jaloux*, book 3 (1728), air 'Som[m]eil, vien soulage', opening *Symphonie* (with added editorial inner parts), bars 1–7. Violins originally in G1 clef.	250
10.1	Albinoni, cantata *Lontan da te, mia vita,* opening recitative.	260
10.2	Pistocchi, cantata *Su la riva del mar tutto dolente*, second recitative.	264
10.3	Vivaldi, cantata *Tremori al braccio e lagrime sul ciglio*, RV 799, opening recitative.	267
10.4	Brusa, cantata *Però che scende in petto*, opening recitative.	270
11.1	Gasparini, cantata *Ed ecco in fine, oh Dio*, aria 'Congiurati ecco a miei danni', bars 1–4.	278
11.2	Polani, cantata *Verrà un dì che la mia bella*, aria 'Quando sarai senz'onde', bars 21–24.	281
11.3	Gasparini, cantata *Andate, o miei sospiri*, aria 'Se vedrete il cor di lei', bars 67–91.	283
11.4	Scarlatti, cantata *Il Nerone*, aria 'Vuò che tremi', bars 1–3: realization anticipating the voice.	287
11.5	Scarlatti, cantata *Il Nerone*, aria 'Vuò che tremi', bars 1–3: realization amplifying the bass.	288
11.6	Vivaldi, cantata *Fonti del pianto*, RV 656, opening aria, bars 1–8, with simple realization.	288

11.7	Vivaldi, cantata *Fonti del pianto*, RV 656, opening aria, bars 1–8, with complex realization.	289
11.8	Marcello, cantata *L'usignolo che il suo duolo*, opening aria, bars 1–11, with realization.	290

List of Tables

2.1	Giacomo Simonelli, cantata *Sotto quest'empie mura*.	47
2.2	Ercole Bernabei, serenata *Amor, re de' tiranni*.	49
2.3	Giovanni Battista Vulpio, cantata *Doppo lunga stagione*.	50
4.1	Non-Venetian publications of vocal chamber music, 1628–59.	82
4.2	Vocal chamber music published in Bologna in the 1670s.	85
4.3	Vocal chamber music published in Bologna in the 1680s.	89
4.4	Vocal chamber music published in Bologna by Pier-Maria Monti, 1690–95.	92
4.5	Vocal chamber music published in Amsterdam, 1691–98.	94
4.6	Vocal chamber music published in Modena by Fortuniano Rosati, 1695–1702.	94
4.7	Vocal chamber music published in Bologna by Marino Silvani, 1696–98.	95
4.8	Vocal chamber music published in Bologna by Marino Silvani, 1700 onwards.	96
4.9	Vocal chamber music published in Venice by Giuseppe Sala, 1706 onwards.	96
4.10	Cantata publications in Amsterdam and London after 1700.	99
8.1	The contents of ms. I-Nc, 34.5.23 (Cantate 304).	212
8.2	Leonardo Vinci's Neapolitan cantatas in I-Nc, ms. 34.5.23 (Cantate 304) and their concordances.	214
8.3	Compositions indexed on f. 95 of I-Nc, ms. 34.5.23 (Cantate 304).	222
9.1	The orchestra of the Académie Royale de Musique, 1713–38.	241

List of RISM Sigla

A-Wgm	Vienna, Gesellschaft der Musikfreunde in Wien
A-Wn	Vienna, Österreichische Nationalbibliothek
B-Bc	Brussels, Conservatoire Royal de Musique
B-Br	Brussels, Bibliothèque Royale Albert Ier
B-Lc	Liège, Conservatoire Royal de Musique
D-Bsb	Berlin, Staatsbibliothek Preussischer Kulturbesitz
D-Dl	Dresden, Sächsische Landesbibliothek – Staats- und Universitätsbibliothek
D-LEm	Leipzig, Musikbibliothek
D-Mbs	Munich, Bayerische Staatsbibliothek
D-MÜs	Münster, Santini-Bibliothek
D-ROu	Rostock, Universitätsbibliothek
D-SHs	Sondershausen, Schlossmuseum
D-WD	Wiesentheid, Musiksammlung des Grafen von Schönborn-Wiesentheid
E-Mn	Madrid, Biblioteca Nacional
E-Zac	Zaragoza, Catedrale
F-Pa	Paris, Bibliothèque de l'Arsenal
F-Pc	Paris, Bibliothèque du Conservatoire (in F-Pn)
F-Pn	Paris, Bibliothèque Nationale
F-Po	Paris, Bibliothèque-Musée de l'Opéra
GB-ABu	Aberystwyth, National Library of Wales
GB-Bu	Birmingham, University Library
GB-Cfm	Cambridge, Fitzwilliam Museum
GB-Cu	Cambridge, University Library
GB-CDp	Cardiff, Central Library
GB-Er	Edinburgh, Reid Music Library
GB-Lam	London, Royal Academy of Music
GB-Lbl	London, British Library
GB-Lcm	London, Royal College of Music
GB-Lgc	London, Guildhall Library
GB-Mp	Manchester, Henry Watson Music Library
GB-Ob	Oxford, Bodleian Library
GB-Och	Oxford, Christ Church Library
GB-Tenbury	Tenbury, St Michael's College (in GB-Ob)
I-Ac	Assisi, Biblioteca Comunale
I-Bc	Bologna, Museo Internazionale e Biblioteca della Musica
I-Bsp	Bologna, San Petronio

I-Fc	Florence, Biblioteca del Conservatorio di Musica 'Luigi Cherubini'
I-Fl	Florence, Biblioteca Medicea Laurenziana
I-Gl	Genoa, Conservatorio di Musica 'Nicolò Paganini'
I-Mc	Milan, Conservatorio di Musica 'Giuseppe Verdi'
I-MC	Montecassino, Biblioteca
I-MOe	Modena, Biblioteca Estense
I-Nc	Naples, Conservatorio di Musica 'S. Pietro a Majella'
I-Pca	Padua, Biblioteca Antoniana
I-PAVu	Pavia, Biblioteca Universitaria
I-PLcon	Palermo, Conservatorio di Musica 'Vincenzo Bellini'
I-Rli	Rome, Accademia Nazionale dei Lincei e Corsiniana
I-Rsc	Rome, Conservatorio di Musica 'S. Cecilia'
I-Rvat	Rome, Biblioteca Apostolica Vaticana
I-REm	Reggio Emilia, Biblioteca Panizzi
I-Tn	Turin, Biblioteca Nazionale e Universitaria
I-Vnm	Venice, Biblioteca Nazionale Marciana
RUS-KAu	Kaliningrad, Nauchnaya Biblioteka Kaliningradskogo Gosudarstvennogo Universiteta
S-L	Lund, Universitetsbiblioteket
US-Cn	Chicago, Newberry Library
US-CAh	Cambridge (MA), Harvard University, Houghton Library
US-FAy	Farmington, Lewis Walpole Library
US-IDt	Independence (MO) Harry Truman Library
US-NH	New Haven (CT), Yale University, Irving S. Gilmore Music Library
US-NHub	New Haven (CT), Yale University, Beinecke Rare Book and Manuscript Library
US-Wc	Washington (DC), Library of Congress

Notes on Contributors

Marco Bizzarini holds a research post at the University of Padua. His main area of research is Italian music and poetry of the Renaissance and Baroque periods. In 2003 Ashgate published his book on Luca Marenzio. He has also edited (for the Fondazione Levi, Venice) the complete poetic texts of Benedetto Marcello's cantatas. His study of Benedetto Marcello appeared in Italian in 2006. He is a collaborator of the Istituto Italiano Antonio Vivaldi.

Norbert Dubowy has been a Visiting Professor at the Universities of Cincinnati and Michigan, having earlier held posts at the Universities of Vienna and Heidelberg, among others. He has published extensively on Italian vocal music of the late seventeenth and early eighteenth centuries, and his books include a widely cited study of the structural relationships between arias and concerto movements. He is currently preparing a book on Alessandro Scarlatti and the *dramma per musica*.

Reinmar Emans gained a doctorate at the university of his birthplace, Bonn, in 1982, with a thesis on the cantatas and canzonets of Giovanni Legrenzi. Since 1983 he has held a research post at the Johann-Sebastian-Bach-Institut, Göttingen, of which he was Acting Director up to 1996. In recent years he has taught in Bochum, Detmold, Cologne and Marburg and has also been active as a reviewer of recordings of both classical and popular music. His publications and research lie mainly in the areas of Italian vocal music of the seventeenth century, the stylistic evolution of J. S. Bach's music, source criticism and the history of German music during the eighteenth century.

Carolyn Gianturco is President of the Editorial Board of the *Edizione Nazionale dell'Opera Omnia di Alessandro Stradella*, to which she has personally contributed two volumes to date. She is the author of a major monograph on Stradella's life and works, and the co-author of the standard thematic catalogue of the composer's works. She is General Editor of sixteen volumes of seventeenth-century Italian cantatas in facsimile, which also offer editions of the texts. She founded and directs the research and music series *Studi Toscani Musicali* and was the National Advisory Editor for Italy of the revised (2001) *New Grove Dictionary of Music and Musicians*. For many years she was Associate Professor of Music History at Pisa University, Italy.

Lowell Lindgren is Professor of Music and MacVicar Faculty Fellow at the Massachusetts Institute of Technology. His recent publications include twenty-five entries in the second edition of the *New Grove Dictionary of Music and Musicians*, a two-volume edition of the 'Complete Sonatas' of Nicola Francesco Haym, a co-authored study (with Colin Timms) of Agostino Steffani's correspondence in the *RMA Research Chronicle*, and an article, 'The Great Influx of Italians and Their Instrumental Music into London, 1701–1710', published in the conference proceedings *Arcangelo Corelli fra mito e realtà storica*.

Giulia Nuti has appeared as a harpsichord soloist, accompanist and ensemble player in concerts and festivals throughout Europe. She has published on the performance of basso continuo in the Italian manner, and her monograph *The Performance of Italian Basso Continuo* was published by Ashgate in 2007. Since 2002 she has taught harpsichord and continuo performance at the Scuola di Musica di Fiesole in Florence, where she also directs the early music department.

Graham Sadler is Emeritus Professor of Musicology at the University of Hull. He has written extensively on French Baroque and pre-Classical music, his research focusing particularly on Rameau and on matters of performance and notation. He is a member of the editorial committee of *Jean-Philippe Rameau: Omnia Opera* (Bärenreiter), for which he has prepared editions of the operas *Zaïs* and *Zoroastre*.

Hendrik Schulze holds a research post at the University of Heidelberg and until recently was a lecturer at the University of Salzburg. He specialises in Italian music of the seventeenth and early eighteenth centuries: principally, opera and lute music. His book *Odysseus in Venedig* (*Ulysses in Venice*), which discusses character portrayal and the choice of subject in seventeenth-century Venetian opera, was published in 2004. The Society for Seventeenth-Century Music has appointed him as its Corresponding Member for Europe.

Michael Talbot is Emeritus Professor of Music at the University of Liverpool. He is the author of several books on Italian music of the late Baroque period and has made special studies of the life and works of Vivaldi and Albinoni, the latest product of which is a recently published book on Vivaldi and fugue. He is also active as an editor of Italian music from the same period and is co-editor of the yearbook *Studi vivaldiani*.

Colin Timms is Peyton and Barber Professor of Music at the University of Birmingham. He has edited cantatas and duets by Agostino Steffani and published a prize-winning book on the composer – *Polymath of the Baroque* (2003). He has also published on Corelli, Vivaldi, Handel and Marcello, and contributed forty articles to *The New Grove Dictionary of Music and Musicians*. His most recent publication is a critical edition of Handel's oratorio *Theodora* for the Hallische Händel-Ausgabe. He is currently collaborating on the *Edizione Nazionale dell'Opera Omnia di Alessandro Stradella* and the *Nuova edizione delle opere di Antonio Vivaldi*.

Roger-Claude Travers, who is a practising physician, chose as the subject of his doctoral thesis (1980) the much-debated illness from which Vivaldi was a lifelong sufferer. In his 'second' role as a musicologist and music critic, he is a member of the advisory board of the yearbook *Studi vivaldiani*, for which he writes an annual column evaluating all the recordings of Vivaldi's music issued during the previous year. Since 1978 he has worked as a critic for the French journal *Diapason*. He takes a special interest in the history of recordings of Baroque music.

Giulia Veneziano teaches the history of music at the Conservatorio 'Gesualdo da Venosa' in Potenza. She has published widely on Italian Baroque music with Neapolitan connections (including entries in the *New Grove Dictionary of Music and Musicians*) and has completed a critical edition of arias for Farinelli composed by Duni. She is currently working on a doctoral thesis on Vinci's cantatas at the University of Zaragoza.

Preface

'Sonate, que me veux-tu?' was, famously, Bernard Le Bovier de Fontenelle's reaction to the eighteenth-century instrumental sonata, which he found difficulty in assimilating to the concept of music as an imitation of nature. Today, as Ellen Harris has very recently remarked, we are more likely to pose the question 'Cantate, que me veux-tu?', remote as we have grown from the literary values and aesthetic frame of reference of secular vocal music of the late Baroque period.[1] How ironic that the link to words, once seen as the key to musical understanding, should over time have become the barrier. This barrier is, of course, raised even higher whenever the words are in a foreign language, which is certainly the case for most music-lovers worldwide, including anglophones, who encounter the Italian (and French) cantata.

The situation is even worse for the chamber cantata than for the contemporary opera or even the serenata, since whereas dramatic works contain elements such as dialogue, movement, scenery and lighting that can be exploited (even if not always wisely) to bring the music to life for modern audiences, an orotund narration in recitative of the non-reciprocation of Fileno's amorous feelings for Fillide, punctuated by passages of mawkish direct speech making up the arias, is apt to fall rather flat today. The storms in cantatas too easily appear teacup-sized, incapable of genuinely involving an audience. The *da capo* aria, too, is seen as a drawback: less a vehicle allowing a singer to display his or her command of improvised variation than a facile expedient for lazy composers. In short, everything still conspires to marginalize the Baroque cantata, even in an age when the Early Music Movement has elsewhere made great strides unimaginable a quarter-century ago. It is easy to forget that just before 1700 the chamber cantata within Italy and even in some places beyond its borders was a dominant genre, equalling if not surpassing its instrumental counterpart, the sonata, in the volume of works produced and, albeit more briefly, in the volume of works published. It became, moreover, a musical laboratory where interesting experiments that still have the capacity to startle by their originality and novelty could take place.

A lack of public and even scholarly interest probably explains why even today there remains only one general survey of the Baroque chamber cantata in any language equivalent to, say, William S. Newman's compendium on the sonata or

---

[1] Ellen T. Harris, '"Cantate, que me veux-tu" or: Do Handel's Cantatas matter?', in Melania Bucciarelli and Berta Joncus (eds), *Music as Social and Cultural Practice: Essays in Honour of Reinhard Strohm* (Woodbridge, 2007), pp. 159–84, at p. 159.

Arthur Hutchings's introduction to the Baroque concerto.[2] And this book, Eugen Schmitz's *Geschichte der weltlichen Solokantate*, was first published as long ago as 1914. True, there have been any number of academic theses devoted to the cantatas of individual composers[3] – but this efflorescence is potentially misleading inasmuch as young scholars gravitate naturally (or are directed by their supervisors) towards certain areas precisely because they have *not* been properly investigated before. What is more significant is the paucity of book-length studies aimed at a reasonably wide readership arising from these dissertations, at least as regards the Italian repertory.[4] And there remains, naturally, the problem of moving beyond the confines of the oeuvre of a single composer to embrace the totality of the genre, something that can be achieved satisfactorily only via a more widely ranging study than a monograph on 'The Cantatas of Composer X'.

Fresh from writing just such a study of the chamber cantatas of a composer in whom I have for many years specialized, Antonio Vivaldi,[5] I conceived the present volume as an opportune means of redressing the balance between the general and the particular, of providing a showcase for some of the excellent work on the cantata being carried out today in several countries and, most important, of winning new friends for the genre. My approach was not prescriptive: I simply invited the present contributors to write about some aspect of the Italian chamber cantata in its mature form (running, roughly, from Legrenzi and Stradella in the 1660s to Porpora and Hasse in the 1740s) that would make an interesting essay. As things have turned out, the result is, I think, a fairly comprehensive overview of the genre in its 'classic' phase, or *Blütezeit* (period of efflorescence), as Schmitz aptly termed it. Like every pack of cards, the present offering contains a Joker: Graham Sadler's discussion of the scoring of French cantatas. On first consideration, such a subject might seem out of place: after all, this essay's focus on the French rather than the Italian repertory makes it an exception. But I think it is useful to have, within the same two covers, a comparator for the Italian cantata. And the sheer originality of Sadler's thesis, which could, if accepted by the performing community, transform

---

[2] William S. Newman, *The Sonata in the Baroque Era* (Chapel Hill, 1959), and companion volumes for later periods; Arthur Hutchings, *The Baroque Concerto* (London, 1961).

[3] See the surveys of scholarly work on the cantata in Teresa M. Gialdroni, 'Bibliografia della cantata da camera italiana (1620–1740 ca.)', *Le fonti musicali in Italia. Studi e ricerche*, 4 (1990): 31–131, and Colin Timms, 'The Italian Cantata since 1945: Progress and Prospects', in Francesco Fanna and Michael Talbot (eds), *Cinquant'anni di produzioni e consumi della musica dell'età di Vivaldi* (Florence, 1998), pp. 75–94.

[4] For the French repertory, in contrast, one has David Tunley, *The Eighteenth-Century French Cantata* (London, 1974), and Gene E. Vollen, *The French Cantata: A Survey and Thematic Catalog* (Ann Arbor, 1982). The French cantata repertory, of course, is much smaller than the Italian.

[5] Michael Talbot, *The Chamber Cantatas of Antonio Vivaldi* (Woodbridge, 2006).

the way in which these cantatas are presented in concert, makes one feel privileged to offer it hospitality.

A few words on the individual contributions and their interconnections are in order. Carolyn Gianturco's opening chapter marks the chronological boundary backwards in time by discussing the cantatas of Stradella, a composer on whom she has published extensively. By focusing closely on Stradella's ariosos – that is, those sections of Stradella's cantatas that could, on account of their poetic metre and content, be set as ordinary recitative but instead are treated in a more extensive, patterned way reminiscent of aria (hence their description as 'arioso') – Gianturco both addresses a type of vocal writing little explored for any composer in the literature on the cantata and draws attention to the exceptional feeling for, and education in, poetry possessed by Stradella.

Colin Timms remains with Stradella, examining a late seventeenth-century manuscript of Italian secular vocal music in the library of the University of Birmingham that contains, besides two 'serenatas' of Stradella, secular vocal compositions by his contemporaries Giovanni Battista Vulpio, Giacomo Simonelli and Ercole Bernabei. Timms argues that this previously ignored manuscript belongs to the important group of contemporary Stradella sources known as the 'original Stradella collection'. Since the compositions collected in the volume are named variously 'serenata' and 'cantata', he takes the opportunity to examine the generic implications of each title.

Hendrik Schulze takes as his subject the solo cantatas (preserved in the Op. 12 and Op. 14 collections) of Stradella's most eminent contemporary active in the vocal domain in Venice, Giovanni Legrenzi. His prime concern is to show how, although not formally dramatic compositions according to the usual rules of thumb applied either in the seventeenth century or today, Legrenzi's cantatas do indeed possesses dramatic properties tailored to a chamber, hence non-theatrical, genre – properties that in some cases parallel very closely the dramatic strategies practised in his operas and in others are *sui generis*. Schulze reminds us that although a solo cantata is, by definition, sung by only one person, it may carry within itself several 'voices' (including the authorial), whose interaction has dramatic potentiality.

Reinmar Emans's chapter examines the published cantata repertory in the later seventeenth century, concentrating on the two leading centres, Bologna and Venice. While in the second half of the seventeenth century the two cities vied for hegemony in the publication of cantatas, now one and now the other being dominant, both largely abandoned the genre in the early eighteenth century. Emans examines carefully the reasons for this decline and proposes, albeit circumspectly, some answers. One of his important findings is that while cantatas circulating only in manuscript (the vast majority) tended towards an ever-increasing uniformity in the last decades of the Settecento, a trend that accelerated in the next century, the printed repertory to some extent resisted this standardization and for that reason is of especial musical interest and value.

Norbert Dubowy considers the significance of Alessandro Scarlatti's cantatas and their place in the composer's oeuvre. His chapter addresses in turn various key aspects: their number, typology and chronology; their patrons, poets (sometimes the same person) and circumstances of performance; their interaction with, and depiction of, the poetic text; Scarlatti's position in the history of the genre. One particular cantata, the celebrated *Al fin m'ucciderete, o miei pensieri*, is singled out for close examination. This would, incidentally, be a good chapter for any reader less familiar with the Baroque cantata repertory to read first, since it contains a wealth of general background information.

Lowell Lindgren focuses his attention on Giovanni Bononcini, who was perhaps the most celebrated composer of continuo cantatas after Alessandro Scarlatti in the late Baroque period. The centrepiece of his chapter is a census of Bononcini's cantatas for single voice, in which, wherever possible, each cantata is assigned to a specific phase of this much-travelled composer's career. The sources and the conflicting attributions are carefully examined and evaluated. Lindgren complements this investigation with a study of the composer's reception – especially in France, where Bononcini became an object of contention during the *querelle* between François Raguenet and Jean Laurent Le Cerf de la Viéville regarding the relative merits of French and Italian music (this episode makes an interesting connection to Graham Sadler's later chapter) – and with analytical commentaries on selected cantatas that shed light on the composer's perceived pre-eminence in the genre during his lifetime.

Marco Bizzarini discusses a hitherto unnoticed adaptation of his own music by Benedetto Marcello, by which the cantata *Dove fuggisti, o dio* became transformed into the setting of Psalm 21 (in Italian paraphrase) *Volgi, volgi, mio Dio, deh volgi un de' tuoi sguardi*. The borrowing is used to illustrate the distinction between the *genus humile* and the *genus sublime*, important aesthetic concepts in the music of the early eighteenth century and ones that Marcello took great pains to differentiate.

Giulia Veneziano re-examines the validity of a much-abused general concept – that of 'Neapolitan' music – by focusing closely on a group of cantatas by Leonardo Vinci. Vinci's meteoric career as a composer of operas in the 1720s has been the object of much study and comment recently, and it is useful to see an evaluation of his cantatas, which are relatively few but enjoyed high regard in his lifetime. Veneziano also pays attention to the reception of Vinci's cantatas in Spain and the *contrafacta* they inspired.

Graham Sadler begins by describing the late arrival of the Italian cantata in France towards 1700 and the swift rise of an indigenous counterpart, the *cantate françoise*. It has long been recognized that, right from the start, the French cantata distinguished itself from the Italian by more often than not accompanying the solo voice not only with a continuo bass but also with an obbligato treble part, typically for violin. Sadler has now discovered that the difference is in reality even more profound, since the French sources usually transmit cantatas in the form of a *partition réduite*: a type of score, most familiar from prints of native operas, in which middle parts are suppressed for the sake of economy and convenience. The cantatas are therefore to be classed as 'orchestral' works – by virtue of their full instrumental texture, if not necessarily in terms of part-sharing. The implications of this conclusion for modern performance are naturally very significant.

Michael Talbot considers a single technical aspect of cantata recitative, traditionally treated as the 'poor relation' of the aria. Since late-Baroque cantata recitative employs advanced techniques of modulation that enable it to navigate back and forth through the circle of fifths very rapidly, it has more than enough capacity to fulfil its basic task of providing tonal linkage from one aria to the next. Accordingly, this 'surplus' is able to be used for expressive and artistic ends. This proposition is examined via examples taken from Albinoni, Pistocchi, Vivaldi and Brusa.

Giulia Nuti brings a practitioner's experience and expertise to bear on a particularly problematic aspect of performance practice in relation to continuo arias: what the accompanist should play, in addition to the bass, during those introductory, concluding and intermediate passages (describable as 'ritornellos') where the voice pauses. Her conclusion, based on contemporary testimony, close analysis of the sources and pragmatic deduction, is that accompanists – in the first instance, harpsichordists, although her recommendations apply equally to lutenists and players of other harmony instruments – should make maximum use of melodic and thematic elements present in the vocal line before thinking of inventing new material.

The volume closes, appropriately, with a study of the reception history of the Baroque cantata. This account, by Roger-Claude Travers, traces not the history of its publication or of its concert performance in modern times but that of its appearance on disc. Inevitably, its revival in this domain, as elsewhere, has been bound up with wider questions and currents affecting the Early Music Movement. Some problems are peculiar to the genre, but most are common. Travers identifies three periods in the revival of these cantatas on disc, which he defines as those of 'emergence', 'analysis' and 'synthesis', respectively. It will be interesting to see whether this interesting, and I think apt, tripartite classification is taken up by other commentators. The chapter concludes with an extensive discography.

* * *

The conventions employed in this book will be familiar to most readers. Musical notes not associated with any particular octave register (such as those denoting keys or chords) are represented as capital letters in Roman type, whereas notes of fixed pitch, italicized, follow the so-called Helmholz system where c' is Middle C, c the octave below, and so forth.[6] The names of libraries appear, where convenient, in abbreviated form, employing the sigla created for them by the international organization RISM (see the list immediately preceding this Preface). Music examples, tables and plates are numbered separately for each chapter. Thus

---

[6] Lowell Lindgren, in Chapter 6, employs in addition a system differentiating pitch in a relative manner, lower-case and upper-case letters representing notes in adjacent octaves.

'Example 3.1' is the first music example in the third chapter. Footnotes run from '1' in each chapter.

The bibliographical apparatus of every chapter is self-contained. This means that complete publication details are given for each item referenced, irrespective of the possible appearance of the same item in an earlier chapter. This will meet the needs of readers who – let us hope only initially! – choose to consult individual essays rather than the whole book. As for the music examples, I have left authors some latitude to decide whether to retain or to replace original clefs and whether or not to draw attention to editorial emendations (for instance, the correction of errant notes or the removal of accidentals redundant in modern notation). In these examples, Italian and French poetic texts, whether transcribed in the text of the essays or underlaid to the notes in music examples, appear with lightly normalized orthography that respects phonic and lexical deviations from the modern language but otherwise aims to conform to modern practice.[7] Unless otherwise specified, translations into English are by the authors themselves.

I have done my best to produce a reasonably comprehensive general index, bearing in mind the different terminological preferences of the authors. There is no separate glossary of specialized terms such as *endecasillabo* or *rima baciata*, but the index subheading 'defined' will lead readers straight to the page or pages on which the appropriate definition occurs.

This book is inscribed to the memory of Nigel Fortune, whose long advocacy of Italian vocal chamber music and important contributions to the literature concerned with it will be as familiar to many readers as they are to most of the contributors. Otherwise, thanks and acknowledgements begin with the team of contributors, whose eager co-operation and constructive advice have made the preparation of this book a real pleasure. As ever, I thank the University of Liverpool and my colleagues within the School of Music for countless little acts of generosity – most notably, my continued access (even as an 'Emeritus') to the photocopying room. To my wife, Shirley, I offer thanks for not only living with my constant disappearances to my study but also plying me with countless refreshing cups of tea.

Michael Talbot
Liverpool, 2009

---

[7] There is a special problem with an obsolete silent 'H' standing at the head of the first word, as in Legrenzi's cantata *Havete il torto a fé* (discussed in Chapter 3 by Hendrik Schulze). Ordinarily, I would modernize to 'Avete', but since this would alter the alphabetical position of the incipit, the temptation has been resisted.

Chapter 1
The When and How of Arioso in Stradella's Cantatas

Carolyn Gianturco

To understand Stradella's cantatas, one must first know his unusual – for a musician – background. The Stradellas, besides being nobles, were a cultured family, and several of their members held noteworthy official posts.[1] Matteo Stradella, a citizen of Fivizzano but the son of Giovanni Marco Stradella of Borgo Tarro, was a party to the section of the agreement of 1475 whereby Fivizzano agreed to be ruled by Florence in exchange for its protection – an arrangement that assured Fivizzano of a privileged position during the rule of the Medici dynasty: it was accordingly laid down that a 'foreign' captain (*capitano*) should reside there; that public and private schools should be established in the city; that theatres and academies should be founded; and that artisans concerned with printing and the making of musical instruments should be permitted to work there to their personal financial advantage. Matteo Stradella's sixteenth-century descendants continued to occupy positions of importance: Ciro, an imperial and Florentine notary, was involved in local politics; Caterina became the second wife of Romulo Malaspina; Giovanbattista, a lawyer, became governor of various cities in the Papal States and had a hand in making changes to the statutes of Fivizzano; Giannettino was appointed governor of Melfi in the Kingdom of Naples; Fulvio became chancellor to Prince Doria of Melfi; and another Matteo was the same prince's doctor for at least thirty years. Still more important, however, was yet another member of the family: Alessio Stradella.[2]

Ordained in the Augustinian seminary of Genoa around 1530, Alessio acquired a reputation as an intellectual and responsible clergyman. A gifted orator, he was invited to preach at the installation of Giovanni Angelo Medici as Pope Pius IV in 1559, as well as at the Council of Trent on 30 May 1562, and again in 1566 in the presence of Maria of Austria; a volume of his sermons was published in 1567. Alessio was also a teacher, first at the Augustinian seminary of Milan and

---

[1] For information regarding the Stradella family, as well as a documented biography of Alessandro Stradella, see Carolyn Gianturco, *Alessandro Stradella (1639–1682): His Life and Music* (Oxford, 1994), especially Part I, 'The Life', pp. 3–60.

[2] Alessio Stradella's biography is related in many sources, among which are Emanuele Gerini, *Memorie storiche di illustri scrittori e di uomini dell'antica e moderna Lunigiana* (Massa, 1839), pp. 136–7, as well as Gianturco, *Alessandro Stradella*, p. 4.

later in that of Bologna – today, the site of the Conservatorio di Musica (Museo Internazionale e Biblioteca della Musica di Bologna). In 1570 and 1575 he was made procurator of his order, and during the same period he taught theology in Rome, where Philip Neri was one of his pupils. Although it was not common for a member of a religious order to assume an important ecclesiastical position, Alessio was consecrated Bishop of Sutri and Nepi on 20 July 1575 by Pope Gregory XIII, Ugo Boncompagni. He established his seat in Nepi, bringing his brothers Giovanbattista, Matteo and Fulvio with him. A few years later, in 1580, Alessio died while on a diplomatic mission, representing the pope, to Charles of Austria.

In this same year a son was born to Fulvio Stradella: Marc'Antonio, the future father of the composer Alessandro. After the death of Fulvio in 1587 or 1588 his widow married Domenico Balada, former secretary to the bishop. At Nepi, belonging to the Papal States, Marc'Antonio would have drawn educational advantage not only from his uncles and stepfather but also from the men who had studied in the seminary founded by Alessio. Already in 1601 he was able to enter into a financial venture with Balada, and in 1603, having reached the legal age of majority, twenty-five, he began to handle such affairs on his own, buying and selling property and assuming political responsabilities as a member of the General Council of Nepi and, later, of the Council of Eight. In addition, for several years he managed the properties of Duke Pietro Altemps in Gallese and in Rome. During the War of Castro he was made Vice-Marquis of Vignola by Ugo Boncompagni, whose dukedom lay in the region of Modena. Marc'Antonio's intelligence and his financial and political astuteness emerge in these several positions, but his musical culture, too, is attested in the assembly and publication of Johannes Hieronymus Kapsberger's *Libro primo de madrigali a cinque voci* that he financed in Rome in 1609 (at the age of twenty-eight or twenty-nine).[3]

It was into this family of professionals, of men engaged in activities requiring education and intelligence, that Alessandro Stradella was born in 1639. Among his closest living relatives, two aunts became vicars in their nunnery, and a stepbrother was an Augustinian who held positions of importance in the order. His maternal grandfather was Simone Bartoli of Bagnoreggio (although the Bartoli were a noble family originally from Florence), a lawyer and governor of various cities in the Papal States who was married to Isabella Alberi from an illustrious family of Orvieto. It was their daughter Vittoria who married Marc'Antonio after his first wife died. It is possible that for some years Alessandro studied not only in Nepi but also in Bologna; certainly, at least eight of his adolescent years (1653–61) were spent at the Roman court of Duke Ippolito Lante, where – after the death of Marc'Antonio – his mother moved with two of her sons, assuming the position of 'lady to the duchess'.

Palazzo Lante is situated in the Piazza de' Caprettari in the parish of Sant'Eustachio in the centre of Rome. As remarked earlier, Marc'Antonio

---

[3] See Emil Vogel, *Bibliothek der gedruckten weltlichen Vokalmusik Italiens aus den Jahren 1500–1700*, 2 vols (Berlin, 1892), vol. 1, p. 335.

managed the properties of Pietro Altemps, Duke of Galese, who, at the death of his first wife, Angelica de' Medici, married Isabella Lante della Rovere: the relationship between the Stradella and Lante families must therefore have been formed through their common earlier connection with the Altemps. In addition to this noble connection, the Lantes were related to the grand dukes of Tuscany, the dukes of Modena and of Parma, the princess of Rossana (Olimpia Aldobrandini Pamphilj), Duke Caffarelli, Marquis Marino of Genoa and Cardinal Boncompagni of Bologna. The fact that many of these figures later became patrons of the composer suggests that the youth had been introduced to them by the Lantes. As well as offering him contacts with these and the many other nobles to whom the Lantes were related, the connection gave him access to writers, theologians, artists and musicians with whom they were involved. Without doubt, the eight years that Alessandro spent as a member of the Lante household (initially as a page) would have served to foster his intellectual enrichment, his general education befitting a gentleman and, not least, his musical training.

That Stradella's general education was excellent is manifested in several ways. The most immediately noticeable is his calligraphy. In a period when not all knew how to read and write – and when among those who did not all regularly exercised the skill of writing – Stradella's autograph pages reveal that he handled a pen with ease and rapidity, producing a script that was consistently uniform. In short, Stradella was highly accustomed to writing and performed the task in the manner of one who has studied and perfected the art of calligraphy. Moreover, one who writes, however neatly, only according to the perceived sound of the letters can easily commit spelling errors, whereas the absence of such errors in the writing of Stradella confirms that he had learned well the rules of contemporary Italian orthography. Finally, Stradella's phrases exhibit a clarity and a logic that are not those of someone who is simply intelligent, but belong, rather, to one who is also accustomed to think independently and to formulate ideas.

The composer's numerous letters[4] written to patrons offer yet another element confirming that he was an educated man: this concerns his relationship with these aristocrats. While Stradella is always courteous according to the conventions of the period, he does not express himself with the exaggerated obsequiousness typical of one who considers himself inferior or who works under the heel of another. Rather, he recounts with easy friendliness his successes and his problems, and any favours requested are solicited in the same vein, without the embarrassment of begging. It was in fact on account of his scholarly and social education, coupled with the self-assurance – neither rudely egotistic nor falsely humble – acquired through these endowments that he attained the status of a true 'gentleman of letters'. As such, and because of the keen interest taken among the educated classes of seventeenth-century Italy in literature and in *poesia per musica*, he was encouraged to write

---

[4] Stradella's twenty-four extant letters are transcribed and translated in Gianturco, *Alessandro Stradella*, pp. 262–99.

texts for music himself as well as to modify without hesitation – in fact, with authority – those of other poets.[5]

Proof of the former activity is found in four of his extant Latin motets: *Care Jesu suavissime* – joyous lines in honor of Philip Neri; *Dixit angelis suis iratus Deus* – filled with God's anger towards sin and ending with a plea from Mary for humankind to be forgiven; *Exultate in Deo, fideles* – with its promise of peace at Christmas; and *O vos omnes, qui transitis* – an intensely religious prayer possibly intended for a girl's investiture as a nun. The texts for all of these are directly attributed, on their scores, to Stradella.[6]

As for his modification of texts provided him by others, there is the documented example of his 1674 cantata *Il duello* (which begins 'Vola, vola in altri petti'), where Stradella intervened eleven times, most often with radical cuts or with the insertion of a substantial number of additional lines.[7] The author of the original text was Sebastiano Baldini, a well-known and highly respected poet of verses for music that were set by almost every composer operating in Rome at the time (and by many elsewhere).[8] Baldini complained bitterly about Stradella's changes – but to no avail.[9] Similar treatment was given by Stradella to another Baldini text, this time that of the serenata *Lo schiavo liberato*, a reworking for music of an episode from Tasso's epic poem *Gerusalemme liberata*. Here, Stradella made nine cuts of lines as well as adding numerous lines of his own.[10] Because of these known literary proclivities, the otherwise fairly inexplicable second versions of both text and music for the serenatas *La forza delle stelle* (text again originally by Baldini)[11] and *La Circe* (by Giovan Filippo Apolloni) may possibly also be laid at Stradella's door.[12] Certainly, the mad scenes for his opera *La forza dell'amor paterno*, added

---

[5] A counterpart from a slightly later period is the Venetian nobleman Benedetto Marcello, who similarly expressed his versatility and the breadth of his culture by writing the music and texts for cantatas either separately or in combination.

[6] See Carolyn Gianturco and Eleanor McCrickard, *Alessandro Stradella (1639–1682): A Thematic Catalogue of His Compositions*, Thematic Catalogue Series, 16 (Stuyvesant, NY, 1991), 'Sacred Vocal Works with Latin Texts, Nonliturgical Settings (Motets)', pp. 199–204.

[7] For sources of, and related information on, all the Stradella cantatas mentioned in this chapter, see Gianturco and McCrickard, *Alessandro Stradella*, pp. 1–116, *passim*.

[8] On Sebastiano Baldini, see the several references in Gianturco, *Alessandro Stradella*, especially p. 27, n. 38, and in Giorgio Morelli and Flavia Cardinale, *Sebastiano Baldini (1615–1685): Le poesie per musica nei codici della Biblioteca Apostolica Vaticana* (Rome, 2000).

[9] These changes are discussed in Carolyn Gianturco, *Stradella, 'uomo di gran grido'* (Pisa, 2008), pp. 128–9.

[10] For the changes, see Gianturco, *Stradella, 'uomo di gran grido'*, pp. 124–5.

[11] Ibid., pp. 116–23.

[12] Ibid., pp. 107–10. On the nature of the serenata genre (also called the 'dramatic cantata'), see Chapter 2 of this volume by Colin Timms.

to Nicolò Minato's libretto for performances in Genoa in 1678 and to which no other poet can be linked, were quite likely by Stradella.[13]

From what has been asserted so far, it will come as no surprise to learn that the music Stradella composed for voice was tied intimately, in style and structure, to its text. This was true of all his vocal music, including his many extant cantatas. It is therefore important to establish the point at which Italian poetry for music had arrived by the time Stradella began to compose. As one knows, Italian poets originally wrote in Latin, the language of the educated, and only gradually began to adopt their native tongue, Dante providing indelible proof of how fine poetry written in the vernacular could be. Because it is a harmonious metre offering rhythmic variety, he and other writers opted for regular lines of eleven syllables (*endecasillabi*), such as had been employed by classical writers including Horace; this metre therefore came with the sanction of poetic tradition. In fact, even some later writers used exclusively eleven-syllable lines, as did Ludovico Ariosto (1474–1533) in his epic poem *Orlando furioso* and in his series of dialogues entitled *Satire*. In his epic poem *Gerusalemme liberata* Torquato Tasso (1544–95) likewise relied entirely on hendecasyllables for narration, description, reported speech and direct speech alike.

However, occasional signs of change are evident in early plays in which the poet knew that vocal music was to be included, as did Agnolo Ambrosini, known as Poliziano (1454–94), in *La favola d'Orfeo*, the first Italian-language play on a secular subject (1471). Here, a mixture of eleven-syllable and seven-syllable lines (*settenari*) is encountered, and stanzas of six or eight lines are formed using either or both of these metres. Tasso, alongside others, experimented similarly with mixed-metre lines, which in his case were generally left unrhymed or at least were not rhymed according to a consistent pattern: in Italian, these are called *versi sciolti* (meaning lines 'not bound' to a poetic scheme), a concept that one could liken to blank verse in English. Tasso's most famous play, *L'Aminta*, on a pastoral subject, is made up almost entirely of *versi sciolti*. For his play *Il pastor fido* Giambattista Guarini (1538–1612) adopted *versi sciolti* but included also rhyming, strophic canzonas for the choruses; in addition, for the chorus 'Cieco Amor, non ti cred'io' Guarini used lines of variously five, seven, eight and eleven syllables, explaining (excusing?) his departure from previous practice by saying that this chorus was also to be danced.

A fine example of how poets worked contemporaneously in the older and the newer styles is offered by Giambattista Marino (1569–1625). In Part I of Marino's *Rime*, a collection of sonnets, each poem is constructed from fourteen hendecasyllabic lines; in Part II, however, there are single-stanza madrigals and strophic canzonas of variable length and mixing heptasyllabic and hendecasyllabic lines. This period's 'liberation' of poetry was carried a stage further by Gabriello

---

[13] See Mariateresa Dellaborra and Carolyn Gianturco, *Alessandro Stradella, 'La forza dell'amor paterno'*, Edizione Nazionale dell'Opera Omnia di Alessandro Stradella, Series II, vol. 2, 'Introduzione' and 'Introduction', pp. v–vii and xv–xvii, respectively.

Chiabrera (1552–1638), who advocated the acceptance of a variety of versification in serious Italian poetry: for instance, Chiabrera proposed that *versi sciolti* be employed for the composition of epic poems. Moreover, he praised the variety of rhythm that exploiting all the possible metres could offer poets – especially, he affirmed, those writing poetry to be set to music. As a matter of fact, he, too, wrote much poetry of this kind, contained in his *Canzonette* (1591) and his *Maniere, scherzi e canzonette morali* and *Maniere de' versi toscani* (both 1599). This, then, was the expanded and varied literary scene at the turn of the sixteenth and seventeenth centuries of which Ottavio Rinuccini (1562–1621), in his *Dafne*, *Euridice*, *Arianna* and *Narciso*, took advantage – as did all those after him who wrote *poesia per musica*.

Rinuccini's works belonged to the new poetic-musical genre – opera – but the other genres that were offshoots of it – oratorio and cantata – followed the same outlines in their poetry. And all responded to the *versi sciolti* with a new and especially free musical style, that of recitative, and to the structured stanzas of text with music that was equally structured: that is, with arias, duets and terzets as required by the text. This parting of the ways becomes evident as early as the collections of 1620 and 1626 by Alessandro Grandi (?1575/80–1630), whose polystrophic canzona and balletto and monostrophic madrigal and fourteen-line sonnet – i.e., the 'closed' forms – do not possess the poetic and musical variety of his cantatas.

By 1702, the secretary of Arcadia and historian of Italian literature Giovan Mario Crescimbeni was able to define cantatas as being 'composed of lines and short lines rhymed without rule [*versi sciolti*], with a mingling of arias [stanzas of poetry], sometimes for one voice, sometimes for more; and that were and are made with dramatic and narrative [elements] mixed together'.[14] Writing in the same period, Sébastien de Brossard made it clear that the cantata was considered an established Italian genre even by those living outside the country: 'It is a large-scale piece, the words of which are in Italian, varied with recitatives, ariettas and different tempos'.[15]

Cantatas by composers just prior to Stradella, and by those who came immediately after him, help to determine his position in the shaping of the genre;

---

[14] Giovan Mario Crescimbeni, *Comentarj intorno alla storia della volgar poesia*, 5 vols (Rome, 1702–20), vol. 1, p. 240: 'composte di versi, e versetti rimati senza legge, con mescolamento d'arie, e talora ad una voce, talora a più; e se ne sono fatte, e fanno anche miste di drammatico, e di narrativo'.

[15] Sébastien de Brossard, *Dictionaire de musique* (Paris, 1703; repr. Amsterdam, 1964): 'C'est une grande piece, dont les paroles sont en Italien; variée de *Recitatifs*, d'*Ariettes*, & de mouvemens différens'. The relationship between text and music is presented in greater detail in Carolyn Gianturco, 'The Italian Seventeenth-Century Cantata: A Textual Approach', in John Caldwell, Edward Olleson and Susan Wollenberg (eds), *The Well Enchanting Skill: Music, Poetry, and Drama in the Culture of the Renaissance: Essays in Honour of F. W. Sternfeld* (Oxford, 1990), pp. 41–51.

they also reveal important changes in the preferences for subjects and for poetic styles and forms. In the works of the composer Luigi Rossi (c.1597–1653)[16] one often finds a quite irregular poetic structure (as in *Ombre, fuggite e voi, notturni orrori*), allied to a tendency not to distinguish neatly between *versi sciolti* and closed form; and many of these works remain anchored in the serious, often introspective, narrative–descriptive–dialoguing tradition of poetry that was not intended from the outset to be set to music, as evidenced by the long texts of Rossi's *Con occhi belli e fieri*, *Al soave spirar d'aure serene* and *Tutto cinto di ferro*, or still more by that of the exceedingly lengthy – with its 256 lines – *Sotto l'ombra d'un pino*.

Giacomo Carissimi (1605–74) set more articulated texts, but still ones containing a great number of *versi sciolti* (*Olà, pensieri, olà*; *Come, ahi come cadeo*) and occasionally conforming to the longer, narrative type (*Poiché lo Sdegno intese*).[17] With Antonio Cesti (1623–69), however, the structure gravitates towards alternation between *versi sciolti* and strophically structured poetry (*Chi non prova star lontano*, *Partite dal mio sen*); the subjects are most often amorous, if sometimes humorously so (*A battaglia vi sfida Cupido*), although the narrative mode retains its currency (a highly dramatic example being *Del famoso oriente*).[18]

Variety is in fact the key characteristic of Stradella's cantatas: variety of subject matter (amorous, historical, humorous, sacred, moral, etc.); of poetic structure; of musical response. It is the cantata in the genre's unrepeatable moment of complete realization, before stylization starts to take precedence over dramatic and musical innovation and freedom.[19] Alessandro Scarlatti (1660–1725)[20] is stationed already at the next moment, when the text, although still taken into careful consideration, is not always the factor that ultimately determines the nature of the composer's music. George Frideric Handel (1685–1759) arrives at the period of maximum stylization, when texts are usually – to put it mildly – no longer so very individual, either in structure or content. Handel writes above all for his singers, providing them with good recitative and very beautiful and showy music for the arias and duets, which by now most often employ a virtually obligatory form – commonly known to music historians as the 'grand da capo' form – that permitted performers to exhibit all their technical skills and to demonstrate their ability to improvise

---

[16] *Cantatas by Luigi Rossi (c.1597–1653), Selected and Introduced by Francesco Luisi*, vol. 1 in the series *The Italian Cantata in the Seventeenth Century*, general editor Carolyn Gianturco (New York, 1986).

[17] *Cantatas by Giacomo Carissimi (1605–74) ... by Günther Massenkeil*, vol. 2 (1986) in the series *The Italian Cantata in the Seventeenth Century*.

[18] *Cantatas by Antonio Cesti (1623–1669 ... by Stephen Bonta*, vol. 6 (1986) in the series *The Italian Cantata in the Seventeenth Century*.

[19] Reinmar Emans, in Chapter 4 of this volume, develops the point about the cantata genre's progressive loss of variety and individuality from the end of the seventeenth century onwards.

[20] *Cantatas by Alessandro Scarlatti (1660–1725) ... by Malcolm Boyd*, vol. 13 (1986), in the series *The Italian Cantata in the Seventeenth Century*.

embellishments on Handel's musical line. With his period, the Baroque cantata – and almost the cantata *tout court* – ends.

* * *

As stated earlier, Stradella's cantatas display a wide variety of subject matter within the three general categories of a secular, sacred or moral nature; they also exhibit various scorings.[21] Of his 142 extant secular cantatas with basso continuo accompaniment, 128 are for solo voice, ten for two voices and four for three voices. There are also 22 secular cantatas requiring from one to seven solo voices and featuring some form of instrumental accompaniment: leaving aside the continuo, this may consist of two violins; of one violin and two violas; of a *concertino* and a *concerto grosso*; or of two separate *concertini* and a *concerto grosso*.[22] And the five sacred and eight moral cantatas exhibit a similar variety of vocal and instrumental scoring. In his cantatas of every species it is often apparent that certain lines are assigned to a narrator who describes the scene and events, whereas other lines constitute the direct speech of the named or unnamed protagonist(s). In solo cantatas the same singer assumes all these roles, which of course calls for dramatic as well as musical ability on the singer's part in order to interpret these works adequately.

The patron who requested a cantata would have made known the occasion and site of the performance, and might even have suggested the subject of the work. He could have stipulated how many musicians were to sing and play, even naming those who were to take part. The poet's task was to comply with these guidelines in his writing of the necessary verses, and the composer's to decide on the most suitable music for the text in the light of the performers' capabilities and with regard to the place of performance (indoors or outdoors, small hall or large, etc.): both poet and composer, of course, had to take into consideration the importance of a singer when deciding upon the number of arias to assign him or her.

The structure of a portion of text in a closed form determined by the poet is generally respected, indeed reinforced, by Stradella's music. Although the poets of his cantatas wrote textual portions with one, two, three or four strophes, most comprise two. When these were of identical structure (the same number of lines, the same metres, the same rhyme scheme) Stradella usually set them to the same music: that is, in AA form. The presence of a refrain formed by a line or a whole

---

[21] For a discussion of all Stradella's cantatas, see Gianturco, *Alessandro Stradella*, pp. 77–139, and Gianturco, *Stradella, 'uomo di gran grido'*, pp. 85–149, and the notes on pp. 278–81.

[22] A *concerto grosso*, literally meaning a 'large' ensemble, conforms to its name not merely by having a relatively large number of independent parts but also by permitting part-sharing – what we would today term an orchestral mode of performance. In contrast, a *concertino*, or 'small' ensemble, normally has fewer parts and does not permit such doubling.

strophe in the poetry could lead to ABA form. Of course, for special dramatic and/or musical reasons Stradella could in theory have decided not to set *versi sciolti* as recitative, or else not to follow the poet's implications regarding form and structural division, but such instances are relatively rare. However, what is always a clear and frequent sign of the music's dominion over the structure of the poetry is the employment, where the text is bistrophic, of ABB′ musical form: here, it is Stradella alone who decides to repeat (although perhaps with variation) the second strophe of poetry and music. For no cantata was there a specific poetic or musical structure that was pre-established and had at all costs to be adhered to. Moreover, there was no rule or even common practice regarding the number of alternations of recitative text with text in a closed form, nor governing which type of text began or ended a cantata – nor even suggesting how long each section should be. Stradella's was a period of wonderful freedom and flexibility.

The style of Stradella's cantata poetry was generally akin to that of Giambattista Marino, who is still today considered one of Italy's greatest poets. As I have noted elsewhere, Marino's skilful use of rhetoric, combined with a rich vocabulary and an intimate knowledge of classical literature and history, resulted in verses calculated to appeal objectively to the intellect although professing to deal passionately with emotions. The aim of such poetry was to simulate more desperation or anger than the described situation would reasonably call for, such as occurs in Stradella's cantata *L'avete fatta a me*, where the female beloved is accused in the lines 'Intanto crudele, | ingrata, infedele, | vantatevi, gloriatevi | d'aver tradito e non saper perché' ('Meanwhile, cruel, ungrateful, unfaithful one, you pride yourself, praise yourself for having betrayed, but without knowing why'). Or in *Già languiva la notte*, where Medea has just wished for the death of the unfaithful Giasone but then repents and calls out wildly to the gods: 'Ah no, fermate, o numi! | Lasciate pur in vita | lo spergiuro, l'ingrato, | l'infedel adorato, | ché s'egli è la mia vita, egl'è il mio core: | viver già non poss'io s'egli sen more' ('Ah no, o gods! Let live the liar, the ungrateful, the unfaithful adored one, since, if he is my life, he is my heart: I cannot live if he dies').

Contrasts in quick succession are typical, and frequent reference is made to eyes, which are alluded to via an immense variety of metaphors. Imagery is employed with telling skill to create a desired atmosphere, and water, with all its possibilities for suggesting the fluctuations of passions or of life's troubles in need of rescue or respite, is so omnipresent that one is tempted to identify it as the chief element (in every sense of the word) evoked by poets.

* * *

Stradella's desire to have the texts he sets understood, as well as his ability to highlight any significant wording or structure, is immediately obvious from the care he takes in his settings. First of all, he makes certain to have the accents in the music coincide with the stressed syllables of the text. Phrases of music are also made to outline verbal phrases; note-values mirror those of the text when read aloud; and the rise and fall of the musical line, articulated with pauses, are governed by his understanding of how one might, when declaiming the words, interpret them. This, then, is not at all the result of a mechanical response to the text but stems, rather, from Stradella's appreciation of the significance of each word, coupled with his insight as a dramatist into how to interpret the sense of the words meaningfully and his ability as a composer to translate the sense into sound and thus communicate both aspects in a clear and interesting poetic-musical dramatic

Example 1.1 Stradella, cantata *Sono in dubbio d'amar*, bars 1–11.

piece. Even his choice of the words or lines to repeat (either of the text proper or of an emphatic series of 'no' or 'sì' exclamations interjected by the composer into the text), whether in recitative or aria, is a musical decision based on a keen awareness of the dramatic content of the individual text.

As examples of Stradella's habitual care that his music should preserve the correct declamation, and therefore promote a clear understanding, of the text, one may cite the setting of the opening recitative of *Sono in dubbio d'amar*, which

Example 1.2 Stradella, cantata *Già languiva la notte*, bars 1–11.

is able to reveal Tirsi's doubts about his love of Lidia (Example 1.1), just as the opening recitative of *Già languiva la notte* describes the waning of night and the first flutterings of early morning breezes (Example 1.2); the opening aria of *Io non vuò più star così* allows Lidia to show her annoyance at love's instability (Example 1.3); and, by stressing the first word of the aria opening *Noiosi pensieri, fuggite dal seno*, the 'nuisance' of troubling thoughts is brought out (Example 1.4), before, in the ensuing phrases, they are commanded to fly away.

Example 1.3 Stradella, cantata *Io non vuò più star così*, bars 1–4.

Example 1.4 Stradella, cantata *Noiosi pensieri, fuggite dal seno*, bars 1–10.

As will already have been realized, Stradella's style in general follows the principle of one note per syllable – another proof of his willing recognition that the cantata was a poetic-musical genre obedient to the injunction 'prima la poesia e poi la musica'. Accordingly, in his vocal music Stradella formed his ideas, small or large, in response to a particular text. At the same time, there were moments when florid music was the natural result of this same process.

After more than a century of similarly manneristic poetry written in the form of the madrigal, to which composers had responded with ever-increasing creative inventiveness in order to interpret via music such passions and imagery, it is no wonder that composers of cantatas continued to employ similarly descriptive music for single words of the same sort. Stradella's cantatas are filled with them. As typical examples of word-painting to be found in his cantatas may be mentioned: the long sustained note to suggest *sempre* ('always' – in the aria 'Si creda più tosto che 'l mare' of the cantata *Ch'io ami, o questo no*); and the series of erratically changing patterns of semiquavers to express *furor* ('rage' – in the aria 'Vincerò di tua fierezza' of the cantata *Ferma, ferma il corso*: Example 1.5).

Example 1.5   Stradella, cantata *Ferma, ferma il corso*, aria 'Vincerò di tua fierezza', bars 192–7.

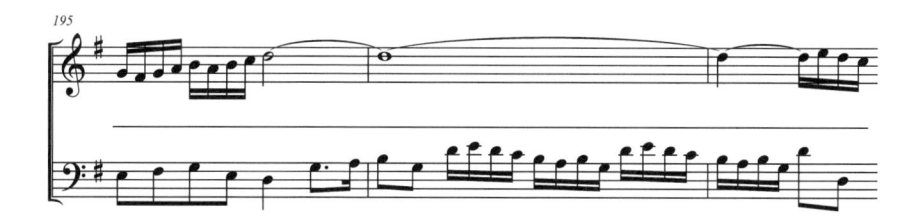

Stradella does not confine such examples, however, to arias. He is, in fact, equally apt to single out pertinent words during a recitative. In an otherwise typical syllabic recitative setting, in order to communicate *lontananza* ('distance'), after an initial descending sixth he writes two rising and falling arpeggios, one reaching up further than the other (the first spanning a tenth, the second an eleventh), then a descending phrase outlining the interval of a twelfth and another ascending an eleventh, before coming to rest at the final cadence (in the recitative beginning 'Non mi lasciar speranza' from the cantata *Sì, ch'io temo*).

A remarkable text by Giambattista Marino begins with the line 'Apre l'uomo infelice all'or che nasce' ('Unhappy man, from the moment he is born'). 'Apre' ('he opens') refers to the conclusion of a later line, which affirms that 'he opens his eyes to pity before he even sees the sun'. To match the weight of this philosophical thought, even though the lines are *versi sciolti* and therefore intended for recitative, Stradella offers a striking beginning to the recitative (and to the cantata itself). He seems to imitate the baby's slow, tentative attempts to open its eyes through three sustained rising notes, and then – as the child continues to persevere and finally sees the world – there is a more active semiquaver fioritura (Example 1.6). The next phrase of text is given a simple syllabic setting; thereafter and throughout this opening recitative meaningful words are set in musical relief.

Example 1.6 Stradella, cantata *Apre l'uomo infelice all'or che nasce*, bars 1–8.

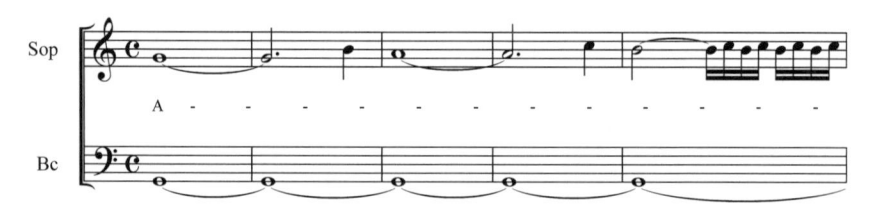

A more dramatic example occurs in a recitative of *Sopra un'eccelsa torre*, which narrates the burning of ancient Rome while Claudio (Nerone/Nero) laughs: Stradella mirrors the hysteria of the emperor by setting the verb *rida* (laughs) with a downward cascading florid phrase, heard several times in the course of the cantata.

* * *

Another, rather more subtle, intervention by Stradella results from his continual scrutiny of recitative text to decide when there can be musical enhancement to strengthen the dramatic interpretation of a line, while still keeping it as recitative and thus allowing the described event or situation to move forward. One notes that at certain moments he interrupts the syllabic style, but not in order to give a particular word a florid treatment. Rather, it is to set a line of recitative text in an entirely different manner: in the style not of recitative but of aria. In Italian usage of the period the resulting section would still be called a recitative, but with the qualifying adjective 'arioso'; today, it would be labelled in any language simply 'arioso'.

In these instances, the recitative text would be repeated, contrary to normal recitative practice, in which words are stated only once: for example, the eleven-syllable line 'che degno è di perdono un cor pentito' ('a repentant heart that is worthy of forgiveness') in the cantata *Genuflesso a tue piante* is stated twice; 'Tu non sorgi mai più se un dì tramonti' ('You will never rise again, if one day you disappear'), again of eleven syllables, in the cantata *In quel sol che in grembo al Tago* is stated three times; 'Perché sol per penar nasce un amante' ('Because a lover is born only to suffer'), of eleven syllables, in *Costanza, mio core* is repeated four times. The vocal line of such recitative sections would also not be that of simple recitative: rather, it would be more melodic than usual in recitative; and the normally static rhythm of the basso continuo would be quickened and become even quite regular, sometimes utilizing a recurrent rhythmic figure. However, as in the usual sort of recitative, the section would modulate: it would begin in one key and end in another. Besides the fact that incomplete sentences or thoughts are not set as independent and complete closed musical forms (arias, duets, etc.), its propensity for modulation is perhaps the most crucial characteristic distinguishing an arioso from an aria – certainly in the case of the longer ariosos, which otherwise could seem at first to be arias, especially when highly organized, as are those of 'Che i confini del riso occupa il pianto' ('That tears take the place of a laugh') in the cantata *Amor, io son contento* and the opening line of *Udite, amanti, un prodigio novello* ('Listen, lovers, extraordinary news'), both treated sequentially. Upon closer examination, however, it becomes obvious that Stradella was composing a recitative, albeit a special sort of recitative.

In connection with the above examples it was mentioned that the line of recitative treated in aria style (NB: not aria form) was of eleven syllables. It was also explained earlier that this line length was traditionally important in Italian literature: always in literature without music but also in poetry designed to be set to music. In fact, it was usually an hendecasyllabic line that concluded a section of recitative: it was at this point that the description or narration or monologue or dialogue of the recitative would have ended. The entire foregoing recitative would have prepared the way and set the scene for the considerations to be set forth in the following closed form, and therefore its last line would have been most particular – a moment of certainty, as it were, since it was designed to call forth the sentiments of the aria, duet or ensemble and as such could have warranted increased musical affirmation.

When Stradella deemed that such a line needed to be highlighted, he set it as an arioso. A typical example of a concluding hendecasyllable of recitative set as an arioso occurs in the above-mentioned cantata *Noiosi pensieri, fuggite dal seno*. After worrying and suffering, the lover concludes: 'Or applaude fortuna a' miei desiri' ('Now fortune applauds my desires'). This thought, to Stradella's mind, is so meaningful and happy that to express it the lover must break into song: that is, into arioso. He therefore changes the metre from common time to 3/2, and writes 16 bars of lively melody, in part sequentially organized and modulating from E minor to B minor, with a continuo accompaniment that accentuates the rhythm and allows the lover to dwell, through repetion, on his good fortune (Example 1.7).

Example 1.7 Stradella, cantata *Noiosi pensieri, fuggite dal seno*, bars 20–35.

While this end position is most typical for the appearance of an arioso, it is not the only one. Equally, the opening line of a recitative may be a meaningful hendecasyllable, and one that Stradella believes should be set in relief. This is the case with the opening line of the cantata *Forsennato pensier, che far poss'io*. Here, a lover has an 'infuriating/wild thought' and wonders 'What can I do?' if the one he adores is denied him. This is the question that dominates the whole work and is even restated later on in the cantata (also as an integral part of an aria). Therefore, the words must be understood and their importance realized by the listener immediately at the outset. Stating the line once in simple recitative would clearly not have achieved that aim, and so Stradella sets it as an arioso: the choice of 3/2 metre makes it evident straight away that this is not simple recitative; the voice presents a true melody; the instrumental bass is rhythmically regular and supportive of the metre; the harmony urges the phrases forward (E major modulating to B major); and the text, with internal word repetitions, is stated twice during the twelve bars assigned to it.[23]

In the cantata *Già languiva la notte*, Medea discovers that Giasone has betrayed her and fled. At the beginning of the scene there are ten lines of *versi sciolti* to describe the dawning of that very day, after which eleven lines narrate Medea's discovery and her resulting wild anger and desire for revenge. The eleventh line is, in fact, 'quando Medea tradita' ('when the betrayed Medea'), going on to relate her passionate reactions. The opening ten lines, however, give no warning of what is to take place; moreover, the line that finally announces the dawning of day is the tenth: 'dell'adorato sol i rai nascenti' ('the emerging rays of the adored sun'). In order to impress listeners sufficiently with the beauty of daybreak and thereby augment its contrast with the ugly tragedy announced directly afterwards, as well as to create the calm of unawareness before the drama that is about to occur, Stradella sets this tenth line as an arioso. It begins in 3/2, a metre very often employed by the composer for his ariosos; the first three words are pronounced twice to very florid music (first in E minor and then in B minor); but then Stradella celebrates the 'rays' in a long fioritura and moves to common time for their exquisite birth in 'i rai nascenti', a glorious six-bar fioritura. Only now does simple recitative take over and the tale of betrayal begin. In this case, the arioso is not the concluding line of a section of recitative, nor is it the opening line; it is, instead, a line situated in the middle of several *versi sciolti* and has been singled out by the composer for special treatment in order to heighten the drama described in the text. This could have all been set as simple recitative and the story adequately told in this manner; but the insertion of the arioso – its length, its loveliness, its distracting embellishments for the voice, its wandering modulation – is the touch of genius that the composer, as interpreter of the drama, has added and which raises to a new level the aesthetic quality of the cantata.

An even more dramatic cantata, because it narrates the personal tragedy of an historical human figure, is that which presents Seneca during the awful preparations for his suicide concluding with the terrible act itself. The text begins with his very words: 'Se Nerone lo vuole, | se lo soffron gli dèi, Seneca mora!' ('If Nero wishes it, if the gods allow it, let Seneca die!'). The opening section is long: thirty lines of *versi sciolti*. During the first seventeen lines Seneca begins by telling his friends not to mourn his tragic fate and then goes on to accuse Nero of burning Rome and betraying those close to him. But, he says, Nero 'sa che più d'ogni strazio odio il suo regno' ('knows that more than any atrocity I hate his [entire] reign'). This revelation of Seneca's condemnatory opinion of Nero's rule is made to emerge

---

[23] As an indication of Stradella's predilection for variety, it should be noted that although recitative text that returns in a cantata may be set as an arioso each time, the music itself may be different. This is true of the line 'Nascon le gioie ad arricchirmi il petto' ('Joys that enrich my heart are born') in the cantata *Vaganti pensieri*, and of the opening line of *Sprezzata mi credi, ma non tradita* ('You believe me despised but not betrayed'), thus enabling the text to be heard again, but in a fresh musical setting.

by Stradella's decision to set the line of recitative in arioso style. The metre now becomes 3/2; the first five words are stated twice; Seneca then says 'odio' ('I hate') four times, concluding with a single statement of the rest of the line with its explanation of what it is he hates; and finally the entire setting of the line is repeated, but with 'odio' on a higher (by a fourth), therefore more striking, tonal level (Example 1.8).

Example 1.8 Stradella, cantata *Se Nerone lo vuole*, bars 59–71.

Similar arioso treatment is given to the last of the *versi sciolti* of the section – the thirtieth line, wherein Seneca affirms: 'maggior della sua rabbia è la mia gioia' ('greater than his [Nero's] anger is my joy'), the joy being that of freeing himself of Nero by dying. Here the usual metre for simple recitative, common time, is maintained, but the text is presented four times, with 'la mia gioia' ('my joy') heard twice each time, in lively, exuberant music modulating from F major to E flat major over a total of 17 bars (Example 1.9).

After a two-strophe aria there are seventeen further lines of *versi sciolti*. In the tenth of these lines Seneca repeatedly declares his innocence and his moral freedom: 'Vissi innocente, so morir invitto' ('I lived innocent, I know how to die unvanquished'). This line, so necessary for evaluating the horror of Nero's dictate, is likewise set as an arioso by Stradella. It is worth noting that Seneca begins affirmatively in the major mode (C major), but ends his emphasis on dying in the minor mode (F minor), as if the full awareness of what is to take place has struck him only at this point. Now, in simple recitative, a narrator relates Seneca's burial, affirming that the philosopher's fame and virtue will live on. He concludes with the hendecasyllable 'si può vantar d'aver la morte vinto' ('he [Seneca] can pride himself on having conquered death'), which Stradella sets as an arioso in common time and repeats insistently for seventeen-and-a-half bars: the oft-presented bouncy dotted-note figure in the continuo and voice and the prevalence of the major mode throughout give an assurance that Seneca has indeed triumphed over Nero and death.

Example 1.9 Stradella, cantata *Se Nerone lo vuole*, bars 149–56.

* * *

In his works with instrumental accompaniment, Stradella very often has a short instrumental piece, called a 'ritornello', played before and/or after a closed vocal form scored with only basso continuo accompaniment. Such instrumental sections were independent pieces based on motives from the closed form, which might be an aria, a duet, a terzet or a chorus. In a few cases, such a ritornello is associated by Stradella with an arioso: this occurs in his motets *Locutus est* and *Sistite sidera* and, in connection with two different ariosos, in his *a 2* cantata *Misero amante*.[24]

This last work presents a discussion between a 'Fido amante' ('Trusting lover') and an 'Infido amante' ('Untrustworthy lover'), their sexes left unspecified by the poet. The situation and setting of the cantata is described by the Fido amante in recitative: he is looking for his beloved before dawn; and 'mentre che festeggianti | trionfano le stelle | della già spenta luce | e, scintillando ognor coi suoi splendori, | rendon chiari dell'ombre i foschi orrori' ('while celebrating, the stars triumph over the already extinguished light and, still shining with their brightness, make visible the gloomy horrors of the shadows'). The five lines of *versi sciolti* describing the lingering light of the stars begin with three of seven syllables and one of eleven syllables – all matter of fact and set as simple recitative by the composer. But then the poet observes, in another hendecasyllable, that the light of the stars is

---

[24] I am grateful to Barbara Nestola for having kindly sent me a copy of this cantata.

sufficient to make worrying shadows visible – a surprise not only with regard to the strength of the stars at that hour, but also concerning what 'horror' might have been illuminated. The different emotional quality of the last line is noted by Stradella, who writes a different sort of music for it: that of an arioso. The metre remains common time but now marked 'a tempo'; the rhythm of both voice and continuo is regular; the vocal line is organized into phrases based on two different ideas, each presented sequentially, the second being a fioritura. Both ideas are then taken up in a six-bar ritornello by the two violins and continuo – the first

Example 1.10   Stradella, two-voice cantata *Misero amante*, recitative 'Ché ardendo per beltà fida e severa', bars 1–19 and concluding ritornello.

homophonically and the second as a point of imitation between the strings, in A minor, the key of arrival of the preceding modulatory recitative.

The following aria (accompanied by instruments) explains that in the shadows one sees the suffering lover who is never at peace, after which the poet sums up the situation in two hendecasyllabic lines: 'Ché ardendo per beltà fida e severa, | la crudeltà non la pietade ei spera' ('Since he is burning with desire for trusting and serious beauty, he can expect [only] cruelty, not compassion'). The first line, which describes the lover's supposedly foolish desire, is set as simple recitative, but the second, with its harsh evaluation of what the lover may instead experience, is set differently: as a 3/2 arioso. Once again, Stradella has the violins take up the vocal motive in a succeeding ritornello, this time of eight bars, in the closing key (A minor) of the modulatory recitative (Example 1.10).

It is obvious that by assigning a ritornello to an arioso Stradella was indicating that this particular section was a noteworthy musical entity in the cantata, one that matched the importance – textually and dramatically – of a much longer and more hallowed closed form. These two instances may equally be viewed as yet further occasions when Stradella approached the structure of the poetry subjectively: not by writing closed forms when the poet's lines were *versi sciolti*, which would have meant elaborating the sections perhaps beyond what he thought they warranted in these specific dramatic situations, but by composing somewhat shorter pieces in aria style – ariosos – which he then amplified in significance by extending the life of their motives via added ritornellos, in this way granting what he regarded as adequate attention to the text.

* * *

Going a step further, Stradella is known to have used instruments to accompany an arioso directly. In his Christmas cantata *Si apra al riso ogni labbro*, scored for two violins and continuo, after the First Shepherd sings the aria 'Con insoliti e chiari splendori', he has simple recitative for the following line, 'Le caligini oscure il ciel disgombra' ('Of sombre fog the sky is cleared'). However, he continues in arioso style (and thereby concludes this section of recitative) for the next hendecasyllable, 'all'apparir del sol sparisce ogn'ombra' ('at the appearance of the sun, all shadows vanish') – alluding here to the birth of Christ, the subject of the entire cantata and the culminating point of the three shepherds' previous extended conversation, and therefore a moment of great relevance. This twenty-nine-bar arioso in 3/2 metre is composed in Stradella's favourite manner, imitative phrases being passed from violin to violin to voice, even with some suggested participation by the continuo. As usual for ariosos, this one also modulates (from G major to D major) (Example 1.11).

The cantata *Se del pianeta ardente* provides another example of a cantata where an arioso is accompanied by instruments – in this case, a setting of the concluding line of the piece. The poem was in truth a series of praises adressed to the *Madama Reale* (the duchess regent) of the court of Savoy at Turin, Maria Giovanna Battista, which are organized in alternating *versi sciolti* and closed forms and scored for soprano accompanied by violin, two violas and basso continuo. One has no idea of the occasion for which the cantata was intended, but since Stradella hoped to become one of the Savoyard court musicians he would have wished his music to add noticeably to the glory of the duchess expressed in the text. That this was so is confirmed by his decision to compose an attractive two-movement sinfonia to open the cantata – something that not all his cantatas with instruments were given – and thereby proclaim the importance of the work and occasion.

Example 1.11   Stradella, three-voice cantata *Si apra al riso ogni labbro*, aria 'Le caligini oscure il ciel disgombra', bars 1–12.

The poetry concludes with six *versi sciolti*: 'Ma che dico, che tento? | Non può l'umil mio canto | sollevarsì tant'alto; | onde tacendo, | al vostro eccelso scettro | consagro i carmi, il cor, la voce e il plettro' ('But what am I saying, what am I trying to do? My simple song cannot rise very high; therefore in silence, to your lofty sceptre I consecrate my songs, my heart, and my music'), which could certainly have been the composer's own humble and flattering sentiments – and perhaps were even his very words. To have set all these lines as simple recitative, however, would have dimished the effect of what was intended as a glowing homage to the duchess. Therefore, after the previous aria (the last in the cantata), which was accompanied by instruments, Stradella relaxes the atmosphere by setting the first five lines as simple recitative (beginning in F major); he then moves to arioso for the last line with its dedication to her of his heart, his voice and his music. It is here that the instruments return, at first being employed to echo or to present vocal motives, and then accompanying the voice directly in the last phrase of the nine-bar section (cadencing in D major), which makes a fitting conclusion to an important cantata.

Two further examples of simple recitative followed by an arioso accompanied by instruments are found in a Stradella cantata composed to a text by Sebastiano Baldini based on a scenario by Queen Christina of Sweden, *La forza delle stelle* (also known by the incorrect title *Il Damone*).[25] In Damone's aria 'Mira mai di me', the protagonist asks his beloved, Clori, if she ever thinks of him. Uncertain of her feelings and jealous of the attention of others, he now attempts to control her, first with a line regarding possible suitors: 'Vadan del loro incendio altri superbi' ('Let others be proud of their fire'), which Stradella sets as simple recitative; but to Damone's ensuing ultimatum to Clori – 'purché tutto il tuo foco a me riserbi' ('as long as you keep all of your fire for me') – Stradella adds emphasis by changing the metre to 3/2, bringing in the two violins to increase musical interest, having them dialogue with the voice (supported of course by the continuo) and making Damone – whose unrest is emphasized by the modulating harmony (G major to F major) – tell Clori several times what he expects of her: in short, Stradella sets the line as an accompanied arioso.

The second time that an arioso is accompanied by instruments in the cantata occurs after the aria 'Disperarsi è vanità', whose text urges lovers not to despair. The eleven-syllable line 'Possente incantatrice è la preghiera' ('Prayer is a powerful enchantress') is set as simple recitative, but the following scolding and moralistic *endecasillabo*, 'indegno è di gioir chi si dispera' ('he who is without hope does not deserve to rejoice'), is an accompanied arioso with the following features: 3/2 metre; textual repetition; imitation between the two violins and the voice, supported by descending, quasi-ostinato phrases in the basso continuo; modulation from B minor to D major (Example 1.12).

---

[25] The following discussion refers to the Turin version of the work (I-Tn, Foà 12, ff. 1–104v).

Example 1.12 Stradella, serenata *La forza delle stelle*, recitative 'Possente incantatrice è la preghiera', bars 1–17.

Because simple recitative and arioso recitative were both present in Stradella's composing vocabulary, it was not difficult for him to use either in works with continuo accompaniment: of course, according to his aesthetic musical sense, but also following his sensitivity for what would best serve the dramatic content of the text. In those vocal pieces with instrumental accompaniment that contained recitative text requiring setting, he used both types of recitative, but now with instrumental accompaniment. Unfortunately, most of Stradella's cantatas are undated, making it impossible even to attempt a chronology of his arioso writing or of his novel approach to accompaning recitatives.

Although, in the absence of sufficient documentation concerning such procedures, one is not able to attribute the actual invention of the arioso accompanied by continuo alone or by string instruments to Alessandro Stradella, it must be allowed that he wrote both sorts of recitative more frequently and more inventively than his Italian predecessors and contemporaries. This was undoubtedly due to his musical skill and creativity, but I believe it also owed much to his thorough education and excellent cultural background, which made his understanding of the texts he set deeper and more refined than that of most others.

After Stradella, singers and their audiences began to demand greater and more extended scope for exhibiting the wonders of a now highly developed vocal art. This greater attention paid to the closed forms on the part of the composer resulted in longer arias. It was here that composers devoted their maximum attention. As a result, there was less time to repeat recitative text as required for arioso, and less interest in doing so. Even accompanied recitative came increasingly to resemble rapid simple recitative with instruments added more than recitative of the arioso variety with added instruments.

The compositional freedom and individuality enjoyed by Stradella in his cantatas – the results of which are to be seen so splendidly also in his ariosos, whether accompanied by continuo alone or by other instruments in addition – was sacrificed in the eighteenth century, which preferred a musical art that was perhaps more brilliant but less thoughtful – certainly richer in texture but more stylized, even stereotyped, in form. Stradella's ariosos epitomize the cantata tradition at its most vital, marrying musical invention to respect for the poetry as a conveyor of drama.

Chapter 2
A Lost Volume of Cantatas and Serenatas from the 'Original Stradella Collection'

Colin Timms

This chapter draws attention to a neglected late seventeenth-century manuscript of Italian secular vocal music in the library of the University of Birmingham (UK). There are at least three reasons why the manuscript deserves to be better known. First, it appears to be one of the volumes missing from the 'original Stradella collection' – an important early group of sources of music by Alessandro Stradella (1639–82) – and sheds new light on the scope and compilation of that collection. Second, since the manuscript contains unique copies of five pieces – two by Stradella and one each by Giovanni Battista Vulpio, Giacomo Simonelli and Ercole Bernabei – it adds to the work lists of three known composers and contributes a substantial piece by one (Simonelli) who otherwise appears to be virtually unknown. Finally, since each work is identified as a 'cantata' or a 'serenata', the manuscript also raises questions about the relationship between these genres in the late seventeenth century.

***

The largest surviving collection of manuscripts of music by Stradella is found in the Biblioteca Estense e Universitaria at Modena (I-MOe) and stems from the library of Francesco II D'Este, duke of Modena from 1664 to 1694.[1] Some of the manuscripts in this collection – those with a shelfmark beginning 'Mus. F.' – may have been acquired from the composer himself or, very soon after his death, from his step-brother, Padre Francesco Stradella;[2] other volumes – those bearing a 'Mus. G.' shelfmark – were added later, though early enough to appear

---

[1] The Modena collection has been catalogued many times: see Carolyn Gianturco and Eleanor McCrickard, *Alessandro Stradella (1639–1682): A Thematic Catalogue of His Compositions* (Stuyvesant, NY, 1991), pp. xi–xiii; Pio Lodi, *Catalogo delle opere musicali: Città di Modena, R. Biblioteca Estense* (Parma, 1923; facsimile repr. Bologna, 1967); and Alessandra Chiarelli, *I codici di musica della raccolta estense. Ricostruzione dall'inventario settecentesco* (Florence, 1987).

[2] Carolyn Gianturco, *Alessandro Stradella (1639–1682): His Life and Music* (Oxford, 1994), pp. 64–5.

in an inventory dated 1755.³ Another substantial collection of Stradella's works – and the largest group of his autograph scores – is housed in the Biblioteca Nazionale Universitaria at Turin (I-Tn). These manuscripts once belonged to the Venetian senator and bibliophile Jacopo Soranzo (1686–1761) and later passed to the Genoese count Giacomo Durazzo (1717–94), sometime director of theatrical performance in Vienna, who purchased them around 1778–80, when he was Imperial ambassador to Venice;⁴ having been divided into two parts in 1895, the collection was reunited in Turin in 1930 and has since been thematically indexed.⁵ Sources of Stradella's music are found also in some fifty other libraries in Europe and the USA.⁶

The phrase 'original Stradella collection' was coined by Owen Jander, who argued that Stradella's surviving autograph music manuscripts belonged to a single collection that had been bound as a matching set in numbered volumes.⁷ He identified ten of the manuscripts today in Turin and one in the Biblioteca Nazionale Marciana, Venice (I-Vnm), as part of this collection. The eleven manuscripts are as follows (the four described as autograph are largely, but not entirely, in Stradella's hand):

---

[3] Elisabeth J. Luin, 'Repertorio dei libri musicali di S. A. S. Francesco II D'Este nell'Archivio di Stato di Modena', *La bibliofilia: Rivista di storia del libro*, 38 (1936): 418–45.

[4] Gianturco, *Alessandro Stradella*, pp. 66–7.

[5] Isabella Fragalà Data and Annarita Colturato, *Biblioteca Nazionale Universitaria di Torino, I: Raccolta Mauro Foà, Raccolta Renzo Giordano* (Rome, 1987); see also Alberto Gentili, 'La raccolta di rarità musicali "Mauro Foà" alla Biblioteca Nazionale di Torino', *Accademie e biblioteche d'Italia*, 1 (1927–28): 36–50; same author, 'La raccolta di antiche musiche "Renzo Giordano" alla Biblioteca Nazionale di Torino', *Accademie e biblioteche d'Italia*, 4 (1930–31), pp. 117–25; Gabriella Gentili Verona, 'Le collezioni Foà e Giordano della Biblioteca Nazionale di Torino', *Accademie e biblioteche d'Italia*, 32 (1964): 405–30; reprinted with English summary in *Vivaldiana*, 1 (1969): 31–56.

[6] See Gianturco and McCrickard, *Catalogue*, pp. 303–11.

[7] Owen Jander (compiler), *Alessandro Stradella (1644–1682)*, Wellesley Edition Cantata Index Series, 4 (Wellesley, MA, 1969), fascicle 4a: Reliable Attributions, pp. 25–31.

Vol. no.	Library and shelfmark	Musical contents[8]
vol. 3	I-Tn, Foà 15	incidental music to *Il Biante*
vol. 4	I-Tn, Foà 12	*Il Damone* (1.4–6)
vol. 10	I-Tn, Giordano 14	*L'accademia d'amore; Lo schiavo liberato*
vol. 11	I-Tn, Foà 14	*Il Damone* (1.4–7) *Vola, vola in altri petti*
vol. 15	I-Tn, Giordano 12	3 sacred cantatas and a trio sonata
vol. 19	I-Vnm, Cod. It. IV. 560 (=9840) (autograph)	6 secular cantatas with instruments, arias, a duet and a trio
vol. 22	I-Tn, Foà 16 (autograph)	opera *La forza dell'amor paterno*
vol. 31	I-Tn, Giordano 11 (autograph)	opera *Moro per amore*
vol. 32	I-Tn, Giordano 13 (autograph)	prologues, intermezzos and an aria
vol. 36	I-Tn, Giordano 10	*Il barcheggio*
vol. 37	I-Tn, Foà 11	sacred cantata *Esule dalle sfere* and instrumental music

Since one of the manuscripts has the figure '37' stamped on its spine, Jander deduced that the set originally comprised at least this number of volumes. He went on to suggest that after Stradella's death his brother sold 'a set of fair copies' of the composer's music to the duke of Modena and sold the 'less legible' autograph manuscripts and performance scores – the 'original Stradella collection' – to 'a collector in Genoa, who valued them sufficiently to have them handsomely bound as a large and impressive set':

> These volumes were all bound in the same shop, presumably at the same time. The style of the bindings is typical of late 17th-century Italian work. Although different colors of morocco are employed, the ornamental work was stamped with the same dies, and the same decorative paper is found on the inside of the covers (a paper made in Augsburg, as is revealed in one of the sheets). Clearly these volumes were all part of the same Seicento library – but whose?[9]

Jander also wondered whether this collector 'was perhaps one of Stradella's Genoese patrons at the time of his death: very possibly Anton Brignole-Sale (but this is mere speculation)' and whether 'some musical enthusiast of the Durazzo family' bought the volumes from him or from one of his descendants.

Jander's remarks stand in need of qualification. To judge from the *Thematic Catalogue* of Stradella's compositions by Gianturco and McCrickard, while it is true that all of the composer's known autograph manuscripts are found in the 'original Stradella collection', they account for less than half of the set: as

---

[8] Numbers in parentheses refer to entries in Gianturco and McCrickard, *Catalogue*; the detailed content of the manuscripts can be reconstructed via the Index of Sources on pp. 303–11.

[9] Jander, *Alessandro Stradella*, p. 25.

Jander observed, most of the music was written by 'several scribes' on 'a great variety of papers of different origins'. Since the scribal and the autograph copies show signs of revision, they may have been intended for performance rather than for a nobleman's library. The well-known librettist Anton Giulio Brignole-Sale (1605–62), marquis of Groppoli, had a grandson named Anton Giulio (II) who was Genoese ambassador to Naples in 1702 and ambassador extraordinary to France in 1704,[10] but even if this is the person whom Jander had in mind, there is no evidence that he or any member of the Brignole-Sale family purchased or owned the 'original Stradella collection'. The decorations on the spines of the volumes are not identical in every respect, but there are many similarities between them, suggesting that the manuscripts were indeed bound in one and the same shop. The inclusion of autograph manuscripts by Stradella could mean that binding took place soon after his death, but it could also indicate that the owner of the 'original Stradella collection' enjoyed a close relationship with the composer.

The origins and history of the surviving Stradella collections have continued to attract attention. David Allen suggested that the composer, when he died, possessed a working collection of his manuscript music, comprising autograph and scribal copies of scores and parts (all of them, probably, unbound or wrapped in temporary covers), and that this was the real 'original' Stradella collection.[11] Maybe this doubtless untidy collection of 'musical compositions' is what Francesco Stradella, acting for his nephew Marc'Antonio, offered to Francesco II of Modena in exchange for 600 doubloons: if so, it is easy to see why the price was considered 'exorbitant'.[12] Allen also suggested that this collection provided the models for the 'Mus. F.' manuscripts at Modena, which were copied and transferred to the ducal library in or soon after 1682,[13] and that the remnants of the same collection formed the basis of Jander's 'original Stradella collection'. According to Allen, this 'Genoa' or 'pre-Durazzo' collection, as he renamed it, resembled a 'complete edition' of Stradella's working materials, comprising those of his manuscripts that were legible and new copies of those that were not. This tidied-up collection was subsequently bound as a substantial series of volumes – of which the surviving bindings suggest that the owner must have valued the music itself, since the quality of the calligraphy was variable. Finally, Allen argued that this 'Genoa' collection was later broken up, that some of the volumes went

---

[10] I am grateful to Michael Talbot for this information.

[11] David Allen, 'The "Lost" Stradella Manuscripts and their Relationship to the Estense Holdings of his Music in Modena', in Carolyn Gianturco (ed.), *Alessandro Stradella e Modena: Atti del Convegno internazionale di studi (Modena, 15–17 dicembre 1983)* (Modena, 1985), pp. 125–35.

[12] Gianturco, *Alessandro Stradella*, p. 64.

[13] On 13 March 1683 the Modenese resident in Genoa, Giovanni Busseti, informed Francesco II by letter that he had posted him some 'libri di musica' that had been given to him by the Genoese nobleman Goffredo Marino, and by 10 April the books had arrived: see Gianturco, *Alessandro Stradella*, p. 65. Maybe they included music by Stradella.

(before 1755) to Modena, where they became the 'Mus. G.' series, and that other volumes were dispersed, some of them eventually being bought by Durazzo.

The suggestion that Stradella possessed a working collection of his own music is supported by a letter of 30 January 1688 to Francesco II from Domenico Bratti, the court organist at Modena. Writing from Genoa, Bratti suggested that the duke might temporarily exchange part of his Stradella collection with part of the collection of Stradella's 'most recondite chamber compositions' that was in the house of Giuseppe Maria Garibaldi, so that both parties could commission copies of works that they lacked; Bratti also stated that 'the originals' were with the man named Domenico ('quel Domenico') whom he had presented to the duke.[14] According to Gianturco, Garibaldi was a Genoese nobleman (died 1700) who had helped to distribute Stradella's possessions to his heirs but must also have colluded with Francesco Stradella in excluding the composer's music from the inventory.[15]

The most extensive discussion of Jander's 'original Stradella collection' (Allen's 'Genoa' collection) is found in Alberto Basso's 'Introduzione' to the Fragalà Data–Colturato catalogue of the Foà and Giordano collections. In addition to the volumes in Turin and Venice, listed above, Basso regarded both the Birmingham manuscript and Genoa, Biblioteca del Conservatorio 'N. Paganini', MS A.7.13 (= B.2.20), as part of this original collection. Like Allen, he was convinced that the Modena MSS Mus. G. 207, 208, 209, 210, 211, 285, 286 and 287 had come from the same collection.[16] But although he gave a fascinating account of Soranzo and of how this part of his collection was eventually bought by Durazzo, Basso could not convincingly explain how the collection passed from Garibaldi to Soranzo. He suggested that Soranzo received it from the Contarini family, to whom he was intimately related by marriage; that the Contarini may have acquired it from Polo Michiel, who was related by marriage to them ('è possibile allora [...]'); and that Michiel had been given it by Garibaldi. These suggestions are supported only by the statement that Michiel had frequently asked Stradella for copies of his music.[17] Now, although Michiel had been a patron and friend of Stradella since the early 1670s, if not before, he died in 1686, by which time some, at least, of Stradella's collection was presumably in the house of Garibaldi.[18]

---

[14] The relevant portion of Bratti's letter is published in Marta Lucchi, 'Stradella e i duchi D'Este: Note in margine a documenti d'archivio e agli inventari estensi', in Gianturco (ed.), *Alessandro Stradella e Modena*, pp. 107–15, at 111. The date of the letter is given in Gianturco, *Alessandro Stradella*, p. 66.

[15] Gianturco, *Alessandro Stradella*, pp. 60 and 64.

[16] Alberto Basso, introduction to Fragalà Data and Colturato, *Biblioteca Nazionale Universitaria di Torino*, pp. lxii, lxiv and lxvi. Basso does not appear to have seen the Birmingham manuscript.

[17] Basso, in Fragalà Data and Colturato, *Biblioteca Nazionale Universitaria di Torino*, p. lxv, based on unpublished letters in Venice, Museo Civico Correr.

[18] For biographical information on Polo Michiel, see Gianturco, *Alessandro Stradella*, pp. 21–2, note 13.

Garibaldi, finally, is the subject of an intriguing remark in Carolyn Gianturco's book on Stradella. As well as suggesting that Garibaldi and Francesco Stradella excluded the composer's music from the inventory of his estate, Gianturco states that 'the two men probably privately divided many more [of Stradella's] belongings among themselves'.[19] The implication seems to be that they also divided up Stradella's collection of music: this interpretation would be compatible with her explanation of how the 'Mus. F.' manuscripts found their way to Modena (via Francesco) and with Allen's suggestion that the working materials in the possession of the composer (and later of Garibaldi) formed the basis of the 'original' Stradella collection. Irrespective of these insights and suggestions, however, the early history of the collection is still rather shrouded in mystery.

* * *

The Birmingham manuscript – Barber Music MS 5019 – was purchased in 1987 from Richard Macnutt.[20] Although its two Stradella pieces have recently been published in a critical edition,[21] the source and its implications have not yet been thoroughly explored. The oblong manuscript is full bound in beautiful red-brown morocco, with gilt tooling on the front and back boards and on the spine. A double rule round the edge of the covers frames a decorative design in the centre and, in each corner, a device featuring human figures, possibly cherubs, playing musical instruments. The spine has five panels, and the decorative device in the corners of these panels is identical to one found in the same place on many of the volumes in Jander's 'original Stradella collection' (see Figure 2.1a).[22] The second panel down on the Birmingham spine bears the gilt numeral '25', indicating that the volume was once part of a set: vol. 25 is one of those regarded as missing from the 'original Stradella collection'. It is true that the Birmingham manuscript lacks the decorative endpapers found in the Turin sources and that it includes music by composers other than Stradella; but the endpapers are absent also from the Venice volume, and sonatas by Arcangelo Corelli and Carlo Mannelli appear together with instrumental music by Stradella in I-Tn, Foà 11. So there seems little reason to doubt that the Birmingham manuscript was vol. 25 in the 'original Stradella collection'.

---

[19] Ibid., p. 64.

[20] [Richard Macnutt], *Catalogue 114: A Small Selection from our Stock of Printed, Manuscript and Autograph Music, Dance & Theatre* (Withyham, Sussex, 1987), entry no. 80.

[21] Colin Timms and Catherine Wyatt (eds), *Alessandro Stradella: Tre Cantate profane con accompagnamento strumentale*, Edizione Nazionale dell'Opera Omnia di Alessandro Stradella, serie I, vol. 13 (Pisa, 2007).

[22] For photographs of the spines of all the volumes in the 'original Stradella collection', see Jander, *Alessandro Stradella*, pp. 28, 29 and 31. The spine of I-Vnm, Cod. It. IV. 560 (= 9840), is reproduced also in Timms and Wyatt (eds), *Alessandro Stradella: Tre Cantate profane con accompagnamento strumentale*.

Figure 2.1　Spines of (a) GB-Bu, Barber Music Library, MS 5019, and (b) I-Tn, MSS Foà 12, Foà 14, Giordano 13 and Foà 11 (by permission, respectively, of Special Collections, Library Services, University of Birmingham, and the Biblioteca Nazionale Universitaria di Torino).

The volume comprises 234 numbered folios of thick, white music paper in oblong quarto format. The leaves, which are gilt-edged, measure approximately 22.4 by 15.9 cm. Two watermarks were noticed by Macnutt: one, consisting of 'a lamb with flag [Paschal Lamb] within a double circle, letters A above, N below', is identical to Heawood 2838, which is found in Rome throughout the third quarter of the seventeenth century (and possibly later than that); the other, comprising 'a fleur-de-lis within a double circle beneath a slender letter G', does not correspond exactly to any of the watermarks illustrated in Heawood or Churchill.[23] Most of the leaves have music on their recto and verso, and the staves and notes are written in jet black ink, typical of Roman music manuscripts of the period.

Although the gatherings of music paper are predominantly in fours, they are not numbered, and the collation of the manuscript is somewhat irregular. Moreover, at the front of the volume there are four additional, unnumbered leaves of inferior-quality paper, of which the recto of f. [i] is stuck to the inside of the cover and thus acts as an endpaper; a list of contents is written on the recto of f. [ii]. A similar gathering is found at the back of the volume, where the verso of the fourth additional leaf (f. [238]v) is glued to the cover and an index appears on f. [235]. The make-up is as follows:

Front 'endpaper' and ff. [ii–iv verso]		1 binio
ff. 1–50v	Stradella, 'serenata' *Chi resiste al dio bendato*	12 binios and 1 bifolio
ff. 51–52v	blank (no staves)	1 bifolio
ff. [53][24]–84v	Stradella, 'serenata' *Lasciate ch'io respiri, ombre gradite*	8 binios
ff. 85–86v	blank (no staves)	1 bifolio
ff. 87–120v	G. B. Vulpio, 'cantata' *Doppo lunga stagione*	8 binios and 1 bifolio
ff. 121–122v	blank (no staves)	1 bifolio
ff. 123–178v	G. Simonelli, 'cantata' *Sotto quest'empie mura*	14 binios
ff. 179–180v	blank (no staves)	1 bifolio
ff. 181–234v	E. Bernabei, 'serenata' *Amor, re de' tiranni*	13 binios and 1 bifolio
ff. [235–238] and final 'endpaper'		1 binio

The blank bifolios appear to have been inserted at the time of binding in order to make clear where one piece ends and the next begins; this would explain why

---

[23] See Edward Heawood, *Watermarks mainly of the 17th and 18th Centuries* (Hilversum, 1950); William Algernon Churchill, *Watermarks in Paper in Holland, England, France, etc., in the XVII and XVIII Centuries and their Interconnection* (Amsterdam, 1935).

[24] Folio 53 is wrongly numbered '52', even though the preceding (blank) folio is also numbered '52'; the sequence is 52, 52, 54.

there is no blank bifolio after the last composition in the book, Bernabei's *Amor, re de' tiranni*. Since these bifolios utilize the same high-quality paper as the music pages, we may conclude that binding took place soon after the music had been copied, and probably in the same city or region.

Most of the pages of music paper have eight staves, ruled apparently by two passes of a four-stave rastrum. An extra stave was added at the foot of f. 137, so that the folio could accommodate three systems of three staves each; although some of the lowest stave (and its music) was cropped by the binder, the score can be reconstructed with little difficulty. Space was left at the beginning of each work for a decorated initial letter – but only in the cantatas by Vulpio and Simonelli was this initial added.

A number of scribes assisted in the preparation of the manuscript. The compositions were written out either by a single hand (A) or, if the music and underlay were copied by different people, by two (A1 and A2); hand A or A2 also wrote the headings above Stradella's *Chi resiste al dio bendato* and Vulpio's *Doppo lunga stagione*. A second (or third) hand (B) was responsible for the list of contents on f. [ii] and the heading of Stradella's *Lasciate ch'io respiri, ombre gradite*, and a third (or fourth) hand (C) added the headings above the items by Simonelli and Bernabei. Once the volume had been bound, it was foliated by a further individual (D), who also compiled the index.

Figure 2.2   Giovanni Battista Vulpio, cantata *Doppo lunga stagione*, beginning of first recitative, GB-Bu, Barber Music Library, MS 5019, f. 91r (by permission of Special Collections, Library Services, University of Birmingham).

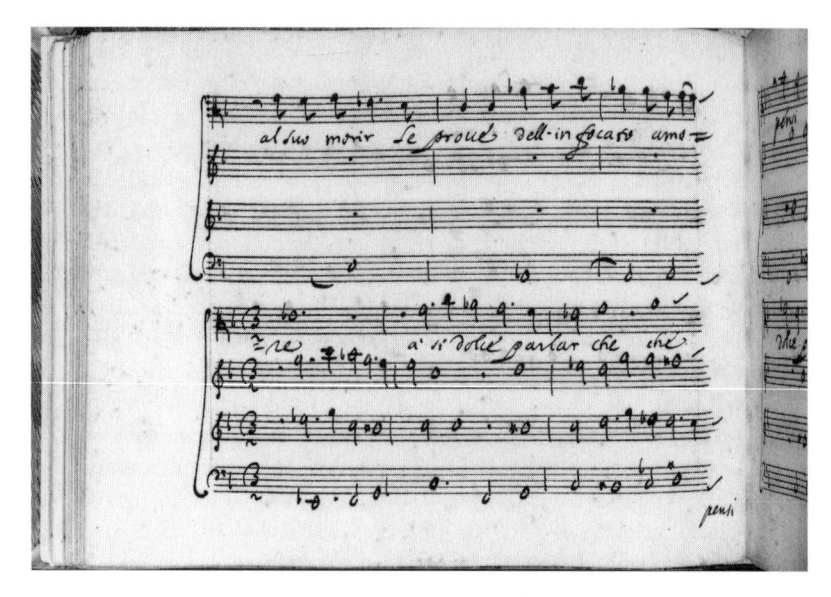

Figure 2.3 Alessandro Stradella, cantata *Da cuspide ferrate* (extract), GB-Cfm, Mu MS 655, f. 32v (by permission of The Fitzwilliam Museum, Cambridge).

Figure 2.4 Alessandro Stradella, opera *Moro per amore*, beginning of Act III, I-Tn, MS Giordano 11, f. 124r (by permission of the Biblioteca Nazionale Universitaria di Torino).

Scribe A (or scribes A1 and A2) appears to have been a fluent exponent of the late seventeenth–century Roman style of musical calligraphy. The hand (see Figure 2.2) is virtually indistinguishable from that of Jander's 'Roman Scribe C', who copied the principal manuscripts of Stradella's oratorio *San Giovanni Battista* (1675: I-MOe, Mus. F. 1136) and his large-scale sacred cantata *Esule dalle sfere* (?1680: I-Tn, Giordano 12, ff. 95–149v) and who also made the only surviving copy of another of his sacred cantatas, *Da cuspide ferrate* (GB-Cfm, Mu. MS 655, ff. 17–34: see Figure 2.3).[25] This hand is also very similar to that of a copyist who worked with the composer on a manuscript of his opera *Moro per amore* (I-Tn, Giordano 11: see Figure 2.4). Gianturco suggested that the latter was the composer Vulpio,[26] who was mentioned by Stradella in a letter of 24 May 1681 to the work's librettist, Flavio Orsini, duke of Bracciano: enclosing a score of his setting, the composer asked Orsini to have it copied and to return the original to him by means of Vulpio, who would bring it back from Rome to Genoa.[27] If Vulpio was also the copyist of the Birmingham manuscript, this might explain why his cantata and the first of the Stradella serenatas are the only works in the volume that are ascribed to a composer by the main copyist (A or A2).

Special interest attaches also to the identity of hand B. In the list of contents this scribe attributed the words of Vulpio's *Doppo lunga stagione* and Simonelli's *Sotto quest'empie mura* – the two cantatas with decorated initial letters! – to the duke of Bracciano, the poet and librettist Flavio Orsini:

f. [ii]: List of Contents
Serenata à 3. con Violini
Serenata à 2. con Violini
Del Sig' Aless[andro] Stradella
Cantata à Solo con Violini dell'Abb[ate] Gio[vanni] Batt[ist]a Vulpio
Parole del Sig' Duca di Bracciano
Cantata à 4. p[er] la Vittoria di Vienna del Sig' Giacomo Simonelli

---

[25] For reproductions of pages from these manuscripts, see Jander, *Alessandro Stradella*, p. 65; Eleanor F. McCrickard (ed.), *Alessandro Stradella: Cantate sacre*, Edizione Nazionale dell'Opera Omnia di Alessandro Stradella, series I, vol. 20 (Pisa, 2004), pp. lxxii and lxxiv, respectively; and same author (ed.), *Alessandro Stradella. Esule dalle sfere: A Cantata for the Souls of Purgatory* (Chapel Hill, 1983), title page.

[26] Carolyn Gianturco (ed.), *Alessandro Stradella: Moro per amore*, Edizione Nazionale dell'Opera Omnia di Alessandro Stradella, serie II, vol. 1 (Pisa, 2003), pp. cxiv and 274.

[27] Stradella's letter is given in Italian and English in Gianturco, *Alessandro Stradella*, pp. 295–8. The only other text by Orsini that is known to have been set by Stradella is the prologue *Reggetemi, non posso più* (1666; repeated 1668): see Gianturco, *Alessandro Stradella*, pp. 176–7; Gianturco and McCrickard, *Catalogue*, p. 144. For a brief introduction to Orsini, see Carolyn Gianturco, 'Orsini, Flavio', in Stanley Sadie and Christina Bashford (eds), *The New Grove Dictionary of Opera*, 4 vols (London, 1992), vol. 3, p. 779; and Carolyn Gianturco, 'Introduzione' / 'Introduction' to *Alessandro Stradella: Moro per amore*, pp. v–vi and xvii–xviii.

Parole del Sig.r Duca di Bracciano
con Violini
Serenata à 4. con Violini del Sig.r Ercole Bernabei

The same scribe wrote the ascription to Stradella on the first page of *Lasciate ch'io respiri*. Assuming that these three ascriptions are reliable (and there is no reason to think they are not), scribe B appears to have had inside information about the contributions of Orsini and Stradella and to represent a link between the two men. In his letter to Orsini, Stradella also mentioned a priest with a good hand who had been in Genoa but had recently left the city. Gianturco has suggested that this priest collaborated with the composer on the Turin manuscript of *Moro per amore*[28] and was also the Birmingham scribe B. His identity is presently unknown.

If the physical properties of the manuscript – the paper and the scribal hands – suggest that the volume was copied and assembled in Rome, the names of the composers and librettist imply that its contents were also composed there. While Orsini belonged to one of the oldest and most prominent noble families in the city, all the composers were associated with Rome and probably acquainted personally with one another. Stradella moved there at the age of fourteen, with his mother and brother, and did not leave until February 1677.[29] Vulpio (1630/31–1705) was a papal singer (alto), a friend of Stradella probably from the 1650s and a colleague of his at the Teatro Tordinona in the early 1670s.[30] Bernabei (1622–87) was reported by Francesco Maria Veracini (1690–1768) to have been Stradella's teacher in Rome.[31] From 1653, when Stradella arrived in the city, Bernabei was organist and then *maestro di cappella* of San Luigi dei Francesi, and also *maestro di cappella* at San Giovanni in Laterano (1665–67); in 1672, at the instigation of Queen Christina of Sweden, he was appointed choirmaster of the Cappella Giulia in the Vatican.[32] Giacomo Simonelli was the son of the composer, organist and papal singer Matteo Simonelli (born after 1618; died 1696) and was active himself as an organist and composer in Rome, at the Gesù and at San Giovanni in Laterano.[33]

---

[28] Gianturco (ed.), *Alessandro Stradella: Moro per amore*, p. 272.

[29] For an account of Stradella's career in Rome, see Gianturco, *Alessandro Stradella*, Chapter 2, and same author, 'Stradella, Alessandro', in Stanley Sadie and John Tyrrell (eds), *The New Grove Dictionary of Music and Musicians*, 2nd edn, 29 vols (London, 2001), vol. 24, pp. 451–2.

[30] Gianturco, *Alessandro Stradella*, p. 33.

[31] See ibid., p. 70, and John Walter Hill, *The Life and Works of Francesco Maria Veracini* (Ann Arbor, 1979), p. 81.

[32] Owen Jander with Jean Lionnet, 'Bernabei, (1) Ercole Bernabei', in *The New Grove Dictionary of Music and Musicians*, 2nd edn, vol. 3, p. 423.

[33] Giancarlo Rostirolla, 'La musica nelle istituzioni religiose romane al tempo di Stradella dal Diario n. 93 (1675) della Cappella Pontificia e dalle "Memorie dell'Anno Santo" di R. Caetano, con alcune precisazioni storiche sulla "stagione" di oratori a S. Giovanni dei Fiorentini', in Carolyn Gianturco and Giancarlo Rostirolla (eds), *Atti del*

Given the intersections between the composers' careers, it also seems likely that the pieces in the manuscript were written within the period 1660–85. The date of Simonelli's cantata is implied by its heading and textual content. Entitled 'cantata [...] per la vittoria di Vienna', *Sotto quest'empie mura* was obviously intended to celebrate the Imperial and Christian victory over the Turks at Vienna in 1683.[34] The siege of the city, which had begun on 14 July, was lifted on 12 September, and the cantata was probably written very shortly afterwards. It ends with cries of 'viva Innocenzio' – a reference to Pope Innocent XI, who was to die six years later, on 12 August 1689. Nothing can be said about the date of Vulpio's piece, but Bernabei probably composed his serenata before May 1674, when he left Rome to become Kapellmeister to the Bavarian court at Munich. It also seems likely that Stradella composed his two serenatas before he left Rome in February 1677.

* * *

The Birmingham manuscript prompts further thoughts on the Stradella collection as a whole. Although the volume was clearly part of Jander's 'original Stradella collection', it differs from the other surviving volumes in two important respects. Whereas the volumes in Turin, Venice and Genoa consist overwhelmingly of works by Stradella, which must therefore have been composed before his death on 25 February 1682, the bulk of the Birmingham manuscript is devoted to pieces by other composers, of which Simonelli's cantata cannot have been composed until at least eighteen months later. Thus neither the Birmingham manuscript nor the Simonelli cantata can have belonged to Stradella or have been part of Allen's 'original' Stradella collection. Although it is conceivable that Stradella owned earlier copies of Vulpio's cantata and Bernabei's serenata, there is no reason for believing that he did. The most plausible conclusion, therefore, is that, after his death, Stradella's working collection was augmented by the addition of further items. Maybe it was expanded by Garibaldi: Gianturco states that Garibaldi attempted 'to enlarge his personal collection' of Stradella's music,[35] but she does not say whether he tried to acquire pieces by other composers. Alternatively, maybe Allen's 'original' Stradella collection was amalgamated with another existing collection of similar music to form Jander's 'original Stradella collection', which at some later date was given a uniform binding.

---

convegno 'Alessandro Stradella e il suo tempo' (8–12 settembre 1982), 2 vols [= *Chigiana*, 39, nuova serie, 19 (1982)], vol. 2, p. 796. An organist named 'Simonelli' played in oratorio performances in Rome in 1682 and 1694: see Andreas Liess, 'Materialen zur römischen Musikgeschichte des Seicento: Musikerlisten des Oratorio San Marcello, 1664–1728', *Acta musicologica*, 24 (1957): 137–71, at 160 and 166–7.

[34] On the siege of Vienna, see Kenneth M. Setton, *Venice, Austria, and the Turks in the Seventeenth Century* (Philadelphia, 1991), Chapter 8, especially pp. 260–70.

[35] Gianturco, *Alessandro Stradella*, p. 60.

The second explanation would be irresistibly convincing if it were possible to identify the owner of such an 'existing collection' and the person who had the resulting joint collection bound. Although this collector must have had a special interest in Stradella, the presence in the collection of sonatas by Corelli and Mannelli (1640–97) and of secular vocal pieces by Vulpio, Simonelli and Bernabei suggests that he also was interested in Roman music by composers other than Stradella and that his interest extended at least from the early 1670s to the mid-1680s.[36] Perhaps he himself was a Roman and acquainted with Stradella and his circle. As we have seen, Stradella was in contact with a Roman nobleman in the early 1680s, less than twelve months before he died, and, like Vulpio and Simonelli, composed settings of his verse. Perhaps it was this nobleman, Flavio Orsini, duke of Bracciano, who assembled Jander's 'original Stradella collection'.

According to Crescimbeni, Orsini was 'an incomparable lord in the exercise of every virtue, especially natural philosophy, poetry and music', had a 'partiality' for painting, sculpture and architecture and was a collector of 'pictures, medals, cameos and other precious stones'; above all, he was devoted to poetry, wrote various 'drammi musicali' and had some of them performed in his family theatre.[37] It seems extremely likely, therefore, that Orsini possessed a library that included a quantity of music; indeed, the presence of a bear rampant (Italian 'orso'), the family crest, on the binding of British Library, Hirsch III.1116, an anthology of secular Italian vocal music by Bernabei, Stradella, Francesco Vulpio, Carlo Caproli and Lelio Colista, suggests very strongly that he did. If this is the case, it is also conceivable that he assembled the 'original Stradella collection', in whole or in part. Even if he did, however, he is probably not the person who had it

---

[36] Four of the sonatas in Mannelli's *Sonate a tre*, op. 2 (Rome, 1682) are named after prominent composers associated mainly with Rome (Foggia, 'Melani', Pasquini and Stradella): see Claudio Sartori, *Bibliografia della musica strumentale italiana stampata in Italia fino al 1700* (Florence, 1952), pp. 500–501.

[37] Giovan Mario Crescimbeni (ed.), *Notizie istoriche degli Arcadi morti*, 3 vols (Rome, 1720–21), vol. 3, p. 174: 'Fu Signore incomparabile nell'esercizio d'ogni Virtù, e singolarmente nella Filosofia naturale, Poesia, e Musica [...] Nè, benchè dedito all'acquisto delle scienze più sublimi, si dimenticò egli di riguardare con parzialità le altre men signorili, cioè la Pittura, Scultura, ed Architettura, come attesta il nobilissimo studio di Quadri, di Medaglie, di Cammei, e d'altre gioie preziose, lasciato nella Galleria del suo Palazzo [...] Ma spezialmente mostrossi egli affezionato alla nostra Poesia, nella quale produsse varj Drammi Musicali, de' quali fece rappresentarne alcuni nel suo Teatro dimestico' ('He was an incomparable lord in the exercise of every virtue, especially natural philosophy, poetry and music [...] Nor, although devoted to the acquisition of the most sublime sciences, did he forget to look favourably on the less lordly [accomplishments], that is, painting, sculpture and architecture, as is attested by the most illustrious studio of pictures, medals, cameos and other precious stones left in the gallery of his palace [...] But above all he demonstrated a partiality for our [Italian] poetry, in which he wrote various dramas for music, some of which he had produced in his private theatre').

bound, for if the volumes had been destined for his library, the bindings would presumably have sported a bear.

Another person who must be considered, surprising as this may seem, is Giovanni Battista Vulpio. Vulpio was not only a close friend of Stradella: he also amassed a substantial collection of music and was intimately connected with the Orsini family.[38] Described as a 'musico del Sig. Duca di Bracciano' (i.e., Flavio's father, Ferdinando Orsini) in 1652, Vulpio was a guest of the family in their palace 'a Pasquino' on the Piazza Navona in 1657, moved in with them in 1661 and was reported to be still there after Flavio's death in 1698 (the Lante palace, where the Stradellas were guests from 1653 for at least seven years, was situated close by). Vulpio was also a member of the papal chapel for over 25 years (1656–83), enjoyed a successful career as a freelance singer and composer, bought a house in Rome and inherited a vineyard and house at Bracciano. When he died at Bracciano, on 26 November 1705, he left a collection of approximately two hundred music manuscripts. A list of them, compiled after his death, mentions their valuable bindings, the numbering of the volumes and folios, and the accuracy of the copies. It also includes the names of 43 composers and three poets or librettists, and lists over fifty numbered volumes of music by Stradella, bound in leather, among them *La forza dell'amor paterno*, *Moro per amore* and 'Prologhi e Intermedi'. Since these works correspond to three of Stradella's four surviving autograph manuscripts (which belong to the 'original Stradella collection'), it seems possible that the 'original Stradella collection' formed part of Vulpio's estate. The latter's collection was recatalogued on 22 July 1706 and moved into storage in Rome. What happened to it thereafter is unknown, but perhaps some or all of it passed eventually to Soranzo.

Vulpio must have assembled his collection of music from a variety of sources over a period of time. As a singer, he probably liked to retain a copy of any work that he performed, especially of pieces by Stradella; indeed, he may have been given copies by the composers themselves. Arias by Stradella were clearly in his house in Rome in 1692, when Flavio Lanciani went there and made a copy of them for Cardinal Pietro Ottoboni.[39] Vulpio almost certainly inherited some of his collection from his slightly older brother, the tenor and composer Francesco Vulpio (died 1699), who, like Giovanni Battista, had probably collected his own repertory. It is conceivable, also, that Vulpio was given some of his music manuscripts by Flavio Orsini, who died in 1698. Such a gesture would have accorded with the

---

[38] See Eleonora Simi Bonini, 'Giovanni Battista Vulpio: cantore pontificio, compositore e collezionista', in Patrizia Radicchi and Michael Burden (eds), *Florilegium musicae: Studi in onore di Carolyn Gianturco* (Pisa, 2004), pp. 927–66, esp. pp. 927–39.

[39] See Hans Joachim Marx, 'Die Musik am Hofe Pietro Kardinal Ottobonis unter Arcangelo Corelli', *Analecta musicologica*, 5 (1968): 104–77, at 132–3, item 37: 'Arie del Sig[no]r Stradella copiate in Casa del Sig[no]re Vulpio'.

(possibly rather sycophantic) sketch of Orsini's character given by Crescimbeni.[40] If these suggestions are correct, then some of Vulpio's manuscripts may have come directly from Stradella and other composers of the period, while others may have passed through the hands of Francesco Vulpio or Flavio Orsini. Vulpio may also have been the person who eventually had the collection bound – which would explain why the surviving volumes display no bear.

* * *

The contents of the Birmingham manuscript give a confusing impression of the serenata as a genre. The three works in the volume that are described as serenatas call for instruments in addition to basso continuo, but so, too, do the pair of so-called cantatas. The serenatas are for three, two and four voices, respectively, the cantatas for one and four. While the words of the solo cantata by Vulpio are a monologue, those of Simonelli's cantata and of the three serenatas involve two or more characters, and in all but one of these pieces (the serenata *Chi resiste al dio bendato*) the characters are expressly identified. These four works recall Aristotle's conception of the dramatic: a kind of poetry in which characters address each other in direct speech without narration.[41] The Simonelli cantata is an occasional piece, but this does not appear to be true of the other works in the manuscript.

---

[40] Crescimbeni (ed.), *Notizie istoriche degli Arcadi morti*, p. 174: 'Per ultimo non dee tacersi la singolar prudenza di lui nell'operare, la destrezza nel maneggio degli affari più rilevanti, la dolcezza del costume, l'affabilità nel tratto, e sopra tutto l'incomparabile sua fortezza, e costanza d'animo' ('Finally, we must not pass over the singular prudence of his behaviour, the skill with which he managed the most difficult affairs, the gentility of his bearing, his affability of manner and, above all, his incomparable strength and constancy of spirit'). A rather different portrait was painted by Pompeo Litta and others, *Famiglie celebri italiane*, 13 vols (Milan, 1819–74), vol. 7 (1844), f. 63, Tavola XXIX: 'Ricco di titoli, ricco d'onori, la sua casa [Orsini] era una corte da sovrano, e l'esservi ammesso si riputava una distinzione. Non aveva però alcun merito personale, anzi modello d'indolenza e di trascuratezza, e non avendo mai servito lo stato, spendendo molto, e non entrando mai capitali in casa, finì la famiglia più qualificata degli Orsini a decadere, e si spense. I debiti erano eccessivi, e si dovette vendere' ('Rich in titles, rich in honours, his [Orsini's] house was like a sovereign's court; to be admitted was considered a distinction. But he was devoid of any personal merit – indeed, a model of indolence and carelessness. Having never served the state, spending heavily with never a penny coming into the house, the most distinguished family of Orsini fell into decadence and spent itself. The debts were excessive, and they had to sell up'). Bracciano was sold in 1697 to the Odescalchi.

[41] Aristotle, *Poetics*, ed. and trans. Stephen Halliwell (Chapel Hill, 1987), p. 33: 'Beside the two already cited [media and objects], there is a third distinction: namely, the mode in which various objects are represented. For it is possible to use the same media to offer mimesis of the same objects in any one of three ways: first, by alternation between narrative and dramatic impersonation (as in Homeric poetry); second, by employing

In view of these somewhat contradictory factors, the volume inevitably poses the question: when is a cantata a serenata? The simplest answer to this question is: when it is performed outdoors, for the word 'serenata' derives from the Italian noun 'sereno', meaning a clear or starlit sky. In 1691 the situation was summarized as follows:

> When a serenata is for solo voice, it does not differ from a cantata, except in that it is called a serenata because foolish lovers sing it under a clear sky – although when it rains, they may sometimes place themselves under arches. It is often written, also, for more than one [voice], *i.e.*, for two, three, four, five or as many as the poet likes. The serenata by me, mentioned above, is for five interlocutors, *viz*. Disdain, Love, Hope, Sleep and A Lover, so it is larger than an ordinary serenata. But it is common for cantatas, also, to be written in dialogue and to be extended [works]. Wherefore, recognizing that it [a serenata] can be classified as a cantata, we shall leave it.[42]

So a late seventeenth-century serenata was a piece of vocal music performed *al fresco*, possibly in the calm of the evening, on land (often in a courtyard, square or garden) or on water, sometimes with the aid of artificial light.

The definition of the genre was gradually sharpened, however, by the accretion over time of additional features required or prompted by the practice of outdoor performance. The most important of these was the use of instruments other than continuo to generate the volume of sound required to enable the music to be heard. Since neither solo instrumentalists nor orchestral musicians came cheap, the expense of engaging them was justified by ensuring that a serenata was a substantial composition. And since a solo vocalist could not perform for a substantial period of time without taking a rest, it became normal for a serenata to be conceived for two, three, four or more singers and for the poetical text to be cast in the dramatic mode. Singers, also, could command astronomical fees,

---

the voice of narrative without variation; third, by a wholly dramatic presentation of the agents'.

[42] Giuseppe Gaetano Salvadori, *La poetica toscana all'uso* (Naples, 1691), Chapter 9, cited in Paolo Fabbri, 'Riflessioni teoriche sul teatro per musica nel Seicento: "La poetica toscana all'uso" di Giuseppe Gaetano Salvadori', in Gianfranco Folena, Maria Teresa Muraro and Giovanni Morelli (eds), *Opera & Libretto. I* (Florence, 1990), pp. 1–32, at 29–30: 'Quando la serenata si fa a solo, non è differente da una cantata, se non che si chiama serenata, perché i folli amanti la cantano a cielo sereno, benché quando piove talvolta si pongano sotto le volte. Suole adunque farsi a più, cioè a due, tre, quattro, cinque e quanto piace al poeta. La mia serenata sopra addotta è a cinque interlocutori, cioè Sdegno, Amore, Speranza, Sonno, Amante. Allora è più che una serenata ordinaria. Ma anche le cantate sogliono farsi in dialogi et esser lunghe. Donde conoscendo potersi collocare tra le cantate, la lasceremo'. See also Michael Talbot, 'Serenata', in *The New Grove Dictionary of Music and Musicians*, 2nd edn, vol. 23, pp. 113–15, and same author, 'The Serenata in Eighteenth-Century Venice', *R. M. A. Research Chronicle*, 18 (1982): 1–50.

so a serenata performance could be an extremely expensive undertaking. For this reason, among others, serenatas were normally commissioned *ad hoc* by wealthy or aristocratic patrons to celebrate a special occasion such as a wedding, birthday, victory or state visit.

The serenata acquired its most characteristic features during the later seventeenth and early eighteenth centuries. It was cultivated mainly in Italy and at Catholic courts in Austria and Germany. At court it was normally given a private performance before an invited audience, although if passers-by stopped to watch or listen, the performance could become a semi-public event. As a court entertainment a serenata could be part of a longer and more elaborate celebration that might also comprise a banquet, ball, religious service, play or opera. The importance of the occasion being celebrated was reflected in the scale of the serenata and its performance – the number of singers or characters involved and the size of the accompanying ensemble. The plot is less likely to have been a story or an intrigue, as in an opera, than a debate about the relative merits of, say, beauty and virtue, or a contest between Mars and Venus. The characters are not historical but allegorical or mythical: the librettos are peopled by personifications, pastoral figures, gods and demigods; and in the interests of balance and decorum the participants are usually given the same number of closed movements to sing. In these respects, and in its frequent moralizing purpose and (eventually) bipartite structure, the serenata was the secular equivalent of the contemporary oratorio. Like opera, it was often performed in costume and with scenery or a backdrop, but the singers did not necessarily come and go, or act; as in a chamber cantata, they usually sang from a book. The serenata was thus a distinctive genre that shared features with oratorio, opera and cantata.

Since the earliest examples of such serenatas (cited by Talbot) date from the 1660s, those of Stradella and his contemporaries belong to the first and second decades of the genre's history and for this reason occasionally lack one or more of the features mentioned above. Most of Stradella's serenatas are known or assumed to have been composed in Rome before February 1677, although *Sciogliete in dolci nodi* and *Se del pianeta ardente* were written in Turin and *Il barcheggio* was created for Genoa in 1681.[43] The serenatas by him in the Birmingham manuscript are discussed in the introduction to the recent critical edition,[44] so attention is focused here on the other three works in the volume.

Perhaps the most pressing question, in the context of this chapter, is why Simonelli's *Sotto quest'empie mura* is designated a cantata rather than a serenata. It is, after all, an occasional work on a large scale, scored for several singers and instruments. The answer seems to lie in the nature of the poetical text. The guiding principles are illustrated by the texts of the other two works. Bernabei's serenata, which likewise is scored for several singers and instruments, is based on

---

[43] See Gianturco and McCrickard, *Catalogue*, pp. 67–105.

[44] Timms and Wyatt (eds), *Alessandro Stradella: Tre Cantate profane con accompagnamento strumentale*.

a dialogue between Cupid and three Lovers, who launch the work by denouncing the god as a pitiless tyrant. Lover 1 is unhappy because his affection goes unrequited; Lover 2 advises that the only remedy is disdain ('sdegno'); to which Lover 3 replies that this merely fuels Cupid's fire: the only answer is to suffer. The scene is thus set for an extended dialogue between Lover 1, who has the largest role, and Cupid himself. While the Lover bemoans his suffering and despairs of finding happiness, Cupid repeatedly urges hope. In a concluding ensemble all the participants caution that there is 'no gain without pain'. The essential point about this text, however, is that it is dramatic in the sense that the characters address each other: this is the reason, presumably, why the work is designated a serenata.

The text of Vulpio's cantata, by contrast, is a lyrical monologue. It is not dramatic in any sense, and it does not include any dialogue. The subject-matter, again, is unrequited love, but the emotional effusion is delivered entirely by the lover himself. In both of these respects the text is wholly characteristic of the secular Italian chamber cantata in the seventeenth and early eighteenth centuries and amply justifies the copyist's decision to identify the setting as an example of that genre.

The text of Simonelli's *Sotto quest'empie mura* differs in kind from those of Bernabei's serenata and Vulpio's cantata. Prompted by the victory at Vienna, it paints a picture of the final battle of the siege, from preparation to engagement and aftermath. There are two principal characters – the Grand Vizier ('Primo Visir') and Count Ernst Rüdiger von Starhemberg ('Starembergh'), the leaders of the Turkish and Imperial armies, respectively; these characters are supported by choruses of their troops. The first person to speak – or sing! – is the Vizier, who hopes for victory and the end of the Austrian empire:

Sotto quest'empie mura […]	Under these impious walls […],
spero con le mie schiere	baptized in blood,
sì gloriose e forti,	I hope, with my troops
di sangue battezzato,	so glorious and strong,
tutta l'Austria inondar fra stragi e morti.	to engulf all Austria in slaughter and death.
Oggi fia ch'estinta cada	Today let this proud imperial residence
questa reggia così altera […]	fall and die […]

In his first utterance Starhemberg hopes for military assistance from the pope, which arrives in due course:

[…] Ma del roman pastore, che qual Argo fedel veglia al suo gregge, spero aita e soccorso: in lui confido perché cada svenato il duce infido […] Ma già di schiere elette Leopoldo assistito dell'Innocenza in Vatican trionfante […]	[…] But I am hoping for aid and succour from the Roman shepherd, who guards his flock like faithful Argus: in him I trust, so that the infidel leader will fall and die […] But now, [Emperor] Leopold is assisted by the crack troops of [Pope] Innocent [XI], triumphant in the Vatican […]

Both leaders exhort their men to combat, and the battle is portrayed in a chorus. When Starhemberg sees the Turkish army flee, his troops rejoice, and in a concluding chorus the victors, including the pope, are praised.

Although the text consists of words uttered by principals and choruses, there is no real dialogue among them: the characters do not address each other but speak, as it were, in parallel. In the absence of dialogue, there is no real drama either – only action, excitement and the narration of events (the fact that narration is delivered by the participants, not by an 'external' *Testo*, does not change the situation). And the absence of dialogue and drama is presumably the reason why the work is not described as a serenata. *Sotto quest'empie mura* is hardly typical of the seventeenth-century cantata, but it is difficult to think of any other word that could then have been used to describe it. Indeed, the piece is rather more reminiscent of the late eighteenth and early nineteenth centuries, when 'the term "cantata" seems to have been particularly favoured for commemorative or occasional works on a fairly large scale and with a strong sense of public involvement' – such as Beethoven's *Der glorreiche Augenblick* (for the Congress of Vienna, 1814).[45]

The music of *Sotto quest'empie mura* comprises five arias, two duets, four choruses, two sinfonias and seven portions of recitative (see Table 2.1). It is scored for two soloists, a four-part choir (soprano, alto, tenor and bass), two violins and continuo; a trumpet is added for the sinfonia following the first chorus because that instrument is mentioned in the text,[46] and is used again in the last three choruses. The part of the victorious Starhemberg (soprano) was presumably sung by a castrato, while that of the defeated Vizier was taken by a villainous bass. In 'Si che benigne arrisero' Starhemberg needs a top b'' (more than once); in 'Oggi fia ch'estinta cada' the Vizier covers two octaves in the space of five crotchets. As one might expect, Starhemberg has the larger part – three arias as against two, and much more recitative. Each of the principals begins with an introductory aria preceded by a

---

[45] Malcolm Boyd, 'The Cantata since 1800', in *The New Grove Dictionary of Music and Musicians*, 2nd edn, vol. 5, pp. 40–41, at p. 40.

[46] 'Nobil fama già rimbomba / al fulgor delle nostr'armi, / dian terrore invitti carmi / al sonar di nostra tromba.' (Already noble fame resounds / to the splendour of our arms; / may our invincible songs strike terror / at the sound of our trumpet.)

recitative with cavata;[47] none of the subsequent recitatives, however, ends with a cavata. The Vizier's introductory 'Oggi fia ch'estinta cada' is the only aria in the work in 3/4 time, and the only one accompanied by continuo alone – although the violins do contribute a ritornello after each of the two strophes. All the other arias are in common time and accompanied by violins as well as continuo. Triple time reappears in the first duet ('A ribatter/reprimer l'empio orgoglio') and the second chorus ('Si affronti, si assaglia'), and the duet is also the only other movement to omit the violins.

Table 2.1   Giacomo Simonelli, cantata *Sotto quest'empie mura*.

Character(s)	Music	Verbal incipit	Metre	Key[48]
—	Sinfonia	—	C	D
Vizier	Recit	Sotto quest'empie mura	C	G
	Aria	Oggi fia ch'estinta cada	3/4	G
Starhemberg	Recit.	Già le ottomane squadre	C	G–a
	Aria	Di tant'armi guerriere all'orrore	C	C
Vizier	Recit.	Di miei guerrieri audaci	C	e–d
[His troops]	Chorus	Nobil fama già rimbomba	C	D
—	Sinfonia	—	C	D
Starhemberg	Recit.	Ma già di schiere elette	C	b–d
	Aria	Quel timore che nel core	C	g
Vizier	Aria	O miei fidi, e che s'aspetta	C	F
Viz./Star.	Duet	A ribatter/reprimer l'empio orgoglio	3/4, C	d
Starhemberg	Recit.	Guerrieri, a voi conviene	C	a–e
Viz./Star.	Duet	Si corra all'assalto	C	a
[All]	Chorus	Si affronti, si assaglia	3/4	D
Starhemberg	Recit.	Ma già nel proprio sangue	C	(e)–D
[His troops]	Chorus	Vittoria, vittoria	C	D
Starhemberg	Aria	Sì che benigne arrisero	C	b
Starhemberg	Recit.	Al Cesare regnante	C	(A)–D
[His troops]	Chorus	Viva, vivan gl'eroi	C	D

[47]   For a brief introduction to the cavata, see Colin Timms, 'Cavata', in *The New Grove Dictionary of Music and Musicians*, 2nd edn, vol. 5, p. 315.

[48]   In all three tables for this chapter major keys are denoted by upper case and minor keys by lower case. Whenever a letter appears in parentheses, the movement begins with the dominant chord of the stated key.

The lack of variety in Simonelli's time signatures and scoring is offset to some extent by his handling of tonality. From this point of view the work's 20 movements may be divided into three roughly equal groups: 1–6, 7–14 and 15–20. The tonic key, D major, is established by the opening Sinfonia and revisited in the first chorus and second Sinfonia (movements 7 and 8), and it achieves dominance in the final third of the work; the structure derives partly from the use of the trumpet. Movements 2–6 and 9–14 explore both related and unrelated keys on the flat side of the tonic, which they reach by a variety of means. Every aria and duet is in a different key; most of these keys are minor, although both of the Vizier's arias are in major keys. His first aria is in G major but includes a surprising modulation to F sharp minor. There are surprises also in Simonelli's handling of rhythm. From the positioning of semiquavers in the bass line of the Vizier's 'O miei fidi, e che s'aspetta' it would appear that the composer liked to create somewhat disconcerting effects (Example 2.1), whereas the first vocal entry in Starhemberg's 'Quel timore che nel core' looks as though it has been misbarred (Example 2.2). *Sotto quest'empie mura* includes other examples of harmonic or rhythmic insecurity, suggesting that Simonelli was not the most accomplished composer of his day.

Example 2.1 Giacomo Simonelli, cantata *Sotto quest'empie mura*, aria 'O miei fidi, e che s'aspetta, bars 1–5.

Example 2.2 Simonelli, cantata *Sotto quest'empie mura*, aria 'Quel timore che nel core', bars 7–12.

The same could not be said of Bernabei, although in *Amor, re de' tiranni* the vocal polyphony barely conceals its roots in the *stile antico*, and the potential of the instruments is hardly exploited at all. The words of the serenata are cast in the form of a substantial series of recitative and aria texts (see Table 2.2), beginning and ending with aria (the basis of the opening and closing ensembles). As was usual in secular Italian vocal music of this period, the recitatives consist of *versi sciolti* employing seven- and eleven-syllable lines, occasionally rhymed, while the arias employ diverse metres and regular rhyme schemes. Most of the aria texts are strophic, but two of them are not, and the musical settings enrich or even disguise the poetical structures.

Table 2.2   Ercole Bernabei, serenata *Amor, re de' tiranni*.

Character(s)	Verse type	Incipit	Key
—	—	[Sinfonia]	C
Lovers 1–3	aria	Amor, re de' tiranni	C
Lover 1	*sciolti*	Notte tacita e bruna	C–c
	aria	Sconsolate pupille	c
Lover 2	*sciolti*	Amante sfortunato	B♭
	aria	Giusto sdegno e nobil ira	B♭
Lover 3	*sciolti*	O troppo audaci e poco saggi amanti	G–D
	aria	Al soffrire, al penare	D
Lover 1	*sciolti*	Dunque chi vive in pene	D–a
	aria	Amor pien d'amarezza	a
Cupid/Lover 1	*sciolti*	Chi temerario e vano	G–C
Cupid	aria	Sulla nave di Speranza	C
Lover 1/Cupid	*sciolti*	Che giova a me d'incenerir col guardo	B♭–G
Cupid	aria	S'un bel guardo ti ferì	G
Lover 1	*sciolti*	Amor, son vinto, hai trionfato, io cedo	C
All	aria	No no no, senza pianti e sospiri	C

In the opening ensemble each of the two strophes is set in four contrasted musical sections, in C, 3/2, C and 3/4 metre, respectively; the sections in C are homophonic in texture, while the others are imitative. 'Sconsolate pupille' begins with a quasi-ostinato bass that is subsequently abandoned; each verse is in C minor but includes a surprising modulation to B flat minor, as well as a recitative setting of its penultimate two lines (the recitative is slightly varied in verse 2). The strophes of 'Giusto sdegno e nobil ira' are divided into two musical sections, each followed by a ritornello. The text of 'Al soffrire, al penare' is a single stanza of six lines, of which the last two are a rhyming couplet of seven and eleven syllables. Lines 1–4 are set in 3/2, line 5 as recitative (in C) and line 6 as a cavata in 3/4; the entire structure is sung first by Lover 3, then by all three Lovers together. A similar rhyming couplet concludes the text of 'Amor pien d'amarezza', which comprises two contrasting stanzas of four and six lines, respectively. The first stanza and the final couplet are set in 3/2, while the bulk of stanza 2 is in C; both stanzas are followed by a similar five-bar ritornello. Three contrasted ritornellos frame the two musical sections into which each strophe of 'Sulla nave di Speranza' is divided in the setting.

The concluding ensemble is an intricate structure, based on six-syllable lines of verse, in which strophes for various of the characters are framed by a refrain for Cupid and Lovers 1 and 2 (and, on its final repeat, Lover 3). The second, third and fourth statements of the refrain are followed by a ritornello, but in the fifth and final statement the instruments enter earlier, accompanying the voices in the closing bars. This is the only place in the work where singers and players are combined. Although the serenata begins and ends in C major, it does not remain in that key. The first recitative ends in C minor, ready for 'Sconsolate pupille', and the next recitative begins in B flat major. Within recitative movements, the explorations are much more adventurous. Perhaps the most striking moment, however, is the B flat opening of Lover 1's recitative 'Che giova a me d'incenerir col guardo' after the C major of Cupid's aria 'Sulla nave di Speranza'. The plunge into a lower and flatter key seems to symbolise Lover 1's desperation, suggesting that Bernabei saw tonality as an affective resource. It is also a reminder that this work is dramatic.

Table 2.3   Giovanni Battista Vulpio, cantata *Doppo lunga stagione*.

Music	Verbal incipit	Metre	Key
Sinfonia	—	C	D
Recit.	Doppo lunga stagione	C	D
Aria	Consigliatemi, pensieri	C, 3/2, C	A
Recit.	Fuggo dal regno infido	C	b–G
Aria	Son miserabile	3/2	G
Recit.	Ma qual magica forza	C	B–D
Aria	Sete voi, pupille amate	C	a
Recit.	Di quante pene, o cieli	C	E–b
Aria[49]	Consigliatemi, pensieri	C	E–D

The text of Vulpio's cantata is a heartfelt lament of an unrequited lover who, tormented both by continual rejection and by his beloved's enticing eyes and lips, looks to his conscience for guidance ('Consigliatemi, pensieri'). The poem includes three arias, each framed by *versi sciolti*, and thus begins and ends with verse for recitative (see Table 2.3). Most of the recitative lines are rhymed (rather unusually), but the rhyme scheme is far from regular. All the arias comprise two quatrains, but only the last is strophic. The quatrains of 'Consigliatemi, pensieri' are composed, respectively, of eight- and six-syllable lines, but the contrast of metre is offset by a linking rhyme (abba/cdda). 'Son miserabile', by contrast,

---

[49] The last line of the preceding recitative ('di due begl'occhi arcieri?') rhymes with 'Consigliatemi, pensieri' and thus prompts a repeat of the aria.

consists of six five- and two (very unusual) nine-syllable lines; the quatrains are thus linked by metre (*quinari sdruccioli*) rather than by rhyme (abab/ccdd).

This interesting text prompts an equally interesting setting, scored for soprano, two instruments [violins] and continuo. The prefatory Sinfonia comprises three sections – a homophonic *Adagio* (not so marked: 4 bars), a fugal *Andante* (14 bars) and a fugal *Allegro* (58 bars). In the *Andante* the contrapuntal texture is confined to the violins, but in the *Allegro* it employs all three parts and diverse kinds of stretto. A single piece of melodic material is the source of the two fugue subjects and also of the first vocal phrase ('Doppo lunga stagione'). At the last line of this recitative ('d'empio fato e d'amor nuove vicende': 'new vicissitudes of impious fate and love') Vulpio brings in the instruments and composes an accompanied cavata followed by a six-bar postlude. 'Consigliatemi, pensieri' comprises three distinct sections. The opening line is set in common time and repeated (in varied form) at the end in the manner of a refrain – a procedure prompted by the rhyme in the text; the rest of the first stanza is set in 3/2, and the whole of the second stanza in C: the structure is therefore ABCA'. As in the opening recitative, the last lines of 'Fuggo dal regno infido' and 'Ma qual magica forza' are set as cavatas-with-postlude, although here the instruments are not used simultaneously with the voice. 'Son miserabile' contains two surprises: although the aria is accompanied only by continuo, the setting of the first quatrain is followed by an eight-bar postlude for the instruments, and the last line of the second quatrain – the exclamation 'Sorte, stelle, destin, pietà!' ('Fate, stars, destiny, have mercy!') – is set as simple recitative. The violins are more prominent in 'Sete voi, pupille amate', but less in combination with the singer than between the vocal phrases; notwithstanding the aria's structure, the passage-work is varied in the second strophe. The final recitative presumably ends with a *tierce de Picardie* to lead smoothly into the repeat of 'Consigliatemi, pensieri', an extended version of the first aria's beginning; this section falls into two halves, one modulating from E major to A, the other from A to D.

The vocal writing in *Doppo lunga stagione* provides ample evidence that the composer of this cantata was also a singer. It is full of idiomatic features, both virtuoso and expressive. In 'Consigliatemi, pensieri' the word 'piagarmi' ('injure me') is set to an extended, decorated cadence, with violins, followed by a slower, chromatic cadenza-like passage for voice and continuo only (Example 2.3). 'Son miserabile' is characterised by ingratiating appoggiaturas, syncopations and dissonances (Example 2.4). Fanfare-like figures appear at appropriate moments throughout. In addition to chromaticism, abrupt changes of chord are used in recitative to draw attention to changes of mood; for example, the first two lines of 'Doppo lunga stagione' are set over a pedal D in the bass, but the third line ('d'amorosa tenzone': 'of amorous combat') is harmonized by chords of F sharp major and B. Although none of the arias is in the tonic key, the cantata is tonally closed.

Doppo lunga stagione is certainly the finest of the three works discussed in this chapter: it would be fitting if its composer, Giovanni Battista Vulpio, could eventually be shown also to have acted as the principal copyist of the Birmingham manuscript or as a major player in the creation of the 'original Stradella collection'.

Example 2.3 Vulpio, cantata *Doppo lunga stagione*, aria 'Consigliatemi, pensieri', bars 71–80.

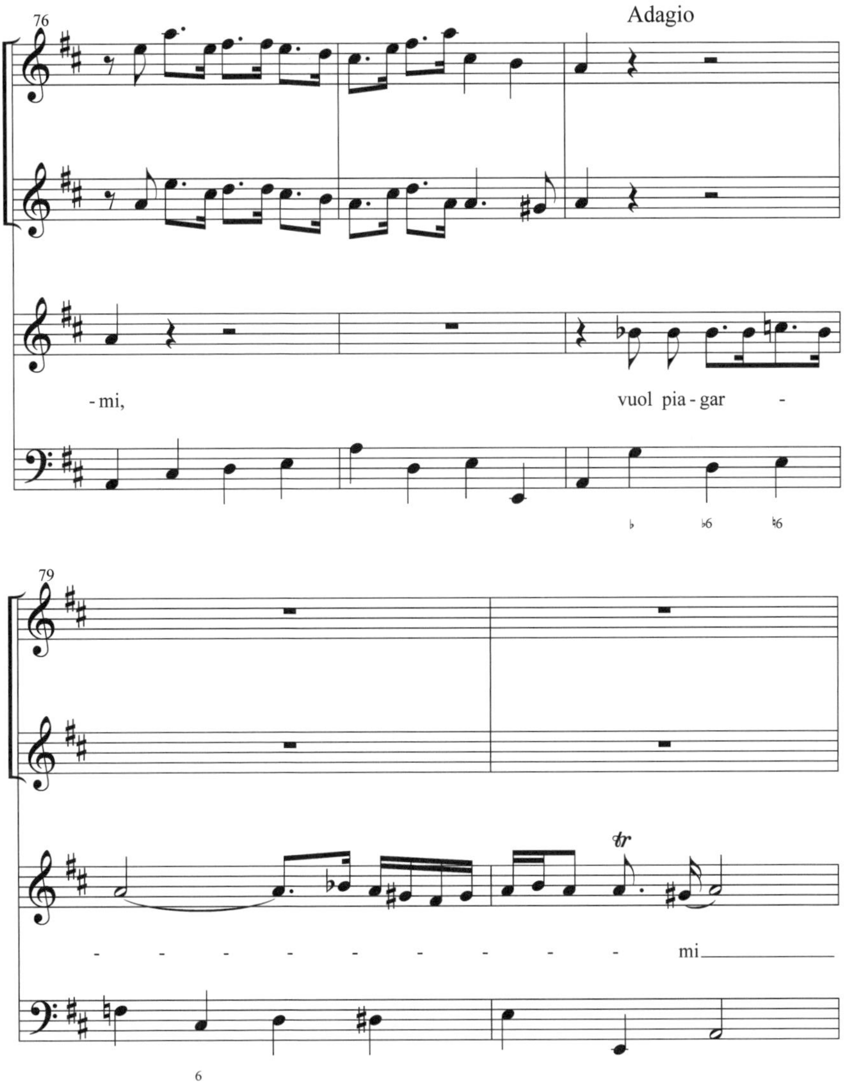
76
Adagio
- mi,
vuol pia - gar -
79
- - - - - - - - - mi

Example 2.4 Vulpio, cantata *Doppo lunga stagione*, aria 'Son miserabile', bars 26–39.

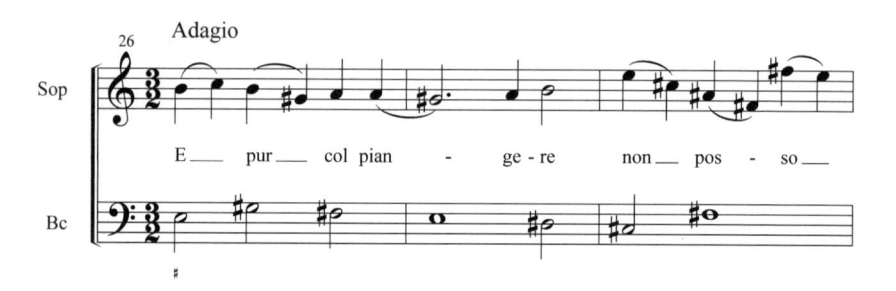

Chapter 3

Narration, Mimesis and the Question of Genre: Dramatic Approaches in Giovanni Legrenzi's Solo Cantatas, Opp. 12 and 14

Hendrik Schulze

Drama, according to Aristotle, is mimesis 'employing the mode of enactment, not narrative' by making use of certain agents, who by their actions, consisting of diction and song, recount a plot.[1] According to this notion, a text or piece of vocal music was essentially dramatic when its plot was entirely driven by the monologues and dialogues of the characters represented; in other words, a drama should consist exclusively of character speech.[2]

Since Aristotle's *Poetics* were taken as the basis of all operatic theory in Italy throughout the entire seventeenth century, librettists and composers drew their idea of what constituted drama directly from these principles – many of them implicitly. But would they apply with equal force to a genre such as the solo cantata, which by definition seems not to fit into the category of drama at all? One would almost intuitively answer in the negative: the genre's reliance on a single singer appears to exclude any possibility of narrating a plot in the form of dialogue, while its designation as chamber music clearly prohibits any use of theatrical devices that might constitute a staging in the sense of the Aristotelian 'enactment'. In the eighteenth century writers such as Johann Adolph Scheibe acknowledged what they saw as an inherent lack of drama in cantatas in their theoretical writings.[3]

---

[1] Aristotle, *Poetics*, ed. and trans. Stephen Halliwell (Cambridge, MA, 1999), Part VI, pp. 46–7.

[2] I use the phrase 'character speech' as a technical term denoting direct speech placed in the mouth of an identifiable character. It differs from 'direct speech' in general in that it refers only to speeches within an enactment; the speakers are agents representing specific characters. In contrast, 'direct speech', as used, for instance, in epic, has the quality of a citation, and as such, in order to have mimetic qualities, neither relies on a specific speaker nor needs to be part of an enactment.

[3] Johann Adolph Scheibe, *Critischer Musikus. Neue, vermehrte und verbesserte Auflage* (Leipzig, 1745), pp. 381–2; see Colin Timms, 'The Dramatic in Vivaldi's Cantatas', in Lorenzo Bianconi and Giovanni Morelli (eds), *Antonio Vivaldi. Teatro musicale, cultura e società* (Florence, 1982), pp. 97–129, at pp. 101–104.

During the seventeenth century, however, the problem was not reflected upon from a theoretical standpoint, at least not in Italy.

On the other hand, as Colin Timms points out, commentators have always remarked on the similarities between cantata and opera.[4] These comprise not just the formal parallels between the two genres, which by the late seventeenth century were alike dominated by a clear distinction between recitative and aria, the latter preferably cast in *da capo* form. Writers have frequently noted the similarity in the mode of narration, which Eugen Schmitz terms 'dramatisch' or representative (in the sense of *rappresentativo*).[5] In the case of Cavalli, Schmitz even states that some of the scenes in this composer's early operas could successfully be removed from their operatic context and pass as self-sufficient cantatas.[6] His judgements, however, seem to be based upon twentieth-century ideas of representation, and his treatment of the terms 'operatic' and 'dramatic' as synonymous is highly questionable. It is therefore necessary to distinguish a number of dramatic strategies used in solo cantata and opera and to compare them. These include: modes of embodiment or staging; verisimilitude or (to use the more appropriate Italian term) *verosimiglianza*; the distinction between narrative, monologue and dialogue; a dramaturgy of aria; and the mixing of comic, pastoral and tragic styles that is a distinguishing feature of seventeenth-century opera, as opposed to spoken drama.

The solo cantatas of Giovanni Legrenzi provide a good example of the ways in which a number of these strategies could be employed within the domain of the cantata. His collections *Cantate, e canzonette a voce sola*, Op. 12,[7] and *Ecchi di riverenza di cantate, e canzoni*, Op. 14,[8] were printed in Bologna in 1676 and 1678, respectively. Their publication thus coincides with a period during which the composer was involved in a number of operatic projects in his city of residence, Venice. The opera *Totila*, composed on a libretto by Matteo Noris and first performed in Venice in 1677, can therefore serve as a point of comparison – all the more so because it opens with a solo *scena* that displays all the formal aspects of recitative and aria that are be found equally in Legrenzi's solo cantatas.[9]

---

[4] Timms, 'The Dramatic in Vivaldi's Cantatas', pp. 122–4.

[5] Eugen Schmitz, *Geschichte der weltlichen Solokantate* (Leipzig, 1955), p. 64.

[6] Ibid., p. 115.

[7] Francesco Passadore and Franco Rossi, *La sottigliezza dell'intendimento. Catalogo tematico di Giovanni Legrenzi* (Venice, 2002): no. 58. Modern edition: *Giovanni Legrenzi, Cantatas and Canzonets for Solo Voice*, ed. Albert Seay (Madison, WI, 1972).

[8] Passadore and Rossi, *Catalogo*, no. 60. Published in facsimile as: *Giovanni Legrenzi, Echi di riverenza di cantate e canzoni, Bologna 1678*, ed. Piero Mioli (Florence, 1980); David Burrows and Stephen Bonta (eds), *Cantatas by Antonio Cesti and Giovanni Legrenzi* (New York, 1986).

[9] Passadore and Rossi, *Catalogo*, no. 17. Score published in facsimile as: *Giovanni Legrenzi/Matteo Noris, Totila*, ed. Howard Mayer Brown (New York and London, 1978).

Staging and embodiment

From its designation as a chamber genre, it follows that the solo cantata cannot employ even the simplest modes of enactment, embodiment and staging that are proper to opera. In operatic texts, these features are usually confirmed by stage directions, as at the start of the first scene of *Totila*, where the score describes the setting as 'Clelia con pugnale alla mano in atto di svenare il proprio figlio'[10] ('Clelia with a dagger in her hand, in the act of killing her son'). The use of the term 'in atto' is very telling, for although this may be perceived as an (albeit not very common) way, in Italian, of indicating the present continuous tense, it likewise refers directly to the generic form of narration via action. It is simple, even for someone unfamiliar with any particular stage production of this opera, to picture the character of Clelia, her hand raised above her head, ready to stab the little bundle that represents her child. In any case, this opening of the opera is already 'dramatic' in the Aristotelian sense by virtue of the action-based nature of the first moment. One would surmise that no further words are needed to set the scene.

Interestingly, though, this assumption turns out to be false. The character Clelia is given the following text as her first words: 'Figlio, sul molle seno | già pende il ferro; ecco t'uccido e sveno' ('Son, over your tender breast already hangs the dagger; behold, I kill you, I murder you'). The authors of the opera evidently felt that a verbal description of the physical action was needed. Where a nineteenth-century librettist would first try to set the scene by portraying the psychological state of the heroine, Noris and Legrenzi are eager to absorb the physical aspects of the scene into the soliloquy of the character depicted on stage, employing a technique that seems almost akin to epic strategies of narration.

Clelia's second sentence appears to be more in line with the genuinely dramatic, for it addresses her inner feelings: 'Clelia, che tenti, o stelle [...]' ('Clelia, what are you attempting? O ye stars [...]'); but, again, a certain amount of authorial content (i.e., information from the author directed at the audience, as opposed to information deriving from the character) is present in this passage of direct speech. Her addressing herself by name in the second person serves not only to heighten the pathos of her words but also to reveal her identity to the audience; it thus conveys the one piece of information contained in the stage directions that has not yet been passed on to the audience. So Noris and Legrenzi squeeze all the relevant information about the situation on stage into the first two sentences spoken by the character: the specific nature of the action being performed in this sequence and the name of the principal agent concerned. In contrast, no information is conveyed about the space in which the scene takes place – a fact consistent with the score, where no locale is mentioned, either.[11] As the remainder of that scene reveals, the space is not important to the plot; hence the omission of this information in

---

[10] Ibid., f. 2r.
[11] Interestingly, the printed libretto describes the scene: Matteo Noris, *Totila* (Venice, 1677), p. 11.

Clelia's speech does not render the authorial information contained in the first two sentences spoken incomplete in a dramatic sense.

It can be argued that this technique of introducing a situation on stage and a character in fact derives from the epic, for it is found right from the earliest years of Venetian opera, when epic models of narration were actively discussed and employed by such librettists as Giacomo Badoaro and Gian Francesco Busenello.[12] In these operas virtually nothing happens on stage that is not at the same time described and evaluated via character speech. Even though other librettists such as Giovanni Faustini and Nicolò Minato (no doubt by agreement with the composers of the operas) did away with most of the instances where such verbal descriptions were introduced in favour of more dramatic ways of introducing sets and subjects,[13] the mode of introduction via descriptions placed in the mouths of characters remained a well-established and much-used technique. In the opera *Artemisia* by Nicolò Minato and Francesco Cavalli, for instance, several changes of stage set as well as some actions confined to the extras are introduced by arias commenting on their distinctive features and sung by a character who seems to have been introduced into the opera almost entirely for that single purpose.[14]

In *Totila*, however, this technique is used more openly and artlessly than in most of the Venetian operatic repertoire from the mid-1640s onwards, where characters and settings are introduced chiefly in the course of dialogue (which makes the identification of both the characters' names and their role in the action narrated much easier). But Noris and Legrenzi chose to begin their drama with a solo scene, which, with its presentation of the character's intense emotional dilemma, is very well designed to capture the audience's attention. The price that they apparently felt they had to pay was the large amount of authorial content that they had to include in the first lines spoken; obviously, they did not trust the ability of the audience to grasp readily what was going on without the additional authorial information supplied in the recitative. Despite all the mimetic and stage techniques available to opera, they therefore found themselves, when opening their drama, in a similar situation to the author of a solo cantata, needing to convey the same kind of authorial content to the audience.

In many of Legrenzi's solo cantatas, the problem of introducing the setting is solved by resorting to simple description by a narrator 'standing in' for the author. The Cantata Op. 12 no. 13, *Ad altro amante in seno*,[15] for example, commences with a five-line description of the setting and the relationship of the characters involved:

---

[12] See Norbert Dubowy, 'Bemerkungen zu einigen Ulisse-Opern', in Silke Leopold and Joachim Steinheuer (eds), *Claudio Monteverdi und die Folgen* (Kassel, 1998), pp. 215–43, at pp. 225–6; Silke Leopold, *Die Oper im 17. Jahrhundert* (Laaber, 2004), pp. 134–5.

[13] These techniques include modes of verbal representation through dialogues, as well as musical representations by use of certain musical figures with emblematic or metaphoric qualities.

[14] Nicolò Minato/Francesco Cavalli, *Artemisia* (Venice, 1657); cf. scenes I.1; I.10; II.5.

[15] Passadore and Rossi, *Catalogo*, no. 58: 13.

Ad altro amante in seno,	To the embrace of another lover
ir notturna e furtiva scorse Alinda;	went at night, and with furtive gazes, Alinda;
Fileno s'impalidì,	Fileno grew pale
gelò tra suoi martiri.	and then, frozen in his agonies,
Questi poscia esalò mesti sospiri:	uttered these sad sighs:
'Ahi che veggio? Ahi che miro?	'Woe is me, what do I see? What do I behold?

One can readily see why Reinmar Emans calls this technique 'epic':[16] the entire passage opens as a piece of authorial speech; it is the author of the text who personally narrates the circumstances leading up to the little scene that follows. Extended use of rhetorical figures such as chiasmus – expressed by the fourfold sequence action–name–name–reaction (furtive departure–Alinda–Fileno–sad sighs), which is how the first five lines are organized – appears to establish firmly the literary aspects of this passage through the way in which it uses this formal device to suggest the difference in personality and affect between the two characters.[17] As a result of this epic technique of narration, Fileno's lament assumes the nature of a quotation within the author's account rather than those of a character's speech. At the level of the text, no embodiment occurs, the perspective remaining always that of the narrator. The text is accordingly void of any dramatic intent.

However, Legrenzi's setting (see Example 3.1) establishes, at least in partial guise, a sense of genuine drama. Via a process that can be described only as staging, he takes advantage of the chiasmus and its positioning of the names of the two characters involved. Where, in the text, the juxtaposition created by the chiasmus sets the two characters apart from each other by much more than just the end of a line, Legrenzi's composition almost forcibly rejoins them; instead of the customary pause that translates the (anonymous) poet's line-division into its musical equivalent, the word 'Fileno' is linked seamlessly to the preceding 'Alinda' (bars 4–5). The protagonists are thus visibly (for the reader of the music)[18] and audibly (for the listener) brought together as a couple, as if they were being presented on stage.

---

[16] Reinmar Emans, *Die einstimmigen Kantaten, Canzonetten und Serenaden Giovanni Legrenzis* (Bonn, 1984), p. 349.

[17] The recounting of Alinda's actions before even revealing her name establishes her as the strong, active partner in the plot, while Fileno's reaction, the report of which is delayed both by the mention of his name and by the description of his frame of mind, identifies him as weak and passive. Thus the two characters are juxtaposed as total opposites.

[18] In a genre such as the solo cantata, which is basically *published* music (as opposed to *public* music, such as opera), even the mere visual appearance of the music has a performative quality, since its intended primary recipient is not just a passive group of spectators but the performers themselves, who thus become part of the audience.

Example 3.1   Legrenzi, cantata *Ad altro amante in seno*, bars 1–14.

Despite the similarities of the epic technique of verbally introducing characters and their names in *Ad altro amante in seno* and *Totila*, there are striking differences in the approach taken: Legrenzi's musical device for linking the names of Alinda and Fileno is an effect quite unnecessary in an opera such as *Totila*, where Clelia and her son are actually visible on stage but need to be named and to have their social relationship defined – hence the injection of authorial content into the character's words. The device as used in *Ad altro amante in seno* is clearly dramatic, since by means of unalloyed authorial narration it constructs a virtual scene that, without any problems, can support narration by character speech. But it is not in the least *theatrical*: it is a different mode of mimesis: one based more on virtual staging than on actual enactment.

As his second task, Legrenzi has accordingly to ensure that what follows the introduction can in fact be perceived as character speech – again, something quite unnecessary in opera. He achieves this end by means of two different techniques. At a textual level, he repeats the expletive 'ahi' (bars 10–11) on a higher note of the chord, thereby creating the naturalistic impression of a person's rising consciousness of spiritual agony. In order to ensure that this is not perceived as a purely poetic form of mimesis common to epic and drama alike, Legrenzi, at a musical level, has recourse to a tonal effect by moving from a chord of D minor at the end of the authorial introduction to one of E major at the point where direct speech takes over. This not only represents a change in tonality (which turns out to be merely a rather simple shift from D minor to the closely related A minor), but, more importantly, it alters the underlying hexachord from one with two flats,[19] emphasized by the E♭ in bar 8, to the natural hexachord, expressed by both the E major chord in bar 10 and the Phrygian cadence on the note E in bars 13–14. This device is one that in the contemporary operas is often used to connote stark contrasts of affect, setting or perspective – most frequently, on the word 'ma' ('but'). In the context of the solo cantata, this hiatus ensures that the singer – who up to that point has embodied the voice of the author – is now perceived as embodying the voice of the character. The musical narration switches from the epic to the dramatic mode, in which it will remain until the end of the cantata. Once again, Legrenzi has used a device familiar to opera in a way that differs from its application there; it has become a dramatic instrument peculiar to the solo cantata.

Verosimiglianza and dialogue

A further aspect of drama that is central to seventeenth-century Venetian aesthetics is the concept of *verosimiglianza*. It has to be pointed out that this is a concept with application not only to drama but equally to other forms of narrative, such as epic, romance and even historiography. In the consideration of dramatic approaches to the solo cantata, it therefore suffices to concentrate on the one purely dramatic aspect of the concept of *verosimiglianza*, which is the naturalistic imitation of speech. In Legrenzi's operas this is the main characteristic of recitative, where the composer seeks to achieve a precarious balance between mimesis of speech and expression of affect. In this task he is aided by the librettist, whose *versi sciolti* are designed to produce a feeling of a less metrically organized, and thus less poetically contrived, language. Matteo Noris's particular invention in this regard is a cross-talk technique of very short (sub-sentence-length) interventions

---

[19] I have coined for this hexachord the description 'bismolle', for lack of a better term (Hendrik Schulze, *Odysseus in Venedig. Sujetwahl und Rollenkonzeption in der venezianischen Oper des 17. Jahrhunderts* (Frankfurt, 2004), p. 91).

by different characters in dialogues that he uses to create an image of a group of people all talking at the same time.[20] Even though the technique is clearly intended to create a comic effect, Noris uses it in serious contexts as well, as Scene 11 of Act I of *Totila* demonstrates: the servant Desbo tries to inform his master Publicola that the latter's wife Clelia, in the face of the advance of the Vandals, has committed suicide. Dreading bad news, Publicola attempts (inaccurately) to second-guess what Desbo is about to tell him, interrupting and thereby delaying the servant's message.

Des. Signor, Signor!	*Des.* Sir, Sir!
Pub. Chi sei?	*Pub.* Who are you?
Des. Desbo, il tuo fido.	*Des.* I am your faithful Desbo.
Pub. Desbo!	*Pub.* Desbo!
Des. Non mi ravvisi?	*Des.* Don't you recognize me?
Pub. Parla tosto, ch'arrechi?	*Pub.* Speak quickly, what [news] do you bring?
Il Vandalo ...	The Vandal ...
Des. No	*Des.* No.
Pub. La fiamma ...	*Pub.* Fire ...
Des. Né meno ...	*Des.* Nor that ...
Pub. I martiri ...	*Pub.* The tortures ...
Des. No, in mal punto ...	*Des.* No, it is getting worse ...
Pub. Le madri ...	*Pub.* The mothers ...
Des. Peggio: il figlio ...	*Des.* Worse: the son ...
Pub. Il figlio? (Ah, ah sì), il figlio morì? Ti fu rapito?	*Pub.* the son? (Oh, yes), the son has died? Or was stolen from you?
Des. No	*Des.* No.
Pub. ... Ma dov'è, di tosto?	*Pub.* ... But where is he? Quick!
Des. È custodito.	*Des.* He is well guarded.
Pub. E Clelia?	*Pub.* And Clelia?
Des. Entro gli Elisi va con l'ombre sepolte [...]	*Des.* In the Elysian Fields she goes with the buried shades [...]

Such a *verosimile* treatment of dialogue seems an impossibility for the solo cantata, where there would have to be a linking narrator introduced between the protagonists of the discourse in order to ensure that the change of identity of the character represented by the speaker was recognized by the audience. Since this introduces the author, as a third party, into the dialogue, a text made up of brief interventions such as the one just cited would engender a significantly higher sense of confusion. Moreover, the confusion would not be *verosimile*, since it would constitute not only a confusion in the realistic sense of imitating everyday

---

[20] See ibid., pp. 334–8. This corresponds to the dramatic-poetic device known as *stichomythia* (I thank Michael Talbot for pointing this out).

situations (which is dramatic, and therefore permissible according to the operatic canons of *verosimiglianza*), but also one at another level of narration: a confusion between character speech and authorial speech.

The cantata *A povero amator* from Op. 12[21] attempts to solve that problem. It depicts a little scene in which the shepherd Aminta is seeking a kiss from Lilla, a greedy and vain girl who tells him that he is not rich enough to enjoy her favours. Her first intervention consists of eight lines, while his answer is even longer; but then a series of questions and responses ensues, whereby the interventions of the narrator become reduced to a few, brief words:

'[…]	'[…]
E che dunque far poss'io?'	And so what can I do?'
Disse Lilla: 'Io non lo so'.	Said Lilla: 'I don't know'.
'Cangierasti il tuo desio?'	'Would you change your desire?'
Li rispose: 'O questo no'.	To which she replied: 'Oh no, not that'.
'La mia fé non gradirai?'	'My fidelity does not please you?'
Disse Lilla: 'Ed a che pro?'	Said Lilla: 'And to what end?'
'E pietade non m'avrai?'	'And you will not take pity on me?'
Li rispose: 'Non si può'.	To which she replied: 'I can't'.

As is obvious from the *ottonario* metre and the regular rhyme scheme, this passage is not intended to be set in recitative; hence already in its textual form it lacks the most basic ingredient of dramatic *verosimiglianza* typical of opera. Legrenzi sets the stanza as an aria, but one consisting of numerous tiny sections assigned to one or other of the protagonists (Example 3.2). Reinmar Emans, who cites this passage as an instance of a 'strange tendency towards the dramatic',[22] points out how Legrenzi carefully distinguishes between the two characters by metre (duple metre for the serious Aminta, triple metre for the fickle Lilla), while he fences off the text of the authorial narrator by employing for it repetitions of a single note placed in a lower tessitura.[23] The harmonic treatment contributes to that differentiation, introducing unexpected progressions at exactly those moments where the character changes. In effect, Legrenzi's composition demonstrates that the interventions from the narrator (which to the poet must seem inevitable)[24] become actually superfluous if

---

[21] Passadore and Rossi, *Catalogo*, no. 58: 2.
[22] Emans, *Die einstimmigen Kantaten*, p. 110.
[23] Ibid., p. 113.
[24] The (anonymous) poet took a great risk by omitting any prior announcement, by the narrator, of Aminta's interventions. At a poetic level, this works only by virtue of the regularity of structure – the parallelism between Aminta's questions and Lilla's replies. By means of this device, the reader is encouraged to take Aminta's point of view; the technique is thus not one of poetically enhancing the dramatic potential of the scene, but rather one of exercising authorial influence over the reader's judgements.

64   *Aspects of the Secular Cantata in Late Baroque Italy*

the passage is treated musically in a certain manner: Legrenzi thus states that the passage is even more intrinsically dramatic than Emans allows.

The composer's solution to the problem of dramatic dialogue is thus a formal one standing in sharp contrast to the recitative dialogue found in operas such as *Totila*. Whereas the cantata aria distinguishes between speakers with the aid of clear formal devices, the operatic recitative presents its quickfire dialogue in a virtually amorphous musical space (Example 3.3), a method that would not work for the unstaged genre of the solo cantata.

Example 3.2 Legrenzi, cantata *A povero amator*, bars 86–127.

Example 3.3 Legrenzi, opera *Totila*, I.11, bars 1–22.

PUB. DES. PUB.
4
De - sbo? Non mi rav - vi - si? Par - la to - sto, ch'ar - re - chi? Il
DES. PUB. DES. PUB.
7
Van - da - lo... No. La fiam - ma... Né me - no... I mar - ti - ri...
DES. PUB. DES. PUB.
10
No, in mal pun - to... Le ma - dri... Peg - gio: il fi - glio... Il
13
fi - glio? (Ah, ah sì), il fi - glio mo - rì? Ti fu ra - pi - to?
DES. PUB. DES.
17
No. Ma do - v'è, di to - sto? È cu - sto - di - to.
PUB. DES.
20
E Cle - lia? En - tro gli E - li - si va con l'om - bre se - pol - te...

In this instance, it is obvious how the requirements of the chamber genre prevent any pretence at *verosimiglianza* in the above-mentioned sense. The naturalistic effect of changing the tessitura in order to distinguish between speakers is employed exactly at the points where this is not dramatic at all: where authorial narration changes to character speech. The dramatic distinction between the speech of different characters is effected instead by means of non-naturalistic formal features. Even though Legrenzi uses these in a manner consistent with the concept of *verosimiglianza*, in that he captures important distinctions of personality in the respective musical characteristics of the two protagonists, he does so only in that sense of *verosimiglianza* which is not limited to drama.

A second species of dialogue is more intrinsic to the solo cantata. This is a musical dialogue between solo voice and bass line. Trivial as this may sound, the observation has to be made that this type of dialogue is not *verosimile* in the above-mentioned sense, since everyday conversation lacks continuo accompaniment. The addition of the instrumental bass part and the setting of the text to a melody would therefore appear to belong strictly to the authorial domain and by that token to be entirely non-dramatic. However, this mode of dialogue is encountered as frequently in opera as in the cantata, so a brief discussion of the phenomenon is needed.

A perfect instance of the use of this technique occurs in *Non ho che lagnarmi* from Op. 14.[25] Throughout this cantata, which is of considerable length, Legrenzi plays with the effect of imitating distinctive phrases of the voice in the bass (see Example 3.4). The fact that this is not just a simple musical imitation of a melodic line is emphasized by the exact replication of the rhythm even when applied to repeated notes; in fact, it is the rhythm rather than the exact melodic line that is most often shadowed. Almost as in a vocal duet, the text of the voice is implicit also in the bass part during these exchanges, and its echoing of vocal phrases is heard as reinforcing and assenting comment. The bass is thus perceived to intervene as an independent voice in a dialogue.

Example 3.4 Legrenzi, cantata *Non ho che lagnarmi*, bars 205–21.

---

[25] Passadore and Rossi, *Catalogo*, no. 60: 2.

[Musical notation: mm. 209–220, with text "mor-te o la mia vi-ta. Di due so-le pa-ro-le da l'aura favo-ri-ta pen-de-rà la mia mor-te o la mia vi-ta, pen-de-rà la mia mor-te o la mia vi-ta."]

The next cantata in the collection, *A piè d'un fonte*,[26] uses the same technique in order to emphasize the final punchline: after a lengthy plea from the quintessential shepherd to the nymph who is the object of his hopeless adoration, the cantata ends with a short couplet:

| La Ninfa udillo, e con acerbo volto | The Nymph heard him, and with an acerbic expression |
| disse: 'Va, ché sei stolto'. | said: 'Go away, for you are stupid'. |

In this instance, the intervention of the bass line precedes the quotation of the Nymph's words (see Example 3.5). After the listener has become used to this technique as an affirmation of the text just sung, the anticipation has the force of a joke: the author (who is addressing his audience via the bass line) knows the story already; he blurts out the punchline before the narrator comes to it, almost spoiling the effect. This impression is enhanced by the textual disposition: by placing the pause that customarily separates the lines after the word 'disse' instead of before it, Legrenzi not only signals a separation between the narrator's speech and that

---

[26] Passadore and Rossi, *Catalogo*, no. 60: 3.

of the character: he also obtains a sense of acceleration, as if the singer were trying to beat the continuo in a race for the punchline. Here, the dialogue between singer and bass line becomes genuinely dramatic. This is, however, a different drama from the one narrated in the text: what Legrenzi is in fact dramatizing is the process of narration itself.

Example 3.5 Legrenzi, cantata *A piè d'un fonte*, bars 142–7.

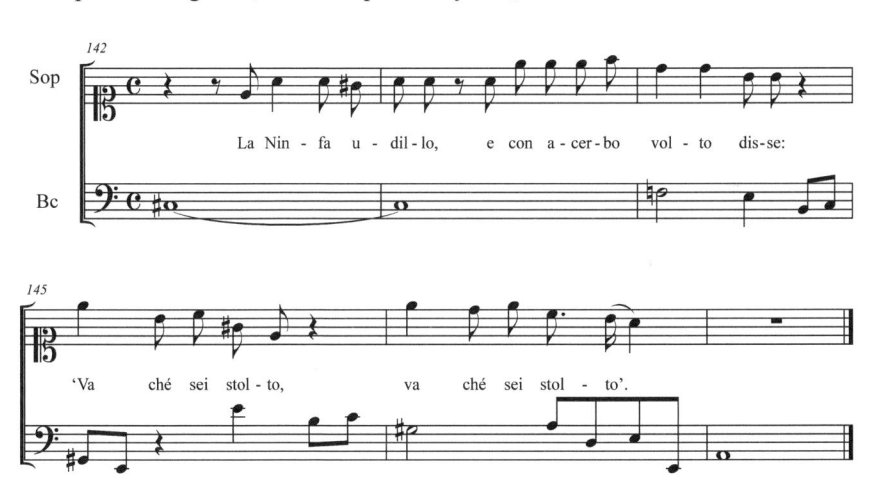

[Musical notation: Soprano and Basso continuo, bars 142–147. Text: "La Nin-fa u-dil-lo, e con a-cer-bo vol-to dis-se: 'Va ché sei stol-to, va ché sei stol-to'."]

Once again, we are confronted by a dramatic technique impossible in opera. Because of opera's nature as a staged genre, such reflections on the method of narration itself are made much more difficult. In the opera of Legrenzi's time the distinction between different layers of authorial voice and character speech was too complex to be used in such a way. The employment of a narrator in the solo cantata, on the other hand, allows the composer to play this kind of trick and make a personal appearance in something that turns out to be a narrative about narrating.

Monologue and aria dramaturgy

As already noted, *Totila* commences with a solo *scena* for one of the main characters, which I have described as formally similar to a solo cantata. To be more specific, it consists of two arias, embedded in sections of recitative (RARAR). While this particular form is rare in the solo cantatas of Legrenzi, it can nevertheless be found. The text of *A povero amator*, for instance, is clearly suggestive of such a structure, with seven lines of *versi sciolti* without a strict rhyme scheme followed by two four-line stanzas of *ottonari* with the rhyme scheme abab; next come fourteen lines of *versi sciolti* without any discernible rhyme scheme followed by the eight lines of *ottonari* cited above. The cantata closes with three lines of *versi sciolti*:[27]

Così'l misero apprese	Thus the miserable [shepherd] had to learn
Tra le sue doglie estreme,	amid his extreme anguish
Ch'Amor e povertà stan male insieme.	That Love and poverty do not go well together.

The difference between *A povero amator* and the first scene of *Totila* becomes apparent, however, in the dissimilar use of the poetic metre for dramatic purposes. *A povero amator* does not depict a solo scene. Rather, it presents two characters and contains passages of purely authorial narration. The narrator's introduction to the scene is delivered in *versi sciolti*, as proper recitative narration should be. The first voice of a character to be heard is that of Lilla, the vain and greedy shepherdess. Fittingly, her speech occupies the whole of the two stanzas making up the first aria. This not only enables her lines to be set to a light triple metre, lending her an air of flimsiness, but also enables the poet to use a language laden with ambivalence and sexual innuendos that would be out of place in the more straightforward recitative.

In contrast, the response of Aminta is once again almost entirely set as *versi sciolti*. The formal simplicity of these lines marks him out as a simple and truthful shepherd, in contrast to the artificial and contrived language employed by Lilla; at the same time, his over-use of mythical allegories to describe his anguish borders on parody and introduces a tone of irony that is apparent in the final *sentenza* of the poem.

The second aria is the dialogue analysed above (Example 3.2). It is followed by the short recitative section that closes the cantata with a moral observation. In this ending, however, the author has planted, like a bomb, an ironic twist, for the expectation of a moral that endorses the shepherd's romantic notion of honest love is not fulfilled. Instead, the poet reiterates the position of Lilla, declaring love to be a negotiable commodity. By his doing so, the seriousness of all that is said by Aminta in the preceding recitative is called into question; the formal distinction that at the time appeared to be a means of character depiction thus turns out in the end to be a vehicle for ironic comedy. This final paradox is, in its turn, an effective way of clinching the argument of the whole scene. There is no need for continuation: the punchline has been delivered (a fact underlined by Legrenzi's setting, which takes the last line as the text for a short cavata). The formal layout of the cantata thus serves the dramatic purpose of identifying and depicting the characters, as well as the authorial purpose of extracting a moral message and bringing closure to the narration.

---

[27] Unfortunately, the poetic structure of the text is rather confused in Seay's otherwise praiseworthy edition (cf. *Giovanni Legrenzi, Cantate e canzonette*, ed. Seay, p. 15).

The solo scene at the beginning of *Totila* has a different purpose. It is the introduction to the plot. Therefore, the task of closing the scene in a satisfying way does not apply, and, in fact, the scene simply breaks off when another character arrives. But the dramatic purpose of distinguishing formally between characters is also absent, since there is only one character on stage. As noted above, Clelia's character is depicted not by formal means but by the rather simpler method of giving her authorial text delivered as character speech. As a result, the distinction between aria and recitative in this scene is not one of truly dramatic plot narration.

This is, to be more precise, a strategy employed to depict the scene rather than the character. As things turn out, there is no inherent reason, in the content of Clelia's speech, to justify a switch from recitative to aria. On top of that, the arias themselves do not appear, in formal terms, to be any more regular than the recitatives: one aria consists of the extremely rare *decasillabi* in conjunction with a weak rhyme scheme, while the other is made up of three lines, a *nonario*, a *decasillabo* and an *ottonario*. This appears to be madness, and that is just what the action is depicting! After all, the scene is one of a mother about to kill her child, which in the context of seventeenth-century values has to be read as one of the highest representations of disorder. Random mixing of musical and poetic forms is here *verosimile* in the sense that it mimics a momentary turbulence in the inner state of the character. So whereas in *A povero amator* the form was part of the technique of embodiment, in the first scene of *Totila* it is part of the staging.

Of quite a different character is *Havete il torto a fé* from Op. 12.[28] The cantata consists entirely of the reflections of an unnamed person on the effects that the eyes of his[29] beloved have upon him. No action is narrated, so the cantata can dispense with a narrator and, indeed, with changes of perspective: it is entirely in character speech. In this respect, it resembles the solo scene from *Totila* much more than it does *A povero amator*. However, this cantata functions without using any techniques of staging or of embodiment, because the situation is topical and easily inferred from the text. The character whose speech the cantata reproduces remains unidentified and unspecific throughout the piece; his name is given merely as 'io' ('I'), and thus one identifies him just with a stereotypical poetic persona from the pastoral realm.

Interestingly, Legrenzi does not follow the suggestions of his poet for a strict formal distinction between recitative and aria. Even though the text is clearly divided in passages of *versi sciolti* and stanzas in more regular metre, Legrenzi's composition ignores this simple dichotomy, creating instead a more polyvalent

---

[28] Passadore and Rossi, *Catalogo*, no. 58: 2.

[29] In the seventeenth century the language of love is expressed in such a way that it is usually quite easy to discern the speaker's gender even in cases such as the present one where no definite gender designations appear. However, the metaphor of a pair of eyes taken as *pars pro toto* of a beloved person appears to be gender-neutral. The gender perspective of *Havete il torto a fé* is hence to be inferred from the gender of the composer.

structure that admits several grades of structural organization intermediate between recitative and aria.

In this context, the question arises whether the combination of poetic and musical form in the way discussed here is to be regarded as an aspect of character speech (which would make it a dramatic strategy), or whether it is a further authorial layer added to the simple character speech. For the purpose of the present argument, it is necessary to establish whether the arias are indeed used as a means to support a specific dramaturgy, and, if they are, in exactly what ways. Since the author of a solo cantata has powerful non-dramatic means at his or her disposal, such as the use of a narrator, any use of the aria as a vehicle for adding authorial comment in this genre might appear to be superfluous. On the other hand, the apparent lack of theatricality in a cantata might compel a special emphasis on the dramaturgy of arias as a means of creating dramatic situations, should the author be interested in these.

For the contemporary Venetian opera, this question is not easily answered. During the 1660s and 1670s its aesthetic premises changed drastically: from an aesthetic based on the chronicling of the process of change (either of situations or emotional states) to one centred more around a representation of an almost encyclopaedic wealth of typified emotions. As a result, the function that arias possessed within the plot narrative became radically altered. Whereas in earlier opera they had been a means of informing the audience about the inner state of individual characters in individual situations created by the plot and hence had to be very flexible in formal respects, they now became the main vehicle whereby the authors spoke to the audience about general ideas of how the world was organized – mainly of how certain types of person typically reacted under certain types of circumstance. In such a sense are the arias of Clelia in the first scene of *Totila* to be understood: not as the individual expression of Clelia as a person, but as the author's description of a typical reaction of a mother who, through particular circumstances, is forced to consider killing her child.

At the level of plot narration, this cannot possibly be considered dramatic. It is pure authorial comment – a fact emphasized by the rise, in the 1660s, of a type of reflective aria to be sung in the presence on stage of other characters, who do not, however, appear able to hear them. Such arias quickly became typified not only with regard to their representation of content, but also formally: the establishment of the *da capo* aria as the almost exclusive type of aria used in opera was possible only within the premises of such an aesthetic turn. Other effects included the emergence of the 'number opera', the interchangeability of arias of similar type (aria borrowing),[30] and a new virtuosity on the singer's part, which at times causes the aria to assume the characteristics of a full-blown concerto within the opera. But in losing their basis within the physical plot, reflective arias began to form their own context: a level of authorial reflection and comment. On

---

[30] See Jennifer Williams Brown, 'Con nuove arie aggiunte. Aria Borrowing in the Venetian Opera Repertory, 1672–1685', PhD dissertation (Cornell University, 1992).

this level, a different discourse is possible: one based not on the character speech but on different perspectives arising from the text, the music and a set of shared ideas current in Venetian society. This discourse in itself holds the possibility of becoming dramatic at the level of a meta-structure, and may for instance develop techniques such as the dialogue between singer and bass line described above, which in a sense compensate for the lack of dramatic character speech.

Legrenzi's solo cantatas do not subscribe to this kind of operatic aesthetic. In fact, a cantata such as *Havete il torto a fé* does not need any differentiation between action and reflection, since it consists only of the latter. It already is the stereotypical response of a stereotypical person to a stereotypical situation – which, after all, was the reason why the poet could omit the part of the narrator. The cantata in its entirety thus resembles an aria of the type belonging to the newer operatic aesthetic.

Interestingly, it does not follow that such a cantata should display all the characteristics of reflective arias discussed above: virtuosity, concertante solo voice and *da capo* form. In contrast, *Havete il torto a fé* resembles perfectly, in its appearance, a solo scene from the older operatic tradition, where form and construction are flexible and adapted closely to the dramatic context. Legrenzi (and to a lesser extent the poet) thus deliberately dramatizes the purely authorial content of the cantata. In doing so, he not only goes against the prevailing current of contemporary operatic practice but also affirms his intention to include dramatic features in the genre of the solo cantata in a manner that is totally independent of operatic practice. For Legrenzi, the solo cantata, though certainly non-theatrical, is clearly a dramatic genre in its own right.

Mixing styles

At least since the time of Badoaro's and Monteverdi's opera *Il ritorno d'Ulisse in patria* (1640) Venetian opera had become established as a mixed genre mingling elements of the comic, the tragic and the pastoral styles.[31] As a result, character depiction is usually less typified than contemporary ideas of *verosimiglianza* appear to advocate. Serious characters thus at times display comic traits or exhibit a simplicity bordering on the bucolic. A good instance occurs in the dialogue between Desbo and Publicola from *Totila* cited above, where Publicola is not behaving in accordance with the *gravitas* prescribed both for elevated characters in tragedy and for eminent figures in Venetian public life.

By the 1670s this mixture of styles had become a very distinct style of its own. Its function was manifold. It stretched from the simple accommodation of diverse public tastes in this public genre to the exposition of certain very specific political views concerning the difference between monarchies and republics. The one function that is arguably the most dramatic, however, is the comic

---

[31] Cf. Schulze, *Odysseus in Venedig*, pp. 141–3.

one. In using characterizations taken from the repertoire of different styles, it is possible to introduce a comic effect into the plot that works within the dramatic framework. This relies less on the content of what is said than on the way in which it is delivered. Such a comic effect is conducive to laughter about the individual speaker and his or her language rather than about the subject matter; it is thus inherently dramatic.

As the examples of *A piè d'un fonte* and *A povero amator* cited above demonstrate, such mixing of styles for comic effect appears in Legrenzi's solo cantatas as well.[32] In these instances, it is a mixture of the pastoral and the comic that occurs. The comic effect derives from a confrontation between the emotional sincerity of the pastoral lover and his rejection for baser motives: in one case, because he is not rich enough; in the other, because he is 'stupid' (no shepherds in classical pastoral are ever 'stupid': they are 'honest'). *A povero amator* even plays with an allusion to a classic of pastoral drama, Torquato Tasso's *Aminta*.[33]

The difference between opera and solo cantata in this instance lies in the way in which the styles are mixed. Whereas in opera the mixture operates at the level of each individual character, creating the ambivalent character types required for that genre,[34] in the solo cantata the characters are not at all similarly ambivalent, and the clash of styles has to unfold via the confrontation of two different characters. Aminta remains throughout the typical naïve but sincere shepherd of pastoral drama, while Lilla remains throughout the frivolous and manipulative girl drawn from comedy. In fact, one may argue that if it is to be perceived as dramatic, the genre needs its characters to be one-dimensional, just as opera needs them to be ambivalent; for if a distinction between different characters within a solo cantata is to be a practical proposition, there must be no danger whatsoever of confusing them.

Why dramatic?

Giovanni Legrenzi's solo cantatas thus employ a variety of different dramatic strategies. As shown in the discussion of aria dramaturgy, the decision to employ these strategies must have been a conscious one. These are not just strategies of effective narration taken over more or less mindlessly from opera but are used to make the cantatas themselves dramatic. A comparison with the dramatic strategies employed in opera reveals also that those used in the solo cantata differ from them in every aspect under consideration here: embodiment; staging; *verosimiglianza*; the distinction between narrative, monologue and dialogue; the dramaturgy of the aria; the mixture of styles. The treatment as synonyms of the words 'dramatic' and 'operatic' by Schmitz and others is unsustainable on close scrutiny. There

---

[32] Emans views the comic as constitutive for the 'bucolic cantatas' of Giovanni Legrenzi (Emans, *Die einstimmigen Kantaten*, p. 353).

[33] Cf. ibid., p. 110.

[34] See Schulze, *Odysseus in Venedig*, passim.

exists a generic dramaturgy of solo cantata in its own right, just as there exists a dramaturgy of opera. One of the genres – opera – is theatrical; the other is not. As a dramatic genre, solo cantata is thus independent of opera, not merely a condensed variety of it.

In view of the generic restrictions that at the outset of our considerations appeared to preclude a dramatic approach to the solo cantata, the question inescapably arises: what purpose could the dramatizing of the genre serve? Statements such as those by Erdmann Neumeister and Christian Friedrich Hunold (Menantes) – that a cantata was like a small piece of opera, because it consisted of recitative and aria[35] – seem to suggest that it was the use of the operatic musical idiom that brought with it a dramatic setting of the narration. However, in the case of Legrenzi this theory cannot be upheld, since, as shown above, it is precisely in the non-operatic application of musical idioms that dramatic strategies can be found.

Another possible theory is that of the cantata as a surrogate or a preparatory exercise for opera. This indeed seems to be the case with Barbara Strozzi, who, as a woman operating within the contemporary Venetian social structure, could neither compose operas nor direct their performances.[36] But with regard to Legrenzi this is highly unlikely, because he certainly was able to compose and perform his operas in Venice regularly and by the 1660s had no need to exercise himself in other domains in the dramatic style.

A related theory would be that the dramatic properties were introduced into the solo cantata to provide opera singers with an opportunity to display their dramatic talents in a chamber environment.[37] Leaving aside the thorny issues of who sang these cantatas on what occasion, and for whom they were initially composed, as well as the problem of distinguishing between published and non-published music with regard to purpose (all of which factors would deserve investigation in their own right), the answer may once again lie in aesthetic considerations. As in the case of its musical and poetic idioms, the particular dramaturgy of the solo cantata seems ill-adapted to operatic forms of embodiment equally in respect of the mimetic art.

Since the genre is specifically non-staged, histrionic elements such as gesture and posture would presumably have to be those of an orator rather than of an actor. The need to impersonate multiple characters and (in most cases) also the authorial narrator would on one hand enable singers to display a wealth of contrasting modes of expression, but on the other hand run into the same problems discussed above in relation to monologue and dialogue. As a vehicle for showcasing outstanding operatic talents, solo cantatas such as represented by Legrenzi's Opp. 12 and 14 would seem somewhat inept; the performance of a solo *scena* such as the first

---

[35] Cf. Schmitz, *Geschichte der weltlichen Solokantate*, pp. 260–61.

[36] Cf. Antje Tumat, 'Barbara Strozzi: Würdigung', in: *Musik und Gender im Internet*, http://mugi.hfmt-hamburg.de/grundseite/mehrzu.php?id=stro1619&text=Wuerdigung (consulted on 15 July 2007).

[37] I wish to thank Michael Talbot for bringing this issue to my attention.

scene of *Totila* would certainly be much more effective in that regard. But as a means of displaying mastery of a multitude of diverse mimetic concepts, the solo cantata may have held some value for operatic singers.

A further solution to the problem may be found in Legrenzi's dedications for the prints of Op. 12 and Op. 14. Both are designed to celebrate a wedding: Op. 12, that of Marquis Giovanni Giuseppe Orsi with Marquise Anna Maria Castracani; Op. 14, that of the Duke Johann Wilhelm, Count Palatinate-Neuburg, with the Archduchess Maria Anna Josepha of Austria. The latter took place on 25 October 1678 – hence only a week before the date of the dedication, which is 1 November of the same year.

Judging from the fact that the solo cantatas are Legrenzi's only publications specifically connected to weddings, it appears that he deemed the genre to be particularly well suited to such an occasion. As he states in the dedicatory letter of Op. 12, the cantatas represent the harmony existing between the couple.[38] This stands in marked contrast to the dedicatory letter of the chamber duets of Op. 13, which are dedicated to Charles II of England. Here, Legrenzi stresses the function of the music as entertainment for the ruler in the form of concerts.[39] In fact, the duets of Op. 13 cannot in any way be described as dramatic; they simply do not contain narrative.[40]

There seems, indeed, to be an intrinsic connection between dramatic music and wedding ceremonies. Of course, in court environments weddings were a common occasion for opera; in fact the wedding of Johann Wilhelm and Maria Anna Josepha was celebrated with both an *Applauso per musica* and an opera specially composed for that event.[41] Since in this case there cannot be any question of a substitution of solo cantata for opera (in the sense that the solo cantata was perceived as the 'opera of the poor', as it were), it follows that both cantata and opera serve the same purpose in providing a dramatic reflection upon an occasion such as a wedding. In fact, Legrenzi implies as much when, in the context of pondering the suitability of his work, he states that the couple to whom he is dedicating Op. 12 has in the past applauded both his theatrical compositions and his cantatas; he takes this as a promise that they will be pleased similarly by the new collection.[42]

In light of these ideas, it becomes clear that the initial question was actually the wrong one. The problem is not why, for Legrenzi, the solo cantata is dramatic but, rather, why, in a given instance, the drama is presented in the form of a solo

---

[38] Passadore and Rossi, *La sottigliezza dell'intendimento*, p. 609.

[39] Ibid., p. 620.

[40] Giovanni Legrenzi, *Idee armoniche estese per due e tre voci, Venice, 1678*; facsimile edition, ed. Clifford Bartlett (London, n.d.).

[41] *La forza dell'Allegrezza* and *Enea in Italia*, the latter being a subject already presented in Venice in 1675 – see Herbert Seifert, *Die Oper am Wiener Kaiserhof im 17. Jahrhundert* (Tutzing, 1985), p. 494.

[42] Passadore and Rossi, *La sottigliezza dell'intendimento*, p. 609.

cantata. The answer is simple: an opera is not appropriate for every context, since there are occasions where a chamber genre is required – e.g., as a private gift for a wedding, at a social gathering in a private house, for performance during Lent, or to gratify the wish of a singer to display a different kind of histrionic art. The difference is one of environment. Opera is intended for the theatre, solo cantata for the chamber. But, at least in the case of Legrenzi, both are perceived equally as dramatic genres in their own right.

Chapter 4

A Tale of Two Cities: Cantata Publication in Bologna and Venice, c.1650–1700

Reinmar Emans

In his *Geschichte der weltlichen Solokantate* Eugen Schmitz made the point that early cantatas survive primarily in printed form. Yet he noted 'in the fourth decade' ('im vierten Dezennium'), by which he probably meant the years around 1650, a clear 'shift from printed sources to manuscript ones' ('Zurücktreten der Druckliteratur gegenüber der handschriftlichen Überlieferung').[1] This view was probably too sweeping, for not a few composers from the second half of the seventeenth century are represented by cantatas surviving overwhelmingly in printed, and only marginally in manuscript, form. This is largely true of those composers whose field of activity lay directly within the orbit of the two major publishing centres, Venice and Bologna – figures such as Giovanni Legrenzi and Giovanni Battista Bassani.[2] For Maurizio Cazzati, who in any case committed most of his compositions to print – among them at least two collections of cantatas and further volumes containing secular vocal music of other kinds – the relationship of published to unpublished cantatas is similar.

Like works transmitted via autograph manuscripts, published works derive an enhanced significance from the simple fact that the authorial intention can be conveyed by them much more strongly than through manuscript copies, which have a rather incidental character and have not always been accurately executed. For that reason alone, one has much higher expectations of finding precise instructions for performance in a published collection. A published cantata rises above the level of an 'occasional composition' and thereby acquires up to a certain point the status of a 'work'.

The physical form of publication was, admittedly, anything but fixed. True, the choice usually fell on oblong format and a production without frills, but one immediately comes up against the problem of what actually constitutes a 'cantata print'. The earliest published cantatas like to bury themselves in collections featuring a number of very diverse genres. Thus Alessandro Grandi (*Cantade et arie a voce sola*, Venice, Alessandro Vincenti, 1620) employs what are at first

---

[1] Eugen Schmitz, *Geschichte der weltlichen Solokantate* (Leipzig, 1914; facsimile repr. Hildesheim, 1966), p. 69.

[2] Schmitz evidently had no knowledge of Bassani's numerous cantata publications, which he fails altogether to mention.

sight unambiguous generic descriptions; but presented under the rubric 'Cantade' are compositions in strophic variation form that we today would not recognize as cantatas, since they do not exhibit the expected alternation of recitative and aria. The same applies (with only a single exception) to Giovanni Pietro Berti's *Cantade et arie ad una voce sola con alcune a doi*, published in Venice by Alessandro Vincenti, and to Domenico Crivellati's *Cantate diverse a una, due e tre voci* (Rome, Giovanni Battista Robletti, 1628). On the other hand, in some early collections we encounter pieces bearing different generic labels that are classifiable as cantatas by virtue of their polymetric texts and mixed musical style. In *Da grave incendio* from Pellegrino Possenti's *Accenti pietosi d'Armillo, canzonete et arie a voce sola* (Venice, Bartolomeo Magni, 1625), for instance, the alternation of recitative and aria is clearly observable – more so than in Girolamo Frescobaldi's *Primo libro* and *Secondo libro d'arie musicali* [...] *a una, a dua* [sic], *e a tre voci*, which appeared in Florence from Giovanni Battista Landini in 1630, or in Giovanni Felice Sances's *Cantade* [...] *a voce sola* (Venice, Bartolomeo Magni, 1633). Almost all pre-1650 collections containing secular vocal music display terminological ambivalences of this kind. In this early period it is not uncommon to find indications in the title that only one or other of the pieces was regarded as a cantata; such pieces were placed for preference at the end of the collection, as occurs in Giovanni Rovetta's *Madrigali concertati a 2, 3,* [...] *voci*, (Venice, Francesco Magni, 1636), where, following the title, we read: 'Con dialogo nel fine et una Cantata a voce sola'.

At all events, we cannot speak of genuine cantata collections before this time, even if the early prints laid the groundwork for the consolidation of the cantata's form: already in the previously mentioned collections of Frescobaldi and Sances the alternation of the two styles of writing, taking its cue from the polymetric verse structure, is clearly delineated.[3] Succeeding prints take over this form, at least in part, and reproduce its properties ever more firmly.[4] Important in this respect are the three collections by Benedetto Ferrari that appeared in Venice from Bartolomeo Magni between 1633 and 1641 – *Musiche varie a voce sola*, *Musiche varie a voce sola* (*Libro secondo*) and *Musiche e poesie varie a voce sola* (*Libro terzo*) – in which the alternation of recitative and arioso sections has a very planned appearance.

---

[3] On this subject, see Piero Mioli, *A voce sola. Studio sulla cantata italiana del XVII secolo* (Florence, 1988). Mioli largely confines himself to the early history of the cantata and, in geographical terms, to Rome. His overview of the early prints containing secular music for solo voice does not need restatement here, allowing us to deal only cursorily with the prehistory of the cantata as this is apparent from published works.

[4] For instance: Martino Pesenti, *Arie a voce sola* [...] *Con una cantata nel fine*, Op. 3 (Venice, Alessandro Vincenti, 1636); Filiberto Laurenzi, *Concerti et arie a una, due e tre voci con una serenata a 5* (Venice, Alessandro Vincenti, 1641); Nicolo Fontei's three collections *Bizzarrie poetiche a 1. 2. 3. voci* (respectively, Venice, Bartolomeo Magni, 1635 and 1636, and Alessandro Vincenti, 1639).

Barbara Strozzi, in her four published collections for solo voice, joins seamlessly in this evolution of form but widens the dichotomy still further, while at the same time retaining both the terminological inexactitude and the old forms in modified guise. With regard to content, too, her Op. 3 remains true to tradition by mixing genres (*Cantate, ariete*) and vocal specifications (*a una, due e tre voci*), whereas Opp. 6–8 are uniformly conceived for solo voice.

These prints appeared in Venice from Francesco Magni in 1657, 1659 and 1664, respectively. Only in Op. 7 is the juxtaposition of cantatas and arias still practised. Cantatas such as *Donna di maestà* stand out from the works in other genres not only by virtue of their polymetric texts but also on account of their larger scale. The differentiation of musical styles, which certainly, as Carolyn Gianturco has pointed out, derives in principle from the character of the text,[5] is employed by Strozzi in this volume even for the *lamenti*. Normally, the metre employed for *lamenti* uniformly employs hendecasyllables and *settenari* and therefore does not readily accommodate excursions in the shape of an aria.[6] In the second cantata of Op. 7, *Appresso a i molli argenti*, superscribed 'Lamento', a fairly extended recitative section is followed by a clearly demarcated aria, whose textual basis is an *ottonario* ('A miei danni congiurato'). A second aria, 'Chiare stelle in cielo ardenti', is likewise based on an eight-syllable line. An equally polymetric layout occurs in the lament *Lagrime mie a che vi trattenete*. Further, the poets of these two laments were respectively Giovanni Pietro Monesi and Pietro Dolfino. That these men, conceivably for the first time ever, chose to cast their *lamenti* in polymetric verse is probably connected in an important way with the Venetian Accademia degli Unisoni, which took a close interest in textual matters. The fact that both of the poets just mentioned were members of this academy strengthens the supposition that, for them and their milieu, the definitive cantata form was viewed as a conglomerate of different metrical and stanzaic types. Incidentally, this print features an omission that occurs even as late as 1700 in Bernardo Gaffis Op. 1, *Cantate da cammera* [sic] *a voce sola* (Rome, Mascardi): for strophic arias the text of the stanzas after the first is printed separately at the end of the cantata, forcing the performer to underlay these words (if he is to rely on more than memory!) in his own hand. This point emerges clearly from a facsimile of Strozzi's Op. 7,[7] as well as from the solitary strophic aria in Gaffi's collection ('Sino quando' from the first cantata). Strozzi's Op. 7 contains, in addition, directions for *da capo* repetition, although these

---

[5] On this point, see Carolyn Gianturco, 'The Italian Seventeenth-Century Cantata: A Textual Approach', in John Caldwell, Edward Olleson and Susan Wollenberg (eds), *The Well Enchanting Skill: Music, Poetry, and Drama in the Culture of the Renaissance: Essays in Honour of F. W. Sternfeld* (Oxford, 1990), pp. 41–51.

[6] On this point, see also Carlo Guaita, 'Le cantate-lamento della seconda metà del diciasettesimo secolo', in *La cantata da camera nel barocco italiano* (Milan, 1990), pp. 40–57, at p. 42.

[7] Published at Stuttgart in 1999/2003 by Cornetto-Verlag.

refer not to the repetition of the opening section of an aria but to that of the opening of the cantata itself. As a rule, one or two bars of the portion to be repeated are printed.

If Strozzi's Op. 7 fulfils, in essence, all the conditions that one would today require in order to classify it as a book of cantatas, this same volume also marks the end, for a while, of Venice's pre-eminence in the domain of the published cantata. Up to that point, only a handful of volumes containing vocal chamber music that were worthy of description, in the wider sense, as 'cantata publications' had appeared outside Venice, as Table 4.1 shows:

Table 4.1   Non-Venetian publications of vocal chamber music, 1628–59.

Crivellati, Domenico	*Cantate diverse a una, due, e tre voci*	Rome – Giovanni Battista Robletti	1628
Frescobaldi, Girolamo	*Primo libro d'arie musicali* [...] *a una, a dua, e a tre voci*	Florence – Giovanni Battista Landini	1630
Frescobaldi, Girolamo	*Secondo libro d'arie musicali* [...] *a una, a dua, e a tre voci*	Florence – Giovanni Battista Landini	1630
Sabbatini, Pietro Paolo	*Il terzo libro*	Rome – Paolo Masotti	1631
Sabbatini, Pietro Paolo	*Il quarto di villanelle a una, due, e tre, voci*	Rome – Giovanni Battista Robletti	1631
Sabbatini, Pietro Paolo	*Prima scelta di villanelle a due voci*	Rome – Vitale Mascardi	1652
Boccella, Francesco	*Primavera di vaghi fiori musicali, overo Canzonette ad una, due, e tre voci*	Ancona – Ottavio Beltrano	1653
various authors	*Canzonette amorose a una, doi, tre, voci*	Rotterdam – Giovanni van Geertsom	1656
Natali, Pompeo	*Madrigali a tre voci pari*	Rome – Mauritio Balmonti	1656
Cazzati, Maurizio	*Cantate morali, e spirituali a voce sola,* Op. 20	Bologna – Vittorio erede Benacci	1659

It was certainly not by chance that, alongside other cities, Rome in particular still played a relatively important role in the dissemination of prints, for it had provided, thanks to Carissimi and Rossi, an important early centre for the cultivation of the cantata. But the products of the Roman school – except for the five listed above – were in the main transmitted via manuscript copies. That these five were entrusted to four different publishers is perhaps a symptom of their limited economic success, which indeed becomes reflected in the following decades in the reluctance of Roman publishers to bring out similar collections. Up to 1695, only four further collections of vocal chamber music appeared in Rome, and these were all for more than one voice and contained no true cantatas.[8] The expansive domain of the chamber cantata was left, evidently quite deliberately, for publishers in Venice and Bologna to exploit.

Bologna emerged as a place of publication for secular vocal music only in 1659. The initial impetus for this initiative clearly came from the print-hungry Maurizio Cazzati, who between 1659 and 1667 sent to the presses no fewer than five well-stocked volumes. The series was inaugurated with his Op. 20 – which one may perhaps regard as a cautious attempt to interest Bolognese publishers in the repertory of chamber music for voice – brought out in 1659 by Benacci. This collection not only features the word 'cantata' in its title but even expands this, with sub-generic precision, to become *Cantate morali e spirituali a voce sola*. This was in itself a novelty, since up to then no collections had appeared in Venice with a similarly edifying content. Already the dedication 'All'Illustrissima Signora Donna Maria Domitilla Ceva, Monaca dell'Insigne Monastero di S.ta Redegunda di Milano' proclaims unmistakably that a new clientèle was being sought. In this way, Cazzati circumvented competition – and evidently also achieved commercial success, for the collection was reprinted exactly twenty years later by Giacomo Monti, this time with a dedication to the celebrated nun–musician Isabella Leonarda. Since vocal music that could find a place not only in the sacred but also in the secular sphere was, presumably, even easier to sell, Cazzati essayed this in his *Diporti spirituali per camera o per oratorii a uno, due, trè e quattro*, which came out in 1668 in partbooks – but not in score, like his Op. 49; this print was dedicated, evidently very astutely, to Laura d'Este.[9] Eight years previously, Cazzati had gained experience of publishing similar music in partbooks when he entrusted his *Madrigali e canzonette per camera, a due e tre parte con violini, e parte senza con un Lamento di tre amanti per il gran caldo*, Op. 26, to Antonio Pisarri.

Whereas in the 1670s the publication of vocal chamber music enjoyed a boom in Bologna, Venice produced after Barbara Strozzi's Op. 8 of 1664 only one further comparable collection (Francesco Magni, 1668): the *Scherzi amorosi a due e tre voci con violini a beneplacito* of Francesco Petrobelli, who was *maestro di cappella* at the cathedral of Padua. And even this Op. 7 is only a continuation of Petrobelli's similarly titled Op. 4, which may have been what persuaded Francesco Magni to try his luck once more with secular vocal music. The choice

---

[8] Mario Savioni, *Concerti morali e spirituali a tre voci differenti* (Rome, Jacomo Fei, 1660); Pompeo Natali, *Madrigali e canzoni spirituali e morali a due et a tre voci* (Rome, Jacomo Fei, 1662); Mario Savioni, *Madrigali morali e spirituali a cinque voci* (Rome, Amadeo Belmonte, 1668); and Domenico da'l Pane, *Secondo libro de' madrigali a cinque voci* (Rome, 'Successor al Mascardi', 1678).

[9] See Carrie Churnside, 'Images of Crying in Bolognese Sacred Cantatas: the Jesuit Influence', at http://www.bpmonline.org.uk/bpm8/Churnside.html (accessed 27 August 2007).

of a prominent dedicatee, the Venetian doge Niccolò Sagredo, may naturally have lessened the risk of a marketing failure. To this collection may be added the *Sacre ariose cantate a voce sola*, Op. 4, of Carlo Grossi (Venice, Francesco Magni *detto* Gardano, 1663), which, however, comprises only settings of sacred texts. Symptomatic of the greater perceived attractiveness that Bologna had earned in the meantime as a place of publication is the fact that of the nine collections of vocal chamber music, predominantly sacred in nature, that the organist at S. Petronio, Carlo Donato Cossoni, committed to print between 1665 and 1670, only the first came out in Venice. Cossoni's *Libro primo delle canzonette amorose a voce sola*, which appeared from Giacomo Monti as Op. 7 in 1669, provides a still relatively early indication of the incipient turn of Bolognese publishers towards cantata publication. In contrast, Venetian publishers retrenched massively during those years, at least with regard to the publication of secular vocal music. Meanwhile, in Bologna Cazzati filled the market to saturation point. During the 1660s he published his Opp. 23–55 as well as a long series of further works, highly diverse in genre, that bear no opus number. New editions of his older works also appeared. Four of these collections contain secular chamber music for voice: the *Canzonette per camera a voce sola*, Op. 27 (Antonio Pisarri, 1661); *Arie e cantate a voce sola*, Op. 41 (Bologna, without publisher's name, 1666); *Il quarto libro delle canzonette a voce sola*, Op. 43 (ditto, 1667); *Il quinto libro delle canzonette a voce sola con violini a beneplacito*, Op. 46 (ditto, 1668). In publishing terms, such a series is plausible only if the individual volumes sell well and yield a profit. Cazzati clearly caught the mood and taste of his time so well that the market opened up for other composers as well. In particular, the cantata collections of Giovanni Battista Mazzaferrata, all for more than one voice but containing solo recitatives and ariosos, evidently filled this void. Mazzaferrata's success is evidenced by that fact that his Op. 2 (*Il primo libro de madrigali a due, a tre, amorosi e morali*), first published in 1668, was reprinted in 1675 and 1683, while his Op. 3 (*Canzonette e cantate a due voci*), dating from the same year, enjoyed reprints in 1675 and 1680.

The floodgates opened in Bologna with the anthology *Canzonette per camera a voce sola* compiled by Marino Silvani, which Giacomo Monti brought out in 1670. After a rather hesitant, but clearly well-targeted and commercially well-planned, start, publications containing cantatas and cognate vocal compositions grew after only a few years to become a torrent. In this development Giacomo Monti was the undisputed leader, as Table 4.2 shows.

Table 4.2   Vocal chamber music published in Bologna in the 1670s.

various authors	*Canzonette per camera a voce sola*, compiled by Marino Silvani	Bologna – Giacomo Monti	1670
Grossi, Carlo	*La cetra d'Apollo*, Op. 6	Venice – Francesco Magni detto Gardano	1672
Mazzaferrata, Giovanni Battista*	*Il primo libro delle cantate da camera a voce sola*, Op. 4	Bologna – Giacomo Monti	1673
Petrobelli, Francesco	[*Musiche da camera a due, tre, et quattro voci con violini in alcune obbligati, et in altre a beneplacito*, Op. 9][10]	Bologna – Giacomo Monti	1673
Nascimbeni, Maria Francesca	*Canzoni, e madrigali morali, e spirituali a una, due, e tre voci*	Ancona – Claudio Percimineo	1674
[Mazzaferrata, Giovanni Battista]	[*Canzonette, e cantate a due voci*, Op. 3]	Bologna – Giacomo Monti	1675
[Mazzaferrata, Giovanni Battista]	[*Il primo libro de madrigali a due, a tre, amorosi, e morali*, Op. 2]	Bologna – Giacomo Monti	1675
Grossi, Carlo	[*L'Anfione, Musiche da camera, ò per tavola a due, e trè voci*, Op. 7]	Venice – Francesco Magni detto Gardano	1675
Bianchi, Giovanni Battista (Padre)	[*Madrigali a due, e tre voci*, Op. 1]	Bologna – Giacomo Monti	1675
Petrobelli, Francesco	*Cantate a una, e due voci*, Op. 10	Bologna – Giacomo Monti	1676
Legrenzi, Giovanni	*Cantate, e canzonette a voce sola*, Op. 12	Bologna – Giacomo Monti	1676
Bononcini, Giovanni Maria	*Cantate per camera a voce sola libro primo*, Op. 10	Bologna – Giacomo Monti	1677
Cazzati, Maurizio	[*Duetti per camera*, Op. 66]	Bologna – Giacomo Monti	1677
[Mazzaferrata, Giovanni Battista]	*Il primo libro delle cantate da camera a voce sola*, Op. 4	Bologna – Giacomo Monti	1677
Bononcini, Giovanni Maria	*Cantate per camera a voce sola libro secondo*, Op. 13	Bologna – Giacomo Monti	1678
Legrenzi, Giovanni	*Ecchi di riverenza di cantate e canzoni*, Op. 14	Bologna – Giacomo Monti	1678
Legrenzi, Giovanni	[*Idee armoniche estese per due e tre voci*, Op. 13]	Venice – Francesco Magni detto Gardano	1678
Bononcini, Giovanni Maria	[*Partitura de madrigali a cinque voci*, Op. 11]	Bologna – Giacomo Monti	1678

Pane, Domenico da'l	[Secondo libro de' madrigali a cinque voci]	Rome – Successor' al Mascardi	1678
Cazzati, Maurizio	Cantate morali, e spirituali a voce sola, Op. 20	Bologna – Giacomo Monti	1679
[Legrenzi, Giovanni]	Ecchi di riverenza di cantate, e canzoni, Op. 14	Venice – Francesco Sala	1679
Coya, Simone	L'amante impazzito con altre cantate, e serenate a solo, et a due con Violini, Op. 1[†]	Milano – Fratelli Camagni	1679
various authors	Scelta di canzonette italiane	London – Godbid and Playford	1679
[Mazzaferrata, Giovanni Battista]	[Cantate morali e spirituali a due, e tre voci, Op. 7]	Bologna – Giacomo Monti	1680[‡]
[Mazzaferrata, Giovanni Battista]	[Canzonette, e cantate a due voci, Op. 3]	Bologna – Giacomo Monti	1680
Bassani, Giovanni Battista	L'armonia delle Sirene, Cantate amorose musicali à voce sola, Op. 2	Bologna – Giacomo Monti	1680

Notes:

[*] Bracketed composers' names indicate a reprint; bracketed titles refer to music for more than one voice.

[†] Coya's cantatas contain strange instructions to the effect that certain dances should be played as well as sung ('Si sona la Pugliese' – 'Si canta la Pugliese', p. 29 and elsewhere).

[‡] A second edition came out in 1690 from Pier-Maria Monti.

The 1670s reproduced the pattern of the 1660s very closely, for other Italian cities engaged only sporadically in the business of publishing secular vocal music,[10] while Venice now clearly contented itself merely with scraps left over. Only Carlo Grossi's publications of 1673[11] and 1675 prove – like his Op. 4 of 1663 – exceptions to this rule, and only Op. 6, *La cetra d'Apollo*, contains pieces corresponding to the genre of the chamber cantata. Here, too, the dedication to no less illustrious a person than emperor Leopold I may have had its effect.

This volume exhibits some peculiarities. Not only its enormous length of 387 pages – unparalleled, so far as I can tell, among cantata publications – but also its engraved title page bearing the inscription 'SIC FATA TRAHUNT' show that

---

[10] The publication of Maria Francesca Nascimbeni's *Canzoni e madrigali morali e spirituali a una, due e tre voci* in 1674 remained a unique case of the involvement of the Ancona publisher Claudio Percimineo in music of this kind.

[11] The example of this publication that I consulted in Venice bore the date '1672' on its title page; however, all relevant work-lists, including the on-line ICCU catalogue, give 1673 as the year of appearance.

Francesco Magni was making a calculated attempt to rise above the simple, by then almost standardized, make-up of similar volumes. Grossi's allusion to this fact in his preface with the words 'che distintamente gl'offro manuscritti [...]' ('for I manifestly offer you manuscripts') is likewise a singular case among published works. In its contents, too, the print possesses some peculiar features. Thus the concluding *tavola* contains not merely the text incipits but also, in every instance, short descriptions of the subject. Also, the two cantatas for baritone that bring up the rear of the volume are absolutely untypical of collections of this kind. Their tempi are unusually precisely specified ('Presto', 'Tardo', 'Adagio', 'Alegrissimo', 'Vivace', 'Spirituoso'); moreover, ariosos (as on p. 100, at the words 'se non cangi pensier', and in the section in 3/2 metre on p. 130, which changes dynamic level at intervals of a bar) and also cavatas (see, for instance, p. 55) are frequently identified explicitly as such. Detailed descriptions of movements such as 'Aria infernale' to characterize 'Numi dell'Erebo' in the cantata *Già l'auriga splendente*, 'Passacaglio' (p. 103) and the direction 'con tutta bizzaria' evidence the effort taken to exceed normality. Another peculiarity is that in some ritornellos instrumental parts are sketched – as in the great aria 'Al celeste armato nume' of the cantata *Chi batte al mio core*.[12] The instruction 'si suona' clarifies the composer's intention.

The impression of great care that characterizes this publication is only increased by the fact that the text of the second stanza is not – as customarily happens in strophic arias – printed separately, but is underlaid to the notes; this caused great difficulties for the typesetting from which Magni on this occasion did not shrink. The typographical problems were recognized clearly enough, as Grossi acknowledges in his preface when he writes: 'Devo poi altro aggiungerti, che rittrovando in queste mie Cantate qualche fiachezza al tuo spiritoso intendimento, scusi, con gl'errori inevitabili della stampa, anco la mancanza in essa dell'intavolatura, che rende imperfetti alcuni passi composti co Bassi dopij' ('I must further inform you that if your keen understanding discovers in these cantatas of mine any weakness, you must pardon, in addition to the inevitable printing errors, the limitations of the notation in score, which renders imperfect certain passages composed with two bass parts').

In the light of this collection, Grossi's Op. 7, which contained polyphonic settings and was consequently issued as a set of partbooks, follows a more traditional path. Nevertheless, this newly acquired interest by a Venetian

---

[12] The example of the cantata *Amanti curiosi* in the Biblioteca Nazionale Marciana, Venice, contains a second upper part added by hand, a fact that carries implications for performance. Michael Talbot has observed, in commenting on this chapter, that inked corrections made by printers themselves were not unusual – see, for example, Bartolomeo Magni's edition of Rigatti's *Musiche concertate*, Op. 2 (1636), preserved at the Fondazione Cini, Venice – so there is a good possibility that this addition stemmed from the publisher, in which case the substitution of ink for print will probably have been made for technical reasons. Giulia Nuti discusses 'sketched' ritornellos in Chapter 11.

publisher in secular vocal music may have ridden on the back of the success of Grossi's *Cetra d'Apollo*. The impression is strengthened by Francesco Magni's return three years later to the same field of activity. Giovanni Legrenzi's *Idee armoniche estese per due e tre voci*, Op. 13, was issued not in the form of separate parts but as a score, which registers a further novelty in the publication of polyphonic secular vocal music. Legrenzi was naturally no stranger to the Venetian publisher, having entrusted his Opp. 1–10 variously to Francesco Magni and to Francesco Sala. Only through the reprint of his Op. 8 in Bologna did Legrenzi open up contact with Giacomo Monti, who then went on to produce his own edition of the *Acclamationi divote*, Op. 10.[13] Shortly afterwards, Monti brought out the two double volumes containing cantatas and canzonets, Opp. 12 and 14. It is surprising that these did not appear in Venice, since the frequency with which Legrenzi's earlier prints were reissued indicates that they were in heavy demand there. But, regarding the place of publication, further developments were to occur.

In 1679 the Venetian publisher Giuseppe Sala turned his attention for the first time to the repertory of secular vocal music. It seems a little like an astute chess move that he began by reprinting Legrenzi's *Ecchi di riverenza di cantate, e canzoni*, Op. 14, which Monti had brought out the year before. Although in the following decade only a few prints of substance appeared from Sala (Carlo Grossi, *Il divertimento de grandi*, Op. 19, in 1681; Giovanni Benedetto Vinaccesi, *Il consiglio degli amanti, overo Cantate da camera a voce sola*, Op. 3,[14] in 1688; and Andrea Paulato, *Cantate a voce sola*, in 1689), they suffice to show that the Venetian publishing industry was becoming active once more in the evolution of the cantata repertory, albeit without challenging, still less ending, Monti's primacy in this domain.

Turning again to Bologna, we find that in the 1680s at least fifteen substantial collections were published, with the entry into the lists in 1687 of a new name, that of Gioseffo Micheletti, who brought out prints by Alveri and Tosi (see Table 4.3). Of these fifteen collections, two (Mazzaferrata's Opp. 2 and 4) were reprints, which again leads one to believe that secular vocal music remained in vogue. With the exception of Viviani, all the composers for this repertory published in Bologna were active in either Bologna or Ferrara.

A single composer, Giovanni Battista Bassani, committed to print in the space of five years no fewer than five substantial collections (including his Op. 1 of 1679) and followed these in 1687 with a further offering. Until then, no composer had chosen to concentrate his efforts so emphatically on the cantata genre.

---

[13] According to the numbering adopted in Stephen Bonta, 'The Church Sonatas of Giovanni Legrenzi' (dissertation, Harvard University, 1964), this is Op. 10a.

[14] On this lost print, see Michael Talbot, *Benedetto Vinaccesi: A Musician in Brescia and Venice in the Age of Corelli* (Oxford, 1994), pp. 33 and 294.

Table 4.3   Vocal chamber music published in Bologna in the 1680s.

Bassani, Giovanni Battista	*L'armonia delle Sirene, Cantate amorose musicali à voce sola*, Op. 2	Bologna – Giacomo Monti	1680
Bassani, Giovanni Battista	*Il cigno canoro, Cantate amorose*, Op. 3	Bologna – Giacomo Monti	1682
Bassani, Giovanni Battista	*La moralità armonica, Cantate à 2, e 3 Voci*, Op. 4	Bologna – Giacomo Monti ad istanza di Marino Silvani	1683
Bassani, Giovanni Battista	*Affetti canori, Cantate et ariette*, Op. 6*	Bologna – Giacomo Monti	1684
Albergati, P. Pirro	*Cantate morali a voce sola*, Op. 3	Bologna – Giacomo Monti	1685
various authors	*Melpomene coronata da Felsina, Cantate musicali à voce sola, date in luce da Signori Compositori Bolognesi*	Bologna – Giacomo Monti	1685
Alveri, Giovanni Battista	*Cantate à voce sola da camera*, Op. 1	Bologna – Gioseffo Micheletti	1687
Albergati, P. Pirro	*Cantate da camera a voce sola*, Op. 6	Bologna – Giacomo Monti	1687
Perti, Giacomo Antonio	*Cantate morali e spirituali a una, & à due voci, con violini, e senza*, Op. 1	Bologna – Giacomo Monti	1688
Cherici, Sebastiano	*Componimenti da camera a due voci*, Op. 5	Bologna – Giacomo Monti	1688
Bassani, Giovanni Battista	*Eco armonica delle Muse, Cantate amorose à voce sola*, Op. 7	Bologna – Giacomo Monti	1688
Tosi, Giuseppe Felice	*Il primo libro delle cantate da camera a voce sola*, Op. 2	Bologna – Giuseffo Micheletti	1688
Viviani, Giovanni Bonaventura	*Cantate a voce sola*, Op. 1	Bologna – Giacomo Monti	1689

Notes:
* The publication claims Bassani also as the author of the words.

Albergati's Op. 3 diverges from the other collections not only by naming the poets of the individual texts set – hardly a unique occurrence but certainly not a common one – but also, more significantly, by making a topical reference in a cantata for bass, *Fallacia del pensiero descritta con le vane speranze del Turco nella presente guerra*, which comments on the war then raging between Venice and the Ottomans. Albergati also set a text by Giovanni Battista Neri dealing with the four seasons, an equally unconventional subject. Albergati's Op. 6 can make a similar claim to originality. It contains a comic cantata, entitled *Musico raffreddato* (The Singer Suffering from a Cold), which, besides putting the singer

Example 4.1   Albergati, cantata *D'Acheronte errini horribili* (*Musico raffredato*), aria 'Non posso cantare', bars 1–16.

[Musical example: Lento / Allegro, with text: "-re. Io son raf-fred-da-to, son me-zo_a-ma-la-to, mi sfor-zo_a par-la-re, son mez-zo_a-ma-la-to, mi sfor-zo_a par-la-re. Non" — D. C. al fine]

through his paces, earns a place as a rare instance of humour in the wide expanses of the published cantata (see Example 4.1).[15]

For the 1680s, similarly, it is instructive to make a comparison with cantata publications in other centres in order to illustrate the primacy enjoyed by Bolognese publishers. Besides the three Venetian prints from this decade that have been mentioned, we have Cataldo Amodei's *Cantate a voce sola*, Op. 2 (Naples, Novello De Bonis, 1685) and Antonio del Ricco's *Urania armonica. Cantate a voce sola*, Op. 1 (Florence, alla Condotta, 1686). But these are genuine exceptions, which occupy a completely isolated place within the publishing landscape of Naples and Florence, if one may discount the slightly later Op. 7 of Giovanni

---

[15] The last recitative holds the nub of the argument: 'O quante altre ragioni introdurre potrei per tal difesa; ma le tosse non vuole, che scorda il canto, e stropia le parole' ('O how many other reasons I could adduce in my defence; but my coughs do not allow me, for I sing out of tune and mangle my words').

Bonaventura Viviani, *Veglie armoniche a una, due e tre voci con violini e senza*, which appeared in 1690 from the same Florentine publisher.

Table 4.4   Vocal chamber music published in Bologna by Pier-Maria Monti, 1690–95.

Antonii, Pietro degli	*Cantate da camera a voce sola*, Op. 6	1690
[Bassani, Giovanni Battista]*	[*La moralità armonica, Cantate à 2, e 3 Voci*, Op. 4]	1690
Gabrielli, Domenico	*Cantate a voce sola*, Op. 2	1691
Bononcini, Giovanni	[*Duetti da camera*, Op. 8]	1691
Brevi, Giovanni Battista	*Le forze d'Amore, Cantate a voce sola*, Op. 1	1691
Porfirii, Pietro	*Cantate da camera a voce sola*, Op. 1	1692
[Bassani, Giovanni Battista]	*L'armonia delle Sirene, Cantate amorose musicali à voce sola*, Op. 2	1692
[Bassani, Giovanni Battista]	*Eco armonica delle Muse, Cantate amorose à voce sola*, Op. 7	1693
Alghisi, Paris Francesco	*Cantate*	1694
Bassani, Giovanni Battista	*La Musa armonica. Cantate amorose musicali à voce sola*, Op. 16	1695

Notes:

* Bracketed composers' names indicate a reprint; bracketed titles refer to music for more than one voice.

In the last decade of the century the composer boasting the greatest number of published cantatas, Giovanni Battista Bassani, changed publishing location. True, in 1690 a reprint of his collection *La moralità armonica, Cantate a 2 e 3 voci*, Op. 4, appeared, as expected, in Bologna. But in this same year, following the death of Giacomo Monti, the business passed to his son Pier-Maria Monti, who had already taken responsibility for a number of published books in the preceding years. Although Pier-Maria Monti continued to publish volumes of cantatas vigorously, and in the first five years of his control produced new editions of Bassani's Opp. 2, 4 and 7, the change of ownership seems somehow to have disrupted Bassani's relationship with the publishing house. At all events, Bassani entrusted his Opp. 14, 15 and 17 – *Amorosi sentimenti di cantate a voce sola* (1693), *Armoniche fantasie di cantate amorose a voce sola* (1694) and *La Sirena amorosa, Cantate a voce sola con violini* (1699) – to the Venetian Giuseppe Sala, who in addition brought out reprints of two of these publications: Op. 14 (1696) and Op. 15 (1701). The attempt made in 1695 to revert, for Op. 16 (*La Musa armonica, Cantate amorose musicali a voce sola*), to Monti seems to have brought problems, for Op. 17 came out again in Venice. Bassani's later cantata collections did in fact return to Bologna – but to Silvani rather than to Monti. Since the composer's sacred publications exhibit a similar pattern of change between publishers,[16] it would probably be correct to impute the cause to difficulties with Monti rather to a progressive disenchantment on Monti's part with the cantata genre. Although the latter remained active as a music publisher probably until 1709,[17] his involvement with cantatas ended in 1695 with Bassani's Op. 16. Nevertheless, between 1690 and 1695 he brought out a not inconsiderable number of substantial collections of vocal music (see Table 4.4).

Of especial interest for performance practice are Brevi's cantata collections, which contain exceptionally full dynamic markings, notably in connection with the performance of *Devisen* (repeated motto statements), which were clearly expected always to be performed in loud–soft alternation, as illustrated in Example 4.2.

Example 4.2 Brevi, cantata *Rendimi un sguardo solo*, first aria, bars 1–5.

That this struggle for supremacy in cantata publication does not become any simpler to characterize, even though a new generation of gifted cantata composers came to join the ever-productive veterans such as Bassani, is due to the growing interest in the cantata genre shown by publishers in other cities.

---

[16] Thus Opp. 9, 10, 12 and 20–24 appeared in Venice; to these may be added new editions of Opp. 11 and 13, previously published by Pier-Maria Monti. Opp. 18, 25–8 and 30 were entrusted, like the cantata collections of the same years, to Silvani in Bologna.

[17] See Luca Casagrande and Filippo Emanuele Ravizza, 'Giovanni Battista Bassani – Serenata – Cantate', at http://www.luca-casagrande.com/it/production/lib/lib_gbassani. pdf (consulted on 27 August 2007), p. 4.

In Amsterdam, first P. and I. Blaeu in 1691 and then Estienne Roger in 1696, 1697 and 1698 staked their claim to this segment of the market, initially with anthologies containing music by several composers and subsequently with the more customary collections by a single composer (see Table 4.5).

Table 4.5   Vocal chamber music published in Amsterdam, 1691–98.

various authors	*Scelta delle più belle ariette, e canzocnine* [sic] *italiane de' più famosi autori*	Amsterdam – P. and I. Blaeu	1691
various authors	*Recueil d'airs serieux et a boire – livre second*	Amsterdam – Estienne Roger	1696
various authors	*Recueil d'airs serieux et a boire – livre troisième*	Amsterdam – Estienne Roger	1697
Le Grand, Nicolas Ferdinand	*Cantate e ariette a voce sola*, Op. 1	Amsterdam – Estienne Roger	1698
Le Grand, Nicolas Ferdinand	*Cantate e ariette a voce sola*, Op. 2	Amsterdam – Estienne Roger	1698
Pistocchi, Francesco Antonio	*Scherzi musicali* [...] *cantate*, Op. 2	Amsterdam – Estienne Roger	1698

This involvement was certainly very purposeful, yet it ended rather abruptly in 1702 (see Table 4.10, below).

In Rome Mascardi brought out in 1695 and 1700, respectively, two substantial cantata collections (Francesco Gasparini, *Cantate da camera a voce sola*, Op. 1, and Bernardo Gaffi, *Cantate da cammera* [sic] *a voce sola*, Op. 1).

Between 1695 and 1702 the Modenese publisher Fortuniano Rosati tried his hand at issuing cantatas (see Table 4.6). Three out of the four publications of Rosati were of secular vocal music by Giovanni Battista Brevi, which is made more surprising by the fact that the composer resided not in Modena but in Milan.

Table 4.6   Vocal chamber music published in Modena by Fortuniano Rosati, 1695–1702.

Brevi, Giovanni Battista	*I Delirii d'amor Divino, Cantate morali a voce sola*, Op. 5	1695
Brevi, Giovanni Battista	*Cantate ed' ariette da camera a'voce sola*, Op. 7	1696
Brevi, Giovanni Battista	*La catena d'oro, Ariette da camera a voce sola*, Op. 6	1696
Albergati, P. Pirro	*Cantate spirituali a una, due, e trè voci con strumenti*, Op. 9	1702

Bartolomeo Gregori, brother of the composer Giovanni Lorenzo Gregori, was for a short time active as a publisher in Lucca. He started by reprinting the *Cantate da camera a voce sola*, Op. 1, of Francesco Gasparini, published in 1695 by Mascardi in Rome. This was followed before the end of the century by three collections of cantatas, one of which was issued in separate parts: Giovanni Lorenzo Gregori's *Arie in stil francese a una e due voci* (1698), Agostino Bonaventura Coletti's *Armonici tributi*, Op. 1 (1699) and Gregori's *Cantate a voce sola*, Op. 3 (1699). The series was concluded in 1701 with Azzolino Bernardino Della Ciaia's *Cantate da camera a voce sola*, Op. 2, and Giovanni Antonio Canuti's *Cantate da camera a voce sola* (without opus number). The connection with Lucca of all these composers is evident, even if Coletti was by then working in Venice. Coletti clearly profited from, and perhaps deliberately cultivated, his links to his native city when he chose to have his twelve cantatas published there.

Even in distant Nürnberg an attempt was made at the end of the century (1699) by Johann Christoph Weigel to publish a set of cantatas. These were the *Tributi armonici* of Carlo Agostino Badia.

Meanwhile, back in Bologna, Marino Silvani raised his profile considerably, starting in the closing decade of the century to supplant Monti as the leading publisher. During these years he vied with Giuseppe Sala in Venice for pole position in the marketplace. Between 1696 and 1698 he republished three collections of Bassani (Opp. 1, 3 and 6) as well as producing four further prints, as shown in Table 4.7.

At the start of the eighteenth century Silvani's market share rose even more: of the forty-three collections containing secular vocal music known to have been published in that century, no fewer than ten emerged from his printing shop (see Table 4.8).

The one Italian publisher who could even half keep pace with Silvani during this period was Giuseppe Sala in Venice, whose productions are listed in Table 4.9.

Table 4.7 Vocal chamber music published in Bologna by Marino Silvani, 1696–98.

Predieri, Giacomo Cesare	*Cantate morali a 2 e 3 voci*, Op. 1	1696
Pistocchi, Francesco Antonio	*Cantate*, Op. 1	1698
Cherici, Sebastiano	*Componimenti da camera a due voci*, Op. 5	1698
Bassani, Giovanni Battista	*Languidezze amorose, Cantate a voce sola*, Op. 19	1698

Table 4.8   Vocal chamber music published in Bologna by Marino Silvani, 1700 onwards.

Aldrovandini, Giuseppe	*Cantate a voce sola*, Op. 2	1701
[Bononcini, Giovanni]*	*[Duetti da camera*, Op. 8]*	1701
Bassani, Giovanni Battista	*Corona di fiori musicali – Tessuta d'ariette con varij stromenti*, Op. 29	1702
Bassani, Giovanni Battista	*Cantate et arie amorose a voce sola con violini unissoni*, Op. 31	1703
Braibanzi, Francesco	*Cantate da camera a canto solo*, Op. 2	1703
Motta, Artemio	*Cantate a voce sola*, Op. 2	1704
various authors	*Cantate varie per musica*	1704
Silvani, Giuseppe Antonio	*Cantate morali e spirituali a 1, 2 e 3 voci*, Op. 5	1707
Albergati, P. Pirro	*Cantate et oratorii spirituali a una, due e tre voci con strumenti*, Op. 10	1714
Albergati, P. Pirro	*Corona de' pregi di Maria. Cantate a voce sola*, Op. 13	1717

Table 4.9   Vocal chamber music published in Venice by Giuseppe Sala, 1706 onwards.

[Bassani, Giovanni Battista]*	*Armoniche fantasie di cantate amorose a voce sola*, Op. 15	1701
Bassani, Giovanni Battista	*Cantate a voce sola*, Op. 28	1701
Albinoni, Tomaso	*Cantate a voce sola*, Op. 4	1702
Altogiri, Abate	*Cantate a voce sola*	1705
Ruggieri, Giovanni Maria	*Cantate con violini e senza*, Op. 5	1706

Notes:

* Bracketed composers' names indicate a reprint; bracketed titles refer to music for more than one voice.

There is some bibliographical uncertainty over Sala's edition of Bassani's Op. 28, recently cited by Michael Talbot.[18] Although this collection appears as item 39, 'Cantate a voce sola, di Gio: Battista Bassani. Opera 28', in Sala's well-known catalogue of 1715, no example appears to survive.[19] But since Sala sometimes acted as a stockist for works issued by other publishers – his catalogue

---

[18] Michael Talbot, *The Chamber Cantatas of Antonio Vivaldi* (Woodbridge, 2006), p. 4. Talbot provides, moreover, a tabular survey of cantata prints (pp. 3–7) that essentially provides the starting point for the present contribution.

[19] Sala's 1715 catalogue, together with transcriptions of many other seventeenth- and eighteenth-century Italian catalogues listing cantata publications discussed in this chapter, is consultable in Oscar Mischiati, *Indici, cataloghi e avvisi degli editori e librai musicali italiani dal 1591 al 1798* (Florence, 1984), pp. 339–44.

Example 4.3 G. B. Bassani, cantata *Ha più foco un sen ferito*, aria 'Non mi far più languir', bars 6–14.

lists as item 94, without special distinction apart from the exceptionally steep price, the Op. 6 violin sonatas of Tomaso Albinoni published only by Roger in Amsterdam – the possibility remains that there was no independent Sala edition. Equally fruitless was the search for an example of Altogiri's cantatas.

That Bassani, the sheer number of whose cantata publications is apt to produce a negative reaction, was not, as has been claimed, a composer content to remain within the bounds of conventional harmony[20] is shown by his soprano cantata *Ha più foco un sen ferito* from his Op. 19, from whose aria 'Non mi far più languir' a few bars are quoted as Example 4.3.

The remainder of the cantata collections published in Italy in the eighteenth century are attributable to: Mascardi in Rome (Bernardo Gaffi, *Cantate da cammera* [sic] *a voce sola*, Op. 1, 1700); Bartolomeo Gregori in Lucca (see above); Fortuniano Rosati in Modena (Giacomo Cattaneo, *Trattenimenti armonici da camera* [...] *con due brevi cantate a soprano solo*, Op. 1, 1700), and P. Pirro Albergati, *Cantate spirituali a una, due e tre voci con strumenti*, Op. 9, 1702); Antonio Bortoli in Venice (the new edition of Giovanni Battista Brevi's *I deliri d'amor Divino, Cantate morali a voce sola*, Op. 5, 1706, and Alessandro Marcello, *Cantate da camera a voce sola*, 1708); Giuseppe Montuoli in Bologna (various authors, *Cantate a voce sola e basso continuo*, 1720); an anonymous publisher in Brescia (Fortunato Zuchini, *Cantate*, 1722); bringing up the rear are the Neapolitan editions, dating from the 1730s, of cantatas by Pergolesi.[21]

All the other prints appeared – and this heralds the end of cantata publication within Italy – north of the Alps. Those of Estienne Roger are bunched at the very beginning of the eighteenth century. In the period 1721–35 London, thanks to the efforts of Smith and Atkins (and others unknown), became almost the only active location of cantata publication, as Table 4.10 shows.

The sporadic involvement of publishers in other non-Italian cities – Hamburg (Keiser, 1713), Köthen (Stricker, 1715) and Lisbon (d'Astorga, 1726) – leaves the impression of a time-lag in the acknowledgement of the cantata's decline as a genre. If we survey cantata manuscripts, we find that after 1720 most such pieces were written in the south of the peninsula, where the genre appears to have enjoyed greater longevity than in the north. In Germany and England the Italian cantata did not establish itself strongly enough to generate imitations (with Italian or vernacular texts) by native-born composers until the eighteenth century. It therefore hardly surprises that in these two lands the publication of cantatas started at a time, paradoxically, when it had almost ceased in Italy itself.[22]

---

[20] See, for example, Peter Smith (adapted from), 'Bassani, Giovanni Battista', in Ludwig Finscher (ed.), *Die Musik in Geschichte und Gegenwart*, 2nd rev. edn, 21 vols (Kassel etc., 1994–2007), *Personenteil*, vol. 2, pp. 447–51, at p. 451.

[21] These are the *Cantate quattro*, reissued in revised form in 1738 as *Quattro cantate da camera*.

[22] France was a case apart. The cultivation of the cantata genre by native-born composers began earlier in France than in either England or Germany, but its rise to

Table 4.10   Cantata publications in Amsterdam and London after 1700.

Scarlatti, Alessandro	*Cantate a 1 e 2 voci*, Op. 1	Amsterdam – Estienne Roger	1701
various authors	*Cantate a 1 e 2 voci con trombe e flauto*	Amsterdam – Estienne Roger	1702
various authors	*Cantate e ariette a voce sola con violini*	Amsterdam – Estienne Roger	1702
various authors	*Cantate e ariette a voce sola senza violini*	Amsterdam – Estienne Roger	1702
Bononcini, Giovanni	*Cantate e duetti*	London	1721
Kelleri, Fortunato	*Cantate e arie con stromenti*	London – Smith	1727
Sandoni, Pietro Giuseppe	*Cantate da camera e Sonate per il Cembalo*	London	1727?
D'Alay, Mauro	*Cantate e suonate*	London	1728
Ariosti, Attilio	*Six Cantatas and Six Lessons for the Viola d'amore*[*]	London	1728
Arrigoni, Carlo	*Cantate da camera ...*	London – Atkins	1732
Duni, Antonio	*Cantate da camera ...*	London – Smith	1735?
Porpora, Nicola	*... nuovamente composte opre di musica vocale*	London	1735

Notes:
[*] This collection lacks a regular title page, so this wording is not original.

The reasons for the decline and, finally, cessation of cantata publishing in Italy are a matter for speculation. Michael Talbot's hypothesis of a connection with practical difficulties of typesetting and with unfavourable economic conditions that made published music in general and cantatas in particular hard to market profitably may be valid.[23] The ever-increasing partiality in cantatas for virtuosity and, especially, rhythmic differentiation may also have played its part: these factors make the performers' vertical alignment of the notes harder, thereby discouraging sight-reading. In other countries the preference for the more flexible process of engraving (which Italian music publishers adopted only sporadically during the period under consideration) mitigated the problem very considerably.

Further, the cantata prints show that the traditional small dimensions and oblong quarto format used for collections became disadvantageous as the cantata's scale expanded in the eighteenth century. Since the chosen format permitted only two systems per page, it was impossible without significantly reducing the font to avoid multiplying the page-turns inordinately. In 1676 Giacomo Monti experimented with a larger size of page that allowed three systems for Legrenzi's

---

indigenous status was both more rapid and more thoroughgoing.

[23] Talbot, *The Chamber Cantatas of Antonio Vivaldi*, p. 2.

Op. 12, repeating the innovation for the same composer's Op. 14 and Petrobelli's Op. 10. But he reverted thereafter to the conventional size and layout. Only very occasionally, as with Pietro Porfirii's *Cantate da camera a voce sola*, Op. 1, did his successor, Pier-Maria Monti, revive this layout. In the last case, the increased page size was necessary, since Porfirii repeatedly writes arias with an additional bass part, as occurs in 'È gran pena amar chi teme' from the cantata *O ch'io son pur sfortunato*, which is headed 'Aria con il Violoncello' (see Example 4.4).

The strong resemblance of this aria to ones with obbligato cello found in contemporary opera – the aria 'Sperar deggio', employed in several operas of the time is a prime example[24] – brings out the modish character of this print. Undeniably, however, virtuoso arias of this kind expose the limitations of the small format, which was much better suited to briefer arias, often employing chromatic formulas, such as 'Flebil sono i suoi lamenti' from Porfirii's first cantata, *Dal Zodiaco stellato*.

Other publishers, among them Novello De Bonis in Naples and Mascardi in Rome, tried, with the help of the three-system layout, to accommodate more music on a page, as their editions of cantatas by Cataldo Amodei and Bernardo Gaffi, respectively, show.

Example 4.4   Porfirii, cantata *O ch'io son pur sfortunato*, aria 'È gran pena amar chi teme', bars 1–33.

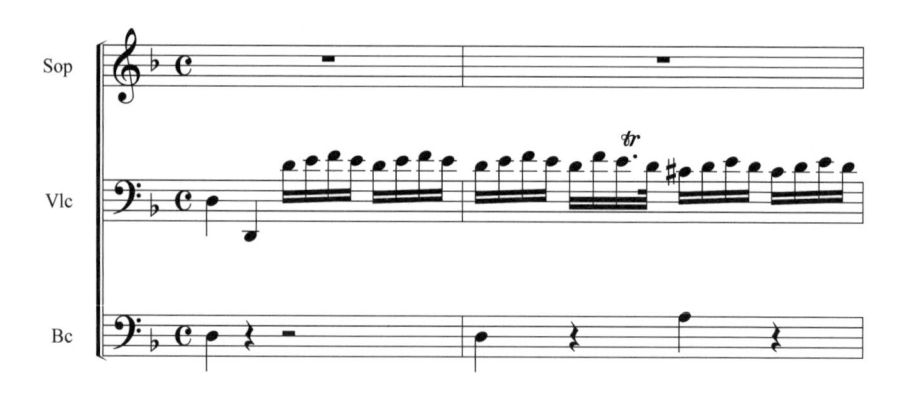

---

[24] On this aria, see Norbert Dubowy, 'Pollarolo e Ziani a Verona. Annotazioni in margine a tre partiture ritrovate', in Alberto Colzani, Andrea Luppi and Maurizio Padoan (eds), *Seicento inesplorato. L'evento musicale tra prassi e stile: un modello di interdipendenza. Atti del III Convegno internazionale sulla musica in area lombardo-padana del secolo XVII* (Como, 1993), pp. 509–35, esp. pp. 523–4, as well as Reinmar Emans, 'Giovanni Legrenzis Oper *Eteocle e Polinice* in der Bearbeitung Antonio Gianettinis. Ein Beitrag zur musikästhetischen Entwicklung der Arie', in Colzani, Luppi and Padoan, *Seicento inesplorato*, pp. 559–90, esp. pp. 570–71, 573 and 585–90.

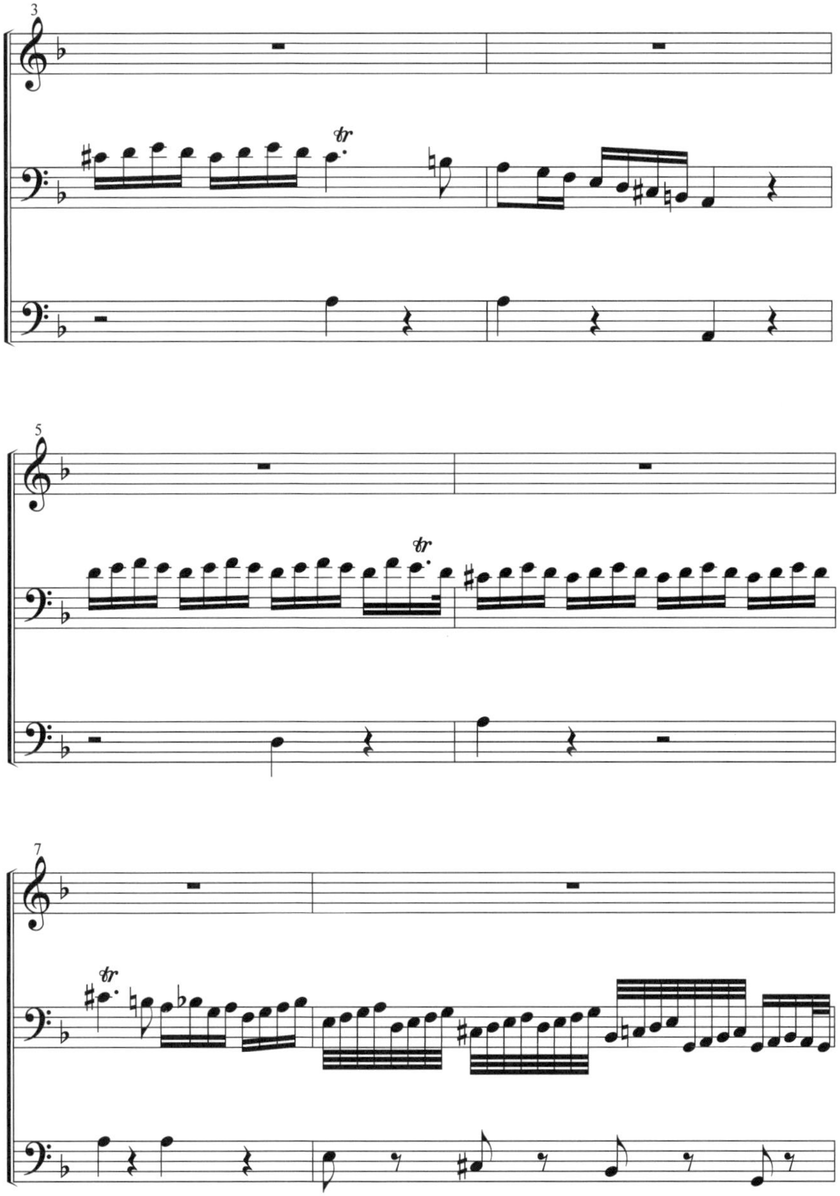
3
tr
5
tr
7
tr

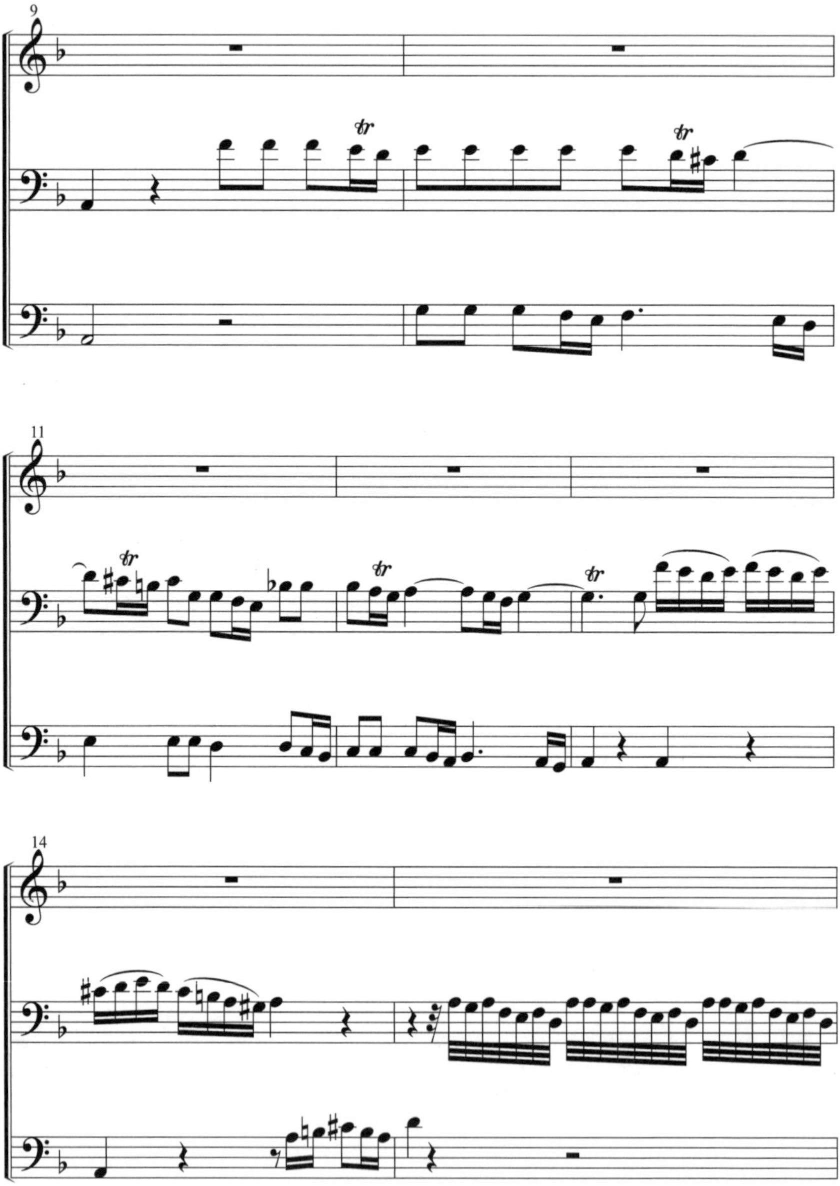
9
11
14

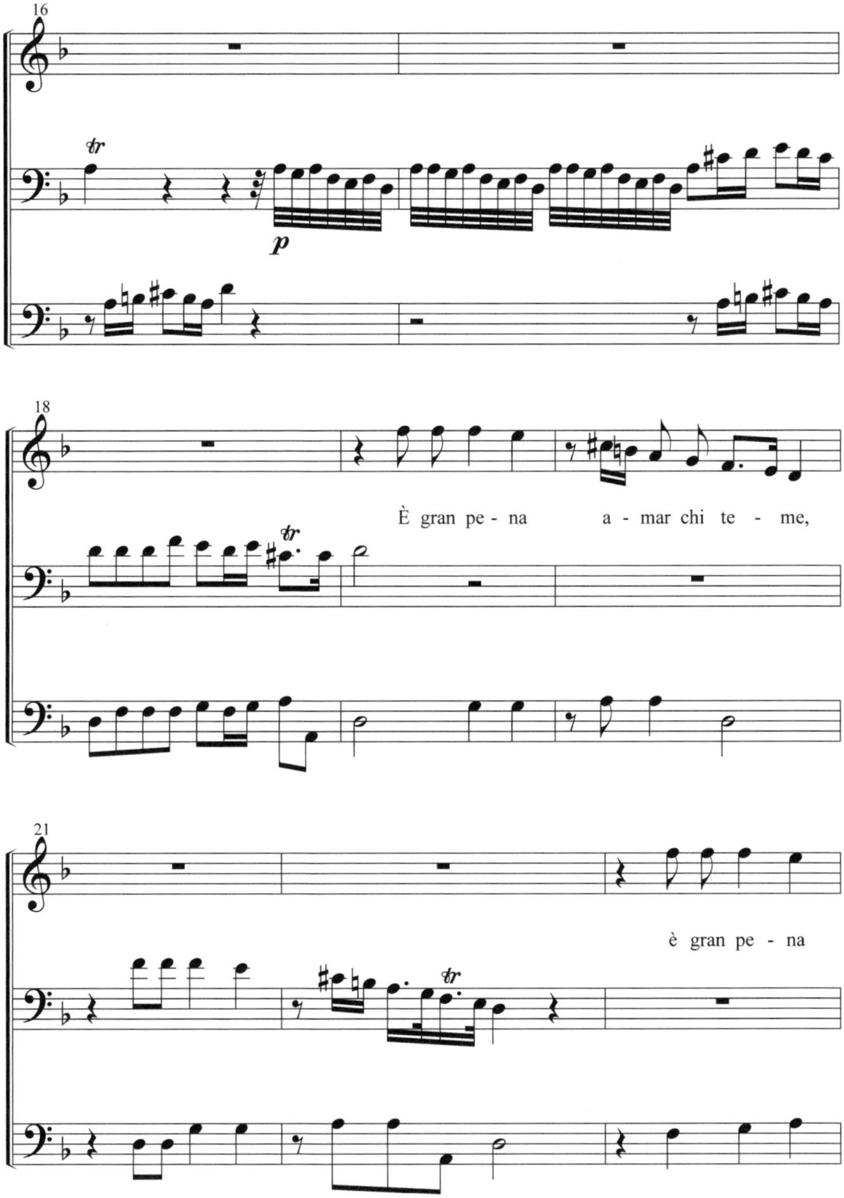
È gran pe - na a - mar chi te - me,
è gran pe - na

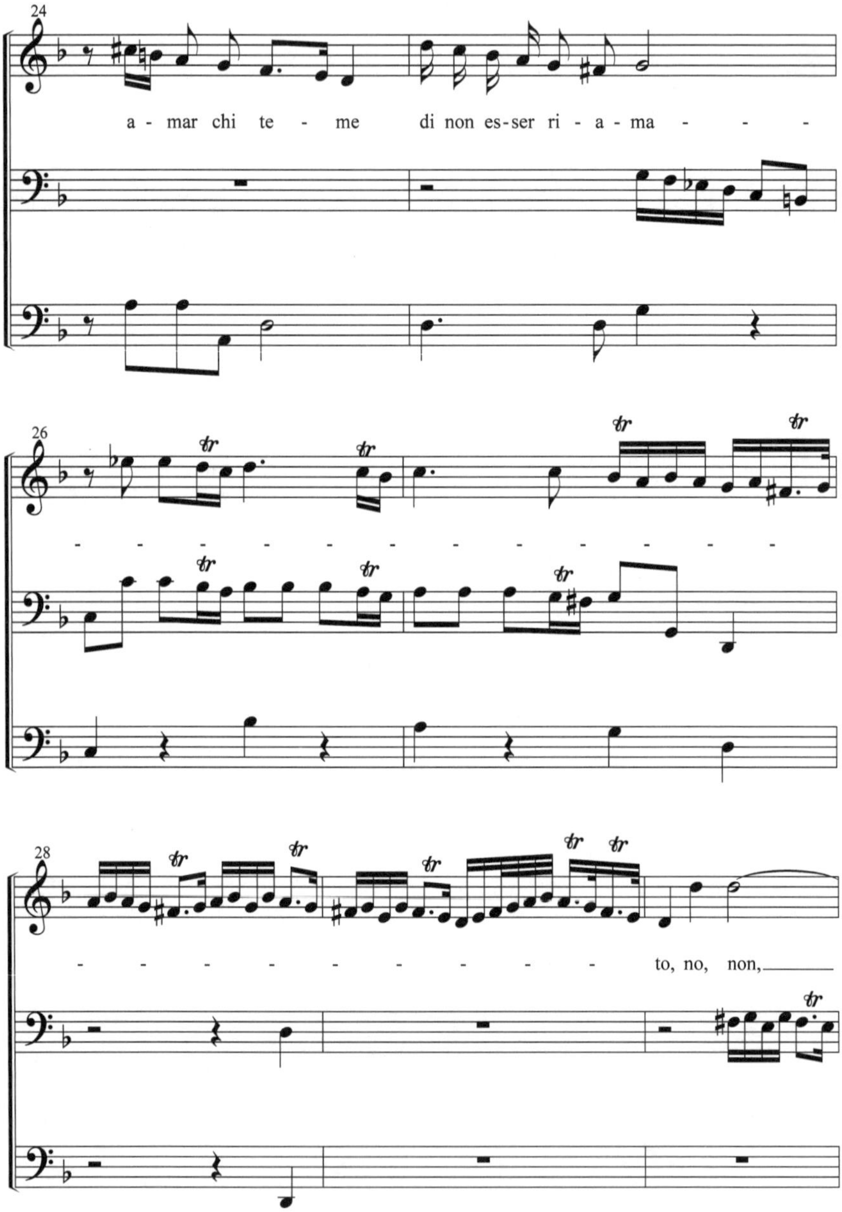
24
a - mar chi te - me di non es-ser ri - a - ma - - -
26
28
to, no, non,

After 1700 the larger dimensions become somewhat commoner, matching, up to a point, the expanded scale of the music. The only print to abandon oblong in favour of upright format is Attilio Ariosti's collection published in London in 1728, and this may be on account of the sonatas (lessons) for the viola d'amore with which the cantatas share the volume. Upright format was generally preferred for music of all kinds for more than one voice and also for solo cantatas with instrumental accompaniment. In this respect, the collections by Tosi (1688), Zanata (1695), Gasparini (1695) and Gregori (1698) seem to deviate from the principle, but the explanation is that they require the extra staff only for certain items. Zanata employs the third staff every so often for violins; Gregori uses it sometimes for an extra vocal part; and the two other composers reserve it for the harpsichordist's right hand. Tosi does not specify the nature of the part on the third staff, but Gasparini provides a detailed description: 'You will find in some arias two basses, one for ease or facility of accompaniment, having had also to adapt itself to the printing process, which has not been fully able to show my intention. However, wherever soprano or treble clefs are found above the bass, [the notes] will be played with the right hand in the fashion of a keyboard score. Alternatives are an archlute or a cello'.[1]

The existence of these diverse sizes and layouts shows that the small oblong quarto format, however practical for the user in terms of portability, eventually grew to be inadequate for the purpose. Even if, despite its shortcomings, this miniature format managed to survive for a very long time, the increasing mismatch between content and page size may, one surmises, have finally caused demand to

---

[1] Preface (headed 'A gl'Amatori della Musica') to *Cantate da camera a voce sola* (Rome, 1695), reprinted in facsimile with an introduction by Piero Mioli (Florence, 1984): 'Trovarete in alcune Arie dui Bassi uno per comodo, ò facilità di accompagnare; essendo stato necessario anche accomodarsi alla Stampa, che non hà potuto totalmente dimostrar la mia intenzione. Però doue si trovano sopra il Basso alcune chiavi di Canto, ò Violino si soneranno con la mano destra in forma d'intavolatura. Ivi potranno ancora sodisfarsi l'Arcileuto, e Violoncello'.

shrink. Manuscript copies permit much a more flexible organization of the notes on a page, and between pages, and their superiority in this respect must have been perceived as a notable advantage.

A further possible reason for the decline of the published cantata in the eighteenth century is that fewer patrons were willing to lend their names to, and to pay or defray the costs of, such volumes. During the *Blütezeit* of cantata prints hardly a volume appeared without a dedication, and patrons from outside the region of publication – such high-ranking persons as Francesco II, Niccolò Sagredo, Ranuccio Farnese, Ferdinand III, Charles II and Leopold I – were increasingly chosen. From around 1690 dedicatees of this degree of eminence appear – at least, in connection with works published in Italy – to have become less readily available. Conspicuous among them was Leopold I, to whom, as late as 1701, Giovanni Bononcini (who had the advantage of being in the emperor's service) dedicated a set of duets. But most dedicatees of Italian cantata prints from this period were persons of local rather than national or international importance, and composers and publishers often dispensed altogether with patronage of this kind. Only in London did composers manage to interest the higher nobility in their projects.

One is right to ask the question whether the over time increasingly standardized form of the cantata contributed to loss of interest in it. If cantatas from the second half of the seventeenth century derived their musical vitality in the first instance from the relative brevity of the musical sections, their increasingly precise tempo markings, aiming at strong contrasts, and their frequent changes of dynamic level show that this contrast-dominated style of writing was viewed as a normative element of this chamber genre, whereas it was exceptional in the contemporary opera. Standardization of any kind means, however, that this vitality risks becoming weakened or even lost altogether. That this was evident, at least in part, to contemporaries can be inferred from the fact that numerous collections from the very end of the seventeenth century retain the older, mosaic-like structures. Indeed, a few prints contain predominantly or even exclusively *Sujetkantaten* (cantatas dealing with well-known historical or mythological episodes), which as a rule possess a more generous scale and a freer structure (as found in Giovanni Maria Bononcini's Op. 1 and Albergati's Op. 6), while also retaining connecting ariosos and expressive tempo changes. As late as 1690 Pietro degli Antonii's cantatas have the *da capo* text repeat set to varied music, and feature, besides arioso insertions, strophic repetition. The latter device is encountered also in Bassani's aria 'Mi far più languir' from the 1698 cantata *Ha più foco un sen ferito*, which shows that published cantatas for a long time largely remained aloof from the simplifying developments in form attested by countless contemporary cantatas preserved only in manuscript. In these circumstances, it comes as no surprise that Eugen Schmitz, whose investigations centred on the repertory preserved in manuscript, was able to describe 'die Mehrzahl der Stücke in den Cantate à voce sola von Giov. Batt. Alveri (Bologna 1687)' ('most of the pieces in the *Cantate a voce sola* of Giovanni Battista Alveri') as 'ziemlich reaktionär' ('fairly reactionary'). Despite this, Schmitz did not remain immune to Alveri's expressive power, quoting the opening bars, with their chromatic descent, of this composer's cantata *Mia vita, mio bene*.[25] But even an aria such as the first of Albergati's alto cantata *D'Acheronte errini horribili* (see Example 4.5) cannot be dismissed *tout court* as backward-looking.

Example 4.5 Albergati, cantata *D'Acheronte errini horribili*, first aria, bars 1–10

---

[25] Schmitz, *Geschichte der weltlichen Solokantate*, p. 110.

[musical notation: "-de - - - - te il mi - - o fu-ror."]

From the perspective adopted by Schmitz, who viewed the so-called Neapolitan School as *the* stylistic, or at least *a* stylistic, end-point, this patchwork structure, which can indeed be a positive feature insofar as it promotes a highly flexible and text-responsive manner of writing, had to be regarded as a deficiency. But also musicians and music-making amateurs of the eighteenth century probably no longer found this contrast-based style fashionable – especially since they would certainly have based their judgement on the contemporary manuscript repertory.

When passing judgement on Schmitz's book on the cantata, we must not forget that it was the pioneering work in its field. This fact makes his in many respects highly detailed and in many parts still valid account all the more praiseworthy. An example of a minor correction that has to be made to his overall picture arises from the vocal registers employed in the published cantatas. Although a preference for the soprano voice is not to be denied, an astonishingly high number of prints contain cantatas for alto and bass. The fact that only the *Cantate spirituali* of Cazzati (1659) and Albergati (1702) include pieces explicitly for tenor voice can be explained by the tradition among tenors of singing soprano parts an octave lower, a tradition mentioned and approved by several collections. Similarly, Schmitz is not wholly correct when stating, as he does on more than one occasion, that cantatas were usually published in sets of twelve. It is true that twelve is the most common number, but this convention did not take root until the 1680s. And there are numerous collections that contain only ten items. Now and again, 'double' volumes with twenty or twenty-four cantatas were published. Less common were 'half' volumes with six cantatas, such as Zanata's Op. 2. Now and again, we encounter volumes with a less regular number: Porfirii's Op. 1 has seven cantatas, Gabrielli's op. 2 eleven, Cazzati's Op. 41 thirteen. So generalization is once again dangerous. Perhaps it will come as no surprise that cantatas featuring the 'classic' scheme Recitative – *Da capo* Aria – Recitative – *Da capo* Aria are rather exceptional in the published repertory, being outnumbered by relatively freely devised schemes, to the great benefit of the portrayal of the *affetto*. For despite (or because of?) the rather conservative content of the cantata publications, one encounters at almost every turn highly subtle and also musically convincing individual solutions that give the lie to any over-generalized assessment of the repertory as a whole. Schmitz was very clear-sighted when, on the basis primarily of the manuscript repertory, he summarized the direction in which the cantata was headed in these words: 'Admittedly, such stereotyping, even if it has the advantage of clarity, is artistically very questionable, and thus we see its entry into our genre as the first sign of decay'.[26] It is precisely flexibility of form that enables the composer to attain a stronger connection between music and form; it is through this feature that the most convincing solutions were obtained. The wish remains that the cantata repertory will be researched in the future more comprehensively and more thoroughly than could be achieved in the present short study.[27]

---

[26] Schmitz, *Geschichte der weltlichen Solokantate*, p. 67: 'Freilich, solche Stereotypisierung, mag sie auch den Vorteil der Klarheit haben, ist künstlerisch stets bedenklich, und darum sehen wir sie in unserer Kunstgattung auch erst mit dem Beginne des Verfalls eintreten'.

[27] A longer study of cantata publications by Sara Dieci (Modena) is reported at the time of writing to be in preparation.

Chapter 5
'Al tavolino medesimo del Compositor della Musica': Notes on Text and Context in Alessandro Scarlatti's *cantate da camera*

Norbert Dubowy

Scarlatti outdid his contemporaries by the sheer quantity of his compositions in the genre of the chamber cantata. Even though quantity does not necessarily translate into quality, importance or historical significance, there is general agreement that the genre of the *cantata da camera* reaches a peak in the work of Scarlatti: quantity is just an external indicator of this fact. Writers of the eighteenth century such as Heinichen or Burney, critical though they are about specific details of Scarlatti's style, acknowledge his achievement in the genre.[1] Music historians of the twentieth and twenty-first centuries unanimously accord Scarlatti a prominent position in the history of the genre. This is sufficiently demonstrated by the obligatory inclusion of one of his cantatas in virtually every music history textbook or modern teaching anthology covering his period.

In relation to Alessandro Scarlatti's cantatas, research has up to now concentrated on the development of their form, some peculiarities of the composer's style, the chronology of the works, certain sub-groups within them and some selected sources. Several proposals have been made over the past hundred years – more or less, since the publication of Eugen Schmitz's pioneering *Geschichte der weltlichen Solokantate* – for appropriate systems for periodizing Scarlatti's immense output in the domain: Schmitz himself divided them into three periods grouped around the axis of a central Roman period, 1703–08;[2] Malcolm Boyd laid emphasis on

---

[1] Johann David Heinichen, *Der Generalbass in der Composition* (Dresden, 1728), pp. 797–836; English edition by George J. Buelow, *Thorough-Bass Accompaniment according to Johann David Heinichen* (Berkeley, 1966). Charles Burney, *A General History of Music, from the Earliest Ages to the Present Period*, 4 vols (London, 1776–89); Burney unequivocally characterizes Scarlatti (vol. 4, pp. 164–5) as 'The most voluminous and most original composer of cantatas that has ever existed, in any country to which my enquiries have reached'.

[2] Eugen Schmitz, *Geschichte der weltlichen Solokantate* (Leipzig, 1914), pp. 146–7; see also Maria Caraci, 'Le cantate romane di Alessandro Scarlatti nel fondo Noseda', in

three distinct Roman periods (1672–84, 1703–08 and 1722–25),[3] and in an earlier article singled out one specific turning point: the year 1697;[4] Hanley identified a long period of transition and formation (up to 1704).[5] Different as these approaches are, they are all still taken as reference points in recent scholarship. They all have to deal with two problems: Scarlatti's personal stylistic development and the wider paradigmatic change in the structure and poetic of the chamber cantata.

It is time to take a second look at some of these issues in order to identify the place of the cantata in Scarlatti's oeuvre, to connect his work with certain moments of his creative life and to look in particular at the changing poetics and aesthetics in the genre around 1700 as reflected in cantata poetry and music.

Any consideration of Scarlatti and the cantata has to take into account the sheer number of cantatas he composed, which can easily prove a deterrent to the modern scholar. At the present time, it is impossible to say how many cantatas he wrote.[6] He outstrips every other composer of his generation, even without attaining the quantity implied by a report in Quantz's autobiography: 'a certain Neapolitan courtier boasted of possessing 4,000 examples of Scarlatti's work, mostly solo cantatas'.[7] After subtracting around 140 doubtful attributions, there are still in the region of 700 chamber cantatas. The numbers are as impressive as they are imprecise. The nature of the transmission of the chamber cantata, which is often preserved in collective manuscripts compiled by copyists who generally had scant interest in the consistent and reliable assignment of authorship, leaves the door wide open to problematic attributions. While sources described in some earlier studies have disappeared, new sources have meanwhile come to light; in some cases, the re-emergence of sources

---

Nino Pirrotta and Agostino Ziino (eds), *Händel e gli Scarlatti a Roma. Atti del Convegno Internazionale di Studi, Roma 1985* (Florence, 1987), pp. 93–112, at p. 98.

[3] Malcolm Boyd, 'Cantata: §1, 6. Alessandro Scarlatti', in Stanley Sadie (ed.), *The New Grove Dictionary of Music and Musicians*, 20 vols (London, 1980), vol. 3, pp. 698–9.

[4] Malcolm Boyd, 'Form and Style in Scarlatti's Chamber Cantatas', *Music Review*, 25 (1964), pp. 17–26.

[5] Edwin Hanley, 'Scarlatti, Alessandro', in Friedrich Blume (ed.), *Die Musik in Geschichte und Gegenwart*, 14 vols (Kassel, 1948–68), vol. 11, coll. 1501–1503.

[6] The central point of reference for any bibliographical study of Scarlatti's cantatas remains Edwin Hanley's impressive catalogue 'Alessandro Scarlatti's Cantate da camera: A Bibliographical Study' (PhD dissertation, Yale University, 1963). In the present study, cantatas are identified by the number in Hanley's catalogue. See also Giancarlo Rostirolla, 'Catalogo generale delle Opere di Alessandro Scarlatti', in Roberto Pagano and Lino Bianchi, *Alessandro Scarlatti* (Turin, 1972), pp. 317–595: cantate da camera, pp. 377–494.

[7] Paul Nettl, *Forgotten Musicians* (New York, 1951), pp. 280–319, at p. 304. The original text appeared as 'Herrn Johann Joachim Quantzens Lebenslauf, von ihm selbst entworfen', in Friedrich Wilhelm Marpurg (ed.), *Historisch-kritische Beyträge zur Aufnahme der Musik*, 8 vols (Berlin, 1754–78), vol. 1, part 1, pp. 197–250, at p. 229. For a critical examination of these numbers, see Hanley, 'Alessandro Scarlatti's Cantate da camera', p. 13.

that have not been accessible for a while causes the absolute number of the cantatas as well as the number of sources transmitting them to fluctuate.[8]

The majority of these cantatas are written for one solo voice, most often a soprano, with basso continuo. In about one cantata in ten Scarlatti adds obbligato instruments to the accompaniment. There is also a smaller group of cantatas for two voices.[9] Some of the latter may more aptly be described as chamber duets, however. Excluded from consideration here are the large-scale celebratory cantatas with orchestral accompaniment that are more suitably categorized as serenatas.[10] The preservation and circulation of cantatas has occurred in the form of manuscripts: either contained within anthologies bearing cantatas by various composers or in collections containing compositions by Scarlatti alone. Autograph scores are found in various libraries, but detailed source criticism of this repertory is still lacking.[11]

A glance at Scarlatti's catalogue of compositions shows a prolific composer working in all areas – in particular, in the dramatic genres of opera, serenata and oratorio, in secular vocal chamber music, in sacred music for large and small ensembles and also in instrumental music. The unequal distribution of these domains in terms of quantity (instrumental music, for instance, forms a relatively small part of Scarlatti's oeuvre) needs to be viewed in the light of the shifts in interest and emphasis that, as more recent research has shown, occurred over the lifetime of the composer. To give one example: most of Scarlatti's surviving sacred music seems to date from after 1700. This general picture holds true even when we take into account the possibility that the lack of earlier pieces is simply due to the vagaries of transmission and preservation. These shifts of focus within

---

[8] On the disappearance of manuscripts, see Hanley, 'Alessandro Scarlatti's Cantate da camera', p. 14, note 25. On some recent findings, see Lawrence Bennett, 'A Little-known Collection of Early-Eighteenth-Century Vocal Music at Schloss Elisabethenburg, Meiningen', *Fontes artis musicae*, 48 (2001): 250–302; and Hans Joachim Marx and Steffen Voss, 'Unbekannte Kantaten von Händel, A. Scarlatti, Fago und Grillo in einer neapolitanischen Handschrift von 1710', in Bianca Maria Antolini, Teresa M. Gialdroni and Annunziato Pugliese (eds), *"Et facciam dolçi canti"*. *Studi in onore di Agostino Ziino in occasione del suo 65° compleanno* (Lucca, 2003), pp. 797–806.

[9] Cantatas with obbligato instruments as well as duet cantatas are studied in Cecilia Kathryn Van de Kamp Freund, 'A. Scarlatti's Duet Cantatas and Solo Cantatas with Obbligato Instruments' (PhD dissertation, Northwestern University, 1979); Freund, p. 1, counts 72 cantatas with obbligato instruments and 28 duet cantatas. Cf. Rostirolla, 'Catalogo generale delle Opere di Alessandro Scarlatti', pp. 377–92.

[10] A representative selection of cantatas is found in Malcolm Boyd (ed.), *Alessandro Scarlatti. Cantatas, The Italian Cantata in the Seventeenth Century*, vol. 17 (New York, 1986). The anthology includes the large-scale cantata *Al fragor di lieta tromba*.

[11] Some discussion occurs in Reinhard Strohm, 'Scarlattiana at Yale', in Pirrotta and Ziino (eds), *Händel e gli Scarlatti a Roma,* pp. 113–52, and in Laura Damuth, 'Alessandro Scarlatti's Cantatas for Soprano and Continuo' (PhD dissertation, Columbia University, 1993).

the oeuvre often come about through a combination of various influences, which include changes in the composer's biographical circumstances, in the patronage he enjoyed and in his institutional affiliations.

For the cantata, this kind of spadework still has to be done, but a reassessment of the material and other considerations may help to redefine some moments of Scarlatti's engagement with the cantata. How do life and career steps, and exposure to social and intellectual groupings, interact with his production of cantatas? The outline of Scarlatti's career in terms of institutional affiliations and service to noble patrons is relatively clear-cut. The first Roman period starts with his apprenticeship (1672), leads to his first position as *maestro di cappella* in 1678 and ends in 1684, when he is appointed *maestro di cappella* of the viceregal chapel in Naples. After his decision to leave the service of the Neapolitan court in 1702, he spends the next few years in Rome in various positions. In 1708 he is reinstated as chapel master in Naples and holds this position until the end of his life. However, even during his long periods of service in Naples, Scarlatti maintained strong relationships with Roman patrons and was frequently in Rome for the production of operas and oratorios.

It is a remarkable fact that Scarlatti evidently kept a precise tally of his operas and similar dramatic works.[12] Such numbers first appear in printed librettos in the mid-1690s and are later quoted in autograph scores. The numbering is in many ways problematic, since Scarlatti's criteria for including a musical work in that series are not clear. However, the fact is in itself noteworthy: it bespeaks personal pride and betrays a consciousness of working in a distinct musical domain. It testifies to the supreme importance the dramatic genre held in Scarlatti's self-assessment as a composer. No document of the same kind exists for the domain of the cantata; Scarlatti did not – so far as we know – count or number his cantatas. But he may have kept a log of them, and it is also very likely that the practice of dating and gathering cantatas in volumes covering a year of production (a *Jahrgang*) that Strohm observed in one of the autograph manuscripts, may well extend beyond that single specimen.[13] This evidences Scarlatti's meticulous tracking of his own production. However, while it speaks for his personal organization and hints at how he ordered his cantata manuscripts, this record-keeping cannot be interpreted, unlike the figures for the operas, as a public statement revealing his estimation of the genre.

There is one other item that may be regarded as a document of self-esteem. Various writers have noted that in one of his known portraits Scarlatti is shown with one of his cantatas. The painting in question is preserved in the Museo Internazionale e Biblioteca della Musica, formerly known as the Civico Museo Bibliografico

---

[12] Other composers of the time known to have kept a running total of their operas are Albinoni and Vivaldi.

[13] Osb. 2 in US-NH; see Strohm, 'Scarlattiana at Yale', p. 135. Similar but less organized is the manuscript D-MÜs, Sant. 3987; see Damuth, 'Alessandro Scarlatti's Cantatas for Soprano and Continuo', pp. 42–50.

Musicale, in Bologna, and has been reproduced in various publications concerning the composer.[14] It shows Scarlatti in half-profile, slightly turned towards the spectator. He wears the cross of the Papal order on his coat, which indicates that the portrait has been made after his receipt of the title of 'Cavaliere' from Pope Clement XI: thus after 1716. In the background, towards the left, a piece of music is depicted that at first sight seems nothing more than a conventional iconographic attribute of a composer.[15] The scene, however, has its own dynamic and a certain intimacy, with an inkwell and quill placed in front of the sheet music representing the composer's desktop: 'il tavolino del compositore'. We seem to be witnessing the composer just when he has interrupted his work for a brief moment in order to greet his visitors.

The text and music of the composition in the background are clearly and doubtless very deliberately legible. The piece can be identified as the cantata *Al fin m'ucciderete, o miei pensieri* (H 21).[16] In Scarlatti's cantata manuscript in US-NH, this cantata bears the date 20 July 1705; it thus comes from the central period of the composer's life.[17] Unfortunately, the picture preserved in Bologna is not an authentic contemporary painting but the work of a Neapolitan artist active in the second half of the eighteenth century who executed portraits also of Feo, Durante and Leo.[18] The portraits of Scarlatti and Leo follow the same pictorial schema that shows a piece of music – in both cases a cantata – in the background. So the painter may simply have put together, in the manner of a capriccio, a portrait of Scarlatti and an available representative example of his compositions. *Al fin m'ucciderete* enjoyed a wide circulation. It is one of the twelve cantatas on which Francesco Durante based his twelve duets, which went on to serve as didactic material throughout the eighteenth and much of the nineteenth century. Music-lovers in the later eighteenth century may well have associated Scarlatti with this piece in particular.

On the other hand, when we pay regard to the careful composition of the picture, it is more likely that the painting is simply a copy of an older painting (indeed, it is normally described in the literature as such). In this case, we may claim, it is

---

[14] See, for example, the reproduction in Pagano and Bianchi, *Alessandro Scarlatti*, after p. 304; also Donald Jay Grout, *Alessandro Scarlatti: An Introduction to his Operas* (Berkeley, Los Angeles and London, 1979).

[15] On the traditional accoutrements of composers in formal portraits, see Werner Braun, 'Arten des Komponistenporträts', in Ludwig Finscher and Christoph-Hellmut Mahling (eds), *Festschrift für Walter Wiora zum 30. Dezember 1966* (Kassel etc., 1967), pp. 86–94.

[16] Hanley no. 21. There are several different manuscripts and versions of this cantata in circulation; the painting shows the commonest version, in G minor. See the facsimile reproduction of GB-Lbl, Add. 31,508 in Boyd (ed.), *Cantatas*, no. 18, pp. 137–45.

[17] Strohm, 'Scarlattiana at Yale', p. 134. This author advances the hypothesis that the cantata was written before 1705.

[18] Information as well as illustrations can be found at Museo Internazionale e Biblioteca della Musica di Bologna, *Iconoteca*, http://badigit.comune.bologna.it (accessed 10 March 2008).

likely to have been Scarlatti himself who selected the composition visible in the background. If so, further questions arise. If the original was executed after 1716, why did Scarlatti choose a piece that was by that time at least eleven years old? Is there a meaning behind his choice, and what is the significance of this particular cantata? Is it a statement of personal significance that the composition is a cantata rather than an operatic aria or a sacred composition? And does the particular piece bear any message or autobiographical reference? Is 'Al fin m'ucciderete, o miei pensieri' Scarlatti's dialogue with his Muse?

It cannot but be speculative to talk about a painting whose original is lost and whose purpose and circumstances of creation are not known to us. It is a fact, however, that the portrait is quite different from the earlier paintings of the composer known to us. Both of these – a portrait of the young Scarlatti normally ascribed to Nicola Vaccaro[19] and a recently published portrait by Scarlatti's friend, the painter Francesco Solimena[20] – show Scarlatti in a very different guise. In both cases, he is dressed opulently; the statuesque pose in the earlier picture becomes a livelier one in the later representation. In Vaccaro's picture we see the young *maestro di cappella* likewise holding a piece of music. Judging from the number of staves that are visible, this is a polyphonic composition, perhaps a sacred piece. By being juxtaposed with such a piece, Scarlatti places himself in a specific tradition: he defines his position and profession by reference to a long-established style corresponding to the duties expected from a *maestro di cappella*. The difference of the late painting from Bologna is striking: there, we see Scarlatti in a domestic setting, in everyday dress and at work: contemplating and composing a cantata – the most intimate and private genre one could imagine at that time.

There is some reason for believing that Scarlatti's second Roman period, stretching from January 1703 to December 1708 – the period to which *Al fin m'ucciderete* belongs – was a peak period in his cantata production.[21] This perception may be influenced by the availability of the dated autograph manuscripts, which give insight into the pace of Scarlatti's compositional process, and the possible social environment in which he was working.[22] If Scarlatti's composition of cantatas in 1704/05 resulted in an annual production of approximately 35–40 cantatas, an estimate for the years 1702 to 1708 would bring us up to a total of c.210–40 cantatas.[23] This may be an over-estimate, since changing duties and working environments may have at times reduced the request for new cantatas. At any rate, there are still up

---

[19] See the illustration in Pagano and Bianchi, *Alessandro Scarlatti*, before p. 33.

[20] Roberto Pagano, *Alessandro and Domenico Scarlatti: Two Lives in One*, translated by Frederick Hammond (Hillsdale, NY, 2006), p. 27.

[21] As stated in George J. Buelow, *A History of Baroque Music* (Bloomington, 2004), p. 134. Buelow identifies two further periods of intense activity: Rome before 1684 and Naples after 1722, in accordance with Boyd's periodization (see above, note 3).

[22] See the remarks on the 'Cantata Diary' in Strohm, 'Scarlattiana at Yale', pp. 132–9.

[23] A similar calculation is made in Damuth, 'Alessandro Scarlatti's Cantatas for Soprano and Continuo', pp. 24–5.

to 500 cantatas that need to be distributed over the remaining periods. Who were the patrons and consumers, and what was the context in which they were composed?

Exactly when Alessandro Scarlatti began writing cantatas may seem a futile question to answer. Given the enormous number of cantatas produced, we may presume that their writing covered the entire span of his creative life. This would mean that the earliest cantatas were composed around the time when Scarlatti held his first official positions and which gave birth, so far as we know, to his earliest dramatic and sacred compositions: in other words, going back to 1678/79, when he held the positions of *maestro di cappella* at S. Giacomo degli Incurabili (from December 1678) and *maestro di cappella* to Queen Christina of Sweden (February 1679). Given the long tradition of the cantata in Rome and the functional association of the genre with academic and aristocratic social gatherings, it seems logical that Scarlatti wrote cantatas for the queen (and her academy). However, this inference is not confirmed by the sources, since almost all Scarlatti's musical activities in the service of the queen remain in obscurity.[24] There is no evidence that he provided her with vocal *musica da camera* in any appreciable quantity.

A different picture can be drawn from another of Scarlatti's early patrons, Cardinal Benedetto Pamphilj (1653–1730). The music-loving cardinal is a key figure in the patronage of the late seventeenth and early eighteenth centuries. In his youth, Pamphilj was associated with the Accademia degli Umoristi, under whose auspices he sponsored the performance of dramatic works in his palace. Later, his patronage shifted towards sacred genres, but the cantata always occupied an important place in his musical interests. A personal connection with Scarlatti is documented as early as 1680, when the cardinal became godfather to Scarlatti's second son, Benedetto Bartolomeo (born 24 August 1680). The cardinal's account books show expenses for the copying of music by Scarlatti and other composers for a period lasting over three decades.[25]

The earliest instance of a cantata written by Scarlatti for Pamphilj could be *Sarei troppo felice*, which is set to a text by Pamphilj himself. The incipit appears in the cardinal's household accounts of 10 February 1682 (an additional aria being copied on 14 February 1682). Copies of a cantata with the same incipit are listed several times between 1682 and 1703; only the copy of 30 June 1704, however, is clearly associated with Alessandro Scarlatti.[26] The unique manuscript of Scarlatti's *Sarei troppo felice* (H 631) is a dated autograph. As is true of a series of other cantatas from the same period, the date has been corrected and is presumably to be read as 30 April 1701.[27] The records in the account books from 1685 and 1689 list

---

[24] See Arnaldo Morelli, 'Mecenatismo musicale nella Roma barocca. Il caso di Cristina di Svezia', *Quaderni storici*, 95, n. 2 (1997): 387–408, especially p. 399.

[25] Hans Joachim Marx, 'Die "Giustificazioni della Casa Pamphilj" als musikgeschichtliche Quelle', *Studi musicali*, 12 (1983): 121–87.

[26] Marx, 'Die "Giustificazioni della Casa Pamphilj"', 167, doc. 110.

[27] All the cantatas are found in the manuscript D-MÜs, Hs 3987; see Damuth, 'Alessandro Scarlatti's Cantatas for Soprano and Continuo', pp. 42–50.

Sarei troppo felice as a cantata with violin accompaniment, whereas the Scarlatti manuscript employs only basso continuo accompaniment. The cardinal enjoyed having his poetry set to music and he evidently enjoyed hearing different musical versions over time. So Pamphilj's text may have been set at least twice – whether by Scarlatti or by one or more composers close to the cardinal – before Handel set the text again in the autumn of 1707. As Hanley already notes apropos of Scarlatti's setting, 'It is possible that in 1701 he modified an older work or that he set the text for a second time; it is unlikely that he merely recopied an older composition'.[28] Dent discusses the cantata in extensive detail and emphasizes Scarlatti's ingenious treatment of the refrain and the setting of the arias.[29] One small detail may in fact support the assumption that the cantata preserved under Scarlatti's name is not the composition mentioned in 1682. It is the use of the *alla breve* metre for the setting of the third aria, 'Il pensiero è un prato ameno'.[30] When we look at his operas for comparison, it is noticeable that he begins using this metre only in the late 1690s, generally for melodies with a lively and fluid character.

Among the early copies of Scarlatti cantatas for Cardinal Pamphilj, three others deserve specific attention. These are *Lasciato haveva l'adultero superbo* (*La Lucretia Romana*, H 378), *La fortuna di Roma* (*Il Coriolano*, H 359) and *Già di trionfi onusto* (*Il Germanico*, H 297), copied in 1688, 1689 and 1690, respectively. All three are cantatas with separate titles – a phenomenon that is not uncommon and often encountered in mid-seventeenth-century printed collections. Among Scarlatti's cantatas, we find around 130 such titles, which range from more generic descriptions (*Cantata notturna*, H 276) or characterizations of the subject treated in the text (*L'infedeltà*, H 641) to an evocation of the amours of imaginary pastoral characters (*Clori a Lisa compagne*, H 311 and H 386). Some titles reflect the sententious inscriptions found in Baroque poetry (*Bella dama di nome Santa*, H 743). The three cantatas for (and also by) Pamphilj belong to a type of cantata based upon mythological or historical characters best known from the older cantata repertory through the works of Luigi Rossi and Alessandro Stradella. While these cantatas within Scarlatti's work seem to be merely a continuation of an older tradition soon to become extinct, they require evaluation as a group in its own right. The predominance of narrative elements and the extended sections in recitative style are characteristic of this type. They pose a particular challenge to the composer, as does the typical situation depicted in those cantatas, where the protagonist is often the victim of tragic circumstances leading to his or her death.[31] Marina Mayrhofer emphasizes the importance of these cantatas for Scarlatti as

---

[28] Hanley, 'Alessandro Scarlatti's Cantate da camera', p. 437.

[29] Edward J. Dent, *Alessandro Scarlatti: His Life and Works* (London, 1905), pp. 76–87.

[30] See the music example in Dent, *Alessandro Scarlatti*, p. 82.

[31] See the editon of *Lucretia Romana* by Rosalind Halton, Society for Seventeenth-Century Music, web library.

a study in a heroic musical language.[32] Dent may seem to belittle these cantatas when he terms them 'lectures on Roman history set to recitative with an occasional aria',[33] but this is essentially what they are. The consecutive dates of copying – and we will assume that the dates of copying follow those of composition closely – suggest that they are intended to form a series of historical miniatures, or a 'gallery' of *huomini e donne illustri* of Roman antiquity.

Cantatas such as *Sarei troppo felice* on one hand and the *Germanico* and *Lucretia* works on the other represent two archetypical layouts of cantatas that go right back to the historical foundations of the genre.[34] One characteristic of *Sarei troppo felice* is the presence of a textual refrain treated in conventional manner also as a musical refrain. The repetition creates a cyclic structure, where the refrain has the added semantic function of a motto, or a reminder that leads the discourse back to a principal subject: the opinion or attitude expressed in the refrain. The function of the device is to create unity while allowing a temporary relief from the other sections. Another text of the same type is *Siamo in contesa, la bellezza ed io* (H 660), again by Pamphilj, whose only surviving setting by Scarlatti is from 1702. A more elaborate example is Scarlatti's *Prima d'esservi infedele* (H 578), where the refrain 'Prima d'esservi infedele', | luci belle, io morirò' frames the entire cantata, while another refrain, 'Ah che non è possibile', occurs in the central recitative section.[35]

The device displayed in the *Lucretia* and *Germanico* cantatas is that of narrative. Cantata poetry is often described schematically as a lover's monologue whose subject is unrequited love. However, many cantatas are marked by the presence of a narrator employed to introduce the characters or protagonists of the little scene represented in the cantata, who thereafter act in direct speech. The narrator, whose text, in recitative verse, opens the cantata, also often concludes it, in such a way that the composition is provided with a narrative frame. This explains why a simple recitative may close the cantata, and not an aria or cavata. The narrator uses formulas such as 'disse' and 'dicea' (both meaning 'he/she said') to introduce the direct speech of the protagonists. The narrative device occurs also in cantatas of other types, such as in *Già lusingato appieno* (H *deest*), which foresees the return of the exiled King James II to England.[36] Other examples are the pastoral

---

[32] Marina Mayrhofer, 'Sei cantate napoletane di Alessandro Scarlatti anteriori al 1694', in *Händel e gli Scarlatti a Roma. Atti del Convegno Internazionale di Studi, Roma 1985*, pp. 155–63, at pp. 159–60.

[33] Dent, *Alessandro Scarlatti*, p. 12.

[34] Norbert Dubowy, '"Una nuova foggia di componimenti": sulla formazione dei caratteri del testo della cantata italiana', *I Quaderni della Civica Scuola di Musica*, 19–20 (1990): 9–18.

[35] Boyd, *Cantatas*, no. 4.

[36] Boyd's hypothesis (*Cantatas*, introduction) that the 'anglico eroe' referred to in the opening of the cantata was James II is confirmed in Teresa Chirico, 'Il fondo dei Campello di Spoleto: autografi Ottoboniani e altri testi per musica', *Analecta musicologica* 37 (Studien zur italienischen Musikgeschichte, 16), ed. Markus Engelhardt (Laaber, 2005),

miniature *Fra mille semplicetti augei canori* (H 292) and Scarlatti's cantata in Neapolitan dialect *Ammore, brutto figlio de pottana* (H 40), which reveals at its end in the words 'Così diceva Cicco' that this was a story reported by a narrator.

A different approach to Scarlatti's early cantatas is to look at the authors of his cantata texts. Pamphilj, as a patron-cum-poet, belongs to a special category, along with a few other noble *dilettanti* such as Flavio Orsini, Antonio Ottoboni and the latter's son Pietro Ottoboni. Antonio Ottoboni was a prolific writer of cantata texts whose poetry is well represented in Scarlatti's catalogue of works.[37]

We can get yet another perspective by looking at one other 'producer' of cantata texts: Francesco Maria Paglia, who is identified – like Pamphilj – in a manuscript of poetry as the author of cantata texts for Scarlatti and others.[38] To describe Paglia as a professional writer may be a misnomer. He probably called himself a *letterato* – shorthand for an intellectual with strong literary interests who probably exercised a completely different profession, working perhaps as a lawyer, a court functionary or an ecclesiastic. Essential to the existence of the *letterato* was his membership of the social and intellectual network of an academy, and in some instances his closeness to a noble patron (possibly his employer), to whom he supplied poetry for various occasions. Such is the case with the *abate* Francesco Maria Paglia.[39] He was not Neapolitan, as Strohm believed, but Roman.[40] In 1686 he is documented as being a member of the Roman *Infecondi* Academy, one of the institutional forerunners of the *Arcadia*.[41] He was also a member of the *Accademici disuniti*, a group founded and led by the young Pietro Ottoboni in the late 1680s, when he had not yet been made a cardinal.[42] The younger Ottoboni was soon to become one of Scarlatti's main supporters and later, in 1705, even a patron to him. The *Disuniti* were active during the first years of Ottoboni's cardinalate. The connection between Ottoboni, Paglia and Scarlatti is confirmed by Ottoboni's

---

pp. 85–178, at p. 163; the separately preserved text gives the title as *Pel ritorno di Giacomo II al Regno d'Inghilterra*.

[37] On Antonio Ottoboni's *poesia per musica*, see Michael Talbot and Colin Timms, 'Music and the Poetry of Antonio Ottoboni (1646–1720)', in *Händel e gli Scarlatti a Roma. Atti del Convegno Internazionale di Studi, Roma 1985*, pp. 367–438.

[38] Hanley, 'Alessandro Scarlatti's Cantate da camera', p. 6. In addition, an 'Abbate Paglia' is named as the poet of Agostino Steffani's chamber duet *Io mi parto, o cara*.

[39] An *abate*, literally 'abbot', was a secular priest belonging neither to the diocesan clergy nor to a religious order and therefore free to take up any respectable employment. Among musicians, Vivaldi belonged to this stratum.

[40] Strohm, 'Scarlattiana at Yale', p. 129.

[41] See *Le pompe funebri celebrate da' signori Accademici infecondi di Roma per la morte dell'illustrissima Signora Elena Lucrezia Cornara Piscopia* (Padua, 1686).

[42] Michele Maylender, *Storia delle Accademie d'Italia*, 5 vols (Bologna 1926–30), vol. 2, p. 213. In 1688 the *Disuniti* published *Applausi poetici al valore del Serenissimo Francesco Morosini Generalissimo dell'Armi venete*.

household expenses; in fact, on 1 July 1692, Flavio Lanciani submitted a bill for the copying of *A voi che l'accendeste* (H 9), a cantata on a text by Paglia.[43]

In addition to his affiliation with Ottoboni and the *Disuniti*, Paglia belonged to the entourage of Francisco Luis de La Cerda, Marquis Cogolludo and Duke of Medinaceli, the Spanish Ambassador to the Holy See. Paglia moved to Naples only in 1696, when the Duke became Spanish-appointed viceroy of the Kingdom of Naples (and as such Scarlatti's automatic patron). While in Rome, Paglia wrote cantata and serenata texts for the duke's family. These include *La notte, il giorno ed il merito* (1688; music by Severo de Luca) and *Applauso musicale* (1693; music by Giovanni Lorenzo Lulier and Arcangelo Corelli).[44] Paglia continued to write texts for serenatas and *drammi per musica* while he remained in Naples, and he updated opera librettos for the Neapolitan stage, most of them set by Scarlatti.[45]

Paglia's early cantata texts – those associated with cantata manuscripts copied in 1693 or earlier – show how rooted his poetic style is in the aesthetics of Seicento poetry following in the tradition of Marino. *Morirei disperato* (H 443) is a good example; its first recitative section runs thus (English translation on the right):

Morirei disperato	I would die a desperate man
se credess', idol mio, d'averti offeso.	if I thought, my idol, that I had offended you.
Vorrei ch'il core acceso	I would wish that my burning heart
si struggesse in faville	were consumed in sparks
distillate nel pianto	distilled in tears
e il tempo della pena	and that the time of the penitence
lacerasse i momenti a poco a poco	tore apart the moments little by little,
onde poscia contenta	after which you would happily see
vedresti naufragar l'acqua nel foco.	water shipwrecked upon the fire.

The text excels on account not of its absolute literary quality but of its functionality in the service of music that allows the application of word painting or of specific

---

[43] Marx, 'Die Musik am Hofe Pietro Kardinal Ottobonis unter Arcangelo Corelli', *Analecta musicologica* 5 (1968): 133, no. 37e.

[44] *La notte, il giorno, ed il merito*, cantata per musica, Rome 1688, for Lorenza de La Cerda Colonna. See Thomas Griffin, 'The Late Baroque Serenata in Rome and Naples: A Documentary Study with Emphasis on Alessandro Scarlatti' (PhD dissertation, University of California at Los Angeles, 1983), p. 147. There are also a *Componimento a quattro voci* in celebration of the birthday of Maria de Giron y Sandoval, the ambassador's wife (Rome, [5 August] 1689, with music by Severo de Luca), and the above-mentioned *Applauso musicale a quattro voci*, for the same occasion (Rome, 1693: vocal sections by Giovanni Lorenzo Lulier, instrumental pieces by Arcangelo Corelli). See Griffin, 'The Late Baroque Serenata', p. 196.

[45] The serenatas are *Venere, Adone et Amore* and *Il trionfo delle stagioni* (both July 1696); Paglia's opera librettos for Scarlatti include *Il prigioniero fortunato* (1698), *Il pastor di Corinto* (1701) and the adaptation of Eustachio Manfredi's *Dafni* (1700).

musical figures. It abounds in poetic images and some stereotypical combinations ('core acceso', 'strugesse faville', 'distillate nel pianto') that appear one after the other in an almost senseless paratactic arrangement that is often difficult to follow. The poem works, however, if it is seen as a functional text for music. In the first recitative the implied hesitation of 'a poco a poco' gives the composer the opportunity to interrupt the flow – something Scarlatti promptly does – while in the arias the text gives ample opportunity for the application of musical topoi, such as the obligatory sustained notes on the word 'costanza' in the third aria, 'S'io credessi ch'un anima amante'.

If Scarlatti's style in the early cantatas makes extensive use, as has been claimed, of arioso writing, especially at the transition from recitative to aria, Paglia's text is supportive towards this device. The poem betrays its functionality as a cantata text by placing the strongest *concetto* at the end of the first recitative: 'vedresti naufragar l'acqua nel foco'. A key device of Baroque poetics of the seventeenth century is the *concetto*: a forced, unnatural combination or a paradox that arouses through this very association a new and unexpected meaning. The word 'naufragar' (to be shipwrecked or drown) implies the presence of water, so that according to the phrase 'naufragar l'acqua' water would itself 'become shipwrecked' in water. To this paradox another is added: that water would become shipwrecked in fire: a paradox, because we expect water to extinguish the fire – but here it is the fire that prevails. Scarlatti realizes this passage through the use of runs and leaps in the voice and basso continuo parts that are apparently the musical representation of a violent and chaotic action. In reality, however, the voice and basso continuo become strictly co-ordinated via canonic treatment, first at the fifth and then at the octave.[46] In this depiction and imagination of a situation involving violence and confusion Scarlatti exercises a maximum of control through the employment of contrapuntal procedures. This procedure foreshadows the direction in which Scarlatti will go in his future stylistic development: towards control of the musical substance, often via the exploitation of contrapuntal technique.[47] The ultimate shape this takes may be seen in the arias *in canone* in cantatas such as *Qui dove alfin m'assido* (H 618, *Il rosignuolo*; last aria, 'Quel bel canto è si grato') and *Farfalla che s'aggira* (H 256, *La Pazzia* or *La Stravaganza*; last aria, 'Tenta la fuga').

Paglia was a respected member of Roman literary circles of the late 1680s and early 1690s. Scarlatti's cantatas written to Paglia's texts fulfil the expectations of a certain clientèle in Rome, even though he himself resided at the time in Naples. As mentioned above, Paglia collaborated with Scarlatti on various operas and serenatas between 1696 and 1702. He may well have provided texts for chamber cantatas that Scarlatti wrote during that period. He is not identified by name in any of the compositions, and it is impossible to say if and how he was influenced by the newer literary trends that arose at the end of the seventeenth century.

---

[46] See Boyd, 'Form and Style', p. 19.

[47] See Brian Daw, 'Alessandro Scarlatti's Cantatas for Solo Soprano and Continuo, 1708–1717' (PhD dissertation, University of Southern California, 1984), pp. 111 and 139.

The new literary trends in the 1690s are epitomized in the Roman Arcadia, whose goal was the renewal of Italian poetry and literary genres through purification of the poetic language. In reaction against seventeenth-century *concettismo*, the poets of Arcadia and their imitators promoted a return to a more natural and psychologically comprehensible expression of emotions that found its outlet in the adoption of pastoral imagery. The pastoral ideal also pervaded the social manners within the Academy, best represented by the adoption by its members of shepherd- or nymph-like pseudonyms. The Arcadia, which rose after its foundation in 1690 to become one of the leading academies in Rome and the world, subsequently spread rapidly through the Italian peninsula (like-minded academies in other cities affiliated to it as so-called colonies) and was a driving force behind the evolution of Italian literature of the eighteenth century. Mayrhofer has identified Arcadian tendencies as early as 1693 in Scarlatti's cantata texts.[48]

Scarlatti himself was admitted to the Academy in 1706 (as Terpandro Politeio) and already before that had enjoyed close contact with several Arcadians, among whom were his patrons Pietro Ottoboni (Crateo Ericinio), who was instrumental in Scarlatti's admission to the academy, the latter's father Antonio Ottoboni (Eneto Ereo) and the Spanish viceroy, the Duke of Medinaceli (Arconte Frisseo), who is himself not known to have had any literary aspirations. The librettist of several of Scarlatti's Neapolitan and Florentine operas, Silvio Stampiglia – like Paglia, a protégé of the viceroy – was a declared Arcadian (Palemone Licurio), but only one of his cantata texts, *Talor per suo diletto*, was set to music by Scarlatti (H 713).[49]

Another representative of the new trends, institutionalized via his membership of the Arcadian Academy, is Giovan Battista Felice Zappi (1667–1719), in Arcadia 'Tirsi Leucasio'. The lawyer ('L'avvocato') Zappi – as he was frequently called – was a native of Imola who came to Rome in 1685. He was a member of the *Infecondi* and the *Intrecciati* prior to becoming a founding member of the Arcadia in 1690.[50] He is considered one of the most talented writers of the first generation of Arcadians.[51]

---

[48] Mayrhofer, 'Sei cantate napoletane di Alessandro Scarlatti anteriori al 1694', pp. 161–2, with reference to *Sopra le verdi sponde che la Brenta superba* and *Di cipresso funesto*.

[49] See Teresa M. Gialdroni, 'Silvio Stampiglia autore di testi di cantata', in Gaetano Pitarresi (ed.), *Intorno a Silvio Stampiglia. Librettisti, compositori e interpreti nell'età premetastasiana. Atti del Convegno internazionale di Studi (Reggio Calabria, 5–6 ottobre 2007)* (forthcoming).

[50] See the biography by Francesco Maria Mancurti, 'Vita del Poeta Gio. Battista Zappi', in Giovan Mario Crescimbeni (ed.), *Le vite degli Arcadi illustri*, Part 4 (Rome, 1727), p. 68.

[51] Bruno Maier, *Rimatori d'Arcadia. Giambattista Felice Zappi, Faustina Maratti Zappi, Eustachio Manfredi, Carlo Innocenzo Frugoni* (Trieste, 1971), p. 10: 'The twin currents of Petrarchism and Anacreontism converge in the lyric poetry of Giambattista Felice Zappi, which is marked by a pathetic, gracious, genteel and miniaturistic melodramaticism,

The episode of the meeting of Scarlatti and Zappi during an extraordinary session of the Academy is well known and often cited.[52] The account is published in *Arcadia*, a novelistic report written and published for the first time in 1708 by the leader (*custode*) and main ideologist of Arcadia, Giovan Mario Crescimbeni (Alfesibeo Cario). Music was not a primary concern of the Arcadia; therefore, this was not an official session of the academy but a kind of concert ('Accademia di musica', as Crescimbeni calls it).[53] The meeting at *abate* Domenico Riviera's residence took place on an unspecified date in or after 1706, when Scarlatti, together with Corelli and Pasquini, had already joined the academy.[54]

It has often been overlooked that on this occasion Crescimbeni makes mention of a much earlier contact and collaboration between Zappi and Scarlatti. The important biographical datum emerging from the account is that Scarlatti and Zappi met in Naples during the reign of Viceroy Francisco de Benavides, Conde de Santisteban (in Italian sources normally described as Conte di Santo Stefano).[55] Benavides ruled Naples from January 1688 to March 1696, which provides us with an overall time-frame; but I would suggest that Zappi's visit to Naples is more likely to have occurred in the early to mid-1690s rather than in the late 1680s – in other words, after Zappi was famous enough to be received at court. In fact, Zappi's biographer Mancurti reports that the poet was honoured by the viceroy for his talent in poetic improvisation.[56] According to Crescimbeni, Scarlatti and Zappi

---

from which is not missing, here and there, the favoured pastoral content or a certain salutary Pindarism and songlike spirit, in association with the duty to celebrate, in a public and worldly sphere, and mostly using a pastoral-idyllic code, various Arcadian festivals and celebrations' ('I due aspetti del petrarchismo e dell'anacreontismo si avvicinano nella lirica di Giambattista Felice Zappi, contraddistinta da un patetico, grazioso, gentile e miniaturistico melodrammatismo, nella quale non manca qua e là la prediletta tematica bucolica, come non sono assenti certo salutario pindarismo e canzonettismo, insieme con l'impegno di celebrare, in una sfera sociale e mondana, e in chiave per lo più idillico-pastorale, talune solennità e cerimonie d'Arcadia').

[52] Dent, *Alessandro Scarlatti*, p. 90.

[53] On the role of music in the Arcadia, see Fabrizio Della Seta, 'La musica in Arcadia al tempo di Corelli', in Sergio Durante and Pierluigi Petrobelli (eds), *Nuovissimi studi corelliani. Atti del terzo congresso internazionale (Fusignano, 4–7 settembre 1980)* (Florence, 1982), pp. 123–50.

[54] Giovan Mario Crescimbeni, *L'Arcadia*, Libro settimo, Prosa v (Rome, 1708), pp. 286–93. Published in part in Mario Rinaldi, *Arcangelo Corelli* (Milan, 1953), p. 271. See also Pagano, *Alessandro and Domenico Scarlatti*, pp. 167–8.

[55] Crescimbeni, *L'Arcadia*, p. 289.

[56] Mancurti, 'Vita del poeta Gio. Battista Zappi': 'He was then for his pleasure in Naples, where, on account of this very rare gift of his [his talent in impovised poetry] he was honoured by the viceroy, the Conte di S. Stefano, in whose service Scarlatti was at the time' ('Trovavasi egli allora per suo divertimento in Napoli, ove per questo suo rarissimo

met several times during Zappi's visit to Naples, where they collaborated on the writing and composing of cantatas.[57]

These reports are important, since they document Scarlatti's preoccupation with the cantata in the 1690s and may even be viewed as an indication of the still very much unexplored place of the cantata in the musical culture of Naples.[58] While some of the poetry by Zappi may have been heard at the viceregal court in the form of cantatas, Zappi's words 'when we were at the countryside of lovely Partenope' hint at a more private setting, where the cantata, written almost *ad hoc* in close collaboration between poet and composer, serves as a literary and musical pastime: a delightful entertainment that engages both the intellect and the senses at the same time.

What Zappi and Scarlatti did in Naples was very much the same as is described in the informal Arcadian meeting: Crescimbeni explains that poet and composer may sit at the same table when writing a cantata, producing the words without polishing (*studio*) and in an improvised manner.[59] This collaboration and improvisation of the poetry is practised at the Arcadian gathering itself: Zappi improvises two aria texts, 'Dolce udir sull'erbe assiso' and 'Amor con me, con voi', which are immediately set to music by Scarlatti.

In addition, Crescimbeni reports on two cantatas to words by Zappi sung during sessions of the Academy:[60] *Dunque, o vaga mia Diva* (aria 'Benché la pallidetta | La vaga violetta') and the cantata for the characters Daliso and Silvia *Vorrei un zeffiretto*. I believe Dent misreads the report when he gives Pasquini as the composer.[61] It is Scarlatti who plays, together with Zappi, the main role in this chapter, and he is the one who provides the vocal pieces performed on this

---

pregio [his talent in impovised poetry] fu onorato dal Vicerè Conte di S. Stefano, al di cui servigio stava in quel tempo lo Scarlatti').

[57] Crescimbeni, *L'Arcadia*, p. 289: In Zappi's words: 'when we were in the countryside of lovely Partenope [Naples]' ('quando eravamo nelle Campagne della deliziosa Partenope'); Crescimbeni adds in a footnote: 'The lawyer Zappi, finding himself in Naples, had the opportunity to collaborate on many occasions with Scarlatti, who was in the service of the viceroy, the Conte S. Stefano, and to write [...]' ('Trovandosi in Napoli l'Avvocato Zappi ebbe occasione di trattar più volte collo Scarlatti, che stava al servigio del Vicerè Conte S. Stefano, e comporre [...]').

[58] See Damuth, 'Alessandro Scarlatti's Cantatas for Soprano and Continuo', p. 26.

[59] Crescimbeni, *L'Arcadia*, p. 289: 'similar [literary] compositions written solely for the sake of music' ('simili componimenti, fatti solamente in grazia della Musica') and 'they are produced on the spot without any polishing, and for the most part at the desk of the composer of the music, as you yourself have witnessed and experienced several times' ('si producono senza alcuno studio all'improvviso, e per lo più al tavolino medesimo del Compositor della Musica, come più volte avete voi stesso e veduto, e sperimentato').

[60] Crescimbeni, *L'Arcadia*, pp. 290–93.

[61] Dent, *Alessandro Scarlatti*, p. 90.

occasion.[62] The first cantata, consisting of a single recitative–aria pair, is probably a fragment lacking at least one more such pair.

The second cantata, *Vorrei un zeffiretto*, is more elaborate, being a dialogue between two pastoral characters. The title is particularly interesting, since 'Vorrei un zeffiretto' is part of the eclogue *Il Ferragosto*, written by Zappi and Crescimbeni and recited during a meeting of the Arcadia on 15 August 1701, under the sponsorship of Pietro Ottoboni.[63] Five musical pieces on texts by Zappi and Crescimbeni were interspersed throughout the eclogue. In his *Comentarj*, Crescimbeni reveals the names of the composers as Magini and Bencini.[64] These are most likely the little known Francesco Magini from Fano, active in Rome in the first decade of the eighteenth century as the composer of cantatas, oratorios, sonatas and a set of *solfeggiamenti*, and the much acclaimed Pietro Paolo Bencini (c.1670–1755).[65]

Scarlatti thus used a text that was not improvised but had already been used several years earlier. *Vorrei un zeffiretto* is a dialogue cantata structured as: aria (Daliso) – recitative – aria (Silvia) – recitative – duet. The layout resembles that of other duet cantatas by Scarlatti, in particular *Lisa, del foco mio* (H 386) and *Il ciel seren, le fresche aurette* (H 311);[66] the first of these was written in 1706, close to the time when the Arcadian meeting took place. Zappi's poetry for music, as seen in the few examples published by Crescimbeni in his *L'Arcadia*, relies strongly on Arcadian imagery – a view of nature that is peaceful, filled with colours and flowers; his verses are more appropriate for the evocation of a pastoral atmosphere and make less use of conventional word combinations.

Dunque, o vaga mia diva,	So, o my fair goddess,
voi mi gradite men, perché in sembiante	you like me less, for you see

---

[62] Crescimbeni, *L'Arcadia*, p. 289: 'After that, Terpandro [Scarlatti] took from his knapsack a few musical songs' ('Dopo ciò trasse Terpandro del zaino alcune Canzoni per musica').

[63] See Della Seta, 'La musica in Arcadia al tempo di Corelli', p. 136.

[64] Crescimbeni, *Comentarj intorno all'istoria della poesia italiana*, vol. 2, ed. T. J. Mathias (London, 1803), p. 252 [reprint of Crescimbeni, *Comentarj ... intorno alla sua istoria della volgar poesia* (Rome, 1702–11)]: 'set to music by Magini and Bencini, two of the leading masters at the [papal] court of Rome' ('sopra le note musicali del Magini e del Bencini, due de' più scelti maestri della corte di Roma').

[65] On Bencini's secular vocal music (he is better known for his church music), see Michael Talbot, '"Loving without Falling in Love": Pietro Paolo Bencini's Serenata *Li due volubili*', in Nicolò Maccavino (ed.), *La serenata tra Seicento e Settecento: musica, poesia, scenotecnica. Atti del Convegno Internazionale di Studi (Reggio Calabria, 16–17 maggio 2003)* (Reggio Calabria, 2007), pp. 373–95.

[66] See Freund, 'A. Scarlatti's Duet Cantatas and Solo Cantatas with Obbligato Instruments', pp. 301–27.

pallido mi vedete.	that my face is pale.
Ah se non lo sapete	Ah, if you did not know it,
questo è il color d'ogni più fido Amante:	this is the colour of every faithful lover:
questo è il color, che Amore	this is the colour that Cupid
di sua man tinge, e segna;	dyes and marks with his hand;
nè vanno i suoi guerrier sott'altra insegna:	nor do his warriors go under any other banner.
[A] Benché sia pallidetta	Although the fair violet
la vaga violetta,	is pale,
non è che non sia bella.	it is not lacking in beauty.
[B] La coglie dal terren	The shepherdess
e se la pone in sen	plucks it from the ground
la Pastorella.	and places it in her bosom.
[A] Benché non sia vermiglio	Although the white lily
il candidetto giglio	is not vermilion,
v'è chi se v'innamora.	some people fall in love with it.
[B] Lo coglie sul matin,	Fair Aurora
e ne fa serto al crin	plucks it in the morning
la vaga Aurora.	and makes it into a wreath for her hair.

From a formal perspective, we notice that in the cantata *Dunque, o vaga mia diva* Zappi provides a strophic aria with two stanzas – an astonishingly old-fashioned design. Each of the stanzas is suitable for an aria in *da capo* form, having two matched textual sections (respectively indicated as A and B).

According to Crescimbeni's report, Scarlatti and Zappi had a sincere appreciation for one another.[67] We may conclude that Zappi was one of Scarlatti's main poets. However, none of the compositions mentioned by Crescimbeni is known to exist today, and nowhere is Zappi identified as the author of one of Scarlatti's cantata texts.

In general, it is difficult to identify literary authors in the cantata repertory, but in this particular case one reason is that Zappi is trying to distance poetry for music from higher-ranking forms of literature. He is very explicit when he says that his literary compositions 'are written solely for the sake of music' and could therefore offend the good taste of the audience. It is clear that Zappi considers *poesia per musica* a minor branch of the art. He also assigns it a decisively functional quality and, for all practical purposes, a subordinate role.

---

[67] Crescimbeni, *L'Arcadia*, p. 289. Scarlatti calls Zappi 'greatly esteemed by me' ('grandemente da me venerato'). Zappi probably also witnessed the performance of Pietro Ottoboni's oratorio *Giuditta* set to music by Scarlatti. One of Zappi's sonnets has the title *Per un'Oratorio dell'Emin. Ottoboni intitolato Giuditta* ('Alfin col teschio d'atro sangue intriso').

The classicist and restorative tendencies propagated by the Arcadia resulted in a dismissive attitude towards penned poetry for music that may explain to some extent why so many cantata texts remain anonymous. Even though Crescimbeni acknowledges the cantata as a literary form in his *Comentarj*, sensitive readers may detect a hint of reproof when he compares the cantata, an invention of the seventeenth century (regarded by Arcadians as a century of decline), defined by its generally unrhymed *versi sciolti* mixed with arias, with the well-ordered poetry of the sixteenth century.[68]

Another reason lies in the strictly functional character of the poetry: in other words, in many cases the poetry was conceived 'al tavolino del compositore' – at the composer's desk and by the composer himself.

Speculation that Scarlatti penned some of the texts he set to music is not new.[69] One – highly problematic – source is the same report by Quantz about the incredible number of '4,000 examples of Scarlatti's work, mostly solo cantatas' to which Quantz appends the remark 'and in many instances the texts were also written by Scarlatti'.[70] Perhaps we should take this remark more seriously. It is well known that Scarlatti was admitted to the Arcadia not only as a musician but also as a poet ('professore anche di Poesia').[71] We know of five poetic essays by Scarlatti, all in the classical form of the sonnet,[72] but no cantata texts bear his signature.

Cantata texts are often very conventional, sharing a repertory of poetic terms and often predictable combinations of words. Many cantatas have their complete first line in common without this identity extending to the rest of the text. Thus, Scarlatti's *All'hor ch'il dio di Delo* (H 31) is not identical textually to Francesco Mancini's cantata with the same incipit.[73]

---

[68] Crescimbeni, *Comentarj*, pp. 253–4: 'certain kinds of poetry commonly called today cantatas, which are composed of long and short lines not subject to rules, with an admixture of arias [...] This sort of poetry was invented in the seventeenth century, because in the preceding one madrigals and other compositions governed by rules fulfilled musical needs' ('certe maniere di poesia, che comunemente oggimai si chiaman Cantate, le quali sono composte di versi e versetti rimati senza legge, con mescolamento d'arie [...] Questa sorte di poesia è invenzione del secolo decimosettimo, perciocché nell'antecedente per la musica servivano i madrigali, e gli altri regolati componimenti').

[69] Damuth, 'Alessandro Scarlatti's Cantatas for Soprano and Continuo', pp. 68–9.

[70] Nettl, *Forgotten Musicians*, p. 304.

[71] Della Seta, 'La musica in Arcadia al tempo di Corelli', p. 127.

[72] Four sonnets appear in Della Seta, 'La musica in Arcadia al tempo di Corelli', pp. 143–5. One sonnet (on the death of Corelli) appears in Franco Piperno, '"Su le sponde del Tebro": eventi, mecenati e istituzioni musicali a Roma negli anni di Locatelli. Saggio di cronologia', in Albert Dunning (ed.), *Intorno a Locatelli. Studi in occasione del tricentenario della nascita di Pietro Antonio Locatelli (1695–1764)* (Lucca, 1995), pp. 793–877, at pp. 801–2.

[73] Hanley, 'Alessandro Scarlatti's Cantate da camera', p. 35, lists six different cantatas that all start with 'Stanco di più soffrire'.

In some cases, however, the similarity persists beyond the first line. Scarlatti's *Notte ch'in carro d'ombre* (H 480) borrows the complete first recitative from the Venetian serenata *La fedeltà consolata dalla speranza* by Nicolò Beregan and Antonio Giannettini (Venice, 1685).[74]

A more intricate case is that of Scarlatti's *Poiché la bella Clori* (H 570), written in or before 1699. The protagonist of the cantata is Fileno, abandoned by Clori, who is leaving on a ship. The story of this cantata is practically the reverse of the Olimpia and Bireno episode in Ariosto's *Orlando furioso*. In the epic poem, princess Olimpia is abandoned on an island while she is sleeping; when she gets up, she can see only Bireno's ship departing from the shore. Scarlatti treats this very story in *Su la sponda del mare per un ingrato* (H 698). The abandonment of Olimpia also constitutes the first scene of the opera *L'Olimpia vendicata* set by Scarlatti in 1685 to a libretto by Aurelio Aureli. *Poiché la bella Clori* can best be understood with the opening scene of the opera in mind. The text of the cantata picks up individual words from the libretto; the third aria, 'Torna, o cara, in questo lido', paraphrases 'Torna, infido, a questo lido' from the opera, which serves as a subtext to the cantata.

The examples cited do not provide confirmation that Scarlatti wrote their texts. In particular, the literary maladroitness of *Poiché la bella Clori* makes one hope that the poem is not by Scarlatti. However, these few cases show that Scarlatti could potentially draw on a vast reservoir of texts that he had under his belt as a composer of cantatas and operas.

As mentioned near the beginning of this chapter, Scarlatti's wrote his cantatas during a period in which the genre was affected by a fundamental change in form and style. This change has often been described in the literature, since it pertains to the overall musical structure as well as to the form of the aria and the use of recitative and arioso. Boyd illustrated the process in an influential article in which, as already said, he offered a precise point of chronological orientation: the year 1697 as a watershed in Scarlatti's treatment of the cantata form.[75] Even though Boyd never really explained the reason for his choice of this particular year, it has become widely adopted in musical historiography as a convenient landmark. Ellen T. Harris, using the same criteria as Boyd, has noted a similar stylistic shift in Handel's cantatas dating from 1707–08 and refers to a comparable development in Mancini.[76] It is possible to divide the criteria listed by Harris into two different categories.

The first category concerns the intervallic structure and shape of the melody in general and the use, where present, of arioso style. The second concerns the choice

---

[74] On this serenata, see Norbert Dubowy, 'Ernst August, Giannettini und die Serenata in Venedig (1685/86)', *Analecta musicologica*, 30 (= Studien zur italienischen Musikgeschichte, 15), ed. Friedrich Lippmann (Laaber, 1998), pp. 167–235.

[75] Boyd, 'Form and Style', 18.

[76] Ellen T. Harris, *Handel as Orpheus: Voice and Desire in the Chamber Cantatas* (Cambridge, MA, 2001), pp. 64–5.

of aria form (binary, *da capo*, other) and the overall structure of the cantata (i.e., an alternation that is not standardized vs. a regular pattern such as RARA). Whereas the elements of the first category are completely under the control of the composer, both aspects of the second category generally remain outside his control.

Italian composers of the seventeenth century set to music not merely words but more specifically poetry, and their secular vocal music not only respects but also reflects the principles of Italian poetry and in particular the basic elements of versification, which are rhyme and metre.[77] Certain cues in the poetry suggest, or even generate, a specific realization on the part of the composer. This is true at the level of the complete cantata, where the choice of recitative, aria and, to some extent, even arioso style is triggered by the poet's choice of verse type (according to the number of syllables), grouping and rhyme. Metrical cues influence the musical setting at the level of the aria as well. The presence of rhyme between the last words of two semistrophes (which may then become the A and B sections of an ABA, or *da capo*, aria), signals to the composer the preferred option of an ABA setting, which Scarlatti only occasionally overrides.[78]

Thus the establishment of the RARA formal scheme and the use of da capo design for arias is less a musical development than a development in poetry. Scarlatti did not 'choose' the RARA pattern, nor did he impose such a pattern on his compositions, but he was confronted more and more often with texts that suggested the RARA structure, texts that abandoned the older constructive principles.[79]

It is difficult to say what role the composer played in this process and whether composers actively asked their poets for poetry fashioned according to modern principles. In a situation of intimate collaboration between poet and musician, such as we saw in the case of Zappi and Scarlatti described above, the composer must have been able to influence the poet. But direct control of both poetry and music was guaranteed only when the composer wrote the poetry himself. Scarlatti was able to do so – but, as we saw, we have no proof that he actually composed his own texts.

If we acknowledge that a switch from a freer and more diverse design to the standard RARA pattern was preceded, or at least accompanied, by a change in musical poetry, the immediate questions are: why did this happen; what makes the new design superior or at least more desirable; and what is the meaning of the form?

---

[77] Carolyn Gianturco, 'The Cantata: A Textual Approach', in John Caldwell, Edward Olleson and Susan Wollenberg (eds), *The Well Enchanting Skill. Music, Poetry, and Drama in The Culture of the Renaissance: Essays in Honour of F. W. Sternfeld* (Oxford, 1989), pp. 41–51.

[78] This *rima chiave*, as it is called in Italian, is hardly ever absent, being the single most important basis for the division of the stanza into two semistrophes. Poets (and, after them, printers) often also show the division visually through indentation.

[79] Stanzas comprising two semistrophes preceded the advent of *da capo* form (they were commonly set by the composer in binary, AB, form), but in this earlier phase they did not anticipate – and often would not have made good sense with – a reprise of the 'A' semistrophe.

In a cantata of the older type such as *Sarei troppo felice* the refrain, prescribed by the poet, acts as a unifying moment that brings the discourse back to the theme expressed in it and establishes a 'cyclic' structure. In contrast, an RARA type cantata lacks any overall cyclical nature (but the cyclic element is integrated on a lower level into the repetition within the *da capo* aria) and tends towards an asymmetrical design: the logic of RARA implies a clear difference of nature between the two arias and the two RA pairs.

Scarlatti's *Al fin m'ucciderete, o miei pensieri* illustrates the state of the art.[80] This is, finally, the lover's monologue that we are programmed to expect in the cantata. The lyrical self, a male, is declaiming, almost deliriously, about the absence of his beloved Clori. The text is carefully constructed. The opening line, 'Al fin m'ucciderete, o miei pensieri', is a statement that assails the listener with its subject of death: 'In the end, you will kill me, o my thoughts'. Without any transition, a second statement is added: Clori is far away. There follows a threefold wish, all enunciated with a piercing phonetic quality underlining the torture that the lyrical self is suffering by its use of the sibilant-rich imperfect subjunctive mood (*ramentasse – incontrasse – pensasse*): 'If Clori could remember my constant love, her sighs may meet my sighs, and she may think of me, since I think of her'. This self-centred discourse about 'me and her' changes with the interpolation of a 'but' that introduces the thought that Clori could be with someone else ('Ma chissa, forse adesso | ragiona con altrui'). A short outburst of jealousy is quickly dispelled by the insight that she could be unfaithful to him as well as to the speaker. The discourse changes a second time, switching back to the lyrical self, tormented by its suspicion that the beloved is unfaithful.

The cantata is in some ways in a hybrid form. It has a clear RARA design, but the first recitative portion is framed by one line of refrain: 'Al fin m'ucciderete, o miei pensieri'. Musically, the first line is a unit within itself, starting in G minor and falling back to the tonic after the voice has reached the melodic peak, E flat, in bar 3. In earlier cantatas, such as *Io morirei contento* (H 340),[81] Scarlatti had the habit of repeating the refrain literally. This is not the case here: he reshapes the melody of the section when it is repeated at the end of the recitative. This is no mechanical repetition but rather a psychological interpretation: the situation has changed, and the music changes accordingly, shifting the emphasis from 'm'ucciderete' to 'al fin'.

The first aria, 'Io morirei contento', picks up the subject of the lover's death prepared in the recitative and, starting from a passive suffering of death inflicted on the lover ('m'ucciderete' – you will kill me), turns this into an acceptance of death as a way to escape constant pain ('morirei' – I would die happily, if pain would cease). Curiously enough, not only does the aria borrow its first line from the previously mentioned cantata with the same text incipit that was written

---

[80] Boyd, *Cantatas*, no. 18; text on p. 271.
[81] Published in Giampiero Tintori (ed.), *A. Scarlatti. 4 cantate inedite* (Milan, 1958).

more than ten years previously,[82] but the basic idea of the recitative in the earlier cantata ('I would die happy, if she could behold my fidelity') now transmutes into: 'I would die happy; I would just like to behold her once more'. Scarlatti may well have written the new cantata text himself, using and reworking some of the poetic ideas from the earlier cantata, of which he still had a clear recollection. There are even some similarities in the melodic contours of the respective ariosos and arias.[83]

The aria displays Scarlatti's mastery of the musical material. Its first musical element is the main motive derived from the line 'Io morirei contento', which consists of a *cambiata* (changing-note) figure, two leaps (of a fourth and a sixth) and a short descending progression spanning a third. The second element, set to 'per non penar così', expands the progression to a sixth. The traditional topos of suffering is brought out by syncopation, inspired by the word 'penar'. These elements, first exposed in the vocal part, permeate the basso continuo as well. The aria is in *da capo* form with a motto opening, but the formal scheme is treated with a freedom typical of Scarlatti's mature compositions. In the second statement of the text in the A section, the word-order is changed, and segments are repeated in order to explore every possibility of textual expression.

Interestingly, the lyrical self changes perspective several times over the course of the cantata. With the lover haunted by visions of an unfaithful Clori and initially tormented by jealousy, the story acquires a new twist in the central section of the first aria. As it begins to focus on Clori's departure and absence ('e poi da me partì'), it becomes a *cantata di lontananza* (cantata about lovers' separation): a theme and typology explored over and over again in Scarlatti's cantatas. In the second recitative, where the lover addresses Clori directly, several pictures emerge as memories of the past, when the lovers were still united. Unbearable torment and death return in the final lines of the recitative – not as a possibility but as a certainty (that is relayed through a change in the grammatical form from the conditional, 'morirei', to the present indicative, 'moro'), even though the last line ('in one single day I die several deaths') does not refer to a literal death but is, rather, a metaphor expressing heightened suffering.

---

[82] The cantatas published by Tintori – more correctly three cantatas and one extended aria ('Fermate, omai fermate'; see Hanley, 'Alessandro Scarlatti's Cantate da camera', p. 227) from Scarlatti's opera *La Psiche* (1683) – are based on manuscript I-PAVu, Aldini 423. Two of the cantatas in the manuscript are dated 1694 (*Elitropio d'amor*, H 244; *Speranze mie, addio*, H 683); an additional source for *Io morirei contento*, I-MOe, F 1362, is listed in the catalogue of music owned by Duke Francesco II of Modena compiled on his death in 1694 and can thus be dated 1694 or earlier; see Elisabeth J. Luin, 'Repertorio dei libri musicali di S. A. S. Francesco II D'Este nell'Archivio di Stato di Modena', *La bibliofilia: Rivista di storia del libro*, 38 (1936): 418–45, at p. 429, no. 76.

[83] The similarity is close enough to have induced the RISM team to list the copy of H 340 in D-MÜs, Sant HS 869, erroneously as 'Al fin m'ucciderete. Excerpt' (see RISM A/II 451.002.66).

Example 5.1a Scarlatti, cantata *Al fin m'ucciderete, o miei pensieri*, first recitative, bars 1–4 (first version of the refrain).

Example 5.1b Scarlatti, cantata *Al fin m'ucciderete, o miei pensieri*, first recitative, bars 27–32 (second version of the refrain).

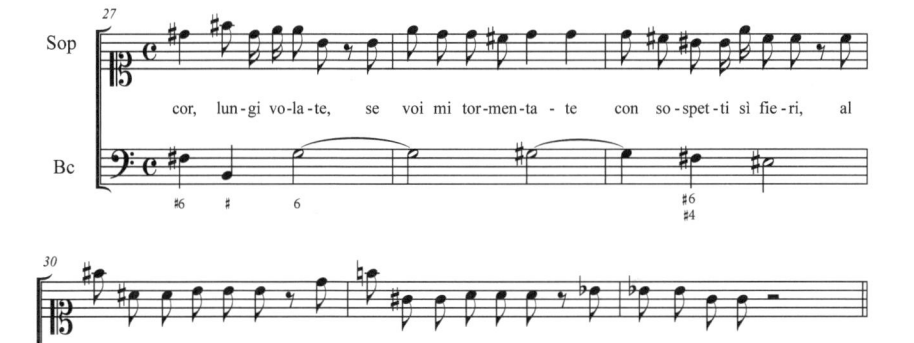

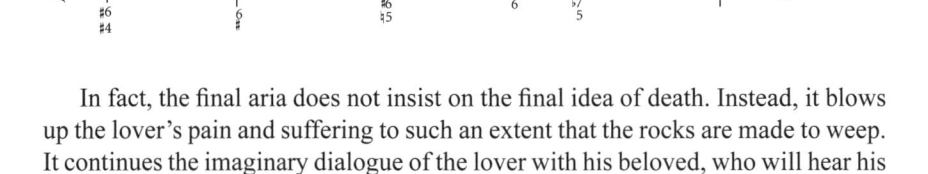

In fact, the final aria does not insist on the final idea of death. Instead, it blows up the lover's pain and suffering to such an extent that the rocks are made to weep. It continues the imaginary dialogue of the lover with his beloved, who will hear his sighs and languish, wherever she may go.

It is important to recognize that this cantata does not rely on a single affect, even though there are recurrent literary motives that act as unifying devices. There is a narrative curve extending over a cantata with two very different parts that are different in subject and in the way that the lyrical self acts. The switch, as we saw, occurs within the central section of the first aria. The disjunction between the first and second parts of the cantata becomes a justification for making the two arias distinctively different from one another or, in some respects, even starkly contrasting. The first aria, in C minor and common time (*a tempo giusto*), is complemented by a second aria in G minor (the home key of the cantata), in 12/8 metre and Largo tempo. The second metre is the one that Scarlatti uses from the late 1690s onwards predominantly for lyrical, melancholic arias that replace the formerly dominant *lamento* type. Despite these differences in their character and expression, the two arias exhibit some similarities. The same manipulation of the text described for the first aria is encountered in the second, as well as the same close interaction between the vocal part and the bass. In the melodic shape of the vocal part there is common substance in the head-motives, and in the ensuing descending progression ranging over a sixth that unites the two arias in purely musical respects. So this cantata is able both to present a highly differentiated trajectory of poetic images and perspectives and a convincing musical unity.

This brief and far from exhaustive survey of Scarlatti's cantatas from the first half of the composer's creative life has had as its primary focus the context of his early production, his identification of certain standard types and the manner in which these relate to the textual and literary basis. As we observed at the beginning, any consideration of Scarlatti's cantata inevitably has to address the question of the formal and stylistic changes within his oeuvre.

It becomes increasingly clear that this development is not simply a question of stylistic and formal choices made in the music. The evolution goes hand in hand with a change in poetry, in form, in language and in the fundamental spirit of the genre. There is no other way of thinking of the cantatas of Scarlatti and his musician colleagues than as a joint achievement of poets and musicians working in close collaboration – perhaps often quite literally at the composer's desk.

Chapter 6
Bononcini's 'agreable and easie style, and those fine inventions in his *basses* (to which he was led by an instrument upon which he excells)'

Lowell Lindgren

During the first three decades of the eighteenth century solo cantatas by Giovanni Bononcini (1670–1747) were frequently performed throughout Europe. The appendix to this chapter (Appendix 6.1) provides text incipits for the 270 works that he is known to have written for a solo voice.[1] It excludes 34 solo works with conflicting attributions,[2]

---

[1] In Stanley Sadie and John Tyrrell (eds), *The New Grove Dictionary of Music and Musicians*, 2nd edn (London, 2001), vol. 3, pp. 875–6, 280 solo cantatas, the overwhelming majority with simple continuo accompaniment, are attributed to Bononcini. Four more must be added: *All'arco tuo fatale* (US-NHub, Misc Ms 273, ff. 25–36v: 'Gio. Bononcini'); *Clori, dal colle al prato* (A-Wn, 17576, ff. 3v–7: 'Giovanni Bononcini', and GB-Er, P 1422, pp. 17–26: 'Bononcini'); *O frondoso arboscello* (*Cantate e duetti di Giovanni Bononcini* (London, 1721), pp. 43–7); and *Pastor d'Arcadia, è morta Clori* (Parma, private collection; see Sara Dieci, 'Due "Clori" di Giovanni Bononcini ritrovate', *Rivista italiana di musicologia*, 38 (2002): 249–64). Three must be deleted: *Erano ancora immote*, which is placed among Antonio Bononcini's cantatas in its only known source (I-Nc, Cantate 69, ff. 40–43v); *Perché dar non ti posso*, which is printed in Caldara, *Cantate da camera*, Op. 3 (Venice, Giuseppe Sala, 1699), no. 5; and *Torna il giorno fatale* (not extant), which must be by the youngest Bononcini brother, Giovanni Maria (called Angelo), since he was serving cardinal Pamphili in 1707, when the latter commissioned the work (see Hans Joachim Marx, 'Die "Giustificazioni della casa Pamphilj" als musikgeschichtliche Quelle', *Studi musicali*, 12 (1983): 121–87, at 134 and 177–82).

[2] *The New Grove*, 2nd edn, vol. 3, p. 876, lists 20 solo cantatas with conflicting attributions. Another 11, which are listed among Bononcini's own works in *The New Grove*, must be moved to the 'conflicting' group, because sources with credible attributions to other composers have been found: *Allor che in dolce oblio* (Fago); *Amarissime pene* (Albinoni or Ariosti); *Amor, che far deggio* (d'Astorga); *Brama d'esser amante* (d'Astorga); *Dalle ingiuste querelle* (Pietragrua); *È un martirio della costanza* (Caldara); one of the two settings of *Genio che amar volea* (Ariosti); *O quanto omai diverso* (Fago); *Se ferirmi sapesti* (Gasparini); *Sia* [recte: *Già*] *tornava l'aurora* (Albinoni); and *Vi conosco, occhi bugiardi* (Handel, 1718). Three further cantatas, with newly found attributions to Bononcini, also belong in the 'conflicting' group: *Ah no, che non si more* (A. Scarlatti); *Amor, Amor vincesti: ho già perduto il core* (d'Astorga); and *Tortorella al monte, al piano* (B. Marcello).

13 vocal duets and 28 serenatas.[3] While residing in Rome from 1692 to 1698, Bononcini composed the 141 solo cantatas listed in section A-1 of Appendix 6.1. A hundred and one of these are extant in more than one source: 23 survive in sources that number between 11 and 31, 17 in 8–10 sources, 21 in 5–7 sources and 40 in 2–4 sources. At that time, solo cantatas with simple continuo accompaniment, solo sonatas, vocal duets and trio sonatas were the 'daily bread' of Italian musicians, prelates and princes.[4] Such works must have been far less common at the imperial court, where Bononcini may have written only two solo cantatas during his dozen years of service, then three more during the following year.[5] The 65 extant solo works placed in section C-1 were probably composed before 1712, when

---

[3] *The New Grove*, 2nd edn, vol. 3, p. 875, lists 26 of the serenatas. The 27th is *Il trionfo degli dèi*, 'serenata a 4 voci, due chori e 60 stromenti', which was performed in Messina on 8 August 1695 to mark the birthday of the Vicereine of Sicily. Giuseppe Prescimone's printed libretto is extant, but Bononcini's score does not survive. See Anna Tedesco, 'La serenata a Palermo alla fine del Seicento e il duca di Uceda', in Nicolò Maccavino (ed.), *La serenata tra Seicento e Settecento: Musica, Poesia, Scenotecnica: Atti del convegno internazionale di studi (Reggio Calabria, 16–17 maggio 2003)* (Reggio Calabria, 2007), pp. 547–98, at pp. 577–84 and 593–4. The 28th is 'Cantata a 3: Egeria, Dorinda e Amarilli', which was conjecturally performed in Rome on 4 November 1715, the name-day of emperor Charles VI. Bononcini's score is preserved in A-Wn, 18283. See Lowell Lindgren, 'Vienna, the "natural centro" for Giovanni Bononcini', in Alberto Colzani, Norbert Dubowy, Andrea Luppi and Maurizio Padoan (eds), *Il teatro musicale italiano nel Sacro Romano Impero nei secoli XVII e XVIII. Atti del VII Convegno internazionale sulla musica italiana nei secoli XVII–XVIII, Loveno di Menaggio (Como), 15–17 luglio 1997* (Como, 1999), pp. 365–420, at pp. 371, 374–81, 405 and 410–20.

[4] According to Roger North (c.1651–1734), Italian instrumental genres played a similar role in the daily life of a British musician around 1700: 'Then came over Corelly's first consort [Op.1, Rome, 1681], that cleared the ground of all other sorts of musick whatsoever. By degrees the rest of his consorts, and at last the conciertos came [Op.6, Amsterdam, 1714], all which are to the musitians like the bread of life' (John Wilson (ed.), *Roger North on Music* (London, 1959), pp. 310–11).

[5] See Appendix 6.1, section B-2, for the two Austrian manuscripts that preserve his five cantatas. The likelihood that the three in A-Wn, 17567, were composed in 1712, the year after Bononcini's employment in Vienna ended, is convincingly argued in Lawrence Bennett, 'The Italian Cantata in Vienna, 1700–1711: An Overview of Stylistic Traits', in Brian W. Pritchard (ed.), *Antonio Caldara: Essays on His Life and Times* (Aldershot, 1987), pp. 183–211, at 208–209. In this article, and in his PhD dissertation of the same title from New York University, 1980 (published Ann Arbor, 1980), Bennett summarizes the stylistic features of 100 cantatas by five composers. He bestows abundant praise on the 13 richly scored works written – mainly in 1708 – by Antonio Maria Bononcini. Each of Antonio's Viennese works survives in only a single source: A-Wn, 17587, 17607 or 17637 (Bennett, dissertation, pp. 586–7 and 590–91), which implies that works written for the imperial court were not permitted to circulate. Yet it should be noted that as many as 32 of Antonio's 40 solo cantatas survive in only one source. They clearly did not have the widespread appeal of those composed by his elder brother.

Bononcini's employment at the imperial court ended. Many of them may have been written for patrons such as Queen Sophie Charlotte, whom he served at Berlin in 1702–03. Nearly two-thirds (42) of them survive in only one source, while a mere 15 are found in two sources, and 8 in three or four. As noted in section C-1, a dozen attributions to Bononcini are questionable, because the sources that contain them are considered untrustworthy. The 53 extant works listed in section D-1 were written either at Rome in 1713–19 or at London in 1720–32.[6] More than two-thirds of them (37) survive in only one source, whereas ten are found in two sources and six in three to six sources.

Under the heads A-2, B-2, C-2 and D-2, Appendix 6.1 lists nearly three-quarters of the known musical sources for Bononcini's solo cantatas. These are identified by RISM sigla and placed after the name of the country in which they were certainly or conjecturally copied.[7] As shown in section A-2, the cantatas written in Italy during the 1690s (Phase 2 of Bononcini's career) survive mainly in 57 Italian sources, some of which – for example, B-Bc, F 15325 ♦5; D-Dl, 1-I-2: 1-2 ♦4; GB-CDp, MS 2 ♦5; and US-NHub, Misc Ms 273 ♦7 – were presumably copied in Rome shortly after they were written.[8] Favour towards Bononcini's works around 1700 is suggested by the contents of a printed miscellany of twelve cantatas by seven composers: Scarlatti, Corazza, Montuoli and Canuti are each represented by one cantata, Mancini and Gregori by two, and Bononcini by four (including the first two in the volume).[9] Esteem for the latter's works around 1700 is further evinced by five substantial Italian collections of his cantatas: I-Fc, B 2376 ♦18; I-

---

[6] On 5 December 1731 Bononcini finished composing or compiling for Count Kinsky, imperial ambassador to Britain, a collection of twelve *cantate co' stromenti* – six for soprano and six for alto – that does not survive; see Lindgren, 'Vienna, the "natural centro" for Giovanni Bononcini', pp. 392–3 and 407, and idem, 'Musicians and Librettists in the Correspondence of Gio. Giacomo Zamboni (Oxford, Bodleian Library, MSS Rawlinson Letters 116–138)', *Royal Musical Association Research Chronicle*, 24 (1991): 1–194, at 135–6. The only extant cantata conceivably composed by Bononcini after 1732 is *Correa dietro a spocori*, which survives in A-Wn, SA 67 A 25, pp. 56–62.

[7] Only a more detailed study concerning each source could solve the many problems concerning their placement. For example, a source with a dozen cantatas might have been written by as many as a dozen copyists, who worked in several different countries. Further study could also place each Italian source within the region in which it was copied. Corrections to the current placement of sources will all be welcomed and acknowledged by the author.

[8] Following the RISM siglum and shelfmark, I indicate the quantity of cantatas contained in each source by appending the appropriate number preceded by the symbol ♦.

[9] The only known copy of this edition, preserved in I-Bc, V 194, lacks pp. 1–4 (i.e., the title page, the prefatory material, and the beginning of the opening recitative for Bononcini's *D'un mirto all'ombra*). The anthology was presumably printed at Lucca by Bartolomeo Gregori, since the cantatas for *canto* end with two by his brother, Giovanni Lorenzo Gregori, and those for *alto* end with one by another Lucchese, Giovanni Antonio Canuti.

REm, 31 Mus Prof ♦18; D-Bsb, Landsberg 35 ♦24; I-Mc, Noseda C 65 7 ♦27; and I-MC, 1 C 9/1 + 1 C 10 + 1 C 11 ♦32.[10]

The 16 English manuscripts listed in section A-2 of Appendix 6.1 preserve the most popular cantatas that Bononcini composed in the 1690s. The suave curlicues of the same elegant professional scribe adorn four substantial volumes that contain nothing but his works: 18 appear in GB-Ob, Mus. d. 20; a different 18 appear in both GB-Ob, Mus. d. 21, and GB-Lbl, Add. 31,545; and 24 – including 16 from Mus. d. 20 and seven from Mus. d. 21 – appear in US-Cn, Case VM1532 B69L. The Garland facsimile edition of 1985 includes 16 from GB-Ob, Mus. d. 20 and eight from Mus. d. 21: eighteen of these cantatas are extant in 11–31 sources, three in 8–9, and three in 5–6.[11]

Another four English volumes attribute spurious works to Bononcini, conceivably because of a great demand for cantatas by him in the early 1700s. The first two were copied by the 'curlicue' scribe, who provided them with a deceptive title page: 'Libro delle cantate del sig[nor] Giov[anni] Bononcini'. Within the first volume, GB-Lgc, G Mus 449 (listed in section C-2), the scribe placed Bononcini's name at the head of only the first of 25 pieces – and even that is a questionable attribution.[12] Within the second volume, GB-Cfm, Mu Ms 46 (listed in A-2), the sole work headed with Bononcini's name is followed by twelve anonymous works, six of which include a part, marked 'viol di gamba', that ranges virtuosically through bass, tenor and treble clefs. Since Bononcini was known to be an excellent cellist, the implication that he composed them all may at the time have seemed entirely reasonable. The cantatas were, however, the work of Tommaso Bernardo

---

[10] A fourth Montecassino manuscript, I-MC, 1 C 9/2 a–k, is listed in section D-2, because its eleven cantatas were conjecturally composed in 1713–19, when Bononcini served Count Gallas, the imperial ambassador in Rome. Perhaps various Montecassino manuscripts (and not only those with cantatas by Bononcini) were utilized for entertainments sponsored by ambassador Gallas. For a thematic catalogue, see Giovanni Insom et al., *Il fondo musicale dell'Archivio di Montecassino*, 2 vols (Montecassino, 2003).

[11] The only two works in GB-Ob, Mus. d. 20 that are not in US-Cn, Case VM1532 B69L, or the Garland edition are *Giacea di verde mirto* (extant in three manuscripts) and *Sventurato Fileno siedeva un dì* (in one manuscript). The Garland edition includes only one work from GB-Ob, Mus. d. 21, *Clori, mio ben, mia vita* (in eight manuscripts), that is not also in US-Cn, Case VM1532 B69L, which replaced it with *Del suo fedel e taciturno ardore* (in ten manuscripts).

[12] See Appendix 6.1, note 142. The 'curlicue' scribe was presumably a German, since he copied the score of Steffani's *I trionfi del fato* (Hamburg, 1699) in 'deutsche Schrift', as discussed and illustrated in Colin Timms, 'The Dissemination of Steffani's Operas', in Alberto Colzani, Norbert Dubowy, Andrea Luppi and Maurizio Padoan (eds), *Relazioni musicali tra Italia e Germania nell'età barocca. Atti del VI convegno internazionale sulla musica italiana nei secoli XVII–XVIII, Loveno di Menaggio (Como), 11–13 luglio 1995* (Como, 1997), pp. 323–49, at 334–6 and 348–9.

Gaffi, constituting his *Cantate da camera*, Op.1 (Rome, 1700).[13] The scribe for the final two manuscripts was Johann Sigismund Cousser, who presumably copied them in 1705–07, when he resided in London.[14] In GB-Cfm, Mu Ms 649 ('Cantate de diversi Maestri, Libro 3^{zo}'), Cousser misattributed seven of Gaffi's and one of Caldara's cantatas to Bononcini.[15] In US-Wc, M1614 A2 B944, all 12 of Gaffi's cantatas, as well as the same Caldara cantata, are misattributed to Bononcini.[16]

The 13 substantial manuscripts delineated in the last three paragraphs may all have been copied around 1705, when the 35-year-old Bononcini was the pre-eminent composer in the service of the new, 27-year-old emperor Joseph I, who reigned until 1711. Francesco Gasparini, who had worked alongside Bononcini at Rome during the 1690s, praised his cantatas and referred to his lofty position at the end of chapter 11, 'Del diminuire o rifiorire il fondamento', in *L'armonico pratico al cimbalo* (Venice, Bortoli, 1708):

> Molti e varij di questi motivi potrai osservare nelle cantate di molti virtuosi professori, ma particolarmente in quelle del Sig. Giovanni Bononcini, degnissimo virtuoso di Sua Maestà Cesarea, in cui scorgerai non meno della

---

[13] In Cfm, Mu Ms 46, the only piece attributed by the 'curlicue' scribe to Bononcini is *Lungi dal ben ch'adoro* (ff. 9–12v), which is scored for S/bc. It later reappears (ff. 50–55v) among the anonymous twelve in a scoring for S/gamba + bc. In his preface 'a gl'amatori della musica' Gaffi did not call for a viola di gamba, but named three other ways of performing the 'arie con due bassi': 'potranno sodisfarsi il violino o violone [presumably a cello], e alla mancanza di questi potrà supplirle la virtù di un buon sonatore di cembalo con fare l'uno e altro basso, cioè la chiave di violino con la mano destra, e le altre con la sinistra'; cited in François Lesure and Claudio Sartori, *Il nuovo Vogel: Bibliografia della musica italiana vocale profana pubblicata dal 1500 al 1700* (Pomezia, 1977), p. 692, no. 1051. See Appendix 6.1, note 122, for the only piece by Bononcini in GB-Cfm, Mu Ms 46.

[14] See Lowell Lindgren, 'J. S. Cousser, Copyist of the Cantata Manuscript in the Truman Presidential Library, and Other Cantata Copyists of 1697–1707, who Prepared the Way for Italian Opera in London', in Bianca Maria Antolini, Teresa M. Gialdroni and Annunziato Pugliese (eds), *'Et facciam dolçi canti'. Studi in onore di Agostino Ziino in occasione del suo 65° compleanno* (Lucca, 2003), pp. 737–82, especially pp. 746–7.

[15] See Appendix 6.1, note 123. Five of the seven Gaffi cantatas in GB-Cfm, Mu Ms 649, include 'arie con due bassi'. Cousser wrote the added part between the voice and continuo and specified an instrument for three of the arias: 'violoncello' for the first aria and 'violino' for the second in *Lunghi dal ben ch'adoro* (pp. 59–67), and 'violoncello' for the aria 'con due bassi' in *Qual oggetto* (p. 110).

[16] In US-Wc, M1614 A2 B944, scribes other than Cousser wrote 'Bononcini' on the verso of the flyleaf and the first page of music and also provided a singing translation for 'Lunghi dal ben ch'adoro' ('Far of[f] from my adored'). Any cover that might once have carried Bononcini's name in Cousser's handwriting is no longer present. Four of Gaffi's cantatas in this manuscript are briefly discussed (as examples of *Bononcini's* style!) in Robert B. Morris, 'A Study of the Italian Solo Cantata before 1750' (DME dissertation, Indiana University, 1955), published Ann Arbor, 1978, pp. 128–30. Morris transcribes Gaffi's *Nel petto ho sol un core* (which he attributes to Bononcini) on pp. 135–7.

bizzaria, la vaghezza, l'armonia, lo studio artificioso e la capricciosa invenzione, che perciò con giustizia incontra l'applauso di un mondo intiero ammiratore del suo bellissimo ingegno.[17]

Two comprehensive volumes of cantatas assembled by the French court copyist in 1705 insinuate that the most highly favoured Italian composer in his land was Bononcini.[18] Both volumes of F-Pn, X 118 (listed in section C-2) are entitled 'Cantate da molti illustrissimi maestri italiani, raccolto per [André Danican] Philidor, il maggiore ordinario della musica del re, guardi[a]no della sua biblioteca della musica, 1705'. Each contains 18 cantatas, and the first also has five arias, one of which was composed by 'Sua Maestà Leopoldo Imperatore' (d. 1705). According to the title, Philidor's primary intention was to represent 'many illustrious Italian masters'. His attributions (some of which are incorrect) signify that 14 composers are represented by one cantata and only four by more than one: Giovanni Paolo Colonna and Antonio Maria Bononcini each by two, Francesco Mancini by four (plus one that Philidor attributed to Giovanni Bononcini), and Giovanni Bononcini by 14 (minus one composed by Mancini and one that is elsewhere credibly attributed to Albinoni).[19] Two cantatas attributed to Giovanni

---

[17] Cited from a reprint (Bologna, Silvani, 1722) that has been printed in facsimile with an introduction by Luigi Ferdinando Tagliavini (Sala Bolognese, 2001), p. 79. An English translation of this passage is given in Tagliavini's introduction, p. 38.

[18] This is also suggested by US-CAh, Ms Mus 63, the source for Figs. 6.1 and 6.2. Its 15 cantatas include seven by Bononcini, four by Mancini, two by Scarlatti and one each by Torri (a duet) and Bencini. According to Barbara Mahrenholz Wolff, *Music Manuscripts at Harvard: A Catalogue of Music Manuscripts from the 14th to the 20th Centuries in the Houghton Library and the Eda Kuhn Loeb Music Library* (Cambridge, 1992), pp. 212–13, this manuscript was copied in '(France?), c. 1750'. It could, however, have been copied as early as 1705, when its five composers were already aged between 33 and 55 years.

[19] Philidor's attribution of *Va sospirando il core* to Giovanni Bononcini in F-Pn, X 118B, pp. 149–64, is incorrect, because it is ascribed to Mancini in six sources. See Josephine Wright, 'The Secular Cantatas of Francesco Mancini (1672–1736)' (PhD dissertation, New York University, 1975), published Ann Arbor, 1976, p. 411, no. 195. Philidor's spellings suggest that Magini, Mangini and Mancini were different composers. This may be true, because the works he ascribes to Magini and Mangini are not listed in Wright's catalogue of Mancini's works. *Rondinella vaga e bella*, the cantata attributed to Mangini in F-Pn, X 118A, pp. 10–23, is known to survive in ten other manuscripts. Five attribute it to Giovanni Bononcini (although in GB-Lbl, Add. 62,102, p. 39, a second hand crossed out his name and wrote 'Mancini' above it), three are anonymous; one ascribes it to 'C Magini', and one to 'Bencini.' It is listed among questionable attributions to Bononcini in Stanley Sadie and John Tyrrell (eds), *The New Grove Dictionary*, 2nd edn, vol. 3, p. 876. One that is now being moved to the questionable category is *Già tornava l'aurora* (see earlier, note 2); Philidor ascribed it to 'Bononcini' in F-Pn, X 118A, pp. 99–112, but it is attributed to 'Albinoni' in D-SHs, Mus B 1:2, pp. 161–79, and it is anonymous in D-Bsb, Mus. ms. 30188, no. 16, according to Harald Kümmerling, *Katalog der Sammlung Bokemeyer* (Kassel, 1970), p. 141, no. 1389. Philidor incorrectly attributed *Perché mai, nume adorato* to 'Carolo

and one attributed to his brother Antonio Maria survive nowhere else, and the text for one of Giovanni's unique pieces was given a different setting by Antonio Maria at Vienna in 1708.[20]

Philidor's implication – that the Italian cantatas most highly favoured in France in 1705 were those composed by Giovanni Bononcini – is corroborated by a well-known literary battle of 1704–06. This was generated by the *Paralele des italiens et des françois, en ce qui regarde la musique et les opéra* (1702), in which François Raguenet delineated particular ways in which the French surpassed the Italians (pp. 5–23), then richly described the compelling means by which the Italians outstripped the French (pp. 23–124).[21] Raguenet exemplified some points by reference to the operas and the oratorio he had seen at Turin in 1697 and at Rome in 1697–98, but does not mention the word cantata. One Bononcini work he had seen in Rome was *La rinovata Camilla*, and he exemplified the unparalleled Italian alliance of 'la tendresse avec la vivacité' with 'Mai non si vide ancor', the aria with which Turno – a soprano castrato – ends Act I. Its tune 'est le plus doux & le plus tendre du monde', while its orchestral accompaniment 'est la plus vive & la plus picquante qui se puisse entendre'.[22]

In 1704 Jean Laurent Le Cerf de la Viéville, seigneur de Freneuse, published the first part of his *Comparaison de la musique italienne, et de la musique françoise*,

---

Ambrogio Lunati' in F-Pn, X 118A, pp. 75–87; it had been printed in Domenico Gabrielli, *Cantate a voce sola* (Bologna, Monti, 1691; facsimile repr. Florence, 1980), pp. 1–19.

[20] Giovanni's unique pieces, *Sopra l'orme d'Irene* and *Chi vide mai, ch'intese*, are in F-Pn, X 118A, pp. 87–98 and 121–31, respectively. Antonio Maria's setting of the former text for alto, *violino primo di concerto*, *violoncello di concerto* and a *concerto grosso* group, is in A-Wn, 17607, ff. 103–20. Antonio's unique piece, *Con non inteso affanno*, is in F-Pn, X 118B, pp. 191–207. It has a text similar to one set by Alessandro Scarlatti, listed in Edwin Hanley, 'Alessandro Scarlatti's Cantate da camera: A Bibliographical Study' (PhD dissertation, Yale University, 1963), published Ann Arbor, 1973, pp. 162–3, no. 142.

[21] Paris, Jean Moreau, 1702. A facsimile reprint (Geneva, 1976) also includes Raguenet's *Défense du parallèle* (Paris, Veuve de Claude Barbin, 1705). The *Paralele* reappeared as *A Comparison between the* French *and* Italian *Musick and Opera's. Translated* [anonymously] *from the* French *with Some Remarks* [by Nicola Francesco Haym] (London, William Lewis, 1709), facsimile repr. Farnborough, 1968. In *A Comparison* French opera is lauded on pp. 2–12, Italian opera on pp. 12–61.

[22] *Paralele*, pp. 49–50, translated in *A Comparison*, pp. 25–6. In his *Défense du parallele*, p. 135, Raguenet asserts that he had never heard, in any role, a *taille* better than the one who portrayed Mezio in the *La rinovata Camilla* produced at the Teatro Capranica in Rome in 1698. Mezio's part in the scores for Naples 1696 is written for a tenor; see, for example, *Il trionfo di Camilla, regina de' Volsci*, facsimile reprint of the manuscript in GB-ABu, Powell Collection, introduction by Howard Mayer Brown (New York, 1978). In the scores for Rome 1698, however, it is transposed up a third or fourth and written in the alto clef. Since women were not allowed to appear on the Roman stage, the singer whom Raguenet heard was presumably an alto castrato. See Lowell Lindgren, 'I trionfi di Camilla', *Studi musicali*, 6 (1977): 89–159, at 100, 135 and 150–51.

which lauds various aspects of French culture, especially poetry. It refers to music infrequently, and, indeed, it is in the midst of a discussion of the 'détestables' Italian poets that it classifies Anton Giulio Brignole-Sale (1605–62) as a 'demi poëte [...] un cuisinier à épice & à sausses. C'est *Cavallo*, c'est *Cesti*, c'est *Buononcini*'.[23] In other words, these three composers are ranked alongside a 'demi poëte' whose works consist basically of spice and sauce. In his *Défense du parallèle* (1705) Raguenet ridiculed the first part of Le Cerf's *Comparaison* – page by page! When he came to attack the above-cited passage, he staunchly defended Bononcini,

> duquel nous avons plus de deux cens cantates à Paris, & même des opéra entiers, M. le Chevalier ne pouvoit pas échoir plus mal, car il n'y a nul maître de musique en Italie dans les ouvrages duquel il y ait si peu de ces endroits picquans & recherchez que M. le Chevalier compare aux épices, qu'il y en a dans les ouvrages de *Buononcini*; tous les maîtres de France le citent comme un modele pour le gracieux, & c'est le seul qu'ils citent en ce genre; il n'y a point de si petit musicien françois qui ne le connoisse sur ce pied, & qui ne fache que c'est là son caractére.[24]

Raguenet's *Défense* was not published until November 1705, and Le Cerf did not publish the second and third parts of his *Comparaison* until after the *Défense* appeared.[25] In part two, at the point where he objected strenuously to the exalted placement of Bononcini and the exclusion of older masters (such as Rossi and Carissimi), he admitted that he had seen only one of Bononcini's works: the *Duetti da camera* (Bologna, 1691):

> C'est *Buononcini* qu'elle cite par préference: c'est celui qu'elle met à la tête de ces admirables modernes. Il est le héros, de l'Italie & le sien. [...] Je n'ai jamais

---

[23] Brussels, François Foppens, 1704–06; facsimile repr. Geneva, 1972, part 1, pp. 40–41.

[24] *Défense*, pp. 43–4, translated in Don Fader, 'Philippe II d'Orléans's "chanteurs italiens", the Italian cantata and the *goûts-réunis* under Louis XIV', *Early Music*, 35 (2007): 237–49, at 249, note 23. Defending the expressive capability of Italian music, Raguenet cites 'la belle Plainte de *Scarlati* qui commence par ces paroles *Povero afflitto cor, come à tanto dolor tu duri ancora &c!* Celle de *Buononcini* sur ces paroles *Ah nò, che non si more per duolo ò per amore &c!* & tant d'autres dont les expressions douloureuses & gémissantes percent le cœur, & sont par conséquent bien au de-là du *sérieux* & de la *gravité* dont vous dites que les Italiens sont incapables' (*Défense*, p. 96). Raguenet's incipits (which I have not found) are presumably for recitatives or arias within operas or cantatas.

[25] The *Défense* ends with Fontenelle's 'approbation' dated 1 June, a 'privilège du roi' dated 23 August, and publishers' documents dated 4 September and 6 and 10 November 1705. Le Cerf's volumes, which were published in Brussels, have no such official dates. Le Cerf himself provided *'Le 16. Aoust* [1706]' in part 3, p. 212. This precedes a separately paginated section: 'Réponse a la Défense du Paralelle [*sic*]' (pp. 1–38) and 'Eclaircissement sur Buononcini' (pp. 39–53).

vû de lui, que ses *duo* imprimez à Boulogne, mais je vous avouë que là-dessus je n'en aurois pas une si haute opinion à plus de la moitié prés. […] Malheur dans lequel est tombé Mr l'Abbé R[aguenet] qui n'a nommé *Buononcini* que dans la foule. Vous voudrez bien avertir de même tous les François Italiens de vôtre connoissance de n'estimer que les compositeurs qui ont brillé depuis 20 ans. Vous avez à Paris & sur tout dans les provinces quantité de jeunes adorateurs de la musique d'Italie, qui admirent souvent sur le nom de l'auteur en *i* ou en *o*.[26]

Since Le Cerf had seen no works by Bononcini other than the *Duetti* of 1691, which marked the culmination of the first phase of his career (spent in Modena and Bologna), one may infer that he had neither seen nor heard any solo cantatas or other works that Bononcini had composed in Rome or Vienna. He remedied this lack of acquaintance in Paris during the summer of 1706, when he heard a sufficient quantity of Bononcini's complete cantatas to speak with confidence about them, and, accordingly, to end his *Comparaison* with an 'Eclaircissement sur Buononcini':

J'entendis cét eté à Paris un assez grand nombre de ses cantates entieres, pour en parler à present avec assurance. Elles me semblerent véritablement dignes d'être loüées de ceux qui les loüent, rafinées, piquantes. […] Mais les musiciens qui les chantoient, quoique musiciens de profession, paroissoient souvent détonner, tant les tons étoient transposez, hors du mode, dissonans. […] Je trouvai que le caractere de Buononcini a beaucoup de raport à celui de Corelli. Ils font tous deux peu de fugues, de contrefugues, de basses contraintes, beautez fréquentes dans les autres ouvrages Italiens: & ils font l'un & l'autre leurs délices ordinaires de tous les intervales les moins usitez, les plus faux & les plus bizares, en quoi je pourrois ne les pas reconnoître pour si sçavans.[27]

Judging from this introduction to the 'Eclaircissement', one would imagine that the ensuing discussion of four cantatas would focus on their bizarre melodic intervals, dissonant harmonies, unstable modes and keys and lack of both fugal writing and ostinato basses,[28] as well as on the deficiencies of the professional

---

[26] *Comparaison*, part 2, pp. 80–81.

[27] Ibid., part 3, section 2, pp. 39–40. In his 'Réponse a la Défense du Paralelle', pp. 19–22, Le Cerf had lambasted the sevenths in the *Preludio* of Corelli's Op. 4, no. 11.

[28] The equivalence of *basses contraintes* and *ostinato* basses is made clear in Sébastien de Brossard, *Dictionaire de musique* (Paris, Ballard, 1703; facsimile repr. Amsterdam, 1964), s.v. 'perfidia': 'il veut dire *ostination*, c'est à dire une *affectation* de faire toûjours la *même chose*, de suivre toûjours le *même dessein*, de continuer le *même mouvement*, le *même chant*, le *même passage*, les *mêmes figures* de nottes, &c. Ainsi *contrapunto perfidiato*, *fuga perfidiata*, ce sont des contrepoints, & des fugues où l'on s'obstine à suivre toûjours le même dessein, telles sont les basses *contraintes* ou *obligées*, comme celles des *chacones* & un infinité d'autres manieres'.

singers he heard,[29] but Le Cerf focuses instead on melismas. With regard to 'Mai non è d'Amor la face', the initial aria of *Lontan dal tuo bel viso*, he objects to the long melismas on 'lonta*nanz*a' and 'co*stanz*a', the words ending sections A and B, respectively, then to the active bass line, which 'fait un tintamarre merveilleux'.[30] Likewise, when discussing [*Quando parli e*] *quando ridi*, he remonstrates mightily against the four lengthy 'roulades' on the verb '*scocc*a', the final word of the closing arioso. In the case of *Amore, e come mai d'un sguardo*, he objects to a bass line of 20 bars in 4/4 metre, where 'la vîtesse est violente', because the bass has nothing but demisemiquavers, while the voice moves slowly, in order to portray 'ardenti sospiri'.[31]

Before Le Cerf discusses a fourth cantata, he tells us that he has borrowed and examined 'quelques cantates de Buononcini. [...] Ce héros de l'Italie répand les richesses des ornemens de sa musique avec une telle profusion, que la simplicité ne sçauroit être une vertu de sa connoissance'.[32] He then exaggerates the general points made at the beginning of his 'Eclaircissiment', culminating with an outcry: 'La rapsodie de toutes les duretez, les bizarreries, les affectations possibles, s'appellera-t-elle une musique agréable & gracieuse? Gracieuse & agréable donc pour des gens yvres ou furieux'. Le Cerf admits that the best Italian airs, though inexpressive, 'ont un beau chant'; but this, he alleges, is not true of those occurring in Bononcini's cantatas, which 'presque toûjours' have 'un chant aigre & rompu, que fait cruellement souffrir'.[33] He goes on to discuss *Arde il mio petto amante*, which – like *Quando parli e quando ridi* – was published in Lucca c.1700. He finds that it, 'marquée du nom du Dieu des Cantates, nous ennuyera moins qu'un autre', because it is 'trés courte & des plus sages', therefore 'une des meilleures'. Near the end of the opening recitative, he took pleasure in the upward leap of an augmented fourth to a seventh and ninth followed by a descent to a sixth and

---

[29] Le Cerf gives no indication concerning the identity of the performers. In the excellent article by Don Fader, 'Philippe II d'Orléans', we learn that Philippe not only imported fashionable Roman/Neapolitan music but had established an ensemble of Italian performers in Paris by 1703. It consisted of two castrati, two violinists and a cellist. If Le Cerf heard Italian cantatas performed by this ensemble, his criticism must be unwarranted.

[30] Throughout the aria, the 'terrible racket' in the continuo is a two-beat pattern consisting of a quaver followed by six semiquavers (g – g a | b♭ g a b♭), which provide nothing more than an adornment of the first note. In its melismas, the voice frequently doubles or imitates this 'terrible racket'. (Here, and later, I have adopted the convention of italicizing the syllable or syllables that are set apart, for example, by means of a melisma, a leap, or a chromaticism.)

[31] Ibid., pp. 40–43. I have not seen *Amore, e come mai d'un sguardo*, which is presumably the work attributed to 'Rignatti' in D-Bsb, Mus. ms. 30197, no. 18, listed in Kümmerling, *Katalog der Sammlung Bokemeyer*, p. 142, no. 1437. In this manuscript the surrounding works (nos. 17 and 19–20) as well as nos. 7–8, 12–14, 22–3, 27 and 29 are by 'Bononcini'. This is the only work attributed to 'Rignatti' in the Bokemeyer collection.

[32] *Comparaison*, part 3, section 2, p. 43.

[33] Ibid., pp. 44–5.

fourth; here, he more or less agreed with Raguenet that Bononcini provided a 'modéle pour le gracieux'.[34] This recitative ends with a first falling and then rising roulade that – for Le Cerf – painted 'joliment l'action d'une belle personne, qui abaisse & releve ses yeux sur quelqu'un'. Throughout the ensuing aria, he heard the cry of a cuckoo, which also pleased him (though this has nothing to do with the text). At the end of his 'Eclaircissiment', Le Cerf expressed the hope that Raguenet would honour him with a second reply. If one was prepared, it was never published, perhaps because Le Cerf died in 1707.[35]

Two years later, *A Comparison between the* French *and* Italian *Musick and Opera's, translated from the* French, *with Some Remarks* (by Nicola Francesco Haym, in 40 long-spun-out footnotes)[36] was published in London. Since Raguenet's knowledge of Italian style was the result of his trip to Rome in 1697–98, Haym was an ideal annotator, because he had worked as a musician in his native Rome until the duke of Bedford called him to London in 1701. At London Haym adapted two operas in which he had probably performed as a cellist at Rome: Bononcini's *Camilla* (Rome, 1698; London, 1706) and Scarlatti's *Pyrrhus and Demetrius* (Rome, 1694; London, 1708). Both were very successful in London.[37] In a summary statement Haym notes that '*Bononcini*'s instrumental musick, that accompanies the voice, is as much superior to *Scarlatti*'s, as *Scarlatti*'s vocal musick is superior to *Bononcini*'s, so that they are both excellent in their way, and may be look'd on as

---

[34] Ibid., pp. 46–9. Since the bass moves up stepwise when the voice leaps up an augmented fourth, the intervals identified as a seventh and ninth by Le Cerf are in fact a sixth and an octave.

[35] Ibid., pp. 50–53. Le Cerf's 'Eclaircissement sur Buononcini' is termed a 'senseless libel, for it deserves no better a name', in John Hawkins, *A General History of the Science and Practice of Music* [1776], 2nd edn (London, 1853; repr. New York, 1963), pp. 836–7. Hawkins was not, however, impartial, because he believed that 'the general sense of mankind' had for a long time settled the question 'and given to the Italian music that preference, which upon principles universally admitted, is allowed to be its due' (ibid., p. 837). According to Hellmuth Christian Wolff, 'Bononcini oder die Relativität historischer Urteile', *Revue belge de musicologie*, 11 (1957): 3–16, at 5, Le Cerf's commentary 'ist für uns heute von grossem Interesse, weil hier an Hand genauer Analysen von Kantaten Bononcinis die Wirkung solcher italienischer Musik auf die Zeitgenossen geschildert wird' ('is of great interest for us today, because by means of precise analyses of Bononcini cantatas the effect of such Italian music on its contemporaries is depicted'). Wolff's statement is, however, misleading, because Le Cerf's analyses are far from 'precise' and – since he was staunchly defending French culture – he was far from being a typical listener in 1704–06.

[36] 'Seignior *H[aym]* or some Creature of his' was identified as the author of the remarks in Charles Gildon, *The Life of Mr Thomas Betterton, the Late Eminent Tragedian*, (London, 1710); facsimile reprint in *Eighteenth Century Shakespeare*, 4 (London, 1970), p. 166. See also Lowell Lindgren, 'The Accomplishments of the Learned and Ingenious Nicola Francesco Haym (1678–1729)', *Studi musicali*, 16 (1987): 247–380, especially 291–2.

[37] The spectacular success of Bononcini's opera is traced in Lowell Lindgren, '*Camilla* and *The Beggar's Opera*', *Philological Quarterly*, 59 (1980): 44–61.

the greatest masters in the world in their different characters'.[38] Haym listed both among the composers who were giving 'the last hand to the perfection of *Italian musick* for opera's and cantata's',[39] but only Scarlatti was named 'a prodigy of musick',[40] and 'artful harshness in musick' was best conveyed in 'some of the recitative in *Scarlatti's cantata's*, where he makes use of all sorts of dissonance to express the force of the words, and afterwards resolves 'em so well that indeed the most beautiful concords are hardly so sweet and harmonious as his discords'.[41]

Thus far, comments made about Bononcini's style in 1705–09 by two amateurs, Raguenet and Le Cerf, and two professionals, Gasparini and Haym, have been cited. In 1716, the musician Johann Ernst Galliard accurately summarized the judgements of his predecessors:

> At present, there are in *Italy, cantata's* innumerable, but those that deserve to be taken notice of, as well as the composers of them, may be reduc'd into a very narrow compass. [...] Of late years, *Aless. Scarlatti* and *Bononcini* have brought *cantata's* to what they are at present; *Bononcini* by his agreable and easie style, and those fine inventions in his *basses* (to which he was led by an instrument upon which he excells) and *Scarlatti* by his noble and masterly turns'.[42]

Galliard thus concurred with Raguenet[43] and opposed Le Cerf, who had said that anyone calling Bononcini's music 'agréable & gracieuse' was drunk or mad. By referring to Bononcini's 'fine inventions in his *basses* (to which he was led by an

---

[38] *A Comparison*, p. 36, note 23.

[39] Ibid., p. 32, note 20.

[40] Ibid, p. 29, note 19. Scarlatti had set 'near a hundred opera's' and 'an infinite number of *oratorio's, cantata's* and *serenades* to musick, [...] with such an incredible quickness, that it's impossible for any cop[y]ist to write so fast as he composeth, and yet he varies so much in his style, that ev'ry new opera seems the work of some new composer. [...] We shou'd not imagine them to be his, was it not for a certain sublimity in his design, which distinguishes him from all the rest of the world besides'. Haym was apparently 'proselytizing' for Scarlatti, whose works – unlike Bononcini's – were little known to Londoners. In other words, he was 'propagandizing' for his own adaptation of Scarlatti's *Pyrrhus and Demetrius* for the London stage.

[41] Ibid., p. 16, note 12.

[42] 'To the Lovers of Musick' is a two-page address within *Six English Cantatas after the Italian Manner Compos'd by M' Galliard* (London, J. Walsh and J. Hare, [1716]). This two-page address is in GB-Lcm, II F 27. It is not in GB-Lam, 3/9; GB-Lbl, H 117 b; or US-CAh, Mus 780 6 605 F*.

[43] Bononcini's name follows Scarlatti's in the lists of a few contemporary Italian composers in Raguenet, *Paralele*, p. 66, and *Défense*, p. 159, but neither he nor Le Cerf focuses upon works by Scarlatti. In *A Comparison*, p. 32, Scarlatti's name was (inadvertently?) omitted from the list given in the *Paralele*, p. 66; therefore, Bononcini's name appears first.

instrument upon which he excells)' and to Scarlatti's 'noble and masterly turns', he echoed points made by Gasparini and Haym.

After a brief discussion of Bononcini's Op. 8 duets, the following pages will summarize the stylistic features of nine Bononcini cantatas that Raguenet and Le Cerf may well have heard and Gasparini, Haym and Galliard may well have performed, since they were widely available in copies made around 1700. Eight of these cantatas appear in the facsimile publication (Garland, 1985) that contains 24 of his cantatas and one serenata. Bononcini's 21 extant serenata scores will not be treated herein, since they were typically commissioned for a single celebration, chronicled in a printed libretto, sung by 2–10 characters (so that scores were often headed 'cantata a 2 [or any number up to 10] voci'), and played by a large group of treble as well as bass instruments. Unlike solo cantatas, they were rarely copied for anyone outside an immediate circle of family and friends.[44]

Bononcini's earliest datable cantata-like works, his ten *Duetti da camera*, Op. 8 (Bologna, Monti, 1691), form a climax to his compositional activity during the first stage of his career. In 1685, the year when Corelli published his Op. 2 and Handel, Bach and Domenico Scarlatti were born, the fifteen-year-old Bononcini published 24 secular trio sonatas in Opp. 1–2 and twelve church sonatas in five to eight parts in Op. 3. In 1686–88, 36 church sonatas and four *Messe brevi a 8 voci piene* appeared in Opp. 4–7.[45] In 1687–90 Bononcini composed three oratorios.[46] During this first phase, while 'sotto la disciplina di Gio. Paolo Colonna, di lui maestro, apprese l'arte del contrap[un]to. Fu aggregato all'Accad[emi]a de' Filarmonici di Bologna l'anno 1688. Sotto il principato del Colonna in qualità di compositore, nella quell'arte fece tali progressi, che si rese celebre il suo nome

---

[44] A score and libretto for *La nemica d'Amore fatta amante* are printed in facsimile in the Garland edition, no. 25, pp. 131–258 and 269–73. This 'Serenata a 3 del sig[no]r Gio[vanni] Bononcini, canto, alto e basso, Clori, Tirsi e Fileno', with text by Silvio Stampiglia, is accompanied by solo and tutti strings. It was produced *al fresco* on 10 August 1693, the name-day of the dedicatee, Lorenza de La Cerda Colonna. A fine recording by Ensemble 415, directed by Chiara Banchini, was released in 2003. *La costanza non gradita nel doppio amore d'Aminta*, the work by Bononcini and Stampiglia that celebrated Lorenza's nameday in 1694, can also be heard on a fine recording, released in 1996 by Lautten Compagney, directed by Wolfgang Katschner. In the score at D-Bsb, Mus. ms. 2191/10, *La costanza non gradita* is headed 'cantata a 3, Filli, Dori e Aminta, del Bononcini'. This is one of the four Bononcini serenatas preserved in D-Bsb (Mus. mss. 2191, 2191/10, 2192 and 2192/10) that the composer probably revised for performances sponsored by Henrietta, duchess of Marlborough, in 1724–31. These four manuscripts appear in Sotheby's *Catalogue of a Selected Portion of the Valuable Library at Hornby Castle, Bedale, Yorkshire, the Property of His Grace the Duke of Leeds* (London, 2–3 June 1930), lot 425. For further information, see Lindgren, 'Vienna, the "natural centro" for Giovanni Bononcini', pp. 387–8 and 406.

[45] Title pages, dedications and tables of contents for Opp. 1–6 are cited in Claudio Sartori, *Bibliografia della musica strumentale italiana* (Florence, 1952), pp. 516–19, 532–3 and 538–9.

[46] Scores survive for two of them (see *The New Grove*, 2nd edn, vol. 3, p. 876).

per tutto l'Europa'. The biographical summary from which the above quotation is taken is followed by a list of published works, which includes a comment only for the *Duetti da camera* of 1691: 'Opera che riportò grande applauso, e da professori e da dilettanti di musica'.[47] The sustained success of Op. 8 is implied by its reprint in 1701[48] and the many handwritten copies made in the 1700s.[49]

If Le Cerf had examined Op. 8 carefully, he could have seen ample evidence of the contrapuntal and fugal writing that he did not hear in Bononcini's solo cantatas. In 1787 Giordano Riccati published his analysis of dissonant chords, modulations, subjects and countersubjects in three duets by Handel and four by Bononcini.[50] Riccati affirmed: 'i duetti del Bononcini non la cedono per lo

---

[47] Giambattista Martini, ed. Gaetano Gaspari, 'Miscellanea musicale', in I-Bc, UU 12, vol. 1: 'Scrittori e professori di musica modenesi', pp. 277–8.

[48] Five copies of the 1691 edition and nine of the 1701 reprint are listed in Karl-Heinz Schlager (ed.), *Einzeldrucke vor 1800*, International Inventory of Musical Sources (RISM), series A, 15 vols (Kassel, 1971–2003), vol. 1, p. 372, nos. B 3613–14. The title page, table of contents, names of the poets and same five copies of the 1691 edition are listed in *Il nuovo Vogel*, p. 249, no. 395. Op. 8 and Bononcini were extolled by Sébastien de Brossard, who commented on his copy of the 1701 reprint in his manuscript 'Catalogue des livres de musique' (1724), p. 205: 'Ce sont des chansons ou airs Italiens pour deux voix dont le travail est exquis et des plus admirables, aussi cet auteur passe pour le plus habile des Italiens modernes' (Yolande de Brossard (ed.), *La collection Sébastien de Brossard, 1655–1730: Catalogue (Département de la Musique, Rés. Vm 8 20)* (Paris, 1994), pp. 296–7, no. 467).

[49] Manuscript copies include A-Wn, 17579 (elegant copy of the entire print, partly autograph?); B-Bc, F 581, ff. 1–24 (1691, nos. 3, 8 and 9); D-Bsb, Amalien-Bibliothek, nos. 295 (1691, nos. 1–10), 296 (1691, nos. 1–3, 5–6 and 8–10) and 297 (identical with no. 296); D-Bsb, SA (Sing-Akademie) 1227, nos. 1–3 (1691, nos. 3, 6 and 8); SA 1458, no. 6 (1691, no. 10); SA 1459, nos. 2–9 (1691, nos. 1–3, 5–6 and 8–10); SA 1460, nos. 2–9 (identical with 1459); and SA 1503, no. 15 (1691, no. 9); D-Mbs, 2776 (1691, nos. 1, 5 and 7); D-MÜs, Hs 599 (1691, nos. 1–10); GB-Cu, Add. 7063 (1691, nos. 1–2, 4–5, 7 and 9–10; nos. 4 and 7 are transposed up a fourth); GB-Lbl, Add. 14,187 (1691, nos. 1–10); GB–Lcm, MS 81 (1691, nos. 1, 3–5, 7 and 9–10; nos. 4 and 7 are transposed up a fourth); I-Bc, X 130 (1691, nos. 1–10?); I-Gl, A 7 29 (1691, nos. 1–10); and I-Nc, 33.4.30 (Cantate 38) (1691, nos. 1–2, 4–5, 7, 9–10). The copy in RUS-KAu, 15879 (1691, nos. 1–3, 5 and 8–10) was apparently destroyed during World War II. I-Bc, X 134 (Martini 1 21), has 'Passi per li duetti del sig. Bononcini, fatti dal sig. Carlo Benati'. Benati wrote ornaments – mainly stepwise passages – for 1691, nos. 1–2, 4–5, 7 and 9–10. He wrote out the da capos and provided new ornaments for them. The opening versetto of no. 7 (*Sempre piango e dir non so*, which has a *basso ostinato*) is printed with Benati's ornaments in Ernst T. Ferand, *Improvisation in Nine Centuries of Western Music*, Anthology of Music, 12 (Cologne, 1956), pp. 118–22, no. 30.

[50] 'Lettere del co[nte] Giordano Riccati al dottissimo padre D. Giovenale Sacchi, professore d'eloquenza nel Collegio Imperiale di Milano', *Nuovo giornale de' letterati d'Italia*, 36 (1787): 172–200. The three by Handel – *Sono liete, fortunate*; *Troppo cruda, troppo fiera*; and *Amor gioje mi porge* – were probably written in Italy before 1711. The four by Bononcini are *Prigionier d'un bel sembiante*, *Se bella son io*, *O che lacci io sento*

meno a quelli dell'Handel, e che gli uni, e gli altri gareggino coi famosi duetti di Monsignor Agostino Steffani'.[51] Bononcini – unlike Handel – provided each singer with a centrally situated 'aria a voce sola' in six of his duets. According to Riccati, these arias are 'scritte con ottimo contrappunto, e con melodie a quel tempo aggradevoli', yet he does not discuss any of them, since they 'riescono presentemente di gusto antico'.[52] One or both of the arias within a duet is in a minor key, is marked Allegro or Vivace, and is characterized by unbridled rhythmic drive. The continuo part maintains the drive by introducing and imitating vocal motives or by playing patterned figuration in quavers or semiquavers.

Riccati mentions the imitative role of the bass in the closing duet of no. 2, *Il nume d'Amore*, which he terms an 'elegante versetto': *alto*: 'Che lusinga et inganna' / *soprano*: 'Che consola e diletta' / *a2*: 'è l'alma e il core' ('What entices and betrays / What consoles and delights / are the soul and the heart'). It is marked 'vivace e à battuta' and has 'tre diversi soggetti, modulando da tuono a tuono. [...] In più luoghi colloca nel basso il primo soggetto'.[53] In the first section the voices introduce the subject (f c a | – g – | – fg ab | c – –) over a contrapuntal bass. The continuo begins each of the eight remaining sections by reintroducing the subject. The bass takes an even more active role in *Chi d'Amor tra le catene*, the first duet in the volume, which begins and ends in A minor. In the opening 3/2 Largo, the bass imitates two vocal leaps: up a fourth to 'd'A-*mor*' and down a diminished seventh to 'l'a-*bis*so'. During the ensuing three duple-metre duets (Allegro in F major, Presto in D minor and Presto in C major), patterned figuration is featured in the bass, which, however, pauses seven times in order to imitate the vocal motive in the D minor duet and introduces, punctuates and terminates the C major duet with the vocal motto. In the closing 3/2 Largo, 'Non conosce piacer cor che non ama' ('Pleasure is unknown to a heart not in love'), the voices intertwine seven times in chains of suspensions that feature descending dotted semibreves for 'cor che non ama'; during these passages the bass plays sequences employing the opening vocal motive, five stepwise-rising crotchets.[54] In all of Bononcini's Op. 8

---

al core and *Il nume d'Amore*. Riccati was presumably working from a manuscript copy of Bononcini's duets, because his numbers for them do not correspond to those in the print.

[51] Ibid., p. 183.

[52] Ibid., pp. 179 and 184. The addressee of the letters, Giovenale Sacchi, questioned the validity of the appellation 'gusto antico'. Thus Riccati's second letter (pp. 184–200) is not concerned with Bononcini's duets, but instead with the virtues of 'la musica moderna' and the defects of 'lo stile dei duetti del Clari [1677–1754], dello Steffani [1654–1728] e degli altri antichi' (p. 198).

[53] Ibid., p. 182.

[54] Giovanni Bononcini wrote two more duet cantatas: *Luci barbare, spietate* and *Pietoso nume arcier*, published in his *Cantate e duetti* (London, 1721), pp. 48–54 and 95–9. Another two, *Quando voi, amiche stelle* and *O penosa lontananza*, are attributed to him in I-Nc, Cantate 38, ff. 185v–198v, and GB-Lcm, MS 81, nos. 8–9. *Quando voi* is apparently by Bononcini, while *O penosa* is by Scarlatti, to whom it is attributed in four eighteenth-

duets youthful fire is combined with academic texture. In other words, their well-wrought counterpoint may not manifest an 'agreable and easie style', but it does at least provide plentiful illustrations of 'fine inventions in his *basses*'. Confirmation that Bononcini (and presumably also his teacher Colonna) greatly valued these vocal duets is their dedication to emperor Leopold I.

The second stage of Bononcini's career – when he wrote all of his most popular solo cantatas – began before the end of 1691 in Rome, where he composed at least 20 arias for the premiere on 12 January 1692 of a pasticcio revival, *Eraclea, o vero Il ratto delle Sabine*. In 1692–96, he composed six serenatas, set to libretti by Silvio Stampiglia, for the August name days of Lorenza, wife of Filippo Colonna and sister of the Spanish ambassador, Luis Francisco de La Cerda y Aragón, duke of Medinaceli. During the 1690s Bononcini undoubtedly wrote most of his cantatas for his patrons, the Colonna and de la Cerda families.[55] He undoubtedly went to Naples to oversee the premiere, on 27 December 1696, of his most successful opera, *Il trionfo di Camilla, regina de Volsci*, dedicated to the wife of Luis Francisco de La Cerda y Aragón, who had just become the Spanish viceroy, a post he held until 1702. Bononcini presumably returned to Rome before the premiere, on 4 February 1697, of *La clemenza d'Augusto*, for which he composed the final act. During the 1690s his last opera for Rome was the 'renewal' of his Neapolitan opera for its production on 12 January 1698 as *La rinovata Camilla, regina de Volsci*.[56]

The nine cantatas for soprano and basso continuo to be examined below are *Ch'io ti manchi di fede, idolo mio*? in E flat ♦31 sources, *Vado ben spesso* in C ♦25, *Impara a non dar fede* in B flat ♦23, *Bei crini d'oro* in B flat ♦20, *Cieco Nume, tiranno spietato* in F sharp minor ♦20, *Lumi, vezzosi lumi* in C minor ♦9, *Luci, siete pur quelle* in A minor ♦18, *Peno e l'alma fedele* in A ♦17 and *Amo, peno, gioisco* in B

---

century sources, listed in Hanley, 'Alessandro Scarlatti's Cantate da camera', p. 360, note 497. The collection of solo cantatas in US-NHub, Misc Ms 273, *Cantate diverse di canto del s[igno]r Gio[vanni] Bononcini*, ends with four duets on ff. 63–109v. As noted by Reinhard Strohm, 'Scarlattiana at Yale', in Nino Pirrotta and Agostino Ziino (eds), *Händel e gli Scarlatti a Roma. Atti del convegno internazionale di studi (Roma, 12–14 giugno 1985)* (Florence, 1987), pp. 113–52, at pp. 141–2 and 149, the duets are written by a second scribe and are not included in the attribution given on the title page. Since one of them, *E ti par poco che t'ho dato il cor*, is attributed to Severo de Luca in D–MÜs, Hs 862, no. 7, de Luca might be the composer of all four.

[55] The only two cantatas known to have been written for someone else are listed in Appendix 6.1, A-2, '57 Italian', I-Nc, 33 4 30 (Cantate 38): 'composta per l'em[inentissimo] sig[no]r cardinal Ottoboni, 1696'. Cardinals Pietro Ottoboni and Benedetto Panfili (or Pamphilj) commissioned many cantatas. In 1703–06, 24 cantatas by Bononcini were copied for Panfili (see Marx, 'Die "Giustificazioni della casa Pamphilj" als musikgeschichtliche Quelle', nos. 99, 100, 110, 114, 116 and 149). It is not known, however, whether Panfili commissioned any Bononcini cantatas during the 1690s.

[56] For a biography and list of works, see Stanley Sadie and John Tyrrell (eds), *The New Grove Dictionary*, 2nd edn, vol. 3, pp. 872–7.

flat ♦16. Each has been published only once: eight in the Garland facsimile of 1985, and one – *Impara a non dar fede* – in J.-B.-C. Ballard, *Meslanges de musique latine, françoise et italienne* (1725), pp. 46–54.[57] In *Il teatro alla moda* [Venice, 1720] Benedetto Marcello informed 'cantatrici' that *Impara a non dar fede* was 'la solita cantata' sung during an audition for the impresario and composer of an opera.

The nine chosen cantatas correspond stylistically to the 24 printed in the Garland volume. Two-thirds of them are in major rather than minor keys, begin with a recitative rather than an aria, and contain two rather than three arias. Seventeen arias are in da capo form, and four in binary form. Some have second strophes, which are eliminated in many copies.[58] Fifteen are in 4/4, three in 3/4, two in 3/8, and one in a mixture of 4/4 ('A' section) and 3/8 ('B' section). The section lengths of da capo arias average ten bars in 4/4, 30 bars in 3/4 and 45 bars in 3/8. Five feature a key signature of one or two flats (two or three in modern notation), while four have a void key signature or two sharps (three in modern notation). Keys on both the major (A and E flat) and minor (F sharp and C) boundaries are represented. Unless a source transposes a cantata – usually by a fifth – for a different vocal register, it maintains what is presumably the original key. The outstanding exception is *Vado ben spesso*, which survives in six keys: D, C and A for soprano clef, and G, F and E flat for alto clef.

All nine works are found in Italian, French and English MSS. Nearly all of the comments made by Gasparini, Raguenet, Le Cerf, Haym and Galliard (cited above in the original language and below in English) refer to Bononcini's cantatas *in toto*. The best example is Gasparini's praise for their '*bizzarria*, beauty, harmony, artful study and fanciful invention, because of which they justly receive the applause of the whole world in admiration of his most delightful talent'.[59] Only Le Cerf exemplified his remarks by reference to specific works. When he discussed four cantatas, he focused on their vocal melody, harmony and instrumental bass.

---

[57] François Lesure, ed., *Recueils imprimés, XVIIIe siècle*, International Inventory of Musical Sources (RISM), B II (Munich–Duisburg, 1964), p. 233. The first section of each aria is shown in Figures 6.1 and 6.2. A CD of *Impara* that features exquisite dialogues between the voice and continuo is performed by Sally Sanford, soprano, Brent Wissick, cello, and Andrew Lawrence-King, harp, on Centaur CRC 2630 (recorded in 2001 and pressed in 2003). A CD of *Cieco Nume*, another of the chosen nine cantatas, features superb *rubati* performed by Cristina Miatello, soprano, Andrea Fossà, violoncello, and Guido Morini, clavicembalo, on Tactus TC 672701 (recorded in 1989 and pressed in 1999); reissued on Brilliant Classics 93349.

[58] The second arias have second strophes in four of the nine chosen cantatas: *Bei crini d'oro*, *Ch'io ti manchi di fede*, *Lumi, vezzosi lumi* and *Impara a non dar fede*. Cantatas 1–3 appear in the Garland edition: no second strophe is given for the first, but second strophes are written after (rather than under) the first strophes for the second and third. Two or more strophes were quite common in the seventeenth century but quite rare in the eighteenth.

[59] Gasparini, *The Practical Harmonist at the Harpsichord*, trans. Frank S. Stillings (New Haven, CT [1963]), p. 94.

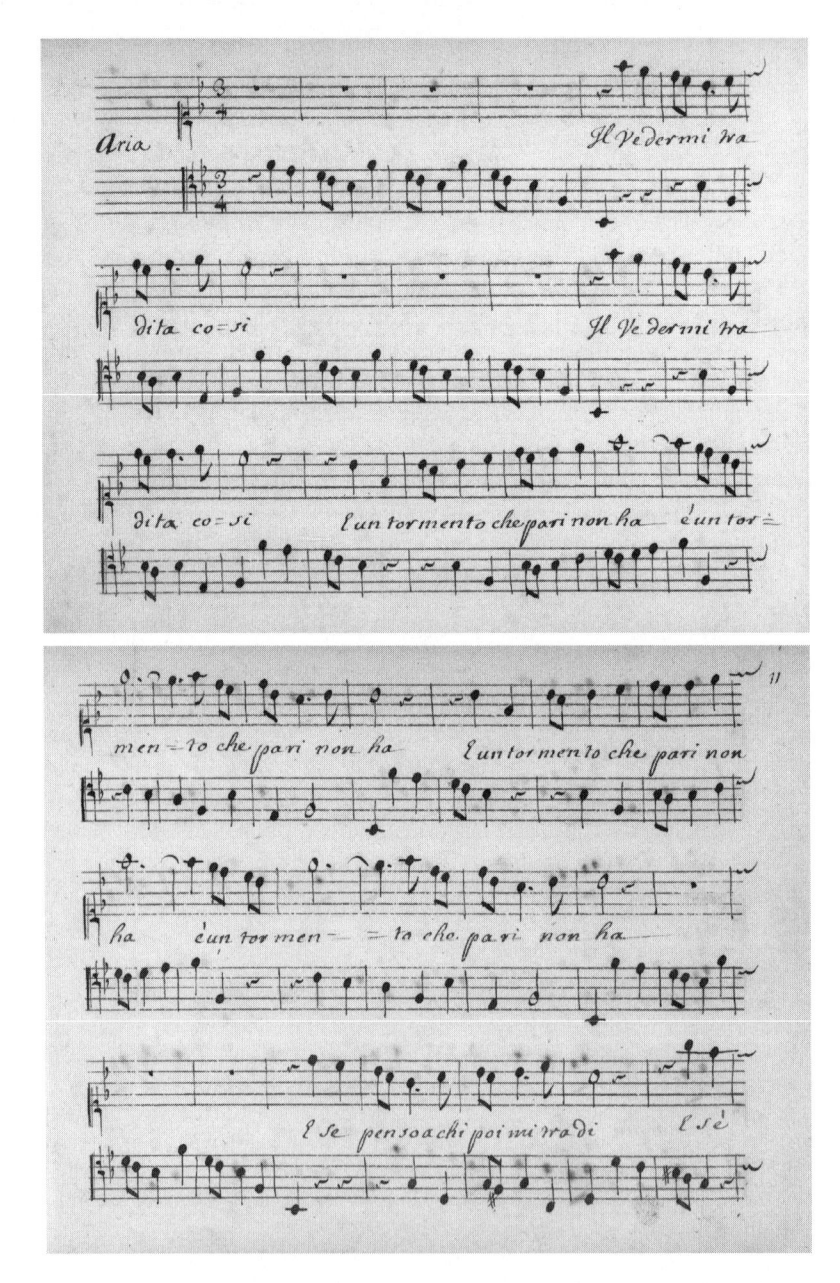

Figure 6.1 Giovanni Bononcini, the 'A' section of 'Il vedermi tradita così', first aria of the cantata *Impara a non dar fede*, US-CAh, Ms Mus 63, ff. 10v–11r (by permission of the Houghton Library, Harvard University, Cambridge, MA).

Figure 6.2 Giovanni Bononcini, the 'A' section of 'Benché speranza, sia mensogniera', second aria of the cantata *Impara a non dar fede*, US-CAh, Ms Mus 63, ff. 14r–14v (by permission of the Houghton Library, Harvard University, Cambridge, MA).

These aspects will serve also as the focal topics for the ensuing survey of melodic meaning within five arias, harmonic spice within four recitatives and inventive adornments within a dozen bass lines.[60]

Le Cerf's assertion that the best Italian airs have a 'pleasing melody' is presumably based on his knowledge of mid-Baroque tunes, such as the stepwise, four-bar phrases of Luigi Rossi (1598–1653).[61] If so, it is little wonder that Bononcini's arias 'nearly always' seemed to have 'an acerbic and broken-up melody', which made him 'cruelly suffer'. This is particularly true of the initial arias in Bononcini's cantatas, and the best example is found in Bononcini's most frequently copied cantata, *Ch'io ti manchi di fede, idolo mio?*, entitled *Bella donna costante*. The 'A' section of the first aria, 'Se mai tento col solo pensiero, di tradirvi pupille adorate' ('If I am ever tempted by a single thought to betray you, adored eyes'), begins with a continuo motto consisting of a four-note followed by a five-note motive (e♭ d | e♭ – b♭ – | – e♭ d c | b♭ – B♭ –); the pair are repeated sequentially twice at lower pitches before they cadence two octaves lower.[62] The four-note motive begins all three vocal phrases in the 'A' section, and the submissiveness of the 'bella donna costante' is illustrated by the stepwise fall in each vocal phrase. Underneath, the continuo reiterates its motives in dialogue with the voice, somewhat like a *basso ostinato*, and conceivably represents the beloved's reciprocated thoughts for the 'bella donna'. The sentence begun in the 'A' section is completed in the 'B' section: 'faccia splendere il fato più fiero, tutte contro di me le stelle irate' ('fierce Fate will order irate Destiny to oppose me unreservedly'). Here, the metre changes from 4/4 to 3/8, the tempo from *Adagio* to *Presto assai*,[63] the key from E flat major to C minor, the vocal line from syllabic to melismatic, and the continuo figuration from motivic to patterned. This total change of nature would undoubtedly have enraged Le Cerf, whose anger would have climaxed when the vocal line dwelled twice on 'ir*a*to'. The first '*ra*' is set by nine bars of sustained notes, then by a nine-bar roulade of 50 semiquavers, while the second contents itself with a nine-bar roulade of 50 notes. Since Le

---

[60] 'Mi basterà l'amarvi' and 'No, che non è bastante', the second arias in *Amo, peno, gioisco* and *Luci, siete pur quelle*, respectively, will not be mentioned. Their opening 9–17 bars are printed in Fader, 'Philippe II d'Orléans', pp. 244–5. Fader illustrates how two Italians who served the duke of Orléans – the violinist Antonio Guido and the cellist Jean-Baptiste Stuck – followed Bononcini's model 'quite closely' in their compositions.

[61] Fourteen references to Rossi are listed in Le Cerf, *Comparaison* [...] *françoise: Index*, compiled and annotated by Carl B. Schmidt (Geneva, 1993), p. 56. Rossi's *Io lo vedo*, in which each text line is set with four bars of music, is printed in Archibald T. Davison and Willi Apel, *Historical Anthology of Music*, II: *Baroque, Rococo and Pre-Classical Music* (Cambridge, MA, 1950), pp. 40–41, no. 203, and in Richard Jakoby, *The Cantata*, trans. Robert Kolben, Anthology of Music, 32 (Cologne, 1968), pp. 38–9, no. 4.

[62] Garland edition, pp. 16–18 and 263.

[63] The 3/8 section is marked *Presto assai* in GB-Lbl, Add 14,184, f. 17, *Presto* in I-REm, 31 Mus Prof, p. 128, and *Prestissimo* in A-Wgm, Q 4563, f. 7.

Cerf's 'Eclaircissement' objects to two thirty-note roulades (on '*scoc*ca' and 'lonta*nan*za') as well as to one of fifty notes (on co*stan*za), the repeated roulade on '*ira*to' would undoubtedly have doubly distressed him.

None of the other arias in the chosen group of nine cantatas interrupts the flow with a total change of stylistic components in its 'B' section. Indeed, the 'A' and 'B' sections usually employ the same motives. One example is 'Bei crini, bei crini d'oro, per voi mi moro, chiego pietà' ('Fair hair, fair golden hair, for you I die, I call for pity').[64] This A text begins the cantata, without any introduction from the continuo. All four text segments are set syllabically, with rests on either side – a style that conveys a broken-up, arioso-like sense of sorrow. During each section ('A' and 'B'), the continuo 'walks' during the opening bars, then intensifies – by doubling it a sixth lower – the five-note motive treated sequentially in two of the text segments.

An aria opening a cantata in which the vocal and continuo lines have nothing in common is 'Cieco Nume, tiranno spietato, chi ti posa il bel nome d'Amore' ('Blind God, ruthless tyrant, who assumes the fair name of Love').[65] Its 'B' section completes the sentence: 'Tu sei l'empio flagello del Fato, crudo mostro d'atroce rigore' ('You are the pitiless scourge of Fate, cruel monster of atrocious severity'). A stepwise descent of a fifth sets each pair of words in line 1. A repeated-note motive is stated three times in order to stress line 2. Another repeated-note motive is stated twice for line 3, which begins the 'B' section. The climax is reached when the repetition of line 4 begins with a chromatic ascent on '*cru*do' and ends with a melisma on 'ri*go*re'. In the totally unrelated continuo motto, a single bar (with a rest on beat 4) is repeated twice in sequence before cadencing an octave lower in bar 4. It serves as a *basso ostinato* for the entire aria, and clearly represents the 'cruel monster of atrocious severity', since it clashes dissonantly with the voice, for example, on both syllables of 'Nume' (bar 4) and the final two of 'spietato' (bar 6). It thus provides fine illustrations of the harmonic 'spice' that dismayed Le Cerf and of the ground bass (*basses contraintes ou obligées*) that he declared to be absent from Bononcini's works. This aria is followed by fifteen bars of recitative that merge (without an intervening ritornello) into a second *da capo* of its 'A' section. Ordinarily, such a merger would lead to a new arioso rather than to a previously heard aria. This extraordinary return confirms that great expressive power resides in the 'A' section of 'Cieco Nume'.

A different method of conveying expressiveness is illustrated by the arias in *Peno e l'alma fedele*.[66] During the first aria, 'Siete barbare, siete pur belle, care luci ch'ogn'or m'affliggete' ('You are barbarous, yet are beautiful, dear eyes that continuously afflict me'), Le Cerf would undoubtedly have been 'afflicted' by the pair of roulades on 'affligg*e*te' at the end of the 'A' section and the similar pair on 'com*e*te' at the end of B. He would have been equally distressed by the threefold or fourfold repetition of a four-note vocal motive, with overlapping imitations in the

---

[64] Garland edition, pp. 126–7 and 268.
[65] Ibid., pp. 11–12 and 263.
[66] Ibid., pp. 48–53 and 265.

continuo, during each of the four roulades. He would undoubtedly have preferred the syllabic tune of the second aria, 'Se al morir fosse concesso' (– c♯ d | e – – | f♯ d c♯| B E –),[67] but would perhaps not have noticed that this is basically the melody for 'Siete barbare, siete pur belle' (c♯ d | e – f♯ e | d – c♯ d | B – E –). Perhaps Le Cerf would have been most strongly attracted to the closing minuet, 'Mia speranza lusinghiera', which features hemiola and an almost exclusive employment of stepwise motion (A B – | c♯ – d |¹ e E – | F♯ ̄ G♯ :||² c♯ B – | A – –), which the continuo doubles a tenth below.

The aria that may well have pleased Le Cerf the most is 'Vado ben spesso cangiando loco, ma non so mai cangiar desio' ('I very often wander, changing location, but I never change the object of my desire').[68] Its four-bar motto is the basis for the entire aria, and its phrases are all two, four or six bars in length. An 'obstinate' rhythmic pattern, crotchet to dotted-quaver and semiquaver, is sung and/or played on almost every strong–weak succession of beats. It clearly represents a frolicsome wanderer, who climaxes with a sustained high note – on f'', then e'' – near the end of each section. Charles Burney found this cantata in a manuscript that he purchased at Rome in 1770. The painter and poet Salvator Rosa (1615–73) might have been the original owner, but 'Vado ben spesso' is among the later additions. Burney printed bar 9 to the end of the 'A' section, noted that it 'begins with such a spirited air as the last century seldom produced', and incorrectly attributed the text and music of the entire cantata to Rosa.[69]

Gasparini listed harmony as a praiseworthy feature of Bononcini's cantatas. Le Cerf disagreed, because for him the substance of Bononcini's works consisted

---

[67] The melodic outline and accompaniment pattern of 'Se al morir fosse concesso' reappeared with the text 'Sion now her head shall raise' in revised versions of Handel's *Esther* (1757) and *Judas Maccabaeus* (1757 or 1758). According to a comment in the copy of *Peno e l'alma fedele* at GB-Cfm, Mu Ms 52, ff. 43–45v, this borrowing was already noted by the bass James Bartleman (1769–1821), who was a celebrated collector of music. Handel's use of 'an alto song by Bononcini' is further discussed in Winton Dean, *Handel's Dramatic Oratorios and Masques* (London, 1959), pp. 213 and 468–9.

[68] Garland edition, pp. 74–6 and 266.

[69] Burney, *A General History of Music, from the Earliest Ages to the Present Period* (1789), 2 vols, ed. Frank Mercer (London: Foulis, 1935; facsimile repr. New York, 1957), vol. 2, pp. 625–6. He annotated the 'Libro, Musica di Salvator Rosa' that he purchased. It is now at F-Pn, Rés Vmc ms 78, and 'Vado' is on ff. 59–63v. Burney's tempo for aria 1, 'spirited', agrees with *Vivace*, the tempo in D-MÜs, Hs 858, ff. 103–109v, a Roman MS copied c.1700, in which the piece is attributed to 'Giovanni Bononcini'. Burney's excerpt from the aria was reprinted with the tempo *Maestoso* at the close of an anonymous article: 'Salvator Rosa as a Musician', *The Harmonicon*, 2 (1824): 62–4 and 83–7, at 86. Burney believed that he was also publishing parts of 'the other two airs in the same cantata, […] well accented and pleasing'; but the 'Libro, Musica di Salvator Rosa', contains only one bar from the third air of the cantata, so the third air given in Burney, vol. 2, p. 627, is the next piece in F-Pn, Vmc ms 78, which is an anonymous aria. A detailed discussion of Vmc ms 78 occurs in Frank Walker, 'Salvator Rosa and Music', *Monthly Musical Record*, 79 (1949): 199–205.

of 'spice and sauce'. Raguenet contradicted Le Cerf: 'there is no other Italian composer whose works have so few piquant and recondite passages. [...] All French composers name Bononcini as a model of grace, and he is the only one whom they cite in this respect'. In his 'Eclaircissement sur Buononcini', Le Cerf replied that professional singers 'often seem stunned by the many notes in unexpected keys and modes and by dissonances. [...] Can such a rhapsody of every kind of harshness, peculiarity and affectation be called pleasing and gracious music? Gracious and pleasing for people who are drunk or insane'. Among those who were pleased by 'artful harshness' in recitatives was Haym, who named Scarlatti as the greatest master of such writing. Bononcini utilized it less often, yet he frequently illustrated textual anguish by 'many notes in unexpected keys and modes and by dissonances'.

There are nineteen recitatives in the nine cantatas being discussed. The average length of the ten shortest (4–11 bars) is eight bars and of the nine longest (12–21 bars) is 16 bars. Ten begin with a phrase of 4–5 bars, nine with one of 6–11 bars.[70] Seven consist of a single phrase, while eight contain two phrases and four have three or four. The cadences of successive phrases nearly always occur in closely related keys. With regard to the ensuing aria, eight recitatives end with a full cadence in its key, four with a half cadence in its key,[71] three in the relative major or minor key,[72] and three in the subdominant.[73] Since these are customary rather than unexpected traits, the recitatives are structurally 'agreable and easie'.

Bononcini employs 'artful harshness' in passages 'where he makes use of all sorts of dissonance to express the force of the words, and afterwards resolves 'em so well that indeed the most beautiful concords are hardly so sweet and harmonious as his discords'. For example, 'Peno, e l'alma fedele, costante nel penar, soffre gl'affanni' ('I grieve, and my faithful soul, constant in its grief, suffers torments') begins with a major ninth dissonance and does not reach a root position consonance until 'pe*nar*' in bar 4.[74] In 'Amo, peno, gioisco, soffro, spero, pavento, dalla gioia e tormento. Agitato, languisco [...]' ('I love, I grieve, I rejoice, I suffer, I hope, I fear, because of joy and torment. Agitated, I languish [...]'), dissonances of a seventh result from leaps of a seventh on 'a*mo*, *pe*no' and 'pa*vento*' and scalewise

---

[70] Each phrase ends with a V–I cadence, in which the continuo moves 5–1. Imperfect cadences have been tallied only when they end a recitative (see next note).

[71] See the Garland edition, pp. 13, 33 and 121, for three customary imperfect cadences, and p. 80 for a pseudo imperfect cadence. The only recitative that returns to an earlier passage is the opening one in *Impara a non dar fede*. A half-close precedes its repeat of the first phrase at the end.

[72] Ibid., pp. 34–5, 50–51 and 122.

[73] Ibid., pp. 22, 53–4 and 128. The cadence on p. 48 has not been tallied, because the recitative ends in C sharp minor, the relative minor of E major, which is the dominant of the ensuing aria in A major.

[74] Ibid., pp. 47 and 265.

motion on 'tor*mento*'.⁷⁵ This leads to a demisemiquaver melisma that descends a minor ninth on 'agi*ta*to' and a syncopated beginning for the slow crotchets on 'languisco'.

Modulatory as well as dissonant 'spice' enhances the second recitative in *Ch'io ti manchi*: 'Prima d'essert'infida, di cento spade e cento incontrerò la tirannia crudele; ed io, con qual contento direi: "moro per te, moro fedele!"' ('Before being unfaithful to you, I will face the cruel tyranny of one, even two hundred swords; then I [Lidia], with some contentedness, will say: "I die for you, I die faithful!"').⁷⁶ In the first two bars, a ninth on '*t'infida di*' leads immediately to a seventh on '*cento spa*de'. In bar 3, the voice reaches its highest note – g'' – on 'ti*ran*nia'. After a cadence in E flat major in bar 4, the bass moves chromatically up for the new sentence, expressing 'qual contento' with a first-inversion C-major chord, which resolves to F minor on 'moro per *te*' before moving chromatically to an A natural on '*mo*ro fedele' and cadencing in C minor. Five bars later, Lidia vows to tell the world that she will die rather than be unfaithful, and Bononcini cadences, as he does in many such distraught situations, in B flat minor.

The most strident text expression in these nine cantatas occurs in the final recitative for Lidia in *Ch'io ti manchi di fede*.⁷⁷ She begins with a metaphoric statement regarding her strength: 'Balze immote al soffrir d'empi aquiloni, scogli che frangon sempre gl'assalti d'onda impetuosa e ria, deboli paragoni sono alle tempre della fede mia' ('Immobile crags withstanding vicious north winds, rocks breaking the assault of impetuous waves, are weak comparisons to the fibres of my faith'). After the continuo plays an A flat major chord, the voice leaps from $e♭''$ to $e♭'$, then to repeated dissonant $d♭''$ for 'balze immote', then to $b♭'$, $d♭''$ and g' for 'al soffrir d'empi', thus maintaining its dissonant character until it finally reaches $a♭'$ on '*a*quiloni'. In the next two phrases Lidia manifests her strength via melodic lines that begin very high (on f'' and g''), descend an octave or a major seventh, and cadence in C minor. She then addresses her lover: 'Se provaste un istante l'amorose tempeste e i miei tormenti, tutte vi frangereste, o voi che resistete all'onda, ai venti' ('If for an instant you experienced the amorous storms and my torments, you would break them all, you who resist the waves and the winds'). This segment begins and remains in B flat minor for four bars, which include a descent by whole steps from g'' to $d♭''$ on 'miei tormenti'. The power of the final 'onda' is portrayed by a seventeen-note melisma that ascends to $a♭''$, the highest note found in the cantata.⁷⁸

In his penultimate chapter, 'Diminution or Adornment of the Bass', Gasparini, a keyboardist who had worked alongside Bononcini at Rome during the 1690s,

---

⁷⁵ Ibid., pp. 53 and 265.
⁷⁶ Ibid, pp. 18–19 and 263.
⁷⁷ Ibid., pp. 21–2 and 263.
⁷⁸ The only higher pitch found in the Garland volume is $b♭''$. In *Presso allo stuol pomposo*, it occurs once near the end of the 'B' section of aria 1, in the midst of a melisma on 'stende' (p. 44), and twice near the end of aria 2, for the phrase 'mi fa più bella' (p. 46).

recommends 'how to play with grace and without confusion'. After exemplifying diminutions with the arpeggios notated in the ritornello that opens the first cantata in his own *Cantate da camera a voce sola*, Op.1 (Rome: Mascardi, 1695),[79] Gasparini writes: 'many such motifs, of various kinds, may be observed in the cantatas of many excellent composers – but especially in those cantatas by Giovanni Bononcini, most worthy virtuoso of His Imperial Majesty.'[80] The violoncellist Haym, who had also played alongside Bononcini in Rome, termed him 'indisputably the first' among violoncellists as well as 'the greatest master in the world' for writing 'instrumental musick that accompanies the voice'.[81] Galliard had presumably performed many of Bononcini's cantatas by 1716, when he praised 'those fine inventions in his *basses* (to which he was led by an instrument upon which he excells)'. In the nine cantatas under discussion, 18 of the 21 arias begin with a motto played by the continuo for at least two bars before the voice enters.

'Walking' bass lines and continuo arpeggiations are effective ways of engendering rhythmic drive. In the nine chosen cantatas a 'walking' continuo line is found throughout three sombre opening arias: 'Quante volte io vi mirai' in *Luci, siete pur quelle*, 'Questo è troppo a tanta fede' in *Lumi, vezzosi lumi*, and 'Bei crini d'oro'.[82] Arpeggiated bass lines are utilized in only two arias. One has already been discussed: the 'B' section of 'Se mai tento col solo pensiero' (the initial aria

---

[79] Facsimile reprint in Archivum Musicum, *La cantata barocca*, no. 19 (Florence, 1984), p. 1.

[80] Gasparini, *The Practical Harmonist*, p. 94.

[81] As shown in Appendix 6.1, sections A-1, B-1 and C-1, only seven of Bononcini's 215 cantatas conjecturally written before 1712 are accompanied by an instrument additional to the continuo, which is the most significant component of the 'instrumental musick that accompanies the voice' during the Baroque period. Yet 'instrumental musick' undoubtedly refers to treble as well as continuo parts. In the Garland volume, the final piece is a Roman serenata, *La nemica d'Amore fatta amante* (1693). Its 17 set pieces include two duos and seven solos with continuo alone, but all seven solos are followed by a TrTrAB string ritornello; the other eight solos include five with TrTrAB and one each with TrTrB ('concertino solo'), TrB ('violino solo') and TB ('violoncello') accompaniments. In *Il trionfo di Camilla* (Naples, 1696), the 57 set pieces include 35 with continuo alone, but 25 of them are followed by a TrTrAB string ritornello; the remaining 22 have TrTrAB (13), TrAB (3) or TrB (6) accompaniments. The only wind instrument is 'cornetto solo', utilized with strings for the final arias in *Camilla*, Acts II and III: Turno's 'Tiranna gelosia' and Prenesto's 'Tutte armate di flagelli'. The score in GB-ABu – one of 14 extant for the Naples 1696 production – is reproduced in facsimile in *Italian Opera: 1640–1770* (New York, 1978). Haym arranged *Camilla* for its London production of 1706, which had 54 arias; he presumably also abbreviated it for a private performance (Queen Anne's birthday at court in 1707?), which had 36 arias. The arias and instrumentations in the London sources are nearly all by Bononcini. On the instrumentation of *Camilla*, see Lindgren, 'I trionfi di Camilla,' p. 96, and idem, Introduction to Giovanni Bononcini, *Camilla: Royal College of Music, MS 779*, Music for London Entertainment, 1660–1800, ser. E, vol. 1 (London, 1990), pp. xiv–xix.

[82] Garland edition, pp. 33–4, 121–2, 126, 264 and 268.

in *Ch'io ti manchi di fede*), which has patterned semiquaver figuration (marked *Presto assai*) for 3/8 chord changes. The second is 'Infante volante', the closing aria in *Cieco nume*, which has patterned semiquaver figuration (marked *Presto assai*) for the chord changes at minim intervals throughout both of its sections.[83]

Repeated notes are a third way to produce rhythmic drive, and four arias exemplify their use. In 'Se al morir fosse concesso', the second aria in *Peno e l'alma fedele*, the motto in quavers consists of a repeated dominant pitch (E, B or F♯) placed between stepwise crotchets.[84] In the mottos for 'Per non offendere', the initial aria in *Amo, peno, gioisco*, 'A quest'alma inamorata', the second aria in *Ch'io ti manchi di fede*, and 'L'empio arciero accesso dardo', the final aria in *Bei crini d'oro*, three repeated-note quavers replace a dotted crotchet.[85] The repeated-note group is played two to four times within the motto, which becomes a *basso ostinato* in the last two arias: it is heard six times in each strophe of 'A quest'alma inamorata' and ten times in 'L'empio arciero'. In both sections of 'Per non offendere', the voice begins most of its phrases with the motto; the continuo intensifies many of these mottoes by doubling them a third or sixth lower, and it further intensifies the first two in each section by playing them in double stops.

Stepwise adornment is a fourth way to enliven the rhythm, and it is employed in the final arias of three cantatas. In 'No, ch'in amor non è' (from *Ch'io ti manchi di fede*) and 'Benché speranza sia mensogniera' (from *Impara a non dar fede*), crotchets become triplet quavers (i.e., e♭ | d and d | d become e♭ f e♭ | d c d and d c b♭ | d c b♭).[86] In both arias, the opening motto already utilizes the adorned version, which both parts employ and develop throughout both sections of the aria. 'Sì che fedele' (from *Lumi, vezzosi lumi*) is undoubtedly marked *Andante* (significantly slower than the *Presto* for 'No, ch'in amor non è') because the crotchets in its bass line become triplet semiquavers, so that six notes supplant a crotchet.[87] The continuo plays this diminution in all but a few bars, while the voice employs it only for the two 13-note melismas on 'lascierò' at the end of the 'B' section.

A *basso ostinato* is the fifth and by far the most effective way to propel the rhythm. Bononcini employed it in eight of the arias under discussion. In each one, the length and completeness of single statements varies. An excellent example is the initial aria of *Impara a non dar fede*: 'Il vedermi tradita così è un tormento che pari non ha' ('Seeing myself thus betrayed [by Tirsi] is a torment without equal').[88] Its motto begins with three stepwise or nearly stepwise descents (f e♭ | dc B♭ f | dc B♭ f | dc B♭ F | BB♭) and ends with a cadence in bar 4. Throughout the

---

[83] Ibid., pp. 14–18 and 263.

[84] Ibid., pp. 51–2 and 265. Handel borrowed this accompaniment motto (see earlier, note 67).

[85] Ibid., pp. 19–21, 54–5, 128–9, 263, 265 and 268.

[86] Ibid., pp. 21–2 and 264 for 'No, ch'in amor non è', and Figure 6.2 (p. 153) for 'Benché speranza sia mensogniera'.

[87] Ibid., pp. 122–5 and 268.

[88] Shown in Figure 6.1 (p. 152).

aria, the motto – which must represent betrayal and torment – recurs 'obstinately' in overlapping imitation between the continuo and voice. Sometimes the motto is abbreviated to a two- or one-bar segment in the continuo. If each abbreviation is given a number, there are eleven *ostinati* in the bass during the 'A' section and ten during the 'B' section. Such constantly overlapping imitation and reiteration may well have 'tormented' Le Cerf, who would presumably have been equally disturbed by the sustained high notes on 'tor*men*to' and 'ha' at the end of the 'A' section and on 'pe*na*' and 'fa' at the end of B.

Seven more arias that utilize *ostinato* basses have already been discussed. Three more in which the two performers share the *ostinato* motive are 'Sei mai tento col solo pensiero' ('A' section only) and 'No, ch'in amor non è', the first and last arias in *Ch'io ti manchi di fede*, and 'Se al morir fosse concesso', the second aria in *Peno e l'alma fedele*. The four in which the singer does not perform the *ostinato* motive are the first aria of *Cieco Nume*; 'A quest'alma inamorata', the second aria in *Ch'io ti manchi di fede*; 'Si che fedele, pupille amate', the final aria in *Lumi, vezzosi lumi*; and 'L'empio arciero acceso dardo', the final aria in *Bei crini d'oro*.

Vado ben spesso deserves special consideration, because it survives in at least 25 complete copies – the second-highest number – and its opening aria has undoubtedly been the most popular piece derived from a Bononcini cantata.[89] As noted above, Burney and countless others have become attached to its frisky rhythm. In the ensuing 3/8 aria in A minor, 'Ne men ti lascierò quando mi moro' ('I will not abandon you, even when I die'), the 18-bar motto features three descending quaver scales, each with a range of a sixth. During the 'A' section the voice sings the scale three times, aptly ending each on either 'lascierò' or 'moro', and the continuo plays it four times. The voice begins the 'B' section, which is entirely in C major, with a bouncy new motive (g | c g c | d g d | e d c) that is repeated (not as a sequence!) in each of the first four phrases, with overlapping imitation in the continuo: 'Ché l'alma mia costante, sempre fedele amante, intorno a te verrà, e spesso ti dirà' ('Because my enduring soul, always a faithful lover, will come to surround you, and will often say'). The climax and cadence (f – – | – e d | e d – | c – –) are provided by the fifth phrase: 'Cara, t'adoro' ('Darling, I adore you'). The final aria, 'Ricordati, ben mio', has no introductory ritornello, and the bass is subservient throughout. This joyful cantata, which contains little that is inventive in its continuo line, is far from the contrapuntal laments that otherwise seem ubiquitous in Bononcini's cantatas.

The most exquisitely composed lament in our group of nine cantatas is *Ch'io ti manchi di fede, idolo mio?* Bononcini's contemporaries obviously prized such

---

[89] Garland edition, pp. 74–81 and 266. It was, needless to say, Burney's misattribution that made the aria 'Vado ben spesso' a famous piece. Liszt set this 'Canzonetta del Salvator Rosa' in his *Années de pèlerinage, deuxième année, Italie* (Mainz, 1858), no. 3. It is also the basis of the musical score (by Alessandro Cicognini) for a swashbuckling film of 1939–40, *Un'avventura di Salvator Rosa*, starring Gino Cervi and directed by Alessandro Blasetti.

gems, since this work survives in 31 sources – a significantly higher number than that for any of his other cantatas. The expressive features of its last two recitatives and all three of its arias – including an ostinato bass in each one of them – have been discussed above. They confirm what Le Cerf wrote near the beginning of his 'Eclaircissement': 'This Italian hero scatters a wealth of adornments over his music with such profusion that simplicity does not seem to be a virtue known to him'. Before Le Cerf provided his final examination of a work by Bononcini, he observed that it was 'branded with the name of the God of Cantatas'. By bestowing this title, he was undoubtedly taunting Raguenet and the numerous Frenchmen who would concur with this label. Indeed, Bononcini seems to have been the most popular composer of Italian cantatas in France around 1705, and the elegant volumes of Bononcini's cantatas copied in England before 1710 imply that he enjoyed similar popularity in London. He was also the favourite composer of the young emperor, Joseph I, who unfortunately died of smallpox in 1711, at the age of 32. Bononcini may well have remained the most highly favoured Italian composer of cantatas much longer if Fate had not intervened in his life, just as it does in the lives of the primary characters in his 'agreable and easie' cantatas, which feature 'fine inventions in his *basses* (to which he was led by an instrument upon which he excells)'.

Appendix 6.1: Text incipits and significant musical sources for Giovanni Bononcini's solo cantatas, listed alphabetically within four chronological sections

After each incipit, any known title, librettist and accompanying instruments (if they exceed basso continuo) are listed in sections A-1, B-1, C-1 and D-1. If a cantata is extant in two or more Baroque sources, the number of sources containing it is entered after the symbol ♦. As in the *New Grove Dictionary of Music*, 2nd edition (2001), an 'L' in section A-1 identifies the 24 solo works reproduced in facsimile in *Cantatas by Giovanni Bononcini, 1670–1747*, selected and introduced by Lowell Lindgren (New York, 1985). '*Ad*' (= Autori diversi) in section A-1 identifies the four works by Bononcini in a collection of twelve *Cantate a voce sola* [Lucca, Bartolomeo Gregori, c.1700]; facsimile repr. Florence, 1980. '*Cd*' in section D-1 identifies the 12 cantatas in Bononcini's *Cantate e duetti* (London, 1721; facsimile repr. Sala Bolognese, 2008). An inventory of significant seventeenth- and eighteenth-century musical sources, comprising three printed editions and 130 manuscripts, is given in sections A-2, B-2, C-2 and D-2. Each source entry begins with a RISM siglum. The number of cantatas in each musical source is placed after the symbol ♦. About 50 manuscripts (each containing one cantata or very few cantatas) are not inventoried, but their contents are included in the numbers placed after the text incipits. Phases 1 and 6 of Bononcini's career – 1670–91 and 1733–47 – are not listed below, because no extant solo cantata can be securely dated to either phase.

A-1: 149 works composed in 1692–98 (= phase 2, in Rome and Naples)

A voi che l'accendeste (F. M. Paglia);[90] *Ah, non havesse, no, permesso il fato* ♦18 L; *All'arco tuo fatale*; *Alla beltà d'un volto* (*Le vicende d'amore*) ♦6; *Alle sue pene intorno* (S/TrB); *Allor che il cieco nume* (F. M. Paglia) ♦4;[91] *Amai ed amo ancora*; *Amo e l'ardor ch'io sento* ♦12; *Amo e ridir no'l posso* ♦14 L ('1698' in I-MOe, Mus F 2024); *Amo ma poco io spero* ♦6; *Amo, peno, gioisco* ♦16 L; *Amo sì, ma non so dire* ♦4; *Amor, non ho più core*; *Amor, tiranno Amor, fanciullo traditor* ♦3; *Amore, e come mai d'un sguardo* (set by Rignatti?);[92] *Amore è quel tiranno* ♦4; *Anche i tronchi, anche le rupi* ♦9; *Arde il mio petto amante* ♦6 + Ad; *Aure che sussurranti* ♦2; *Aure, voi che mormorando*; *Aure, voi che sì liete*; *Bei crini d'oro* ♦20 L; *Celinda, anima mia* ♦6; *Ch'io canti mi dicesti*; *Ch'io ti manchi di fede, idolo mio?* (*Bella donna costante*) ♦31 L ('1701' in I-Gl, B 2 23); *Che tirannia di stelle* ♦13 L; *Chi non prova amor in petto* ♦4; *Chi non sa che sia tormento* ♦12 L; *Cieco Nume, tiranno spietato* ♦20 L;[93] *Clori, dunque mi lasci*; *Clori, mi sento al core* ♦8; *Clori, mio ben, mia vita* ♦8 L; *Clori, saper vorrei, qual sia maggiore in te*; *Col arco d'un ciglio* (A. Ottoboni) ♦5;[94] *Come siete importuni, amorosi pensieri*; *D'ogni puro candore* ♦4; *D'un mirto all'ombra* ♦ Ad (incomplete);[95] *Da che Tirsi mirai un occulto piacere* ♦2; *Dal dì ch'il ciel severo* ♦8 ('composta per l'em[inentissimo] sig[no]r cardinal [Pietro] Ottoboni, 1696' in I-Nc, Cantate 38); *Dal dì ch'io non vi veggio*; *Dal geminio splendor di due pupille*; *Dal giorno fortunato ch'io vidi il vostro lume* (F. M. Paglia)[96] ♦10; *Dall'incurvato ferro*; *Del suo fedel e taciturno ardore* ♦10; *Del Tebro antico in su la verde sponda* ♦3; *Del Tebro in su la riva*; *Della beltà* – see *Alla beltà*; *Di Venere dolente insanguinata prole*; *Ditemi, o care selve* ♦3; *Dopo lunga tempesta*; *Dove bambino rivo* (*Il pastore disperato*) ♦2;

---

[90] Paglia's text is in I-Rvat, Vat lat 10204, f. 81v. D-Dl, Mus. 1-I-2: 2, contains five settings of his text, one each by Giacomo Antonio Perti, Giovanni Bononcini, Giovanni [Lulier] del Violone, Antonio Mangiarotti and Alessandro Scarlatti.

[91] Francesco Maria Paglia's text is preserved in I-Rvat, Vat lat 10204, ff. 50–51. This source contains the texts for 72 'cantate per musica a voce sola di Fran[cesc]o Maria Paglia'.

[92] See earlier, note 31.

[93] Bononcini's *Cieco Nume* was copied for cardinal Pietro Ottoboni on 'fogli reali n. 2', according to a bill dated 18 June 1693; see Teresa Chirico, 'L'inedita serenata alla regina Maria Casimira di Polonia: Pietro Ottoboni committente di cantate e serenate (1689–1708)', in Nicolò Maccavino (ed.), *La serenata tra Seicento e Settecento*, pp. 397–449, at 407, note 33.

[94] Michael Talbot and Colin Timms, 'Music and the Poetry of Antonio Ottoboni (1646–1720)', in Nino Pirrotta and Agostino Ziino, *Händel e gli Scarlatti a Roma*, pp. 367–437, at p. 411, no. 65. The 264 texts inventoried in their study include 236 solo cantatas.

[95] See earlier, note 9..

[96] Paglia's text is preserved in I-Rvat, Vat lat 10204, f. 79.

Dove le pianto giro ♦11; *È bella Irene e vanta un indole modesta* ♦3; *È la rosa regina dei fiori*; *Ecco da me partita l'alma mia* ♦3; *Ferma l'ardita prora?*; *Filli, del tuo partire* ♦11 L; *Filli vezzosa, oh dèi* ♦3; *Fillide mia, se t'amo* ♦2; *Gelosia, so che t'affanna*; *Genio, che amar volea* ♦9; *Già fugavan le stelle (A b[ella] d[onna] crudele*, F. M. Paglia);[97] *Giacea di verde mirto all'ombra in giorno* ♦3; *Il mio cor fu sempre mio* (A. Ottoboni) ♦6;[98] *Impara a non dar fede* ♦22 ('1701' in I-Gl, B 2 23) + *Meslanges* 1725; *In due luci vezzosette* ♦13; *In siepe odorosa* ♦6; *In una valle amena* ♦3; *Incominciate a piangere*; *Infelice quel cor che vi crede* ♦7; *Io che a Filli lontano*; *Io son lungi alla mia vita (Lontananza)* ♦7 ('1701' in I-Nc, Cantate 69); *Irene, idolo mio, Irene, addio*[99] ♦17 L; *Langue accesa d'amore* ♦5; *Lascia di tormentarmi, tiranna gelosia* ♦3; *Lidia, tu sai ch'io t'amo* (F. M. Paglia) ♦2;[100] *Lidio, schernito amante di Lucilla* ♦10; *Lontan dal tuo bel viso* (F. M. Paglia) ♦10;[101] *Lontananza crudel, se tu pretendi* ♦7 ('composta per l'em[inentissimo] sig[no]r cardinal [Pietro] Ottoboni, 1696' in I-Nc, Cantate 38); *Luci, siete pur quelle* ♦18 L; *Lumi, vezzosi lumi (Costanza non gradita)* ♦19 L; *Lunghi da te, mio bene*; *Lunghi dalla mia Filli* ♦7; *Mentre l'ascoso ardor*; *Nell'orror più profondo* (S/TrTrB, 'in Roma' in GB-Lam, 126) ♦4; *Nella stagion che di viole e rose (La primavera)* ♦2; *No, più non vi crede, no* ♦7; *Non ho pace nel mio core (Amor sfortunato)* ♦3; *Non sarei de'fior reina (La rosa regina dei fiori*, B. Panfili) ♦5;[102] *O d'affetto gentil, figlia crudele (Gelosia*, A. Ottoboni);[103] *O Fileno, Filen crudele, ingrato sì* ♦11; *O foriera del giorno (Nel partire per restituirsi alla S[ua] D[onna]*, A. Ottoboni) ♦4;[104] *O Irene, Iren* – see *O Fileno, Filen*; *O tu che sì fastosa*; *Ohimè*

---

[97] Paglia's text, in I-Rvat, Vat lat 10204, f. 27, is headed 'Musica di Sev[er]o de Luca'.

[98] Talbot and Timms, 'Antonio Ottoboni', p. 417, no. 112.

[99] In F-Pn, D 14440, pp. 71–85, *Filli, già che la sorte*, headed 'Cantata a voce sola del sig[no]r Gasparini', is followed by *Irene, idolo mio*, headed 'La risposta del sig[no]r Bononcini'. The text of the first is by Antonio Ottoboni (Talbot and Timms, p. 415, no. 99). Gasparini's work also survives in I-Rli, Fondo Caetani, 208 A 4, ff. 43–4; see Fabio Carboni, Teresa M. Gialdroni and Agostino Ziino, 'Cantate ed arie romane del tardo Seicento nel Fondo Caetani della Biblioteca Corsiniana: Repertorio, forme e strutture', *Studi musicali*, 18 (1989): 49–192, at 80, 82, 93–4 and 111, note 64.

[100] Paglia's text is preserved in I-Rvat, Vat lat 10204, f. 62.

[101] Ibid., ff. 76v–77v.

[102] Panfili's text is preserved in I-Rvat, Vat lat 10205: 'Cantate di S[ua] E[ccellenza] P[adro]ne', ff. 34–36. According to Hans Joachim Marx, 'Die Musik am Hofe Pietro Kardinal Ottobonis unter Arcangelo Corelli', *Analecta musicologica*, 5 (1968): 104–77, at 137 and 140, nos. 47c and 66a, *Non sarei de'fior* was copied for Ottoboni on 25 May 1693 and 7 March 1694. A different setting of *Non sarei de'fior* survives in I-Rsc, A Ms 3710, ff. 1–15; since it is anonymous in the manuscript, it should not have been attributed to Giovanni Bononcini in Annalisa Bini, *Il fondo Mario nella biblioteca musicale di Santa Cecilia di Roma: Catalogo dei manoscritti* (Rome, 1995), pp. 413–14, no. 827/4.

[103] Talbot and Timms, 'Antonio Ottoboni', p. 424, no. 166.

[104] Ibid., p. 425, no. 170.

chi mi risveglia ♦3; *Partenza che parti in pezzi il mio core* ♦2; *Parto, sì parto, mio bene*; *Pende dal sen di Fille* ♦3; *Peno e l'alma fedele* (*A Tirsi che pena e tace*, S. Stampiglia) ♦17 L;[105] *Per sollevar quest'alma* ♦6; *Per un colpo di sorte maligna* (*In morte d'un rosignuolo*); *Piango in van dall'idol mio* ♦10; *Più dell'Alpi gelato* ♦14 L; *Presso allo stuol pomposo* (*La violetta*) ♦9 L; *Pur vi riveggio ancora* ♦5 L; *Quando la finirai di tormentarmi*; *Quando m'innalza Amore*; *Quando mai, Cupido ingrato* (F. M. Paglia, S/TrTrB) ♦2;[106] *Quando mai, vermigli labri* ('1702' in I-Nc, Cantate 69) ♦9; *Quando, o bella, io ti viddi* ♦4; *Quando parli e quando ridi* ♦Ad; *Quanto peno e quanto piango* ♦2; *Quanto sarei felice* ♦4; *Scherza meco il destino* (F. M. Paglia) ♦5;[107] *Sconsigliato consiglio* ♦5; *Se dal indiche arene*; *Se di Tantalo si dice* ♦2; *Se per soverchio duolo* (*Non ardisce di scoprirsi amante*, P. A. Bernardoni) ♦4;[108] *Sorge l'alba e torna il dì* ♦16 L; *Sospirato ben mio, dolcezza del mio core*; *Sovra il famoso fiume*; *Sovra un bel poggio assisa* ♦14 L; *Stanca di più penar Clori la bella* ♦6 L; *Stanco del tuo gran duolo* ♦2; *Sulla sponda d'un rio afflitta e mesta* ♦5 + Ad; *Sulle ripe dell'Ebro* ♦3; *Sventurato Fileno siedeva un dì*; *Sventurato Mirtillo, e che farai?*; *Titolo di costante non merta quel amante* ♦4; *Tormento del mio seno* ♦9; *Tra catene haver il piede* ♦8; *Tra dubbiosi pensieri* ♦4;[109] *Tra i raggi d'un bel volto* ♦8;[110] *Tra l'amene delitie* (*Eurilla dolente in un giardino*) ♦6 L; *Tra mille fiamme ardenti* (*Il Nerone*) ♦2; *Un dì che nel mio core* ♦2; *Va, credi e spera, mio cor traditor* (S/TrTrB, 'in Roma' in GB-Lam, 126) ♦8; *Vado ben spesso cangiando loco* ♦25 L; *Vantar alma di gelo* ('1701' in I-Gl, B 2 23); *Vidi in cimento due vaghi Amori* ♦8 L; *Viver e non amar fora delitto* ♦2; *Voglio senza speranza* (S. Stampiglia)[111] ♦4; *Voi che tutto dolente* ♦11 L.

---

[105] 'Delle rime di Palemone Licurio [i.e., Silvio Stampiglia], Pastore Arcade, tomo V, che si divide in due libri, il primo di cantate ad una sol voce, il secondo di cantate a due voci, in Roma 1718', cantata 26, pp. 36–7. I am truly grateful to Teresa M. Gialdroni, who sent me a facsimile of this I-Fl manuscript in 2007.

[106] Paglia's text is preserved in I-Rvat, Vat lat 10204, f. 68.

[107] Ibid., f. 71.

[108] Pietro Antonio Bernardoni, *Rime varie, consagrate alla S. C. R. Maestà di Giuseppe I* (Vienna, Giovanni van Ghelen, 1705), pp. 178–9.

[109] Bononcini's *Tra dubbiosi pensieri* was copied for cardinal Pietro Ottoboni on 'fogli reali n. 2', according to a bill dated 18 June 1693; see Teresa Chirico, 'L'inedita serenata alla regina Maria Casimira di Polonia', in Nicolò Maccavino (ed.), *La serenata tra Seicento e Settecento*, p. 407, note 33.

[110] Five reliable sources ascribe *Tra i raggi* to 'Giovanni Bononcini'. Two others – GB-CDp, MS 2, ff. 9–16, and D-SHs, Mus B 1:2, pp. 179–85 – attribute it to 'Gasparini', and one – I-MC, 1 C 11, ff. 9–15v – is anonymous.

[111] 'Delle rime di Palemone Licurio', tomo V, cantata 7, pp. 11–12.

A-2: 80 significant musical sources for phase 2 cantatas

57 Italian

Ad ♦4;[112] B-Bc, F 15325 ♦5; D-Bsb, Landsberg 35 ('Cantate a voce sola in soprano, di Gio[vanni] Bononcini, II') ♦24; D-Dl, Mus. 1-I-2: 1–2 ♦4; D-LEm, III 5 5 ♦8;[113] D-Mbs, 695 ♦3; D-MÜs, Hs 865 ♦3; D-MÜs, Hs 3915 ♦6; D-MÜs, Hs 3977 ♦2; F-Pn, Rés Vmc ms 78 ♦1;[114] F-Pn, Vmc ms 88 ♦3; GB-Cfm, Mu Ms 45 ♦2; GB-Cfm, Mu Ms 231 ♦1 ('Franc° Mª Bononcini'!); GB-CDp, MS 2 (M C 1 2) ♦5; GB-Lam, 126 ♦7; GB-Lbl, Add. 14,184 ♦7; GB-Lbl, Add. 14,211 ♦9; GB-Lbl, Add. 14,228 ♦9; GB-Lbl, Add 31,518 ♦10; GB-Mp, Q544 Bk51 ♦1; GB-Och, 993 ♦2; I-Bc, DD 45 ♦1; I-Bc, DD 48 ♦3; I-Bc, DD 199 ♦1; I-Bc, X 132 ♦1;[115] I-Bsp, Lib B 3 ♦4; I-Bsp, P 69 36 ♦2; I-Fc, B 2376 ('Bononcini' is on the spine) ♦18; I-Gl, B 2 23 ('raccolte dal sig. Biagio de Avitabile in quest'anno 1701'[116]) ♦3; I-Mc, Noseda A 50 5 + A 50 6 + C 65 1 + C 65 3 + C 65 4 + C 65 5 + C 65 6 ♦7; I-Mc, Noseda C 65 7 ♦27; I-Milan, Professor Giovanni Pini ♦3; I-MC, 1 C 9/1 (a + c–f) + 1 C 10 (a–g + j–q) + 1 C 11 (a–b + e–f + h–k + m + p–q + s) ♦32;[117] I-MOe, F 1379 ♦6;[118] I-MOe, 2024 ♦4 ('1698' precedes *Amo e ridir*); I-Nc, 60 2 49 (Cantate 18) ♦8; I-Nc, 60 2 52 (Cantate 24) ♦6; I-Nc, 34 6 33 (Cantate 32) ♦3; I-Nc, 33 4 30 (Cantate 38) ♦12 ('Cantata a voce sola composta per l'em[inentissimo] sig[no]r cardinal [Pietro] Ottoboni, 1696' precedes *Dal dì ch'il ciel* and *Lontananza crudel*); I-PLcon, Arm 1 Pis 2 + Arm 1 Pis 4 + Arm 1 Pis 5 + Arm 1 Pis 6 + Arm 1 Pis 32 ♦14;[119] I-Rli,

---

[112] See earlier, note 9. Two of the cantatas in *Ad*, *Quando parli* and *Sulla sponda*, have been edited by Alejandro Garri, assisted by Kent Carlson, in *Canti di Terra: An Anthology of Secular Vocal Music*, vols 28 and 43 (Frankfurt am Main, 2005).

[113] A list of contents is provided in Wolff, 'Bononcini oder die Relativität historischer Urteile', p. 16. I am very grateful to Peter Wollny, who examined this manuscript for me.

[114] See earlier, note 69.

[115] This is a sacred retexting of *Vado ben spesso*. A facsimile of its first page, headed 'Cantata Sacra, S[an]ta M[ari]a Maddalena in viaggio alla solitudine', faces p. 108 in Bianca Becherini, 'Dal "barocco" all'oratorio di Giovanni Bononcini', in Adelmo Damerini and Gino Roncaglia (eds), *Musicisti della scuola emiliana* (Siena, 1956), pp. 97–110.

[116] Salvatore Pintacuda, *Catalogo del fondo antico, Genova, Biblioteca dell'Istituto Musicale 'Nicolò Paganini'*, Bibliotheca Musicae, 4 (Milan, 1966), pp. 467–8.

[117] For a thematic catalogue, see Insom et al., *Il fondo musicale dell'Archivio di Montecassino*, vol. 1, pp. 126–31, nos. 994–1025 and 1028–31; and pp. 449–50, no. 3428; vol. 2, p. 1053, no. 7783; p. 1057, no. 7799; p. 1061, nos. 7835–6; p. 1194, no. 8810; p. 1226, no. 9168; p. 1242, no. 9320; and p. 1255, no. 9459.

[118] Alessandra Chiarelli, *I codici di musica della Raccolta Estense: Ricostruzione dall'inventario settecentesco* (Florence, 1987), pp. 45–6, no. 61.

[119] For a thematic catalogue, see Nicolò Maccavino, *Catalogo delle cantate del Fondo Pisani del Conservatorio 'V. Bellini' di Palermo* (Palermo, 1990).

Fondo Caetani 208 A 1 + 208 A 5 + 208 A 8 ◆7;[120] I-REm, 31 Mus Prof ◆18; US-NHub, Misc Ms 273 ('Cantate diverse di canto del s.r Gio: Bononcini') ◆7.[121]

16 English
GB-Cfm, Mu Ms 46 ('Libro delle cantate del sig[nor] Giov[anni] Bononcini' [*sic*], almost entirely copied by the 'curlicue' scribe) ◆1;[122] GB-Cfm, Mu Ms 649 ('Cantate de diversi maestri, Libro 3^{zo}', copied by J. S. Cousser) ◆8;[123] GB-Lam, 34 ◆13;[124] GB-Lam, 37 ◆9; GB-Lbl, Add. 31,545 ('Libro delle cantate dell sig[no]r Giovanno Bononcini', copied by the 'curlicue' scribe) ◆18;[125] GB-Lbl, Add. 31,546 ◆17;[126] GB-Lbl, Add. 31,547 ◆6; GB-Lbl, Add. 38,036 ('Libro delle cantate de diversi gran maestri', copied by the 'curlicue' scribe) ◆1;[127] GB-Lbl, Add. 62,102 (from the library of the duke of Chandos) ◆8, GB-Lbl, R. M. 24. c. 17 ('Cantate del sig[nor] Giovanni Buononcini', from the library of Queen Caroline, wife of George II) ◆23; GB-Ob, Mus. d. 5 ('Libro delle cantate dell diversi gran maestri') ◆1;[128] GB-Ob, Mus. d. 20 ('Libro delle cantate dell sig[no]r Giov[ann]i Bononcini', copied by the 'curlicue' scribe) ◆18 (facsimiles of 16 cantatas are in

---

[120] For an analytical study and a thematic catalogue with concordances, see Carboni, Gialdroni and Ziino, 'Cantate ed arie romane', pp. 49–192.

[121] Strohm, 'Scarlattiana at Yale', pp. 126–8, 141–2 and 149.

[122] The 'curlicue' scribe wrote the title page for his collection of 19 cantatas, but the only piece composed by Bononcini, *Peno e l'alma fedele*, stands alone in a manuscript copied by someone else and appended to the first scribe's collection. See earlier, note 13.

[123] Mu Ms 649 also contains eight works that are misattributed to 'Gio. Bononcini'. Seven were published in Gaffi, *Cantate*, Op. 1 (1700), nos. 1–2, 6, 8–9 and 11–12. The eighth is *È un martirio della costanza* for B/bc, ascribed to Antonio Caldara in Italian sources. All but one of the 26 works in Mu Ms 649 were in Cousser's 'cantate tomi primi', which included 30 works. Its contents are listed in his Commonplace Book: US-NHub, Osborn Music Ms 16, p. 180, which is reproduced in facsimile in Lindgren, 'J. S. Cousser, Copyist', p. 779.

[124] The 13 in GB-Lam, 34, are found in the same order in GB-Lbl, Add. 31,546, GB-Ob, Mus. d. 22 and US-Cn, VM1532 B69L.

[125] Its contents are identical to those in GB-Ob, Mus. d. 21.

[126] The first, *Non sa dir*, was copied by a Roman scribe. The remaining 16 are found in the same order in GB-Ob, Mus. d. 20, GB-Ob, Mus. d. 22, and US-Cn, Case VM1532 B69L. The same copyist wrote GB-Lbl, Add. 31,546 and GB-Ob, Mus. d. 22.

[127] The same 30 cantatas by 17 composers are found in Add. 38036 and GB-Ob, Mus. d. 5. All 30 are contained in Cousser's Commonplace Book, US-NHub, Osborn Music Ms 16, pp. 180 (1 cantata), 181 (28 cantatas) and 183 (1 cantata). The year when Add. 38036 was copied may be revealed by an inscription at the bottom of f. 3: 'P. F. An[no] Dom[ini] 1706'. Another inscription is found on the rear flyleaf: '1712, Monday, 27 October [O. S.], Mr Cousser came. From ye 14 Dec. he comes but twice a week'. The 'curlicue' scribe wrote relatively few figures under the bass part, but Cousser added profuse figures above it, presumably when he was teaching a harpsichordist.

[128] Its contents are identical to those in GB-Lbl, Add. 38,036.

L); GB-Ob, Mus. d. 21 ('Libro delle cantate dell sig[no]r Giov[ann]i Bononcini', copied by the 'curlicue' scribe) ♦18 (facsimiles of eight cantatas are in L); GB-Ob, Mus. d. 22 ('Cantatas by Bononcini') ♦16;[129] GB-Ob, Mus. Sch. E. 396 ♦4; US-Cn, Case VM1532 B69L ('Libro delle cantate dell sig[no]r Giovanno [*sic*] Bononcini', copied by the 'curlicue' scribe) ♦24.

5 French
Meslanges 1725 = *Meslanges de musique latine, françoise et italienne* (Paris, Ballard, 1725) ♦1; F-Pn, D 14440 ♦12; F-Pn, X 115 ♦3; F-Pn, Vm^7 30/IV + V ♦9; F-Pn, Vm^7 52 ♦10.

2 German
D-Bsb, Mus. ms. 2226 ♦8; D-ROu, XVIII 73, nos. 29–30 + 33–8 ♦8.

B-1: Five works composed in 1699–1711 = phase 3, in Vienna, Charlottenburg and Venice

Clori, svenar mi sento (A/TrTr, flute solo, bc) ♦2; *Non ardisco pregarti, anima bella*; *Or nel bosco ed or nel prato*; *Rompi l'arco, rompi i lacci*; *Sento dentro del petto*.

B-2: Three significant musical sources for phase 3 cantatas

2 Austrian
A-Wn, 17567 ♦3;[130] A-Wn, 17721 ♦2.

1 English
F-Pn, Rés Vma ms 967 ('Airs italiano a chanter', copied by Charles Babel) ♦2.[131]

---

[129] See notes 124 and 126, above.

[130] See earlier, note 5.

[131] Babel's career as a professional musician and copyist is discussed in Bruce Gustafson, 'The Legacy in Instrumental Music of Charles Babel, Prolific Transcriber of Lully's Music', in Jérôme de La Gorce and Herbert Schneider (eds), *Jean-Baptiste Lully: Saint-Germain-en-Laye and Heidelberg 1987* (Laaber, 1990), pp. 495–516. The Bononcini cantatas in F-Pn, Rés Vma ms 967, include one in category A (*Piango in van dell'idol mio*, ff. 213v–215, no. 235) and one in category B (*Clori, svenar mi sento*, ff. 156v–159, no. 186). Babel's elegant hand can be seen in two facsimile editions: 'La Camilla Triomfante, Opera del Signor Gio. Bononcini' (GB-ABu, Powell Collection), in *Italian Opera, 1640–1770*, introduced by Howard Mayer Brown (New York, 1978), and *Recueil de pièces choisies pour le clavessin, 1702* (GB-Lbl, Add. 39,569), in *17th Century Keyboard Music: Sources Central to the Keyboard Art of the Baroque*, vol. 19, introduced by Bruce Gustafson (New York, 1987).

C-1: 69 works composed in 1692–1711 = phase 2 or 3[132]

A piè della sua Clori (set by Antonio Bononcini?); *Acceso da bei lumi* ♦2; *Allor che in mille petti* (questionable); *Amato tesoro che dolce ristoro*; *Anima del cor mio, volami o cara in sen* ♦3; *Antri romiti e solitarie selve*; *Api che raccogliete dell'alba il dolce amor* ♦2; *Bionde crini, chiome vaghe* ♦3; *Care fonti, erbette e fiori* ♦2 (questionable); *Che Dori è la mia vita* ♦2; *Chi disce che Amore* (questionable) ♦4; *Chi vide mai, ch'intese*; *Clori, bell'idol mio, or che dura*; *Clori, perché mi fuggi*;[133] *Clorinda, mio core, con sommo dolore*; *Con che fasto in sen di Flora* ♦2; *Con lusinghiero inganno, mascherate*; *Con trasparente velo* ('1702' in I-Nc, Cantate 69) ♦3; *Da quel dì che per voi, amorosa saetta* ♦2; *Dalisa, oh Dio, Dalisa, che novità, che bizzarie*; *Daliso, m'intendi, non voglio ti prendi* (questionable); *Deh, tu m'insegni, Amore, come fugar poss'io*; *Di smringa la bella un dì s'accese*; *Di sovrana bellezza* (incomplete); *Dove sei, mia bella Irene*; *Entro d'ombrosa valle*; *Filli mia, mio bel tesoro*; *Filli mio ben, mia speme*; *Già tra l'onde il sol t'asconde* ♦2; *Già tutti i miei pensieri* (*Contrasto di pensieri amorosi*, P. A. Bernardoni);[134] *Godea dolce sapore Tirsi sopra l'arene*; *In tante pene e in così acerbo duolo*;[135] *Incredule Amarilli* (lost); *Ingrata Lidia, [h]a vinto il tuo rigor* ♦2 (questionable); *Io vi chiedo, o selve amene* (A/TrTrB) ♦4; *Irene, idolo mio, in questo a me fatale*; *Irene mia che tanto bella* (GB-Lbl, Add. 14,217, f. 74: 'Fra[nces]co Ant[oni]o Izzarelli s[cripsit] alli 18 di Agosto 17' [year cropped]); *L'infelice Fileno assiso* ♦4; *Lidia, bell'idolo mio* (lost); *Luci belle, pupille adorate* ('1702' in I-Nc, Cantate 69) ♦2; *Mai non vidi il sol più adorno*; *Nelle scuole erudite* ♦3; *Ninfe, pastori, ahimé* (lost); *Non per anche disciolta* (set by Antonio Bononcini?); *Non sa dir che*

---

[132] Twelve listed in section C-1 are labelled 'questionable' in the Table, because the attributions to Bononcini occur only in untrustworthy sources: D-Bsb, Mus. ms. 30074; D-Bsb, Mus. ms. 30186; and GB-Lgc, G Mus 449.

[133] Alfred Wotquenne (1867–1939) saw *Clori, perché mi fuggi* in D-Dl, Mus. 1-K-22 (*olim* 101), one of many Dresden manuscripts destroyed during World War II. (His handwritten card index of cantatas can be viewed at B-Bc.) A newly found copy of *Clori, perché mi fuggi* is discussed in Dieci, '"Due "Clori" di Giovanni Bononcini ritrovate', pp. 249–54 and 262. Wotquenne also saw another five Bononcini cantatas in Dresden manuscripts that were destroyed: *Incredule Amarilli* in Mus. 1-K-22; *Lidia, bell'idolo mio* in Mus. 1-K-37 (*olim* 101ᵃ); and *Ninfe, pastori, ahimé, Passan i giorni e l'ore* and *Soave libertade* in Mus. 1-K-10 (*olim* B 13ᵃ). In Appendix 6.1, all of these except *Soave libertade* have been placed in section C-1. I found a copy of *Soave libertade* in GB-Er, P 1425, pp. 13–23, and have placed it in section D-1.

[134] Bernardoni, *Rime varie* (1705), pp. 232–3, where the title is *Propone di perseverare nell'amor suo quando anche debba divenirne più sventurato*.

[135] *In tante pene*, attributed to 'Gio. Bononcini' in I-Nc, 60 1 47 (Cantate 33), no. 14, is concordant with the setting in D-Mbs, 679, ff. 7–10v, attributed to 'G. B.' These initials presumably refer to Giovanni Bononcini rather than to 'Bacci', the composer of the surrounding pieces in Mbs, 679. I am grateful to Lawrence Bennett for information concerning Mbs, 679.

pena sia ♦3; *Partirò ma con qual core* (S/vc + bc); *Passan i giorni e l'ore* (lost); *Pastor d'Arcadia, è morta Clori*; *Pensier che ti nutrisci*; *Perché non dirmi un sì del cor tiranna*; *Prigionier di bionde chiome*; *Qual più cercando ai bella tiranna mia*; *Quella speranza, o Dio* ♦2;[136] *Sappia e pianga ogni core*; *Sciolto in placidi umori*; *Se parti io morirò, dolce mia vita* (A. Ottoboni)[137] (questionable); *Sì, t'intendo, tu vuoi ch'io non pensi* (questionable); *Son tradita e pur non moro*; *Sono amante e due tormenti* ♦2 (questionable); *Sopra l'orme d'Irene*; *Su tapeto odoroso d'erbe* ♦2 (questionable); *Sulla sponda odorosa* (set by Antonio Bononcini?); *Tortorella che priva*; *Tra i smeraldi di prato gentile* (questionable); *Tu volgesti altrove i vanni*; *Tutti li miei* – see *Già tutti i miei*; *Vago prato, ben ristori* ♦2 (questionable); *Varie pene d'amore*; *Voi carbonchi animate* ♦2; *Voi ch'io dica che t'adoro* (questionable).

C-2: 29 significant musical sources for phase 2 or 3 cantatas

11 English
A-Wn, 17576 ♦5; A-Wn, 17748 ♦17;[138] D-Mbs, 11882 ♦15;[139] D-SHs, Mus B 1:1 + Mus B 1:2 + Mus B 1:3 ♦11 (same scribe as for I-MOe, Mus F 99);[140] GB-Lgc, G

---

[136] The opening page of the copy in D-Bsb, Mus. ms. 30136, no. 4, is reproduced in Kümmerling, *Katalog der Sammlung Bokemeyer*, p. 233, no. 58.

[137] Talbot and Timms, 'Antonio Ottoboni', p. 431, no. 216.

[138] The contents of A-Wn, 17748 and 17750, are listed and discussed in Rita Steblin, 'Did Handel meet Bononcini in Rome?', *Music Review*, 45 (1984): 179–93. The English origins of A-Wn, 17576 and 17748, are briefly discussed in Bennett, 'The Italian Cantata in Vienna, c. 1700–c. 1711' (Ann Arbor, 1980), pp. 245–6.

[139] D-Mbs, 11882 is a copy of A-Wn, 17748, nos. 1–15. Many of the two sources' attributions are questionable. D-Mbs, 11882, is the source for four cantatas attributed to Bononcini in Garri Editions (GE), *Canti di Terra* (2006–07). The only other known sources for *Del Tebro antico in su la verde sponda* (GE, vol. 76) and *Nelle scuole erudite* (GE, vol. 81) also attribute them to Bononcini; the former is found only in a reliable source, I-PLc, Arm I Pis 2, pp. 197–208, while the latter is transmitted only by an unreliable source, D-Bsb, Mus. ms. 30186, pp. 249–56. *Ecco il sole ceppi di gelo* (GE, vol. 70) is ascribed to Pistocchi in D-Bsb, Mus. ms. 30197, nos. 10 and 30; see Kümmerling, *Katalog der Sammlung Bokemeyer*, p. 142, nos. 1429 and 1449. *Mi tormenta il pensiero* (GE, vol. 128) is assigned to Scarlatti in five sources, listed in Hanley, 'Alessandro Scarlatti's Cantate da camera', p. 319, no. 427, second setting.

[140] According to Ernst Ludwig Gerber, *Neues historisch-biographisches Lexikon der Tonkünstler*, 4 vols [1812–14], ed. Othmar Wessely (Graz, 1966), vol. 1, col. 81, s.v. 'Alveri', the Sondershausen collection consists of about 20 beautifully copied manuscripts brought from London around 1720. Each volume contains an entire Italian opera or up to 25 cantatas, duets and/or tercets. The cantata volumes undoubtedly include D-SHs, Mus B 1:1–3. A cognate volume is I-MOe, Mus F 99.

Mus 400 (mainly copied by J. S. Cousser) ♦2;[141] GB-Lgc, G Mus 449 ('Libro delle cantate dell: sig[nor] Giov[anni] Bononcini' [*sic*], copied by the 'curlicue' scribe) ♦5–11;[142] GB-Ob, Mus. Sch. D. 223 ('Rac[c]olta di molte cantate di diverse autorÿ – appartenente alla signora [struck through: 'Isabella Aubert'] Anno 1714') ♦8[143]; I-MOe, Mus F 99 (on the binding: 'Cantat[e] del sig[no]r [G]iovan Bononc[ini]) ♦17 (same scribe as for D-SHs, Mus B 1:1 + B 1:2 + B 1:3); US-IDt (mainly copied by J. S. Cousser) ♦8.[144]

8 Italian
D-MÜs, Hs 856 ♦2; F-Pn, Rés Vmc ms 74 ♦6; F-Pn, Rés Vmc ms 81 ♦4; GB-Lbl, Add. 29,963 ♦10; GB-Lbl, Add. 31,503 ♦6;[145] I-Bc, DD 44: Cantate per la

---

[141] This manuscript is a disorderly compilation including about 16 cantatas and about 50 arias. All but one of the cantatas appear in lists in Cousser's Commonplace Book, US-NHub, Osborn Music Ms 16, pp. 180 (11 cantatas), 182 (1 cantata) and 183 (3 cantatas).

[142] GB-Lgc, G Mus 449 contains 25 cantatas, five of which are known to be by Bononcini. Only seven of the works have attributions on their first page: A. Scarlatti and T. Albinoni are each named twice, while G. Aldrovandini, G. Bononcini and H. Wilderer are each named once. Bononcini is named only for *Chi disce che Amore*, the first piece in the source, which is not known to survive elsewhere. It is accordingly listed in Appendix 6.1, section C-1, as a 'questionable' attribution. Five further cantatas that are described as '(questionable)' include four that are also contained in D-Bsb, Mus. ms. 30074, and a fifth that is also in D-Bsb, Mus. ms. 30186 (see below, notes 149–50). The attributions in these manuscripts are considered untrustworthy.

[143] GB-Ob, Mus Sch D 223, is discussed in Colin Timms, '"Prendea con man di latte": A Vivaldi spuriosity?', *Informazioni e studi vivaldiani*, 6 (1985): 64–72. Timms lists the incipits for 16 of the 37 cantatas in the manuscript. One credited to Bononcini, *Dalle ingiuste querelle*, has been removed from the list given in *The New Grove*, 2nd edn (2001) on the grounds that it is ascribed to 'Carolo Grua' in S-L, Samling Wenster Lit. Ä N° 1, ff. 101–103v. Aubert's singing career in London, spanning 1715–1720, is summarized in Philip H. Highfill, Jr, Kalman A. Burnim and Edward A Langhans, *A Biographical Dictionary of Actors, Actresses, Musicians, Dancers, Managers & Other Stage Personnel in London, 1660–1800*, 16 vols (Carbondale, IL, 1973–93), vol. 1, pp. 174–5.

[144] The concordances for each work are listed in Lindgren, 'J. S. Cousser, Copyist', pp. 770–77, nos. 2, 11, 15–17, 24, 27 and 32. The volumes listed in Cousser's Commonplace Book, US-NHub, Osborn Music Ms 16, pp. 180–83, contain 13 of the 24 cantatas in US-IDt, including five of the eight by Bononcini.

[145] In Add. 31,503 11 works are attributed to 'Bononcini' or 'Antonio Bononcini'. They include two by other composers, three by each brother and three *unica*. The latter are described in section C-1 of appendix 6.1 as 'set by Ant[onio] Bononcini?'.

serenis[si]ma sig[no]ra princip[es]sa Amalia ♦1;[146] I-Nc, 33 4 29 (Cantate 69) ♦9;[147] I-Parma, private collection ♦2.[148]

---

[146] I-Bc, DD 44, opens with a cantata by Giovanni Bononcini from Modena and continues with four by Francesco Peli (from Modena?) plus one each by Fiorè, Lotti and Pistocchi. It might have been compiled in Modena for princess Amalia Guglielmina, who resided there in 1697–99, visiting her sister, princess Carlotta Felicità, who had married duke Rinaldo I of Modena in 1696. In mid-January 1698, *Endimione* was staged at the small court theatre, and in mid-November 1698 emperor Leopold granted permission for his elder son, Joseph, to marry princess Amalia. Bononcini might be the composer of the Modenese *Endimione*, because his setting for Vienna 1706, which is dedicated to Amalia and was among the first dramatic works to be staged after she became empress, has many textual similarities. See Lowell Lindgren, 'A Bibliographic Scrutiny of Dramatic Works Set by Giovanni and His Brother Antonio Maria Bononcini' (PhD dissertation, Harvard University, 1972), published Ann Arbor, 1974, pp. 54–6 and 779–81, and Claudio Sartori, *I libretti italiani a stampa dalle origini al 1800*, 7 vols (Cuneo, 1990–94), nos. 8838 and 8842. Activities at the Modenese court in the period 1695–1702 are summarized in Elisabeth J. Luin, 'Antonio Giannettini e la musica a Modena alla fine del secolo XVII', *Atti e memorie della R. Deputazione di storia patria per le provincie modenesi*, ser. 7, vol. 7 (1931): 145–230, at 193–207. Peli's oratorio *L'ultima persecuzione di Saule contro Davidde* (1708) was sung at the Modenese court on the name-day of Benedetta, duchess of Braunschweig-Lüneburg, who was the mother of duchess Carlotta and empress Amalia (Sartori, *I libretti italiani*, no. 24228). His career is summarized in Robert Münster, 'Peli, Francesco', in Stanley Sadie and John Tyrrell (eds), *The New Grove Dictionary*, 2nd edn, vol. 19, p. 295.

[147] I-Nc, Cantate 69, is a compilation of manuscripts containing works by the Bononcinis. It begins with nine cantatas and one aria (from *Endimione*, Naples, 1721) by Antonio Bononcini. The next cantata, *Brama d'esser amante*, is attributed here and in I-MOe, Campori γ L 10 10, to 'Gio. Bononcini', but in B-Bc, 15154, no. 4, and GB-Lbl, Add. 64,960, no. 3, to d'Astorga. I have therefore placed it among the questionable attributions to Bononcini. The remainder of the manuscript consists of works by Giovanni Bononcini: nine cantatas (three dated 1702 and one dated 1701) and one aria (from *Abdolomino*, Naples, 1711).

[148] Dieci, 'Due "Clori" di Giovanni Bononcini ritrovate', pp. 249–64.

5 German
D-Bsb, Mus. ms. 30074 ♦9;[149] D-Bsb, Mus. ms. 30182 ♦6; D-Bsb, Mus. ms. 30186 ♦9;[150] D-Bsb, Mus. ms. 30188 ♦21; D-Bsb, Mus. ms. 30197 ♦13.

3 French
F-Pn, H 659/II + IV + V ♦5;[151] F-Pn, X 118A + 118B: 'Cantate da molti illustrissimi maestri italiani, raccolto per Philidor, il maggiore ordinario della musica del re, guardi[a]no della sua biblioteca della musica, 1705' ♦12.[152]

1 Austrian
A-Wn, E. M. 178 ♦3.

---

[149] D-Bsb. Mus. ms. 30074, was copied by Georg Österreich (1664–1735), who mainly worked as a composer and tenor at the court in Braunschweig-Wolfenbüttel; he also was the chief copyist of a collection of over 1,800 compositions and 24 treatises, which he sold to Heinrich Bokemeyer in 1718 (Kerala J. Snyder and Geoffrey Webber, 'Österreich, Georg', in Stanley Sadie and John Tyrrell (eds), *The New Grove Dictionary*, 2nd edn, vol. 18, pp. 778–80). As noted in Kümmerling, *Katalog der Sammlung Bokemeyer*, pp. 136–43, Österreich was also the chief copyist of the other cantata manuscripts that include works by Bononcini: D-Bsb, Mus. mss. 30182, 30186, 30188 and 30197. (I am grateful to Lawrence Bennett for providing information about these Berlin manuscripts.) D-Bsb, Mus. ms. 30074 and GB-Lgc, G Mus 449 are closely related (see earlier, note 142). These two manuscripts alone credit Bononcini with four cantatas found nowhere else: *Care fonti, erbette e fiori*, *Ingrata Lidia*, [*h*]*a vinto il tuo rigor*, *Sono amante e due tormenti* and *Vago prato, ben ristori*. They are described as 'questionable' in section C-1 of Appendix 6.1. They alone misattribute two cantatas to him: *Per due vaghe pupille* (by Fregiotti) and *Sentite, o tronchi* (by Sarro or Scarlatti).

[150] Eleven cantatas in D-Bsb, Mus. ms. 30186 are attributed to Bononcini or Giovanni Bononcini. The settings of *Già fra l'onde il sol t'asconde* and *Presso allo stuol pomposo* differ from those by Bononcini. Six settings – described as 'questionable' in section C-1 of Appendix 6.1 – have been found nowhere else: *Allor che in mille petti*, *Daliso, m'intendi*, *Se parti io morirò*, *Sì, t'intendo, tu vuoi*, *Tra i smeraldi* and *Voi ch'io dica*. *Su tapeto odoroso* – also labelled 'questionable' – is found only here and in GB-Lgc, G Mus 449 (see earlier, note 142).

[151] F-Pn, H 659, is a set of seven well-organized volumes prepared for the court of the exiled British king James II around 1700; see Jean Lionnet, 'Innocenzo Fede et la musique à la cour des Jacobites à Saint-Germain-en-Laye', *Revue de la BN*, no. 46 (Winter, 1992): 14–18. The bass parts for vols. II, IV and V are preserved in F-Pn, Rés F 1675 (5, 7 and 9). They were formerly in GB-Tenbury, 240, 242 and 244. See Catherine Massip, 'La collection musicale Toulouse-Philidor à la Bibliothèque nationale', *Fontes Artis Musicae*, 30 (1983): 181–207, at 198–201 and 206.

[152] The bass parts for all of F-Pn, X 118A, and for the second half of X 118B, are in F-Pn, Rés F 1675 (2 and 3). These volumes were formerly GB-Tenbury, 238–9. See Massip, 'La collection musicale Toulouse-Philidor', p. 206.

1 Swedish
S-L, Samling Wenster Lit. Ä N° 1: '32 cantate preciosissimi, senza stromenti, composte dalli più famosissimi authori d'italiani, raccolte con gran fatica' ♦5.

D-1: 55 works composed in 1713–32 = phases 4 and 5, in Rome, London and Paris

Ad onta del timore (voice/TrTrB; lost);[153] *Ai begli occhi del mio bene* (S/TrTrB, incomplete); *Barbara ninfa ingrata* (S. Stampiglia, S/TrTrB) ♦1 + *Cd*;[154] *Belle labra porporine* (S/TrTrB); *Care luci del mio bene* (A/TrTrB) ♦1 + *Cd*; *Cento pastori e cento*; *Clori, bell'idol mio, fido amator* ♦3 ('1720' in I-Nc, Cantate 32bis); *Clori, dal colle al prato* ♦2; *Combattuta alma mia*; *Corre dal monte al prato* (S/TrTrB); *Correa dietro a spocori affannato Filen*; *Da quel dì, da quel ora*; *Da te che pasci ogn'ora* ♦1 + *Cd*; *Di virtude s'è armata ragione*; *Dolente e mesta vo sospirando* ♦*Cd*; *Dove con ampio giro*; *Ecco, Dorinda, il giorno* (S/TrTrB) ♦3 + *Cd*; *Ferma, Borea, che tenti?* (B. Panfili);[155] *Fissai, caro mio bene*; *Già la ridente aurora* (*Diana e Apollo*, S/TrTrB); *Già la stagion d'Amore* ♦*Cd*; *Il partir del caro bene*; *L'infelice tortorella* (set by Antonio Bononcini?) ♦2; *Lasciami un sol momento* ♦2 + *Cd*; *Le tenui ruggiade* (*Il lamento d'Olimpia*, S/TrTrB) ♦*Cd*; *Lo sapete, occhi lucenti*; *Mai non s'udì cred'io* (S/TrTrB) ♦2; *Mercé d'amico raggio* (*Doglianze d'Irene*) ♦2; *Misero e che far deggio* (S/TrTrB); *Misero pastorello ardo di sete* (S. Stampiglia, A/TrTrB) ♦*Cd*;[156] *Nice, mia cara Nice*; *O Fille, amata Fille* (S/TrTrB); *O frondoso arboscello* ♦*Cd*; *O mesta tortorella* ♦*Cd*; *Pastor, come diverso* (S/TrTrB); *Poiché Fille superba* (S/TrTrB); *Poiché speme non v'è* (*Moderazione d'amore*, Bernardoni);[157] *Quanto piace agl'occhi miei* ♦6; *S'io piango e tu non m'odi*; *Se v'è chi amante peni* (S/TrTrB); *Sei nata a farmi piangere*; *Siedi, Amarilli mia* (A/TrTrB) ♦*Cd*; *So d'essermi d'Amor* (S/vn, vc, bc); *Soave libertade, nasci, è vero* (*Amor privo di libertà*); *Son'io barbara donna, infida Clori*; *Sulla sponda del mar stava Fileno* (Conte di C[hiaromonte?]; apparently in the hand of Pietro Sigismondo);[158] *Sventurato pastor* (voice/TrTrB; lost);[159] *Torna, torna alla capanna*; *Torno a voi, piante amorose* (A/fl, fl, bc) ♦3; *Un dì tre pastorelle* (written-out cembalo part for

---

[153] *Ad onta del timore* is listed in Sotheby's *Catalogue of* [...] *the Property of His Grace the Duke of Leeds* (London, 2–3 June 1930), lot 428.

[154] 'Delle rime di Palemone Licurio,' tomo V, cantata 5, pp. 7–8.

[155] Panfili's text is preserved in I-Rvat, Vat lat 10205: 'Cantate di S[ua] E[ccellenza] P[adro]ne', ff. 9–10, where a title is given: *La viola gialla*.

[156] 'Delle rime di Palemone Licurio,' tomo V, cantata 4, pp. 5–7.

[157] Bernardoni, *Rime varie* (1705), p. 184.

[158] Augustus Hughes-Hughes, *Catalogue of Manuscript Music in the British Museum*, 3 vols (London, 1906–09; photolithographic repr. 1964–66), vol. 2, p. 582.

[159] *Sventurato pastor* is listed in Sotheby's *Catalogue of* [...] *the Property of His Grace the Duke of Leeds* (London, 2–3 June 1930), lot 428.

aria 2); *Usignol che col mio pianto* ♦2; *Vago augelletto al patrio nido* (S/TrTrB); *Vanne sì, ruscelletto contento* ♦5; *Veggio la bella Dori*; *Viver lungi dal suo bene è un tormento* (*Lontananza*) ♦2.

D-2: 18 significant musical sources for phase 4 or 5 cantatas

8 Italian
B-Lc, 503-2 L-IX ♦2; D-Dl, Mus. 1-I-3: 1 ♦1; F-Pn, D 1350 ♦4; F-Pn, D 4338 ♦3; F-Pn, X 914 ♦2; I-MC, 1 C 9/2 (a–k) ♦11; I-Nc, 65 4 29 (Cantate 32bis) ♦3; I-Pca, D I 1367 ('Cantate all virtù della Signora Maria Pignatelli') ♦5.[160]

7 English
Giovanni Bononcini, *Cantate e duetti*, printed by subscription (London, 1721; reprint 1727) ♦12 + 2 duet cantatas; GB-Er, P 1422 ♦9; GB-Er, P 1425 ♦6; GB-Lcm, MS 698 ♦2, GB-Lcm, 1102 ♦4; I-Rsc, 3710 ♦2; US-Wc, M1497 H13 Case ♦2.

2 French
F-Pn, X 115 ♦3; US-CAh, Mus Ms 63 ♦7.[161]

1 Austrian
A-Wn, Fonds Kiesewetter SA 67 A 25 ♦2.

---

[160] I am grateful to Beatrice Barazzoni for sending me valuable information concerning this source.

[161] See note 18 above, and see Figs. 6.1 and 6.2. The manuscript is written scrupulously, so that it looks like an engraving. No watermark is visible. The first identifiable owner is identified by a stamp on fol. 1: enclosed within the circular frame is 'St Martin's Hall Library, 1850'. This 3,000-seat music hall was built in Covent Garden, Long Acre, London. The foundation stone was laid on 21 June 1847 and the first concert was given in the unfinished hall on 11 February 1850; see 'Hullah's New Music Hall' and 'St Martin's Hall' in *The Musical Times and Singing Class Circular*, vol. 2, no. 39 (1 August 1847): 113–14, and vol. 3, no. 70 (1 March 1850): 292–3. Inside the circular frame is a ladder with a letter on either side: 'I[ohn] H[ullah]'. Hullah was a singing teacher (see Bernarr Rainbow, 'John Hullah', in Stanley Sadie and John Tyrrell (eds), *The New Grove Dictionary*, 2nd edn, vol. 11, p. 815) and may have utilized the manuscript when he gave lessons; but the only signs of use are the pencil and red crayon markings that provide occasional position markings for the cellist (ff. 1v–3v and 94) and detailed continuo figuration for three items (a recitative and a duet by Torri on ff. 57–58v and 63–66v, and an aria by Bononcini on ff. 82v–84). Hullah may have added the index at the end of the manuscript, or at least the six 'plus' and nine 'minus' signs placed there. The 'plus' signs, signifying favour, are bestowed upon the cantata by Bencini, two cantatas by Mancini and three by Bononcini, one of which is *Impara a non dar fede*.

Chapter 7

The 'Humble' and 'Sublime' Genres, the Pastoral and Heroic Styles: Rhetorical Metamorphoses in Benedetto Marcello's Cantatas

Marco Bizzarini

In musical history the categories of the pastoral and the heroic bring to mind the titles of two of the most popular symphonies of Beethoven, on the shoulders of which rests, however, an ancient and complex rhetorical doctrine. There exist various ways of expressing ideas (*res*) via words (*verba*): this stylistic multiplicity is reflected in the so-called *genera elocutionis* or *genera dicendi*, to which, among others, Cicero, in his *Orator* (VI, 20–21), and Quintilian, in his *Institutio oratoria* (XII, 10.10), make reference. In particular, Cicero, borrowing the terminology of the *Rhetorica ad Herennium*, classifies the three *genera dicendi* as *grave*, *medium* and *tenue*.

In the middle of the thirteenth century the English grammarian John of Garland elaborated in his turn a tripartite scheme that was destined to enjoy great favour in Western culture: the *rota Vergilii*. The main works of Virgil – the *Bucolics*, the *Georgics* and the *Aeneid* – became, respectively, the paradigms of the *stilus humilis*, the *stilus mediocris* and the *stilus gravis*. To each of these styles were assigned particular places, proper names, plants, animals and social classes: to take an example from the field of botany, the beech tree (*fagus*), named right at the start of Virgil's first eclogue, belonged to the *stilus humilis*, the apple tree (*melus*) to the *mediocris*, the laurel (*laurus*) and the cedar (*cedrus*) to the *gravis*.

One text of fundamental importance to Italian poetry and music in the Renaissance was Pietro Bembo's *Prose della volgar lingua*, in which the threefold classification of the *rota Vergilii* was changed into a bipartite one comprising the categories of the *piacevole* (pleasing) and the *grave*.[1] The concept of the *sublime* arrived later, in the seventeenth or eighteenth century, with the modern reception of the treatise *Perì hypsous*, composed in Greek by an unknown author of the Imperial era, today conventionally named Pseudo-Longinus. In 1674 Nicolas Boileau, in his successful French translation, chose to render the Greek adjective

---

[1] Pietro Bembo, *Prose di M. Pietro Bembo nelle quali si ragiona della volgar lingua* (Venice, 1525).

hypsos as 'sublime' (as shown in the work's title, *Le traité du sublime ou du merveilleux dans le discours*), a word already encountered occasionally in Latin literature (for example, in Quintilian's *Institutio oratoria*, in the phrase 'genus sublime dicendi') with the significance of a style that was not only serious and elevated but also capable of generating perturbation and exaltation. Boileau himself traced the source of everything 'sublime' back to the poetry of Homer.[2] In the following century, with Edmund Burke's work *A Philosophical Enquiry into the Origins of our Ideas of the Sublime and Beautiful*, the concept of the sublime was counterposed systematically to the beautiful, implying an overthrowing of harmonious order by the forces of nature, by the lower depths or by the infinite.[3]

So the classification of the *genera elocutionis* as *humile*, *medium* or *sublime*, as we find it in the treatises on rhetoric of the twentieth century (one thinks of Heinrich Lausberg's fundamental work *Elemente der literarischen Rhetorik*), is the product of a centuries-old stratification that certainly has its roots in classical Latin literature but has received important increments from later periods.[4] In the musical domain, the polarity of the *Pastoral* and *Eroica* symphonies of Beethoven certainly goes back to the Virgilian archetype codified by John of Garland, but implies a conversion of the threefold ordering into a twofold one: the world of the shepherds clearly corresponds to the *Bucolics*, that of the heroes to the *Aeneid*. To the first is assigned a *genus elocutionis humile*, to the second a *genus grave* or – following the terminology of Pseudo-Longinus as revisited by Boileau – a *genus sublime*.

The same distinction observed in Beethoven finds an interesting precedent in the Italian cantata repertory of the early eighteenth century. There exist, indeed, *ordinary* compositions, the poetic texts of which pursue amorous themes in pastoral contexts, but there are also *extraordinary* compositions – those for which Eugen Schmitz coined the felicitous term *Sujetkantaten*[5] – in which the protagonist is a hero or heroine drawn from mythology or history. It goes without saying that the *genus humile* is naturally suited to the first type, while the second inclines towards the *genus grave* or *genus sublime*.

Benedetto Marcello (1686–1739), one of the most productive composers of chamber cantatas alongside Alessandro Scarlatti, orients his own musical language in both directions, according to the poetic text and the choice of subject. His *genus humile* tends towards musical simplicity, small dimensions and regular *da capo* form for arias. In contrast, his *genus sublime* privileges complexity, artifice, monumental proportions and departures from the norm. In this specific repertory

---

[2] Nicolas Boileau (trans.), *Le traité du sublime ou du merveilleux dans le discours* (Paris, 1674).

[3] Edmund Burke, *A Philosophical Enquiry into the Origins of our Ideas of the Sublime and Beautiful* (London, 1757).

[4] Heinrich Lausberg, *Elemente der literarischen Rhetorik* (Munich, 1967).

[5] Eugen Schmitz, *Geschichte der weltlichen Solokantate* (Leipzig, 1914), pp. 151–4.

harmonic solutions may assume the most unconventional and unpredictable features, while forms tend to become asymmetrical and open-ended.

Although he was active also as a *letterato* and as a theorist of music, Marcello unfortunately left no treatise dealing specifically with the *genera elocutionis* as applied to cantatas.[6] Be this as it may, his musical oeuvre conforms very well – perhaps more exactly than that of any other contemporary composer – to the theoretical matrices described above: so much so that Giovenale Sacchi, one of the Venetian composer's earliest biographers, used the adjective 'eroico' to denote the subgenre of the *Sujetkantate*, clearly distinct from cantatas of an Arcadian-pastoral character.[7]

It is worth mentioning that this polarity between the 'pastoral' and the 'heroic' finds application, albeit in different terms and with the numerical proportions reversed, also in the operatic repertoire of the same time, where *pastorali* constitute a subsidiary genre alongside the more mainstream, 'heroic' *drammi per musica*. A letter of the poet Apostolo Zeno dating from his period of residence at the Viennese court refers explicitly to these two different theatrical genres.[8]

If it is true that the aspiration towards the *genus sublime* implies an abandonment of stylistic conventions in favour of exceptional solutions, it follows that views of an artistic creation conceived in this fashion will oscillate between enthusiasm on the part of some and rejection and incomprehension on the part of others. Charles Burney, in the course of his travels in Italy, described vividly the disorientation he experienced when listening to Marcello's cantata *Cassandra*, whereby the latter – in Burney's words – 'entirely sacrificed the music to the poetry, by changing the time or stile [*sic*] of his movement at every new idea which occurs in the words; this may, perhaps, shew a composer to be a very sensible man, but at the same

---

[6] Among the bibliographical sources cited by Marcello in the prefaces to the volumes of his *Estro poetico-armonico* we find Cicero's *De oratore*. For a complete list of these sources, see Marco Bizzarini, *Benedetto Marcello* (Palermo, 2006), p. 127.

[7] [Francesco Luigi Fontana and Giovenale Sacchi], *Vita di Benedetto Marcello patrizio veneto* (Venice, 1788), p. 86: 'Altro libro pur di cantate tutte eroiche senza strumenti'. This old biography of Marcello was originally written in Latin by Francesco Fontana, but on the basis of notes assembled by Giovenale Sacchi. The Italian-language version, though published anonymously, was probably prepared for the press by Sacchi.

[8] *Lettere di Apostolo Zeno cittadino veneziano*, 3 vols (Venice, 1752), vol. 2, p. 373 (letter from Apostolo Zeno to Luisa Bergalli dated 26 May 1725): 'Altri studi più sodi mi chiamano a sé nel declivio in cui sono; e debbo omai pensare ad altro sviluppo che a quello di pastorali e di drami'. Reinhard Strohm observes apropos of the librettos written in the late seventeenth and early eighteenth centuries: 'Pastoral themes, and their characteristic kind of stage decoration, were popular throughout this period, and to alternate them with heroic plots was a frequent strategy of impresarios in Italy as well as abroad'. See Reinhard Strohm, 'Apostolo Zeno's *Teuzzone* and its French Models', in *Dramma per musica: Italian Opera Seria of the Eighteenth Century* (New Haven, CT and London, 1997), pp. 121–33, at p. 124.

time it must discover him to be of a very phlegmatic turn, and wholly free from the enthusiasm of a creative musical genius'.⁹

An opposite opinion to Burney's was held, in the mid-eighteenth century, by the Italian scholar Francesco Algarotti, who was a cosmopolitan figure, a friend of Voltaire, a traveller in Germany and Russia, a connoisseur of the figurative arts and a popularizer of the most recent scientific theories of Newton. In his *Saggio sopra l'opera in musica* (Venice, 1755), which anticipates ideas later developed in the *Alceste* of Calzabigi and Gluck, Algarotti observed:

> Who ever was more animated with a divine flame in conceiving and more judicious in conducting his works than Marcello? In the cantatas of Timotheus and Cassandra and in the celebrated collection of psalms he hath expressed in a wonderful manner, not only all the different passions of the heart, but even the most delicate sentiments of the mind. He has, moreover, the art of representing to our fancy things even inanimate.[10]

But the imposing corpus of cantatas composed by Benedetto Marcello, of which over two hundred specimens survive, is not in the least monolithic: the *genus humile* and the *genus sublime* confront one another repeatedly, and there are occasional opportunities for mediation between musical expressions that appear by turns extremely simple and extremely complex.[11]

It was noted earlier that in Marcello's cantatas the *genus sublime* is often identified with those works dealing with heroes and heroines of Antiquity. The catalogue of this Venetian composer offers a rich collection of them: classical epic – including Virgil – is represented by Andromache, Cassandra, Medea and Dido; Roman history by Cato, Lucrece and Cleopatra; biblical lore by

---

[9] Charles Burney, *The Present State of Music in France and Italy* (London, 1771), p. 160.

[10] The quotation reproduces the text of an anonymous English translation of Algarotti's Saggio given in Oliver Strunk, *Source Readings in Music History* (New York, 1950), p. 672.

[11] For Benedetto Marcello, as for many other composers of the period, we are still far from possessing a truly complete list of the surviving cantatas, despite the all efforts that have so far been made, among which the authoritative catalogue in Eleanor Selfridge-Field, *The Music of Benedetto and Alessandro Marcello. A Thematic Catalogue* (Oxford, 1990), stands out. After Vivaldian musicology has managed in recent years to announce the exciting discovery of several new works, we ought, by the same token, to expect that a much less exhaustively studied composer such as Marcello could give rise to future discoveries of some significance. For an overview of Marcello's cantatas, the reader is referred to the following studies: Marco Bizzarini (ed.), *Benedetto Marcello. Le cantate profane: i testi poetici* (Venice, 2003); *Benedetto Marcello*, pp. 148–76. On Marcello's *Sujetkantaten*, see Colin Timms, 'The Cassandra Cantata of Conti and Marcello', in Claudio Madricardo and Franco Rossi (eds), *Benedetto Marcello: la sua opera e il suo tempo* (Florence, 1988), pp. 127–59, and Michael Talbot, 'The Effects of Music: Benedetto Marcello's Cantata Il Timoteo', in Madricardo and Rossi, *Benedetto Marcello*, pp. 103–25.

Herod. Indeed, the psalms of Marcello's *Estro poetico-armonico*, especially in their frequent sections scored for single voice and continuo (with the possible accompaniment of concertante instruments), share not a few stylistic traits with the secular *Sujetkantaten*.

The present essay aims to examine more closely the process of metamorphosis that in Marcello's vocal music leads from the *genus humile* to the *genus sublime*. In particular, we will see how the composer, in the act of transforming, at the levels of structure and function, the poetic and musical material of a cantata on the subject of love manages successfully to adapt it to the needs of a composition of an elevated and heroic stamp.

The cantata in question is *Dove fuggisti, o dio* (SF A97),[12] preserved in a version for alto and continuo in manuscript in the Biblioteca Nazionale Marciana, Venice.[13] Cast in the simple form aria–recitative–aria (ARA), with *da capo* repetition prescribed for both arias, the composition has a poetic text on the well-worn subject of the separation of lovers. In the first aria a female character, presumably a shepherdess, bewails the mysterious departure, which could be a deliberate desertion, of her lover, Tirsi. In the recitative the protagonist adds to her personal grief a note of bitterness expressed in three urgent questions. Love and nostalgia, at any rate, prevail in the concluding aria, which transmutes the last utterance of the recitative into a heartfelt prayer – 'ricordati di me' – without giving in to possible thoughts of revenge.

Dove fuggisti, o dio![14]	Where are you fleeing, o God!
speranza del cor mio,	hope of my heart,
Tirsi adorato?	beloved Tirsi?
Se muovi lunge il piè,	When you travel afar,
no che del mio non v'è	there is no unhappier
cor infelice	heart
più sventurato. (*Da capo*)	than mine.
Ah Tirsi, ah caro ben, questa mercede	Ah Tirsi, ah my beloved, is this
si rende alla mia fede?	the reward paid to my fidelity?
Ove son le promesse e i giuramenti	Where are the promises and the oaths you swore
di pria morir che mai lasciarmi? Oh dio!	to die before leaving me? Oh God!

---

[12] The sigla 'SF' refer to the catalogue by Eleanor Selfridge-Field cited in the preceding note.

[13] Shelfmark: Cod. It. IV n. 968 (= 10751), ff. 35r–36v.

[14] I am happy to accept the suggestion made by Bruno Brizi to use lower case for the transcription of the casual exclamatory phrase 'o dio!' in order to distinguish it from the preface to a prayer addressed to the (or a) Deity, 'o Dio!'. This distinction has significance also for the metamophosis from the *genus humile* to the *genus sublime* that we shall describe shortly.

perché fuggi, amor mio?	why are you fleeing me, my love?
Vanne, ma sappi almeno	Go, but know at least
che dell'afflitto seno	that I find for my torments
altra pace or non sento a' miei martiri	no peace in my wounded breast
che il pensar dove sei, dove t'aggiri.	but the thought of where you are and what you do.
Sin che lontano sei,	As long as you are far from me,
ho tutto il mio piacer,	I gain all my pleasure,
caro, in pensar a te.	dearest, from thinking of you.
Tu ancora per mercede	Show pity for
di mia costante fede	my steadfast constancy
ricordati di me. (*Da capo*)	by still remembering me.

The manuscript in the Marciana, which in terms of the music paper employed and the style of handwriting is visibly different from musical sources of the early eighteenth century, dates perhaps from the end of that century.[15] The work is headed by an illuminating remark: 'Confrontisi questa cantata col Salmo XXI del Marcello!' ('Compare this cantata with *Salmo XXI* of Marcello!'). On this point, it is very easy to verify that the 'A' section of the cantata's first aria bears surprisingly strong musical resemblances to the setting of the first lines of *Salmo XXI*, as published in the fourth volume of the *Estro poetico-armonico*.[16] We clearly have here a case of self-borrowing processed via a series of adaptations – starting with a completely new poetic text – that effect a transition from the *genus humile* to the *genus sublime*.

The transformation of the text at the opening of the two works seems to recall the traditional procedures of *contrafactum* or *travestimento spirituale*:[17]

Cantata SF A97	*Cantata SF A97*
Dove fuggisti, o dio!	Where are you fleeing, o God!
speranza del cor mio,	hope of my heart,
Tirsi adorato?	beloved Tirsi?
Salmo XXI	*Psalm XXI*
Volgi, mio Dio, deh volgi un de' tuoi guardi	Turn, my God, pray turn one of your glances
e ti piaccia mirar da quali e quante	towards me and behold by what, and by how many,
miserabili angustie io sono oppresso:	miserable tribulations I am oppressed:
perché così mi lasci in abbandono?	Why do you abandon me so?

---

[15] The watermarks of this manuscript are not visible.

[16] The eight volumes of Marcello's work were published in 1724 and 1726 by the Venetian printer Domenico Lovisa. Tomi 1–4 came out in the first year, Tomi 5–8 in the second.

[17] A *travestimento spirituale* is a religious paraphrase of a secular original.

In reality, the genesis of the two poetic texts was completely unconnected. Girolamo Ascanio Giustiniani, the author of the Italian-language verse paraphrases of the first fifty psalms, set to music by Marcello, merely translated and elaborated in poetic fashion the Latin text of the Vulgate Psalm XXI, the first verse of which reads: 'Deus Deus meus, respice in me: quare me dereliquisti?'.

Marcello and Giustiniani themselves regarded this psalm as 'venerando fra tutti' ('to be venerated among [them] all') since, according to an established theological tradition, 'Davidde in mezzo alle sue miserie ed alle sue afflizioni profeticamente e maravigliosamente descrive la morte, la sepoltura, la risurrezione di Gesù Cristo in figura di lui, la vocazione de' gentili e lo stabilimento della Chiesa' ('David, amid his tribulations and afflictions, prophetically and marvellously prefigures the death, burial and resurrection of Jesus Christ, the vocation of the Gentiles and the establishment of the Church').[18] It would have been difficult for the anonymous author of the text of the cantata *Dove fuggisti, o dio* to have thought of taking holy scripture as his literary model; it would have seemed to him out of place, if not actually blasphemous, to adapt the words of the crucified Saviour as reported by the Gospels (Mark 15.34; Matthew 27.46) to become the lovelorn lament of a simple shepherdess. Nevertheless, despite their different genesis, the two texts have in common the theme of abandonment, and it was probably for this reason that Marcello deemed it opportune to re-use the same musical ideas, founded on the same *affetto*, while organizing them according to a different *genus elocutionis* implying changes in the composition's morphology and instrumentation.

If we compare the cantata in the late Venetian manuscript with the printed edition of *Salmo XXI*, a difference of scoring leaps to the eye: the cantata employs alto and continuo, while the psalm has alto, two concertante *violette* (violas) and continuo. Closer inspection of the cantata suggests, however, that the apparent absence of instruments is deceptive: in the opening ritornello, indeed, the continuo part contains too many rests to be viable on its own. We therefore have to conclude that the musical text, in the form transmitted to us for alto and continuo alone, is manifestly incomplete right from its opening bars. A rapid survey of the other cantatas contained in the manuscript supports the idea that this musical source is simply a short score, or a copy for the use of singers (the description 'Parte che canta' appears, indeed, at the head of the volume), that transcribes only the vocal part and the continuo and omits the obbligato instruments.[19]

The original scoring is impossible to establish with certainty. One might start, with the example of the psalm to hand, by hypothesizing the presence of two violas and continuo, but this solution would be too recherché for a secular cantata and unparalleled in the rest of Marcello's cantatas known at present. A more standard ensemble would be that of two violins, viola and continuo, as used for most of

---

[18] The Gospel of St John (19.24) refers in an explicit way to the text of Psalm 21 (which corresponds to Psalm 22 in the Hebrew and Protestant numbering).

[19] On the nature and purpose of a short score in this repertory, see Michael Talbot, *Tomaso Albinoni. The Venetian Composer and His World* (Oxford, 1990), pp. 118 and 193.

the arias in Marcello's serenatas and oratorios. This form of ensemble would also allow, if desired, the addition of a concertante cello.

The solution to the problem proved easier than expected. Selfridge-Field's catalogue lists a second source of the cantata *Dove fuggisti, o dio*: the manuscript B. 2849 in the library of the Conservatorio 'Luigi Cherubini', Florence. From what the catalogue tells us, this would be the same collection of cantatas contained in the Venetian manuscript, and scored, similarly, for voice and continuo (i.e., in short score); but in reality the Florentine volume contains the full scores, complete with all the instrumental parts omitted from the Marciana source. The cantata *Dove fuggisti, o dio* appears at the end of the volume, at ff. 233–246: in this instance, without any annotated reference to the psalm. Its instrumental component is scored, apart from the continuo, for just a pair of violins without viola. The instrumental parts of the cantata and those of the psalm are very similar, with the difference that the two violins yield their place to two violas, causing the music often to be transposed down an octave. The *genus sublime* here obviously implies a lowering of the tessitura.

Marcello himself, his the preface to readers (headed 'a' leggitori') in the fourth volume of his *Estro poetico-armonico*, supplies a reasoned argument for his choice of scoring:

> Il Salmo vigesimoprimo *Deus Deus meus respice in me &c.*, siccome concorda la maggior parte de' sacri interpreti e spositori esser una profezia ed una figura del Redentore del mondo spirante sopra la Croce, così non si è giudicato disconvenevole, anzi creduta si è precisa necessità, di comporlo ad una sola voce, e colle maniere più flebili e più adatte a tanto lugubre compassionevole avvenimento, cui per rendere espresso in più efficace maniera e per isvegliare negli ascoltanti lo possibile più forte dolore nel riflesso del gran mistero, si è accompagnato colle violette, stromento per sé medesimo (quando trattato sia egli da esperta mano) atto ad indurre agevolmente commuovimento e tristezza. Perciò ben rifletta qualunque virtuoso cantore debba eseguire esso Salmo a ciò ch'egli esprime e che rappresenta; quindi piuttosto colla pia tenerezza del cuore che coll'artifizioso vagar della voce schiettamente 'l pronunzi, che non saravvi chi l'oda, e pe' gravissimi dolorosi sensi e per la melodia lamentevole ond'espresso ne viene, che internamente non si contristi non poco e non senta parte di quel necessario compungimento che si richiede a così alto e doloroso mistero.[20]

---

[20] *Estro poetico armonico. Parafrasi sopra li primi venticinque salmi, poesia di Girolamo Ascanio Giustiniani, musica di Benedetto Marcello, patrizi veneti*, vol. 4 (Venice, 1724), pp. 1–2: 'Since the Twenty-first Psalm, Deus Deus meus respice in me etc., is agreed by the majority of sacred interpreters and commmentators to be a prophesy and prefiguration of the Redeemer of the World dying on the Cross, it has not been deemed unseemly – indeed it has been thought necessary – to compose it for a single voice and in a very mournful manner best suited to such a lugubrious and compassion-arousing event. In order to express this in the most effective way and to stimulate in listeners the greatest possible grief in the contemplation of this great mystery, it is accompanied by violas,

Example 7.1   B. Marcello, Opening aria of the cantata *Dove fuggisti, o dio* (source: Florence, Biblioteca del Conservatorio 'Luigi Cherubini', Ms. B. 2849, ff. 233r–234v).

instruments that in themselves (when played by expert hands) readily induce compassion and sadness. Therefore, any practised singer who has to perform this psalm should think carefully about what he is expressing and depicting; thus he should enounce it simply with tenderness of heart rather than with artificial vocal flights, so that there will be none who hears it, with its feelings of the deepest grief and the dolourous melody that expresses it, who does not grow not a little sad inside himself and does not experience the necessary remorse required by such an exalted and sorrowful mystery'.

6
f p
Do - ve, do - ve fug - gi - sti,‿o di - o!, spe -
8
- ran - za del cor mi - o, Tir - - - si‿a - do - ra - to? Do - ve,
10
do - ve fug - gi - sti,‿o di - o!, spe - ran - za del cor mi - o, Tir -

12
- si‿a - do - ra - to, Tir - - - - si‿a-do-ra - - - - - - -
14
- - - - to, Tir - - - - si‿a-do-ra - to?
16
Do - ve?
Do - ve fug-gi - sti,‿o

18
di - o!, spe - ran - za ___ del cor mi - o? Do - ve,
20
do - ve fug-gi - sti, o di - o?, spe - ran - za del cor mi - o, spe -
22
- ran - za del cor mi - o? Do - - - ve fug - gi - sti,‿o di - o? Do - ve,

24
do - - - - ve fuggi - sti,‿o di - o!, do - ve, Tir - si‿a -do - ra -
26
- to, do - ve, Tir - si‿a - do - ra - to, do -
28
- ve, spe - ran - za, fug - gi - sti, cor mi - o, Tir -

Aspects of the Secular Cantata in Late Baroque Italy

36
cor in - fe - li - ce più, più sven - tu - ra - to, no, __
38
__ che del mio non v'è cor ______ in - fe - li - ce più, più ______
40
D.C.
__ sven - tu - ra - to, più ______ sven - tu - ra - - - to.

It is clear that, chronologically speaking, the secular cantata precedes the psalm, which, in certain aspects, constitutes its *travestimento spirituale*: this explains the change from conventional instrumentation with two violins to the unconventional one with two violas. Seeing that the psalm was published in 1724, the cantata must have been composed earlier, even if present knowledge does not allow us to be more precise.

Between the Venice manuscript (which we will hereafter call VE) and the Florence manuscript (FI), ignoring the string accompaniment, there is a substantial identity of musical text. FI is in every instance anterior to VE: this can be gleaned not only from the general appearance of the manuscript but also from the *usus scribendi*, or notational style. For instance, in VE the key signature has three flats as opposed to the two in FI (and in the cognate movement contained in the *Estro poetico-armonico*), which one may take as further evidence that the Venetian source is the work of a copyist of a later date who found a need to modernize the key signature for C minor, whereas Marcello, like many other Italian composers of the same period, followed the traditional practice going back to the *tuoni salmodici* of the seventeenth century, which normally required one flat fewer. FI is also more copiously endowed with tempo and dynamic marks: among other things, VE opens with the simple tempo mark *Ad[agi]o*, whereas FI directs: *Adagio assai, schietto sempre*. The idea of *schietto sempre* brings clearly to mind the preface to the psalm mentioned earlier, where the singer is enjoined to avoid 'artifizioso vagar della voce' in order to set in relief 'schiettamente'– that is, in an unadorned manner – the expressive content of the poetic paraphrase. The vocal part, originally notated in the alto clef, appears here in the treble clef.

Example 7.2   B. Marcello, *Salmo XXI* (B621), bars 1–29.

Marco Bizzarini

10
quan-te mi-se - ra - bi-li an-gu - stie io so - no, so-no op-pres - so, e ti piac -
Vlc solo
12
- cia, ti piac - cia mi-rar da qua - - li e quan - te mi - se - ra - bi - li an-
14
f
f
- gu - - - stie io so - no, so - no op-pres - so.
Tutti
Vlc solo

16
p
f
p
f
Per - ché,
per - ché co - sì mi
f
Tutti
[Vlc solo]
Tutti
18
p
[p]
la - sci, mi la - sci in ab - ban - do - no?
deh, mio
20
Dio, vol - gi, vol - gi un de' tuoi guar - di,
deh, per - ché,
deh, per - ché co - sì mi

22
la - sci in ab - ban - do - no, per - ché, mio
[Vlc solo]
24
Di - o, per-ché mi la - sci, per-ché mi la - sci in ab-ban-do - no, in ab - ban-
26
f
f
-do - - - - no?
Tutti

Let us now attempt to compare in detail the 'A' section of the first aria of the cantata – following the text given in FI (see Example 7.1) – with the opening section of *Salmo XXI* (see Example 7.2). At a macrostructural level, one notes the suppression in the psalm of the 'B' section of the aria and of the consequential *da capo*. The 'A' section of the aria, which runs to 33 bars in common time, is slightly pared down – to 29 bars – in the psalm. It was stated earlier that the two poetic texts, apart from their shared subject of abandonment, have nothing in common.

The sequence, in the aria, of two *settenari piani* in *rima baciata* followed by a *quinario piano* is changed in the psalm to become four *endecasillabi sciolti*.[21] But the metrical structure of the two poetic texts is less important than the 'cantilena'– the configuration of the words, with their various repetitions, in the musical setting. The aria follows the practice that, by the second decade of the eighteenth century, has become routine, and is followed regularly by Marcello, of setting twice in succession, in two discrete periods, or *intercalari* (as these were called in the eighteenth century), the lines of the first semistrophe.[22] This is how the 'cantilena' works out in the two periods of the 'A' section of the aria; in the right-hand column the corresponding number of syllables for each section of text appears:

---

[21] *Settenari*, *quinari* and *endecasillabi* are, respectively, lines of seven, five and eleven syllables. A *piano* line places the final accent on the penultimate syllable. *Rime baciate* follow the pattern AABB etc. *Sciolto* means unrhymed.

[22] An aria stanza is commonly dived into two semistrophes that correspond, respectively, to the 'A' and 'B' sections.

First period	(total of 52 syllables)
Dove, dove fuggisti, o dio,	9
speranza del cor mio,	7
Tirsi adorato,	5
dove, dove fuggisti, o dio,	9
speranza del cor mio,	7
Tirsi adorato, Tirsi adorato, Tirsi adorato.	5+5+5
Second period	**(total of 85 syllables)**
Dove, dove fuggisti, o dio,	9
speranza del cor mio,	7
dove, dove fuggisti, o dio,	9
speranza del cor mio, speranza del cor mio,	7+7
dove fuggisti, o dio, dove, dove, fuggisti, o dio,	7+9
dove, Tirsi adorato, dove, Tirsi adorato,	7+7
dove, speranza, fuggisti, cor mio,	11
Tirsi adorato.	5

The systematic repetition of the word 'dove', which creates an effective expressive intensification, often transforms the original *settenari* into effective *novenari*. One notes how, in the penultimate line of the table ('dove, speranza, fuggisti, cor mio'), the composer freely reorders words drawn from the first two lines of poetry, creating a synthetic *endecasillabo*. In the second period, however, the delivery of the lines becomes even more artificial and complex. The syllable-count reaches a total of 52 syllables for the first period and 85 for the second: a grand total of 137 syllables.

The 'cantilena' of the psalm is laid out very differently:

First period	(total of 63 syllables)
Volgi, volgi, mio Dio, deh volgi un de' tuoi guardi	13
e ti piaccia, ti piaccia mirar da quali e quante	14
miserabili angustie io sono oppresso	11
e ti piaccia, ti piaccia mirar da quali e quante	14
miserabili angustie io sono oppresso.	11
Second period	**(total of 57 syllables)**
Perché, perché così mi lasci in abbandono?	13
deh, mio Dio, volgi, volgi un de' tuoi guardi	11
deh perché, deh perché così mi lasci in abbandono?	15
perché, mio Dio, perché mi lasci?	9
perché mi lasci in abbandono?	9

First and foremost, the distinction between the two periods is subtler: it no longer arises from textual restatement but, rather, from applying the musical technique of the *Devise*, with its opportune repetition of the first word ('Volgi, volgi' in the first period, 'Perché, perché' in the second).[23] It is clear that the interrogative element 'Dove, dove?' that characterized the aria through its insistent iterations finds its counterpart in the psalm less in the colourless 'Volgi, volgi' than in the much more urgent 'perché, perché?' The syllable-count shows that the first period acquires, in the psalm, a slight supremacy, inverting the situation in the aria, where the second period enjoys a marked preponderance.

In re-using the music of the aria, Marcello had to solve the problem of providing two texts of such radically different lengths (7+7+5 syllables in the first vis-à-vis 11+11+11+11 in the second) with a similar musical treatment. Rather than presenting in succession two settings of the same semistrophe, as required by the compositional practice of the 'double period', the composer divided up the four cumbrous *endecasillabi* of the psalm paraphrase into two groups: the first comprising the first three lines, and the second comprising only the fourth, followed by a reprise of the opening line. In so doing, he achieved a very well-balanced distribution of lines, since each line could count on at least one complete repetition.

Let us now compare the length in bars of the respective sections:

Aria	Psalm
Instrumental ritornello: 5 bars (+ 3/4)	Instrumental ritornello: 5 bars (+ 3/4)
First period: 9 bars (+ 2/4)	First period: 9 bars (+ 2/4)
Second period: 15 bars	Secondo period: 11 bars
Ritornello (coda): 3 bars	Ritornello (coda): 3 bars

The bar-count confirms similarly that in his psalm Marcello sought to rebalance the length of the two periods by taking out a few bars from the second.

Although they have the same length, the introductory instrumental ritornellos are not identical. The lowering of the tessitura caused by the replacement of the violins by violas inspired Marcello to introduce a further tone-colouring effect: the addition of a part for *violoncello solo* in the bass that constantly alternates with the assembled *tutti* instruments (cellos, contrabasses and harpsichord). In the continuo part of the cantata, separated by long rests, there were only *tutti* entries. The solo cello, which matches the timbre of the violas well (it was clearly better not to leave them exposed), creates, throughout the introductory ritornello, a three-part contrapuntal texture fuller than that employed in the cantata. Then there is an important musical variation in the second bar. In the cantata there was a simple echo repetition by the violins, *piano*, in the lower octave, rounded off by a phrase in dotted rhythm over a dominant in the bass; but the psalm presents a contrasting consequent leading to the dominant of F minor. The latter solution not only seems more elegant but, more especially, relieves the violas of the need to descend below their available range; change was therefore unavoidable.

---

[23] A *Devise* (German for a heraldic device) is a short, detachable opening motto. It is commonly heard first alone and then, after an instrumental interruption, together with its continuation.

The first vocal period exhibits fewer changes than the preceding ritornello. Beyond the necessary adjustments to the vocal line caused by the wholesale replacement of the poetic text and the changed number of syllables, one remarks once more the addition to the continuo part of passages for solo cello that on occasion (for instance, in bars 12 and 13) fill in what were originally, in the cantata, rests in the bass line. Another point to note is that the viola parts here largely retain the register of the earlier violins, except when, as occasionally happens, they are taken down an octave, as in bars 13 and 14.

As for the second vocal period, we have already seen that in the psalm Marcello effects a noticeable contraction. In particular, the composer cuts the passage running from the last crotchet of bar 20 to the third crotchet of bar 23, which is based on the same motif as the opening ritornello: in the *genus sublime* superfluous repetitions tend to disappear. Marcello additionally remodels bars 27–30,[24] removing a cadential phrase of four crotchets coincident with the words 'Tirsi adorato', between bars 26 and 27. This melodic formula was in fact too predictable and too firmly linked to a closed form to be retained in the new context. For a similar reason, the composer rewrites the final cadence of the vocal part in the psalm. Whereas, in the cantata, this drove in time-honoured fashion towards the tonic ('Tirsi adorato'), in the sacred composition it creates a sense of suspense matching the question mark of the text ('perché mi lasci in abbandono?') by ending on B♮ and dominant harmony: this melodic–harmonic incompleteness is clearly tailored to an open form. The same interrogative character is captured at the start of this period by the new *Devise* on the word 'perché?', which, with its rising fifth, is very different from the earlier setting of the equivalent 'dove', with its falling octave (Example 7.1, bar 16).

In the concluding ritornello, largely unchanged, the first violin in the cantata becomes the second viola in the psalm, its notes taken down an octave except in the final bar. At this point, the two paths diverge. The cantata continues with a brief 'B' section for the aria (nine-and-a-half bars), based throughout on the same musical materials. Starting in E flat major, this passes via various modulations to G minor. The psalm, however, proceeds to an entirely new movement (Adagio, 3/4, E flat major), at the end of which no *da capo* occurs.

* * *

To conclude: the cantata and the psalm share a metre (C), a key (C minor) and a basic *affetto* (a lament over abandonment); both works employ a battery of expressive resources that include dissonant suspensions and melodic chromaticism. But the change of register arising from the move from a secular to a sacred context

---

[24] During this passage, in the Florentine manuscript of the cantata, the continuo is silent, the second violins playing a bassetto notated in the bass clef. In contrast, the psalm normalizes the writing by retaining the bass in the continuo.

has necessitated some rhetorical transformations in conformity with the *genera elocutionis*, thus:

Cantata *Dove fuggisti, o dio*	**Salmo XXI**
Genus humile	*Genus sublime*
two *settenari* plus a *quinario*	four *endecassilabi*
rhymed verse	unrhymed verse
Adagio assai	Grave
violins in a high register	violas transposed to the lower octave
no solo–tutti contrast in the continuo	solo–tutti contrast in the continuo
predominantly 'a 2' in the ritornello	'a 3' in the ritornello
closed form (ABA) with *da capo*	open form (A) without *da capo*
overt division into two periods	less overt division into two periods
unequal length of the two periods	similar length of the two periods
frequent motivic repetition	less frequent motivic repetition
standard melodic formulas	fewer standard melodic formulas
'Dove, dove?'	'Perché, perché?'

In the mid-eighteenth century the composer and musical theorist Charles Avison made explicit mention of the category of the sublime and of Marcello's *Estro poetico-armonico*. In his *Essay on Musical Expression* of 1752 Avison proposes a classification of the fifty *Psalms* under three 'styles in musical expression': Grand, Beautiful, Pathetic. Each of the three styles is in its turn subdivided into three sub-categories: the Grand into the Sublime, Joyous and Learned; the Beautiful into the Chearful, Serene and Pastoral; the Pathetic into the Devout, Plaintive and Sorrowful.[25] In comparison with the twin categories of the Pastoral and the Heroic with which we began, Avison's system appears rather cumbersome, but it is clear that the Pastoral belongs to the Beautiful, while the Heroic – at least, by implication – should be assigned either to the Grand or to the Pathetic, according to whether the expression is grandiloquent or more intimate. In every case, this is a distinction that primarily concerns musical expression, or the *affetti*, rather than the *genera elocutionis* in any strict sense. This is why Marcello's *Salmo XXI* is not placed by Avison in the category of the Sublime but instead in the sub-category (within the Pathetic category) of the Sorrowful – a destination to which he would probably also have consigned the secular cantata *Dove fuggisti, o dio*.

Since the musical quality is elevated in both of the compositions studied, leaving aside their respective *genera*, it is not out of place to end with a laudatory quotation taken from Antonio Eximeno's book *Dell'origine e delle regole della*

---

[25] See Charles Avison, *An Essay on Musical Expression* (London, 1752), as reprinted in facsimile from the second edition of 1753 (New York, 1967); see also Roger Barnett Larsson, 'Charles Avison's "Stiles in Musical Expression"', *Music & Letters*, 63 (1982): 242–61.

musica (1774). Let these words act as a stimulus to rediscover in our modern age the value of the vocal chamber music not only of Benedetto Marcello but also of all his more interesting contemporaries:

> Nelle composizioni del Gasparini, Bononcini, Marcello e Clari appare già posto a chiaro lume il vero scopo della musica col difficile accordo dell'espressione del contrappunto. Solamente mancarono a questi compositori le parole del Metastasio; ma compensarono questa mancanza con altre bellezze, che a poco a poco vengono ora mai in disuso; eglino non erano troppo vaghi di quei tritumi di note, che senza effetto particolare straccavano le braccia de' sonatori; ma ogni nota era una pennellata di maestro, che richiedeva nell'esecutore somma esattezza, abilità e buon gusto.[26]

---

[26] Antonio Eximeno, *Dell'origine e delle regole della musica, colla storia del suo progresso, decadenza e rinnovazione* (Rome, 1774), also reprinted in facsimile (Hildesheim, Zürich and New York, 1983), p. 439: 'In the works of Gasparini, Bononcini, Marcello and Clari we already see clearly enunciated the true purpose of music, reconciled with difficulty to the expression of counterpoint. These composers merely lacked the words of Metastasio, but they compensated for this lack with other beauties, which today are passing little by little into disuse; they were not over-enamoured of those floods of notes that, without making any particular effect, used to weary the arms of the players; but every note was a the brush-stroke of a master, which demanded of the performer the highest precision, proficiency and good taste'.

Chapter 8

Investigations into the Cantata in Naples During the First Half of the Eighteenth Century: The Cantatas by Leonardo Vinci Contained in a 'Neapolitan' Manuscript[1]

Giulia Veneziano

The 'Neapolitan' cantata: problems of definition

The abundance of sources related to the operas of Neapolitan composers from the first half of the eighteenth century has tended to place in the shade their contribution to the genre of the cantata, which nevertheless is considerable, to judge from the quantity of surviving manuscripts preserved in libraries all over Europe. Although a portion of this production has received its due consideration in connection with the history of chamber music of the mid-eighteenth century, there remain many cantatas by Neapolitan composers whose purpose and destination are not settled. My research into the secular cantatas of Leonardo Vinci has thrown up a few questions that raise the problem of how these works can be fitted in, in stylistic terms, to what one understands as 'Neapolitan' music. Is there, in fact, a kind of cantata that one may accurately describe as Neapolitan? If so, what are the elements that make this cantata Neapolitan? Is it the place of composition? The place of performance? The place where the composer who wrote it was born or educated? Something about the performance practice applied to it? A distinctive musical style? Regarding the chamber cantata as it existed in Neapolitan salons during the last years of the Spanish vice-regency (up to 1707) and during the ensuing period of Austrian rule (up to 1734), there have not yet been any comprehensive studies, and hardly anything is known about the authorship of the literary texts and the patterns of patronage.[2] In this connection, the case of Leonardo Vinci is especially

---

[1] This chapter arises from my continuing research into the cantata in Naples, and in particular into Leonardo Vinci, which I have undertaken towards a doctoral thesis at the University of Zaragoza under Juan José Carreras, whom I would like to thank warmly for his encouragement of my research. I must also thank Dinko Fabris for a long exchange of ideas, enthusiams and research findings concerning Naples and its siren Partenope.

[2] To the bibliography by Teresa M. Gialdroni, 'Bibliografía della cantata da camera italiana (1620–1740 ca.)', in *Le fonti musicali in Italia. Studi e ricerche*, 4, 1990, pp. 31–

significant, for despite the existence today of competent studies undertaken by experts in the genre, the discovery of some cantatas by Vinci in Spanish archives reveals that much remains to be investigated not only with regard to the original function of these works but also concerning how they were adapted and reused in different contexts.

Preliminary historical considerations

A study of the Neapolitan chamber cantata cannot dispense with a few preliminary historically oriented remarks, especially in relation to the concepts of 'Neapolitan music' and a 'Neapolitan School'. Since the repertory of cantatas was intended for immediate practical use, it is essential to locate it in a well-defined cultural context that was also its original destination.

Any definition of a Neapolitan cantata has, as its first task, to take on board the features that historians have identified as characteristic of music composed in Naples and featuring a distinctive style associated with the city or, slightly more broadly, with a Neapolitan School. This notion has been inseparable, in the past, from an idealization linked to the myth of Naples as a centre of exceptionally intense and fruitful musical activity, a rosy picture that has been challenged, albeit cautiously, by some modern musicologists.[3] Starting with the *General History of Music* of Charles Burney, who wished to draw attention to the musical ferment that he had personally witnessed at Naples in 1770 on his musical tour, the term was used to describe a compositional style, the *stile napoletano*, especially in connection with the operatic domain.[4] After 1961, when, at a conference of the International Musicological Society held in New York, the question was

---

131, must be added the update by Colin Timms: 'The Italian Cantata since 1945: Progress and Prospects', in Francesco Fanna and Michael Talbot (eds), *Cinquant'anni di produzioni e consumi della musica dell'età di Vivaldi, 1947–1997* (Florence, 1998), pp. 75–93, at pp. 87–93.

[3] An examination of the present state of knowledge and opinion regarding the historiographical problems attendant on the so-called Neapolitan School was made by Dinko Fabris and the present writer at a seminar held at the Conservatorio di Musica 'Gesualdo da Venosa' in Potenza, in collaboration with the Menna Foundation of Salerno, during the academic year 2006/07: their resulting paper, 'Mito e realtà della cosiddetta "scuola napoletana"', is published in Fulvio Artiano and Clementina Cantillo (eds), *Forme del linguaggio musicale tra contemporaneità e tradizione* (Potenza, 2009), pp. 33–48.

[4] Indeed, Burney, in his *General History*, entitled his chapter on Naples 'Progress of the Musical Drama at Naples, and Account of the eminent Composers and School of Counterpoint of that city', thereby focusing attention on the common stylistic characteristics of the school of counterpoint (in the wider sense of 'composition') of the Neapolitan conservatories as a collective. This was the *fons et origo* of the idea of a 'Neapolitan School'. See Charles Burney, *A General History of Music from the Earliest Ages to the Present Period*, 4 vols (London, 1776–89), vol. 4, p. 544.

confronted at a round table session devoted to the Neapolitan operatic tradition, scholars began to speak, more cautiously, of a 'so-called' Neapolitan School.[5] Nevertheless, the common milieu shared by the composers who studied, taught and wrote music in the Naples of the four conservatories during the sixteenth to eighteenth centuries offers a scholar of our day the possibility of referring unapologetically to a Neapolitan School in the narrower sense of a model of didactic transmission, a musical-pedagogic tradition passed down within a single city from master to pupil, regardless of any stylistic factors.[6] The Parthenopaean mythography of the nineteenth century reinforced this idea in a decisive way, sometimes distorting – not always unconsciously – its original meaning. Among the most blatant inventions was the identification of Alessandro Scarlatti as the 'father' of the Neapolitan School. However, musicologists of the mid-twentieth century remained by and large comfortable with the concept of a Neapolitan School in the sense that, prior to the studies of Francesco Degrada, they regarded Naples as the home of a well-defined musical style.[7] Wisely, Michael F. Robinson

---

[5] See Dinko Fabris and Giulia Veneziano, 'Mito e realtà', where reference is made, in chronological order, to the studies of, and positions taken by, Francesco Florimo, Salvatore di Giacomo, Ulisse Prota-Giurleo, Guido Pannain, Hugo Riemann, Rudolf Gerber, Robert Haas, Manfred Bukofzer, Helmut Hucke, Edward O. D. Downes, Michael Robinson and Francesco Degrada; also the contributions made at the 1982 conference of the Società Italiana di Musicología published in Lorenzo Bianconi and Renato Bossa (eds), *Musica e cultura a Napoli dal XV al XIX secolo* (Florence, 1983).

[6] This is the point of departure for the innovative conception of the *Scuola napoletana* developed by Dinko Fabris in an impressive monograph centred on Francesco Provenzale: *Music in Seventeenth-Century Naples: Francesco Provenzale (1624–1704)* (Aldershot, 2007).

[7] The historical reality of a Neapolitan school or opera was challenged by Francesco Degrada, who argued that a pedagogical practice or musical style specifically linked to Naples and independent of music produced in other centres, such as Venice, Florence and Bologna, could not be shown to exist. The perceived primacy of Naples, in Degrada's view, was an artifical historiographical construct. He identified as specifically Neapolitan contributions only the locally produced comic opera of the seventeenth and eighteenth centuries, the literary tradition of texts in Neapolitan dialect, the *dramma sacro*, the *Comedia de santos* and the Spanish theatre cultivated in the city. In the final analysis, Degrada proposed no simple solution to the problem but urged the concepts of a Neapolitan school and style to be treated with more circumspection and attention to parallel developments in other important European centres of the time, without losing sight of the prime need to investigate historical and aesthetic fact in its 'peculiare e irripetibile individualità' ('particular and unrepeatable individuality'). See, for instance, Francesco Degrada, '"Scuola napoletana" e "opera napoletana": nascita, sviluppo e prospettive di un concetto storiografico', in Carlo Marinelli Roscioni (ed.), *Il teatro di S. Carlo: la cronologia 1737–1987* (Naples, 1987), pp. 9–20. Other notable sceptics have been Walther Müller, in *Johann Adolf Hasse als Kirchenkomponist* (Leipzig, 1911), who emphasized the pan-Italian dimension of musical style in the eighteenth century, and Hellmuth Christian Wolff, whose influential article 'Das Märchen von der neapolitanischen Oper und Metastasio' ('The Fairy-Tale of Neapolitan

advocated using the term 'Neapolitan' only for composers who had a close, personal and significant contact with the city.[8] In his essay 'The Neapolitans in Venice' (1995), Reinhard Strohm returned to the problem of the term 'school' as commonly used in reference to a peculiarly Neapolitan style, and traced the history of the musicographical and musicological traditions that supported this thesis.[9] The high reputation of music written by Neapolitan composers, according to Strohm, was due to the Europe-wide success among their contemporaries of those of their operas that were performed not necessarily in their native city but at Venice, a musical entrepôt linking Italy to transalpine Europe and a barometer of the artistic climate of the time.

Modern scholars still tend to associate the Neapolitan provenance of music and its most prominent composers with an assumed common style, for which the appropriate term remains, as before, 'Neapolitan'. Indeed, the high quality of the music produced by such composers as Leo, Porpora, Vinci and Hasse has sharpened the image of a Neapolitan School as a hothouse of musical talent trained for composition in a special stylistic manner different from that current in other Italian cities.

The problem of identifying this Neapolitan repertory extends to all genres cultivated in Naples from the second half of the seventeenth century to the end of the eighteenth century, and perhaps beyond. If one concentrates on opera composed at Naples, and in particular on operatic arias, avenues of research are opened up that may possibly lead to the identification of compositional commonalities linking all the composers active in the city and representing the Neapolitan 'brand' throughout Europe. For this purpose, it would be useful to examine the compositional tendencies of Neapolitan composers vis-à-vis those of their contemporaries in an attempt to isolate the stylistic features employed in so universal and basic a musical structure as the aria of an opera, a cantata or a serenata. Quite clearly, an analytical approach[10] enables us to distinguish characteristics relating, for example, to the *concertato* use of the continuo instruments, to the choice of two,

---

Opera and Metastasio'), *Analecta musicologica*, 9 (1970): 94–111, gives away the gist of its conclusion in its very title.

[8] Michael F. Robinson, *Naples and Neapolitan Opera* (Oxford, 1972), also translated into Italian under the provocative title of *Opera napoletana: storia e geografia di un'idea musicale settecentesca* (Venice,1984, trans. Giovanni Morelli and Luca Zoppelli).

[9] Reinhard Strohm, 'The Neapolitans in Venice', in Iain Fenlon and Tim Carter (eds), '*Con che soavità': Studies in Italian Opera, Song, and Dance, 1500–1740* (Oxford, 1995), pp. 249–74.

[10] Of interest is the analytical method employed by Tonino Battista in a paper relevant to Vinci written jointly with Nicolò Maccavino: '*Il ritratto dell'eroe* (Venezia,1726): una serenata di Giovanni Porta dedicata al Cardinale Ottoboni falsamente attribuita a Leonardo Vinci', in Gaetano Pitarresi (ed.), *Leonardo Vinci e il suo tempo. Atti dei convegni internazionali di studi (Reggio Calabria, 10–12 giugno 2002; 4–5 giugno 2006)* (Reggio Calabria, 2004), pp. 339–96. The paper analyses serenata arias by Vinci, Vivaldi, Handel and Porta, comparing statistical data and drawing convincing conclusions.

three or four parts for the accompaniment, or to the instrumental doubling of the voice (or contrapuntal interplay between voice and accompaniment), as we encounter them in the composers under investigation.[11] Carolyn Gianturco has identified certain peculiarities of the Neapolitan style of the Baroque period.[12] These include the employment of the harpsichord not merely in a continuo role but also as a concertante instrument for the purpose of bringing out the meaning of the literary text, thereby giving rise to a melodic line that on many occasions dialogues with the vocal part.[13] The orchestra, too, assigns special functions to the instruments.[14] The vocal part, finally, is very articulated, with *fioriture* and displays of virtuosity sometimes employing surprising and interesting intervals; the line is characterized not so much by the reiteration of melodic fragments as by concatenations of several motives that join forces to create the musical phrase and period. Gianturco emphasizes how wedded the 'Neapolitans' are to dotted rhythmic figures alternating long and short notes, 'producing a characteristic effect peculiar to their music. Rests frequently punctuate phrases, as though to suggest conversation among the vocal and instrumental forces. Because downbeats are not stressed, the result is of lightness and movement, but not the smooth and linear style of Venetian composers'.[15] In her view, it was these characteristics, first brought to wider public notice by alumni of the Neapolitan conservatories, that won the hearts of audiences all over Europe.

Further thoughts leading in the same direction are provided by Michael Talbot, who, writing about the cantatas of Antonio Vivaldi, which have traditionally been described (without too much reflection) as 'Neapolitan' in a general sense, observes: 'Modern musicology is shy of using this label [Neapolitan] with too broad a meaning, especially when the composers in question have no obvious connection with Naples. However, a good case can be made for identifying as genuinely "Neapolitan" the *galant* style in its early phase (the second half of the

---

[11] See Maccavino and Battista, 'Il ritratto dell'eroe', pp. 388–9, for the compositional parameters chosen for analysis and the results obtained; the paper also draws on data published in Michael Collins, 'L'orchestra nelle opere di Vivaldi', in Antonio Fanna and Giovanni Morelli (eds), *Nuovi studi vivaldiani. Edizione e cronologia critica delle opere* (Florence, 1988), pp. 285–312.

[12] Carolyn Gianturco, 'Naples: A City of Entertainment', in George J. Buelow (ed.), *Man & Music: The Late Baroque Era from the 1680s to 1740* (London, 1993), pp. 94–127.

[13] The same characteristic informs the cantatas of certain Neapolitan composers, including those of Francesco Mancini preserved in German sources, according to a paper read by Helen Geyer at the Thirteenth Annual Conference of the Società Italiana di Musicologia (Turin, 2006).

[14] We know, for instance, that four-part writing employing the viola (often named 'violetta' in the manuscripts) was common in Naples, as we indeed discover in several Neapolitan sources containing Vinci's music.

[15] Gianturco, 'Naples: A City of Entertainment', p. 110, which cites, in addition, Lorenzo Bianconi and Thomas Walker, 'Production, Consumption and Political Function of Seventeenth-Century Italian Opera', *Early Music History*, 4 (1984): 209–96, at 247.

1720s and the 1730s), when three masters trained in that city, Leo, Vinci and Porpora, almost overnight achieved dominance over the Italian stage and by so doing imparted a new stylistic inflection to vocal music of all the kinds, including the cantata. According to that criterion, Vivaldi's cantatas written before c.1725 may be regarded as "pre-Neapolitan", and his later cantatas as "Neapolitan"'.[16]

Notwithstanding such methodological precautions, it would appear by today's standards rather unwise to apply the label 'Neapolitan' *tout court* to a cantata composed by a member of the Neapolitan School in the absence of a clear destination made explicit in the source, and without knowledge of who commissioned it and of where and when it was performed – information only rarely provided in cantata manuscripts.

But it is sometimes possible to confirm the Neapolitan identity of a cantata by piecing together all the isolated pieces of information derived from the study of a work, or group of works, and of the composer. A new and convincing investigative approach was recently adopted by Teresa Gialdroni and Agostino Ziino in their study of a new source for a cantata by Hasse, in which a series of observations about the nature of the music, in combination with the latest facts about the composer's period of activity in Naples, enabled them to pinpoint certain characteristics that established the 'Neapolitan-ness' of the works examined.[17] In the light of all these problems, my own work over almost ten years on Leonardo Vinci's cantatas has led me to exercise much caution in viewing them as 'Neapolitan' in any meaningful sense.

Leonardo Vinci's cantatas

The surviving cantatas of Vinci do not match in quantity the production of works in this genre by some of his contemporaries similarly associated with Naples (one thinks of those of the long-lived Alessandro Scarlatti, or of Mancini and Porpora), but, given the brevity of Vinci's life (he was born in Strongoli around 1690 and died at Naples in 1730), this is not surprising. His career took him from Naples to Rome and subsequently to Venice, a city that, over and above the success enjoyed by his operas among the public, launched their export abroad. The salient points of his musical style were accurately appreciated already by his contemporaries, to the extent that the historiographical tradition from Burney onwards has assigned to Vinci a decisive role in the stylistic transformation that Neapolitan (and other) composers underwent in the 1720s. According to Burney

---

[16] Michael Talbot, *The Chamber Cantatas of Antonio Vivaldi* (Woodbridge, 2006), p. 14.

[17] Teresa M. Gialdroni and Agostino Ziino, 'Un'altra fonte per *Povero giglio, oh Dio!* e il problema della datazione di alcune cantate "napoletane" di Hasse', in Michael Jahn and Angela Pachovsky (eds), *Figaro là, Figaro qua. Gedenkschrift Leopold M. Kantner (1932–2004)* (Vienna, 2006), pp. 253–77.

himself, the birth of the Neapolitan school was inseparable from that of the *stile galante*. So the true founding father of the school was to be found not in Scarlatti but in Vinci, whose compositions highlighted the vocal parts, which became much more complex in comparison with those of his predecessors, thereby freeing arias from the tyranny of counterpoint.[18]

The case of Vinci's cantatas is instructive also for the surprises that it has thrown up in the course of my research. Some surviving sources for the cantatas have turned up, sometimes as *unica*, in Spain, in a church archive.[19] The destination of these works, originating in the secular sphere, can be inferred from their 'double' literary text in Spanish: one 'divina' in nature and thus sacred; the other described as 'humano' and thus secular, following the time-honoured practice of Spanish *villancicos*. So these 'Neapolitan' cantatas of Vinci, as a result of the contemporary circulation of musical sources, musicians and performers, penetrated Spain, where their nature as secular compositions underwent change. Becoming adapted to the needs of their new environment, they were used as a vehicle for the importation of Italian music into Spain at the start of the eighteenth century, when, in locally produced *villancicos*, we find the earliest recommendations to adopt a performance style 'al uso del Italia'.[20]

---

[18] See Francesco Degrada, 'L'opera napoletana', in Alberto Basso (ed.), *Storia dell'opera*, 6 vols (Turin, 1977), vol. 1, pp. 237–332, at p. 239, where this scholar shows how, by the very act of making Vinci the harbinger of the new style, Burney presupposed the existence of a stylistic rupture between Alessandro Scarlatti and the Neapolitan composers of the next generation.

[19] This is the archive of the Cathedral (the *Virgen del Pilar*) of Zaragoza (E-Zac), which holds a collection of cantatas by Neapolitan composers, described by the present writer in 'Un Corpus de cantatas Napolitanas del siglo XVIII en Zaragoza: Problemas de difusión del repertorio italiano en España', *Artigrama. Revista del Departamento de Historia del Arte de la Universidad de Zaragoza*, 12 (1996–97): 277–91.

[20] See Álvaro Torrente, 'The Sacred Villancico in Early Eighteenth-Century Spain: The Repertory of Salamanca Cathedral' (PhD thesis, Cambridge, 1997), p. 110, and Tess Knighton and Álvaro Torrente (eds), *Devotional Music in the Iberian World: The Villancico and Related Genres* (Aldershot, 2007). See also Miguel Ángel Marín, *Music on the Margin: Urban Musical Life in Eighteenth-century Jaca (Spain)* (Kassel, 2002), pp. 246–53. The *villancico* genre was one of those native to Spain best suited to absorb foreign elements. In the first years of the seventeenth century 'recitativi' and 'arie' – together with other imports bearing labels such as 'minuetto', 'grave'and 'fuga' – began to be used in combination with the traditional 'introducción', 'estribillo' and 'coplas', thereby inaugurating a transformation in the genre that, in the space of about twenty years, would revolutionize its structure. The question of the reception of Italian music in Spain has been treated by Juan José Carreras in several of his writings, among which are 'Tra la Sicilia e la Penisola iberica: il barone d'Astorga alla corte di Filippo V di Spagna', *Avidi Lumi*, 5 (14 February 2002): 59–67; 'Amores difíciles: la ópera de corte en la España del siglo XVIII', in Emilio Casares Rodicio and Álvaro Torrente (eds), *La ópera en España e Hispanoamérica. Actas del Congreso Internacional (Madrid, 29.XI/3.XII de 1999)* (Madrid, 2001), pp. 205–30; and, for a critical historiographical account, 'Hijos de Pedrell. La historiografía musical

Manuscript 34.5.23 (Cantate 304) of the Biblioteca del Conservatorio 'S. Pietro a Majella' of Naples

The cantatas of a Neapolitan composer such as Vinci therefore embody the problematic nature of the questions raised in previous discussions. In the Biblioteca del Conservatorio di Musica 'S. Pietro a Majella', Naples, we encounter the manuscript 34.5.23 (also known as Cantate 304), a composite volume (or 'binder's collection', to use the appropriate bibliographical term) that contains mostly cantatas and loose arias attributed to Vinci. The source abounds in pieces of information that, when interpreted in the chosen way, allow us to develop hypotheses concerning the existence of a truly 'Neapolitan' cantata. Of the 27 cantatas, both of secure and of insecure attribution, contained in the canon of Vinci's compositions, as many as six are transmitted by this single Neapolitan source, one even in duplicate.[21]

A brief description of the manuscript and some remarks about its history will help to evaluate its content. An anthology, as we said, of arias and cantatas by Vinci, it was identified already in the old Gasperini–Gallo catalogue as follows: 'Cantate a 1 voce con e senza accomp. di Strum. Sono unite a vari pezzi a 1 e a più voci dello stesso Autore ...', to which was appended the textual incipits of the cantatas and detached arias.[22] The title page of the manuscript bears the legend: 'Vinci | Musica div[ers]a | Pezzi 24'. Effectively, the collection contains twenty-four gatherings (fascicles) of diverse provenance brought together between two covers by the archivist Francesco Rondinella in the nineteenth century. Rondinella renumbered the folios of the assembled gatherings consecutively from 1 to 173 (the original foliation is no longer always visible on account of the trimming of the margins in preparation for binding), and he also gave a serial number to the gatherings making up the volume, even though some of them possessed a different original number. Table 8.1 displays the content of the manuscript, giving the old

---

española y sus orígenes nacionalistas (1780–1980)', *Il Saggiatore Musicale*, 8 (2001): 123–73.

[21] In forming a list of Vinci's cantatas, I have cross-checked against several sources: Kurt Markstrom's entry for Vinci in the 2001 edition of Stanley Sadie and John Tyrrell (eds), *The New Grove Dictionary of Music and Musicians*, 2nd edn (London, 2001) vol. 26, pp. 654–7; Teresa M. Gialdroni, 'Vinci "operista" autore di cantate', in Francesco Luisi (ed.), *Studi in onore di Giulio Cattin* (Rome, 1990), pp. 307–29; same author, 'Leonardo Vinci e la cantata spirituale a Napoli nella prima metà del Settecento', in Agostino Ziino (ed.), *Musica senza aggettivi: studi per Fedele d'Amico* (Florence, 1991), pp. 123–43; Giulia Veneziano, 'Un Corpus de cantatas Napolitanas del siglo XVIII en Zaragoza: Problemas de difusión del repertorio italiano en España'.

[22] Guido Gasperini and Franca Gallo, *Catalogo delle opere musicali teoriche e pratiche di autori vissuti sino ai primi decenni del secolo XIX, esistenti nelle biblioteche e negli archivi pubblici e privati d'Italia. Città di Napoli, Biblioteca del R. Conservatorio di Musica di S. Pietro a Majella*, serie X (Parma, 1934), p. 379.

(where ascertainable) and new foliation and the new numbering of the gatherings, with some additional comments in the last column.

In this manuscript at least three different provenances can be identified:

1. Gatherings 5, 6 and 13, formerly numbered 'Nc.' 482, 483 and 486, these marks of identification being written in the same hand and ink, and containing three cantatas.
2. The gatherings running from 16 to 22, inclusive, formerly known as 'Vinci 1–7'. These are all bibliographically similar and contain individual arias taken from a single Vinci opera.
3. The remaining gatherings are of heterogeneous provenance.

The cantatas contained in the volume are listed in Table 8.2, which identifies the concordances and transcribes the original title as it appears at the head of the relevant gathering.

Not many of Vinci's cantatas can be dated on the basis of indications given in individual manuscripts. Ms. 34-5-23 is no exception. But we can derive useful information from the identification of a chronological anchorage point in just a single composition of the collection, which may enable us to date the contents of the volume as a whole approximately.[23] In the present case, however, we know that the volume was put together by the previously mentioned Francesco Rondinella, deputy archivist of the Real Collegio di Musica of Naples from 1826 to 1888 (coincident with the activity there of the librarian Francesco Florimo). Evidence of his hand, as we saw, is recognizable within this manuscript, as it is in many of the anthology-like collections today in the possession of the Conservatorio 'S. Pietro a Majella'.[24] To draw wider chronological conclusions for the contents of the volume as a whole from the dating of a single work is, of course, a risky business when, as here, one is dealing with a binder's collection. The single chronological pointer that we possess in the present instance is a date of composition (readable as either 1703 or 1708) entered at the end of the cantata *Pietosa l'aurora in cielo*, to which we will return shortly.

---

[23] Once more, I refer the reader to the streamlined methodology adopted by Teresa M. Gialdroni and Agostino Ziino in 'Un'altra fonte per *Povero giglio, oh Dio!*', supported by cross-referenced data arising from studies into Hasse quoted in their essay; see also the conclusions of the study of manuscript collections in the library of the Naples Conservatorio in Mauro Amato, 'Le antologie di arie e di arie e cantate tardo-seicentesche alla Biblioteca del Conservatorio "S. Pietro a Majella" di Napoli', (doctoral dissertation, Cremona, Scuola di Paleografia Musicale, 1998, 2 vols).

[24] Many of these manuscripts once belonged to Giuseppe Sigismondo (1739–1826), who was the librarian of the Conservatorio della Pietà dei Turchini, to which institution he donated many of his manuscripts; these later passed to the library of the Real Collegio di Napoli, today the Conservatorio 'S. Pietro a Majella'.

Table 8.1 The contents of ms. I-Nc, 34.5.23 (Cantate 304).*

Gathering number	Old numbering (where extant)	Folios	Old foliation (where extant)	Genre	Title	Scoring	Comments
1		1–16v	cropped	Cantata	*Mesta, oh Dio, fra queste selve*	S, 2 vl, bc	'con violetta' added later, but no staff provided
2		17v–24		Cantata	*Mesta, oh Dio, fra queste selve*	S, 2 vl, violetta, bc	
3		25–27		Aria	*Vò solcando un mar crudele*	S, 2 vl, bc;	[Arbace, *Artaserse*, I.15. Rome, Alibert, 1730]
4		27v–28v		Aria	*Prigioniera abbandonata*		'Pergolese' [*Adriano in Siria*, 1734]
		29–35		Aria	*Vò solcando un mar crudele*	S, 2 vl, vla, bc	[Arbace, *Artaserse*, I.15. Rome, Alibert, 1730]
5	Nc. 482 #2	37–44		Cantata	*È pure un gran portento*	S, bc	
6	Nc. 483	45–48		Cantata	*Veggo la selva e 'l monte*	S, bc	
7		49–62	21–34	Duetto	*Tu vuoi ch'io viva, o cara*	S, S, 2 vl, violetta, bc	'Astroa, Caffarelli [Mandane, Arbace, *Artaserse*, III.7. Rome, 1730, Naples, 1738 and 1743]
8		63–68v	42–48	Duetto	*Tu vuoi ch'io viva, o cara*	S, S, 2 vl, bc	[Mandane, Arbace, *Artaserse*, III.7. Rome, 1730, Naples 1738 and 1743]
9		69–72v		Duetto	*Tu vuoi ch'io viva, o cara*	S, S, 2 vl, bc	[Mandane, Arbace, *Artaserse*, III.7. Rome, 1730, Naples 1738 and 1743]
10	3	73–78v		Aria	*So che godendo vai*	S, 2 vl, vla, bc	[Marzia, *Catone in Utica*, II.13. Rome, 1728; Naples, 1732]
11	4	79–84v		Aria	*Mi credi spietata*	S, 2 vl, vla, bc	[Mandane, *Artaserse*, III.5. Rome, Alibert, 1730; Naples, 1738 and 1743]
12		85–94v		Aria	*Vò solcando un mar crudele*	S, 2 vl, Violetta, bc	[Arbace, *Artaserse*, I.15. Rome, Alibert, 1730]

13	Nc. 486	95–100	1–6	Cantata	Mi costa tante lacrime	S, bc	[Appio, Valeria, *La caduta dei Decemviri*, III.11, Naples, S. Bartolomeo, 1727]
14		101–104	15–18	Duetto	Sarò fedele a te	S, A, 2 vl, bc	terminal annotation: '28 luglio 1708' (or '1703')
15		105–108	19–22	Cantata	Pietosa l'aurora in cielo	S, bc	
16	Vinci 1	109–113v	1–6v	Aria	Barbaro, prendi e suona	A, 2 vl, vla, bc	[Andromaca, *Astianatte*, I.10. Naples, 1725]
17	Vinci 2	114–119v	7–12v	Aria	Luci spietate, voi m'insegnate	A, 2 vl, vla	[Pirro, *Astianatte*, II.3. Naples, 1725]
18	Vinci 3	120–127	13–20	Aria	Al patrio lido ritornerò	S, 2 vl, vla, bc	[Ermione, *Astianatte*, I.8. Naples, 1725]
19	Vinci 4	128–133	21–26	Aria	Un raggio di speme	S, 2 vl, vla, bc	[Oreste, *Astianatte*, I.5. Naples, 1725]
20	Vinci 5	134–139v	27–32v	Aria	Alma grande nata al soglio	A, 2 vl, vla, bc	[Pirro, *Astianatte*, I.3. Naples, 1725]
21	Vinci 6	140–145v	33–38v	Aria	Misera si, non vile	A, 2 vl, vla, bc	[Andromaca, *Astianatte*, I.1. Naples, 1725]
22	Vinci 7	146–151	39–44	Aria	Temi di vendicarti	S, 2 vl, violetta, corni da caccia, bc	[Oreste, *Astianatte*, II.6. Naples, 1725]
23		152–159v	35–42	Duetto	Cara, l'averso [sic] fato	S, A, 2 vl, bc	'Duetto del Sig.' [name deleted]
24		160–173	43–56	Cantata	Dite, vedeste forse	S, 2 vl, bc	

* In the 'Comments' column I note the provenance of each operatic aria, with mention of the act and scene, the character who sings it and the date of the opera's first performance and of any subsequent performances relevant to the investigation.

Table 8.2   Leonardo Vinci's Neapolitan cantatas in I-Nc, ms. 34.5.23 (Cantate 304) and their concordances.*

No.	Cantatas in I-Nc, ms. 34.5.23 (Cantate 304)	Folios	Scoring	Key	Structure	Concordances	Comments	Possible datings
1	*Mesta, oh Dio*	1–16v (no. 1);	S, 2 vl, bc	a	ARA		'Cantata a Voce Sola con VV. Del Sig.r Leonardo Vinci'	1724–29
2	*Mesta, oh Dio*	17–24 (no. 2)	S, 2 vl, bc	a			'Cantata con VV. Del Sig.r Vinci'. 'con Violetta'	
			S	g		I-Bc, DD 46	'Del Sig.r Leonardo Vinci'	
			S	g		E-Zac, 117/870	'Cantata a Voce Sola con stromenti. Del sig. re Leonardo Vinci'. With double text (one in Spanish as *Triste, ausente*)	
			S	a		I-MC, 6-B-20/1a (formerly 126 E 18 op. 1)	'Cantata con VV del Sig.r Leonardo Vinci'. Provenance V. Bovio	
			A	f		I-MC, 6-E-3/14 (formerly 126 F 21, op 13)	'Cantata con strumenti / Sig. Vinci per la Sig.ra Tesi' (viola has staff void of notes). Provenance V. Bovio	
			A	?		A-Wgm, VI 17270		
			S	g		B-Br, Ms II 3952 Mus Fétis 2431, no. 8		
			S	g		D-Bsb, 22383, Nr. 1	'del Sig. Vinci'. Provenance C. D. Ebeling	
			A	f		D-MÜs, Hs 4282	'Del Sig.r Leonardo Vinci'	
			A	f		D-WD, 767 GB-Lbl, Add. 31,604	'Cantata del Sig. Leonardo Vinci' ms. dated 1739	
			A	d		GB-Lcm, Ms. 695	'Cantata con V.V. Del Sig.r Leonardo Vinci'	

			S	g			'Cantata a Solo Del Sig:re Leonardo Vinci'
			S	g		US- FAy, Lewis Walpole coll., Quarto MS 532 MS 3	'Cantata spirituale con V.V. à C. Solo. Vinci. S. Pietro' (text opening: *Dove, oh Dio*)	late
3	È pure un gran portento	37–44 (no. 5)	S, bc	A	RARA	I- Ac, Ms. 324/2	'Del Sig.r Leonardo / Vinci'
4	†*Veggo la selva e 'l monte* Text: P. Metastasio	45–48 (no. 6)	S, bc	e	RARA		'Cantata a Voce Sola'
			S	d		E-Mn, M 2245	'Cantata a voce sola Del Sig. Carlo Benati' (attr. Carlo Benati)
			S	d		D-MÜs, Hs 861 (Nr. 14)	
			S	g		I-Nc, Cantate 335² (formerly 22.2.24)	'Del S.r Benati'
5	*Mi costa tante lacrime*	95–100 (no. 13)	S, bc	E♭	ARA	A-Wn, SA.67.A.25, Nr.8	'Cantata a Voce sola di Soprano / Del Sig.r Leonardo Vinci'
6	†*Pietosa l'aurora in cielo*	105–108 (no. 15)	S, bc	B♭	RARA		at end: '27 luglio 1703' (or '1708')	1703 or 1708
7	*Dite, vedeste forse*	160–173 (no. 24)	S, 2 vl, bc	B♭	RARA		'Cantata a Voce Sola con Violini/del Sig.r Leonardo Leo Vinci' ('Leo' deleted, then replaced by 'Vinci')	172?

*   Where keys are not given, the information has not yet been obtained.
†   The attribution of these cantatas is considered doubtful.

Table 8.2 lists the cantatas in the order in which they appear in the manuscript 34.5.23 (Cantate 304).[25] The cantata *Mesta, oh Dio, fra queste selve*, in both first and second place, does not raise any doubts over authorship: in both copies contained in the Naples manuscript the attribution is to 'Sig. Vinci'. The scoring with violins is augmented by the subsequently entered direction 'con Violetta' in the second copy (gathering 2): in actual fact, the score, with its four staves, does not directly reflect the participation of this instrument, which, following an *ad libitum* practice current in Neapolitan (and other) music of the time, will presumably have doubled the bass part, either at the same pitch or, more often, an octave above.[26] Indeed, the same instrument is called for also in one of two Vinci cantata sources preserved in the library of the abbey of Montecassino, 6-E-3/14 (dating from the first half of the eighteenth century), where the stave for viola is added but left void of notes.[27] *Mesta, oh Dio* is perhaps an exceptional case on account of the number of sources preserving it, as Table 8.2 makes clear. The English source of this cantata, GB-Lbl, Add. 31,604, ff. 2–17, is the only one to offer an approximate date, thanks to an estimate (1739) given in the manuscript containing it (1739).[28] This cannot be a date of composition, Vinci having died in 1730, and must refer instead to a date

---

[25] The shelfmarks of the manuscripts of the library of the Naples Conservatorio have followed a tortuous path as a result of problems affecting the administration of such a precious heritage that have surfaced over the years, and on account of the vicissitudes that it has had to undergo. The shelfmarks composed of three numbers – such as that of the manuscript under present discussion, 35.4.23 – refer to an old system of storage where the first number identified the bookcase (*pluteo*), the second the shelf, and the third the position within the shelf; such numbers were allocated to the manuscripts after their transfer from the Collegio di Musica dal Convento di S. Sebastiano to S. Pietro a Majella in 1826. When the library grew in size, the older material was removed to a new upper floor, where is was reclassified according to genre: in this system, 'Rari' refers to autograph manuscripts, operatic scores, madrigals, librettos and collections of arias from identified works; there are also sections for 'Oratori', 'Musica religiosa', 'Musica strumentale' and 'Arie e Cantate' ordered according to the Gasperini–Gallo catalogue of 1934 (see note 21, earlier). From these groups some manuscripts were kept apart, since they gave rise to problems of classification, not being describable in simple terms either as arias or as cantatas. For them, the special category of so-called 'Cantate Ibride' ('Hybrid Cantatas') was created. But in 1993, as a result of a further updating of the library's catalogue, a portion of the old material was returned to its old classification, with a restoration of the *pluteo* numbers running from 29 to 35.

[26] The term 'violetta' was often used in Naples to denote the alto instrument of the string family. Scoring for a four-part ensemble was very common in chamber music – and not only in Naples – in the first half of the eighteenth century. In the cantatas of the successors of Alessandro Scarlatti in Naples the four-part ensemble with continuo became the standard form of accompaniment.

[27] Giovanni Insom, *Il fondo musicale dell'archivio di Montecassino* ('Biblioteca Cassinese', 3), 2 vols (Montecassino, 2003), vol. 2, p. 1159.

[28] See Augustus Hughes-Hughes, *Catalogue of Manuscript Music in the British Museum*, 3 vols (London, 1906–09), vol. 2, p. 526, and Colin Timms, 'A New Cantata by Domenico Scarlatti (Words by Antonio Ottoboni)', in Patrizia Radicchi and Michael Burden

of copying. One indicator of especial importance for Vinci chronology, and not only for this cantata, is contained in the already mentioned Montecassino source, where, to the right of the first system, we find the words: 'Del Sig. Vinci per la Sig.ra Tesi'. This cantata was therefore written for Vittoria Tesi (Florence, 1700–Vienna, 1775), one of the most sought-after operatic contraltos of her generation. In the absence of a clear indication of the patron for whom the cantata was written or of the author of the text – in the present state of knowledge – the identification of the performer for whom the work was written assumes a special importance. Vittoria Tesi, nicknamed 'la Moretta', was to encounter Vinci and his music on several occasions in the course of her career:[29] the first known time was in 1724, when (as a *virtuosa* in the service of the prince of Parma) she sang the title role of *L'Eraclea* in Naples;[30] in 1725 she took the role of Andromaca in *Astianatte* in Naples; she subsequently interpreted Medea in the production of *Medo* at Parma in 1728 and sang in the reprise of *Farnace* in Naples in 1729, leaving aside her participation in other revivals of Vinci's operas after his death.

The wide dissemination of *Mesta, oh Dio* may be linked to the success of Vittoria Tesi as its interpreter and perhaps, more widely, as a promoter of Vinci's music generally. One thinks of the Spanish source, with Spanish text, of *Triste, ausente, en esta selva*,[31] preserved in Zaragoza (see note 21) – a testimony to the wide circulation and consumption enjoyed by a musical composition. The fourteen sources of *Mesta, oh Dio* preserved in libraries in Europe and beyond give evidence of its popularity, since they include versions transposed from the original key of F minor up to G minor, A minor and even D minor (in GB-Lcm). Vittoria Tesi sang in Madrid in 1739, summoned by Farinelli to take the role of Berenice in the *Farnace* of Francesco Corselli (Courcelle)[32] at the Teatro del Buen Retiro, where she achieved a resounding success. Perhaps she was the conduit via which the Vinci cantata written for her came to be preserved today in Zaragoza, together with other Italian cantatas held by the cathedral archive.[33]

(eds), *Florilegium Musicae. Studi in onore di Carolyn Gianturco* (Pisa, 2004), pp. 967–79. There exists a modern edition of this cantata by Alejandro Garri (Garri Editions, 2004).

[29] For this purpose, the index to singers of Claudio Sartori, *I libretti italiani a stampa dalle origini al 1800*, 7 vols (Cuneo, 1990), is invaluable.

[30] On this occasion Tesi sang opposite Farinelli in the role of Damiro; the pair appeared together the following year in Hasse's serenata *Antonio e Cleopatra*.

[31] This cantata was recorded, together with other 'Spanish' cantatas of Vinci, in connection with a musicological project undertaken in collaboration with the ensemble La Cappella della Pietà de' Turchini di Napoli, directed by Antonio Florio, for the label Opus 111-Naïve (see Chapter 12).

[32] Alongside Vittoria Tesi, in a cast hand-picked by Farinelli, were the celebrated singers Gaetano Majorano Caffarelli, Annibale Pio Fabbri and Anna Peruzzi (Sartori, no. 9750).

[33] Zaragoza was an obligatory point of transit in a journey from Italy to Spain, since it lay half-way between Barcelona and Madrid. We know also that Farinelli, returning to Italy in the aftermath of events that had forced him to leave Madrid, stopped at Zaragoza

Consisting of two arias with independent violin parts and a central recitative, the cantata is a setting of a typical bucolic text, Metastasian in inspiration, that treats of the love of Irene betrayed by Fileno.[34] The recitative, which is accompanied, mirrors the dramatic nature of the text by adopting a kind of *stile concitato* that sets in relief the dialogue between the vocal part, almost arioso-like in its syllabic and very articulated manner of setting, and the instrumental component, characterized by virtuosic passage-work that likewise responds to the sung text, with great descriptive effect.

If *Mesta, oh Dio* was indeed written originally for Vittoria Tesi Tramontini, the time-frame for its composition must be the period 1724–29, with Naples as the place of composition.

A reference to the intended performer occurs also in one other cantata by Vinci, by good fortune dated, which is not included in our Neapolitan manuscript. This is *Parto, ma con qual core*, preserved at the abbey of Montecassino under the shelfmark 6-B-20/8 (formerly 126 E 8), which is signed by its copyist, Nicolò Sche[…], and has the terminal indication 'finis 1723'. A separate title for this cantata is written in a central position at the top of the first page of the source: 'La partenza del [*sic*] Faustina'. Faustina can be no other person but the Venetian-born mezzo-soprano Faustina Bordoni (1700–81), the wife of Johann Adolf Hasse (from 1730) and a leading interpreter of settings of Metastasio's verse. In 1722 Faustina sang in Naples at S. Bartolomeo in Vinci's first serious opera, *Publio Cornelio Scipione*, forming an artistic bond with the composer so close that she was to continue to take the roles of Vincian heroines even after the composer's untimely death.[35] She remained in the city from 1721 to 1723, appearing in at least seven operas, among which were Leonardo Leo's *Bajazete* and the *Partenope* of Domenico Sarro (1722).[36] In the latter opera she sang the title role with great success, prefiguring her equal success in the same role in Vinci's *Partenope* (under the title of *Rosmira fedele*), given at S. Giovanni Grisostomo, Venice, in 1725. The cantata leaves no doubt about the identity of the subject or her activity, since

---

for three weeks in 1759 (see Giovenale Sacchi, *Vita del Cavaliere Don Carlo Broschi detto il Farinello* (Venice, 1784; modern edn Naples, 1994). It is an attractive thought that many sources of Italian music today preserved in Zaragoza may originate from the transit of singers and composers between Italy and Spain.

[34] Pietro Metastasio wrote most of his cantatas in Naples between 1719 and 1724; these were published only later in Nicola Porpora's collection entitled *All'Altezza Reale di Frederico prencipe reale di Vallia e prencipe elettorale di Hanover* (London, 1735). Further cantatas were published in the Parisian edition of Hérissant (1780–82).

[35] See Kurt Markstrom, *The Operas of Leonardo Vinci, Napoletano* (Hillsdale, 2007), pp. 99–100, and Dinko Fabris, '"Adesso se ne conoce il merito, e vivente si lacerava": la fama europea di Leonardo Vinci', in Damien Colas and Alessandro Di Profio (eds), *D'une scène à l'autre l'opéra italien en Europe*, vol. 1: *Les pérégrinations d'un genre* (Paris, 2009), pp. 85–117.

[36] See Winton Dean's entry for Faustina Bordoni in the 2001 edition of the *New Grove* (vol. 3, pp. 894–5).

it contains the phrase 'dite che Rosmira è morta' ('say that Rosmira is dead') – referring to the eventuality of her non-return to Naples. It is a grief-laden farewell to a beloved soil, where the singer declares: 'Io non porto altrove il core, benché porti altrove il pié' ('I will not take my heart elsewhere, even if I take my foot'). Even if she has to frequent other places ('altre arene'), she vows to return within three years, ther period in which 'il sole tre volte indori al Sagittario i dardi' ('the sun thrice gilds the arrows of Sagittarius'). Her parting is unwelcome but necessary: 'Partenza amara, e pur partire conviene'. Here is the complete text:

Parto, ma con qual core,	I leave, but in what state of mind
dir non lo so, se non lo dice amore!	I cannot say unless love says it!
Lungi da queste piagge,	Far from these shores,
dove fan meraviglia agli occhi miei	where nymphs and demigods
e ninfe e semidei,	delight my eyes,
il destino mi tragge in altre arene.	destiny draws me to other parts.
Partenza amara, e pur partire conviene.	A bitter parting, and yet I have to part.
Non vedrò in altro cielo,	I do not see under any other skies
sempre per me sì belle,	so many beautiful stars
scintillar tante stelle	burning so brightly for me,
per me, nemmeno all'ora bella vedrò	nor will I see dawn so resplendent
così splender l'aurora.	at dayrise.
Oh Dio, queste son pene!	Oh God, these are torments!
Partenza amara, e pur partire conviene.	A bitter parting, and yet I have to part.
Chi m'ascolta, chi mi vede,	Whoever listens to me, whoever sees me,
per mercede, si ricordi,	I beg at least
si ricordi almen di me.	to remember me.
Tutta fede, e tutta amore,	I am filled with loyalty and love,
io non porto altrove il core,	I will not take my heart elsewhere,
benché porti altrove il pié.	even if I take my foot
Ecco, mi parto, addio!	So I am leaving, adieu!
Ma, se non è vicino	But if the last of my days
l'ultimo dei miei giorni,	is not close,
far non potrà il destino	fate will not prevent me from returning
che a respirar quest'aure io non ritorni,	to breathe this air,
e se prima che il sole	and if before the sun thrice
tre volte indori al Sagittario i dardi	gilds the arrows of Sagittarius
ella a voi non si porta,	she does not return to you,
allora dite che **Rosmira** è morta.	say then that **Rosmira** is dead.

Qual ruscelletto,	Like a stream
che torna al mare,	that returns to the sea,
a voi tornare	I know that one day
un dì saprò.	I will return to you.
Del mio ritorno	Await the day
il giorno aspetto;	of my return;
tornar prometto,	I promise to return,
e tornerò!	and return I shall.

Faustina Bordoni left Naples in 1723 for Florence, a city where another source for this cantata survives, at the Conservatorio di Musica 'Luigi Cherubini'.[37] This is important evidence of the circulation of music via its itinerant performers. *Parto, ma con qual core* contains in its opening recitative a stylistic feature that links it to one of the cantatas in the Neapolitan manuscript 34.5.23, (Cantate 304[5]), incorrectly deemed spurious by the revised (2001) *New Grove Dictionary of Music and Musicians*, despite the clear indication of authorship in the sole surviving source, that in Naples, which is headed: *È pure un gran portento | Cantata | Del Sig.r Leonardo | Vinci*. As in the previous cantata, where lines 7 and 14 of the opening recitative have the same text, 'Partenza amara, e pur partire conviene', and the same melodic shape, in *È pure un gran portento* lines 6 and 12 of the first recitative and line 8 of the second recitative have almost identical words and music: 'Questa non è già meraviglia, Amore' and 'Questa è tua nuova meraviglia, Amore'('This is no new marvel, Love' and 'This is your new marvel, Love'). The result is a melodic circularity, a kind of 'rondeau-recitative' that interrupts the flow of freely mixed seven-syllable and eleven-syllable lines to introduce a recognizable melodic refrain. Similarly, the two arias of *È pure un gran portento*, one marked *Lento* and the other *Andante*, display the trademarks of Vinci, with a continuo bass that often dialogues with the vocal part, an instrumental introduction that anticipates the opening vocal period and slowly moving harmonies, dotted rhythms, frequent modulations and rather inventive sequences that suggest maturity as a composer.

Some valuable information may be gleaned from the title page of *Mi costa tante lacrime*, which occupies ff. 95–100 of manuscript. 34.5.23 and comprises gathering 13 of the volume. This cantata belongs to group 1 as identified above, where gatherings possess an old identification number preceded by 'Nc'. Surrounding – and even between the two lines of – the title, *Cantata à Voce sola di Soprano | Del Sig.r Leonardo Vinci*, the remainder of the page contains a list of works in a contemporary hand that are not included in the binder's collection, except for the cantatas *Mi costa tante lacrime* and *Pietosa l'aurora in cielo*. This

---

[37] Shelfmark D 336. In the literature, mention is made erroneously of a further source for this cantata in the library of the Naples Conservatorio. In fact, the source in question (Cantate 19, formerly 57.2.30, ff. 21–8) transmits a quite different cantata by Vinci, *Io parto, e con qual core*, thereby adding an extra cantata to Vinci's tally.

was evidently a table of contents prepared by the user of the original collection before its dismemberment. This surviving index makes it possible to form useful ideas about the content and date of the present anthology. Here we find other pieces written 'per la Faustina' (this time, by her husband Hasse) and works that for the most part are known from other, similar miscellanies in the library of the Naples Conservatorio, as Table 8.3 shows.

Altogether, there are fifteen pieces. Apart from the two Vinci cantatas just mentioned (the second of doubtful authorship), no work in the list is contained in manuscript. 34.5.23. The attempt to trace the works described in the index to other collections in the same library has proved successful. One cantata by Porpora and a duet by Vinci (nos. 2 and 3 in Table 8.3) are preserved in another Naples volume, manuscript 34.6.25 (also known as Arie 617); four arias by Hasse (nos. 5, 9, 13 and 14), which can be traced back to their parent operas and on that basis dated between 1732 and 1739, appear in the manuscript Cantate 156; two arias, one by Leo and one anonymous (nos. 10 and 11) are contained in the manuscript Cantate 172 (formerly 33.2.27), which houses works by Leo and also Hasse; an aria by Sarro (no. 6) seems no longer to be extant, while the remaining four pieces (nos. 7, 8, 12 and 15), comprising two arias and two cantatas (one of the latter being by the little-known Tommaso de Cupertinis and bearing in its manuscript the date of 1709), are preserved in Naples individually under separate shelfmarks.

The pieces by Hasse comprise two arias sung, respectively, in the Venetian operas *Euristeo* (San Samuele, 1732) and *Viriate* (San Giovanni Grisostomo, 1739) and a further aria belonging to an opera written for Naples, *Issipile* (San Bartolomeo, 1732). Whereas in *Euristeo* the *prima donna* was Francesca Cuzzoni, Faustina's rival, the leading lady of the other two operas by Hasse was his wife Faustina, as the source numbered 5 in the table discloses through the words: 'Sassone [i.e., Hasse] per la Faustina'. The agency of Faustina Bordoni Hasse is thereby confirmed as decisive not only for the origin but also for the subsequent circulation of music by composers such as Hasse and Vinci.

There is a little more to say about the manuscript 34.5.23. It is necessary to evaluate the remaining compositions listed in Table 8.1 to have a complete overview of the manuscript. The seventh gathering transmits the duet 'Tu vuoi ch'io viva, o cara' for two sopranos, who are named in the source as 'Astroa e Caffarelli'. These are the Turinese singer Giovanna Astroa and the castrato Gaetano Majorano, nicknamed Caffarelli. They sang this duet in the respective roles of Mandane and Arbace in Vinci's *Artaserse* (premiered at Rome in 1730) in a Neapolitan revival of 1743 'accomodata' by Gennaro Manna.[38] The same piece is transcribed in gatherings 8 and 9 without mention of the singers or of the presence of the viola ('violetta') in the ensemble.[39] In addition to this duet, we find in the volume other movements originating from Vinci's *Artaserse*: on three occasions (in gatherings

---

[38] See Sartori, *I libretti*.
[39] The 'violetta' is prescribed by only one of the three copies, which has it doubling the bass an octave higher.

Table 8.3   Compositions indexed on f. 95 of I-Nc, ms. 34.5.23 (Cantate 304).

No.	Transcription of the title	Preserved in ms. 34.5.23	Preserved elsewhere in I-Nc*	Datings
1	Vinci Leonardo Cantata per Soprano: Mi costa tante lagrime col solo Basso per Canto p. 1	no. 13		
2	Porpora Nicola Can.*ta* p[er] Canto: Simile: Ecco l'infausto lido p .7		34.6.25[11]	
3	Vinci Duettino p[er] C, e A, con VV in D. Sarò fedele a te p. 15		Arie 617[19] (olim 34.6.25)	
4	Can.*ta* Anonima per Canto: Pietosa l'aurora p. 19	no. 15		
5	Sassone p[er] la Faustina Eccomi non ferir p. 23		Cantate 156[4]	[Naples: Issipile, 1732]
6	Sarri Domenico Aria: Tortorella abbandonata in F. con VV. p. 27		Lost	
7	Latilla Gaet.° Aria: Và dal superbo, e digli &c in D con VV. p. 35		Cantate 30[27] (olim 22.3.13)	
8	Leo. Aria: Lieto canta su d'un ramo p[er] Canto in ♭B, p. 41 con Flauto obbligato		Cantate 173[8]	
9	Sassone: Aria: Amo, Bramo, e non dispero per Canto in ♭B pag. 47		Cantate 156[5]	[Venice: Euristeo 1732]
10	Leo: Aria: Per forza d'amore: p[er] Canto in ♭B pag: 53		Cantate 172[4] (olim 33.2.27[4])	
11	Aria: Povero Pellegrino: p[er] Canto in B pag: 63. Anon.		Cantate 172[5] (olim 33.2.27[5])	
12	de Cupertinis: Cantata p[er] Soprano con Viol. pag. 69 in Elami: Fille a freggiar di tue bellezze il velo &c		Cantate 104 (olim 34.4.14), '1709'	1709
13	Sassone: Aria: Se fosse il mio diletto: pag 74 in A		Cantate 156[6] (olim 33.2.21)	[Venice: Viriate, 1739]
14	aria: Più infelice sventurato: in C. pag: 81 [Hasse]		Cantate 156[7] (olim 33.2.21)	
15	Sarri: Aria: Cantata p[er] Soprano: su le fiorite sponde. in Alamire Rec.*vo* pag: 85		22.2.11[32] (olim Cantate 51)	

* Superscript numbers denote item numbers within collections containing several pieces.

3, 4 and 12) we encounter one of the most widely disseminated arias from Vinci's *Artaserse*, 'Vo solcando un mar crudele', which is the number with which Arbace closes Act I of Metastasio's drama. Even though in this instance the source names no singer, we know that at the opera's premiere in Naples in 1738 the role of Arbace was taken by Vittoria Tesi, one of the composer's favourite singers. Also from *Artaserse* comes an aria for Mandane, 'Mi credi spietata?' (gathering 11), to which the same observations regarding the singer apply as for the duet discussed above (in the premiere of 1738 the role was taken by Anna Maria Peruzzi). One notes in addition an aria from Vinci's *Catone in Utica* (gathering 10) and a duet from his *La caduta dei Decemviri* (gathering 14). Appended to a copy of Vinci's 'Vo solcando un mar crudele' (gathering 3), is one of 'Prigioniera abbandonata', an aria from the *Adriano in Siria* (1734) of Pergolesi, reputed to have been a pupil of Vinci.

To Vinci's favourite contralto, who took the role of Andromaca in 1725 at San Bartolomeo, can be assigned the arias 'Misera sì, non vile' and 'Barbaro, prendi e suona' from *Astianatte*, in a production that included in its cast also the famous Anna Maria Strada as Ermione and Farinelli as Oreste: these two were the performers of the other movements from *Astianatte* contained in the manuscript (see Table 8.1).

The appearance side by side in this collection (which, as we know, was assembled much later than the period when the individual pieces it contains were copied out) of movements belonging to the Neapolitan and Venetian repertories identifiable within Vinci's career points us in the direction of the interesting conclusions reached, after detailed study, by Teresa M. Gialdroni and Dinko Fabris.[40] The tendency towards a 'topological' organization of Italian vocal music of the eighteenth century along the Naples–Venice axis[41] is evidenced also by manuscript 34.5.23 of S. Pietro a Majella, which reinforces the claim of a close connection between the two metropoles in respect of the circulation of composers, performers, contracts and economic interests.

Conversely, the remaining three cantatas in the manuscript pose various problems. The first of these, *Veggo la selva e 'l monte*, is the only cantata attributed to Vinci for which we have an author of the text: Pietro Metastasio.[42] Unfortunately,

---

[40] Teresa M. Gialdroni, 'Vivaldi, la cantata e gli altri: ancora sul manoscritto di Meiningen Ed. 82e', paper read to the international conference 'Antonio Vivaldi. Passato e futuro' held in Venice at the Fondazione Giorgio Cini in June 2007 and later published in *Studi musicali*, 37, 2008: 359–86. Gialdroni draws attention here to the possible derivation – pernicious but revealing – of some cantata arias from operatic arias, a passage that my own researches into the cantata tend to support. I thank the author for allowing me sight of her paper beforehand. The work by Dinko Fabris is 'Adesso se ne conoce il merito'.

[41] Pioneering in relation to this question is Reinhard Strohm's 'The Neapolitans in Venice'.

[42] Pietro Metastasio, *Tutte le opere*, ed. Bruno Brunelli, 5 vols (Milan, 1951–65), vol. 2, pp. 739–40.

however, this cantata is likely to be spurious, since other manuscripts[43] – still not widely known, even to specialists – attribute it to Carlo Benati,[44] a Bolognese composer who was a prolific writer of cantatas.[45] Its first aria (within the scheme RARA) is an interesting 'tarantella' in duple metre, very Neapolitan in character, while the second, marked 'Vivace' and in 3/8, presents a tripartite strophic form, in which each of the brief sections is marked for repeat. This would be a novelty for Vinci's cantata arias, if the movement were indeed by him.

The last two cantatas in the volume, *Pietosa l'aurora in cielo* and *Dite, vedeste forse*, are respectively anonymous and of doubtful ascription. The first, as we saw earlier, has an important bearing on the dating of the cantatas in that, on its last page, it gives a day, '27 luglio [July]' and then a year, which could be read as either '1703' or '1708'. The earlier year would indicate great precocity on Vinci's part (assuming for the moment that he was the composer), given his date of birth in or around 1690. This would make the composer only thirteen or so years old and predate his admission to the Conservatorio dei Poveri di Gesù Cristo.[46] The two arias of the cantata are very short; both include a 'da capo' and display a frequent characteristic of Vinci's arias: the prefiguring in the instrumental introduction of the opening of the vocal line (rather than, say, of its bass). The second aria is an evocative siciliana in 12/8, similar to ones found in some early cantatas of

---

[43] These are: the manuscript M 2245 of the National Library, Madrid; the manuscript Hs 861 Nr 14 of the Santini Library, Münster; and the manuscript Cantate 335² of the library of the Conservatorio 'S. Pietro a Majella', Naples.

[44] Carlo Antonio Benati is a little-known composer, a Bolognese singing teacher mentioned by Farinelli in a letter of 1739 addressed to Count Sicinio Pepoli (Farinelli's letters addressed to Sicinio Pepoli, his friend and estate manager *in absentia*, have been published by Carlo Vitali, Roberto Pagano and Francesca Boris in *La solitudine amica. Lettere al conte Sicino Pepoli* (Palermo, 2000); the letter in which Carlo Broschi mentions Benati is transcribed on pp. 157–61. Despite the attribution of the cantata to Benati in the Spanish and German sources (see Table 8.1), Rosy Candiani is firm in her belief that it is by Vinci, in which case it would be his only setting in this genre of a Metastasian text (which, incidentally, Porpora also set). See Rosy Candiani, 'Originalità e serialità nella scrittura del Metastasio: l'esempio delle cantate', in Marta Columbro and Paolgiovanni Maione (eds), *Pietro Metastasio: il testo e il contesto* (Naples, [2000]), pp. 111–24, at p. 113.

[45] To cite a curiosity, I would like to draw attention to a cantata (A51 in Eleanor Selfridge-Field's catalogue) that links the name of Carlo Benati to those of Vittoria Tesi and Faustina Bordoni (among many other vocal celebrities): this is the *Lettera del Sig.r Carlo Ant.o Benati | scritta alla Sig.ra Vittoria Tesi a Venezia | Musica dell'Ecc.mo Sig.r Benedetto Marcello | Nobil Veneto* (examples preserved in the Biblioteca Palatina, Parma, the Museo Internazionale e Biblioteca della Musica, Bologna, and elsewhere), a satirical composition of Benedetto Marcello on a text by Benati; see Caroline Sites, 'More on Marcello's Satire', *Journal of the American Musicological Society*, 11 (1958): 141–8.

[46] The present state of knowledge about Vinci's biography, his date of birth and his admission to the Conservatorio dei Poveri di Gesù Cristo is reviewed in Dinko Fabris, 'Adesso se ne conoce il merito'.

Domenico Scarlatti.[47] The other cantata, *Dite, vedeste forse*, is headed 'Cantata a voce sola con violini | del Sig.r Leonardo Leo [deleted] Vinci', with the attribution to Vinci written in a later hand. On the last folio of this cantata, which brings up the rear of the collection, we find an annotated figure '172' at the end of the first system, between the staves for voice and violin; this could well be a date, with the year of the decade not entered. The second of its two arias has a very mobile vocal line with frequent wide skips of up to a tenth. This cantata is not included in the canon of Leo's cantatas,[48] to which one may add that the confusion between the two composers named 'Leonardo' on the part of their contemporaries occurs also in other cantata sources, where the attribution remains similarly indeterminate.

Final remarks

As recent studies have suggested, the cantata had, during the period in question, a relationship of dependency vis-à-vis the opera. Even if its performance took place in more intimate settings and was functionally distinct, it was cultivated by the same aristocratic circles. For this reason, the study of the late-Baroque cantata written for Naples is closely bound up with that of the development of 'Neapolitan' opera and with the persons who were the agents of its Europe-wide dissemination, and at the same time its standardization as a recognizably 'Neapolitan' product. The sources transmitting the cantatas give ample evidence of this close dependency, as we have seen from our examination of the manuscript 34.5.23 (Cantate 304) in Naples. In the light of our knowledge that cantatas ranked as 'leggiadrissima cosa, e il più bello, e gentil divertimento, che mai possa prendersi in qualunque onorata, e nobile conversazione',[49] this fact adds point to a question posed by Colin Timms (concerning the close perceived relationship between chamber cantatas as entertainment for an *accademia* and arias from operas 'in season'):

---

[47] See Dinko Fabris and Giulia Veneziano, 'Le cantate giovanili di Domenico Scarlatti', in Dinko Fabris and Paologiovanni Maione (eds), *Domenico Scarlatti: musica e storia* (Naples, 2009), forthcoming. This is a sequel to the same authors' study of Scarlatti's cantatas published as 'Le cantate da camera di Domenico Scarlatti', in Teresa M. Gialdroni (ed.), *La cantata da camera intorno agli anni 'italiani' di Händel: problemi e prospettive di ricerca* (Rome, 2009), pp. 169–95.

[48] See the entry for Leonardo Leo by Helmut Hucke (revised by Rosa Cafiero) in the 2001 edition of the *New Grove* (vol. 14, pp. 553–6), and Giuseppe A. Pastore, *Don Leonardo. Vita e opere di Leonardo Leo* (Cuneo, 1994), as well as Daniela Quargnolo's unpublished dissertation 'Le cantate di Leonardo Leo (1694–1744)' (*tesi di laurea*, Università degli Studi di Milano, 1993/94).

[49] Giovan Mario Crescimbeni, *Dell'istoria della volgar poesia*, 3rd edn, 6 vols (Venice, 1730–31), vol. 1, pp. 299–300: 'the lightest of things, and the finest and most genteel entertainment ever to be had in any honourable and noble *conversazione*'.

'When an aria from an opera was performed at a *conversazione*, did it become *musica da camera*?'.[50]

If we wish *malgré tout* to describe a cantata as 'Neapolitan', the only valid path to follow, in the case of most of the manuscripts with which we have to deal, is that of taking into account and co-ordinating all the diverse elements – bibliographical, contextual and stylistic – that a source has to offer. Naturally, the pieces of data collected for this purpose in the end rarely lead to unequivocal conclusions, but they can open up promising lines of enquiry and provide good approximations for present needs. The case of Leonardo Vinci, rendered exceptional by the Spanish sources specially adapted for use in their new locale, perhaps opens up a new front in the study of the cantata, showing how, just like the sonata, the genre can, if required, wear 'da chiesa' garb.[51] Viewed in this light, a cantata that is fully 'Neapolitan' by virtue of its place of origin, the patrons who commissioned it, the musicians who executed it and its place of performance may come to appear as a true emblem of the thing that it represents – a symbol of a unique geographical and cultural heritage even when exported to milieux quite unforeseen by the composer and his colleagues. Perhaps it is, in the end, best to reserve the label 'Neapolitan' not simply for a cantata that 'ticks the right boxes' with regard to objective criteria such as compositional origin, style, context, use, performers, destination and poetic text, but, rather, for one that over and above this manages also to represent Naples subjectively, reflecting the peculiar *fascino* that the city, now as then, exerts on everyone who comes into contact with it.

---

[50] Timms, 'The Italian Cantata since 1945', p. 86. Charles Burney informs us, similarly, that in his day the place of cantatas was often taken by operatic *scene* or individual arias preceded by a recitative, since these had the same narrative character of an opening, a development and a conclusion – with the difference that in private performances the music was usually played by a chamber ensemble rather than by a full orchestra. See Burney, *A General History*, vol. 4, p. 179.

[51] A similar practice has been identified by Aníbal E. Cetrangolo in his research on Italian music 'imported' into Guatemala and Bolivia, where he has discovered operatic arias on texts predominantly by Metastasio that have been translated into Spanish – but in a 'sacred' version for use in liturgical contexts.

Chapter 9
The Orchestral French Cantata (1706–30): Performance, Edition and Classification of a Neglected Repertory

Graham Sadler

With that time-lag characteristic of so many French musical borrowings from Seicento Italy, the *cantate françoise* emerged when its Italian counterpart had already been in existence for over half a century.[1] It was not until 1706 that the first published French collections appeared,[2] while the earliest surviving manuscript cantatas predate these publications by only a few years.[3] Yet once launched, as the composer and theorist Sébastien de Brossard noted, the new genre proved a runaway success:

> Among the different kinds of divertissements or concerts whose invention [...] we owe to Italy, there is none which has been received in France with more applause or whose usage has spread so quickly and so widely as that which is now known as the cantata.[4]

The broad outline of the French cantata's gestation has long been clear. By the end of the seventeenth century Italian cantatas (those by Giovanni Bononcini, especially) circulated widely in France,[5] while the peace treaty with Savoy in

---

[1] The present chapter retains the obsolete spelling *cantate françoise* as a convenient shorthand for the French genre in the period 1706–30.

[2] Morin and Stuck each published their first cantatas in 1706. On the dating of Bernier's first book, see note 18.

[3] See, for example, François Turellier, 'Des cantates anonymes attribuables à Jean-Baptiste Morin (1677–1745) dans le manuscrit F-Pc. Rés 1451: "Cantates de Mancin[i]"', *Ostinato rigore: Revue internationale d'études musicales*, 8/9, 1997: 329–39; Turellier dates this manuscript to no earlier than 1703.

[4] Sébastien de Brossard, 'Dissertation sur cette espèce de concert qu'on nomme cantate', F-Pn, ms. fr. n.a. 5269, fol. 75: 'Entre les differentes manieres de divertissemens ou de concerts, dont on doit l'invention [...] à l'Italie; il n'y en a point qui ait esté receu en France avec plus d'aplaudissement, et dont l'usage se soit répandu plus viste ny plus generallement que de celui qu'on nomme maintenant cantate'.

[5] For a discussion of the reception of Bononcini's cantatas in France, see Chapter 6.

1696 facilitated transalpine contacts.[6] The long-suspected role of Philippe II, duc d'Orléans, in this gestation has recently been confirmed with the revelation that the duke employed a hitherto unknown ensemble of Italian or Italian-trained musicians to perform music in the most up-to-date ultramontane styles.[7] Philippe's ensemble, comprising two castratos, two violins and a bass violin (or, later, a cello), was active from 1703 until 1705, the years immediately preceding the earliest French cantata publications. Italian cantatas by two members of this group, Jean-Baptiste ('Batistin') Stuck and Giovanni Antonio Guido, survive in a French manuscript dating from this same period, alongside works by Jean-Baptiste Morin that were to appear in revised form in the composer's first book of *cantates françoises* of 1706.[8] These cantatas by Stuck and Guido, with their modern, Italian idiom, give a flavour of the ensemble's repertory, which would doubtless also have included cantatas by Bononcini and others of the kind circulating in Paris.[9] Although, as Fader points out, 'the members of Orléans's ensemble were certainly not the only Italian musicians in France during this period, they were alone in representing an active group of virtuosos trained in the latest styles'.[10]

This transalpine repertory would thus have been familiar to Philippe's composers when they set about adapting the cantata to French taste. The resultant *cantate françoise* was never designed merely as an Italian cantata with French words, but rather as a manifestation of what Couperin would later christen the *réunion des goûts*. Yet among the Italian characteristics it initially retained was the intimate scoring for small forces. This is immediately clear from the earliest published cantatas, which seldom include more than one obbligato line. Many collections are, in fact, predominantly for one singer and continuo, so that 'with only a solo voice, harpsichord, and bass viol', as Morin puts it, 'one can easily perform most of this

---

[6] On the circulation of Italian music in France at this time, see Jean Duron, 'Aspects de la présence italienne dans la musique française de la fin du XVIIe siècle', in Jean Lionnet (ed.), *Le concert des Muses. Promenade musicale dans le baroque français* (Versailles, 1997), pp. 97–115, and Jean Lionnet, 'Les copies de musique italienne et leur diffusion', ibid., pp. 81–95. For details of an extensive collection, much of it compiled in the seventeenth century and including items by more than 80 Italian composers, see Tula Giannini, 'The Music Library of Jean-Baptiste Christophe Ballard, Sole Music Printer to the King of France, 1750 Inventory of his Grand Collection Brought to Light', *E-Documentation in the Humanities*, Series 1 (Spring 2003) http://rand.pratt.edu/~giannini/ballard.htm (accessed 14 February 2008).

[7] Don Fader, 'Philippe II d'Orléans's "chanteurs italiens", the Italian cantata and the *goûts-réunis* under Louis XIV', *Early Music*, 35 (2007): 237–49; see also Fader, 'Musical Thought and Patronage of the Italian Style at the Court of Philippe II, duc d'Orléans (1674–1723)' (PhD dissertation, Stanford University, 2000), pp. 282–302.

[8] Turellier, 'Des cantates anonymes attribuables à Jean-Baptiste Morin': 329–39.

[9] In *Benedetto Vinaccesi: A Musician in Brescia and Venice in the Age of Corelli* (Oxford, 1994) Michael Talbot comments (pp. 162–3) on a cantata by Vinaccesi (1666–1719) preserved in Ms. Rés 1451, which he links to Philippe's ensemble.

[10] Fader, 'Philippe II d'Orléans's "chanteurs italiens"', p. 246.

music for the chamber'.[11] As late as the mid-eighteenth century the *Dictionnaire de Trévoux* could still describe the French cantata as being 'usually for solo voice with continuo, often with two violins or several instruments'.[12]

It is this 'chamber music' nature that has been stressed in much of the literature on the *cantate françoise*, especially in English – understandably, since this is its predominant character. Indeed, the duc d'Orléans's Italian ensemble, augmented by a flautist or two, could have met the requirements of a substantial proportion of French cantatas of the period, and of the Italian cantata repertory circulating in France.

Yet a significant minority of French cantatas were clearly designed with orchestral forces in mind, since their scoring unambiguously specifies multiple strings (most usually in the designation of individual lines as 'violons', 'basses de violon', etc.) and, on occasion, such manifestly orchestral instruments as trumpets and drums, or *contrebasse*. This is an aspect of cantata instrumentation that has not received the attention it deserves. Although the orchestral nature of certain works has been noted,[13] there has been no published study devoted solely to the orchestral French cantata. Such a study is nevertheless justified, for several reasons. First, modern performances of these works have, in my experience, tended to opt for chamber forces: a legitimate alternative, but one that restricts the range of instrumental colour and sonorities, and affects the balance of voice and accompaniment. Second, there is evidence that some of the accompaniments of orchestral cantatas, like those of many contemporary operas and *grands motets*, survive only in abridged form – evidence which, though rarely mentioned in print, has implications of vital importance for editors and performers, and indeed for our judgement of the artistic worth of such pieces. Third, it becomes clear that the standard classification of cantatas into those with instruments (*avec symphonie*) and those with continuo only (*sans symphonie*) is over-simple and in need of revision.

* * *

---

[11] Jean-Baptiste Morin, *Cantates françoises* [...] *premier Livre* (Paris, 1706), 'Avis': '[...] avec une seule Voix, un Clavecin, & une Basse de Violle, on peut aisement faire une Musique de Chambre'. As noted in Jérôme Dorival, *La cantate française au XVIIIe siècle* (Paris, 1999), the expression *musique de chambre* used in many cantata publications did not have quite its modern sense at that time, since 'la "chambre" qu'il désigne est plus princière que bourgeoise' (p. 4). (The same is, incidentally, true of the contemporary Italian expression *musica da camera*.)

[12] *Dictionnaire de Trévoux* (i.e., *Dictionnaire universelle françois et latin*), 7 vols (Paris, 1743–52), vol. 1, p. 1670: '[...] pour ordinaire à voix seule, avec une basse continue, souvent avec deux violons, ou plusieurs instruments'. This passage paraphrases Sébastien de Brossard, *Dictionaire de musique* (Paris, 1703), art. 'Cantata'.

[13] See, for example, Mary Cyr, 'Performing Rameau's Cantatas', *Early Music*, 11 (1983): 480–89, Catherine Cessac, *Nicolas Clérambault* (Paris, 1998), chapter 8, and Dorival, *La cantate française au XVIIIe siècle*, pp. 72, 79–84 and 89.

One major factor in assessing the instrumentation of the *cantate françoise* is that the vast majority of these works survive in published form. The publication process was expensive, and composers stood a better chance of recouping their costs if the commercial appeal of a publication was as wide as possible. Thus instrumental designations in the scores often include alternatives – 'violon ou flûte', 'trompettes ou hautbois' and so on. On this basis, David Tunley is justified, as far as markings such as 'violons' are concerned, in advising the modern performer that 'while the plural form will be found in the score, the part can be played by a single instrument'.[14]

Elsewhere, however, Tunley stretches this liberal concept too far in stating that 'some large-scale works also include *optional* parts for trumpets, horns, oboes, bassoons and drums' [my italics].[15] In a limited sense, he is right, in that French cantata composers accepted that amateurs would adapt the instrumentation to whatever resources were available. Elisabeth Jacquet de La Guerre, in the Avertissement to her *Cantates françoises* (after 1715), goes so far as to state that the airs may all be sung 'sans symphonie'.[16] But the option of omitting parts would nowadays be considered no more desirable than that of omitting the *ripieno* of Corelli's Op. 6 *Concerti grossi*, described on the title page as *ad arbitrio*.[17] It is one thing to accept that this was a solution of last resort, quite another to suggest that it was what the composer seriously intended. If the scores of *cantates françoises* specify trumpets, drums and other 'orchestral' instruments, this was because the works in question were conceived with such forces in mind.

* * *

Glimpses of the emerging orchestral genre may already be seen in some of the earliest publications of *cantates françoises*. At this stage, it must be stressed, the majority of cantatas retain the chamber scoring of their Italian models. The first books of Bernier, Morin and Stuck, all published in 1706,[18] each contain the customary six cantatas, although each collection places a different emphasis on

---

[14] David Tunley (ed.), *The Eighteenth-Century French Cantata: A Seventeen-Volume Facsimile Set of the Most Widely Cultivated and Performed Music in Early Eighteenth-Century France* (New York, 1990), vol. 2, p. xii. This series includes most, though not all, of the cantatas discussed in the present chapter.

[15] David Tunley, 'Cantata, §III. The French cantata to 1800', in Stanley Sadie and John Tyrrell (eds), *The New Grove Dictionary of Music and Musicians,* 2nd edn (London, 2001), vol. 5, p. 33.

[16] Quoted in Catherine Cessac, *Élisabeth Jacquet de La Guerre: une femme compositeur sous le règne de Louis XIV* ([Arles], 1995), p. 157.

[17] See Richard Platt (ed.), *Corelli: Concerti grossi* (London, 1997), pp. vi and xlviii.

[18] According to Fader, 'Philippe II d'Orléans's "chanteurs italiens"' (p. 248, note 2), ongoing research indicates that Bernier's undated first book appeared in 1706. Jean-Paul C. Montagnier, *Charles-Hubert Gervais: un musicien au service du Régent et de Louis*

instrumental participation. Bernier's, the most typical in this respect, comprises four works for solo voice and continuo, plus two with a single obbligato instrument labelled 'violon' throughout. At the opposite extreme, Stuck's volume is uncharacteristic of the early cantata in consisting entirely of works with obbligato instruments. The three works that include two obbligato lines are labelled 'avec deux violons'; the remaining three are designated respectively 'avec deux violons et une haute-cont[r]e' (i.e., viola), 'avec deux violons, une flute et un hau[t]bois' and 'avec deux violons, une flute et une haute cont[r]e'. That this labelling indicates one-to-a-part performance is confirmed in the scores themselves, where all instrumental designations appear in the singular.[19]

It is in Morin's first book that the earliest evidence of orchestral performance is found. While five of the six cantatas are scored for solo voice (or, in one case, two voices) *sans symphonie*, the remaining work, *Enone*, includes three arias, each with different scoring: the first contains a single obbligato part labelled 'flûte, ou violon seul'; the second is for continuo alone; the third has two obbligato lines, both labelled 'violons'. Thus in what may well be the earliest French cantata publication we already find one work requiring multiple strings.[20] A comparable pattern occurs in Morin's second book, published a year later, in 1707. Four of its six cantatas are for voice and continuo, while a fifth has a single obbligato line marked 'violon ou flûte'; the remaining work, *Bachus*, described at the start as being for 'basse-taille [baritone], avec violons, ou flutes', includes four arias: the first includes a single obbligato part labelled 'violons, ou flutes, à l'unisson'; the second has two obbligato parts merely labelled 'symphonie'; the third is with continuo only; and the last, once again, has two obbligato lines, this time marked 'violons, flutes, ou hautbois'.[21]

Lest it be thought that the use of plural designations here is the result of carelessness or inconsistency, we should note that contemporary French sources

---

XV (Paris, 2001), p. 76, notes that Sébastien de Brossard's manuscript copy of this book is annotated 'Gravé à Paris par Beaussan [en] 1706'.

[19] All but one of the six cantatas nevertheless include passages where the obbligato component is reduced to a single line marked 'violons à l'unisson'.

[20] Morin's employer, the duc d'Orléans, could call on an impressive number of performers when required. According to the *Mercure* of February 1705, p. 64, more than 80 musicians took part in a performance of Orléans's own opera *La Suite d'Armide* at the Palais Royal, his Paris residence, earlier that month. Many of these were doubtless supernumeraries. In the absence of archival records, however, it is impossible to establish the precise size of the duke's musical establishment; see Fader, 'Musical Thought and Patronage of the Italian Style at the Court of Philippe II, duc d'Orléans', pp. 282–91 and Appendix 3 (see p. 242 for the quotation from the *Mercure*).

[21] Don Fader points out, in personal correspondence, that the wind player Jacques-Martin Hotteterre, in dedicating his *Sonates en trio* (Paris, 1712) to the duc d'Orléans, stated that he had heard the duke's 'savantes compositions' in concerts in which he had been invited to play – further evidence of the occasional use of supernumeraries. I am grateful to Professor Fader for this information and for invaluable comments on a draft of this chapter.

normally maintain a distinction between singular and plural to differentiate between solo and multiple instruments (although certain exceptions will be examined in due course).[22] In *Enone*, moreover, the contrasting of a movement involving a solo player ('flûte, ou violon seul') and one with two lines marked 'violons' is typical of the varied French approach to instrumentation in an orchestral context, a subject to which we shall return.

In the years immediately following Morin's first two books the proportion of published cantatas with orchestral characteristics, though still small, reveals a steady growth. Of the sixteen volumes of cantatas issued during the period 1708–13,[23] only five include no hint of orchestral resources: among them are Brunet de Moland's *Cantades et ariettes françoises* (1708), all 'sans symphonie', Bernier's undated second, third and fourth books, and Louis-Nicolas Clérambault's first book (1710), scored throughout for chamber forces.[24] The remaining eleven books all include at least one work with plural designations of individual lines, normally 'violons'. Among these are Clérambault's second book (1713), which includes the highly dramatic *Léandre et Héro*, calling for 'Flûtes allemandes', 'Violons' and 'Contre Basse', and Stuck's fourth book (1714), where *Les festes bolonnoises* is captioned 'avec Violons, Trompettes, ou Haut-bois'. In Philippe Courbois's *Cantates françoises* (1710) the comic cantata *Dom Quichotte* is subtitled 'à voix seule et un violon', but the score itself calls for unison 'violons', 'trompette' and 'hau-bois', as well as 'vielle' [hurdy-gurdy].

The year 1714 marks a turning point in the development of the orchestral cantata. From then until the rapid decline of the *cantate françoise* in the 1730s the number and proportion of works specifying orchestral forces increases hugely, most cantata publications containing at least one work of this kind. Indeed Bernier's fifth book (1715) consists entirely of orchestral cantatas, while publications with two or more include Clérambault's third and fourth books (1716, 1720), Mouret's first (c.1718), Colin de Blamont's first two (1723, 1729) and Campra's third (1728). Several orchestral cantatas were published individually – among them, Destouches's *Œnone* (1716) and *Sémelé* (1719), Clérambault's *La Muse de l'Opéra* (1716) and *Le soleil, vainqueur des nuages* (1721), and Campra's undated *La guerre*.

---

[22] See Lois Rosow, 'Paris Opéra Orchestration, 1686–1713: Deciphering the Code in the Orchestral Parts', in Sarah McCleave (ed.), *Dance & Music in French Baroque Theatre: Sources & Interpretations* (London, 1998), pp. 33–53.

[23] These figures include Bernier's undated books 2–4 (published by 1714) and Bousset's *Cantates françoises* (before 1710).

[24] In Clérambault's *Cantatas françoises à 1. et 11. voix* [...] *livre premier* the treble obbligato of *Orphée* is indicated as 'flûte allemande ou violon' (p. 28), 'violon' (pp. 31 and 42), 'flûte allemande' (p. 36) and 'flute' (p. 40); yet where these instruments have separate parts (p. 38), the lower is marked 'violon' and the upper one 'flûtes'. In such an intimate work, I take this isolated plural to be an engraving error.

From this period, too, evidence emerges that certain works were occasionally performed with orchestra even though instrumental designations in the published score appear in the singular. A set of manuscript partbooks of *L'Amour vainqueur* from Bernier's sixth book (1718) was seemingly intended for multiple strings, since the *basse continue* has cues for 'violons' throughout, even though the single obbligato line in the engraved score merely specifies 'violon'.[25] Another set of partbooks, containing Clérambault's *Le jaloux* (1710), confirms this practice and reveals an implicit *petit chœur–grand chœur* alternation. The set includes three violin parts, respectively labelled 'violon', 'violon de ripienne' and 'violon ripienne' – these last two playing only when the voice rests.[26] The published score shows no sign of this distinction, the single obbligato line being merely labelled 'symphonie' or 'violon'.

By the late 1720s the term *à grande symphonie* began to appear in association with cantatas scored for especially large forces. A press announcement of Colin de Blamont's second and third books in 1729 states that these works were suitable both for private concerts and for ones 'à grande symphonie', since most of them required 'all the different instruments that are normally used in large musical establishments'.[27] When Courbois's *Dom Quichotte* of 1710 was reissued in a revised version (Paris, no date), it was likewise described on the title pages as 'à une voix avec grande Simphonie'. This term, while self-evidently denoting a large ensemble, also indicated that a full body of strings was required, including at least two viola parts. According to Jean-Jacques Rousseau, 'a piece is said to be *en grande symphonie* when, in addition to the bass and treble, it has two other instrumental parts: namely, *taille* and *quinte de violon*'.[28]

* * *

---

[25] F-Pn, Vm⁷ 229, discussed in Mary Cyr, 'Performing Rameau's Cantatas', pp. 480–89, and same author (ed.), *Elisabeth-Claude Jacquet de La Guerre: Three Sacred Cantatas* (New York, 2005), p. 58. I am grateful to Professor Cyr for providing copies of this and other sources, and for her much valued comments on a draft of this chapter.

[26] F-Pn, Vm⁷ 4768, ibid., p. 59.

[27] *Mercure de France*, November 1729, p. 2730: '[…] des differens instrumens dont on se sert ordinairement dans les grandes Musiques'; see also *Mercure de France*, May 1729, p. 1031, where Colin de Blamont's *Le Parnasse lyrique* is described as 'absolument faite pour un grand Concert, étant composée pour tous les differens Instrumens qui y sont ordinairement nécessaires'.

[28] Denis Diderot and Jean le Rond d'Alembert (eds), *Encyclopédie, ou Dictionnaire raisonné des sciences, des arts et des métiers* 35 vols (Paris, 1751–80), art. 'Symphonie': 'On dit d'une piece qu'elle est en grande symphonie, quand outre la basse & les dessus, elle a encore deux autres parties instrumentales ; savoir, taille & quinte de violon'. In fact, the two viola parts were normally referred to as *haute-contre* and *taille* (*de violon*). This definition appears *verbatim* in Jean-Jacques Rousseau, *Dictionnaire de musique* (Amsterdam, 1768), art. 'Symphonie', to which is added: 'La Musique de la Chapelle du Roi, celle de plusieurs Eglises, & celle des Opéra sont presque toujours en grande *Symphonie*'.

The above examples emphasize the fact that cantata publications, like so many others of the period, were designed for a mixed market. If certain works were scored for forces beyond the resources of many users, that is often a consequence of the circumstances in which they were written. As with other genres, cantatas were not necessarily composed expressly for publication. Many, as we shall see, were written some considerable time before they appeared in print, often for concerts mounted by a patron or employer. We have discussed Morin's *Enone* and *Bachus* in the context of the duc d'Orléans's musical establishment, which would have been available to other composers in the duke's entourage: Bernier, Stuck, Campra and Charles-Hubert Gervais. Further orchestral cantatas can be associated with specific patrons or organizations. The strongly orchestral character of Campra's third book (1728), for instance, is a likely consequence of his appointment in 1722 as director of music to the duc de Conti.[29] Similarly, Colin de Blamont's many orchestral cantatas date from his years at Louis XV's court (from 1719) and were designed for the considerable resources of the Musique du Roi.

Cantata publications also contain a number of occasional works. The entire contents of Bernier's fifth book (1715) originated at the duchesse du Maine's extravagant entertainments known as the *Grandes nuits de Sceaux*, as did individual cantatas by Philippe de Courbois, Jean-Joseph Mouret, Philippe Marchand, Thomas-Louis Bourgeois and Colin de Blamont, many with orchestral scoring.[30] While we do not know the exact make-up of the duchess's orchestra at the time when these cantatas were performed, as early as 1704 the entertainments at Sceaux had apparently involved an orchestra of thirty-five.[31]

Among other occasional works with orchestral accompaniment, Stuck's *Les festes bolonnoises* (Book 4, 1714) includes divided 'violons' plus two lines both marked 'tromp. ou hautbois', and was apparently written in honour of the duc d'Aumont, governor of the Boulonnais (hence the cantata's title), on the occasion of his departure on a mission to England in 1712.[32] Clérambault's *Le soleil,*

---

[29] On this 'mélomane distingué' and his support for the Concerts des Mélophites, see Maurice Barthélemy, *André Campra (1660–1744): étude biographique et musicologique* ([Arles], 1995), pp. 154–5.

[30] See Catherine Cessac, 'La duchesse du Maine et la musique', in Catherine Cessac, Manuel Couvreur and Fabrice Prévat (eds), *La duchesse du Maine (1676–1753). Une mécène à la croisée des arts et des siècles* (Brussels, 2003), pp. 97–107, and Benoît Dratwicki, 'François Colin de Blamont à la cour de Sceaux: le jeu des influences et des rencontres', ibid., pp. 109–115.

[31] Renée Viollier, 'La musique à la cour de la Duchesse du Maine, de Châtenay aux grandes nuits de Sceaux, 1700–1715', *La revue musicale*, 20 (1939): 96–105 and 133–8, at 99.

[32] See Maurice Barthélemy, 'Les cantates de Jean-Baptiste Stuck', *Recherches sur la musique française classique*, 2 (1961–62): 125–37. The duc d'Aumont's concerts are mentioned in Joachim Christoph Nemeitz, *Séjour de Paris* (Leiden, 1727), p. 69; Nemeitz attended them before the duke's departure for England.

vainqueur des nuages (1721) celebrates the recovery of the eleven-year-old Louis XV from a serious illness. This work was performed in September of that year at court with the large resources of the Musique du Roi: the scoring specifies oboes (marked 'seuls' at several points), 'Violons' and 'Basses de violons [*sic*], Basson et continüe', while individual movements feature a 'Fluste allemande', solo violin and '[basse de] viole seule'.

Particularly revealing in the present context are those cantatas written specifically for the Paris Opéra (the Académie Royale de Musique), since here we are more fully informed on the available orchestral resources (see Table 9.1). The interaction of opera and cantata manifests itself in different ways. At its simplest, it entailed the performance of cantatas during operatic productions. André Cardinal Destouches, for instance, took advantage of his position as *Inspecteur général* at the Opéra to have his orchestral cantata *Œnone* (1716) performed at the end of Campra's *L'Europe galante* when this work was revived that year. In 1720 Gervais added the cantata *Pomone* to his ballet *Les amours de Protée* during the course of its first run. Unlike Destouches's *Œnone*, which was merely tacked on to Campra's *opéra-ballet*, Gervais's *Pomone* was integrated into the ballet, and it remained part of the work, albeit in abridged form, at the 1728 revival.[33] A further work of this kind is Clérambault's *La Muse de l'Opéra* (1716). The precise event for which it was written is not known,[34] but the score was on sale at the door of the Académie Royale de Musique, and the subject matter involves a guided tour of the marvels one could see there, thereby providing an opportunity to exploit the resources of the Opéra orchestra in such staple operatic scenes as a *bruit de chasse*, a *tempête*, a *sommeil* and a *scène infernale*.

More complex is the case of Clérambault's *Le soleil, vainqueur des nuages*. As noted, this was performed at court in September 1721, when it was described as a 'cantate allegorique'.[35] On 12 October it was staged at the Opéra under the new description of 'divertissement allegorique' and augmented with a sacrificial scene, choruses and ballet.[36] This staging must have been planned from the moment the

---

[33] Greer Garden, 'Réflexions sur les cantates scéniques d'André Campra et sur les cas de *Pomone* de Charles-Hubert Gervais', *XVIIe siècle*, 198 (1998): 29–36. For further evidence of the use of cantatas at the Opéra, see Gene E. Vollen, *The French Cantata: A Survey and Thematic Catalog* (Ann Arbor, 1982), pp. 28–9, and the *Catalogue de l'œuvre de François Colin de Blamont* http://philidor.cmbv.fr/catalogue/oeuvre-blamont-1 (accessed 14 February 2008).

[34] Donald Foster (ed.), *Louis-Nicolas Clérambault: Two Cantatas for Soprano and Chamber Ensemble* (Madison, 1979), p. ix, suggests a connection with the *Bals de l'Opéra*; these public balls do not, however, seem to have included vocal music: see Richard Semmens, *The 'Bals publics' at the Paris Opera in the Eighteenth Century* (Hillsdale, 2004), especially pp. 137–56.

[35] *Mercure de France*, September 1721, p. 56.

[36] *Mercure de France*, October 1721, pp. 124–5.

king's recovery was announced, so the cantata performed at court was presumably an abridged version of the divertissement.

A similar interaction between opera and cantata occurs in Campra's output. Greer Garden reveals that two of the six cantatas in the composer's second book (1714), *Les heureux époux* and *Silène*, are largely borrowed from his ballet *Les amours de Mars et de Vénus* (1712).[37] All the airs are taken from this ballet, and although those in the first are shorn of their obbligato lines, those in the second retain the original scoring for unison 'violons'.[38]

A further work in this same book illustrates the fine dividing line between cantata and divertissement (which in this context normally involved choral and dance movements). The material of the final cantata, *Enée et Didon*, also occurs in *Didon*, a divertissement commissioned for performance at Marseille on October 1714 in honour of Elisabeth of Parma (Isabella Farnese), who was travelling to Spain to marry Philip V.[39] The divertissement, which survives in a manuscript entitled 'Didon de M.ʳ Campra mise en concert',[40] is considerably longer than the cantata, and includes not only the expected choruses and ballet movements but even the occasional stage direction (e.g. 'le jour paraît', fol. 7v). At first sight, the subtitle 'mise en concert' suggests that it was an adaptation of the cantata, which, as we recall, was published that same year. Yet the cantata may well have been extracted from the divertissement. It is among the relatively few *cantates françoises* to contain no narrative: all the recitatives and airs are sung either by Dido or Aeneas, and the duets include both characters. In the cantata score this distribution must sometimes be merely inferred – by no means all the sections are labelled 'Enée' or 'Didon' – whereas in the divertissement it is explicit throughout.[41]

If the cantata *Enée et Didon* did, in fact, derive from *Didon*, then half the works in Campra's second book have their origins in stage works or divertissements. Indeed, Garden suggests that further cantatas in the volume may have had a similar dramatic origin: among other features, she cites a bourrée interrupted by recitative

---

[37] Greer Garden, '*Les amours de Vénus* (1712) et le *Second livre de cantates* (1714) de Campra', *Revue de musicologie*, 77 (1991): 96–107.

[38] Garden (ibid., p. 103) shows that sources of the ballet indicate 'tous' for the obbligato of the air 'Respectez la tranquillité', which suggests oboe doubling of unison violons.

[39] Barthélemy, *André Campra (1660–1744)*, p. 149. Campra himself was involved in organizing these festivities.

[40] F-Pa, M.892 Musique, fols 1–27v.

[41] A comparable case is Clérambault's *Le triomphe de la Paix* (1713), written for the Duke of Bavaria in celebration of the Treaty of Utrecht (1713) but given in 1732 at the Académie de Musique at Dijon with 'grand chœur et symphonie' (Cessac, *Clérambault*, p. 181). The fact that the published version lacks the customary narrative and is sung throughout by three characters – Flore, Pomone and Vertumne – may suggest that it began life as a divertissement rather than a cantata, in which case the version performed at Dijon may have been based on the now lost original.

in *La dispute de l'Amour et de l'Hymen*.[42] In a separate study she examines several cantatas embedded in Campra's stage works, notably *Les festes vénitiennes* (1710) and *Les noces de Vénus* (1740).[43] Indeed, the publisher Christophe Ballard drew attention to such cantatas in order to encourage separate performance: in advertisements and in the score itself, *Les festes vénitiennes* is described as a '*Ballet*, orné de trois *Cantates*'. The second of these became well enough known as an independent work to merit a *parodie*.[44]

* * *

The preceding paragraphs have focused on cantatas that were demonstrably conceived for orchestra – clearly no small number. Many of these works continued to be performed orchestrally once they had been published. As is well known, the heyday of the *cantate françoise* coincided with the emergence of the public concert in France, which in turn built on the experience of extensive concert activity in aristocratic and wealthy households.[45] We should therefore briefly consider the place of the cantata in three concert series – the Concert Spirituel, its sister series known as the Concert Français, and the Concerts de la Reine, all of which involved orchestra. Of these, the first two are best documented; both were inaugurated by André Danican Philidor: the Concert Spirituel in 1725, the Concert Français two years later.[46] The former only occasionally included cantatas, since the terms of its *privilège* precluded music with French words – hence the establishment of the Concert Français, which was not bound by any such restriction. This latter series, which ran from 1727 to 1733, regularly programmed cantatas alongside divertissements, concertos, Italian arias, *grands motets* and other works. Whereas the Concert Spirituel involved about 60 performers from the Musique du Roi, the Opéra and elsewhere,[47] the Concert Français took place on days when the Opéra was open and thus had to compete for performers with this and other organizations. No details of the precise numbers survive, but the orchestral forces must have been substantial enough to do justice to Lalande's *Te Deum*, with its trumpets and drums,

---

[42] Garden, '*Les amours de Vénus* (1712) et le *Second livre de cantates* (1714) de Campra', p. 96.

[43] Garden, 'Réflexions sur les cantates scéniques d'André Campra', pp. 30–33.

[44] See Jérôme Dorival, 'André Campra et la cantate française', in Lionnet (ed.), *Le concert des Muses*, pp. 319–31, at p. 329.

[45] Michel Brenet, *Les concerts en France sous l'ancien régime* (Paris, 1900), pp. 115–57.

[46] On these series, see Constant Pierre, *Histoire du Concert Spirituel, 1725–1790* (Paris, 1975), and David Tunley, *The Eighteenth-Century French Cantata*, 2nd edn (Oxford, 1997), pp. 6–11.

[47] *Mercure de France*, March 1725, p. 614. The figure of 60 performers included the chorus.

woodwind and strings, and to a concerto by Signor Antonio [Guido] for 'trompetes, cors de chasse, hautbois & tymbales, avec les chœurs de toute la symphonie'.[48]

Unlike the works considered so far, cantatas presented at these series were normally drawn from existing published collections (a rare exception is Rameau's *Le berger fidèle*, described as 'une nouvelle Cantate' when performed at the Concert Français in 1728).[49] It is thus noteworthy that, with certain exceptions (Clérambault's *Orphée* and *La musette*, for example), the chosen cantatas were ones whose published scores specify orchestral resources. Several have already been mentioned. Those given at the Concert Spirituel included Clérambault's *Léandre et Héro*, Colin de Blamont's *Didon* and Destouches's *Œnone*, all in 1728.[50] The first two reappeared frequently at the Concert Français, whose programmes between 1727 and 1731 included also the following orchestral cantatas: Clérambault's *Le soleil, vainqueur des nuages*,[51] Colin de Blamont's *La toilette de Vénus*, Destouches's *Sémelé*, Jean-Baptiste Dutartre's *La paix*, Mouret's *Andromède et Persée*, Rameau's *Le berger fidèle*, and Stuck's *Les bains de Toméry* and *Heraclite et Démocrite*. As for Stuck's *Céphale et Procris*, originally a chamber work, this was doubtless chosen on account of its rich textures, which lend themselves to orchestral performance: four-part strings at the start (violins 1 and 2, viola and continuo) and three obbligato parts (flute, violins 1 and 2) in later movements. The formula of these concerts, with its mixture of cantata, divertissement, *grand motet* and orchestral piece, was widely imitated at the 'académies de musique' (concert societies) that thrived in provincial towns.

Orchestral cantatas also featured prominently in music at court. Title pages of many collections proudly bear the phrase 'chanté devant le Roi' or 'devant la Reine'.[52] The latter description usually refers to performance at the Concerts de la Reine, established by Destouches in 1725 at the request of Queen Maria Leszczyńska. These were directed in alternate quarters by Destouches and Colin

---

[48] *Mercure de France*, April 1728, pp. 854–5. The expression 'chœurs de toute la symphonie' may refer to something other than the traditional *petit chœur–grand chœur* division, since a *Mercure* report of an anonymous [?German] chalumeau concerto draws attention to 'les accompagnements de la Simphonie qui forment les Chœurs' (February 1728, p. 386); see Brenet, *Les concerts en France*, p. 135.

[49] *Mercure de France*, November 1728, p. 2511.

[50] On 15 and 16 May 1728 the Concert Spirituel performed a 'Cantate tiré du 2e ballet de Lalande dansé par le roi en décembre 1720 aux Tuileries' – i.e., *Les folies de Cardenio* (see Lionel Sawkins, *A Thematic Catalogue of the Works of Michel-Richard de Lalande (1657–1726)* (Oxford, 2005), p. 573).

[51] Performances in 1728 were of the divertissement, whereas in 1729 the cantata version was used; see *Mercure de France*, December 1728, p. 2726, and ibid., October 1729, p. 2525.

[52] Dorival, *La cantate française au XVIIIe siècle*, p. 36, note 2; see also Vollen, *The French Cantata*, which includes transcriptions of the title pages of most cantata publications of the period.

de Blamont, *surintendants* of the Musique du Roi, and took place four or five times a month in the queen's apartments and elsewhere at Versailles or at other royal residences. The programmes mainly comprised concert performances of the French operatic repertory, but often ended with one or more cantatas. The performers included Opéra stars, as well as singers from the Musique de la Reine and players from the Musique du Roi.

In its reports of the Concerts de la Reine the *Mercure de France* rarely specifies individual cantatas. Those it names had usually appeared at the Concert Français, and the choice of works follows a similar pattern of chamber cantatas (Clérambault's *Orphée*, Blamont's *Le charme de la voix*) and orchestral ones (Clérambault's *Léandre et Héro*, Blamont's *Didon*, *La nymphe de la Seine*, *Le Parnasse lyrique* and *La toilette de Vénus*). Royal household accounts more fully reveal the extent to which cantatas formed part of the repertory of these concerts. The official scribe Le Noble, who was also an oboist in the Musique du Roi, submitted an invoice 'pour toutes les copies et partitions de musique qu'il a fait pour les concerts qui ont été chantés devant Leurs Majestés en 1726', these including scores and parts of the following cantatas:

Bernier:	*Les nymphes de Diane* and *L'Hymen*;
Clérambault:	*Orphée*, *Zéphyre et Flore*, *Alphée et Aréthuse*, *Le soleil, vainqueur des nuages*, *La musette*, *Léandre et Héro* and *L'Amour et Bacchus*;
Colin de Blamont:	*Diane et Endymion* and *La toilette de Vénus*;
Destouches:	*Sémelé*;
Dutartre:	*La Paix*;
Stuck:	*Proserpine* and *Neptune*.[53]

In 1730 Le Noble also supplied a large number of scores of operas and cantatas, the latter including works by Alexandre, Bergiron de Briou, Boismortier, Bourgeois, Burette, Campra, Courbois, David, Destouches, Gervais, Gervais de Rouen, Grandval, Lemaire, Mouret, Néron, Rameau and Renier.[54]

Concerning the number of performers active at the Concerts de la Reine, various archival documents include payments to some seventeen or eighteen players – generally five flutes and oboes (the same players 'doubled' on each), two bassoons, five or six violins, three 'basses d'accompagnement', bass viol and harpsichord.[55] Though relatively small, this ensemble would have proved more than adequate for performances in the royal apartments. It could, moreover, be reduced

---

[53] Marcelle Benoit, *Musiques de cour: Chapelle, Chambre, Écurie* (Paris, 1971), p. 365; for similar payments in 1729, see ibid., pp. 408–411.

[54] Ibid., p. 425; see also pp. 410 (payments for *parties séparées* of cantatas by Lalande and Destouches) and 411 (payments to the printer Ballard for various scores, including cantatas by Morin and Dutartre).

[55] Ibid., pp. 375, 404, 406–407, 420–21, 424.

or augmented when necessary, as illustrated by performances of the same cantata (Blamont's *La nymphe de la Seine*) in two different venues. The first took place in the queen's apartments in the Vieux Louvre on 7 November 1729, when the cantata was accompanied by what the *Mercure* describes as 'une magnifique Symphonie' comprising 'les S.rs Besson, Rebel, le Roux, Francœur, le Noble, Braun, Marchand, Alarius, & Brunel'. This ensemble, whether 'magnifique' or not, is actually quite small: the first four players listed were violinists, the others being, respectively, players of the oboe, flute, *basse de violon*, bass viol and bassoon.[56] The second performance was given two days later in the Salon de la Paix at Versailles. In this larger venue the concert involved 'toute la Musique du Roi', and Blamont's cantata was performed 'avec grande Symphonie, Trompettes, Timballes, &c.'.[57]

Taken together, then, the evidence of orchestral performance of the cantata repertory at the Opéra or in concert series in Paris and at court is extensive. Moreover, the practice of orchestral performance was by no means limited to the organizations we have examined, as is suggested by numerous elaborately scored cantatas that cannot be linked with these series or venues – among them Montéclair's *Le retour de la Paix* (c.1709), Courbois's *Dom Quichotte* (1710), Stuck's *Les festes bolonnoises* (1714), and Bourgeois's *La lyre d'Anacréon* (undated), all requiring trumpets.

* * *

In the *Recueil de cantates* of 1728 Bachelier tempers his praise of the cantatas of Campra with the criticism that they 'sometimes smack a bit too much of the Opéra'.[58] We have indeed noted the strong links between cantata and stage in Campra's output from the second book onwards. But Campra was far from being the only person whose cantatas reveal operatic influences, which is no surprise when so many composers – Stuck, Gervais, Montéclair, Mouret, Colin de Blamont – worked in both areas.

One respect in which French opera proved especially influential in this connection is the manner in which the orchestra was treated. Although the

---

[56] *Mercure de France*, November 1729, p. 2729. The list includes no keyboard player. Blamont's score not only calls for trumpets and timpani but also has obbligato parts for divided flutes and oboes.

[57] Ibid. Accounts for the Concerts de la Reine do not include payments to trumpet or timpani players or, indeed, to players of the viola, since these were brought in, when required, from other departments of the Musique du Roi, such as the Grande Écurie or the Vingt-quatre Violons du Roi. For details of the Musique du Roi personnel at this time, see Yolande de Brossard and Érik Kocevar, 'États de la France (1644–1789). La Musique: les institutions et les hommes', *Recherches sur la musique française classique*, 30 (1999–2000): 323–35.

[58] '[...] elles sentent qu'elquefois un peu trop l'Opera': J. Bachelier, *Recueil de cantates* (The Hague, 1728), p. 6.

cantata can seldom be properly regarded as 'opera in miniature', its appropriation of many operatic *topoi* – storms and sleep scenes,[59] evocations of birdsong, rustic music-making, echoes and the like – usually entailed appropriation of an associated orchestral style. Further, the diverse styles of accompaniment of cantata airs and ariettes often have much in common with their equivalents in contemporary stage works. Operatic influence, though perceptible in chamber cantatas, is naturally more obvious in orchestral ones, not least those originally conceived for the Opéra itself.

This being so, it is worth reminding ourselves of the performing forces available at the Académie Royale de Musique during the period of the orchestral cantata's evolution (Table 9.1).

Table 9.1 The orchestra of the Académie Royale de Musique, 1713–38.[60]

	1713	1719	1725/26	1738
Petit chœur				
Violins	2	2	[2]	4
Transverse flutes	2	2	[2]	—
Theorbos	2	2	1	—
Harpsichord	1	1	1	1
Basses de viole	1–2	2	1–2	—
Basses de violon (later, cellos)[61]	2	2	2–3	3
Contrebasse	1	1	1	1
Grand chœur				
Violins	14	16	14	16
Hautes-contre (viola 1)	3	2	3	2–3
Tailles (viola 2)	2	2	3	3
Quintes (viola 3)	2	2	—	—
Basses de violon (later, cellos)	10	10	10–11	11
Contrebasse	1	1	1	1
Flutes and oboes	6	[4]	5	5
Bassoons	4	5	4	5

---

[59] See Caroline Wood, 'Orchestra and Spectacle in the *tragédie en musique* 1673–1715: oracle, *sommeil* and *tempête*', *Proceedings of the Royal Musical Association*, 108 (1981–82): 25–46, and Michele Cabrini, 'Expressive Polarity: the Aesthetics of tempête and sommeil in the French Baroque Cantata' (PhD dissertation, Princeton University, 2005).

[60] Statistics taken from Jérôme de La Gorce, 'L'orchestra de l'Opéra et son évolution de Campra à Rameau', *Revue de musicologie*, 76 (1990): 23–43; see also Graham Sadler, 'Rameau's Singers and Players: a Little-known Inventory of 1738', *Early Music*, 11 (1983): 453–67.

[61] The replacement of *basses de violon* by cellos occurred during the 1730s; see Graham Sadler, 'Rameau and the Orchestra', *Proceedings of the Royal Musical Association*, 108 (1981–82): 47–68.

The Opéra orchestra was the largest permanently established ensemble that is known to have performed cantatas. During the period that concerns us it maintained the same *concertino–ripieno* distinction we have already glimpsed in some cantata performances. The *petit chœur* included the continuo players plus a pair of violins and flutes, entrusted with solos. The *grand chœur* comprised a substantial string section of between thirty-two and thirty-four players, and nine or ten woodwind. Where required, trumpets, horns and timpani were played either by supernumeraries or by members of the string section. The polarity of the outer parts is noteworthy, with few players on each of the inner parts. The elimination of the third viola part (*quinte*) occurred gradually over a period extending from as early as 1712 until about 1725,[62] a subject to which we shall return.

One striking feature of the orchestration of French opera at this time is the great diversity of sonorities and instrumental combinations. While certain movements utilized standard textures (the overture and many dances, for example, are scored for full strings, with oboes and bassoons doubling treble and bass), the accompaniment of vocal airs is often strikingly imaginative, the composer responding to the particular sentiments or imagery of the text. Here, the *petit chœur* often came into its own: the obbligatos of operatic airs often involve some soloistic combination of flutes, violins and/or bass viol. The influence on the orchestral cantata of this diverse approach to scoring may be illustrated by one such work specifically written for the Académie Royale orchestra, Clérambault's *La Muse de l'Opéra*, in which the successive vocal airs are scored as follows:

1. *Air gay*, 'Au son des trompettes' – four instrumental staves labelled respectively: (i) 'Trompette, et 1.[r] dessus de violon'; (ii) '2.[d] Dessus de violon'; (iii) 'Timballes, et Basses de violon'; (iv) 'Basses de Violes, et continües' (figured). The middle section of this *da capo* movement includes passages in trio texture for divided oboes and unison bassoons.
2. *Tempeste*, 'Mais quel bruit interrompt ces doux amusemens?' – three instrumental staves: (i) unlabelled but intended for unison violins, which descend to their lowest open string; (ii) 'basses de violon'; (iii) 'Contre-Basse, et Basse Continüe' (figured).
3. *Air*, 'Oyseaux, qui sous ces feüillages' – two instrumental staves: (i) 'Flute allemande seule'; (ii) 'Violons' in G1 clef (unfigured).
4. *Sommeil*, 'Vos concerts heureux oyseaux' – two instrumental staves: (i) 'violons'; (ii) figured bass (unlabelled).
5. [*Scène infernale*], 'Mais quels nouveaux accords' – two instrumental staves: (i) 'tous' (i.e., unison violins with oboe doubling, except where the line descends too low); (ii) figured bass (unlabelled).

---

[62] Caroline Wood, *Music and Drama in the* tragédie en musique, *1673–1715* (New York, 1996), p. 167; La Gorce, 'L'orchestra de l'Opéra et son évolution de Campra à Rameau', p. 30.

6. *Air*, 'Ce n'est qu'une belle chimere' – two instrumental staves: (i) a mainly unison line marked 'tous' / 'violons'; (ii) figured bass (unlabelled). The middle section includes passages for 'hautbois seul'.

Such a varied sequence would not be out of place in the contemporary French operatic repertory. As in opera, it is the text that motivates these contrasts. The successive movements of *La Muse de l'Opéra* illustrate the proposition that at the Opéra 'tout l'Univers se decouvre à vos yeux'. If this cantata consequently exploits the principle of text-led orchestral contrasts more than most, the same principle is nevertheless apparent in the majority of orchestral cantatas.

* * *

The engraved layout of Clérambault's score raises one fundamental but largely overlooked question about the orchestral textures. To anyone familiar with French Baroque opera scores, the presentation of *La Muse de l'Opéra* conforms exactly to that of a typical *partition réduite*. By this term is meant, at that period, a score which lacks most or all of the inner parts.[63] A *partition générale*, by contrast, retained these so-called *parties de remplissage*, although publishers produced fewer scores of this kind because of a combination of higher costs and lower demand.

Example 9.1, from the 'Tempeste' in this cantata, demonstrates the bare two-part textures typical of a *partition réduite*. Bar 10 consists almost entirely of a forcefully prolonged tritone; bar 11 begins with bare ninths and includes octave E♭s on the third beat and two open fifths thereafter. Sparse textures of this kind might just be tolerable in a one-to-a-part performance in a small room. At the Opéra, however, this movement would have introduced some sixteen violins on the upper line and an equal number of instruments on the lower line (bassoons, *basses de violon* and *contrebasse*).[64] Such forces would merely emphasize the bareness; the Académie's single harpsichord and two theorbos could never have proved adequate to project the powerful harmonies indicated by the continuo figuring.

---

[63] Italian cantatas did not cultivate 'reduced' scores of this type. However, the 'songs' (arias, plus some duets) from Italian operas published by Walsh in London form a close equivalent. In similar fashion, the reduced format facilitated production, reduced costs and increased practicality for amateur or provincial performers.

[64] Julie Anne Sadie, *The Bass Viol in French Baroque Chamber Music* (Ann Arbor, 1980), pp. 39–43, notes that this cantata is one of eight to include a *tempête* in which the bass line divides (see also Cabrini, 'Expressive Polarity', pp. 117–19). That this is also a feature of many operatic *tempêtes*, among them the highly influential one in Marais's *Alcyone* (1706), is illustrated in Wood, 'Orchestra and Spectacle', pp. 44–5, and the same author's *Music and Drama in the* tragédie en musique, *1673–1715*, pp. 334–45. For a facsimile of the opening of the Marais *tempête*, see James R. Anthony, *French Baroque Music from Beaujoyeulx to Rameau*, rev. 3rd edn (Portland, Oregon, 1997), p. 157.

Example 9.1 Clérambault, cantata *La Muse de l'Opéra* (1716), 'Tempeste' bars 9–11; continuo derived from a second, simplified bass line (here omitted) marked 'Contrebasse, et Basse Continüe'. Violins originally in G1 clef.

Had this been the intended manner of performance, a composer of Clérambault's undoubted skill and sensitivity could easily have adjusted the part-writing to ensure a more self-sufficient treble–bass duet. But the Opéra orchestra, as we have seen, included half-a-dozen viola players, and it is highly unlikely that they remained silent in a movement so clearly intended for the *grand chœur*. We must therefore suppose that Clérambault's original score included inner parts of the kind envisaged by Rousseau in his definition of *en grande symphonie* quoted above (i.e., for *hautes-contre*, *tailles* and possibly *quintes*),[65] but that these inner parts were discarded when the score was prepared for publication as a *partition réduite*.

Example 9.2 presents an editorial reconstruction of the same passage, with added *hautes-contre* and *tailles*. Given the completeness of the continuo figuring, reconstruction is straightforward. Until the 1730s and the appearance of Rameau's operas French inner parts seldom had much melodic interest, since they were performed by so few players in relation to the numbers on treble and bass that their lines could scarcely be distinguished individually. They tend to adopt the rhythm of one or other of the outer parts and are mainly confined to the space between

---

[65] This cantata belongs to the period when the *quinte* was being phased out.

Example 9.2 As Example 9.1, with added viola parts (*hautes-contre* and *tailles*). Violins originally in G1 clef.

violins and bass (though not wholly, especially when the former descend to their lowest register). As the unflattering term *parties de remplissage* suggests, they are primarily harmonic fillers. Yet comparison of Examples 9.1 and 9.2 reveals the huge contribution they can make to a satisfactory performance, and few people would nowadays agree with Jean-Jacques Rousseau that 'in eliminating [such inner parts] the piece is not mutilated'.[66]

I first drew attention to the need for editorial reconstruction in passages of this kind as long ago as 1981 when reviewing an edition of *La Muse de l'Opéra*. Even

---

[66] Rousseau, *Dictionnaire de musique*, art. 'Obligé': '[…] par le retranchement [des parties de remplissage] la Piece n'est point mutilée'.

so, the general principle is still not widely recognized.[67] One reason is that by no means all movements in a typical orchestral cantata lack viola parts. In this, they differ from, say, François Couperin's *Concert dans le goût théatral* (*Les goûts-réünis*, 1724) in which, as Peter Holman has convincingly shown, all movements require editorial completion.[68] In the orchestral cantata repertory, by contrast, the need for inner parts may well be only intermittent. This is demonstrated by another cantata written for the Opéra, Destouches's *Œnone* (1716), where the movements with *symphonie* are scored as follows:

1. *Ritournelle*: four obbligato parts, two marked 'flutes', two marked 'violons', plus 'basse continue'.
2. 'Les plus aimables concerts': two obbligato parts, both marked 'hautbois', plus unlabelled continuo.
3. 'Venez, charmant Paris': two obbligato parts, respectively marked 'flutes' and 'violons', plus unlabelled continuo.
4. 'Vents tumultueux': two instrumental parts, the upper marked 'violons', the lower an unlabelled continuo part.
5. 'Volez, grands Dieux': three instrumental parts, the top two both labelled 'violons', the third a continuo part marked 'tous'.
6. 'Triomphe, tendre Amour': two obbligato parts, both labelled 'violons', plus 'basse-continue'.

The instrumental accompaniments of nos. 1, 2 and 6 are mainly or wholly in trio texture and are clearly intended to be self-sufficient; moreover, there is no reason to suspect that the two- and three-part instrumental writing of no. 3 (and probably no. 5) is incomplete. But no. 4, another tumultuous *tempête*, reveals voice-leading 'defects' similar to those of Example 9.1 above. True, the two-part writing of the *ritournelles* is less consistently bare; but once the voice enters, the three-part textures include root-position diminished triads and frequent octave doublings rather than full triads.

The supposition that Destouches's part-writing does not result merely from faulty technique gains support from the example of another work – one of the 'embedded' cantatas in Campra's *Les festes vénitiennes* discussed earlier. Here, we have a cantata, albeit one untypical in many respects, that exists both in *partition réduite* and in full score. The cantata – untitled, like all those embedded in operas – appears in the *entrée* 'Les Sérénades et les Joueurs' (scene 4). It begins with the air 'Suivez-moy, venez tous', a *sommeil* in all but name. Example 9.3a presents an

---

[67] See *Music & Letters*, 62 (1981), pp. 446–7. To my knowledge, the only other source to note that inner parts may be missing is Cessac, *Nicolas Clérambault*, p. 192 (on this same cantata) and p. 203 (on *Le soleil, vainqueur des nuages*).

[68] Peter Holman, 'An Orchestral Suite by François Couperin?', *Early Music*, 15 (1986): 71–6, argues that this *concert* consists of orchestral sections, published in *partition réduite*, from a now lost stage work.

Example 9.3a Campra, opéra-ballet *Les festes vénitiennes* (1710), air 'Suivez-moy, venez tous', bars 45–53: (a) from *partition réduite* (Paris: Christophe Ballard, 1710), 'Les Sérénades et les Joueurs', pp. 22–3. Violins originally in C1 clef.

248 *Aspects of the Secular Cantata in Late Baroque Italy*

Example 9.3b Campra, opéra-ballet *Les festes vénitiennes* (1710), air 'Suivez-moy, venez tous', bars 45–53: (b) from F-Po, A. 78a (ms full score, c. 1710), p. 122. Violins and *hautes-contres* originally in soprano clef, *tailles* in C2 clef, *quintes* in C3 clef.

extract from this air as it appears in the *partition réduite* published in the year of the opera's premiere (1710); here we see the same kinds of 'defect' identified in the Clérambault and Destouches *tempêtes* – a diminished triad in root position (bar 45), octave doublings rather than full triads in all bars except 45 and 48, and bare octaves and/or fifths (bars 47 and 49). Example 9.3b derives from a manuscript full score that includes Campra's three inner parts.[69] The transformation is immediate: the prevailing sparseness of Example 9.3a is replaced by a full six-part texture, while the approach to the final cadence – frankly, rather unpleasant in the *partition réduite* – emerges as a progression of wonderful richness and invention.

It is instructive to note that, of all the airs in the three cantatas from *Les festes vénitiennes*, this is the only one to include violas. Such parts, important as they are, were certainly not included as standard in movements requiring orchestral violins. This is an essential consideration when debating whether or not a given movement lacks inner parts. By and large, the more italianate the idiom, the less likely it is to require completion. Example 9.4, from Elisabeth Jacquet de La Guerre's sacred cantata *Le temple rebasti* (1711), illustrates the kind of self-sufficient two-part instrumental writing with obvious Italian roots – in this case the *siciliana*. Here the composer has taken evident care to avoid bare or harsh intervals on the main beats, and her simple but elegant *symphonie* may be performed very satisfactorily with the unison 'violons' and continuo indicated. Accompaniments in trio texture with divided violins or other instruments likewise have Italian roots

---

[69] F-Po, A.78.a. Max Lütolf (ed.), *André Campra: Les festes venitiennes* (Paris, 1972), p. xi, shows that this score dates from the year of the premiere.

Example 9.4 Jacquet de La Guerre, cantata *Le temple rebasti* (1711), opening *Symphonie*, bars 1–3. Violins originally in G1 clef.

Example 9.5 Campra, cantata *Le jaloux*, book 3 (1728), air 'Som[m]eil, vien soulage', opening *Symphonie* (with added editorial inner parts), bars 1–7. Violins originally in G1 clef.

and are almost invariably self-sufficient. In any case, French orchestras at this time did not often exploit textures that combined violas with divided violins, at least in secular music.

Between them, such italianate two- and three-part accompaniments account for a large proportion of the *symphonies* in orchestral cantatas of the period. But these works often include movements whose style and derivation are more obviously French – among them *tempêtes*, as we have seen, and *sommeils*. In addition to the examples already discussed, the following cantatas contain *tempêtes* (though not all so named) that arguably lack their original inner parts: Jacquet de La Guerre's *Jonas* (1708) and *Le sommeil d'Ulisse* (1715); Clérambault's *Léandre et Héro* (1713); Colin de Blamont's *Didon* (1723); Louis Le Maire's *L'Été* (1724). The repertory includes fewer *sommeils*, and many of these are self-sufficient. But the *air* 'Som[m]eil, vien, soulage les maux' in Campra's *Le jaloux* (1728) bears most of the tell-tale signs of incompleteness. The opening bars are shown in Example 9.5, in which the outer staves present the two-part texture found in the engraved score. Apparent weaknesses such as prominent open fifths (bars 1, 3, 5), bare octaves (bar 7) and root-position diminished triads (bar 4) are by no means confined to this passage, being evident in other *symphonies* in this cantata. If we accept that Campra's score is a *partition réduite*, however, the 'weaknesses' disappear once the editorial inner parts (middle stave) have been added.

Unlike the typical chamber cantata, the orchestral equivalent often includes independent instrumental movements. These range from fully fledged overtures (vestiges, in some cases, of a previous incarnation as a divertissement) to ballet movements or descriptive *symphonies*.[70] Almost all such movements are presented in *partition réduite* – usually in two-part writing, where the yawning gap between treble and bass, allied to a preponderance of bare intervals, is once again symptomatic of missing inner parts. When the strings are doubled by trumpets, as in the 'Air de triomphe' in Campra's *La colère d'Achille* (1728) or the 'Bruit de trompettes' in Colin de Blamont's *Le Parnasse lyrique*, the impression of bareness is merely reinforced.

A final symptom of *partition réduite* presentation in the *symphonies* is the alternation between two-part writing (treble and bass) and trio passages. French Baroque orchestral music often exploits the contrast between full orchestra and passages in trio texture, whether for the classic *trio des hautbois* or for the violins and/or flutes of the *petit chœur*. In *partitions réduites* the trios survived, but the 'full' passages were normally reduced to treble and bass. Oddly enough, some reduced scores maintained three staves throughout, even when the top two have identical music. Clérambault's *Le soleil, vainqueur des nuages*, which, as we recall, was performed both at court and at the Opéra, provides an example. The opening ritournelle of the air 'Préparons d'eclatantes festes' is headed 'Fanfares'. The top two staves both present an identical melodic line, one designated

---

[70] Here, a parallel with the instrumentally accompanied Italian cantata, which quite often contains a *sinfonia*, is apparent.

'hautbois' and the other 'violons', while the third stave has the figured bass. At bar 10 this two-part writing gives way to an imitative trio texture in which oboes, violins and continuo enter in turn. Eight bars later, the two-part texture returns, but still with separate staves for the treble instruments. Had this been a *partition générale*, we may surmise that it would contain viola parts as far as bar 10, and that these would rest during the eight-bar imitative trio but then reappear at bar 18. This alternating pattern continues throughout the air. In the 'two-part' passages, moreover, Clérambault's continuo figuring indicates some biting dissonances that were doubtless originally supplied by the inner parts. If this air were performed with orchestra but without violas, the continuo could hardly be expected to project such dissonances adequately; and without the spice that these add the piece would seem fairly bland.

* * *

It remains to consider the extent to which the orchestral French cantata may be considered a coherent genre with its own characteristics, over and above the use of an orchestra. Until now, attempts to classify the *cantate françoise* have focused mainly on subject matter (mythological, chivalric, pastoral, anacreontic, comic, sacred, etc.), while the question of instrumentation has been pursued no further than the basic *avec symphonie–sans symphonie* distinction. From the foregoing discussion, however, it should be clear that four types of cantata may be distinguished on the basis of their scoring. At one extreme is the cantata *sans symphonie*. In the period up to 1713 such works form much the most numerous group, comprising well over half of all cantatas. During the period 1714–30, however, the continuo cantata fell out of favour, accounting for scarcely more than a third of the examples published. (In Italy a similar decline occurs after about 1710.[71]) At the other extreme is the cantata *à grande symphonie*. This group includes those performed at the Opéra and many of those at court, especially ones involving trumpets and drums. It also includes the above-mentioned works by Montéclair, Bourgeois, Courbois, Stuck and Campra that likewise include trumpets. Between them, these works *à grande symphonie* form a small but significant proportion of cantatas, the number growing steadily from about 1709 onwards.

The remaining cantatas, all *avec symphonie*, fall into two categories depending on whether chamber or orchestral performance is implied by the instrumental designations. Here, it is sometimes difficult to make a hard-and-fast distinction, since the captioning may be inconsistent or imprecise (e.g., in the use of such terms as *symphonie* or *accompagnement*). Even so, we can estimate that in the period to up 1713 chamber performance is overwhelmingly the original intention. Thereafter, a sudden shift occurs, and from this date cantatas in these two categories occur in roughly equal proportion.

---

[71] See Michael Talbot, *The Chamber Cantatas of Antonio Vivaldi* (Woodbridge, 2006), p. 13.

One consideration concerns the forms displayed by these different categories of cantata. In adapting the Italian cantata to French taste, the poet Jean-Baptiste Rousseau imported one particular scheme in which three recitatives alternate with three arias, and this RARARA pattern became the norm in the early years of the French cantata's development. As the *cantate françoise* evolved, however, exceptions can increasingly be found – most of them occurring in orchestral cantatas and especially in those *à grande symphonie*. Often, these works contain a much larger number of movements, some of them purely instrumental, and they depart more frequently from simple recitative–air alternation. Many begin with a substantial instrumental movement, variously labelled 'prélude', 'symphonie' or 'ouverture'. These diverse features may well be a consequence of the circumstances in which many cantatas were created: as occasional works. The forms of some representative cantatas *à grande symphonie* may be expressed as follows (where P is a free-standing preludial movement and where other instrumental movements are indicated in italics):

Bourgeois, *La lyre d'Anacreon* – P+AAAARARA
Clérambault, *La Muse de l'Opéra* – P+RAARAAARRA
Campra, *La colère d'Achille* – P+R *air de triomphe* RARARARA
Colin de Blamont, *Le Parnasse* – P+RA *air* R *musette* AA *musettes / bruit de trompettes* RA
Colin de Blamont, *La nymphe de la Seine* – P+RAA *air en rondeau*

It must be conceded that the dividing line between the more elaborate orchestral cantatas *à grande symphonie* and the divertissement is often quite fine. Some works, though published as cantatas, should properly be regarded as divertissements in view of their extensive use not just of instrumental movements but also of chorus – a defining feature of the divertissement. This is the case with the two huge works in Bernier's fifth book. The title page makes clear their ambivalent character: *Les nuits de Sceaux, Concerts de chambre ou Cantates françoises [...] en maniere de divertissements*. A further ambivalent work is Pipereau's *L'Isle de Délos* (1715), subtitled 'concert en forme de cantate' and comprising fourteen movements, among them a French overture and four ballet movements.

* * *

For the performer, such niceties of classification may be of less consequence than the fact that a substantial number of orchestral cantatas cannot be performed adequately until the inner parts have been reconstituted. To my knowledge, no score has yet been published in which this has been done. At the same time, orchestral cantatas – especially ones with Opéra or court connections – seem to be less frequently performed today than the chamber cantatas, or are performed with one-to-a-part forces. These observations may not be unconnected: if economic factors doubtless contribute to the comparative neglect of the more elaborately scored works, another reason may well be the unpromising appearance (at least to anyone unfamiliar with the *partition réduite* layout) of those movements that lack their essential harmonic core.

It is not the aim of this chapter to encourage the indiscriminate addition of inner parts in places where they were never intended. In assessing whether a given movement lacks violas, editors must be finely attuned to contemporary French scoring practices. This presupposes a painstaking study of contemporary operas and ballets and, above all, a minute comparison of those works that survive in both *partition réduite* and *partition générale*. If this investigation leads to the renaissance of a long-neglected repertory, it will be worth the effort.

Chapter 10

Patterns and Strategies of Modulation in Cantata Recitatives

Michael Talbot

It is a matter of simple observation that the recitatives of late-Baroque cantatas are discussed less often and less comprehensively in modern writings on the genre than their arias. This relative silence carries the implicit message that in the final analysis recitatives are utilitarian music unworthy of particularly close attention. Such a view has gained support from a long tradition of inattention towards – sometimes verging on alienation from – recitative on the part of audiences, which has had knock-on effects for both composers (who have liked recitatives to be few and short) and singers (who have sung them hurriedly and inexpressively). This sorry state of affairs was described around the middle of the eighteenth century by Francesco Saverio Quadrio in the second volume of his great history of Italian poetry.[1] Quadrio even proposed a limit of six lines for recitative stanzas: an over-pessimistic (and in the event rarely observed) formula that nevertheless illustrates the nature of the problem.[2] Viewing the matter more broadly, the polarization of function between aria and recitative – the first predominantly describing states, the second predominantly recounting actions – guaranteed the survival of the latter. Poets, especially, clung tenaciously to recitative, for the *versi sciolti* to which it was set – lines, mostly unrhymed, freely mixing scansions of seven and eleven syllables – seemed to offer greater possibilities for the display of erudition and poetic art than the shorter metres preferred for arias.

Musical connoisseurs were, of course, kinder towards recitative than lay audiences. Johann Adolph Scheibe commended the great range and freedom of modulation that they permitted,[3] while the imperial *Kapellmeister* Johann Joseph Fux, in his famous treatise on counterpoint (which is really a general manual of composition), showed – convincingly, even to modern eyes – how the forms of cadence used in recitative formed an efficient and coherent system of punctuation

---

[1] Francesco Saverio Quadrio, *Della storia e della ragione d'ogni* poesia, 5 vols (Bologna and Milan, 1739–52), vol. 2, pp. 336.

[2] Ibid., p. 334, quoted in Marco Bizzarini, *Benedetto Marcello. Le cantate profane: I testi poetici* (Venice, 2003), p. xii.

[3] Johann Adolph Scheibe, *Critischer Musikus. Neue, vermehrte und verbesserte Auflage* (Leipzig, 1746), pp. 399–400, quoted in Colin Timms, 'The Dramatic in Vivaldi's Cantatas', in Lorenzo Bianconi and Giovanni Morelli (eds), *Antonio Vivaldi. Teatro musicale, cultura e società* (Florence, 1982), pp. 97–129, at p. 99.

analogous to the full stops, commas and other marks in the written language.[4] True, the comments on recitative by Scheibe and Fux are primarily technical, not aesthetic, in nature, but they do at least serve to remove any misapprehension that composers approached the composition of recitatives unsystematically or with little ambition. Scheibe in fact singled out recitatives in what he termed the 'chamber' (as opposed to the 'theatrical') style for approbation, noting that they gave the composer the freedom to follow the dictates of his imagination in order to create a beautiful effect.[5] (It is important to remember that in cantatas, unlike operas, singers read from the notes and were thereby freed from the burden of memorization. Complexities – for instance, long flights of arioso or enharmonic changes – that would have been out of place on the operatic stage found a natural home in the more intimate and cultivated milieu of the chamber cantata.)

One barrier to the analysis of late-Baroque recitative is that it is – to a greater extent than any other kind of music practised in its day – through-composed. That is to say, its thematic material is not reprised and/or developed (in the ordinary understanding of those terms) in the course of the movement: the music is, strictly speaking, *athematic*. Whereas in the middle of the seventeenth century, when the chamber cantata was still a fairly young genre, one finds some recitatives employing regular patterning for short-range effect (this would include what Roger Freitas has termed 'block sequential repetition' in connection with Carissimi's and Cesti's cantatas),[6] the tendency proved short lived. From the time of Stradella and Legrenzi (roughly, the 1660s) onwards, the characteristic means of putting together a recitative movement is simply additive. The musical material itself is to a large extent centonized: it is pieced together in both its treble (the vocal part) and its bass (the continuo part) from recognizable, already much-used fragments.[7] This high dependence on pre-existent material, although unquestionably a limiting and disciplining factor, does not in any sense stifle creativity, since the combinations and recombinations of the simple formulas contained in the bran tub of recitative are endless. In fact, the very familiarity of the material makes it easier, rather than harder, to achieve striking effects, since these can operate against a background of clear expectations on the listener's part.

Among the many fundamental differences between aria style and recitative style in the cantata repertory from early times is the treatment of tonality. Arias, whether cast in binary or in *da capo* form, are 'closed' tonal structures. That is, the key established at the outset is the one in which the movement ends. Recitatives, in contrast, are in principle 'open' tonal structures with no restriction on the relationship between the first chord (most often classifiable from what follows as a tonic) and

---

[4] Johann Joseph Fux, *Gradus ad Parnassum* (Vienna, 1725), pp. 194–5.

[5] Scheibe, *Critischer Musikus*, pp. 399–400.

[6] See Freitas's introduction to his critical edition of Atto Melani's cantatas (*Atto Melani: Complete Cantatas*, Madison, 2006), p. xvii.

[7] 'To centonize' and 'centonization' come from the Italian word *centone*, meaning a patchwork quilt. This method of invention and construction is widespread in traditional folk musics and is a characteristic feature of plainsong.

the final chord (usually a tonic but occasionally a dominant). The rationale behind the distinction is that an aria is a free-standing structure that needs tonal rounding to complement its thematic rounding,[8] whereas a recitative is a connective structure that, so far as tonality is concerned, takes the movement from the vicinity of the key of the preceding aria to the vicinity of the key of the following aria (or to the key of the cantata as a whole, if the recitative lies in final position).

But the distinction between open and closed structure is not the only one separating aria from recitative in the domain of tonality. There is also a fundamental contrast in what I shall term 'tonal range'. By and large, late-Baroque arias, like all other types of free-standing movement (in sonatas, concertos, suites, etc.), move within a set of six closely related keys comprising (i) the tonic, (ii) its dominant and subdominant, (iii) the relative major or minor key and (iv) the dominant and subdominant of the latter. Another way to visualize this set is to say that the tonic triads of the six keys are the diatonic major and minor triads based on the notes of the home key. Of course, there may be occasional excursions outside the set, but these are usually parenthetical in nature and not wide-ranging.

As Scheibe recognized, recitatives roam with total freedom back and forth around the circle of fifths. To do this, they need techniques of modulation that allow them to cover ground more rapidly than is allowed by those used in arias. Chief among them is what I have elsewhere called the 'modal shift'.[9] This is a change from major to minor, or the reverse, while retaining the keynote. At a stroke, the music thereby advances or retreats three numbers around the clock face of the circle of fifths. Many such shifts employ ellipsis: that is, the altered tonic triad is not present in its own right but is implicit as a central link between two other tonalities. Take, for example, a modulating sequence ascending from the tonic one note at a time. In an aria, such a sequence would progress upwards in the following fashion: C – d – e – F:[10] the choice of major or minor depends on the nature of the diatonic triads within the home key. In a recitative, however, it would be possible to proceed C – D – E – F♯, travelling half-way round the circle of fifths in three equal steps. Were one to insert the missing links suppressed through ellipsis, the progression would appear as C – (d) – D – (e) – E – (f♯) – F♯. For this type of sequential progression, in which not only the interval between successive keys but their modality remains constant, I employ the expression 'modulation chain'. An even more common type of modulation chain proceeds, without change of modality, one step at a time around the circle of fifths (e.g., C – G – D – A). Here, there is arguably no ellipsis but simply continuation by analogy.

---

[8] 'Rounding' refers to the reprise or recapitulation of tonal, thematic or any other features from earlier in the structure. Where rounding occurs in customary locations, as when an introductory ritornello reappears in the original key at the end of the 'A' section of a *da capo* aria, it can provide useful signposts for the listener.

[9] Michael Talbot, 'Modal shifts in the Sonatas of Domenico Scarlatti', *Chigiana*, n.s. 20 (1985): 25–43.

[10] Capitals stand for major keys, lower case for minor keys.

The tonal design of recitatives is governed in the first instance by the keys of the preceding and the following aria or – in cases where the recitative is a first or last movement – by the tonality of the cantata as a whole. Three paragraphs earlier, I was careful to write that a recitative travels from the vicinity of one key to the vicinity of another rather than from one key to another *tout court*. To draw an analogy from daily life, this is like saying that a recitative is not like a taxi travelling from doorstep to doorstep but like a bus travelling from one stop to another, each stop being within easy reach of its respective doorstep. In a recent article I discussed the reason why, in the late Baroque period, recitatives in cantatas (and also in other genres) so rarely begin and end in the key of the adjacent aria.[11] My conclusion was that the progression from the last chord of a recitative to the different chord opening an aria often has affective force, instantaneously establishing its mood. Were a recitative routinely to end on the tonic chord of the following aria, expressive potential would be lost. A similar progression from the last chord of an aria to the first chord of a recitative creates a necessary disjunction that defines the start of the recitative as a new beginning. These conventions provide the composer with a useful margin of flexibility that is often exploited in opera when cuts are made or arias are substituted.

In opera and other large-scale dramatic genres (oratorio, serenata) there are really no rules (other than a preference for variety) governing the succession of keys in consecutive arias. In Albinoni's serenata *Il nome glorioso in terra, santificato in cielo* (1724), for example, the succession of keys for closed numbers (arias and ensembles) is: [first part] B♭ – A – F – D – D [second part] G – B♭ – C – D – C – D. From the point of view of abstract tonal architecture, this is as good as random, but the choices have, of course, been informed by considerations of instrumentation (D major is the 'trumpet' key) and affect. The wide tonal gap between the B flat major of the first aria and the A major of the second is noteworthy but not untypical.

In chamber cantatas, however, where the arias typically number only two or (after 1700) at most three, such freedom is usually curtailed, and instrumentation becomes relevant only on the rare occasions when wind instruments are employed in an obbligato role. In a cantata that adopts the Aria – Recitative – Aria (ARA) plan both arias are perforce in the same key. In a RARA cantata the first aria is customarily in a foreign key. But the choice is generally not much wider than one is accustomed to find in internal slow movements within sonatas or concertos. To take one typical instance: in the largest surviving manuscript collection of Albinoni's cantatas (D-Bsb, Mus. ms. 447), sixteen works begin with a recitative that defines the overall tonality; in all cases the key of the first aria remains within the ambit of the 'closely related' set.[12] Vivaldi is even more conservative in his choice of key for

---

[11] Michael Talbot, 'How Recitatives End and Arias Begin in the Solo Cantatas of Antonio Vivaldi', *Journal of the Royal Musical Association*, 126 (2001): 169–92.

[12] This collection dates from around 1700. In the seven major-key cantatas the scale degrees chosen for the first aria are: vi (twice), V (twice), iii and ii. In the nine minor-key

the first aria following a recitative. As Colin Timms has noted, four of his RARA cantatas place the first aria in the home key itself.[13]

The mutual proximity of the keys of the arias making up a chamber cantata, which constitute its fixed tonal points, has consequences for the tonal design of recitatives. Even if, on average, they are much shorter than the recitatives of operas (the fact that they are monologues would alone virtually ensure this), they are usually longer than is needed to effect the required modulation to the vicinity of the next aria or back to the home key. This surplus of space is, however, not an embarrassment but rather an opportunity to use modulation for expressive purposes. The harmonic rhythm (rate of chord change) and the choice of chord progressions and/or modulation are in fact the principal vehicle for expression in late-Baroque recitative, given the centonized, therefore unavoidably generalized, character of the vocal line. Slow harmonic rhythm, tonal stability and predictability of chord progression are employed to suggest placidity or serenity, while fast harmonic rhythm, tonal instability and outré chord progressions convey, in varying degrees, the opposite.[14] The bass and the continuo harmonies hold up a mirror both to the emotions of the text and to their reflections in the vocal line. So the surplus of space is put to good use for the benefit of musical expression. In a typical longer recitative the music sweeps in wide arcs, alternately moving sharpwards and flatwards. The 'gross' tonal movement is considerable, but the mutual cancelling out of sharpward and flatward modulation ensures that the 'net' movement remains small.

To demonstrate how these principles are realized in practice, we will consider a series of examples. The first is the opening recitative of Albinoni's *Lontan da te, mia vita* (sixth of the cantatas in the Berlin manuscript).[15] Unusually, this recitative ends in its starting key (i.e., the key of the whole cantata) as defined by the first chord, A minor, but the fact that the following aria is in D minor reduces the significance of this tonal event (Example 10.1). The text of the recitative is this:

Lontan da te, mia vita,	When I am far from you, my life,
s'ancor viva son io,	if I still live,
o che dal viver mio	or if the quivered archer [Cupid]
il faretrato arcier forma un portento,	makes a plaything of my life,
o per anima in sen ho il mio tormento;	or if I carry my torment in my breast;
no, che viva non sono	no, I am not alive

---

ones they are: iv (four times), VII (twice), VI, III and i. The 'flatward' bias of the minor-key cantatas is noteworthy.

[13] Timms, 'The Dramatic in Vivaldi's Cantatas', p. 119.

[14] The correlation between heightened activity in the bass and impassioned diction is recognized in Johann Joseph Fux, *Gradus ad Parnassum oder Anführung zur regelmäßigen musikalischen Composition* (Leipzig, 1742), p. 193.

[15] This cantata is consultable in a modern edition prepared by the present author for Edition HH (Launton, 2006).

se il mio cor, la mia vita è sempre teco:	if my heart and my life are always with you:
sì che viva son sempre	even though I live,
alla mia morte a canto,	I am always next to death,
se mi scorge ch'io vivo il duolo e il pianto.	if what I live is grief and lamentation.[16]

Example 10.1   Albinoni, cantata *Lontan da te, mia vita,* opening recitative.

---

[16] All translations of recitative texts are my own.

[Musical notation, bars 12–17, with text underlay:]

si che vi- va son sem-pre a la mia mor-te a can-to, se mi scor-ge ch'io vi-vo il duo-lo, il duo - - - lo e il pian - - - - - - - to.

The principal keyword of the first six lines is 'tormento' rather than 'lontan'; the anonymous poet depicts the agony of a lover grieving at her separation from the beloved. In line 6 the mood becomes calmer and more reflective, albeit still lachrymose, as the protagonist makes her avowal of eternal fidelity. Albinoni expresses the change of mood by creating a musical caesura in the middle of bar 9 and using different harmonic approaches and patterns of modulation to bring out the contrast between the two sections.

From the second harmony, the six-three chord needed for the singer's second note, Albinoni plunges the music into tonal instability by introducing a sequence of alternating six-four-two and seven-five chords (a favourite device of his) that takes the music down by semitonal steps, thereby also alluding to the classic emblem of lament, the *passus duriusculus*.[17] However, in bar 6, having touched on G minor, the composer transfers the chromatic line to the soprano part, reversing its direction; the bass supplies complementary upward, loosely sequential movement. In bars 6–8, to match the mounting agitation of the lover, the harmonic rhythm quickens (chords follow each other at the interval of a crotchet rather than a minim as before) and the tonality passes via E minor to B minor. An arioso flourish on the central syllable of 'tormento' rounds off the first section.

A move to a G major chord in the second half of bar 9, coupled with the straightforwardness of the chord progressions that follow, allowing the music to drift gently flatwards to F major, reflects very effectively the change of mood. In bar 14, corresponding to the start of the last line of the stanza, the mood darkens once again: Albinoni accelerates the harmonic rhythm, restores the minor mode,

---

[17] Ellen Rosand, 'The Descending Tetrachord: An Emblem of Lament', *Musical Quarterly*, 65 (1979): 346–59.

and gives the soprano a second, this time longer, burst of arioso, culminating in the (by 1700) rather archaic cadence-form at the conclusion.[18]

If we examine the multiple modulations of these mere seventeen bars as a whole, we find a characteristic 'snaking' movement. The music first moves flatwards from A minor to G minor and then reverses track, overshooting A minor to reach B minor. It then moves directly to G major, from where it slips down to F major via C major. From F major it moves across to D minor, thence back to A minor. There are thus two flatward-moving phases (bars $1-6_1$ and 9_2-13) balanced by two sharpward-moving phases (bars 6_2-9_1 and 14–17).[19] The major–minor antithesis, which sets off bars 9_2-13 from the rest of the movement, operates in conjunction with these oscillations around the circle of fifths.[20] The 'net' tonal movement turns out to be zero.

The tonal range of this recitative is not especially wide (its 'flat' extremity is D minor, its 'sharp' extremity B minor), and modulation is effected in all cases by linear movement around the circle of fifths or interchange between relative major and minor keys. We shall consider now a recitative in which modal shifts are used to provide additional expressive force and expand the tonal range.

Example 10.2 shows the second recitative from the cantata *Su la riva del mar tutto dolente* by Francesco Antonio Pistocchi (1659–1726). This is the sixth work in his *Scherzi musicali*, Op. 2, published in Amsterdam by Estienne Roger in 1698.[21] At the time, Pistocchi, famous as a contralto and teacher of singing, was *maestro di cappella* at the court of Margrave Georg Friedrich of Brandenburg-Ansbach, to whom the collection was dedicated. Pistocchi's work as a composer has not yet been studied in depth, but his chamber cantatas rank with the best of his time in respect of musical imagination and shapeliness of musical line.

This cantata, which follows the RARA plan, describes the horror of Polyphemus at his discovery that Galatea has spurned him in favour of Acis. In typical fashion, the two recitatives are cast in the 'epic' voice (for the poet's narration), while the two arias adopt the 'lyric' voice (for quotation of the protagonist's utterances). Appropriately for a Cyclops, the voice is a bass – a

---

[18] On this cadence, see Michael Talbot, *The Chamber Cantatas of Antonio Vivaldi* (Woodbridge, 2006), p. 82.

[19] Subscript numbers denote halves of a bar in quadruple metre.

[20] The circle of fifths is best visualized as a clock face comprising not one but two concentric rings (respectively holding the twelve major and twelve minor keys) in which keys sharing a modern key signature stand on the same radius.

[21] No opus number appears on the title page, but Roger's catalogues describe this collection as 'Opera prima'. However, the true Op. 1 is a publication entitled *Capricci puerili* published in Bologna by Giacomo Monti in 1667, when the child prodigy was aged seven or eight. That Pistocchi acknowledged the *Scherzi musicali* as his second opus is implied by the fact that his next published collection, entitled *Duetti e terzetti* (Bologna, Marino Silvani, 1707), is identified as 'Opera terza'. I am grateful to Rashid-Sascha Pegah for sending me a photocopy of the *Scherzi musicali*.

relatively uncommon choice in cantatas for solo voice of the period, where the soprano is supreme and the alto accounts for most of the remaining works.

The first recitative, in which Polyphemus is pictured pining for Galatea, begins on a C major chord (which defines the overall key) and cadences in the same key, having modulated surprisingly little. The relatively static tonality of this movement reflects its expository character. In the following *da capo* aria, in E minor, Polyphemus gives vent to his unrequited passion for the nymph.

It falls to the second recitative (text given below) to advance the action.

Tali accenti esprimea quand'improvviso,	He was speaking thus when suddenly,
volgendo il largo fronte	turning his broad face
vers'il mar, vide, ahi vista!,	towards the sea, he saw, oh the sight!,
con la sua Galatea Aci l'amante,	his Galatea and her lover Acis together
che in stretti nodi avvinti	frolicking in a tight embrace
con le bell'onde insieme	amid the lovely waves
scherzavan per dolcezza e per piacere.	for their sport and pleasure.
Pien di rabbia e furore, il fier Ciclopo	Full of anger and fury, the fierce Cyclops
spezzò la sua zampogna,	broke his pan pipes,
bestemmiò il Ciel, la terra, il mar e Amore,	cursed Heaven, earth, the sea and Cupid,
e così sfogò afflitto il suo dolore.	and poured out his grief in this manner.

The recitative begins calmly enough, the six-three chord on the leading note of B minor providing just the right amount of tonal distance from the final E minor chord of the preceding aria. Although the retention of this bass note for three and a half bars and its orthodox resolution suggest tranquillity, Pistocchi injects a subtle note of disquiet by introducing a series of dissonances in the vocal line: a diminished octave and minor ninth on the last beat of bar 2 and a diminished seventh on the first beat of bar 3. Then, as the poet describes Acis and Galatea frolicking in the sea, the music suddenly brightens by moving to the relative major key of D. Because of the shock that this sight causes Polyphemus, one might have expected the music to be very different at this point. However, this would be to misunderstand the approach to word-painting normal at the time. Pistocchi's prime aim is to express in musical notes the keywords 'scherzavan' (were frolicking), 'dolcezza' (sweetness) and 'piacere' (pleasure), even if this means momentarily redirecting the focus away from Polyphemus and towards the happy couple. Hence, the relaxing effect of the six-three chord on F♯ in bar 6 is calculated and, in terms of the convention within which it operates, effective.

The first jolt arrives in bar 11, when Pistocchi substitutes a tonic D minor chord for the expected D major chord. His evident purpose is, by abruptly dampening the mood, to shift attention back to Polyphemus. The new chord is immediately reinterpreted as the subdominant chord of A minor, on the tonic note of which a pedal is briefly sustained, consolidating the new tonal context. To portray Polyphemus's mounting fury, Pistocchi then embarks on a sequentially unfolding arioso passage: in turn, the notes B♭ (bar 14_2), C (bar 15_2), D♭ (bar 16_2), E♭ (bar 17_2) and finally F (bar 19_1) become tonicized, as the bass rises chromatically in a series of alternating six-three and five-three harmonies. This progression is classifiable as a modulation chain based on major keys a whole tone apart, except that at a crucial moment (bar 15_1) the composer opts to rise by a semitone instead of a whole tone (otherwise, he would have ascended to D major and E major). In bar 19 Pistocchi opts for F minor in place of F major and continues in that key for the rest of the movement. The final chord, however, is indicated by the bass figure as major. This *tierce de Picardie* runs a little counter to the affect, but can be justified, first, as a sign of closure and, second, as a means of bringing the key of the cadence sufficiently near to that of the second and final aria (a lament for Polyphemus), which duly restores the C major tonality of the cantata's opening.

Example 10.2 Pistocchi, cantata *Su la riva del mar tutto dolente*, second recitative.

9
- van per dol-cez - za e per pia-ce - re. Pien di rab - bia‿e fu -
4 ♯3 ♮
12
- ro-re, il fier Ci-clo-po spez - zò la sua zam-po-gna, be-stem - miò‿il Ciel, la ter-ra, il
4
2
15
mar e‿A - mo - re, e co - sì sfo-gò‿af - flit - to, e co -
♭6
♮
[♭]5 [♭]6
17
- sì sfo - gò‿af - flit - to il suo do-lo - - - - - - - -
[♭]6 6 ♭
20
- - - - - - - - - - - - - - re.
♮ ♮6 ♮

The tonal range of this recitative thus encompasses as much as two-thirds of the circumference of the circle of fifths (from B minor to D flat major), through which it navigates deftly, thanks to the devices of modal shift and modulation chain. On this occasion, the tonality does not zigzag in the fashion of the Albinoni example but describes a single, wide arc, first falling from B minor to D flat major and then rising to F major.

The third illustration (Example 10.3) is of a cantata that achieves expression less by operating over a wide tonal range (only once, with its tonicized A♭ in bar 14_2, does it venture fleetingly outside the set of six closely related keys) than by introducing unexpected chord progressions, in some of which the device of ellipsis is employed to good effect. The chosen example is the opening recitative of Vivaldi's cantata *Tremori al braccio e lagrime sul ciglio*, RV 799, which is believed to date from his years in Mantua (1718–20).[22] As its theme the cantata takes the favourite figure of the timid lover, here tormented equally by the thought of confessing, and of not confessing, his love to Elvira:

Tremori al braccio e lagrime sul ciglio,	Tremors in my arms and tears in my eyes,
sospiri al labbro, al volto mio pallore,	sighs on my lips, paleness in my face,
in sua muta favella	in their silent language
parlan teco, o bella, ed a quel core	talk to you, o fair one, and has the report
che quest'anima adora	of my love still not reached that heart
l'avviso del mio amor non giunse ancora?	that this soul worships?
Perché le mie catene	Because I know how
so strascinar con arte, acciò il rumore non si senta de' ceppi	to drag along my chains artfully, so that the sound of the fetters
che mi stringono il core,	that constrain my heart is not heard,
il ciglio del mio ben non le rimira,	the eyes of my beloved do not see them,
e perché tace il labbro	and because my lips are silent,
Amor sen' ride e non m'intende Elvira.	Cupid mocks me and Elvira hears me not.

---

[22] On this fairly recently discovered cantata, see Olivier Fourés and Michael Talbot, 'A New Vivaldi Cantata in Vienna', *Informazioni e studi vivaldiani*, 21 (2000): 99–108, and Talbot, *The Chamber Cantatas*, pp. 118–19. The sole original source is A-Wgm, VI 61340. RV 799 has been published in an edition by Francesco Degrada in the New Critical Edition of Vivaldi's works (Milan, 2002).

Example 10.3 Vivaldi, cantata *Tremori al braccio e lagrime sul ciglio*, RV 799, opening recitative.

Vivaldi's approach to text setting is in general highly manneristic. The trills, angular melodic intervals and fermatas of the opening bars take this tendency to extremes. Harmonic ellipsis appears as early as bar 2, where a six-four-two chord on G passes to another on C without any intermediate chord of D to supply a resolution for the G (on F or F♯). In their chromatic downward slide via alternate six-five and six-four-two chords, bars 2–4 resemble bars 2–5 of Example 1, and their purpose is the same: to express despair and disorientation. Bars 5–6, which have no vivid keyword to illustrate, take the music calmly and diatonically from B flat major to a cadence in F major.

The shift to D minor in bar 7 restores the anxious mood. In bars 9–10, by which time the music has reached G minor, Vivaldi translates the question mark ending the sixth line of the stanza into a standard form of half-close (related to the so-called Phrygian cadence) used for this purpose.[23] But the continuation is anything but orthodox: Vivaldi follows the cadence, in bar 10, with a C minor chord (the G minor chord is suppressed by ellipsis). The most striking case of ellipsis occurs, however, a little further on, in bar 13, where Vivaldi passes directly from a six-five chord on B♮ to a similar six-five chord on G. The second chord is resolved conventionally by the A flat chord in bar 15, but the first chord lacks the resolution to a C minor chord that would have made the progression perfectly sequential and symmetrical. From E flat major the music finds its way back comfortably to the original tonic, G minor, which becomes the launching pad for the aria in C minor that follows.

In a way, Vivaldi is using outré harmonic progressions in this recitative as surrogates for vigorous modulatory movement. They become an alternative way of 'running on the spot': a way of making the music eventful and responsive to the mood of the text without moving more than a short distance from the home

---

[23] See Fux, *Gradus ad Parnassum oder Anführung zur regelmäßigen musikalischen Composition*, p. 195 and Table 56 no. 1.

base. It is interesting that the salient harmonic events never coincide with the most picturesque melodic events, such as the 'dragging' two-note melismas for 'strascinar' in bar 11 or Cupid's mocking phrases in bars 16_2–19_1. There is, so to speak, a give and take of responsibility between the vocal line and the bass. Where one is active, the other is passive. The result is a recitative that is expressive and artful but does not collapse under its own density. Even some rather plain moments (for instance, bars 5–6) are needed to lend perspective to the more recherché ones.

The last movement to be considered, shown as Example 10.4, comes from an instrumentally accompanied cantata, *Però che scende in petto*, by Vivaldi's talented younger Venetian contemporary and possible protégé Giovanni Francesco Brusa (c.1700–68).[24] The work comes from a volume of cantatas by several composers from Venice and Naples compiled for Duke Anton Ulrich of Saxe-Meiningen in 1726 and 1727.[25]

Però che scende in petto, a RARA cantata that dispenses with the strings (apart from those playing continuo) in both recitatives, belongs to the old tradition of the *lezione amorosa*, the 'lesson in love' in which the poet imparts advice to young lovers. The general theme, outlined in the opening recitative, is that love is like a huntsman's anticipated prey that at the last moment, when apparently helpless, slips from his grasp:

Però che scende in petto	Even though he enters our breast
col riso in bocca e col piacer d'appresso,	with a smile on his lips promising pleasure,
folli, crediamo spesso	we foolishly often imagine
che dolce sempre si dimostri Amore;	that Love is always sweet;
l'iniquo traditore,	the wicked traitor
ei prende con inganno,	achieves his ends through deceit,
e di mito signore divien tiranno.	and from being a mild lord turns into a tyrant.
Sta tutto umil da pria:	At first, he is humility itself:
quasi si dà per vinto,	he almost admits defeat,
e del desir vien preda	and he makes himself captive to our desires
finch'egli scorga in suo poter condotte	until he finds himself master over morals,
e ragione e virtude;	reason and virtue;

---

[24] On Brusa's extraordinary biography, see Talbot, *The Chamber Cantatas*, pp. 122–3.

[25] The volume (D-MEIr, Ed 82ᵇ) contains in addition the only known source of Vivaldi's cantata *Che giova il sospirar, povero core*, RV 679. On Duke Ulrich's music collection, see Lawrence Bennett, 'A Little-Known Collection of Early-Eighteenth-Century Vocal Music at Schloss Elisabethenburg, Meiningen', *Fontes Artis Musicae*, 48 (2001): 250–302, and Talbot, *The Chamber Cantatas*, pp. 131–3.

ma poi ché ne siam privi,	but since we are now bereft of these,
scuopre la faccia e il predator delude.	he uncovers his face and eludes his capturer.

There is a gently ironic tone to this admonition, and passion is the last thing required for the expression of the text. So the mood is temperate, and the movement between chords and keys even-paced. More than in any of the earlier examples quoted, the vocal line and bass are centonized from very familiar elements. Notwithstanding this, Brusa's recitative reveals not a few masterly touches.

Example 10.4 Brusa, cantata *Però che scende in petto*, opening recitative.

Sop: Pe - rò che scen - de in pet - to col ri - so in boc - ca e col pia-cer d'ap-pres-so, fol-li, cre-dia-mo spes-so che dol-ce sem - pre si di-mo-stri A - mo - re; l'i - ni - quo tra - di - to - re, ei pren-de con in - gan-no, e di mi - to si - gnor di-vien ti-ran-no. Sta tut-to u-mil da pri - a: qua - si si dà per

[Musical notation: bars 12–17, vocal line with text and bass line]

vin-to, e del de-sir vien pre-da fin-ch'e-gli scor-ga in suo po-ter con-dot-te e ra-gio-ne e vir-tu-de; ma poi ché ne siam pri-vi, scuo-pre la fac-cia e il pre-da-tor de-lu-de.

The movement opens in C minor, which, naturally enough, is also the key of the closing aria. However, the first aria is in E minor, which is sufficiently distant from C minor to force the composer to move sharpwards by several degrees in the course of the opening recitative. Initially, this movement is leisurely, G minor being reached in bar 6. In bar 7 Brusa makes as if to return to C minor: the six-four-two chord on F natural appears to be a dominant seventh in that key. However, the text has just reached the word 'inganno' (deceit), and Brusa has a trick up his sleeve. The next chord is not of C minor but of E major, as a dominant to A minor, which then becomes the subdominant of E minor, in which key the first regular cadence occurs (bar 9). In the remainder of the recitative the music circles around D major and its satellites A major and G major, finally cadencing in the last key. The freely sequential pattern of the chord progressions in bars 11–15 has a pleasing logic about it, and the coincidence of the six-four-two chord over a slightly unexpected C♮ with the expressive word 'privi' (bereft) in bar 16 lends welcome emphasis. The unconventional cadential phrase given to the soprano in bar 17 may possibly be a deliberate illustration of the final word, 'delude' (eludes). Once again, we observe that the vocal line is at its most inventive when the harmony is most conventional, and vice versa.

The reinterpretation of the apparent dominant seventh in C minor as a tonic seventh in G major results in an instant advance of four numbers around the clock face of the circle of fifths. This is a radical species of modulation that was not especially common even in the Classical period and had to wait until the nineteenth century to become popular.[26] Very occasionally, cantatas of the period contain modulations dependent on enharmonic change, as when one or more notes

---

[26] A typical instance occurs in the Scherzo of Schumann's String Quartet in A minor, Op. 41 no. 3, in which bars 1–10, in A minor, are answered by eight bars in E major.

of a diminished seventh are explicitly or implicitly respelt or a German sixth transmutes into a dominant seventh; these sit well with the contemporary taste for *bizzarria*.[27]

Conclusions

Consideration of the four examples discussed above results in five basic propositions regarding modulation in cantata recitatives:

1. Harmonic movement and modulation in Italian cantata recitatives of the period 1700–50 are partly necessary and functional (to establish or return to the home key, or to move to the vicinity of the key of a following aria), partly facultative and expressive.
2. The total length of the recitative in relation to the overall tonal distance to be covered normally creates a *surplus* of available space, which encourages the expressive use of modulation. Such modulation typically moves in wide tonal arcs, in which sharpward and flatward movement compensate for one another, thereby reducing the net tonal distance traversed.
3. The pace and character of modulation are used as an indicator of the emotional temperature conveyed in the text and sometimes (but not invariably) expressed also in the vocal line.
4. By using advanced techniques of modulation (modulation chains, harmonic ellipsis, modal shifts, enharmonic conversion, etc.), recitatives are able to range more widely, and move more freely within the tonal sphere, than arias and other closed types of movement.
5. Composers take care not to saturate the music of recitative with expression: at any given time, either the vocal line or the bass is likely to be relatively neutral and conventional, setting off whatever special effects occur in the other.

A final reflection of a more general character is in order. Although there is no historical link between Baroque recitatives and the development sections of sonata-form movements of the Classical period and later, one cannot help noticing the similarity of the advanced techniques of modulation employed. Would it be too bold to suggest that recitative in chamber cantatas (and, of course, also in dramatic genres) served as a useful laboratory, during the first half of the eighteenth century, for harmonic and tonal processes that became widely applied to closed forms only in the second?[28]

---

[27] For discussion of relevant instances in Vivaldi's cantatas, see Talbot, *The Chamber Cantatas*, pp. 82–3 and 127.

[28] I am grateful to Colin Timms for reading and making comments on a first draft of this chapter.

Chapter 11
'Imitando l'Arietta, ò altro allegro, cantato di fresco': Keyboard Realization in Italian Continuo Arias

Giulia Nuti

Introduction

Of all the musical genres of the Baroque, the cantata for voice and basso continuo offers the greatest scope for continuo players to display their harmonic, rhythmic and compositional skills; the opening and closing bars of a *da capo* aria give the continuo player great exposure and, at the same time, the freedom to construct a realization for the right hand that can be simple or complex, dramatic or understated, and as highly ornamented as the performer dares. This chapter deals with the ways in which it is possible to analyse and treat the composed material within the aria in order to play a stylistically plausible and varied realization during the ritornellos.

Unlike in the other particularly highly regarded genre of chamber music of the time, the instrumental sonata, where the construction of the composition is such that it is most usual for the solo instrument to begin playing together with the bass – or, at the very least, where any introduction in the continuo part is brief –[1] in the cantata the aria ordinarily begins with a short introduction consisting of anything from 2 to 20 bars, depending on the time signature and the tempo. Even in arias where the voice enters immediately for dramatic effect, the aria will almost always end with a short instrumental coda.[2] This makes the relationship between the voice and the continuo uniquely challenging for the continuo player, who must, within the space of a few bars, alternate between leading the aria and accompanying the

---

[1] There are exceptions, of course: among Vivaldi's sonatas, RV 2 and RV 9 for violin and continuo, RV 39 and RV 44 for cello and continuo and RV 53 for oboe and continuo all begin with an instrumental introduction. However, mainstream composers of late Baroque instrumental sonatas rarely opened a movement with a continuo ritornello. In Albinoni's Opp. 2 and 4, Corelli's Op. 5 and Bonporti's Opp. 7 and 10 – to name some major collections of the early eighteenth century – all the movements begin with the two parts playing together. I am grateful to Federico Maria Sardelli for identifying the Vivaldi sonatas with ritornellos.

[2] See, for example, the final aria from Albinoni's cantata *Senza il core del mio bene*.

voice, playing as both soloist and accompanist while taking account of all that is required by these very different performance styles.

Here, 'cantata' refers specifically to the mature form that arose in the last decade of the seventeenth century and flourished at the beginning of the eighteenth century; as a rule, its arias are written in *da capo* form. Cantatas for voice and continuo by some of the genre's most prolific cultivators – Alessandro Scarlatti, Marcello and Vivaldi – will be considered here, along with cantatas by Francesco Gasparini and the less familiar Girolamo Polani.

Structure

The structure of a typical cantata *da capo* aria has been summarized by Michael Talbot:[3]

1. Introductory ritornello.
2. First vocal period, modulating to the dominant or alternative key.
3. Ritornello in the new key (vestigial in solo cantatas).
4. Second vocal period, leading back to the home key. Sometimes capped by a coda.
5. Reprise of introductory ritornello, often abridged.
6. One or two vocal periods cadencing in new keys.
7. 7–11. Recapitulation of 1–5, ornamented *ad libitum*.

The ritornellos where the continuo plays alone occur during the 'A' section (1, 3 and 5), whereas the 'B' section (6) does not leave the continuo uncovered. As can be seen from Marcello's cantata *L'usignolo che il suo duolo* (see Example 11.8), the length of the introductory ritornello, varying in response to tempo and time signature, can be considerable.

In seeking to contribute to the success of the composition by providing maximum impact when realizing the opening of the aria, the accompanist must consider how different kinds of bass line call for correspondingly different styles of realization.

As in cantata arias with an obbligato instrumental part, where the opening ritornello theme of the aria is introduced instrumentally and, after this short introduction, the voice begins to sing – consider the opening of Vivaldi's 'Avvezzo non è 'l core' from *All'ombra di sospetto*, or 'Augelletti voi col canto' from the same composer's *Lungi dal vago volto* – and where, similarly, the aria also ends with an instrumental coda, in continuo arias these instrumental sections are similarly present; but it is left to the continuo player to provide all the melodic and harmonic

---

[3] Michael Talbot, *Vivaldi*, rev. edn (London, 1993), p. 137. Although Talbot is referring specifically to the structure of Vivaldi's arias, this scheme can be applied to the later works considered here.

interest, without any specific indications from the composer concerning how the passages are to be realized. In the entire cantata output of the Italian Baroque there are only a handful of arias where suggestions for right-hand realizations have been sketched in or printed: some of these are considered below.

Although it is most common for treatises of the time to speak in terms of the accompaniment of the voice, rather than the accompaniment of an instrumental line, authors do not expound specifically on the realization of a continuo aria, despite the high level of exposure of the continuo player. The few sentences that do refer to arias, however, offer important guidelines. These will now be discussed.

Realizing the ritornello and accompanying the voice

Of the few writers who do make explicit reference to realization within an aria, Lorenzo Penna is among the earliest. In his instruction manual *Li primi albori musicali*, the first of whose many editions came out in Bologna in 1672, Penna writes:

> During ritornellos, or pauses, introduced [to allow] the singer to rest, the organist should play as he chooses, imitating the arietta, or other allegro, that has just been sung. This is clear enough without supplying an example.[4]

Even though the style to which he is referring is a little earlier than that of the cantatas discussed here, Penna indicates clearly that the continuo player must distinguish in treatment between ritornellos and the accompaniment of the voice, explicitly calling for a more eloquent and 'soloistic' accompaniment during the pauses in the vocal part. Writing a little later, Francesco Gasparini states that imitation – not in the contrapuntal sense but in that of replicating something found elsewhere – is the most appropriate way to realize the bass when the voice is silent (see below for a discussion of imitation).

> [...] the accompanist must be proud of being called a good and solid accompanist, not a lively and fast player, as he can satisfy and express his high spirits when he plays alone, not when he is accompanying [...][5]

---

[4] Lorenzo Penna, *Li primi albori musicali* (Bologna, 1684; facsimile repr. Bologna, 1996), p. 185: 'Che nelli Ritornelli, ò Pause, poste per riposo del Cantante, l'Organista suoni alquanto di suo capriccio, imitando l'Arietta, ò altro allegro, cantato di fresco. È chiaro da se senza dar esempio'.

[5] Francesco Gasparini, *L'armonico pratico al cimbalo* (Venice, 1708), p. 105: '[...] deve chi accompagna pregiarsi del titolo di buono, e sodo Accompagnatore, non di spiritoso, e veloce Sonatore, potendo sodisfarsi, e sfogar il suo brio, quando sona solo, non quando accompagna [...]'.

Gasparini's phrase 'when he plays alone' ('quando sona solo') could at first sight be taken to refer to solo keyboard performance, but that it refers as well to the realization of ritornellos is suggested when he goes on to say:

> As for when these [divisions in the bass] can be made, I give complete licence during the ritornellos, and whenever the voice is silent.[6]

In this respect, at least, Gasparini draws a clear distinction between the style of the realization during the ritornellos and that employed when accompanying the voice.

In the absence of other material specifically referring to cantata arias with continuo, it can be assumed that continuo players would have accompanied the voice always with the discretion described and urged in the treatises of the time, but drawing on their improvisatory and compositional training for the ritornellos.

Improvisation in ritornellos

The *partimenti* of such composers as Alessandro Scarlatti, Durante, Greco and Mattei (among many others belonging to the Neapolitan school, in particular) illustrate how the harpsichordist would gain the skill to improvise securely above a given bass in the absence of a vocal line to accompany.[7] *Partimenti* were exercises in counterpoint and harmony and consisted of bass lines (either figured or unfigured), sometimes with an incipit for the realization of the right hand marked at the beginning of the piece – this theme was to be continued throughout the exercise, a process that would develop the pupil's ability to manipulate these formulas in order to produce a well-structured composition possessing both harmonic and melodic invention starting from the bass alone. Some *partimenti* have more than one suggestion of how to realize the given bass, offering to the pupil various opening ideas for the exercise; surviving books of *partimenti*, most of them in manuscript, rarely contain explanatory text and consist simply of page after page of music. The pupil was taught the correct harmonic principles in order to play from an unfigured bass, as well as the most interesting melodic patterns to associate with a given bass. With training, the most intricate counterpoint above a bass could be performed at sight; the experienced keyboard player who had received such schooling clearly would have no difficulty in improvising the opening of a cantata aria.

---

[6] Ibid., pp. 108–9: 'Circa il praticarle [le diminuizioni] io ne dò assoluta licenza ne i Ritornelli, e quando tace il canto'. For further discussion on divisions in the bass line, see Giulia Nuti, *The Performance of Italian Basso Continuo: Style in Keyboard Accompaniment in the Seventeenth and Eighteenth Centuries* (Aldershot, 2007), pp. 110–26.

[7] Some of the most detailed *partimenti* are those of Francesco Durante: 'Partimenti, ossia intero studio di numerati per ben suonare il cembalo' (I-Bc, EE. 171).

There are other authors[8] who provide examples of how to realize frequently occurring bass designs (see Gasparini, below), showing that this was not a practice confined to the south of Italy; manuscripts containing exercises for the realization of cadences are not uncommon.[9]

Existing realizations

In Chapter 10 of *L'armonico pratico*, Gasparini tries to set down the ways of playing a fine and varied accompaniment; he demonstrates various solutions for the realization of ascending and descending scales in the bass, as well as cadences. The bass line is fully figured, and he specifies that the harmony should be supplied by the left hand, since the right hand is engaged in more detailed passage-work.[10] The space taken up by notes printed with movable type made the printing of chords on a single stave very difficult using this process, and for this reason chordal accompaniments are never encountered in early printed sources. This is a limitation of printed (as opposed to engraved or handwritten) music that has always been an obstacle to the full representation, even for purposes of illustration, of continuo realization, and one that was acknowledged to be a limitation at the time.[11] Gasparini's examples are rather bland realizations of the bass, probably because they are intended to be applicable in a great number of situations; but it is worthwhile to take note of the compass of the right hand, which covers two octaves and reaches as high as *a"*.

---

[8] In particular, the Roman manuscript 'Regole accompagnar sopra la parte N. 1 d'autore incerto' (I-Rli, MS Musica R. 1).

[9] See, for example, I-MOe, MS C311 in lute tablature.

[10] The full participation of both hands in chordal accompaniment, with the increased likelihood of octave-doublings in the part-writing that this introduces, is an indispensable aspect of harpsichord playing; full chords in both hands should be introduced in order to obtain rich harmony from the instrument, since this is a practice widely documented in relation to both basso continuo accompaniment and the performance of solo repertoire. The solo keyboard toccatas of Alessandro Scarlatti exemplify well how opulent the texture produced by the two hands can be. In the sonatas of such later composers as Durante and Cimarosa the keyboard writing is not so rich harmonically, yet calls out for the playing of richer harmonies than those that are written; clearly these were expected in performance. Interestingly, it is in the sonatas of Domenico Scarlatti that the most convincing demonstration of this style of playing can be found, since Scarlatti writes with a precision of notation unequalled by his Italian contemporaries, and the style in which many of his sonatas are written derives from the same tradition. The present-day custom of using the treble clef rather than the soprano clef for notated realizations tends to widen the gap between the two hands, thereby discouraging the co-option of the left hand in chordal playing.

[11] Consider the examples of Penna, whose printed realizations are less full than the figuring implies.

The *partimenti* give a wider and more varied testimony of how bass lines can be realized, while Gasparini's commentary is an essential indicator of how to change the style of playing when the voice is singing: although maximum discretion and elegance must be sought while accompanying the voice, during the ritornellos the continuo player is permitted a display of inventiveness in the right hand, with a full, harmonic accompaniment in the left. Alternatively, the harpsichordist may employ varied diminutions in the left hand accompanying with a harmonically rich right hand.

Gasparini's *Cantate da camera*[12] exemplify the teachings later to be expounded in *L'armonico pratico*. It is most interesting to consider what he notates for the right hand 'in forma d'intavolatura' (as a 'tablature': i.e., fully written out); he writes in a manner that is discreet while the voice sings but imitative where the voice is silent.

Example 11.1 Gasparini, cantata *Ed ecco in fine, oh Dio*, aria 'Congiurati ecco a miei danni', bars 1–4.

---

[12] Francesco Gasparini, *Cantate da camera* (Rome, 1695; facsimile repr. Florence, 1984). Gasparini's use of clefs is retained in the example.

Consider the opening ritornello of the aria 'Congiurati ecco a miei danni' from the cantata *Ed ecco in fine, oh Dio* (Example 11.1), where a rhythmic idea is introduced in the right hand. When the voice begins to sing, the rhythmic feature of a semiquaver rest followed by three semiquavers moves from the right hand to the left. Since the left hand is playing diminutions, it is clear that the right hand must revert to a simpler style, perhaps playing crotchet chords over the bass rests. Both in the middle of the 'A' section and at the end of the 'A' section, the right hand plays semiquavers, once again confirming the distinction that must be drawn between how the continuo player treats the material when playing alone and when accompanying within the cantata aria. A similar use is made of the material in the aria 'Parlami, insegnami, svelami amore' from the cantata *Dove sei, dove t'ascondi*.[13]

Gasparini remains the only composer ever to attempt to explain in words how right-hand flourishes and realizations might be applied; this is possibly because he had published both the cantatas and *L'armonico pratico* by 1708, so that, given the popularity of this primer, it was not thought necessary to expound further on the subject. His advice to imitate the great masters was wholly acceptable for an age when the direct master–pupil relationship was the principal means of instruction and demonstration and was favoured over laborious explanation.

Imitation in extant realizations

Every instance of cantatas where composers, or perhaps performers, have written 'con la mano destra in forma d'intavolatura' has to be evaluated individually. First, it should be remembered that the improvisatory nature of basso continuo makes it, by definition, impossible to annotate; this means that, not unnaturally, composers never even attempted to represent the harpsichordist's part with the fullness of chords, added dissonances and ornamentation that the style required. Written-out improvisation is a contradiction in terms: anything written out (unless expressly marked as optional) achieves obbligato status *ipso facto*.[14] There are examples, however, of cantata aria ritornellos with a melodic guidelines for the right hand, most often written in the singer's stave. All these examples feature imitation, either of the bass or of the vocal part, as Penna explicitly encourages.

Extant melodic suggestions for the right hand can be more or less complex. Sometimes they are predictable and intuitive; quite possibly, these were sketched in by the composer as a guarantee that the imitation would not be missed even by an unimaginative or insecure player. In other instances, they are extended expositions of a whole theme; yet whether they are short snatches of the tune

---

[13] See Nuti, *The Performance of Italian Basso Continuo*, p. 124, for a discussion of this aria.

[14] Alessandro Scarlatti's cantata *Da sventura a sventura* is a unique example for Italy of an obbligato harpsichord part. Discussed in Nuti, *The Performance of Italian Basso Continuo*, pp. 80–81.

or longer episodes, in either case they are exceptional and prescriptive, not just illustrative.

An early example of a simple imitative figure occurs in a cantata from Barbara Strozzi's *Diporti di Euterpe*;[15] in the printed edition of 1659 the opening of the cantata *Basta cosi, vi ho inteso* has suggestions for imitation of the vocal part added, quite possibly at the printer's workshop, in what appears to be pen.[16]

The same figure is written in when the theme returns in the following section. While undoubtedly this imitative figure corresponds to the style of playing that Penna describes, the precision of the notation and the literal nature of the imitation take this passage away from improvised practice and towards the addition of a third obbligato 'voice'. The figuration is written in the bass clef, and can either be played at written pitch, as a tenor voice with a chordal accompaniment in the right hand, or can be played in the right hand, possibly an octave higher, with a chordal accompaniment in the left hand.

Strozzi's simple and intuitive example (not given here) shows how the two parts, voice and continuo, could neatly interlock; if the third part had not been written in, the harpsichordist's immediate reaction should nonetheless be that of imitating the voice in this way, since all the compositional elements of the first six bars suggest such a solution. In the first two bars the bass is static, moving in crotchets and minims; however, the third, fourth and fifth bars imitate the figure of a quaver followed by two semiquavers, indeed, the bass alternates this with the voice – the only instance where this does not happen is in the second half of bars 1 and 2. So while this added figuration is here a necessary part of the composition, it also illustrates a practice that can be profitably carried out in similar circumstances by an improvising accompanist.

Nicola Porpora leaves an indication for the harpsichordist in the engraved edition of his cantata *D'amor il primo dardo*:[17] in the aria 'Ch'io mai vi possa lasciar d'amare' the harpsichordist is required to play a little fragment of the tune of the vocal part; this is printed in the singer's stave and is marked by the words 'si sona'; but the figuration is disappointingly similar to that of the vocal line, and no new insight is gained.

An example of a more complex and interesting imitation for the right hand can be found at the end of the 'A' section of the final aria from Girolamo Polani's 'Cantata quinta', 'Quando sarai senz'onde';[18] in order not to let the player miss the

---

[15] Barbara Strozzi, *Diporti di Euterpe overo Cantate e ariette a voce sola* (Venice, 1659; facsimile repr. Florence, 1980).

[16] Cf. Reinmar Emans's parallel case of inked additions to printed music, described in Chapter 4.

[17] Nicola Porpora, [*Cantate e duetti*] (London, 1735).

[18] I am grateful to Michael Talbot for drawing my attention to this *intavolatura*. Polani was a Venetian soprano and composer who specialized in operatic composition. Documented testimonies to his presence in England occur sporadically from 1717 onwards. The six cantatas, of unexpectedly high quality, represent his sole surviving music. Their

intended stretto imitation, Polani has written it out for the right hand, following the pattern of the stretto that occurs earlier between continuo and voice, in bars 12–13 (Example 11.2).

Example 11.2　Polani, cantata *Verrà un dì che la mia bella*, aria 'Quando sarai senz'onde', bars 21–24.

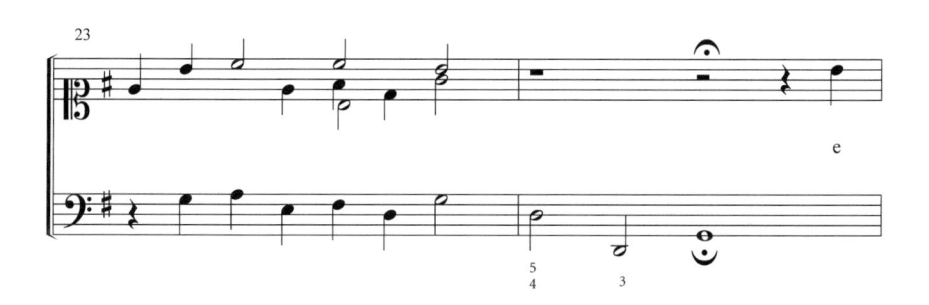

G. B. Pescetti's aria 'Come va l'ape nel prato' from the cantata *Di sì bel faggio all'ombra*[19] provides another example of how the composer may prescribe a melody to be played during the ritornello. As is invariably the case, however, Pescetti does not take the opportunity to compose new material specifically for the harpsichord, but limits himself to writing out a complete exposition of the vocal theme above the bass line; the line is then repeated when the voice enters.

Gasparini includes a few bars of right-hand realization in the aria 'Se vedrete il cor di lei' from his cantata *Andate, o miei sospiri*, which he composed and sent to Alessandro Scarlatti as a present, and which resulted in an exchange of cantatas

---

style is that of the years around 1730. Since they are preserved in the Royal Music Library, GB-Lbl, R.M. 22.m.28. (1–6), they may have been presented in homage to Queen Caroline, wife of George II.

[19]　Musical example in Michael Talbot, *The Chamber Cantatas of Antonio Vivaldi* (Woodbridge, 2006), p. 87.

between the two masters.[20] Scarlatti would certainly not have needed suggestions for right-hand improvisation; nor would Gasparini have presumed to show him how he should set about realizing the ritornellos. Gasparini evidently considers this particular snatch of imitation to be an integral part of the composition, and rather fun to share with another keyboard player.

Gasparini's *intavolatura* begins in bar 81, where 'si sona' is marked; Example 11.3 begins from the singer's preceding passage in order to show how the imitation has been used. My realization in bars 68–80 demonstrates how the chordal accompaniment of the voice can contrast with melodic imitation, which in this instance Gasparini himself has supplied for the ritornello.[21] In addition to the melodies and imitations marked by the composers, the harpsichordist should add chords in both hands, as well as dissonances and ornamentation (discussed below), for the style to be represented fully: both in the realization and while playing the composer's *intavolatura*.

Notating the realization

As the visual appearance of this example demonstrates, the problems associated with writing down an improvisation are almost insurmountable; the desired harmonic fullness that characterizes the Italian style of continuo playing clashes with the established precepts of notated music. It encourages the doubling of parts and results in errors of part-writing, and in consecutive fifths and octaves;[22] the rules of counterpoint are knowingly suspended in order to achieve the greatest contrasts of colour. While it is possible to sketch uncontroversially a purely melodic idea, as was done by the composers themselves in the cases already illustrated, the apparent grammatical errors that result when what is actually improvised in performance is transcribed on paper, evidenced by the opening fourteen bars of Example 11.3, makes the realization appear, to the eye, utterly unacceptable (see also Examples 11.4–11.8, below). This is a problem that was extensively acknowledged at the time and is one of the factors that may explain why so few composers ever attempted – even in a didactic work – to represent in full a realization as it would actually have been heard.[23]

---

[20] See Charles Burney, *A General History of Music from the Earliest Ages to the Present Period*, 4 vols (London, 1776–89), vol. 4, p. 176.

[21] Here, and in other music examples, my realization appears in smaller notes.

[22] See Nuti, *The Performance of Italian Basso Continuo*, pp. 92–4, for a discussion of how contemporary authors addressed the problem.

[23] An attempt to write down the continuo accompaniment of an aria, *Sono un certo spiritello*, was made by the anonymous author of the Roman manuscript 'Regole per accompagnar sopra la parte', f. 66. For a discussion of this aria, see Nuti, *The Performance of Italian Basso Continuo*, pp. 93–4.

Example 11.3 Gasparini, cantata *Andate, o miei sospiri*, aria 'Se vedrete il cor di lei', bars 67–91.

It is worth considering, however, that every apparently egregious feature of Example 11.3 finds a justification in the treatises of the time:

1. The realization occupies the same register as the singer;[24]
2. Dissonances are doubled in both hands wherever possible;[25]

---

[24] See, among others, Bernardo Pasquini, 'Regole del Sig. Bernardo Pasquini per bene accompagnare con il cembalo' (I-Bc, D. 138), p. 2: 'Non coprir la parte che canta; cioè se canta il soprano fare la cadenza in detto Soprano, e toccar le corde del soprano, e se canta il contralto, fare il simile' ('Do not cover [play above] the part which is singing; that is, if the soprano is singing, play the cadence in the soprano [register], and play the notes of the soprano; if an alto is singing, do the same').

[25] See, among others, Gasparini, *L'armonico pratico*, p. 97: '[…] bisogna con estremi d'ambe le mani toccar due tasti con un sol dito, cioè con l'Auricolare, e con il Pollice' ('[…] you must touch two keys with only one finger, using the extremities of both hands, that is with the little finger and the thumb').

3. The E♯ in bar 71, a leading note, takes a 6/5/3 chord;[26]
4. The E in bar 79, implicitly a 6 chord, is realized as 6/4/3;[27]
5. The acciaccaturas, ornamental unprepared dissonances occupying a gap between two thirds in the chord (e.g., G♯ in bars 69 and 72), are normally played short, but, at the player's discretion, can also be long.[28]

Repetition with variety

Another important reason why it was not desirable for the right-hand notes to be written out in the ritornellos was because in a standard *da capo* aria there are three separate instances where the continuo player is called upon to improvise the upper parts in full (each replicated in the *da capo* reprise); the effect is most beautiful if these are varied in style each time.

Given that the continuo player's special training consisted, through the intensive study of *partimenti*, of improvised composition above a prescribed bass, there was no need to write out these short passages. If the ritornellos were fixed, ordinarily 'composed', parts of the aria, the harpsichordist, together with other accompanying instruments such as cello or theorbo, would be unable to respond to the singer, and unable to respond to each other, in the most appropriate manner; moreover, the type of voice being accompanied, the tempo preferred by the singer and the manner of realization of the other instruments playing the bass line are all extra factors that legitimately demand to influence the right-hand realization. As Gasparini concludes:

---

[26] As Gasparini, *L'armonico pratico*, p. 94, advises: 'Quando al Mi, o nota con ♯ vi cade la quinta falsa, vi si unisce la sesta minore, e per acciaccatura tra l'ottava, e la decima si aggiunge in mezzo la nona, che fa buonissimo effetto' ('When, on a Mi or on a note with a ♯ [i.e., a leading note], there is a diminished fifth, to this one can add a minor sixth; [regarding] the acciaccatura, between the octave and the tenth, a ninth should be added in the middle, as it makes a very good effect').

[27] Alessandro Scarlatti, 'Per accompagnare il cembalo', GB-Lbl, Add. 14,244, p. 40, writes: 'È da notare per bella maniera di sonare (e questo è secondo lo stile di chi scrive in questo libro) tutte le volte che accade la consonanza di sesta maggiore, si aggiunge la 4.a sopra la 3.a di detta consonanza, perchè fa bel sentire' ('Note that to play beautifully (following the present writer's style), whenever there is a consonance of a major sixth, the fourth should be added to the third of this consonance, for it is pleasing to hear').

[28] 'Regole accompagnar sopra la parte N. 1 d'autore incerto' (I-Rli, MS Musica R. 1), f. 65: 'Fra le consonanze pongo talvolta alcune dissonanze toccandola e subito lasciandola, e la chiamo mordente quasi un picciol morso d'animaletto, quale appena ponga il dente e poi subito lo toglie, e se ad'alcuno piacesse più tenere, che levare la dissonanza, starà in suo arbitrio' ('Among consonances sometimes I place some dissonances, touching them and releasing them at once; I call this *mordente*, like a little bite from a small animal, who might begin to apply its teeth and then immediately withdraw; though if anyone wishes to hold the dissonance rather than quit it, he may do so at his own discretion').

Many more things could be shown, but in order that they do not end up useless, superfluous or confusing, they are left to the ingenuity, the skill and the good taste of the diligent accompanist, who, when he is able to play most of what I could set down on paper, I judge will have no need of such examples, for he will be able to cope on his own by attentively observing good players and the compositions of the most famed authors and masters.[29]

Gasparini deems his written instruction to be inadequate on its own, both because the medium of print does not allow him to present his thoughts fully (the full richness of the chords required to play in this style cannot be fully represented with movable type, as stated above) and because it would not be possible to exemplify all the thematic recurrences during a single movement. Gasparini is not the only composer of this period to point out the inadequacy of mere words when trying to explain musical style;[30] he advises learning by imitating fine players and by studying actual compositions.

It is infinitely regrettable that these fine players of the Settecento can no longer be heard, but it is still most certainly possible and worthwhile to consider in what ways the arias can be studied in order to provide an input for the realization of ritornellos when no suggestion is given by the composers.

In the following examples, possible ways of realizing certain bass lines are considered, together with the reasons why these might be realized in this way.

Harmony, rhythm, melody

The ritornello's bass line can consist of:

1. the same material used as an accompaniment to the voice part;
2. an anticipation of the vocal theme or material derived from it;
3. material that shapes the bass line throughout and is never developed in the vocal part.

First, it is necessary to ascertain to which category the bass line under consideration belongs, since the style of realization will be different for each of these cases. In the first instance described, for example, inspiration for the realization in the right

---

[29] Gasparini, *L'armonico pratico*, p. 104: 'Molte cose di più potrei dimostrare, ma per non riuscire inutile, o di superfluità, o di confusione le lascio al genio, all'industria, ed al buon gusto dello Studioso Accompagnatore, il quale quando sarà capace di sonar il di più che potrei metter in Carta, stimo, che non averà bisogno di simili Esempij, mentre potrà ingegnarsi da per se, osservando con attenzione i buoni Sonatori, e le Composizioni degli Autori, e Maestri più celebri'.

[30] Alessandro Scarlatti also complains of the difficulty of explaining style in words, in a passage quoted in Nuti, *The Performance of Italian Basso Continuo*, p. 3.

hand can be gained from the vocal line, anticipating the musical text that is to come (see Example 11.4). Where melodic imitation of the voice part is not possible because the theme, or material derived from it, is already present in the bass line (instance 2), it is most appropriate to treat the left hand as the main melodic strand and accompany in a chordal manner with the right hand, rather than think of introducing a second melody (Example 11.6). In the third instance described, it is best to combine chords and countermelodies, depending on the character and length of the ritornello (Example 11.8). In all instances, it is most important to consider the rhythmic and harmonic characteristics of *both* the bass line *and* the vocal line, in order to imitate one or other of these where possible.

The first type of bass line described above is illustrated well by the aria 'Vuò che tremi' from Alessandro Scarlatti's cantata *Il Nerone*.[31] The opening ritornello comprises three bars and introduces the most characteristic feature of the bass line: the dotted rhythm. When this is taken up by the voice, it is revealed to depict trembling ('tremi Giove'). Throughout the aria the bass line does not develop any other rhythmic patterns, whereas the word-painting of 'balenar' ('flashing', as in lightning) in the voice is achieved with triplets. Fortunately for the continuo player, Scarlatti has provided an example of a melodic solution for the right hand during the opening bars: bar 2, where the continuo is alone, has the same bass as bars 11 and 15. In bar 11 the voice moves in contrary motion to the bass line, while in bar 15 the voice rises with the bass in parallel seventeenths (compound thirds) above it; this yields two main possibilities for realizing the opening bars (shown, respectively, in Examples 11.4 and 11.5).

Example 11.4   Scarlatti, cantata *Il Nerone*, aria 'Vuò che tremi', bars 1–3: realization anticipating the voice.

In Example 11.4 the realization takes material from the vocal part, combining contrary and parallel motion and thereby avoiding a literal anticipation of the composed, sung part. However, this manner of realization may be better suited to

---

[31] I am grateful to Elisabeth Scholl for allowing me to use her transcription of this cantata.

the *da capo* rather than to the opening of the aria, in order to allow the descriptive triplets to be introduced by the voice. A different solution for the realization, shown in Example 11.5, is to treat the theme in the bass line as the main feature of these opening bars and to play a chordal accompaniment in the right hand. The rhythm of the bass can also be mirrored, and chords can be filled out in the left hand as well where possible. This alternative realization amplifies the distinctive rhythm of the bass without anticipating the voice's triplets.

Example 11.5 Scarlatti, cantata *Il Nerone*, aria 'Vuò che tremi', bars 1–3: realization amplifying the bass.

Example 11.6 Vivaldi, cantata *Fonti del pianto*, RV 656, opening aria, bars 1–8, with simple realization.

Example 11.7 Vivaldi, cantata *Fonti del pianto*, RV 656, opening aria, bars 1–8, with complex realization.

It is immediately apparent that in both these realizations the number of voices is not regular, and the inner voices are not followed through. This is because these represent attempts to notate what the harpsichordist might play rather than aspiring to the status of thought-through composition. Chords are therefore formed from the notes that fall well under the hand, and regularity of part-writing has low priority. The number of notes in each chord also depends on the accentuation required; by varying the number of notes in the chords, it is possible to emphasize certain beats of the bar more than others (in this instance, the fourth crotchet of the bar – interpreting the double-length bars as being effectively in 6/4 rather than the indicated 3/4 – is made strongest, in order to bring out the triple metre). This need to create clear patterns of stress is one reason why, in performance, it is acceptable to abandon the rules of counterpoint in favour of achieving the most colourful effect. Indeed, the limited dynamic possibilities of the harpsichord make it essential for a player to be able to alter the emphasis in the bar by varying the number of notes in successive chords – and to be able to do this at each new presentation of the ritornello. For example, if a 'hemiola' effect were to be sought in the *da capo* restatement, the chord with the greatest number of notes should occur on the sixth crotchet of bar 2.

This approach to realization is at its most appropriate when the bass line carries the melody (the second case above). In the first aria of Vivaldi's cantata *Fonti del pianto*, RV 656, the opening bars are of the bass are melodic, and are taken up again by the bass when the voice enters (the bass of bars 1–3 is repeated in bars 9–11). However, it would be inappropriate to imitate the voice part in the right hand at the very beginning of the aria, since the long, held note of the voice in bar 9 is extremely unsuited to a plucked instrument. The right-hand accompaniment should therefore be predominantly harmonic; the rhythm of the right-hand chords is dictated by the harmony implied by the bass – in this instance, a minim followed by a crotchet upbeat into the following bar. In its simplest form the realization might look as in Example 11.6. But in a more stylistically correct elaboration (Example 11.7) the harmonies should be enriched and inessential notes added.

In Example 11.6 the added harmony notes (such as the E♭ in bar 3), together with the doubling of dissonances (e.g., on the third beat of bar 2), are undoubtedly 'incorrect' according to normal canons; however, when played on the harpsichord, the gradual addition of notes in both hands through the first three bars gives the desired impression of a crescendo, while the chordal opening contrasts well with the semiquaver movement that ensues in bars 3–6.

Example 11.8 Marcello, cantata *L'usignolo che il suo duolo*, opening aria, bars 1–11, with realization.

When the material used in the bass line is not melodic, and it is inappropriate to imitate the vocal part (the third case enumerated above), it is necessary to improvise new material. Benedetto Marcello's cantata *L'usignolo che il suo duolo* (whose opening ritornello is shown in Example 11.8) exemplifies such an opening. In the first aria the ritornello is unusually long, and the thematic material used in the bass consists of broken-chord figures and descending linear patterns, neither of which features occurs in the vocal part. It is not possible to superimpose the vocal theme on the opening bars: when the voice enters, the bass line changes, and when the bass returns in accompaniment to the vocal part, this theme is not suitable because it moves in crotchets and, as in the Vivaldi example, would sound bare on a keyboard. Simple appropriation of the vocal theme is therefore not a satisfactory option. Furthermore, the bass line, especially in the opening bars, is not so interesting melodically that chords in the right hand would suffice; nor is there any distinctive rhythmic characteristic of the bass that can be imitated in the realization, since the former moves in continuous quavers.

Bars 1–5 receive a new harmony in each bar; bars 6–8 can be treated by playing in sixths with the bass; bars 9–11 form the cadence and are therefore taken care of. So it is the opening five bars that afford the greatest scope for imaginative realization: they are harmonically static, giving space for melodic invention in the passage from one harmony to the next, as Example 11.8 illustrates.

Ornamentation

It was noted earlier, in connection with Example 11.3, how acciaccaturas can be included in chords as ornamental devices. When the realization is melodic in character, trills and other ornamentation can be expected to be added, both in the right hand and in the left, as Gasparini proposes:

> I wish to show you many sorts of diminutions, embellishments, ornaments and manners of giving grace to the accompaniment.[32]

Hence shakes and trills can profitably be included in a realization of the type represented by Example 11.7, just as if this were a solo movement. Gasparini, indeed, regards ornamentation as an essential component of the realization, writing:

> You can use the mordent as well as acciaccaturas in arias and canzonas, since these are most necessary for playing with grace and good taste: the resulting accompaniment will be much more harmonious, and delectable.[33]

---

[32] Gasparini, *L'armonico pratico*, p. 98: 'Sarei desideroso di mostrarti molte sorti di diminuzioni, fioretti, abbellimenti, e maniere di dar grazia all'accompagnare'.

[33] Ibid., p. 97: 'Potrai ancora usare tanto il mordente, come l'acciaccature nelle Arie, o Canzoni; essendo molto necessarie per sonare con grazia, e buon gusto; e riuscirà

Treatises set no limits on the extravagance of ornament that can be indulged when the continuo player is momentarily alone, despite being so insistent on discretion whenever the voice is accompanied. The ritornellos of cantata arias therefore offer an ideal context for playing in the most lavish and ornate manner.

Conclusions

Despite the lack of specific instructions concerning how to realize the material in the ritornellos of *da capo* arias in cantatas, it is reasonable – indeed most desirable – to carry over into the playing of these ritornellos all the advice and concrete illustrations to be gleaned from contemporary authorities, as well as all the inferential evidence on solo playing. As the continuo player is the undisputed soloist during these sections, with licence to realize them at will, the harpsichordist must draw on solo skills in order to introduce ornamentation, diverse passages in the realization and diminutions in either hand, as well as to master the harmonically rich texture in both hands, causing the harpsichord to speak in the most colourful way while being responsive to the inputs from the singer and/or any other continuo players. In the past, the study of *partimenti* would have perfected the ability to vary the musical material at each occurrence; hints for suitable harmony, rhythm, melody, texture and compass pertinent to the aria under consideration can be found in notated material within the composition itself – both in the vocal part and in the bass line. Arias with melodic guides sketched in give an idea of how their composers wished the ritornello to be realized. Revealingly, the composers never use the ritornellos as a pretext for introducing new material, but only in order to show how imitation should be carried out.

It is also essential to recognize the individual strengths and skills of the individual voice and to react accordingly in the accompaniment. The principal means of doing this, on the harpsichord, is by the skilful addition and subtraction of parts. To achieve the flexibility necessary for success in the performance of the aria, the composer is therefore normally best advised to leave the realization of the ritornello entirely to the player. Appropriate ornamentation must be added to the execution: acciaccaturas where the realization is mainly chordal, and mordents and trills where it is melodic. Where possible and appropriate, some of the vocal ornamentation may be imitated in addition.

Modern scholarship has come to accept the essentially improvisatory nature of basso continuo performance, and the more successful notated editorial realizations of today tend towards simplicity, which allows the performer to add freely to a basic harmonic framework. It risks, though, misleading by its very plainness, for the style of accompaniment as it emerges in performance should not at all be simple. It has been shown how the cantata aria, when approached with the right training, contains within itself all the information needed to realize the ritornellos

---

l'accompagnare assai più armonioso, e dilettevole'.

– indeed, it is essential that the material used be derived from within the arias: there are no deficiencies in the notation, for it is the harpsichordist who becomes the 'composer' for the space of a few bars. Although at the time it was most probably the composer of the aria himself who would have been sitting at the harpsichord, it is the duty of – and the challenge to – the modern performer to master the former's skills and take his place.

Chapter 12
The Revival of the Italian Chamber Cantata on Disc: Models and Trends

Roger-Claude Travers

The fortunes of the Italian chamber cantata on disc mirror, at a general level, those of recordings of the late-Baroque repertory as a whole during the post-war period. A closer examination reveals, however, how intimately its revival is linked to the evolving Baroque 'movement' (for which the French have coined a special term: 'baroqueux') of the last quarter of the twentieth century.

A study of the main recordings enables one to identify three fairly well-defined periods in this renaissance spearheaded by recordings, which can be characterized in turn as follows.

The *period of emergence*, where interest in this repertory is sporadic and limited to only a handful of composers, opens with the advent of the long-playing record in the 1950s. It bears the common stigmata of that period, betraying an imperfect knowledge of the genre and, even more, of the style proper to each composer, as well as of the appropriate means to recapture it in performance.

Next comes what we may term the *period of analysis*, beginning in the mid-1970s and thus benefiting from the advances in interpretative knowledge made by specialist ensembles, where the Italian cantata or, rather, a representative selection garnered from the genre, is used to illustrate and provide evidence for experiments in vocal delivery, research into continuo performance or some aspect of editing or historically informed performance. The common feature of this period is that the recording is treated as a means to a greater end than the simple enjoyment of the music itself: in other words, it has a didactic or propagandistic agenda.

Towards 1990 we see the first signs of the *period of synthesis*, which gathers pace in the new millennium. By now, the Italian Baroque cantata has won its natural place in the repertory as a major genre in its own right. This situation benefits both a few well-known composers, whose cantatas can now be recorded in their totality, and a large mass of less well-known ones, thanks to the assiduous combing of manuscript sources by musicologists and, even more, by scholar–performers. This stream of novelties is so great as to risk sating the palate of the music-lover – and it often does not wait for the written discussion of the same music in musicological forums.

The period of emergence

During the first quarter of the twentieth century, in the formative years of phonographic reproduction, as well as in the three succeeding decades – the golden age of the 78 rpm record, when the symphonic and chamber music repertory of the preceding century was so unforgettably preserved in recorded form – the Italian Baroque cantata remained almost unknown to musicians and music-lovers alike. Indeed, modern editions, an almost indispensable requirement for performers of that time, were conspicuously lacking.[1]

The music critic Ivan A. Alexandre, in a brilliant pioneering essay relating the history of the recorded Baroque repertory,[2] has drawn attention to the passionate spirit underlying the words of two works of seminal importance for the revival of this repertory, both published near the start of the twentieth century.

The first of these, which he describes as a 'bible for future generations', was a book first published in 1915 by the British harpsichordist and musicologist Arnold Dolmetsch.[3] According to Alexandre, the influence of this 'perturbateur, [...] révolté, [...] pittoresque fanatique' (a description roughly translatable as 'subversive, rebellious, colourful fanatic') has not yet weakened:

> By considering, in chapter after chapter, the significance of expression, tempo, dance, rhythmic notation, ornamentation, figured bass, fingering and contemporary instruments, Dolmetsch gave proof that the music of the past, 'old' though it might be, was not any less alive.[4]

In a masterly book originally published in 1909, which is to say six years before Dolmetsch, the then still very young Polish harpsichordist Wanda Landowska wrote:

> If I have insisted upon the truism of 'musical progress', it is because I consider it the principal cause of the ignorance of our past and of all the errors in the interpretation of the old masters. It is because of this prejudice, become a religion,

---

[1] A rare exception was the anthology *Auserwählte Kammer-Kantaten der Zeit um 1700* compiled by Hugo Riemann just before the First World War (Leipzig, 1911).

[2] See Ivan A. Alexandre, 'Le printemps des Anciens', in same author (ed.), *Guide de la musique ancienne et baroque*, (Paris, 1993), pp. v–xlviii.

[3] Arnold Dolmetsch, *The Interpretation of the Music of the Seventeenth and Eighteenth Centuries Revealed by Contemporary Evidence*, (London, [1915]).

[4] Alexandre, 'Le printemps des Anciens', p. xi: 'En visitant, chapitre après chapitre, ce que signifient expression, tempo, danse, notation rythmique, ornementation, basse chiffrée,

that music, filled as much as the other arts with beautiful things, is still very poor in its revelation of these things. We are still deaf to the miracles of those beauties which uplift the soul by means of the melodious echo so marvellously remote and by that divine link which 'unites sympathetic hearts across the centuries'.[5]

At the turn of the nineteenth and twentieth centuries, the fire of the nascent passion for old music was being kindled in various European hearths. In France, for example, the composers Charles Bordes and Vincent d'Indy launched a prestigious series of concerts of Baroque music at the Schola Cantorum in rue Saint-Jacques, Paris, reviving the operatic music of Monteverdi, Lully, Destouches, Rameau and their peers, and even taking an interest – relevant to our present purposes – in the cantatas of Clérambault.

The musicologist Jules Écorcheville, an attentive listener, was unconvinced by the performances, observing 'On applaudit à la Schola, sans doute, avec conviction parfois, mais combien mollement!' ('The applause at the Schola is, to be sure, sometimes given with conviction, but how muted it is!').[6] Écorcheville goes on to summarize, apropos of the 'style de Bach', the persuasive arguments that will come to influence interpretations of the inter-war period and will still remain valid, forty years later, for the earliest recordings belonging to the period of emergence:

> [...] the spirit of the archaeologist and of the scholar will always have their place; but the ear and the heart are well and truly sacrificed [...] thereby. Uniformity at any price! That is the watchword. And how do people set about achieving it? Nothing is simpler: it is enough to reduce to a minimum the dynamic and rhythmic nuances of every piece. The effect is unmistakable [...] Above all, no rubato. Rubato is the ultimate sin for our conductors, when they direct old music. They make a good rallentando at cadences, but elsewhere keep the beat firm.[7]

---

doigtés et instruments d'époque, Dolmetsch apportait la preuve que la musique du passé, pour être "ancienne" n'en était pas moins vivante'.

[5] Wanda Landowska, *Musique ancienne. Style-Interprétation/Instruments-Artistes* (Paris, 1909; reprint, 1996), p. 227: 'Si j'ai insisté sur le lieu commun du progrès dans la musique, c'est parce que je le considère comme la cause principale de l'ignorance de notre passé et de toutes les erreurs dans l'interprétation des maîtres anciens. C'est à cause de ce préjugé, devenu religion, que la musique, gorgée autant que les autres arts de belles choses, est encore très pauvre en révélation de ces choses. Nous sommes encore sourds aux miracles de ces beautés qui relèvent l'âme par l'écho mélodieux si merveilleusement lointain et par ce lien divin qui "rattache des cœurs sympathiques de siècle en siècle"'. The English version of the passage given above is taken from the translation of the same book by William Aspenwall Bradley as *Music of the Past* (London, [1926]), p. 175.

[6] Jules Écorcheville, 'La Schola Cantorum et le style de Bach', *Mercure musical*, April 1907: 399–406, at 400.

[7] Ibid., p. 401: '[...] l'esprit de l'archéologue, de l'érudit trouvera toujours son compte; mais l'oreille et le cœur sont vraiment sacrifiés [...] Uniformité avant tout! Tel est le mot d'ordre. Et comment s'y prend-on? Rien de plus simple: il suffit de réduire à

Instead of which, Écorcheville invites performers to:

> restore to old music its free imagination and the expressive emotion that was formerly its attraction [...] The age in which operatic recitative and the bel canto of virtuoso singers flourished knew nothing of this gloomy tyranny of uniformity. On the contrary, it sought, in a thousand different ways, to avoid this defect into which we have so willingly plunged it [...].[8]

Sadly, the initiatives towards the revival of old (including Baroque) music slowed down considerably in the inter-war period, having failed to make its nature and internal logic compatible with the existing musical institutions. If the situation was unpromising for instrumental music, in the particular case of the Italian cantata for voice and continuo the genre remained a virtual *terra incognita* right up to the Second World War,[9] after which it was slow to emerge from general indifference, despite the selective interest in the Baroque repertory that manifested itself in the post-war years. Michael Talbot has pertinently summed up the difficulty, for performers of the period, of including – especially in live performance – music from cantatas in recitals for voice and piano, which were (and still are) traditionally oriented towards the Classical and Romantic periods:

> There are too many obstacles: the accompaniment is wrong in terms of timbre, balance, and (perhaps most of all) atmosphere; the vocal technique demanded differs considerably from that required for Lieder and *mélodies*; the language of the text appears (especially outside Italy) archaic, precious, and far too full of such devices as elision and synaloepha that seem designed to trip up a foreigner. And what is true of the arias is multiplied in the recitatives, for which there seems no right solution: if they are sung in an overly 'dramatic' manner, the chamber-music character of the programme (in terms of the conventions

---

leur minimum les nuances dynamiques et rythmiques de tous ces morceaux. L'effet est immanquable [...] Surtout pas de rubato. Le rubato est la pierre de scandale de nos chefs d'orchestre, lorsqu'ils dirigent la musique ancienne. Un bon ralentissement aux cadences, et la mesure rigide partout ailleurs'.

[8] Ibid., p. 405: 'rendre à la musique ancienne la libre fantaisie, et l'émotion expressive qui fit autrefois son attrait [...] L'époque où fleurit le récit d'opéra et le bel canto des virtuoses n'a pu connaître cette tyrannie morose de l'uniformité. Elle a cherché au contraire, et par mille façons, à éviter ce défaut dans lequel nous la laissons si volontiers tomber [...]'.

[9] The case of Vivaldi is exemplary in this respect. The programme chosen for his spectacular modern revival in the *Settimana Vivaldi* that took place in Siena from 16 to 21 September 1939 included representative works from all the principal instrumental and vocal genres – except the solo cantata.

governing song recitals) is compromised; if they are sung too dispassionately, the result is tedium.[10]

The same conclusion is reached by Alexandre, who observes: 'on n'avait jamais résolu le problème du récitatif (cette "steppe"), jamais trouvé les clefs du style, qu'on croyait si proches au début du siècle' ('no one had ever found a solution to the problem of the recitative (that "steppe") or had discovered the vital key to the style, which, at the beginning of the century, had been thought so close').[11]

However, by 1950 the time had come for what one may describe in humorous and generalizing terms as 'Telemania': a rolling tide that brought to the surface the instrumental music of Telemann, Albinoni and above all Vivaldi – to the indignation of certain members of the progressive intelligentsia.[12] These works were entrusted to chamber orchestras of traditional type, many newly established, and their emergence – which coincided with a new, revolutionary platform for recorded music, the long-playing record – was greeted by the public first with curiosity and then with rapid acceptance.

Amid this discographic plenty, however, Italian *cantate a voce sola* represented merely the end of the tail of the Baroque comet. The masters of the past who had already achieved institutional recognition, Bach and Handel in particular, were naturally the earliest beneficiaries. The German soprano Agnes Giebel, who had come to public attention via her participation, in 1950, in the weekly broadcasts of Bach cantatas by RIAS (Berlin), was the grand priestess of the first years. Musical precision and purity of tone, allied to delicacy and stylistic perfection, characterized every one of her interpretations. However, in her recorded versions of Handel's *Agrippina condotta a morire* (HWV 110), *Pensieri notturni di Filli* (HWV 134) and *Armida abbandonata* (HWV 105)[13] the tragic situation of Agrippina and the torments of Armida were altogether lacking in pathos. Giebel displayed insufficient verbal and dramatic involvement in these works, whose depths she did not really

---

[10] Michael Talbot, *The Chamber Cantatas of Antonio Vivaldi* (Woodbridge, 2006), p. 21. Talbot makes the additional point (ibid.) that Baroque sonatas for violin and continuo, the instrumental equivalent of continuo cantatas, are accommodated much more readily in 'mainstream' recitals for violin and piano.

[11] Alexandre, 'Le printemps des Anciens', p. xv.

[12] See Dave Harker, 'In Perspective: Theodor Adorno', article published on-line by the Centre for Popular Music Research at the Humboldt University, Berlin (consulted January 2008 at www2.hu-berlin.de/fpm/texte/Harker3.htm), where, for example, one reads: 'Adorno knew it was "far more difficult to see why one popular song is a hit and another a flop than why Bach finds more of an echo than Telemann", but he expected his readership to know who Telemann was and to fall into line behind his denunciation of the "banality" and "vulgarity" of the "crudely simple" music of the "screeching retinue of Elvis Presley"'.

[13] OCEANIC OCS 30 / OLYMPIE RECORDS Q 8116 (LP): Agnes Giebel (soprano), Tonstudio Orchester Stuttgart, Rudolf Lamy (*R* 1952).

attempt to plumb. An unpleasant-sounding Neupert continuo harpsichord and a monotonous, rigid Stuttgart orchestra gave her solid support when it could. The future star of Mozartian singing, the American soprano Teresa Stich-Randall, victorious in competitions in Lausanne and Geneva in 1951, took part the following year in the Salzburg Festival, recording with the Camerata Academica Mozarteum, directed by Bernhard Paumgartner,[14] the first version on disc of *Su le sponde del Tebro* by Alessandro Scarlatti.[15] The stiff rhythm hammered out by the Austrian conductor found its counterpart in the staccato manner of the singer, her tendency to fragment the vocal line in detached notes and her inappropriately placed breaths, notwithstanding her superb voice that conveyed authentic emotion. The sluggishness of the recitatives, interspersed with interminable pedal-points and sustained notes, pointed up, once again, the disparity between the enormous potential of these exceptional voices and the basic ignorance of the rhetoric proper to this repertory.

The first decade of the long-playing record (1950–59) was also marked by two important initiatives. In the margins of the prevailing 'Telemania' two cantatas by Vivaldi timidly entered the catalogues. One was an adaptation by Virgilio Mortari[16] of *Cessate, omai cessate* (RV 684), sung by a very average mezzo-soprano and accompanied by the Società Corelli, a local rival of the Musici di Roma, who constituted the rising star of the chamber orchestras that were then devoting themselves eagerly to the concertos of the *Prete rosso*.[17] The other, made one year earlier, was the first-ever recording of a Vivaldi cantata: *Qual in pioggia dorata i dolci rai* (RV 686),[18] sung by another contralto of no especial merit and accompanied by the Orchestra della Scuola Veneziana, the earliest ensemble of its kind in post-war Italy, under the baton of its founder, Angelo Ephrikian.[19] The choice of instrumentally accompanied cantatas (plus two horns over and above the

---

[14] From 1938 to 1945 Paumgartner directed in Florence a research institute of the University of Vienna.

[15] Brilliantly scored for soprano, two violins, trumpet and continuo, the cantata was published in an edition by Paumgartner himself in 1956.

[16] In the manner of *Ingrata Lidia, ha vinto il tuo rigor*, RV 673, a spurious cantata preserved in Florence, of which Mortari had prepared the first modern edition in 1947 for the publisher Carisch (Milan). He went on to publish his own edition of *Cessate, omai cessate*. A member of the Siena circle grouped around the Accademia Musicale Chigiana, Mortari had already pulled apart and reorchestrated *L'Olimpiade* (RV 725) for the first modern performance of any Vivaldi opera, given at Siena during the *Settimana Vivaldi* of 1939.

[17] RCA (Radio e Televisione Italiana) A 12 R-0098 (LP): L. Ribacchi (mezzo-soprano), Società Corelli (*R* 1953).

[18] PERIOD RENAISSANCE RN X58 (LP): G. Borelli (contralto), Orchestra della Scuola Veneziana, A. Ephrikian (*R* 1952).

[19] A founder, in 1947, together with Antonio Fanna, of the Istituto Italiano Antonio Vivaldi, whose artistic director was Gian Francesco Malipiero. Ephrikian was also the editor of the earliest scores in the collected edition of the composer's instrumental music published by Ricordi (Milan) in association with the same institute.

strings in RV 686) was not fortuitous. The aim was to win over music-lovers by a more or less overt identification of the arias with concerto movements. For the miracle of the rehabilitation of Vivaldi as a great composer for the voice to have occurred forty years earlier, one would have needed someone with the intuition of Claudio Scimone, when he had the inspired idea of offering the title role in the opera *Orlando* (RV 728) to Marilyn Horne.

Perhaps the most promising cantata recording of the 1950s was reserved for the most pared-down form of the genre. The recorded versions of *Qui dove alfin m'assido* (*Il rosignuolo*) and *Clori vezzosa e bella*,[20] cantatas by Alessandro Scarlatti for alto and continuo, already contain the features that will characterize the great moments of the succeeding period of analysis. At the head of the record company L'Oiseau-Lyre stood the wealthy, Australian-born benefactress Louise Dyer, who had founded it in 1932.[21] The practice of including, for each recording, musicologically precise details of the works performed, which was to become a priceless source of information for the *aficionados* of this repertory, goes back to this venerable company. The harpsichord in the recording was played by Thurston Dart, a spiritual heir to Dolmetsch in Great Britain, as were August Wenzinger in Germany and Switzerland and Antoine Geoffroy-Dechaume in France. Helen Watts, a member of the Handel Opera Society, produced a tone quality of marble consistency and a supple vocal line, even if she was not entirely free of affectation (notably in her precious pronunciation) – a fault shared with Dart, who imitated the nightingale (*rosignuolo*) a little too closely.

Five years later, Watts overcame these sins of her youth when she made a classic recording of three instrumentally accompanied cantatas by Handel: two for alto – *Carco sempre di gloria* (HWV 87) and *Splenda l'alba in oriente* (HWV 166) – and one for soprano – *Tu fedel? Tu costante?* (HWV 171), in a transcription for alto.[22] In these performances she demonstrated her restrained, classical and full-voiced technique, for which the young Raymond Leppard provided a tasteful and spirited accompaniment. The English conductor revisited Handel in 1967 to make a memorable recording, with the unforgettable Janet Baker, of *Ah! crudel, nel pianto mio* (HWV 78) and *Armida abbandonata* (*Dietro l'orme fugaci*, HWV 105),[23] of which Alexandre wrote an enthusiastic review, remarking:

> Janet Baker is already known as a high-flying Handelian heroine. This vocal timbre that no one has produced since, this astonishing declamation, this

---

[20] L'OISEAU-LYRE 50173 (LP): H. Watts (contralto), D. Dupré (viola da gamba), T. Dart (harpsichord) (*R* 1957).

[21] Dyer was prompted to found the company after having been enraptured by Rameau's *Hippolyte et Aricie* (in the heavily arranged edition of Vincent d'Indy).

[22] DECCA (LP) / 433737-2: H. Watts (contralto), English Chamber Orchestra, R. Leppard (*R* 1961).

[23] EMI ASD 2458 (LP): J. Baker (mezzo-soprano), English Chamber Orchestra, R. Leppard (*R* 1967).

shaping of phrasing and tempo that allows no relaxation in the tension, remain peerless.[24]

even if a price had to be paid by the conscientious conductor:

The assertive but insufficiently attentive support provided by Raymond Leppard gives rise to wrinkles that the singer ignores but to which she can occasionally fall victim.[25]

The Handel cantata had found its voice. In the course of the same decade Elly Ameling, Agnes Giebel and once more Teresa Stich-Randall lent their distinctive soprano voices to *Non sa che sia dolore* (BWV 209) by J. S. Bach, while the baritone Dietrich Fischer-Dieskau, already at the peak of his reputation, placed his huge dramatic understanding and sensitivity to the text at the service of *Amore traditore* (BWV 203).[26] These memorable recitals from the period of emergence before the revolution wrought by the *baroqueux* have two traits in common: they feature 'great voices' (as if to compensate the listener for the unfamiliarity of the genre) and favour, so far as this is possible, the use of orchestral accompaniment and/or the distinctive sound of obbligato instruments. The works are chosen to show off the performers, not the reverse. Handel, Bach and, in an ancillary role, Alessandro Scarlatti – all 'canonized' composers of the late Baroque – represent alone, or almost so, an entire genre. The sole exceptions to this pattern come from Italy. There, Renata Tebaldi and Tito Gobbi took into their repertory, doubtless on account of its pronounced lachrymose mood, the first aria of a cantata believed at the time to be by Vivaldi, *Piango, gemo, sospiro e peno* (RV 675),[27] while the Swiss conductor Edwin Loehrer (to whom we will return later) supplied an elegant and sophisticated continuo to complement the splendid voice, perfectly restrained in style, of the baritone Laerte Malaguti, in transposed versions of RV 684 and RV 675 (once more). This recording was rewarded in France with a Grand Prix du Disque.[28] The passion for Alessandro Stradella shared by the musicologist

---

[24] Alexandre, *Guide de la musique ancienne et baroque*, p. 640: 'Janet Baker s'annonçait déjà comme une héroïne handelienne de haute volée. Ce timbre qu'on n'a pas retrouvé depuis, cette déclamation bouleversante, cette conduite des phrases et des mouvements sans la moindre chute de tension n'ont pas encore rencontré de rivaux'.

[25] Ibid., p. 640: 'Le soutien présent mais inattentif de Raymond Leppard a pris des rides que le chant ignore, mais dont il peut, à l'occasion, devenir la victime'.

[26] EMI Classics (LP) / 5 68 509 2 (LP): D. Fischer-Dieskau (baritone), I. Poppen (cello), E. Picht-Axenfeld (harpsichord) (*R* 1960–62).

[27] Edited for this purpose, in 1956, by John Edmonds for the publisher R. D. Row Music Co. (Boston, USA), together with four other arias taken (how ironic!) from three similarly inauthentic cantatas preserved at the Florence conservatorio.

[28] CYCNUS (LP) / NONESUCH 71.088: L. Malaguti (bass), Società cameristica di Lugano, E. Loehrer (*R* 1963).

Francesco Degrada and the already mentioned conductor Angelo Ephrikian, director of the small record company Arcophon, led them to record the composer's entire instrumental music and a selection of cantata arias.[29] This initiative was based on a revolutionary procedure (improbable though this description may seem to us today) that became common only in the period of analysis that followed. This procedure consisted of undertaking an independent preliminary musicological study specifically linked to the recording. In other respects, the recording shows its age – not so much because of the voices, which are always radiantly beautiful and sensitive, as on account of the instrumental accompaniment, where the string basses cultivate an obsolete heaviness.

The period of analysis

The period of emergence pursued its development in parallel with that of the long-playing record. The fragility of the link forged by this repertory to musical institutions, to everyday concert life, to the record market, and to amateur performers and listeners induced most artists more or less consciously to cast their performing style and material in a traditional mould exemplified by the modern-style chamber orchestra, a creation of the immediate post-war period, which appropriated a repertory stretching from Corelli to Britten and occasionally co-opted voices – frequently very beautiful ones, but not ones trained specifically with old music in mind – in order to venture into the uncharted territories of Baroque opera and, for the more daring, the Italian chamber cantata, in the face of the perils created by simple (*secco*) recitative.

A few artists, 'inquiets et mal consolés de voir leur discipline dégénérer en papier peint' ('restless, and loth to see their discipline degenerate into wallpaper'),[30] made a breach in the edifice of the new certainties as early as the start of the 1950s[31] by inventing, and then elaborating thread by thread, the fabric of what the French call the *mouvance baroque*, on which so many ensembles enthusiastically weave their tapestries today.[32] In the space of three decades much work was accomplished, but not without conflicts with the world of musical institutions, some stylistic dead-

---

[29] ARCOPHON (LP) / HARMONIA MUNDI HMA 322: L. Ticinelli Fattori (contralto), G. Sarti (baritone), Complesso barocco di Milano, F. Degrada (*R* 1965).

[30] Alexandre, 'Le printemps des Anciens', p. vii.

[31] As early as May 1954 an LP of Bach cantatas brought together no fewer than five prophets of the 'mouvance baroque': the counter-tenor Alfred Deller, the organist and harpsichordist Gustav Leonhardt, the violinists Marie Leonhardt and Eduard Melkus and the cellist Nikolaus Harnoncourt.

[32] English possesses no neat equivalent of 'mouvance baroque': one would speak, rather, of the 'Early Music Movement', of which the performance of Baroque music forms just one compartment.

ends,[33] some constructive rivalries and plenty of uncertainties. Finally, a bridge was formed to the universities, which until then (at least in France) had shied away from practical music. The era of 'practice-oriented musicology' had arrived. To quote Alexandre, this called forth 'une armée de chercheurs occupés, non à étudier telle forme ou tel maître, mais à exhumer livres, traités et correspondances dont les interprètes doivent tenir compte s'ils veulent assurer une exécution philologique de tel style ou de telle œuvre' ('an army of researchers busying themselves not with this or that [musical] form or composer but studying books, treatises and written references relevant to performers wishing to give a philologically accurate account of this or that style or work').[34] For each category of performer there were problems – major or minor, particular or general, continuous or sporadic – that had to be overcome. Each new discovery provoked another. Articulation, phrasing, dynamic shading, ornamentation, pitch, intonation, tempo, rhythmic interpretation, the manner of holding and playing the instruments, the way to make them expressive: all these aspects, and many more, engaged the interest of this swarming anthill of tireless searchers and experimenters.

From the middle of the 1970s, when trust in the hegemonic concept of 'modernity' entered its twilight, to the start of the 1980s, which marks the rise of the period of synthesis, Italian chamber cantatas of the late Baroque at last became a favoured terrain of singers specializing in early music performance. The range of works performed did not initially show more diversity or enterprise than those introduced previously, but the works of composers who were 'recognized' (by them)[35] were adroitly selected by the pace-setters of the drive for authenticity in order to illustrate their theories, which were sometimes speculative but nearly always enriching.

The partisans of Early Music, at that time coming mainly from the English-speaking countries or the Low Countries, gravitated naturally towards Handel as a representative composer. The fashion for 'boyish' voices and for dreamy-toned male altos, who sounded unreal but could give eloquence to each word, was born. The dominant figures were sopranos possessing the qualities of agility, transparency and insubstantiality: these singers were uncomfortable in the pathetic style and unsuited to opera, but supreme vocalisers and well versed in certain techniques of Baroque *bel canto* (*affetti*, diminutions, trills, etc.). Such singers as Giebel, Stich-Randall and Ameling now belonged to the ethos of the past. Instead, the public warmed to the childlike charms of 'period voices' trained via the methods laid down by Tosi and Mancini (authors of the singing treatises that

---

[33] See the discussion, below, of the case of Nella Anfuso.

[34] Alexandre, 'Le printemps des Anciens', p. xx.

[35] Naturally excluding Vivaldi, whose operas and other secular vocal works were poorly regarded at the time (and remain so by a rearguard of the Early Music Movement that includes Jacobs, Herreweghe, Gardiner and Christie). The hour of the rehabilitation of Vivaldi's secular vocal music sounded – but how loudly when it finally arrived! – only at the threshold of the twenty-first century.

were most frequently consulted in connection with the Italian repertory).[36] This was the heyday of the sopranos Emma Kirkby and Judith Nelson. But the greatest concern of the *mouvance baroque* was to promote, in music requiring alto, the counter-tenor voice. The voice masterfully revealed in the English repertory by the unforgettable pioneer Alfred Deller remained a model for his followers. The Belgian singer René Jacobs developed a *voce mezzana*: that is, a falsetto voice united to a high natural (chest) voice, with a smooth transition between the two registers.[37] Jacobs's 'head voice' soon gained imitators, such as James Bowman and Paul Esswood in England and the French counter-tenors Henri Ledroit and Gérard Lesne. These experimented with extending their compass downwards, a very risky step. The American Derek Lee Ragin brought virtuosic agility, the German Jochen Kowalski a mastery of the pathetic dimension.

Mi palpita il cor (HWV 132), composed towards 1708 in Rome by Handel, was their almost mandatory test piece. In the version for alto (HWV 132c) René Jacobs[38] adopts the pose of an aesthete, showing undeniable understanding and elegance in his evocation of images and colours. At his ease in virtuosic passages, he lacks warmth in tenderer moments, and his nasal tone-production can be off-putting. The tone and style of the accompaniment provided by Kuijken, Bylsma and Leonhardt, however, deserve only praise. Drew Minter,[39] then at the very start of his career, displays great taste and a natural quality. The tone produced by this American counter-tenor possesses neither roundness nor especial allure. But his flexibility, his comfortableness in the high register, the perfection of his trills and an almost disembodied charm recall the English school founded by Deller. Paul Esswood[40] possesses a superb head register and a rather wide vibrato. Sadly, for all his refinement and facility with ornaments, monotony easily sets in on account of a want of expressive devices. With the soft-toned Gérard Lesne[41] we encounter accurate diction and a theatrical sense applied to the poetic text, as well as captivating diminutions. His accompaniment by the ensemble Seminario Musicale provides

---

[36] Pier Francesco Tosi was the author of the frequently reprinted and translated treatise *Opinion de' cantori antichi e moderni* (Bologna, 1723), Giambattista Mancini of the manual *Riflessioni pratiche sul Canto figurato* (Milan, 1777).

[37] Jacobs expounded the theoretical bases of his approach and technique in *La controverse sur le timbre du contre-ténor* (Arles, 1985).

[38] RCA SEON 303-93 (LP): R. Jacobs (counter-tenor), S. Kuijken (flute), A. Bylsma (cello), G. Leonhardt (harpsichord) (*R* 1980).

[39] HUNGAROTON HRC 183 (LP): D. Minter (counter-tenor), V. Stadler (flute), G. Szilvassy (harpsichord) (*R* 1981).

[40] HUNGAROTON SLPD 12564: P. Esswood (counter-tenor), P. Németh (flute), C. Falvay (cello), P. Ella (harpsichord) (*R* 1984).

[41] VIRGIN VC 7 91480-2: G. Lesne (counter-tenor), Il Seminario Musicale (*R* 1990).

a warm supportive background. Finally, with Jochen Kowalski,[42] we discover mysterious and disturbing tone colours. With limited ability in the high register and possessing only a basic technique, but powerful and moving, Kowalski concludes this catalogue of counter-tenor voices reinvented by the *baroqueux*. Meanwhile, Emma Kirkby,[43] in the version of the same cantata for soprano (HWV 132a), lacks interpretative depth and the kind of humanity needed for the unfolding of this 'chamber drama'; she prefers, it seems, chastity of expression and the decorative arts to the mirroring of human passions.

The Italian composers of the late Baroque were of little interest, in fact, to British and French specialist singers of that time. True, René Jacobs recorded in 1975 and 1979 a few cantatas of Giovanni Bononcini,[44] selected from the published set *Cantate e Duetti dedicati alla Sacra Maestà di Giorgio Rè della Gran Bretagna* (1721),[45] while the Brazilian singer Paulo Abel do Nascimento[46] presented himself, in cantatas by Alessandro Scarlatti, as a 'natural castrato' voice, whose richness in harmonics, facility in passage-work and variety of colours could not compensate for the strangeness of his throat production, the 'clucking' sound heard in melismas and the upsetting changes of timbre. Vivaldi, as ever, constituted a special case, which is well illustrated by the fortunes on disc of *Cessate, omai cessate* (RV 684). René Jacobs[47] recorded it, in 1978, only at the request of his record company, and later spoke of the experience without warmth.[48] The reason why Paul Esswood[49] recorded it owed much to the advocacy of Jean-Claude Malgoire. The sincere enthusiasm of Gérard Lesne,[50] who opened his career with Vivaldi, was little appreciated in France by the *baroqueux*, who questioned his choice of composer. Finally, Italy had then hardly started its 'cultural revolution' in respect of old music – including the genre of the Italian chamber cantata, of which it alone was,

---

[42] CAPRICCIO 10323: J. Kowalski (counter-tenor), K. H. Passin (flute), S. Pank (viola di gamba), C. Schornsheim (harpsichord), Akademie für Alte Musik Berlin (*R* 1988).

[43] L'OISEAU-LYRE 414 473-2: E. Kirkby (soprano), Academy of Ancient Music, C. Hogwood (*R* 1984).

[44] ARCHIV PRODUKTION 2533 450 (LP): R. Jacobs (counter-tenor), S. Kuijken, L. van Dael (violins), W. Kuijken (cello), R. Kohnen (harpsichord) (*R* 1979), and PHILIPS 6575.058 (LP): R. Jacobs (counter-tenor), S. Kuijken (violino), A. Bylsma (cello), G. Leonhardt (harpsichord) (*R* 1975).

[45] The homage to Albion enshrined in the collection perhaps had something to do with this original choice.

[46] LYRINX 062: P. A. do Nascimento (counter-tenor), P. Foulon (cello), J.-M. Hasler (harpsichord) (*R* 1986).

[47] ARCHIV PRODUKTION 2533.385 (LP): R. Jacobs (counter-tenor), Complesso Barocco, A. Curtis (*R* 1978).

[48] As he related to the present writer in 1978.

[49] CBS 74.094 (LP): P. Esswood (counter-tenor), La Grande Écurie et la Chambre du Roy, J.-C. Malgoire (*R* 1979).

[50] ADDA 58.1053 (LP): G. Lesne (counter-tenor), Il Seminario Musicale (*R* 1985).

theoretically, in a position to have a perfect knowledge of the musical and linguistic codes. In the land of *bel canto* (of the nineteenth rather than the seventeenth century) the counter-tenor voice was still regarded as an aberration. However, within this morass of indifference there rose up, like a haughty, slightly intimidating peak, the certitudes of the soprano Nella Anfuso, a self-styled 'musicologist–performer' and of her mentor, Annibale Gianuario. Proclaiming herself the sole specialist in the domain of Italian music from the fifteenth to the eighteenth century, and in particular of its special brand of virtuosity, she deigned to commit to disc her definitive revelations on the right way, at last, to perform Vivaldi.[51] These included a very slow delivery of recitative, irrespective of note values; interminable, and at the very least unconventional, trills on the vowel 'O'; an absence of climaxes; lachrymose lamentos; suspect intonation; impossibly lethargic tempi; cadenzas with something of a clucking hen. This formidable technomane, obsessed with pure virtuosity, contributed in her own way, following an original path that ultimately led nowhere, to the instructive experiments of the period of analysis.

Finally, having attempted for a long time to reach a state of equilibrium via a number of fruitless experiments conducted in the years following the stutterings of the period of emergence, the basso continuo experienced normalization, both in its instrumentation and in its execution. In the words of Michael Talbot:

> Thirty years ago, cantatas were almost uniformly performed with an accompaniment of harpsichord and cello. The harpsichordist read from a carefully prepared realization that not infrequently was far too elaborate for its own good – slowing down the pace and drawing too much attention to itself. The voicing of chords was often unfortunate, leaving too large a gap between the bass and the fistful of notes in the right hand.[52]

More worrying still was the fact that the exchanges between the vocal line and the continuo often remained very formal in character, so that the *affetti* portrayed in the poetic text were conveyed almost exclusively by the singer, while the instruments remained tethered to their subordinate role as accompanists: unvaried in their expression and only rarely venturing, whether in arias or in recitatives, to introduce digressions in rhythm or tempo. Commentaries by the harpsichordist's right hand, scarcely ever imaginative, did not yet dare to draw inspiration from the thematic content of the melodic lines present in aria ritornellos.[53]

Running parallel with research into interpretation, the progress (or lack of it) achieved by instrument-makers played an equally important role here. What would be the use of virtuously applying the principles of accompaniment enounced in

---

[51] ARION ARN 238.032 (LP): N. Anfuso (soprano), Insieme da Camera Fiorentino, E. Sciarra (*R* 1981).

[52] Talbot, *The Chamber Cantatas of Antonio Vivaldi*, p. 192.

[53] See the end of Giulia Nuti's present chapter 'imitando l'Arietta, ò altro allegro, cantato di fresco': *Keyboard Realization in Italian Continuo Arias*, p. 279–82.

Gasparini's treatise if the instrument to which they were applied was a Neupert or Sperhaake harpsichord, complete with its four-foot register, which, with its aggressive, penetrating tone, was the mainstay of the pioneer generation of interpretations?[54] To caress a phrase on a copy of a Hemsch or Dülcken instrument, to polish a sound on a Blanchet or Taskin: such acts would come to make their contribution, during the period of analysis, to the poetry of the discourse.

The delicate balance between the singer and the continuo, the result of a long maturation process, could not yet be taken for granted. The fortunes of the recording of *Piango, gemo, sospiro e peno* (RV 675), attributed at the time to Vivaldi, exemplify this arduous quest. Published[55] five years before its first recording, in 1963,[56] this cantata for alto voice was probably picked by the Swiss conductor Edwin Loehrer[57] on account of the *lamento* character of the opening aria. He transposed the vocal line down an octave to fit it to the compass of the baritone Laerte Malaguti, celebrated at the time for the beauty of his tone, the subtlety of his phrasing and his exquisite sensibility in the Monteverdian repertory.[58] The prime purpose seems to have been to programme 'Vivaldi's *lamento*'. This fine voice was given a solid accompaniment: the rock-firm cello of Edigio Roveda and a modern Neupert harpsichord – bright and pleasantly toned – entrusted to the Bolognese Luciano Sgrizzi, well-known for his Scarlatti playing, whose refined touch sought to illuminate the inflections of the poetic text while maintaining a natural rhythmic flow. Sgrizzi's right hand, discreet but tasteful, followed the lead of the vocal line, sometimes anticipating or punctuating it. Similarly, Loehrer, a visionary musician, achieved a balanced reading, which remains unequalled to this day. The pathetic character of the first aria could not fail also to attract celebrated *dive* such as the Italian soprano Renata Tebaldi[59]

---

[54] As the prototype of such instruments one may mention the Pleyel harpsichord that Wanda Landowska was playing in the 1930s, with its metal frame, two keyboards and seven pedals.

[55] Edited by Franco Floris for Zanibon, Padua (1958).

[56] CYCNUS (LP) / NONESUCH 71.088: L. Malaguti (bass), Società cameristica di Lugano, E. Loehrer (*R* 1963).

[57] One of Loehrer's signal merits is to have brought to light, with a degree of authenticity amazing for the time (starting in the immediate post-war period), the vocal art of Monteverdi and this composer's Italian contemporaries, by means of his choir attached to the Swiss Italian-language radio station in Lugano.

[58] In continuo cantatas, in contrast to instrumentally accompanied operatic arias, the downward transposition, for 'natural' male voices, of a high vocal part is perfectly historical, even though tenors, rather than basses or baritones, were the usual beneficiaries in the seventeenth and eighteenth centuries.

[59] DECCA SXL S629 (LP): (1st aria, transcribed D. Gamley) R. Tebaldi (soprano), New Philharmonia Orchestra, R. Bonynge (*R* 1973).

and the Spanish mezzo-soprano Tereza Berganza,[60] whose interpretations, from 1973 and 1979 respectively, are a belated testimony to the ideas of the period of emergence. In a recital of 'Eighteenth-Century Arias' Tebaldi lends a personal touch to the 'aria antica' *Piango, gemo, sospiro* [*sic*] by surrounding herself with a particularly kitsch realization by Douglas Gamley entrusted to the strings, in four parts, of the sumptuous New Philharmonia Orchestra conducted by her mentor and husband Richard Bonynge. The vocal line is a cloth on which a harmonic world belonging to the eighteenth century is woven. Berganza's approach is quite different. This grand concert aria is turned into a Lied, thanks to the co-operation of her husband Felix Lavilla, who at that time acted as her accompanist, especially in recitals of Spanish songs. Lavilla's piano transcription of the accompaniment, in the recording played by Ricardo Requejo, features a sophisticated embroidery for the right hand traversing almost the full length of the keyboard and in the ritornellos serves up a melodious counter-theme, while the left hand, in contrast, remains largely faithful to the original notes of the bass. Seventeen years after Loehrer, Hans Ludwig Hirsch[61] included the entire cantata in a recording devoted to Vivaldi and Bach that makes claim to 'authenticity', as do so many recitals on disc from the period of analysis. Here, the continuo is supplied by harpsichord alone, without cello. The realization is monotonous and rather uninspired, even if the right hand allows itself a few imaginative touches in the *da capo* repeats. The mezzo-soprano, Gloria Banditelli, and the harpsichord pursue a parallel evolution in which the vocal line neither implies nor inspires that of the realization of the bass. The contralto Caterina Calvi is, together with James Bowman and Gloria Banditelli, one of the few performers familiar with the Baroque repertory to have tackled this famous, albeit spurious, cantata attributed to Vivaldi. Her version of 1989, under the direction of Roberto Gini,[62] appears the most interesting of all. In this, the continuo role is parcelled out among a theorbo (or is it a chitarrone?), which supplies harmonies for the bass in the form of some rather maladroit and confused chords, a dry-sounding bass viol that looks after its rhythmic shape and a harpsichord, which enters only in the 'B' sections of arias and in the recitatives. True, the aesthetic result produced by this schematic division of labour is laboured and colourless, but its boldness of imagination in the treatment of the continuo, a testimony to the propensity for experiment characteristic of the period of analysis foreshadows the successes that were to arrive in the period of synthesis.

As Gustav Leonhardt aptly put it a little later:

> We are going forward; we are going to look more deeply into works, instruments and styles; and we will discover truths that are far richer than the generalities

---

[60] DEUTSCHE GRAMOPHON 2531 192 (LP): (1st aria, transcribed F. Lavilla) T. Berganza (mezzo-soprano), R. Requejo (piano) (*R* 1979).

[61] FREQUENZ VENETIA 1 DVE (LP): G. Banditelli (mezzo-soprano), Accademia Strumentale Italiana, H. L. Hirsch (*R* 1980).

[62] NUOVA ERA 6859: C. Calvi (contralto), Ensemble Concerto, R. Gini (*R* 1989).

that that already attract us enough to cause us to undertake this work. We will rediscover the lost unity of these pieces. Inevitably, our work increases the stature of the compositions themselves, of our knowledge and of ourselves.[63]

The period of synthesis

At the start of the 1990s the long period of initiation finally bore fruit, with a radical change of mentality. The rapidly growing interest in 'heritage', which affected all types of cultural artefact, had brought with it an acceptance of the naturalness of the exploration of old music. As Alexandre saw it, the process of modernity led to the 'destruction of chronological certitude, doubt over whether the past is really past; whether what comes afterwards is really a replacement; whether there is really a modern art and an old art; and whether one of these is livelier, more present or more immediate than the other'.[64] He accepted as reality an insight that had been gaining ground daily in the analytical period of the Early Music Movement: that 'factual authenticity would always remain an illusion'.[65] Handel, Bach and Vivaldi were listened to 'as truly real music, of which we may love the form, the expression, the melodic invention, the rhythmic verve and the harmonic beauty', and of which we may attempt to 'discover the original nature, but of which we will probably never know the reality – as conceived by the composer'.[66]

The concomitants of this evolution have been many. The advent of on-line library catalogues has greatly facilitated access to manuscript sources. Musicological investigations related to the Baroque period have advanced on all fronts, with an explosion in the number of available critical or facsimile editions. Journals and specialized studies have zealously relayed discoveries and new information. Knowledge relating to organology and instrument-making has made great strides, as have the mastery of old instruments and experiments with 'period voices', the technical, expressive and ornamental aspects of which are now much better known to us.

But above all, recorded music has been the decisive conduit in the change, the straight channel marshalling all the participants in the enterprise. The long-

---

[63] *Diapason-Harmonie*, no. 391 (March 1993), p. 27: 'Nous avançons, nous allons voir plus profondément dans les œuvres, les instruments, les styles, et nous découvrons des vérités qui sont beaucoup plus riches que les généralités qui nous séduisaient déjà assez pour que nous entreprenions ce travail. Nous retrouvons l'unité perdue des œuvres. Inévitablement, ce travail agrandit et les œuvres et notre connaissance et nous-mêmes'.

[64] Alexandre, 'Le printemps des Anciens', pp. xxi–xxv.

[65] Ibid., p. xxiii: 'l'authenticité factuelle ne serait jamais qu'une illusion'.

[66] Ibid.: 'comme des musiques bien réelles, dont nous pouvons comprendre et aimer la forme, l'expression, l'invention mélodique, la verve rythmique, la beauté harmonique […] retrouver la forme originelle, mais dont nous ne connaîtrons probablement jamais la réalité – celle que le compositeur a conçue'.

playing record had accompanied the period of emergence, allowing the pioneers to speak, and had subsequently provided a platform for their disciples, stoked controversies, provoked experimental performances, and, via sleeve notes of an often excellent scholarly quality, enabled researchers to make contact with the ever-growing number of music-lovers drawn towards old music, these 'children of the Baroque'.[67] The advent, in the mid-1980s, of a new means of sound recording, the compact disc (CD), only gave the ultimate boost to the movement.[68]

The general enthusiasm for old music played on period instruments gave record companies, in the first years of the new medium, a ready opportunity to re-record, using a digital technology that produced a more true-to-life sound, the masterpieces of Bach, Handel and Vivaldi under the claimed banner of 'authenticity' in order to restock their catalogues. But the insatiable curiosity of record-buyers now demanded the issue of previously unrecorded works, whose appearance was greeted with lively and generally favourable comment. The desired (and often achieved) commercial gain led many companies, even ones previously uninterested in Baroque music,[69] to seek out a new generation of performers reared in the Early Music Movement to become flagships of their label. Among these musicians there developed a kind of chivalric order with its own dignitaries, grades and titles. These newly favoured *baroqueux* eagerly seized their extraordinary opportunity to explore, with a freedom unprecedented in the history of recording, the musical genres closest to their hearts. The Italian solo cantata was among the beneficiaries of this moment.

Why certain composers in this genre flourished on CD, while others, whose merits were recognized by scholars, did not, owed little to chance, conforming to rules that it will be interesting to elaborate.

Material published in modern editions naturally had an important role to play in this, as shown – to take just two examples – by the choice of the Porpora cantatas *D'Amore il primo dardo*, *Idolatrata e cinta*, *Or che una nube ingrata* and *Questa dunque è la selva* for alto and continuo as performed by the counter-tenor Nicholas Clapton,[70] of which a ready-made text exists in the shape of an edition by James Sanderson,[71] and the complete Op. 4 of Albinoni as performed by Barbara Schlick

---

[67] The title (as 'enfants de la Baroque ') of a famous radio programme on the station France-Musique devoted to the 'mouvance baroque' by the music critic Gaëtan Naulleau.

[68] See Roger-Claude Travers, '1947–1997: Vivaldi, les baroques et la critique', in Francesco Fanna and Michael Talbot (eds), *Cinquant'anni di produzioni e consumi della musica dell'età di Vivaldi, 1947–1997* (Florence, 1998), pp. 53–74.

[69] The companies and labels specializing in old music such as *L'Oiseau-Lyre, Deutsche Grammophon Gesellschaft (Archiv Produktion), Telefunken (Teldec), Harmonia Mundi* and *Astrée*, however, continued generally to offer the boldest choices of repertory.

[70] HUNGAROTON HCD31747: N. Clapton (counter-tenor), R. Pertorini (cello), B. Dobozy (harpsichord) (*R* 1990s).

[71] Currently available via the Internet (www.cantataeditions.com).

and Derek Lee Ragin,[72] as well as a selection from this collection's soprano cantatas as sung by Patrizia Vaccari,[73] which are based on Michael Talbot's edition.[74] One needs here to emphasize in passing that the 'critical', scholarly dimension of an edition, as Talbot elsewhere remarks pertinently,[75] has often counted for little among performers, who are inclined on pragmatic grounds to remain faithful to less authoritative editions that happen already to be in their possession. Facsimile publications have likewise served as the basis for recorded recitals, as shown, for instance, by the recordings of *Cantate con istromenti* of Conti by the mezzo-soprano Bernarda Fink[76] and by a selection from Legrenzi's *Ecchi di riverenza di Cantate, e Canzoni* by the Cappella Mauriziana,[77] both of which appear to have used facsimile editions produced by the publisher Studio per Edizioni Scelte (SPES).[78] Cristina Miatello's recording of the Bononcini cantatas *Ah non havesse, no, permesso il fato*, *Che tirannia di stelle*, *Cieco nume, tiranno spietato* and *Vidi in cimento due vaghi amori* for soprano and continuo derived its text from a facsimile edition selected and introduced by Lowell Lindgren appearing as tenth volume in the series *The Italian Cantata in the Seventeenth Century*.[79]

A privileged collaboration between an artist and 'his/her' dedicated researcher, which confers a seal of authority on this performer, is the route taken by, among others, the counter-tenor Gérard Lesne, Antonio Florio (director of the ensemble Cappella della Pietà de' Turchini) and, of course, the soprano Nella Anfuso. Over twenty years the musicologist Sylvie Mamy guided the recordings of Lesne, choosing for him repertory items particularly well suited to his range, timbre and agility, editing and preparing the material from contemporary manuscripts and, finally, writing a scholarly booklet text.[80] Over a similar length of time, Dinko Fabris has given Florio the benefit of his intimate knowledge of old Neapolitan music, which

---

[72] ETCETERA KTC 118: B. Schlick (soprano), N. Selo (cello), R. Shaw (harpsichord) (*R* 1993), and ETCETERA KTC 1204: D. L. Ragin (counter-tenor), N. Selo (cello), R. Shaw (harpsichord).

[73] STRADIVARIUS 33592: P. Vaccari (soprano), Harmonices Mundi, C. Astronio (*R* 2000).

[74] *Tomaso Albinoni. Twelve Cantatas, Opus 4* (Recent Researches in the Music of the Baroque Era, xxxi), ed. Michael Talbot (Madison, 1979).

[75] Talbot, *The Chamber Cantatas of Antonio Vivaldi*, p. 24.

[76] ARCANA A 309: B. Fink (mezzo-soprano), Ars Antiqua Austria, G. Letzbor (*R* 2001).

[77] BELLA MUSICA BM 911016: Cappella Mauriziana, G. Valsecchi (*R* 1993).

[78] Studio per Edizioni Scelte (SPES) (Florence), collection 'Archivum Musicum', series 'La cantata barocca'.

[79] Published in 1985 by Garland Publishing (New York and London).

[80] A good example is a recording devoted to Giovanni Bononcini that contains the cantatas *Già la stagion d'amore*, *Lasciami un sol momento*, *Misero pastorello ardo di sete* and *Siedi, Amarilli mia* on VIRGIN CLASSICS 5 45000 2: G. Lesne (counter-tenor), Seminario Musicale (*R* 1992); a similar single-composer recording presents the Caldara

was largely unknown to music-lovers until the regular appearance, in an almost uninterrupted stream, of unsuspected jewels of the Neapolitan musical tradition.[81] Whatever one thinks of the stylistic criteria embraced by Nella Anfuso,[82] it would be churlish to deny that the material prepared for her by Annibale Gianuario,[83] and justified in a reasoned set of notes, deserves a small plaudit.

Probably rather strange from a commercial viewpoint, but of great musicological interest, has been the decision to devote a recording to a particular musical source. Wolfgang Katschner, director of the German ensemble Lautten Compagney, advised by Helen Geyer of the Weimar-Jena Musicological Institute, has interested himself in this way in the collections of Italian music originating from the princely houses of Meiningen (the collection of Duke Anton Ulrich of Sachsen-Meiningen) and of Sondershausen,[84] conferring on his recordings the honour of bringing musical works to public attention almost simultaneously with their discovery and the related scholarly study.[85]

That a record company itself should identify unknown cantatas to put on disc is perhaps the most unexpected kind of initiative. This happened in the case of a CD devoted to Francesco Gasparini,[86] which contained his *Doppo tante, e sì strane*, *Esci, mio gregge florido*, *Seguir fera che fugge*, *Non v'aprite ai rai del sole*, *Dal stral d'Amore* and *Palesar vorria gl'ardori*, all for soprano and continuo, and was commissioned from local musicians by a small Venetian label that wished to offer passing tourists an exceptional souvenir of their visit to the proprietor's shop.

---

cantatas *D'improviso Amor ferisce*, *Medea in Corinto*, *Soffri, mio caro Alcino* and *Vicino a un rivoletto*: VIRGIN 10 7.91479-2: G. Lesne (counter-tenor), Il Seminario Musicale (*R* 1990).

[81] See, for example, *L'amante impazzito* by Simone Coya and *Marte, ammore, guerra e pace* by Michelangelo Faggioli, recorded on SYMPHONIA SY 96 147: P. de Vittorio (tenor), Cappella della Pietà de' Turchini, A Florio (*R* 1996), and Francesco Provenzale's *Care selve, amati orrori*, *La mia speme è vanità* and *Sui palchi delle stelle* on SYMPHONIA SY 94S29: R. Invernizzi (soprano), Cappella della Pietà dei Turchini, A. Florio (*R* 1994).

[82] See earlier, p. 307.

[83] A creditable example is a recording containing the Porpora cantatas *Oh! Dio! che non è vero* and *Queste che miri, o Nice* on AUVIDIS AV 6116: N. Anfuso (soprano), L. Alvini (harpsichord) (*R* 1986).

[84] The Sondershausen collection had not been examined closely before the work of Helen Geyer, while that of Meiningen had been studied earlier by Lawrence Bennett and Hertha Müller.

[85] For instance, the anthologies 'Dolce moi ben', containing Conti's *Clori, sei tutta bella*, Magini's *Da che vidde il duo sembiante* and Sarro's *Barbara gelosia* on BERLIN CLASSICS 001770 BC: M. Beaumont (mezzo-soprano), Lautten Compagney Berlin, W. Katschner (*R* 2006), and 'Mia vita, mia bene', containing Alveri's *Mia vita, mio bene*, Porta's *Udite, o Cieli*, Fedeli's *Lascamenti al mio duolo speranze adultrici* and Gaffi's *Ditemi che cos'è* on BERLIN CLASSICS 001770 2 BC: D. Andersen (soprano), A. Hallenberg (mezzo-soprano), Lautten Compagney Berlin, W. Katschner (*R* 2006).

[86] NALESSO RECORDS NR 001: M. Tomasi (soprano), C. Ronco (cello), P. Talamini (harpsichord) (*R* 1997).

The case of the French company K 617, which includes cantatas by Zipoli[87] in its remarkable anthology 'Les Chemins du Baroque', devoted to music by composers who emigrated to South America,[88] is again very special, but no less praiseworthy.

But most of the time it is the performers themselves who select the content of their recordings. The decisive voice is often that of a harpsichord-playing leader who, assuming the double duty of continuo player and editor, chooses the works and thinks nothing of spending long hours in libraries in order to read through works and make his or her choice, in consultation with the singer, prior to preparing the material. This perhaps explains why a section of the recorded cantatas of Alessandro Scarlatti still exists only in manuscript form.

However, the very rarefied, codified genre of the *cantata da camera* no longer encounters so many obstacles as it did ten years ago, when Colin Timms could write:

> The pastoral vein seems to pose particular problems [...] the emotional effusions of Arcadian nymphs and shepherds often evince embarrassment or apology. It is true that the pleasures and pains of their loves and jealousies are expressed in conventional language.[89]

And observing with a hint of pessimism that:

> [This] music [...] displays great sophistication of melodic, harmonic, textural and structural skill and sensitivity. Unless the cantata is taken seriously as a field for poetical and musical analysis and criticism, as well as for performance, the full quality of the repertory will never be revealed.[90]

The ever-greater regard shown, both in recorded performances and in the accompanying booklets, for the poetic texts of cantatas is an encouraging sign: recitative is really no longer seen as an obstacle to overcome.[91] One can only rejoice that Albinoni, Aldrovandini, Alveri, Conti, Ferrandini, Gasparini,

---

[87] *Dell'offese a vendicarmi* and *Mia bella Irene* on K617 K 617 037: A. Fernandez (soprano), V. Torres (baritone), Ensemble Elyma, G. Garrido (*R* 1993).

[88] On this repertory, see Alberto Basso, 'Le nuove frontiere del barocco musicale: i repertori ricuperati ai confini dell'Europa e nelle Americhe', in *Cinquant'anni di produzioni e consumi della musica dell'età di Vivaldi*, pp. 401–408.

[89] Colin Timms, 'The Italian Cantata since 1945: Progress and Prospects', in *Cinquant'anni di produzioni e consumi della musica dell'età di Vivaldi*, pp. 75–94, at p. 85.

[90] Ibid., p. 86.

[91] The poetic texts in Italian, correctly laid out as verse (once, it was common to present them as prose, and this particular sin has not quite yet quite died out), are nowadays usually complemented in the accompanying booklets by translations in English, French, German and sometimes also Spanish, even if the quality of these translations often leaves something to be desired.

Legrenzi, Leo, Benedetto Marcello, Melani, Pergolesi, Perti, Domenico Scarlatti and Steffani have made their *entrée* in the catalogue of a genre today accepted and appreciated, and that the chamber cantatas of such recognized specialists as Bononcini, Caldara and Alessandro Scarlatti have multiplied considerably. It is a sign of the times, too, that at last Italian singers are taking an interest in their vernacular poetry.[92] Patrizia Vaccari, Cristina Miatello, Rossana Bertini, Roberta Invernizzi, Patrizia Ciofi, Gemma Bertagnolli and Pino de Vitorio,[93] regardless of the intrinsic qualities of their voices, are, on the evidence of the results, the best placed to achieve in recitative a perfection of diction in a language that they have (naturally!) completely mastered. Curiously, and perhaps fortuitously, the two 'Saxons' – Handel (the most distinguished contributor to the genre, the earliest to earn recognition in it and the best served in terms of the number of recordings) and, less obviously, Hasse – have attracted the most international array of singers and have enjoyed particular success among counter-tenors.[94]

So tastes, in old music, do not remain static. However, two constants remain: the continuing favour accorded to composers whose reputation goes back a long time and the periodic revelation and consecration of new vocal 'stars'. The genre of the Italian cantata does not deviate from this general pattern. The *opera omnia* of J. S. Bach, not surprisingly, has been the earliest repertory to occupy the former category. It will be joined soon by those of Handel and Vivaldi, whose discographies still contain small gaps. The irony in Vivaldi's case is that only certain violin concertos have not been recorded, whereas the entirety of his surviving secular vocal music – chamber cantatas and operas included – has been recorded, often several times over.[95] With Handel, the deficit comprises around fifty of the chamber cantatas.[96] Fortunately, the Spanish record company Glossa is on hand to fill this void, under the most favourable conditions, with a projected complete series of cantatas,

---

[92] It is worth remarking that the early eighteenth century, dominated by Arcadian aesthetics, is commonly seen as a period of decadence in Italian poetry, and consequently one little studied in Italian schools. Even native singers often need a period of orientation before feeling completely at home in the precious and classicizing poetic idiom.

[93] It will be noticed that the singers are mainly female, including – especially – contraltos. Italian counter-tenors remain thin on the ground; indeed, this voice type, whatever the nationality of its possessor, still encounters resistance in the Italian heartland of the cantata repertory.

[94] Alongside Caldara, the works of whose Viennese period seem to be particularly attractive to singers, who do not altogether ignore, however, the cantatas he composed earlier for Rome.

[95] Or will be shortly, with the issue of the incomplete operas *Farnace* (RV 711G) of 1738 and *Armida al campo d'Egitto* (RV 699A).

[96] If one considers each version as a distinct work. At the start of 2008 the following cantatas still awaited their first recording: HWV 86, 93, 94, 95, 100, 101a, 102b, 103, 104, 106, 107, 111b, 114, 120a, 121b, 125a, 126a,b, 127b,c, 128, 133, 135a, 136b, 139a,b,c, 144, 148, 149, 151, 152, 156, 157, 158a,b,c, 159, 160a,b,c, 161a,c, 167a,b, 169, 177.

recently initiated by the ensemble La Risonanza under the harpsichordist Fabio Bonizzoni,[97] who has recruited to his cause some of the leading Italian singers.

As the third millennium draws away, the world of old music remains fixated, as ever, on the production of celebrities. The counter-tenors of yesteryear who wowed their audiences during the period of analysis have now faded from the scene. The new *divi* of this voice type are Andreas Scholl, Max Emmanuel Cencic and – perhaps in pole position – Philippe Jaroussky, who, passionate equally about Vivaldi[98] and Handel, has contributed with greatest distinction to the domain of the *cantata a voce sola*. French though he is, Jaroussky has taken Italian recitative to a level of refinement rarely achieved before him, illuminating each phrase with *affetti* of every kind that lend extra meaning to word after word. *Desio, timor, orrida, preme, terribile tempesta, flagella, prende coraggio, si smorza in me la fiamma*: all these utterances receive their appropriate special colouring.

The young musicians of the Ensemble Artaserse who accompany Jaroussky in his Vivaldi recital take the elaboration of the continuo to a rarely matched level of audacity and refinement. In the first aria of *Alla caccia dell'alme e de' cori* (RV 670), for instance, they dare to add to the attentive cello and rhythmically inventive harpsichord a Baroque bassoon in order to lend colour to the bass line during ritornellos. The recitative is accompanied by lute and bassoon, while in the final aria the rhythmic support is entrusted to a cello, the harmonies to a chamber organ and melodic commentary to a bassoon. In the course of *Qual per ignoto calle* (RV 677) and *Perfidissimo cor! Iniquo fato!* (RV 674) the performers exploit all possible permutations among the bass instruments. But Artaserse opts for a lighter continuo, using only cello and lute, all the way through the cantata *Care selve, amici prati* (RV 671). The singer and the continuo accompaniment, acting in perfect fusion, unite in the expression of the poetic text. This is a model of interpretation whose success has been repeated many times in the period of synthesis.

It is no exaggeration to say that today, after a period of gestation perhaps somewhat longer than one would have expected or wished, the Italian chamber cantata for solo voice has – even purely in quantitative terms – become one of the mainstays of the recorded repertory of older music. The richness of the musical sources still awaiting exploration (or served inadequately in the past) augurs well for the future. Perhaps the peculiar glamour enjoyed by the genre today is the predictable obverse of its former neglect: we have reached that exciting stage where familiarity has just set in and over-familiarity has not yet arrived.

---

[97] Bonizzoni is fortunately able to base his work on reliable critical editions, and in particular on those by Hans Joachim Marx for the Hallische Händel-Ausgabe: *Kantaten mit Instrumenten, I–II* (Kassel etc., 1994–95).

[98] Of whose cantatas he has offered a superb recital on VIRGIN CLASSICS 5 45721 2: P. Jaroussky (counter-tenor), Ensemble Artaserse (*R* 2004).

Appendix 12.1: A list of recordings of Italian-language cantatas for solo voice from the late-Baroque period

The present discography, concluded on 1 December 2007, is a near-complete list of recordings of *cantate a voce sola* composed to Italian-language texts[99] in the late Baroque period. Composers of the early Baroque or commencing their activity around the middle of the seventeenth century (Strozzi, Carissimi, Cesti, etc.), as well as those from the Classical age (Haydn, Paisiello, Zingarelli, etc.) are on principle excluded from the present study, even though the mention of certain composers who were still active around the start of the late Baroque (c.1680) or had already initiated their activity around its close (c.1750) is sometimes a matter of personal judgement.

The identification of the cantatas presented on disc, unproblematic for those by composers lucky enough to have catalogues of their works, becomes less simple for less well-known works, which are often receiving their first modern performance and have been ignored, or almost so, by the literature. In those cases, the identification is dependent on the information supplied with the recording. Similarly, when the manuscript source or original edition has not been available for consultation, the register indicated for the voice and the nature of the accompaniment, possibly including instruments additional to the continuo, correspond to those of the recorded performance. Where the original scoring, listed (with abbreviations) after the title or incipit, differs from that listed for an individual recording (without abbreviations), the explanation is either that the performers themselves have adapted it or that the performing material available to them departs from the original in this way.[100]

For each cantata, the recordings are listed in chronological order. Since reissues of old discs with different couplings selected on the basis of very varied criteria are numerous, I have decided, in order not to overload and complicate the list unnecessarily, to restrict myself to a single discographical reference identified by the name of the label and the order number of the disc, which is unless otherwise specified a CD. Other media (LP, cassette and DVD) are identified within parentheses as appropriate at the first mention of the recording.

---

[99] With the exception of the cantatas of Leonardo Vinci, discussed by Giulia Veneziano in Chapter 8. Discographies are notoriously harder to make absolutely complete than bibliographies, since the circulation of recordings is subject to the vagaries of marketing decisions and distribution agreements valid for individual countries and regions. I am grateful to Reinmar Emans, Carolyn Gianturco and Michael Talbot for informing me of additional items to include.

[100] Note that transposition (e.g., taking a cantata originally for soprano down a fourth for performance by an alto) was widely practised in the continuo cantata repertory of the time and is not in itself, therefore, an historically inappropriate feature.

The year of the recording (prefaced by *R*), when known, is given according to the information on the disc. Otherwise, an approximation such as '1970s' serves as a general guide to chronological position.

Abbreviations

A = alto; B = bass; bc = basso continuo; C = contralto; fl = flute(s); ob = oboe(s); *R* = recorded in; rec = recorder(s); S = soprano; str = strings (usually two violins and viola); T = tenor; tpt = trumpet; vc = violoncello; vn = violin(s).

Tomaso Albinoni (1671–1751)

Amor, Sorte, Destino! (S, bc) (Op. 4 no. 1)
    ETCETERA KTC 1181; B. Schlick (soprano), N. Selo (cello), R. Shaw (harpsichord) (*R* 1993)
    STRADIVARIUS 33592; P. Vaccari (soprano), Harmonices Mundi, C. Astronio (*R* 2000)

Chi non sa quanto inhumano (A, bc) (Op. 4 no. 12)
    ETCETERA KTC 1204; D. L. Ragin (counter-tenor), N. Selo (cello), R. Shaw (harpsichord) (*R* 1998)

Da l'arco d'un bel ciglio (A, bc) (Op. 4 no. 2)
    ETCETERA KTC 1204; D. L. Ragin (counter-tenor), N. Selo (cello), R. Shaw (harpsichord) (*R* 1998)

Del chiaro rio (S, bc) (Op. 4 no. 3)
    ETCETERA KTC 1181; B. Schlick (soprano), N. Selo (cello), R. Shaw (harpsichord) (*R* 1993)
    STRADIVARIUS 33592; P. Vaccari (soprano), Harmonices Mundi, C. Astronio (*R* 2000)

Filli, chiedi al mio cor (A, bc) (Op. 4 no. 6)
    ETCETERA KTC 1204; D. L. Ragin (counter-tenor), N. Selo (cello), R. Shaw (harpsichord) (*R* 1998)

Lontananza crudel, mi squarci il core (S, bc) (Op. 4 no. 5)
    ETCETERA KTC 1181; B. Schlick (soprano), N. Selo (cello), R. Shaw (harpsichord) (*R* 1993)
    STRADIVARIUS 33592; P. Vaccari (soprano), Harmonices Mundi, C. Astronio (*R* 2000)

Mi dà pena quando spira (A, bc) (Op. 4 no. 8)
    ETCETERA KTC 1204; D. L. Ragin (counter-tenor), N. Selo (cello), R. Shaw (harpsichord) (*R* 1998)

Ove rivolgo il piede (S, bc) (Op. 4 no. 7)
    ETCETERA KTC 1181; B. Schlick (soprano), N. Selo (cello), R. Shaw (harpsichord) (*R* 1993)

STRADIVARIUS 33592; P. Vaccari (soprano), Harmonices Mundi, C. Astronio (*R* 2000)

Parti, mi lasci (S, bc) (Op. 4 no. 9)
ETCETERA KTC 1181; B. Schlick (soprano), N. Selo (cello), R. Shaw (harpsichord) (*R* 1993)
STRADIVARIUS 33592; P. Vaccari (soprano), Harmonices Mundi, C. Astronio (*R* 2000)

Poiché al vago seren di due pupille (S, bc) (Op. 4 no. 11)
ETCETERA KTC 1181; B. Schlick (soprano), N. Selo (cello), R. Shaw (harpsichord) (*R* 1993)
STRADIVARIUS 33592; P. Vaccari (soprano), Harmonices Mundi, C. Astronio (*R* 2000)

Riedi a me, luce gradita (A, bc) (Op. 4 no. 4)
ETCETERA KTC 1204; D. L. Ragin (counter-tenor), N. Selo (cello), R. Shaw (harpsichord) (*R* 1998)

Son qual Tantalo novello (A, bc) (Op. 4 no. 10)
ETCETERA KTC 1204; D. L. Ragin (counter-tenor), N. Selo (cello), R. Shaw (harpsichord) (*R* 1998)

Giovanni Antonio Vincenzo Aldrovandini (1671–1707)

Son ferrito d'un labbro di giglio (S, str, bc)
DYNAMIC CDS 106; L. Serafini (soprano), Ensemble Barocco Padovano Sans Souci (*R* 1993)

Giovanni Battista Alveri (c.1670–after 1719)

Mia vita, mio bene (A, bc)
BERLIN CLASSICS 001770 2 BC; A. Hallenberg (mezzo-soprano), Lautten Compagney Berlin, W. Katschner (*R* 2006)

Filippo Amadei (c.1665–c.1725)

Il pensiero che rapido vola (S, bc)
Janiculum JAN D203; A. Elliott (tenor), N. Roberts (cello), J. Clark (harpsichord) (*R* 1999)

Anonymous

Per combater (S, bc)
 HARMONIA MUNDI HMA 190-5.137; J. Nelson (soprano), K. Gohl (cello), G. Murray (harpsichord) (*R* 1983)
Posa sopra d'un faggio (S, bc)
 RENE GAILLY CD 92042; G. de Reyghere (soprano), Telemann Consort (*R* 1998)

Attilio Ariosti (1666?–1729)

Il naufragio (A, bc) (no. 5 of published set)
 NAXOS 8.557573; T. van der Poel (contralto), Musica Solare (*R* 2003)
L'amore onesto (S, bc) (no. 2 of published set)
 DA CAMERA M 92604 (LP): C. Lehmann (soprano), Saarbrücker Kammermusikkreis (*R* 1967)
 NAXOS 8.557573; L. Reviol (soprano), Musica Solare (*R* 2003)
L'olmo (S, bc) (no. 3 of published set)
 DA CAMERA M 92604 (LP); C. Lehmann (soprano), Saarbrücker Kammermusikkreis (*R* 1967)
 NAXOS 8.557573; L. Reviol (soprano), Musica Solare (*R* 2003)
La gelosia (A, bc) (no. 6 of published set)
 NAXOS 8.557573; T. van der Poel (contralto), Musica Solare (*R* 2003)
La rosa (S, bc) (no. 1 of published set)
 DA CAMERA M 92604 (LP); C. Lehmann (soprano), Saarbrücker Kammermusikkreis (*R* 1967)
 CAPRICCIO 10 459; A. Monoyios (soprano), Berliner Barock-Compagney (*R* 1995)
 NAXOS 8.557573; L. Reviol (soprano), Musica Solare (*R* 2003)
Libertà acquistata in amore (A, bc) (no. 4 of published set)
 NAXOS 8.557573; T. van der Poel (contralto), Musica Solare (*R* 2003)
Pur al fin gentil (S, viola d'amore, bc)
 DA CAMERA M 92604 (LP); C. Lehmann (soprano), Saarbrücker Kammermusikkreis (*R* 1967)
 Winter & Winter 910096-2: M. Mauch (soprano), L. Hampe (viola d'amore), Affetti Musicali (*R* 2002)

Johann Sebastian Bach (1685–1750)

BWV 203 *Amore traditore* (B, bc)
 VOX (LP) / ORBIS 21090 (LP); B. Müller (bass), H. Elsner (harpsichord), R. Reinhardt (*R* 1950s?)

EMI Classics (LP) / 5 68 509 2 (LP); D. Fischer-Dieskau (baritone), I. Poppen (cello), E. Picht-Axenfeld (harpsichord) (*R* 1960–62)
TELDEC 3984-25710-2 (LP); J. Villisech (bass), G. Leonhardt (harpsichord) (*R* 1965)
VOX / TURNABOUT TV 4071 (LP); K. Ocker (bass), D. Messlinger (cello), M. Galling (harpsichord), R. Ewerhart (*R* 1966)
ARCHIV PRODUKTION 2533 453 S; S. Lorenz (bass), M. Pfaender (cello), W. H. Bernstein (harpsichord), P. Schreier (*R* 1981)
NUOVA ERA 7099; M. van Egmond (baritone), M. Mencoboni (clavecin) (*R* 1991)
ERATO 8 573880502; K. Mertens (bass), J. ter Linden (cello), T. Koopman (harpsichord) (*R* 1995)
HÄNSSLER CLASSICS 92062; D. Henschel (bass), M. Behringer (harpsichord), H. Rilling (*R* 1998)
EUROARTS / NAXOS 'Ton Koopman plays Bach' (DVD); K. Mertens (bass), T. Koopman (harpsichord) (*R* 2004)

BWV 209 *Non sa che sia dolore* (S, fl, str, bc)
DUCRETET-THOMSON LAG 1074 (LP); G. Weber (soprano), Kammerorchester 'Pro Arte', K. Redel (*R* 1950s?)
VANGUARD CLASSICS CLA 991.021 (LP); T. Stich-Randall (soprano), Orchestra of the Bach Guild, A. Heiller (*R* 1952)
CANTATE (LP) / ORYX (LP); N. van der Spek (soprano), Heidelberger Kammerorchester, H. M. Göttsche (*R* 1960s?)
LE CHANT DU MONDE LCD 278903 (LP); T. Stich-Randall (soprano), Saar Kammerorchester, K. Ristenpart (*R* 1960)
DEUTSCHE HARMONIA MUNDI 37151-2-RG (LP); E. Ameling (soprano), Collegium Aureum (*R* 1964–68)
MHS 1367 (LP); M. Stader (soprano), Cologne Soloists Ensemble, H. Müller-Brühl (*R* 1965)
TELDEC 3984-25710-2 (LP); A. Giebel (soprano), Leonhardt-Consort, G. Leonhardt (*R* 1966)
VOX BOX 3039 (LP); E. Speiser (soprano), Württemberg Chamber Orchestra, R. Ewerhart (*R* 1966)
MELODIYA 12481 (LP); G. Pisarenko (soprano), Kameryj Orkestr, J. Nikolavskij (*R* 1970s?)
ARIOLA EURODISC 80615 (LP); A. Stolte (soprano), Gewandhausorchester Leipzig, G. Bosse (*R* 1971)
EMI Electrola 063-0237 L (LP); E. Ameling (soprano), Academy of St Martin-in-the-Fields, N. Marriner (*R* 1973)
SUPRAPHON 1112 2453 G (LP); J. Jonášová (soprano), Ars Rediviva of Prague, M. Munclinger (*R* 1978)
ARCHIV PRODUKTION 2533 453 (LP); E. Mathis (soprano), Kammerorchester Berlin, P. Schreier (*R* 1979)

PHILIPS (LP); E. Ameling (soprano), English Chamber Orchestra, R. Leppard (*R* 1980s)
CAPRICCIO 10615; I. Poulenard (soprano), Capella Coloniensis, F. Leitner (*R* 1987)
MELODYIA; G. Pisarenko (soprano), Lithuanian Chamber Orchestra [Litauisches Kammerorchester], S. Sondeckis [Sondezkis] (*R* 1987)
L'OISEAU-LYRE 421 728-2; J. Baird (soprano), The Bach Ensemble, J. Rifkin (*R* 1989)
VLČEK MUSIC PRODUCTION; E. Mirgová (soprano), Concertino Notturno Praha, A.Kröper (*R* 1990s)
HARMONIA MUNDI FRANCE HMF 1903010; M. Zádori (soprano), Capella Savaria, P. Németh (*R* 1990)
NAXOS 8.550431; F. Wagner (soprano), Capella Istropolitana, C. Brembeck (*R* 1991)
SLOVART 5R 0003-2-131; K. Zajíčková (soprano), Musica Aeterna Bratislava, P. Zajíček (*R* 1993)
VIRGIN Veritas 7243 5 61644; N. Argenta (soprano), Ensemble Sonnerie, M. Huggett (*R* 1993)
CAROLINA BAROQUE CB 114; T. Radomski (soprano), Carolina Baroque, D. Higbee (*R* 1996)
ERATO 0630-15562-2; L. Larsson (soprano), Amsterdam Baroque Orchestra, T. Koopman (*R* 1996)
HÄNSSLER CLASSICS 92065; S. Rubens (soprano), Bach-Collegium Stuttgart, H. Rilling (*R* 1998)
CAVALLI RECORDS CCD 317; B. Schlick (soprano), Dorian Consort, S. Ad-El (*R* 2003?)

Giovanni Bononcini (1670–1747)

Ah non havesse, no, permesso il fato (S, bc)
TACTUS TC 660002; C. Miatello (soprano), A. Fossa (cello), G. Morini (harpsichord) (*R* 1989)

Care luci del mio bene (A, 2 vn, bc)
ARCHIV PRODUKTION 2533 450 (LP); R. Jacobs (counter-tenor), S. Kuijken, L. van Dael (violins), W. Kuijken (cello), R. Kohnen (harpsichord) (*R* 1979)
TACTUS TC 67012001; G. Banditelli (mezzo-soprano), Ensemble Aurora, E. Gatti (*R* 1989)

Che tirannia di stelle (S, bc)
TACTUS TC 660002; C. Miatello (soprano), A. Fossa (cello), G. Morini (harpsichord) (*R* 1989)

Cieco nume, tiranno spietato (S, bc)
  TACTUS TC 660002; C. Miatello (soprano), A. Fossa (cello), G. Morini (harpsichord) (*R* 1989)
Ecco, Dorinda, il giorno (A, 2 vn, bc)
  ARCHIV PRODUKTION 2533 450 (LP); R. Jacobs (counter-tenor), S. Kuijken, L. van Dael (violins), W. Kuijken (cello), R. Kohnen (harpsichord) (*R* 1979)
Già la stagion d'Amore (A, bc)
  VIRGIN CLASSICS 5 45000 2; G. Lesne (counter-tenor), Seminario Musicale (*R* 1992)
Il lamento di Olimpia (S, bc)
  TACTUS TC 67012001; G. Banditelli (mezzo-soprano), Ensemble Aurora, E. Gatti (*R* 1989)
  ETCETERA KTC 1202; M Zanetti (soprano), Fons Musicae, Y. Imamura (*R* 1999)
Lasciami un sol momento (A, bc)
  VIRGIN CLASSICS 5 45000 2; G. Lesne (counter-tenor), Seminario Musicale (*R* 1992)
Misero pastorello ardo di sete (A, 2 vn, bc)
  ARCHIV PRODUKTION 2533 450 (LP); R. Jacobs (counter-tenor), S. Kuijken, L. van Dael (violins), W. Kuijken (cello), R. Kohnen (harpsichord) (*R* 1979)
  VIRGIN CLASSICS 5 45000 2; G. Lesne (counter-tenor), Seminario Musicale (*R* 1992)
  ETCETERA KTC 1202; P. Bertin (counter-tenor), Fons Musicae, Y. Imamura (*R* 1999)
Siedi, Amarilli mia (A, 2 vn, bc)
  ARCHIV PRODUKTION 2533 450 (LP); R. Jacobs (counter-tenor), S. Kuijken, L. van Dael (violins), W. Kuijken (cello), R. Kohnen (harpsichord) (*R* 1979)
  VIRGIN CLASSICS 5 45000 2; G. Lesne (counter-tenor), Seminario Musicale (*R* 1992)
Torno a voi, piante amorose (S, 2 fl, bc)
  RENE GAILLY CD 92042; G. de Reyghere (soprano), Telemann Consort (*R* 1998)
Vidi in cimento due vaghi amori (S, bc)
  TACTUS TC 660002; C. Miatello (soprano), A. Fossa (cello), G. Morini (harpsichord) (*R* 1989)

Antonio Caldara (1670–1736)

Amante recidivo (A, bc)
    CAPRICCIO 67124; M. E. Cencic (counter-tenor), Ornamente 99, K. E. Ose (*R* 2005)

Astri di quel bel viso (A, bc) (Op. 3 no. 5)
    ETCETERA KTC 1204; D. L. Ragin (counter-tenor), N. Selo (cello), R. Shaw (harpsichord) (*R* 1998)
    RAMÉE RAM 0405; J. Banholzer (counter-tenor), M. Übellacker (salterio), E. Gliozzi (cello), La Gioia Armonica (*R* 2004)

Che dite, o miei pensieri (B, bc)
    CYCNUS CM 016 (LP); J. Loomis (bass), Società cameristica di Lugano, E. Loehrer (*R* 1963)

Clori, mia bella Clori (A, bc)
    DYNAMIC CDS 106; E. Lax (alto) Ensemble Barocco Padovano Sans Souci (*R* 1993)

Clori sdegnosa (A, bc)
    ELY RECORDINGS 007 (audio cassette); G. Coker (counter-tenor), H. Polglase (cello), D. Mews (harpsichord) (*R* 1988)

D'improviso Amor ferisce (A, bc) (Op. 3 no.6)
    VIRGIN 10 7.91479-2; G. Lesne (counter-tenor), Il Seminario Musicale (*R* 1990)
    ETCETERA KTC 1204; D. L. Ragin (counter-tenor), N. Selo (cello), R. Shaw (harpsichord) (*R* 1998)

Da' tuoi lumi (A, bc)
    CAPRICCIO 67124; M. E. Cencic (counter-tenor), Ornamente 99, K. E. Ose (*R* 2005)

Dario (B, bc)
    UNICORN KANCHANA CKPCD 9130; M. Elliott (BASS), Wren Baroque Soloists, M. Elliott (*R* 1991)

Filli pentita (A, bc)
    ELY RECORDINGS 007 (audio cassette); G. Coker (counter-tenor), H. Polglase (cello), D. Mews (harpsichord) (*R* 1988)

Il gelsomino (A, bc)
    UNICORN KANCHANA CKPCD 9130; S. Davies (counter-tenor), Wren Baroque Soloists, M. Elliott (*R* 1991)

Il silentio (A, bc) (Op. 3 no.9)
    ASV GAUDEAMUS 347; J. Lane (mezzo-soprano), The Four Nations Ensemble, A. Appel (*R* 2004)

Irene orgogliosa (A, bc)
    ELY RECORDINGS 007 (audio cassette); G. Coker (counter-tenor), H. Polglase (cello), D. Mews (harpsichord) (*R* 1988)

L'anniversario amoroso (A, bc) (Op. 3 no. 11)
    ASV GAUDEAMUS 347; J. Lane (mezzo-soprano), The Four Nations Ensemble, A. Appel (*R* 2004)

La Cleopatra crudele (A, bc)
    ELY RECORDINGS 007 (audio cassette); G. Coker (counter-tenor), H. Polglase (cello), D. Mews (harpsichord) (*R* 1988)

La fama (A, bc) (Op. 3 no. 8)
    ASV GAUDEAMUS 347; J. Lane (mezzo-soprano), The Four Nations Ensemble, A. Appel (*R* 2004)

La forriera del giorno (A, bc)
    UNICORN KANCHANA CKPCD 9130; N. Jenkin (soprano), Wren Baroque Soloists, M. Elliott (*R* 1991)

La rosa (S, bc) (Op. 3 no. 7)
    DEUTSCHE GRAMMOPHON 000733002 (LP); B. Sills (soprano), L. Parnas (cello), C. Wadsworth (harpsichord) (*R* 1972)

Lungi dall'idol mio (S, bc)
    UNICORN KANCHANA CKPCD 9130; L.-J. Rogers (soprano), Wren Baroque Soloists, M. Elliott (*R* 1991)
    ALBANY RECORDS 705; J. Baird (soprano), E. Comparone (harpsichord) (*R* 2004)

Medea in Corinto (A, str, bc)
    VIRGIN 10 7.91479-2; G. Lesne (counter-tenor), Il Seminario Musicale (*R* 1990)

Non v'è pena (A, bc)
    CAPRICCIO 67124; M. E. Cencic (counter-tenor), Ornamente 99, K. E. Ose (*R* 2005)

Partenza (S, bc)
    ELY RECORDINGS 007 (audio cassette); H. Macdonald, (soprano), H. Polglase (cello), D. Mews (harpsichord) (*R* 1988)

Sempre mi torna in mente (A, bc)
    CAPRICCIO 67124; M. E. Cencic (counter-tenor), Ornamente 99, K. E. Ose (*R* 2005)

Senti, Filli (S, bc)
    ELY RECORDINGS 007 (audio cassette); H. Macdonald, (soprano), H. Polglase (cello), D. Mews (harpsichord) (*R* 1988)

Soffri, mio caro Alcino (A, bc)
    VIRGIN 10 7.91479-2; G. Lesne (counter-tenor), Il Seminario Musicale (*R* 1990)
    RAMÉE RAM 0405; J. Banholzer (counter-tenor), M. Übellacker (salterio), E. Gliozzi (cello), La Gioia Armonica (*R* 2004)

Stella ria (A, bc)
    UNICORN KANCHANA CKPCD 9130; F. Jellard (contralto), Wren Baroque Soloists, M. Elliott (*R* 1991)

Vedrò senz'onde il mare (A, bc)
    CAPRICCIO 67124; M. E. Cencic (counter-tenor), Ornamente 99, K. E. Ose (*R* 2005)

Vicino a un rivoletto (A, str, bc)
    PHILIPS 6575.058 (LP); R. Jacobs (counter-tenor), S. Kuijken (violino), A. Bylsma (cello), G. Leonhardt (harpsichord) (*R* 1975)
    VIRGIN 10 7.91479-2; G. Lesne (counter-tenor), Il Seminario Musicale (*R* 1990)
    CAPRICCIO 10 703; A.Köhler (counter-tenor), C. Huntgeburth (fl), B. Maté (cello), R. Alpermann (harpsichord) (*R* 1995)
    ALBANY RECORDS 705; P. Djerejian (contralto), E. Comparone (harpsichord) (*R* 2004)
    ASV GAUDEAMUS 347; J. Lane (mezzo-soprano), The Four Nations Ensemble, A. Appel (*R* 2004)
    RAMÉE RAM 0405; J. Banholzer (counter-tenor), M. Übellacker (salterio), E. Gliozzi (cello), La Gioia Armonica (*R* 2004)

Francesco Bartolomeo Conti (1681–1732)

Clori, sei tutta bella (A, bc)
    BERLIN CLASSICS 001770 BC; M. Beaumont (mezzo-soprano), Lautten Compagney Berlin, W. Katschner (*R* 2006)

Con più lucidi candori (S, chalumeau, vn, lute, bc) (no. 3)
    TACTUS TC 680 301; R. Bertini (soprano), Ensemble La Signoria (*R* 1998)
    ARCANA A 309; B. Fink (mezzo-soprano), Ars Antiqua Austria, G. Letzbor (*R* 2001)

Lontananza dell'amato (S, ob, vn, lute, bc) (no. 1)
    TACTUS TC 680 301; R. Bertini (soprano), Ensemble La Signoria (*R* 1998)
    ARCANA A 309; B. Fink (mezzo-soprano), Ars Antiqua Austria, G. Letzbor (*R* 2001)

Ride il prato e fra l'erbe (S, vn, lute, flute, bc) (no. 2)
    TACTUS TC 680 301; A. Simboli (mezzo-soprano), Ensemble La Signoria (*R* 1998)
    ARCANA A 309; B. Fink (mezzo-soprano), Ars Antiqua Austria, G. Letzbor (*R* 2001)

Vaghi augelletti che d'amor (S, chalumeau, vn, lute, bc) (no. 4)
    TACTUS TC 680 301; A. Simboli (mezzo-soprano), Ensemble La Signoria (*R* 1998)
    ARCANA A 309; B. Fink (mezzo-soprano), Ars Antiqua Austria, G. Letzbor (*R* 2001)

Simone Coya (17th–18th Century)

L'amante impazzito (T, str, bc)
   SYMPHONIA SY 96 147; P. de Vittorio (tenor), Cappella della Pietà de' Turchini, A. Florio (*R* 1996)

Michelangelo Faggioli (1666–1733)

Marte, ammore, guerra e pace (T, str, bc)
   SYMPHONIA SY 96 147; P. de Vittorio (tenor), Cappella della Pietà de' Turchini, A. Florio (*R* 1996)
Sto poglietta presuntuso (T, str, bc)
   SYMPHONIA SY 91 509; P. de Vittorio (tenor), Cappella della Pietà de' Turchini, A. Florio (*R* 1991)

Ruggiero Fedeli (1655–1722)

Lascamenti al mio duolo speranze adultrici (A, bc)
   BERLIN CLASSICS 001770 BC; M. Beaumont (mezzo-soprano), Lautten Compagney Berlin, W. Katschner (*R* 2006)

Giovanni Battista Ferrandini (c.1710–91)

Ecco quel tronco (S, str, bc)
   ACCENT ACC 24181; E. Scholl (soprano), Echo du Danube (R 2006)
O spettacolo pur troppo funesto (S, str, bc)
   ACCENT ACC 24181; E. Scholl (soprano), Echo du Danube (R 2006)

Tommaso Bernardo Gaffi (c.1667–1744)

Ditemi che cos'è (S, bc)
   BERLIN CLASSICS 001790 2 BC; D. Andersen (soprano), Lautten Compagney Berlin, W. Katschner (*R* 2006)

Francesco Gasparini (1661–1727)

Andate, o miei sospiri (S, bc)
   OPUS 111 OPS 30 182; R. Bertini (soprano), La Venexiana (*R* 1996)

Dal stral d'Amore (S, bc)
    NALESSO RECORDS NR 001; M. Tomasi (soprano), C. Ronco (cello), P. Talamini (harpsichord) (*R* 1997)
Doppo tante, e sì strane (S, bc)
    NALESSO RECORDS NR 001; M. Tomasi (soprano), C. Ronco (cello), P. Talamini (harpsichord) (*R* 1997)
Esci, mio gregge florido (S, bc)
    NALESSO RECORDS NR 001; M. Tomasi (soprano), C. Ronco (cello), P. Talamini (harpsichord) (*R* 1997)
Non v'aprite ai rai del sole (S, bc)
    NALESSO RECORDS NR 001; M. Tomasi (soprano), C. Ronco (cello), P. Talamini (harpsichord) (*R* 1997)
Palesar vorria gl'ardori (S, bc)
    NALESSO RECORDS NR 001; M. Tomasi (soprano), C. Ronco (cello), P. Talamini (harpsichord) (*R* 1997)
Queste voci dolenti (A, bc)
    OPUS 111 OPS 30 182; C. Cavina (counter-tenor), La Venexiana (*R* 1996)
Seguir fera che fugge (S, bc)
    NALESSO RECORDS NR 001; M. Tomasi (soprano), C. Ronco (cello), P. Talamini (harpsichord) (*R* 1997)

George Frideric Handel (1685–1759)

HWV 77 *Ah che pur troppo è vero* (S, bc)
    DHM Quintessence 2 PMC 2714 (LP); E. Ameling (soprano), Collegium Aureum, F. J. Maier (*R* 1966)
    HUNGAROTON SLPD 12564; M. Zádori (soprano), C. Falvay (cello), P. Ella (harpsichord) (*R* 1984)
    MUSICAL OFFERING 9604; E. Hargis (soprano), Seattle Baroque Orchestra (*R* 1997)
HWV 78 *Ah! crudel, nel pianto mio* (S, 2 ob, str, bc)
    EMI ASD 2458 (LP); J. Baker (mezzo-soprano), English Chamber Orchestra, R. Leppard (*R* 1967)
    CLARIUS AUDI CD 29004; P. Macrelli (soprano), instruments, A. Anzalone (cello), F. Ravizza (harpsichord) (*R* 1996)
    EUFODA CDEUF 1297; D. York (soprano), Collegium Instrumentale Brugense, P. Peire (*R* 1999)
    ORF Alte Musik 3001; N. Rial (soprano), La Risonanza, F. Bonizzoni (*R* 2006)
HWV 79 *Diana cacciatrice (Alla caccia)* (S, coro (unison S), tpt, 2 vn, bc)
    BERLIN Classics 11712 BC; M. Spagele (soprano), Virtuosi Saxoniae, L. Güttler (*R* 1996)

EUFODA CDEUF 1297; D. York (soprano), Collegium Instrumentale Brugense, P. Peire (*R* 1999)

HWV 80 *Allor ch'io dissi Addio* (S, bc)
HUNGAROTON HCD 32383; A. Korondi (soprano), R. Pertorini (cello), J. Pétri (harpsichord) (*R* 2005)

HWV 81 *Alpestre monte* (S, 2 vn, bc)
L'OISEAU-LYRE 414 473-2; E. Kirkby (soprano), Academy of Ancient Music, C. Hogwood (*R* 1984)
DORIAN DOR-90147; J. Baird (soprano), Philomel Baroque Orchestra (*R* 1990)

HWV 84 *Aure soavi e liete* (S, bc)
STUDIO MATOUŠ MK00132231; I. Troupová (soprano), S. Mai (violino), J. Freiheit (cello), M. Wilke (harpsichord) (*R* 1990s?)

HWV 87 *Carco sempre di gloria* (A, str, bc)
DECCA (LP) / 433737-2; H. Watts (contralto), English Chamber Orchestra, R. Leppard (*R* 1961)
CHANNEL CLASSICS CCS 0890; D. L. Ragin (counter-tenor), Divitia Köln (*R* 1990)
VIRGIN VC 7 91480-2; G. Lesne (counter-tenor), Il Seminario Musicale (*R* 1990)

HWV 88 *Care selve, aure grate* (S, bc)
HUNGAROTON HCD 32383; A. Korondi (soprano), R. Pertorini (cello), J. Pétri (harpsichord) (*R* 2005)

HWV 90 *Chi rapì la pace al core* (S, bc)
CEDILLE RECORDS CDR 90000 057; P. M. Bedi (soprano), Chicago Baroque Ensemble, J. M. Rozendaal (*R* 2000)
HUNGAROTON HCD 32383; A. Korondi (soprano), R. Pertorini (cello), J. Pétri (harpsichord) (*R* 2005)

HWV 91A *Clori, degli occhi miei* (A, bc)
CENTAUR CRC 2540; J. Gall (counter-tenor), M. Rozendaal (viola da gamba), D. Schrader (harpsichord) (*R* 2004)

HWV 92 *Clori, mia bella Clori* (S, 2 vn, bc)
HYPERION Q A 66155; P. Kwella (soprano), London Handel, D. Darlow (*R* 1984)
ACCORD 10 201102; L. M. Äkerlund (soprano), Ensemble Baroque, A. Wenzinger (*R* 1991)
COLLINS CLASSICS 15032; A. Murray (mezzo-soprano); Symphony of Harmony and Invention, H. Christophers (*R* 1997)

HWV 97 *Crudel tiranno Amor* (S, str, bc)
PHILIPS 6500.008 (LP); E. Ameling (sopano), English Chamber Orchestra, R. Leppard (*R* 1970s)
BERLIN CLASSICS 6157197 (LP); A. Stolte (soprano), Händel-Festspielorchester Halle, T. Sanderling (*R* 1970)

CHANDOS 0583; N. Argenta (soprano), Collegium Musicum 90, S. Standage (*R* 1994)
HUNGAROTON HGR 31534; M. Zádori (soprano), Concerto Armonico, M. Spanyi (*R* 1995)
ARION ARN 68505; S. Haller (soprano), Les Paladins, J. Correas (*R* 2000)
OEHMS OC 599; S. Greenberg (soprano), Wen-Sinn Yang (Cello), E. Krapp (harpsichord) (*R* 2006)

HWV 98 *Cuopre tal volta il cielo* (B, 2 vn, bc)
EMI Classics EMI 7243 5 67345 2 4 (LP); D. Fischer-Dieskau (baritone), A. Nicolet (flute), I. Poppen (cello), E. Picht-Axenfeld (harpsichord) (*R* 1970s)
STRADIVARIUS STR 33425; J. L. Bindi (bass), Artificii Musicali, G. Delvaux (harpsichord) (*R* 1995)
TALL POPPIES TP 173; M. Leighton Jones (bass), C. Shugg, N. Forsyth (violins), R. Hunt (cello), S. Cohen (chitarrone), J. Ogeil (harpsichord) (*R* 2005)

HWV 99 *Il delirio amoroso* (*Da quel giorno fatale*) (S, rec, 3 vn, va, vc, bc)
HUNGAROTON HCD 11653-2 (LP); M. Kalmar (soprano), Ferenc Liszt Chamber Orchestra Budapest, F. Sandor (*R* 1974)
HUNGAROTON HGR 31534; M. Zádori (soprano), Concerto Armonico, M. Spanyi (*R* 1995)
COLLINS CLASSICS 15032; A. Murray (mezzo-soprano), Symphony of Harmony and Invention, H. Christophers (*R* 1997)
ARCHIV PRODUKTION 469 065 2; M. Kožená (soprano), Les Musiciens du Louvre, M. Minkowski (*R* 1999)
EUFODA CDEUF 1297; D. York (soprano), Collegium Instrumentale Brugense, P. Peire (*R* 1999)
GLOSSA 921521; R. Invernizzi (soprano), Ensemble La Risonanza, F. Bonizzoni (harpsichord) (*R* 2005)
VIRGIN CLASSICS 09463438422; N. Dessay (soprano), Le Concert d'Astrée, E. Haïm (*R* 2005)

HWV 101b *Dal fatale momento* (B, bc) – dubious
STRADIVARIUS STR 33425; J. L. Bindi (bass), Artificii Musicali, G. Delvaux (harpsichord) (*R* 1995)

HWV 102a *Dalla guerra amorosa* (B, bc)
CLASSIC CLP 6195 (LP); D. Hollestelle (bass), Netherlands Handel Society Orchestra, J. Loory (*R* 1950s)
EMI Classics EMI 7243 5 67345 2 4 (LP); D. Fischer-Dieskau (baritone), A. Nicolet (flute), I. Poppen (cello), E. Picht-Axenfeld (harpsichord) (*R* 1960s)
MONDIODIS MON 11003 (LP); L. Malaguti (baritone), J. B. Hoffmann (harpsichord) (*R* 1976)
MERIDIAN CDE 84157; J. Shirley-Quirk (baritone-basso), J. Fenton (cello), M. Scully (contrabass), M. Isepp (harpsichord) (*R* 1990)

NUOVA ERA 7099; M. van Egmond (baritone), M. Menceboni (harpsichord) (*R* 1991)
STRADIVARIUS STR 33425; J. L. Bindi (bass), Artificii Musicali, G. Delvaux (harpsichord) (*R* 1995)
ARION ARN 68505; J. Correas (baritone-basso), M. Middenway (cello), E. Haïm (harpsichord), Ensemble Les Paladins (*R* 1999)

HWV 105 *Armida abbandonata* (*Dietro l'orme fugaci*) (S, 2 vn, bc)
OCEANIC OCS 30 /OLYMPIE RECORDS Q 8116 (LP); A. Giebel (soprano), Tonstudio Orchester Stuttgart, R. Lamy (*R* 1952)
EMI ASD 2458 (LP); J. Baker (mezzo-soprano), English Chamber Orchestra, R. Leppard (*R* 1967)
PHILIPS 6539 068 (LP); S.Woytowicz (soprano), Berlin Kammer Orchester, K. Masur (*R* 1973)
TELEFUNKEN 6.42367 (LP); M. Kweksilber (soprano), Musica Antiqua Amsterdam, T. Koopman (*R* 1977)
EMI Reflex CDC 7 49799 2; E. Kirkby (soprano), London Baroque, C. Medlam (*R* 1988)
ACCORD 202 712; M. C. Kiehr (soprano), Il Teatro Armonico, A. de Marchi (*R* 1993)
COLLINS CLASSICS 15032; A. Murray (mezzo-soprano), Symphony of Harmony and Invention, H. Christophers (*R* 1997)
MUSICAL OFFERING 9604; E. Hargis (soprano), Seattle Baroque Orchestra (*R* 1997)
VIRGIN CLASSICS VC545 283 2; V. Gens (soprano), F. Fernandez, M. Glodeanu (violins), Les Basses Réunies (*R* 1998)
TELDEC 3984-24571; E. Mei (soprano), Il Giardino Armonico, G. Antonini (*R* 1999)
CAPRICCIO SACD 71083; V. Winter (soprano), Das Kleine Konzert, H. Max (*R* 2005)
CORO COR 16045; E. Manahan Thomas (soprano), Symphony of Harmony and Invention (*R* 2006)

HWV 108 *Dolce mio ben, s'io taccio* (S, bc)
HUNGAROTON HCD 32383; A. Korondi (soprano), R. Pertorini (cello), J. Pétri (harpsichord) (*R* 2005)

HWV 109a *Dolc'è pur d'amor l'affanno* (A, bc)
CAPRICCIO 10323; J. Kowalski (counter-tenor), S. Pank (viola di gamba), C. Schornsheim (harpsichord), Akademie für Alte Musik Berlin (*R* 1988)
CENTAUR CRC 2540; J. Gall (counter-tenor), M. Rozendaal (viola di gamba) D. Schrader (harpsichord) (*R* 2002)

HWV 109b *Dolc'è pur d'amor l'affanno* (S, bc)
CLASSIC CLP 6195 (LP); D. van Doorn (soprano), Netherlands Handel Society Orchestra, J. Loory (*R* 1950s)
STUDIO MATOUŠ MK00132231; I. Troupová (soprano), S. Mai (violino), J. Freiheit (cello), M. Wilke (harpsichord) (*R* 1990s)

QUERSTAND 0010; G. Näther (soprano), La Voce Umana, J. Fiedler (cello), J. Trinkewitz (harpsichord) (*R* 2001)
HWV 110 *Agrippina condotta a morire* (*Dunque sarà pur vero*) (S, 2 vn, bc)
OCEANIC OCS 30 /OLYMPIE RECORDS Q 8116 (LP); A. Giebel (soprano), Tonstudio Orchester Stuttgart, R. Lamy (*R* 1952)
ASV 10 DCA 766; A. Mackay (soprano), European Community Chamber Orchestra, E. Aadland (*R* 1990)
DORIAN DOR-90147; J. Baird (soprano), Philomel Baroque Orchestra (*R* 1990)
MD+G 10 L 3399; J. Koslowsky (soprano), Musica Alta Ripa (*R* 1990)
HUNGAROTON HGR 31534; M. Zádori (soprano), Concerto Armonico, M. Spanyi (*R* 1995)
VIRGIN CLASSICS VC545 283 2; V. Gens (soprano), F. Fernandez, M. Glodeanu (violins), Les Basses Réunies (*R* 1998)
TELDEC 3984-24571; E. Mei (soprano), Il Giardino Armonico, G. Antonini (*R* 1999)
CORO COR 16045; E. Manahan Thomas (soprano), Symphony of Harmony and Invention (*R* 2006)
HWV 111a *E partirai, mia vita?* (S, bc)
CALLISTO RECORDS CIO 403; A. Pabyan (soprano), M. Marding (cello), P. Erdas (harpsichord) (*R* 2003)
HWV 112 *Figli del mesto cor* (A, bc)
FY FYCD 112 (LP); H. Ledroit (counter-tenor), D. Simpson (cello), N. Spieth (harpsichord) (*R* 1983)
CAPRICCIO 10323; J. Kowalski (counter-tenor), S. Pank (viola di gamba), C. Schornsheim (harpsichord), Akademie für Alte Musik Berlin (*R* 1988)
ASTREE AUVIDIS E 8577; J.-L. Comoretto (counter-tenor), Il Divertimento (*R* 1996)
MUSICIANS SHOWCASE 1090; P. Djerejian (contralto), English Chamber Orchestra, P. Ledger (*R* 2003)
CENTAUR CRC 2540; J. Gall (counter-tenor), M. Rozendaal (viola da gamba), D. Schrader (harpsichord) (*R* 2004)
HWV 113 *Figlio d'alte speranze* (S, vn, bc)
TELEFUNKEN 6.42367 (LP); M. Kweksilber (soprano), Musica Antiqua Amsterdam, T. Koopman (*R* 1977)
CLARIUS AUDI CD 29004 (1996); P. Macrelli (soprano), instruments, A. Anzalone (cello), F. Ravizza (harpsichord) (*R* 1996)
CAPRICCIO SACD 71083; V. Winter (soprano), Das Kleine Konzert, H. Max (*R* 2005)
GLOSSA 921521; R. Invernizzi (soprano), Ensemble La Risonanza, F. Bonizzoni (harpsichord) (*R* 2005)
HWV 115 *Fra pensieri quel pensiero* (A, bc)
FY FYCD 112 (LP); H. Ledroit (counter-tenor), D. Simpson (cello), N. Spieth (harpsichord) (*R* 1983)

CAPRICCIO 10 703; A. Köhler (counter-tenor), B. Maté (cello), R. Alpermann (harpsichord) (*R* 1995)
ANALEKTA FL 2 3161; M.-N. Lemieux (contralto), A. Keesmaat (cello), L. Beauséjour (harpsichord) (*R* 2001)
MUSICIANS SHOWCASE 1090; P. Djerejian (contralto), English Chamber Orchestra, P. Ledger (*R* 2003)

HWV 117 *Hendel, non può mia musa* (S, bc)
STRADIVARIUS STR 33424; R.Invernizzi (soprano), Retablo Barocco (*R* 1997)

HWV 118 *Ho fuggito Amore anch'io* (A, bc)
BERLIN CLASSICS 3104; A. Stolte (soprano), P. Klug (viola da gamba), W. Iwer (harpsichord) (*R* 1995)
CENTAUR CRC 2540; J. Gall (counter-tenor), M. Rozendaal (viola di gamba), D. Schrader (harpsichord) (*R* 2002)

HWV 120b *Irene, idolo mio* (A, bc)
ANALEKTA FL 2 3161; M.-N. Lemieux (contralto), A. Keesmaat (cello), L. Beauséjour (harpsichord) (*R* 2001)
CENTAUR CRC 2540; J. Gall (counter-tenor), M. Rozendaal (viola di gamba), D. Schrader (harpsichord) (*R* 2002)

HWV 121a *La solitudine* (*L'aure grate, il fresco rio*) (A, bc)
CENTAUR CRC 2540; J. Gall (counter-tenor), M. Rozendaal (viola di gamba), D. Schrader (harpsichord) (*R* 2002)

HWV 123 *Languia di bocca lusinghiera* (S, ob, vn, bc)
ASV Gaudeamus CD GAU 192; C. Brandes (soprano), The Four Nations Ensemble (*R* 1999)
EUFODA CDEUF 1297; D. York (soprano), Collegium Instrumentale Brugense, P. Peire (*R* 1999)

HWV 125b *Lungi da me, pensier tiranno* (A, bc)
FY FYCD 112 (LP); H. Ledroit (counter-tenor), D. Simpson (cello), N. Spieth (harpsichord) (*R* 1983)
CHANNEL CLASSICS CCS 0890; D. L. Ragin (counter-tenor), Divitia Köln (*R* 1990)
ASTREE AUVIDIS E 8577; J.-L. Comoretto (counter-tenor), Il Divertimento (*R* 1996)
BONGIOVANNI 5568-2; A. Manzotti (counter-tenor), S. Ruffino (viola di gamba), G. Kiss (harpsichord) (*R* 1997)
ANALEKTA FL 2 3161; M.-N. Lemieux (contralto), A. Keesmaat (cello), L. Beauséjour (harpsichord) (*R* 2001)
OPUS 111 OP 30395; S. Mingardo (contralto), Concerto Italiano, R. Alessandrini (*R* 2004)

HWV 126c *Lungi da voi, che siete poli* (A, bc)
BERLIN Classics 0017192BC; B. Schwarz (contralto), S. Maass (lute) (*R* 2000)

MUSICIANS SHOWCASE 1090; P. Djerejian (contralto), English Chamber Orchestra, P. Ledger (*R* 2003)
HWV 127a *Lungi dal mio bel nume* (S, bc)
ASTREE AUVIDIS E 8577; I. Poulenard (soprano), Il Divertimento (*R* 1996)
HWV 129 *Manca pur quanto sai* (S, bc)
CALLISTO RECORDS CIO 403; A. Pabyan (Soprano), M. Marding (cello), P. Erdas (harpsichord) (*R* 2003)
HWV 130 *Mentre il tutto è in furore* (S, bc)
ACCORD 202 712; M. C. Kiehr (soprano), Il Teatro Armonico, A. de Marchi (*R* 1993)
HWV 131 *Menzognere speranze* (S, bc)
ASTREE AUVIDIS E 8577; I. Poulenard (soprano), Il Divertimento (*R* 1996)
HWV 132a *Mi palpita il cor* (S, bc)
L'OISEAU-LYRE 414 473-2; E. Kirkby (soprano), Academy of Ancient Music, C. Hogwood (*R* 1984)
MERIDIAN CDE 84157; Y. Kenny (soprano), J. Fenton (cello), M. Scully (contrabass), M. Isepp (harpsichord) (*R* 1990)
BNL 112 859; T. Livingstone (soprano), Il Parnasso Confuso, J. Nirouët (*R* 1994)
AEOLUS AE 10046; E. Umbach (soprano), Umbach & Consorten (*R* 1998)
QUERSTAND 0010; G. Näther (soprano), La Voce Umana, J. Fiedler (cello), J. Trinkewitz (harpsichord) (*R* 2001)
HWV 132b *Mi palpita il cor* (S, ob, bc)
VIRGIN CLASSICS 09463438422; N. Dessay (soprano), Le Concert d'Astrée, E. Haïm (*R* 2005)
HWV 132c *Mi palpita il cor* (A, fl, bc)
RCA SEON 303-93 (LP); R. Jacobs (counter-tenor), S. Kuijken (flute), A. Bylsma (cello), G. Leonhardt (harpsichord) (*R* 1980)
HUNGAROTON HRC 183 (LP); D. Minter (counter-tenor), V. Stadler (flute), G. Szilvassy (harpsichord) (*R* 1981)
HUNGAROTON SLPD 12564; P. Esswood (counter-tenor), P. Németh (flute), C. Falvay (cello), P. Ella (harpsichord) (*R* 1984)
CAPRICCIO 10323; J. Kowalski (counter-tenor), K. H. Passin (flute), S. Pank (viola di gamba), C. Schornsheim (harpsichord), Akademie für Alte Musik Berlin (*R* 1988)
KOCH 10 3-7021-2 HI; M. Zakai (contralto), A. Biron (flute), M. Haran (cello), S. Ad-El (harpsichord) (*R* 1988)
VIRGIN VC 7 91480-2; G. Lesne (counter-tenor), Il Seminario Musicale (*R* 1990)
ARTS 47711; W. Matteuzzi (tenor), Münchner Barocksolisten, H. Hoffmann (archlute), H. L. Hirsch (*R* 1991)
CAPRICCIO 10 703; J. Kowalski (counter-tenor), C. Huntgeburth (flute), B. Maté (cello), R. Alpermann (harpsichord) (*R* 1993)

ASV GAU211; M. White (counter-tenor), The Four Nations Ensemble, A. Appel (*R* 1998)
BONGIOVANNI 5568-2; A. Manzotti (counter-tenor), M. Mercelli (flute), S. Ruffino (viola da gamba), G. Kiss (harpsichord) (*R* 1999)
ANALEKTA FL 2 3161; M.-N. Lemieux (contralto), M.-C. Labbe (flute), A. Keesmaat (cello), L. Beauséjour (harpsichord) (*R* 2001)
RAUMKLANG RK 2101; S. Houtzeel (mezzo-soprano), The Bouts Ensemble (*R* 2001)
MUSICIANS SHOWCASE 1090; P. Djerejian (contralto), English Chamber Orchestra, P. Ledger (*R* 2003)
TALL POPPIES TP 173; C. Field (counter-tenor), R. Hillier (flute), R. Hunt (cello), S. Cohen (chitarrone), J. Ogeil (harpsichord) (*R* 2004)
HARMONIA.MUNDI HMC 901957; A. Scholl (counter-tenor), Accademia Bizantina, O. Dantone (*R* 2006)

HWV 132d *Mi palpita il cor* (A, ob, bc)
AMBROISIE AMB 9958; R. Expert (counter-tenor), Amarillis (*R* 2004)
LYRICHORD LEMS 8055 (2006); M. Coid (counter-tenor), M. Heller (oboe), P. Seidenberg (cello), E. Comparone (harpsichord) (*R* 2006)

HWV 134 *Pensieri notturni di Filli* (*Nel dolce dell'oblio*) (S, REC, BC)
CLASSIC CLP 6195 (LP); D. van Doorn (soprano), Netherlands Handel Society Orchestra, J. Loory (*R* 1950s)
OCEANIC OCS 30 /OLYMPIE RECORDS Q 8116 (LP); A. Giebel (soprano), Tonstudio Orchester Stuttgart, R. Lamy (*R* 1952)
DHM Quintessence2 PMC 2714 (LP); E. Ameling (soprano), Collegium Aureum, F. J. Maier (*R* 1964)
HUNGAROTON HCD 11653-2 (LP); M. Kalmar (soprano), Chamber Orchestra Franz Liszt of Budapest, F. Sandor (*R* 1974)
TELEFUNKEN 6.42367 (LP); M. Kweksilber (soprano), Musica Antiqua Amsterdam, T. Koopman (*R* 1977)
PANTHEON D 10680 (LP); B.Valente (soprano), J. Bassett (flute), R. Sylvester (cello), D. Effron (harpsichord) (*R* 1980s)
AULOS PRE 68507 (LP); M. van Altena (tenor), G. M. Klemisch (flute), F. Borstlap (cello), C. Farr (harpsichord), Barockensemble Camerata Amsterdam (*R* 1983)
PEARL SHE 590; V. Masterson (soprano), piano (*R* 1985)
DORIAN DOR-90147; J. Baird (soprano), Philomel Baroque Orchestra (*R* 1990)
MD+G 10 L 3399; J. Koslowsky (soprano), Musica Alta Ripa (*R* 1990)
ACCORD 202 712; M. C. Kiehr (soprano), Il Teatro Armonico, A. de Marchi (*R* 1993)
BNL 112 859; T. Livingstone (soprano), Il Parnasso Confuso, J. Nirouët (*R* 1994)
BONGIOVANNI 5568-2; A. Manzotti (counter-tenor), M. Mercelli (flute), S. Ruffino (viola da gamba), G. Kiss (harpsichord) (*R* 1999)

CALLISTO RECORDS CIO 403; A. Pabyan (Soprano), Lorenzo Cavasanti (flute), M. Marding (cello), P. Erdas (harpsichord) (*R* 2003)
CORO COR 16045; E. Manahan Thomas (soprano), Symphony of Harmony and Invention (*R* 2006)
GLOSSA 921521; R. Invernizzi (soprano), Ensemble La Risonanza, F. Bonizzoni (harpsichord) (*R* 2006)

HWV 135a *Nel dolce tempo* (S, bc)
ACCORD 204 212; M. C. Kiehr (soprano), Il Teatro Armonico, A.de Marchi (*R* 1993)

HWV 135b: *Nel dolce tempo* (A, bc)
FY FYCD 112; H. Ledroit (counter-tenor), D. Simpson (cello), N. Spieth (harpsichord) (*R* 1983)
BERLIN Classics 0017192BC; B. Schwarz (contralto), S. Maass (lute) (*R* 2000)
CENTAUR CRC 2540; J. Gall (counter-tenor), M. Rozendaal (viola da gamba), D. Schrader (harpsichord) (*R* 2002)
HARMONIA.MUNDI HMC 901957; A. Scholl (counter-tenor), Accademia Bizantina, O. Dantone (*R* 2006)

HWV 136a *Nell'africane selve* (B, bc)
OISEAU LYRE DSLO 580 (LP); D. Thomas (bass), S. Sheppard (cello), C. Hogwood (harpsichord) (*R* 1981)
STRADIVARIUS STR 33425; J. L. Bindi (bass), Artificii Musicali, G. Delvaux (harpsichord) (*R* 1995)
ARION ARN 68505; J. Correas (baritone-basso), M. Middenway (cello), E. Haïm (harpsichord), Ensemble Les Paladins (*R* 1999)

HWV 137 *Nella stagion che di viole e rose* (S, bc)
OISEAU LYRE DSLO 580 (LP); J. Nelson (soprano), S. Sheppard (cello), C. Hogwood (harpsichord) (*R* 1981)

HWV 138 *Nice, che fa? che pensa?* (S, bc)
QUERSTAND 0010; G. Näther (soprano), La Voce Umana, J. Fiedler (cello), J. Trinkewitz (harpsichord) (*R* 2001)

HWV 141 *Non sospirar, non piangere* (S, bc)
STRADIVARIUS STR 33424; R. Invernizzi (soprano), Retablo Barocco (*R* 1997)

HWV 142 *Notte placida e cheta* (S, 2 vn, bc)
HUNGAROTON HCD 12981; M. Zádori (soprano), Capella Savaria, P. Németh (*R* 1988)
CHANDOS Chaconne CHAN 0620; C. Bott (soprano), The Purcell Quartet (*R* 1997)
ORF Alte Musik 3001; N. Rial (soprano), La Risonanza, F. Bonizzoni (*R* 2006)

HWV 145 *La Lucrezia* (*Oh numi eterni*) (S, bc)
EMI 2701381 (LP); A. Murray (mezzo-soprano), Scottish Chamber Orchestra, R. Leppard (*R* 1970s)

CAMBRIDGE RECORDS CRS 2773 (LP); C. Bogard (soprano), C. Meints (cello), J. Weaver (harpsichord) (*R* 1972)
PHILIPS 426 450-2 (LP); J. Baker (mezzo-soprano), English Chamber Orchestra, R. Leppard (*R* 1972)
DORIAN DOR 90104; J. Baird (soprano), M. Lutzke (cello), C. Tilney (harpsichord) (*R* 1987)
VIRGIN VC 7 91480-2; G. Lesne (counter-tenor), Il Seminario Musicale (*R* 1990)
STRADIVARIUS STR 33424; R. Invernizzi (soprano), Retablo Barocco (*R* 1997)
VIRGIN CLASSICS VC545 283 2; V. Gens (soprano), Les Basses Réunies (*R* 1997)
ARCHIV PRODUKTION 469 065 2; M. Kožená (soprano), Les Musiciens du Louvre, M. Minkowski (*R* 1999)
ARION ARN 68505; S. Piau (soprano), M. Middenway (cello), E. Haïm (harpsichord), Ensemble Les Paladins (*R* 1999)
TELDEC 3984-24571; E. Mei (soprano), Il Giardino Armonico, G. Antonini (*R* 1999)
CEDILLE RECORDS CDR 90000 057; P. M. Bedi (soprano), Chicago Baroque Ensemble, J. M. Rozendaal (*R* 2000)
QUERSTAND 0010; G. Näther (soprano), La Voce Umana, J. Fiedler (cello), J. Trinkewitz (harpsichord) (*R* 2001)
AVIE 0030; L. Hunt Lieberson (mezzo-soprano), Orchestra of the Age of Enlightenment, H. Bicket (*R* 2004)

HWV 146 *Occhi miei, che faceste?* (S, bc)
MERIDIAN CDE 84189; J. Baird (soprano), J. Dornenburg (viola da gamba), M. Proud (harpsichord) (*R* 1981)

HWV 147 *Partì, l'idolo mio* (S, bc)
HARMONIA MUNDI HMA 1901004 (LP); J. Nelson (soprano), Concerto Vocale, R. Jacobs (*R* 1978)
HUNGAROTON HCD 32383; A. Korondi (soprano), R. Pertorini (cello), J. Pétri (harpsichord) (*R* 2005)

HWV 150 *Ero e Leandro* (*Qual ti riveggio, oh Dio*) (S, 2 ob, str, bc)
HUNGAROTON HCD 12981; M. Zádori (soprano), Capella Savaria, P. Németh (*R* 1988)
ACCORD 10 201102; L. M. Äkerlund (soprano), Ensemble Baroque, A. Wenzinger (*R* 1991)
ORF Alte Musik 3001; N. Rial (soprano), La Risonanza, F. Bonizzoni (*R* 2006)

HWV 153 *Quando sperasti, o core* (S, bc)
BNL 112 859; T. Livingstone (soprano), Il Parnasso Confuso, J. Nirouët (*R* 1994)
CALLISTO RECORDS CIO 403; A. Pabyan (Soprano), M. Marding (cello), P. Erdas (harpsichord) (*R* 2003)

HWV 154 *Quel fior che all'alba ride* (S, bc)
    MERIDIAN CDE 84189 (LP); J. Baird (soprano), J. Dornenburg (viola da gamba), M. Proud (harpsichord) (*R* 1981)
    OISEAU LYRE 595 146 (LP); E. Kirkby (soprano), S. Sheppard (cello), C. Hogwood (harpsichord) (*R* 1981)

HWV 158c *Se pari è la tua fé* (S, bc)
    HELICON HE 1007; F. Robinson (soprano), Brewer Baroque Chamber Orchestra (*R* 1996)

HWV 161b *Sento là che ristretto* (A, bc)
    HARMONIA MUNDI HMA 1901004 (LP); R. Jacobs, Concerto Vocale (*R* 1978)

HWV 162 *Siete rose ruggiadose* (A, bc)
    FY FYCD 112 (LP); H. Ledroit (counter-tenor), D. Simpson (cello), (harpsichord) (*R* 1983)
    CHANNEL CLASSICS CCS 0890; D. L. Ragin (counter-tenor), Divitia Köln (*R* 1990)

HWV 163 *Solitudini care, amata libertà* (S, bc)
    MERIDIAN CDE 84189; J. Baird (soprano), J. Dornenburg (viola da gamba), M. Proud (harpsichord) (*R* 1981)

HWV 164a *Il gelsomino* (*Son gelsomino*) (S, bc)
    HUNGAROTON HCD 32383; A. Korondi (soprano), R. Pertorini (cello), J. Pétri (harpsichord) (*R* 2005)

HWV 164b *Il gelsomino* (*Son gelsomino*) (A, bc)
    CENTAUR CRC 2540; J. Gall (counter-tenor), M. Rozendaal (viola da gamba), D. Schrader (harpsichord) (*R* 2002)

HWV 165 *Spande ancor a mio dispetto* (B, 2 vn, bc)
    CLASSIC CLP 6195 (LP); D. Hollestelle (bass), Netherlands Handel Society Orchestra, J. Loory (*R* 1950s)
    STRADIVARIUS STR 33425; J. L. Bindi (bass), Artificii Musicali, G. Delvaux (harpsichord) (*R* 1995)
    HELICON HE 1007; J. Ostendorf (baritone), Brewer Baroque Chamber Orchestra (*R* 1996)
    TALL POPPIES TP 173; M. Leighton Jones (bass), C. Shugg, N. Forsyth (violins), R. Hunt (cello), S. Cohen (chitarrone), J. Ogeil (harpsichord) (*R* 2005)

HWV 166 *Splenda l'alba in oriente* (A, 2 fl/ob, str, bc)
    DECCA (LP) / 433737-2; H. Watts (contralto), English Chamber Orchestra, R. Leppard (*R* 1961)
    CAPRICCIO 10323; J. Kowalski (counter-tenor), S. Pank (viola di gamba), C. Schornsheim (harpsichord), Akademie für Alte Musik Berlin (*R* 1988)
    VIRGIN VC 7 91480-2; G. Lesne (counter-tenor), Il Seminario Musicale (*R* 1990)
    VIRGIN 5 45737; V. Genaux (mezzo-soprano), Les Violons du Roy, B. Labadie (*R* 2005)

HWV 168 *Partenza di G. B.* (*Stelle, perfide stelle*) (S, bc)
  ACCORD 204 212; M. C. Kiehr (soprano), Il Teatro Armonico, A. de Marchi (*R* 1993)
  HUNGAROTON HCD 32383; A. Korondi (soprano), R. Pertorini (cello), J. Pétri (harpsichord) (*R* 2005)
HWV 170: *Il consiglio* (*Tra le fiamme*) (S, 2 ob/rec, 2 vn, va da gamba, bc)
  BERLIN CLASSICS 6157197 (LP); A. Stolte (soprano), Händel-Festspielorchester Halle, T. Sanderling (*R* 1970)
  L'OISEAU-LYRE 414 473-2 (LP); E. Kirkby (soprano), Academy of Ancient Music, C. Hogwood (*R* 1980)
  DORIAN DOR-90147; J. Baird (soprano), Philomel Baroque Orchestra (*R* 1990)
  CHANDOS Chaconne CHAN 0620; C. Bott (soprano), Purcell Quartet (*R* 1996)
  MUSICAL OFFERING 9604; E. Hargis (soprano), Seattle Baroque Orchestra (*R* 1997)
  ARCHIV PRODUKTION 469 065 2; M. Kožená (soprano), Les Musiciens du Louvre, M. Minkowski (*R* 1999)
  ASTREE E 8674; M. Bayo (soprano), Capriccio Stravagante, S. Sempe (*R* 1999)
  GLOSSA 921521; R. Invernizzi (soprano) Ensemble La Risonanza, F. Bonizzoni (*R* 2006)
  MIRARE 009; N. Rial (soprano), Ricercar Consort, P. Pierlot (viola da gamba and conductor) (*R* 2006)
HWV 171 *Tu fedel? Tu costante?* (S, 2 vn, bc)
  DECCA 433737-2 (LP); H. Watts (contralto), English Chamber Orchestra, R. Leppard (*R* 1961)
  NONESUCH H 71.159; C. Bressler (tenor), New York Chamber Soloists (*R* 1970s)
  L'OISEAU-LYRE 414 473-2; E. Kirkby (soprano), Academy of Ancient Music, C. Hogwood (*R* 1984)
  ACCORD 202 712; M. C. Kiehr (soprano), Il Teatro Armonico, A. de Marchi (*R* 1993)
  RAUMKLANG RK 2101; S. Houtzeel (mezzo-soprano), The Bouts Ensemble (*R* 2001)
  TALL POPPIES TP 173; M. Allan (soprano), C. Shugg, N. Forsyth (violins), R. Hunt (cello), S. Cohen (chitarrone), J. Ogeil (harpsichord) (*R* 2005)
  CORO COR 16045; E. Manahan Thomas (soprano), Symphony of Harmony and Invention (*R* 2006)
HWV 172 *Udite il mio consiglio* (S, bc)
  MERIDIAN CDE 84189 (LP); J. Baird (soprano), J. Dornenburg (viola da gamba), M. Proud (harpsichord) (*R* 1981)
  CHANNEL CLASSICS CCS 0890; D. L. Ragin (counter-tenor), Divitia Köln (*R* 1990)

BONGIOVANNI 5568-2; A. Manzotti (counter-tenor), S. Ruffino (viola da gamba), G. Kiss (harpsichord) (*R* 1999)
HWV 173 *Un'alma innamorata* (S, vn, bc)
TELEFUNKEN 6.42367 (LP); M. Kweksilber (soprano), Musica Antiqua Amsterdam, T. Koopman (*R* 1977)
NUOVA ERA ID 7065; M. Cotterill (soprano), Ensemble Pian e Forte, A. Frigé (harpsichord) (*R* 1991)
BONGIOVANNI 5568-2; A. Manzotti (counter-tenor), S. Ruffino (viola da gamba), G. Kiss (harpsichord) (*R* 1999)
CEDILLE RECORDS CDR 90000 057; P. M. Bedi (soprano), Chicago Baroque Ensemble, J. M. Rozendaal (*R* 2000)
CAPRICCIO SACD 71083; V. Winter (soprano), Das Kleine Konzert, H. Max (*R* 2005)
HWV 174 *Un sospir a chi si muore* (S, bc)
BONGIOVANNI 5568-2; A. Manzotti (counter-tenor), S. Ruffino (viola da gamba), G. Kiss (harpsichord) (*R* 1997)
HWV 175 *Vedendo Amor* (A, bc)
FY FYCD 112 (LP); H. Ledroit (counter-tenor), D. Simpson (cello), N. Spieth (harpsichord) (*R* 1983)
ARION ARN 68046; James Bowman (counter-tenor), J. Bernfeld (viola da gamba), S. Sempé (harpsichord) (*R* 1987)
CAPRICCIO 10323; J. Kowalski (counter-tenor), S. Pank (viola di gamba), C. Schornsheim (harpsichord), Akademie für Alte Musik Berlin (*R* 1988)
ACCORD 204 212; A. Scholl (counter-tenor), Il Teatro Armonico, A. de Marchi (*R* 1993)
BNL 112 859; J. Nirouët (counter-tenor), Il Parnasso Confuso, J. Nirouët (*R* 1994)
ASTREE AUVIDIS E 8577; J.-L. Comoretto (counter-tenor), Il Divertimento (*R* 1996)
BERLIN Classics 0017192BC; B. Schwarz (contralto), S. Maass (lute) (*R* 2000)
HARMONIA.MUNDI HMC 901957; A. Scholl (counter-tenor), Accademia Bizantina, O. Dantone (*R* 2006)
HWV 176 *Amore uccellatore* (*Venne voglia ad Amore*) (A, bc)
CAPRICCIO 10 703; A. Köhler (counter-tenor), B. Maté (cello), R. Alpermann (harpsichord) (*R* 1994)
HWV deest (CB 19.6) *Pastorella vagha, bella* (S, bc) – doubtful
BERLIN CLASSICS 3105; A. Stolte, (soprano), P. Klug (viola da gamba), W. Iwer (harpsichord) (*R* 1995)
LYRICHORD LEMS 8055; J. Baird (soprano), P. Seidenberg (cello), E. Comparone (harpsichord) (*R* 2006)

Johann Adolf Hasse (1699–1783)

Ah, troppo è ver! (A, str, bc)
    MDG 3090944; K. Wessel (counter-tenor), A. Röhrig, U. Bundies (violins), C. Heidemann (viola), J. Teichmanis (cello), B. Lohr (harpsichord) (*R* 2000)

Bella, mi parto, a Dio (A, bc)
    MDG 3090944; K. Wessel (counter-tenor), J. Teichmanis (cello), B. Lohr (harpsichord) (*R* 2000)

Clori, Clori, mia vita (A, 2 vn, bc)
    HUNGAROTON HCD 31843; E. Lax (mezzo-soprano), Affetti Musicali Budapest, J. Malina (*R* 2000)

E pur odo e non moro (S, 2 vn, bc)
    CLARIUS AUDI CA 29006; P. Zanardi (soprano), Parnasus Symphonicus, C. Del Turco, A. Bares (violins), M. Dal Cortivo (cello), F. Ravizza (harpsichord) (*R* 1997)

Fille dolce, mio bene (S, fl, bc)
    CRD 3488; J. Baird (soprano), N. Hadden (flute), E. Headley (viola da gamba), M. Proud (harpsichord) (*R* 1991)

L'armonica (S, glass harmonica, str, bc)
    FSM 10 737 (LP); E. Wiens (soprano), B. Hoffmann (glass harmonica), Orchestre Pro Musica de Stuttgart, P. Angerer (*R* 1970s)
    ADDA 581147; V. Dietschy (soprano), D. James (glass harmonica), Ensemble Stradivaria, D. Cuiller (*R* 1989)

La gelosia (S, str, bc)
    ADDA 581147; V. Dietschy (soprano), D. Cuiller (violino), Ensemble Stradivaria, D. Cuiller (*R* 1989)

La scusa (S, str, bc)
    VIRGIN 5 45737; V. Genaux (mezzo-soprano), Les Violons du Roy, B. Labadie (*R* 2005)

Per palestri appieno (S, 2 fl, bc)
    HUNGAROTON HCD 31843; M. Zádori (soprano), Affetti Musicali Budapest, J. Malina (*R* 2000)

Pur deggio partire (S, 2 vn, bc)
    CLARIUS AUDI CA 29006; P. Zanardi (soprano), Parnasus Symphonicus, C. Del Turco, A. Bares (violins), M. Dal Cortivo (cello), F. Ravizza (harpsichord) (*R* 1997)

Qual nuovo sole è questo (A, str, bc)
    NALESSO RECORDS NR 004; C. Calvi (contralto), F. Missaggia, R. Croce, E. Imbalzano (violins), V. Pedronetto (viola), C. Zanardi (cello), P. Zuccheri (violone), V. Dal Maso (harpsichord) (*R* 1999)

Quel vago seno, o Fille (S, fl, bc)
    CRD 3488; J. Baird (soprano), N. Hadden (flute), E. Headley (viola da gamba), M. Proud (harpsichord) (*R* 1991)

NALESSO RECORDS NR 004; C. Miatello (soprano), A. Dainese (flute), C. Zanardi (cello), P. Zuccheri (violone), V. Dal Maso (harpsichord) (*R* 1999)

Se il cantor trace, oh Dio (A, 2 vn, bc)
HUNGAROTON HCD 31843; E. Lax (mezzo-soprano), Affetti Musicali Budapest, J. Malina (*R* 2000)
MDG 3090944; K. Wessel (counter-tenor), A. Röhrig, U. Bundies (violins), C. J. Teichmanis (cello), B. Lohr (harpsichord) (*R* 2000)

Solitudini campestre (S, 2 vn, bc)
CLARIUS AUDI CA 29006; P. Zanardi (soprano), Parnasus Symphonicus, C. Del Turco, A. Bares (violins), M. Dal Cortivo (cello), F. Ravizza (harpsichord) (*R* 1997)

Vaga madre di cari diletti (S, 2 vn, bc)
CLARIUS AUDI CA 29006; P. Zanardi (soprano), Parnasus Symphonicus, C. Del Turco, A. Bares (violins), M. Dal Cortivo (cello), F. Ravizza (harpsichord) (*R* 1997)

Giovanni Legrenzi (1626–90)

4 Acclamationi divote a voce sola (*Libro Primo*, Op. 10)
BELLA MUSICA BM 911016; Cappella Mauriziana, M. Valsecchi (*R* 1993)

3 Echi di Riverenza di cantate e canzoni (*Libro Secondo*, Op. 14)
BELLA MUSICA BM 911016; Cappella Mauriziana, M. Valsecchi (*R* 1993)

Che fiero costume (S, bc) (*Libro Secondo*, Op. 14)
UNITED ARTISTS UAL-3412; (1st aria, transcribed) J. Peerce (tenor), A. Rogers (piano) (*R* 1964)
DECCA 028942152625; (1st aria, transcribed) L. Pavarotti (tenor), J. Wustman (piano) (*R* 1990)
Eurodisc 28519KK (LP); (1st aria, transcribed) M. Theodore (tenor), Münchner Rundfunkorchester, J. Dünnwald (*R* 1970s)
SONY SNYC 66309SMK; (1st aria, transcribed) R. Tucker (tenor), Columbia Chamber Ensemble (*R* 1999)
CHALLENGE CLASSIC CC 72100; C. Margiono (soprano), Margiono Quintet (*R* 2002)

Leonardo Leo (1694–1744)

Così del vostro suono (*Il Trionfo della Gloria*) (S, str, bc)
TACTUS TC 693701; C. Miatello (soprano), La Confraternita de' Musici, C. Prontera (*R* 2001)

Sorge Lidia la notte (A, str, bc)
TACTUS TC 693701; E. Bianchi (counter-tenor), La Confraternita de' Musici, C. Prontera (*R* 2001)

Splende più dell'usato (S, str, bc)
    TACTUS TC 693701; C. Miatello (soprano), La Confraternita de' Musici, C. Prontera (*R* 2001)

Signor Lignani (17th–18th Century)

Chi sa dove è la speranza (A, str, bc)
    DYNAMIC CDS 106; E. Lax (contralto), Ensemble Barocco Padovano Sans Souci (*R* 1993)

Antonio Lotti (1666–1740)

Pur dicesti, o bocca bella (S, bc)
    KOCH/SCHWANN 3-1164-2 H1; (1st aria, transcribed) E. Berger (soprano), G. Weissenborn (piano) (*R* 1949)
    RCA Red Seal 9026; (1st aria, transcribed) Ramón Vargas (tenor) (*R* 2002)
Ti sento, o Dio Bendato (A, bc)
    DYNAMIC CDS 106; E. Lax (contralto), Ensemble Barocco Padovano Sans Souci (*R* 1993)

Francesco Magini (17th–18th Century)

Da che vidde il duo sembiante (A, bc)
    BERLIN CLASSICS 001770 BC; M. Beaumont (mezzo-soprano), Lautten Compagney Berlin, W. Katschner (*R* 2006)

Francesco Mancini (1672–1737)

Quanto dolce è quell'ardore (S, str, bc)
    DYNAMIC CDS 106; L. Serafini (soprano), Ensemble Barocco Padovano Sans Souci (*R* 1993)

Alessandro Marcello (1673–1747)

D 903 *Contro l'empio Fileno* (*Irene sdegnata*) (S, str, bc)
    ARTS Authentic 47 505 2; S. Pozzer (soprano), Venice Baroque Orchestra, A. Marcon (*R* 1997)

Benedetto Marcello (1686–1739)

A 22 *Amai, no'l niego, una gentil sembianza* (S, str, bc)
    TACTUS TC 68 3801; A. Simboli (soprano), Accademia degli Invaghiti, F. Moi (*R* 2001)

A 51 *Carissima figlia* (A, bc)
    RODOLPHE EUROPA COCEU 008; N. Clapton (counter-tenor), J. Gray (harpsichord) (*R* 1989)

A 61b *Chiuse in placida quiete* (A, bc)
    OPUS 111 OPS 30 149; C. Cavina (counter-tenor), La Venexiana, P. Beier (theorbo), M. Testori (cello), F. Bonizzoni (harpsichord) (*R* 1995)
    BERLIN Classics 0017192BC; B. Schwarz (contralto), S. Maass (lute) (*R* 2000)

A 83 *Deh lasciatemi un momento* (S, bc)
    RODOLPHE EUROPA COCEU 008; C. Bevaqua (soprano), J. Gray (harpsichord) (*R* 1989)

A 98 *Dove, misera, dove lungi da me* (*Arianna abbandonata da Teseo*) (S, str, bc)
    TACTUS TC 68 3801; A. Simboli (soprano), Accademia degli Invaghiti, F. Moi (*R* 2001)

A 127 *Fonti, voi che al mio pianto crescete* (A, str, bc)
    TACTUS TC 68 3801; M. Oro (counter-tenor), Accademia degli Invaghiti, F. Moi (*R* 2001)

A 169 *Lasciato avea l'adultero* (*La Lucrezia*) (A, bc)
    OPUS 111 OPS 30 149; C. Cavina (alto), La Venexiana, P. Beier (theorbo), M. Testori (cello), F. Bonizzoni (harpsichord) (*R* 1995)

A 179 *Lontananza e gelosia* (A, bc)
    FY FYCD 108; H. Ledroit (counter-tenor), D. Simpson (cello), N. Spieth (harpsichord) (*R* 1982)

A 242 *Onda d'amaro pianto* (S, bc)
    OPUS 111 OPS 30 149; R. Bertini, (soprano), La Venexiana, P. Beier (theorbo), M. Testori (cello), F. Bonizzoni (harpsichord) (*R* 1995)

A 248 *Pecorelle che pascete* (S, bc)
    RODOLPHE EUROPA COCEU 008; C. Bevaqua (soprano), J. Gray (harpsichord) (*R* 1989)

Z 316 *Sentite, o tronchi, o sassi* (S, bc)
    FY FYCD 108; H. Ledroit (counter-tenor), D. Simpson (cello), N. Spieth (harpsichord) (*R* 1982)

A 182 *Sento già che nel mezzo al mio core* (B, bc)
    RODOLPHE EUROPA COCEU 008; G. Trew (baritone), J. Gray (harpsichord) (*R* 1989)

A 321 *Senza gran pena non si giunge al fine* (*Stravaganze d'amore: Cantata enarmonica*) (S, bc)
    OPUS 111 OPS 30 149; R. Bertini, (soprano), La Venexiana, P. Beier (theorbo), M. Testori (cello), F. Bonizzoni (harpsichord) (*R* 1995)

Alessandro Melani (1639–1703)

All'armi, pensieri (*Se d'un volto mi struggo all'ardore*) (S, tpt, bc)
    HARMONIA MUNDI HMA 190-5.137; J. Nelson (soprano), D. Ferry (trumpet), K. Gohl (cello), J. Rubin (theorbo), G. Murray (harpsichord) (*R* 1983)
    FSM 10 68908 PAN; L. Shelton (soprano), E. Carroll (trumpet) (*R* 1985)
    NUOVA ERA 7009; E. Gambarini (soprano), G. Cassone (trumpet) (*R* 1990)
    BAYER RECORDS 100329; A. Ruf (soprano), Cantoclarino, P. Leiner (trumpet), M. Eichenlaub (harpsichord) (*R* 2000)
    ALBANY RECORDS ALB TROY555; J. Baird (soprano), D. Kelly (trumpet), S. Alltop (organo) (*R* 2002)

Colà dove rimbomba (S, str, bc)
    DYNAMIC CDS 274; R. Frisani (soprano), Alessandro Stradella Consort, E. Velardi (*R* 1999)

Lunge dal sole amato (S, str, bc)
    DYNAMIC CDS 274; R. Frisani (soprano), Alessandro Stradella Consort, E. Velardi (*R* 1999)

Oratio Coclite (*A ricalcare in Tebro*) (S, 2 vn, bc)
    DYNAMIC CDS 274; R. Frisani (soprano), Alessandro Stradella Consort, E. Velardi (*R* 1999)

Pompeo in Lesbo (*La libertà di Roma*) (S, str, bc)
    DYNAMIC CDS 274; R. Frisani (soprano), Alessandro Stradella Consort, E. Velardi (*R* 1999)

Quai bellici accenti ascolti, mio core? (*La tromba*) (S, tpt, bc)
    NUOVA ERA 7009; E. Gambarini (soprano), G. Cassone (trumpet) (*R* 1990)
    DYNAMIC CDS 274; R. Frisani (soprano), G. Cassone (trumpet), Alessandro Stradella Consort, E. Velardi (*R* 1999)
    ETCETERA KTC 1244 ; D. Wirtz (soprano), Parnassi Musici (*R* 2001)
    ALBANY RECORDS ALB TROY555; J. Baird (soprano), D. Kelly (trumpet), S. Alltop (organo) (*R* 2002)

Qual mormorio giocondo (S, str, bc)
    CAPRICCIO 10 583; R. Siesak (soprano), Budapest Strings, B. Banfalvi (*R* 1996)
    DYNAMIC CDS 274; R. Frisani (soprano), Alessandro Stradella Consort, E. Velardi (*R* 1999)
    ETCETERA KTC 1244 ; D. Wirtz (soprano), Parnassi Musici (*R* 2001)

Giovanni Battista Pergolesi (1710–36)

Chi non ode e chi non vede (S, str, bc)
    TACTUS TC 711601; A. Rossi de Simone (soprano), Ensemble Concerto, R. Gini (*R* 1991)

BONGIOVANNI BG 2185; S. Rigacci (soprano), G. Banditelli (contralto), Complessi in Canto, F. Maestri (*R* 1995)

Dalsigre, ahi mia Dalsigre (S, str, bc)
TACTUS TC 711601; A. Rossi de Simone (soprano), Ensemble Concerto, R. Gini (*R* 1991)
BONGIOVANNI BG 2185; S. Rigacci (soprano), Complessi in Canto, F. Maestri (*R* 1995)

Luce degli occhi miei (S, str, bc)
TACTUS TC 711601; A. Rossi de Simone (soprano), Ensemble Concerto, R. Gini (*R* 1991)
BONGIOVANNI BG 2185; S. Rigacci (soprano), Complessi in Canto, F. Maestri (*R* 1995)

Orfeo (*Nel chiuso centro*) (S, str, bc)
ELECTRECORD 7005 (LP); E. Petrescu (soprano), Rumanian Concertino (*R* 1970s)
TACTUS TC 711601; A. Rossi de Simone (soprano), Ensemble Concerto, R. Gini (*R* 1991)
CAPRICCIO 10517; R. Klepper (soprano), Quatuor Bamberg (*R* 1993)
NAXOS 8 550766; J. Faulkner (soprano), Camera Budapest, M. Halasz (*R* 1994)
BONGIOVANNI BG 2185; G. Banditelli (contralto), Complessi in Canto, F. Maestri (*R* 1995)

Questo è il piano (A, str, bc)
BONGIOVANNI BG 2185; G. Banditelli (contralto), Complessi in Canto, F. Maestri (*R* 1995)

Giacomo Antonio Perti (1661–1756)

Cantate morali e spirituali [a una et due voci], Op. 1
BONGIOVANNI GB 2208/09; R. Frisani (soprano), C. Calvi (contralto), C. Lepore (bass), instrumentalists of the Cappella Musicale di San Petronio, S. Vartolo (*R* 1996)

Francesco Antonio Mamiliano Pistocchi (1659–1726)

Con dolce mormorio (A, bc)
CAVALLI CCD 312; K. Wessel (counter-tenor), G. Darmstadt (cello), U. Wedemeier, (lute, Baroque guitar), S. Erdmann (harpsichord) (*R* 2001)

Dolorosa partenza (S, bc)
CAVALLI CCD 312; B. Schlick (soprano), G. Darmstadt (cello), U. Wedemeier, (lute, Baroque guitar), S. Erdmann (harpsichord) (*R* 2001)

Giovanni Benedetto Platti (c.1690–1763)

Fugge del bosco al prato (S, str, bc)
　AGORA AG 123.1; A. Venturino (soprano), Gli Affetti (*R* 1996)

Nicola Porpora (1686–1768)

Ad onta del timore (A, bc)
　HUNGAROTON HCD 31747; N. Clapton (counter-tenor), R. Pertorini (cello),
　　B. Dobozy (harpsichord) (*R* 1990s)
D'Amore il primo dardo (S, bc)
　ASV Gaudeamus CD GAU 192; C. Brandes (soprano), The Four Nations
　　Ensemble (*R* 1999)
D'Amor la bella pace (A, bc)
　HUNGAROTON HCD 31747; N. Clapton (counter-tenor), R. Pertorini (cello),
　　B. Dobozy (harpsichord) (*R* 1990s)
Dorindo, dormir ancor? (S, str, bc)
　BONGIOVANNI GB 2181/82; R Invernizzi (soprano), Alessandro Stradella
　　Consort, E. Velardi (*R* 1993)
Fille, oh Dio (S, str, bc)
　SYRIUS SYR 14350; E. Crommen (soprano), Ensemble Baroque Le Rondeau,
　　J.-P. Boulet (*R* 1999)
Idolatrata e cinta (A, bc)
　HUNGAROTON HCD 31747; N. Clapton (counter-tenor), R. Pertorini (cello),
　　B. Dobozy (harpsichord) (*R* 1990s)
Oh! Dio! che non è vero (S, bc)
　AUVIDIS AV 6116; N. Anfuso (soprano), L. Alvini (harpsichord) (*R* 1986)
Or che d'orrido verno (S, fl, str, bc)
　BONGIOVANNI GB 5541 2; S. Donzelli (soprano), M. Mercelli (flute),
　　Orchestra da camera 'Benedetto Marcello' Teramo, E. Maschio (*R* 1993)
Or che una nube ingrata (A, bc)
　PHILIPS 6575.058 (LP); R. Jacobs (counter-tenor), G. Leonhardt (harpsichord)
　　(*R* 1975)
　HUNGAROTON HCD31747; N. Clapton (counter-tenor), R. Pertorini (cello),
　　B. Dobozy (harpsichord) (*R* 1990s)
Questa dunque è la selva (A, bc)
　HUNGAROTON HCD 31747; N. Clapton (counter-tenor), R. Pertorini (cello),
　　B. Dobozy (harpsichord) (*R* 1990s)
Queste che miri, o Nice (S, bc)
　AUVIDIS AV 6116; N. Anfuso (soprano), L. Alvini (harpsichord) (*R* 1986)
Speranze del mio cor (A, bc)
　HUNGAROTON HCD 31747; N. Clapton (counter-tenor), R. Pertorini (cello),
　　B. Dobozy (harpsichord) (*R* 1990s)

Giuseppe Porsile (1680–1750)

Cantata sopra arcicalascione (S, bc)
  CYPRÈS 1649; M. Beasley (tenor), Accordone, G. Morini (harpsichord) (*R* 2006)
E già tre volte sorse (S, str, bc)
  RENÉ GAILLY CD 92042; G. de Reyghere (soprano), Telemann Consort (*R* 1998)

Giovanni Porta (c.1675–1755)

*Udite, o Cieli (*A, str, bc)
  BERLIN CLASSICS 001770 2 BC; A. Hallenberg (mezzo-soprano), Lautten Compagney Berlin, W. Katschner (*R* 2006)

Francesco Provenzale (1624–1704)

Care selve, amati orrori (S, str, bc)
  SYMPHONIA SY 94S29; R. Invernizzi (soprano), Cappella della Pietà dei Turchini, A. Florio (*R* 1994)
La mia speme è vanità (S, str, bc)
  SYMPHONIA SY 94S29; R. Invernizzi (soprano), Cappella della Pietà dei Turchini, A. Florio (*R* 1994)
Me sento 'na cosa (S, str, bc)
  SYMPHONIA SY 96147; R. Invernizzi (soprano), Cappella della Pietà de' Turchini, A. Florio (*R* 1996)
Squarciato appena havea (T, str, bc)
  SYMPHONIA SY 91 S09; P. de Vittorio (tenor), Cappella della Pietà de' Turchini, A. Florio (*R* 1991)
Sui palchi delle stelle (S, str, bc)
  SYMPHONIA SY 94S29; R. Invernizzi (soprano), Cappella della Pietà dei Turchini, A. Florio (*R* 1994)

Domenico Natale Sarro (Sarri) (1679–1744)

Andate, o miei sospiri (S, str, bc)
  DYNAMIC CDS 106; L. Serafini (soprano), Ensemble Barocco Padovano Sans Souci (*R* 1993)
Barbara gelosia (A, bc)
  BERLIN CLASSICS 001770 BC; M. Beaumont (mezzo-soprano), Lautten Compagney Berlin, W. Katschner (*R* 2006)

Alessandro Scarlatti (1660-1725)

Ammore brutto figlio de pottana (T, bc)
    TACTUS TC 661901; G. P. Fagotto (tenor), L. Scoppola (rec), P. Pandolfo (viola da gamba), R. Alessandrini (harpsichord) (*R* 1990)
    CYPRES CYP 1649; M. Beasley (tenor), Accordone, G. Morini (harpsichord) (*R* 2006)

Andate, o miei sospiri (S, bc)
    TACTUS TC 660002; C. Miatello (soprano), A. Fossa (cello), G. Morini (harpsichord) (*R* 1989)

Augellin vago e canoro (S, 2 fl, bc)
    AGORA AG 071.1; E. Mari (soprano), Fête Rustique Ensemble, E. Mari (*R* 1996)
    RENE GAILLY CD 92042; G. de Reyghere (soprano), Telemann Consort (*R* 1998)

Bella madre dei fiori (S, 2 vn, bc)
    AUVIDIS 4815 (LP); S. Toczyska (mezzo-soprano), Ensemble Capella Arcis Varsoviensis, M. Sewen (*R* 1970s)
    TACTUS 67012001; G. Banditelli (mezzo-soprano), Ensemble Aurora, E. Gatti (*R* 1988)
    PROPHONE 002.; S. Rydén (soprano), A. Wallström, M. Bergman (violins), A. Akerberg (cello), B. Gäfvert (harpsichord) (*R* 1990)
    CONIFER CLASSICS 75605 51 293 2; C. Brandes (soprano), Arcadian Academy, N. McGegan (harpsichord) (*R* 1996)
    HARMONIA MUNDI HMC 901725; M. C. Kiehr (soprano), Concerto Soave, J.-M. Aymes (harpsichord) (*R* 2000)

Clori mia, Clori bella, ah non più (S, fl, bc)
    TACTUS TC 661901; C. Miatello (soprano), L. Scoppola (rec), P. Pandolfo (viola da gamba), R. Alessandrini (harpsichord) (*R* 1990)

Clori vezzosa e bella (A, bc)
    L'OISEAU-LYRE 50173 (LP); H. Watts (contralto), D. Dupré (viola da gamba), T. Dart (harpsichord) (*R* 1957)
    CONIFER 51 325-2; B. Asawa (counter-tenor), Arcadian Academy, N. McGegan (*R* 2000)
    KAMMERTON KT 2011; G. Schmid (counter-tenor), Ensemble Batzdorfer Hofkapelle (*R* 2001)

Cor di Bruto, e che risolvi? (B, bc)
    HUNGAROTON HCD 32456; P. Fried (bass), P. Vitárius (violino), O. Nagy (cello), Savaria Baroque Orchestra, P. Németh (*R* 2006)

Correa nel seno amato (S, 2 vn, bc)
    HYPERION 66254; L. Dawson (soprano), Purcell Quartet, R. Woolley (harpsichord) (*R* 1987)
    PIERRE VERANY 790013; J. Nicolas (soprano), S. Deeks, X. J. Laferrière (violins), A. Verzier (viola da gamba), P. Ramin (harpsichord) (*R* 1989)

HARMONIA MUNDI HMC 901725; M. C. Kiehr (soprano), Concerto Soave, J.-M. Aymes (*R* 2000)

Deh torna, amico sonno (*Il sonno*) (S, bc)
ADES 202172; V. Dietschi (soprano), Ensemble Gradiva (*R* 1991)

Dove alfin mi traeste? (*L'Arianna*) (S, bc)
CONIFER CLASSICS 75605 51 293 2; C. Brandes (soprano), Arcadian Academy, N. McGegan (harpsichord) (*R* 1996)

Ebra d'amor fuggia (*L'Arianna*) (S, 2 vn, bc)
HARMONIA MUNDI 30591; H. Graf (soprano), Ensemble Ricercare de Zurich, E. Melkus (*R* 1970s)
CONIFER CLASSICS 75605 51 293 2; C. Brandes (soprano), Arcadian Academy, N. McGegan (harpsichord) (*R* 1996)

Elitropio d'amor (S/A, bc)
LYRINX 062; P. A. do Nascimento (counter-tenor), P. Foulon (cello), J.-M. Hasler (harpsichord) (*R* 1986)

Ferma omai, fugace e bella (A, 2 vn, va, bc)
LYRINX 062; P. A. do Nascimento (counter-tenor), P. Foulon (cello), J.-M. Hasler (harpsichord) (*R* 1986)
CONIFER 51 325-2; B. Asawa (counter-tenor), Arcadian Academy, N. McGegan (*R* 2000)
KAMMERTON KT 2011; G. Schmid (counter-tenor), Ensemble Batzdorfer Hofkapelle (*R* 2001)

Filen, mio caro bene (*Filli che esprime la sua fede a Fileno*) (A, 2 vn, fl, bc)
VIRGIN Veritas VC5 45126-2; S. Piau (soprano), Il Seminario Musicale, G. Lesne (*R* 1997)

Filli, tu sai s'io t'amo (*Sconsolato rusignolo*) (S, 2 fl, bc)
AGORA AG 071.1; E. Mari (soprano), Fête Rustique Ensemble, E. Mari (*R* 1996)

Già lusingato appieno (S, 2 vn, bc)
HYPERION 66254; L. Dawson (soprano), Purcell Quartet, R. Woolley (harpsichord) (*R* 1987)
CONIFER CLASSICS 75605 51 293 2; C. Brandes (soprano), Arcadian Academy, N. McGegan (harpsichord) (*R* 1996)

Il genio di Mitilde (S/A, bc)
CONIFER 51 319-2; D. Daniels (counter-tenor), Arcadian Academy, N. McGegan (*R* 1998)

Il rosignolo se scioglie il volo (A/S, bc)
CONIFER 51 319-2; D. Daniels (counter-tenor), Arcadian Academy, N. McGegan (*R* 1998)

Immagini d'orrore (B, 2 vn, bc)
HUNGAROTON HCD 32456; P. Fried (bass), P. Vitárius (violino), O. Nagy (cello), Savaria Baroque Orchestra, P. Németh (*R* 2006)

Io morirei contento (S, bc)
   LYRINX 062; P. A. do Nascimento (counter-tenor), P. Foulon (cello), J.-M. Hasler (harpsichord) (*R* 1986)

L'armi crudeli e fiere (A, bc)
   CAPRICCIO 10 703; A. Köhler (counter-tenor), B. Maté (cello), R. Alpermann (harpsichord) (*R* 1995)
   KAMMERTON KT 2011; G. Schmid (counter-tenor), Ensemble Batzdorfer Hofkapelle (*R* 2001)

Là dove a Mergellina (S, bc)
   EMI 7 54176 2; N. Argenta (soprano), Chandos Baroque Players (*R* 1989)

Lascia più di tormentarmi, rimembranza (S, bc)
   TACTUS TC 660002; C. Miatello (soprano), A. Fossa (cello), G. Morini (harpsichord) (*R* 1989)

Leandro, anima mia (*Ero e Leandro*) (A/S, bc)
   PIERRE VERANY 790013; A. Aubin (counter-tenor), A. Verzier (viola di gamba), P. Ramin (harpsichord) (*R* 1989)

Lontan da la sua Clori (S, bc)
   TACTUS TC 660002; C. Miatello (soprano), A. Fossa (cello), G. Morini (harpsichord) (*R* 1989)

Nacqui a' sospiri e al pianto (S, 2 vn, bc)
   AUVIDIS 4815; S. Toczyska (mezzo-soprano), Ensemble Capella Arcis Varsoviensis, M. Sewen (*R* 1970s)

Nel silentio comune (S, 2 vn, va, bc)
   CONIFER 51 325-2; B. Asawa (counter-tenor), Arcadian Academy, N. McGegan (*R* 2000)

Non so qual più m'ingombra (*Cantata pastorale*) (S, 2 vn, bc)
   CONIFER 51 325-2; B. Asawa (counter-tenor), Arcadian Academy, N. McGegan (*R* 2000)

O pace del mio cor (S/A, bc)
   CONIFER 51 319-2; D. Daniels (counter-tenor), Arcadian Academy, N. McGegan (*R* 1998)

Oh di Betlemme altera povertà (*Cantata pastorale per la nascita di Nostro Signore*) (S, 2 vn, va, vc, lute)
   VSM 063 02058 (LP); J. Baker (mezzo-soprano), English Chamber Orchestra, R. Leppard (*R* 1970s)
   HUNGAROTON 12561 (LP); M. Zádori (soprano), Capella Savaria, P. Németh (*R* 1980s)
   NAXOS 8.545 0483; G. C. Majeric (soprano), Mainzer Kammerorchester, G. Kehr (*R* 1988)
   EMI 7 54176 2; N. Argenta (soprano), Chandos Baroque Players (*R* 1989)
   HYPERION HYP 66875; D. York (soprano), King's Consort, R. King (*R* 1996)

Ombre tacite e sole (S, 2 vn, va, bc)
    CONIFER 51 319-2; D. Daniels (counter-tenor), Arcadian Academy, N. McGegan (*R* 1998)
Or [Hor] che di Febo ascosi (S, 2 vn, bc)
    EMI 7 54176 2; N. Argenta (soprano), Chandos Baroque Players (*R* 1989)
Per un momento solo (*Lo sfortunato*) (S/A, bc)
    TACTUS TC 660002.; C. Miatello (soprano), A. Fossa (cello), G. Morini (harpsichord) (*R* 1989)
Perché tacete, regolati concenti? (A, 2 vn, bc)
    MDG 309 0632 2; K. Wessel (counter-tenor), Ensemble Musica Alta Ripa (*R* 1992)
    CONIFER 51 319-2; D. Daniels (counter-tenor), Arcadian Academy, N. McGegan (*R* 1998)
Piango, sospiro e peno (A, 2 vn, bc)
    CONIFER 51 325-2; B. Asawa (counter-tenor), Arcadian Academy, N. McGegan (*R* 2000)
Poi ché riseppe Orfeo (S, bc)
    CONIFER CLASSICS 75605 51 293 2; C. Brandes (soprano), Arcadian Academy, N. McGegan (harpsichord) (*R* 1996)
    HARMONIA MUNDI HMC 901725; M. C. Kiehr (soprano), Concerto Soave, J.-M. Aymes (*R* 2000)
Quella pace gradita (S, fl, vn, vc, bc)
    EMI 7 54176 2.; N. Argenta (soprano), Chandos Baroque Players (*R* 1989)
    AGORA AG 071.1; E. Mari (soprano), Ensemble Fête Rustique, E. Mari (*R* 1996)
Qui dove alfin m'assido (*Il rosignuolo*) (S, bc)
    L'OISEAU-LYRE 50173 (LP); H. Watts (contralto), D. Dupré (viola da gamba), T. Dart (harpsichord) (*R* 1957)
    PROPHONE 002.; S. Rydén (soprano), A. Wallström, M. Bergman (violins), A. Akerberg (cello), B. Gäfvert (harpsichord) (*R* 1990)
Siete unite a tormentarmi (A, 2 vn, bc)
    KAMMERTON KT 2011; G. Schmid (counter-tenor), Ensemble Batzdorfer Hofkapelle (*R* 2001)
Solitudini amene, apriche collinette (S, fl, bc)
    CLAVES 500604; K. Graf (soprano), P.-L. Graf (flute), R. Altwegg (cello), M. Kobayashi (harpsichord) (*R* 1989)
    AGORA AG 071; E. Mari (soprano), Ensemble Fête Rustique, E. Mari (*R* 1999)
Sovente amore mi chiama (A, bc)
    TACTUS TC 661901.; C. Cavina (counter-tenor), L. Scoppola (flute), P. Pandolfo (viola da gamba), R. Alessandrini (harpsichord) (*R* 1990)
Speranze mie, addio (S, bc)
    LYRINX 062; P. A. do Nascimento (counter-tenor), P. Foulon (cello), J.-M. Hasler (harpsichord) (*R* 1986)

Splendeano in bel sembiante (B, bc)
    HUNGAROTON HCD 32456; P. Fried (bass), P. Vitárius (violino), O. Nagy (cello), Savaria Baroque Orchestra, P. Németh (*R* 2006)

Su le sponde del Tebro (S, 2 vn, tpt, bc)
    ARCHIV 14024 (LP); T. Stich-Randall (soprano), Camerata Academica Mozarteum Salzburg, B. Paumgartner (*R* 1952)
    ERATO 55046 (LP); A. Maliponte (soprano), M. André (trumpet), Società cameristica di Lugano, E. Loehrer (*R* 1969)
    CBS 76 636 (LP); J. Blegen (soprano), G. Schwarz (trumpet), Columbia Chamber Ensemble, G. Schwarz (*R* 1976)
    SCHWANN AMS 3532; R. Yakar (soprano), G. Touvron (trumpet), RIAS Sinfonietta, U. Lajovic (*R* 1980)
    EMI 27 0175 1; H. Donath (soprano), M. André (trumpet), Academy of St Martin-in-the-Fields, N. Marriner (*R* 1985)
    FSM 68908; L. Shelton (soprano), E. Carroll (trumpet), instruments, E. Brewer (harpsichord) (*R* 1985)
    CAPRICCIO 10 221; P. Schreier (tenor), L. Güttler (trumpet), Virtuosi Saxoniae (*R* 1987)
    NUOVA ERA 7009; E. Gambarini (soprano), G. Cassone (trumpet), Ensemble Pian e Forte (*R* 1989)
    DE PLEIN VENT 9006; B. Löcher (soprano), G. Touvron (trumpet), instruments (*R* 1990)
    SONY SK 46672; K. Battle (soprano), W. Marsalis (trumpet), Orchestra of St Luke's, J. Nelson (*R* 1991)
    CAPRICCIO 10 583; R. Siesak (soprano), Budapest Strings, B. Banfalvi (*R* 1996)
    HYPERION HYP 66875; D. York (mezzo-soprano), C. Steele-Perkins (trumpet), King's Consort, R. King (*R* 1996)
    ETCETERA KTC 1244; D. Wirtz (soprano), Parnassi Musici (*R* 2001)
    BONGIOVANNI GB 2327-2; R. Frisani (soprano), G. Cassone (trumpet), Alessandro Stradella Consort, E. Velardi (*R* 2003)

Tu sei quella che al nome (*Bella dama di nome santa*) (A, 2 vn, fl, bc)
    MDG 309 0632 2; K. Wessel (counter-tenor), Ensemble Musica Alta Ripa (*R* 1992)

Domenico Scarlatti (1685–1757)

Amenissimi prati, fiorite piagge (B, bc)
    NUOVA ERA 7099; M. van Egmond (baritone), M. Mencoboni (harpsichord) (*R* 1985)
    REM 10984; Monteverdi Consort, R. Correa (*R* 1986)
    BONGIOVANNI GB 10 2026-2; R. Girolami (bass), C. Cornoldi (violino), G. Catalucci (harpsichord) (*R* 1988)

Bella rosa adorata, cara pompa di Flora (S, bc)
    AUVIDIS AV6.101; N. Anfuso (soprano), J. Gray (harpsichord) (*R* 1985)
Che pretendi, o tiranna (S, bc)
    EX LIBRIS EL 16 993; L. Klay (mezzo-soprano), M. Jappe (viola da gamba), R. Scheidegger (harpsichord) (*R* 1985)
Che si peni in amore (A, bc)
    EX LIBRIS EL 16 993; L. Klay (mezzo-soprano), M. Jappe (viola da gamba), R. Scheidegger (harpsichord) (*R* 1985)
Che vidi, o ciel (S, 2 vn, bc)
    UNICORN Kanchana DKP 9095; K. Eckersley (soprano), Fiori Musicali, P. Rapson (*R* 1990)
    AUVIDIS E 8673; C. Gerstenhaber (soprano), XVIII/21 Musique des Lumières, J. C. Fritsch (*R* 1999)
    TACTUS TC 681901/02; L. Bertotti (soprano), Ensemble Seicento Italiano, D. Boccaccio (*R* 2000)
Con qual cor mi chiede pace (S, bc)
    UNICORN Kanchana DKP 9125; K. Eckersley (soprano), Musica Fiammante (*R* 1991)
    CAPRICCIO 37 173; M. E. Cencic (counter-tenor), Y. Imamura (theorbo), M. Amrein (cello), A. Zylberajch (fortepiano) (*R* 2006)
Crudo mar di fiamme orribili (B, 2 vn, bc)
    BONGIOVANNI GB 2165-2; R. Ristori (bass), Alessandro Stradella Consort, E. Valardi (*R* 1993)
Deh che fate, o mie pupille (S, bc)
    AUVIDIS AV6.101; N. Anfuso (soprano), J. Gray (harpsichord) (*R* 1985)
Di Fille vendicarmi vorrei (S, bc)
    UNICORN Kanchana DKP 9124; K. Eckersley (soprano), Musica Fiammante (*R* 1991)
Dir vorrei, ah m'arrossisco (S, 2 vn, bc)
    UNICORN Kanchana DKP 9119; K. Eckersley (soprano), Fiori Musicali, P. Rapson (*R* 1991)
    TACTUS TC 681901/02; L. Bertotti (soprano), Ensemble Seicento Italiano, D. Boccaccio (*R* 2000)
    CAPRICCIO 67 027; M. E. Cencic (counter-tenor), Ornemente 99, K. E. Ose (2002)
Dopo lungo servire (A, 2 vn, bc)
    EX LIBRIS EL 16 993; L. Klay (mezzo-soprano), M. Lüthi, M. Harras (flutes), M. Jappe (viola da gamba), R. Scheidegger (harpsichord) (*R* 1985)
    MDG 309 0632 2; K. Wessel (counter-tenor), Ensemble Musica Alta Ripa (*R* 1992)
Fille, già più non parlo (S, bc)
    UNICORN Kanchana DKP 9124; K. Eckersley (soprano), Musica Fiammante (*R* 1991)

CAPRICCIO 37 173; M. E. Cencic (counter-tenor), Y. Imamura (theorbo), M. Amrein (cello), A. Zylberajch (fortepiano) (*R* 2006)
Mi tormenta il pensiero (S, bc)
EX LIBRIS EL 16 993; L. Klay (mezzo-soprano), M. Jappe (viola da gamba), R. Scheidegger (harpsichord) (*R* 1985)
REM 10984; Monteverdi Consort, R. Correa (*R* 1986)
No, non fuggire, o Nice (S, bc)
UNICORN Kanchana DKP 9125; K. Eckersley (soprano), Musica Fiammante (*R* 1991)
CAPRICCIO 37 173; M. E. Cencic (counter-tenor), Y. Imamura (theorbo), M. Amrein (cello), A. Zylberajch (fortepiano) (*R* 2006)
O qual meco Nice cangiata (S, 2 vn, bc)
UNICORN Kanchana DKP 9119; K. Eckersley (soprano), Fiori Musicali, P. Rapson (*R* 1991)
AUVIDIS E 8673; C. Gerstenhaber (soprano), XVIII/21 Musique des Lumières, J. C. Fritsch (*R* 1999)
TACTUS TC 681901/02; L. Bertotti (soprano), Ensemble Seicento Italiano, D. Boccaccio (*R* 2000)
Onde della mia Nera (A/S, bc)
AUVIDIS AV6.101; N. Anfuso (soprano), J. Gray (harpsichord) (*R* 1985)
Piangete, occhi dolenti (S, 2 vn, bc)
UNICORN Kanchana DKP 9095; K. Eckersley (soprano), Fiori Musicali, P. Rapson (*R* 1990)
VIRGIN 5455462; P. Ciofi (soprano), Il Complesso Barocco, A. Curtis (*R* 2003)
Pur nel sonno almen tal'ora (S, 2 vn, bc)
REM 10984; Monteverdi Consort, R. Correa (*R* 1986)
UNICORN Kanchana DKP 9095; K. Eckersley (soprano), Fiori Musicali, P. Rapson (*R* 1990)
AUVIDIS E 8673; C. Gerstenhaber (soprano), XVIII/21 Musique des Lumières, J. C. Fritsch (*R* 1999)
CAPRICCIO 67 027; M. E. Cencic (counter-tenor), Ornemente 99, K. E. Ose (*R* 2002)
Qual pensier, quale ardire ti guida? (S, bc)
UNICORN Kanchana DKP 9125; K. Eckersley (soprano), Musica Fiammante (*R* 1991)
CAPRICCIO 37 173; M. E. Cencic (counter-tenor), Y. Imamura (theorbo), M. Amrein (cello), A. Zylberajch (fortepiano) (*R* 2006)
Quando miro il vostro foco (A, bc)
AUVIDIS AV6.101; N. Anfuso (soprano), J. Gray (harpsichord) (*R* 1985)
Rimirai la rosa un dì (A, bc)
AUVIDIS AV6.101; N. Anfuso (soprano), J. Gray (harpsichord) (*R* 1985)

Scritte con falso inganno (S, 2 vn, bc)
>UNICORN Kanchana DKP 9119; K. Eckersley (soprano), Fiori Musicali, P. Rapson (*R* 1991)
>CAPRICCIO 67 027; M. E. Cencic (counter-tenor), Ornemente 99, K. E. Ose (*R* 2002)
>VIRGIN 5455462; P. Ciofi (soprano), Il Complesso Barocco, A. Curtis (*R* 2003)

Se fedele tu m'adori (S, 2 vn, bc)
>BONGIOVANNI GB 10 2026-2; A. Rossi (soprano), C. Cornoldi (violino), G. Catalucci (harpsichord) (*R* 1988)
>UNICORN Kanchana DKP 9095; K. Eckersley (soprano), Fiori Musicali, P. Rapson (*R* 1990)
>TACTUS TC 681901/02; L. Bertotti (soprano), Ensemble Seicento Italiano, D. Boccaccio (*R* 2000)

Se sai qual sia la pena (S, bc)
>UNICORN Kanchana DKP 9124; K. Eckersley (soprano), Musica Fiammante (*R* 1991)

*Se ti dicesse un core (*S, bc)
>UNICORN Kanchana DKP 9124; K. Eckersley (soprano), Musica Fiammante (*R* 1991)

Sospendi, o man, per poco (S, bc)
>UNICORN Kanchana DKP 9124; K. Eckersley (soprano), Musica Fiammante (*R* 1991)

Ti ricorda, o bella Irene (S, bc)
>UNICORN Kanchana DKP 9125; K. Eckersley (soprano), Musica Fiammante (*R* 1991)
>CAPRICCIO 37 173; M. E. Cencic (counter-tenor), Y. Imamura (theorbo), M. Amrein (cello), A. Zylberajch (fortepiano) (*R* 2006)

Tinte a note di sangue (S, 2 vn, bc)
>UNICORN Kanchana DKP 9119; K. Eckersley (soprano), Fiori Musicali, P. Rapson (*R* 1991)
>CAPRICCIO 67 027; M. E. Cencic (controtenoire), Ornemente 99, K. E. Ose (*R* 2002)
>VIRGIN 5455462; P. Ciofi (soprano), Il Complesso Barocco, A. Curtis (*R* 2003)

Tu mi chiedi, o mio ben (S, bc)
>EX LIBRIS EL 16 993; L. Klay (mezzo-soprano), M. Jappe (viola da gamba), R. Scheidegger (harpsichord) (*R* 1985)

Francesco Scarlatti (1666–1741)

O come in un'istante (A, bc)
>MDG 309 0632 2; K. Wessel (counter-tenor), Ensenble Musica Alta Ripa (*R* 1992)

Agostino Steffani (1654–1728)

Fileno, idolo mio (S, str, bc) (*Scherzi musicali*)
    BONGIOVANNI GB 2123-2; Alessandro Stradella Consort, E. Velardi (*R* 1991)
    HUNGAROTON HCD 32078; N. Kiss (soprano), Affetti Musicali, J. Malina (*R* 2001)
    PAN CLASSICS PC 510 131; M. Zanetti (soprano), Fons Musicae, Y. Imamura (*R* 2001)

Guardati a core (S, str, bc) (*Scherzi musicali*)
    CAPRICCIO 10459; A. Monoyos (soprano), Berliner Barock-Compagney (*R* 1993)
    HUNGAROTON HCD 32078; N. Kiss (soprano), Affetti Musicali, J. Malina (*R* 2001)

Hai finto di lusingarmi (S/A, str, bc) (*Scherzi musicali*)
    HUNGAROTON HCD 32078; Affetti Musicali, J. Malina (*R* 2001)

Il più felice e sfortunato amante (A, str, bc) (*Scherzi musicali*)
    BONGIOVANNI GB 2123-2; Alessandro Stradella Consort, E. Velardi (*R* 1991)
    HUNGAROTON HCD 32078; E. Lax (contralto), Affetti Musicali, J. Malina (*R* 2001)
    PAN CLASSICS PC 510 131; P. Bertin (counter-tenor), Fons Musicae, Y. Imamura (*R* 2001)

Lagrime dolorose (S/A, str, bc) (*Scherzi musicali*)
    HUNGAROTON HCD 32078; Affetti Musicali, J. Malina (*R* 2001)

Spezza, amor (S/A, str, bc) (*Scherzi musicali*)
    HUNGAROTON HCD 32078; Affetti Musicali, J. Malina (*R* 2001)

Alessandro Stradella (1639–82)

Ardo, sospiro e piango (S, bc)
    MUSICA OSCURA 070984-2; The Consort of Musicke, A. Rooley (*R* 1984)

Dentro bagno fumante (B, str, bc) – dubious
    ARCOPHON (LP) /HARMONIA MUNDI HMA 322.; G. Sarti (baritone), Complesso barocco di Milano, F. Degrada (*R* 1970)

Ferma, ferma il corso (*L'Arianna*) (S, bc)
    ADDA 581 173; I. Poulenard (soprano), M. Muller (viole de gambe), E. Buckley (harpsichord) (*R* 1989)
    HARMONIA MUNDI HMU 907 192; C. Brandes (soprano), P. O'Dette (lute), I. Matthews (violino), M. Springfels (viola da gamba), B. Weiss (harpsichord) (*R* 1997)

Frena, o Filli, il fiero orgoglio (S, str, bc) – dubious
> HARMONIA MUNDI HMU 907 192; C. Brandes (soprano), P. O'Dette (lute), I. Matthews (violino), M. Springfels (viola da gamba), B. Weiss (harpsichord) (*R* 1997)

Fuor della stigia sponda (S, str, bc)
> HARMONIA MUNDI HMU 907 192; C. Brandes (soprano), P. O'Dette (lute), I. Matthews (violino), M. Springfels (viola da gamba), B. Weiss (harpsichord) (*R* 1997)

Non avea il sole ancora (S, bc)
> HARMONIA MUNDI HMU 907 192; C. Brandes (soprano), P. O'Dette (lute), I. Matthews (violino), M. Springfels (viola da gamba), B. Weiss (harpsichord) (*R* 1997)

Ombre, voi che celate (A, str, bc)
> ARCOPHON (LP) /HARMONIA MUNDI HMA 322/ RIVO ALTO CRA 89161.; L. Ticinelli Fattori (soprano), Complesso barocco di Milano, F. Degrada (*R* 1970)

Quando mai vi stancherete (S, bc)
> COLUMNS CLASSICS WDR 070984; E. Kirkby (soprano), The Consort of Musicke, A. Rooley (*R* 1994)

Si salvi chi può (S, str, bc)
> HARMONIA MUNDI HMU 907 192; C. Brandes (soprano), P. O'Dette (lute), I. Matthews (violino), M. Springfels (viola da gamba), B. Weiss (harpsichord) (*R* 1997)

Sopra candido foglio (S, bc)
> ARCOPHON (LP) / HARMONIA MUNDI HMA 322 / RIVO ALTO CRA 89161; L. Ticinelli Fattori (soprano), Complesso barocco di Milano, F. Degrada (*R* 1970)

Pietro Torri (c.1650–1737)

V'amo sì, care luci (A, str, bc)
> DYNAMIC CDS 106; E. Lax (contralto), Ensemble Barocco Padovano Sans Souci (*R* 1993)

Giuseppe Tricarico (1623–97)

Sdegno, campion audace (T, bc)
> SYMPHONIA SY 91 S09; P. de Vittorio (tenor), Cappella della Pietà de' Turchini, A. Florio (*R* 1991)

Leonardo Vinci (c.1690–1730)

Adónde fugitivo (A, str, bc) (text in Spanish)
  NAÏVE OP 30274; A. Calzolari (contralto), Cappella della Pietà de'Turchini, A. Florio (*R* 2001)
Cuando, infeliz destino (A, str, bc) (text in Spanish)
  NAÏVE OP 30274; R. Invernizzi (soprano), Cappella della Pietà de'Turchini, A. Florio (*R* 2001)
Triste, ausente, en esta selva (S, str, bc) (text in Spanish)
  NAÏVE OP 30274; A. Calzolari (contralto), Cappella della Pietà de'Turchini, A. Florio (*R* 2001)

Antonio Vivaldi (1678–1741)

RV 649 *All'ombra d'un bel faggio* (S, bc)
  STILNOVO SN 8808; N. Anfuso (soprano), E. Baiano (harpsichord) (*R* 1992)
  MONDO MUSICA MM 90011; C. Gasdia (soprano), Barocco Veneziano, C. Ferrarini (*R* 1997)
RV 650 *Allor che lo sguardo* (S, bc)
  STILNOVO SN 8807; N. Anfuso (soprano), E. Baiano (harpsichord) (*R* 1991)
  AGORA AG 101.1 ; R. Invernizzi (soprano), Conserto Vago (*R* 1996)
  MONDO MUSICA MM 90011; C. Gasdia (soprano), Barocco Veneziano, C. Ferrarini (*R* 1997)
RV 651 *Amor, hai vinto, hai vinto: ecco il mio seno* (S, bc)
  SOLSTICE SOL 5 (LP); A.-M. Miranda (soprano), N. Rouillé (viola da gamba), M. Delfosse (harpsichord) (*R* 1977)
  L'OISEAU-LYRE 421.655-2 (LP); E. Kirkby (soprano), Academy of Ancient Music, C. Hogwood (*R* 1980)
  ARION ARN 238.032 (LP); N. Anfuso (soprano), Insieme da Camera Fiorentino, E. Sciarra (*R* 1981)
  FREQUENZ VENEZIA 21012; T. d'Althann (soprano), Accademia Monteverdi di Venezia, H. L. Hirsch (*R* 1988)
  TUDOR 735; Y. Hashimoto (soprano), K. Schickhaus (salterio) (*R* 1988)
  STILNOVO SN 8807; N. Anfuso (soprano), E. Baiano (harpsichord) (*R* 1991)
  AGORA AG 101.1 ; R. Invernizzi (soprano), Conserto Vago (*R* 1996)
  MONDO MUSICA MM 90021; C. Gasdia (soprano), Barocco Veneziano, C. Ferrarini (*R* 1997)
  TACTUS TC 67207; R. Bertini (soprano), Modo Antiquo, F. M. Sardelli (*R* 1997)

HELICON RCORDS HE 1019; R. Wong (sopranista), P. Hale (cello), L. Burman-Hall (harpsichord) (*R* 1998)
OPUS 111 OP 30404; G. Bertagnolli (soprano), L'Astrée (*R* 2000)
ASV Gaudeamus GAU 339; M. Nelson (soprano), The Band of Instruments (*R* 2002)

RV 652 *Aure, voi più non siete* (S, bc)
STILNOVO SN 8808; N. Anfuso (soprano), E. Baiano (harpsichord) (*R* 1992)
MONDO MUSICA MM 90011; C. Gasdia (soprano), Barocco Veneziano, C. Ferrarini (*R* 1997)
TACTUS TC 67207; R. Bertini (soprano), Modo Antiquo, F. M. Sardelli (*R* 1997)

RV 653 *Del suo natio rigore* (S, bc)
STILNOVO SN 8808; N. Anfuso (soprano), E. Baiano (harpsichord) (*R* 1992)
MONDO MUSICA/2CD MM 90011; C. Gasdia (soprano), Barocco Veneziano, C. Ferrarini (*R* 1997)
TACTUS TC 672209; N. Kennedy (soprano), Modo Antiquo, F. M. Sardelli (*R* 1998)

RV 654 *Elvira, anima mia* (S, bc)
SOLSTICE SOL 5 (LP); A.-M. Miranda (soprano), N. Rouillé (viola da gamba), M. Delfosse (harpsichord) (*R* 1977)
STILNOVO SN 8807; N. Anfuso (soprano), E. Baiano (harpsichord) (*R* 1991)
MONDO MUSICA MM 90021; C. Gasdia (soprano), Barocco Veneziano, C. Ferrarini (*R* 1997)
TACTUS TC 67207; R. Bertini (soprano), Modo Antiquo, F. M. Sardelli (*R* 1997)
OPUS 111/CD OP 30358; L. Polverelli (mezzo-soprano), L'Astrée (*R* 2000)
AVIE CKD 281; M. Lawson (soprano), La Serenissima, A. Chandler (*R* 2006)

RV 655 *Era la notte quando i suoi splendori* (S, bc)
MONDO MUSICA MM 90011; C. Gasdia (soprano), Barocco Veneziano, C. Ferrarini (*R* 1997)
TACTUS TC 67208; E. Cecchi Fedi (soprano), Modo Antiquo, F. M. Sardelli (*R* 1997)

RV 656 *Fonti del pianto* (S, bc)
ERATO 2292 45147 (LP); (1st aria) M. Horne (mezzo-soprano), G. Chiampan (cello), E. Farina (harpsichord) (*R* 1977)
NUOVA ERA 6859; A. Ruffini (soprano), Ensemble Concerto, R. Gini (*R* 1989)
FORLANE UCD 16620; (1st aria) E. Podles (mezzo-soprano), Collegium Musicum de Bruges, P. Peire (*R* 1990)
AGORA AG 101.1 ; R. Invernizzi (soprano), Conserto Vago (*R* 1996)

MONDO MUSICA MM 90011; C. Gasdia (soprano), Barocco Veneziano, C. Ferrarini (*R* 1997)

TACTUS TC 672209; N. Kennedy (soprano), Modo Antiquo, F. M. Sardelli (*R* 1998)

OPUS 111 OP 30404; G. Bertagnolli (soprano), L'Astrée (*R* 2000)

RV 657 *Geme l'onda che parte dal fonte* (S, bc)

MONDO MUSICA MM 90011; C. Gasdia (soprano), Barocco Veneziano, C. Ferrarini (*R* 1997)

TACTUS TC 67208; E. Cecchi Fedi (soprano), Modo Antiquo, F. M. Sardelli (*R* 1997)

OPUS 111 OP 30404; G. Bertagnolli (soprano), L'Astrée (*R* 2000)

RV 658 *Il povero mio cor* (S, bc)

FREQUENZ VENEZIA 21012; T. d'Althann (soprano), Accademia Monteverdi di Venezia, H. L. Hirsch (*R* 1988)

STILNOVO SN 8808; N. Anfuso (soprano), E. Baiano (harpsichord) (*R* 1992)

AGORA AG 101.1 ; R. Invernizzi (soprano), Conserto Vago (*R* 1996)

TACTUS TC 67208; E. Cecchi Fedi (soprano), Modo Antiquo, F. M. Sardelli (*R* 1997)

RV 659 *Indarno cerca la tortorella* (S, bc)

SOLSTICE SOL 5 (LP); A.-M. Miranda (soprano), N. Rouillé (viola da gamba), M. Delfosse (harpsichord) (*R* 1977)

STILNOVO SN 8807; N. Anfuso (soprano), E. Baiano (harpsichord) (*R* 1991)

MONDO MUSICA MM 90021; C. Gasdia (soprano), Barocco Veneziano, C. Ferrarini (*R* 1997)

TACTUS TC 67208; E. Cecchi Fedi (soprano), Modo Antiquo, F. M. Sardelli (*R* 1997)

RV 660 *La farfalletta s'aggira al lume* (S, bc)

SOLSTICE SOL 5 (LP); A.-M. Miranda (soprano), N. Rouillé (viola da gamba), M. Delfosse (harpsichord) (*R* 1977)

STILNOVO SN 8807; N. Anfuso (soprano), E. Baiano (harpsichord) (*R* 1991)

MONDO MUSICA MM 90011; C. Gasdia (soprano), Barocco Veneziano, C. Ferrarini (*R* 1997)

TACTUS TC 67208; E. Cecchi Fedi (soprano), Modo Antiquo, F. M. Sardelli (*R* 1997)

HELICON RCORDS HE 1019; R. Wong (sopranista), P. Hale (cello), L. Burman-Hall (harpsichord) (*R* 1998)

EROICA JDT 3099; (Aria 1) E. Mager (soprano), Members of the Four Seasons Orchestra (*R* 2001)

RV 661 *Nel partir da te, mio caro* (S, bc)

STILNOVO SN 8808; N. Anfuso (soprano), E. Baiano (harpsichord) (*R* 1992)

MONDO MUSICA MM 90011; C. Gasdia (soprano), Barocco Veneziano, C. Ferrarini (*R* 1997)

TACTUS TC 67207; R. Bertini (soprano), Modo Antiquo, F. M. Sardelli (*R* 1997)

RV 662 *Par che tardo oltre il costume* (S, bc)

MONDO MUSICA MM 90021; C. Gasdia (soprano), Barocco Veneziano, C. Ferrarini (*R* 1997)

TACTUS TC 672209; N. Kennedy (soprano), Modo Antiquo, F. M. Sardelli (*R* 1998)

BRILLIANT CLASSIC 99562/39; M. Strijk (soprano), Netherlands Bach Collegium, P. J. Leusink (*R* 2000)

RV 663 *Scherza di fronda in fronda* (S, bc)

AGORA AG 147 ; R. Invernizzi (soprano), Conserto Vago (*R* 1997)

MONDO MUSICA MM 90011; C. Gasdia (soprano), Barocco Veneziano, C. Ferrarini (*R* 1997)

RV 664 *Se ben vivono senz'alma* (S, bc)

MONDO MUSICA MM 90021; C. Gasdia (soprano), Barocco Veneziano, C. Ferrarini (*R* 1997)

TACTUS TC 67207; R. Bertini (soprano), Modo Antiquo, F. M. Sardelli (*R* 1997)

RV 665 *Si levi dal pensier* (S, bc)

STILNOVO SN 8808; N. Anfuso (soprano), E. Baiano (harpsichord) (*R* 1992)

MONDO MUSICA MM 90021; C. Gasdia (soprano), Barocco Veneziano, C. Ferrarini (*R* 1997)

TACTUS TC 672209; N. Kennedy (soprano), Modo Antiquo, F. M. Sardelli (*R* 1998)

RV 666 *Sì, sì, luci adorate* (S, bc)

AGORA AG 147; R. Invernizzi (soprano), Conserto Vago (*R* 1997)

MONDO MUSICA MM 90021; C. Gasdia (soprano), Barocco Veneziano, C. Ferrarini (*R* 1997)

BRILLANT CLASSICS 99562/40; M. Strijk (soprano), Netherlands Bach Collegium, P. J. Leusink (*R* 2000)

RV 667 *Sorge vermiglia in ciel la bella Aurora* (S, bc)

ETCETERA KTC 1069; D. L. Ragin (counter-tenor), V. de Hoog (cello), C. Farr (harpsichord) (*R* 1989)

NUOVA ERA 6859; A. Ruffini (soprano), Ensemble Concerto, R. Gini (*R* 1989)

AGORA AG 101.1 ; R. Invernizzi (soprano), Conserto Vago (*R* 1996)

MONDO MUSICA MM 90021; C. Gasdia (soprano), Barocco Veneziano, C. Ferrarini (*R* 1997)

HELICON RECORDS HE 1019; R. Wong (soprano), P. Hale (cello), L. Burman-Hall (harpsichord) (*R* 1998)

TACTUS TC 672209; N. Kennedy (soprano), Modo Antiquo, F. M. Sardelli (*R* 1998)

RV 668 *T'intendo sì, mio cor* (S, bc)
AGORA AG 147 ; R. Invernizzi (soprano), Conserto Vago (*R* 1997)
MONDO MUSICA MM 90021; C. Gasdia (soprano), Barocco Veneziano, C. Ferrarini (*R* 1997)
TACTUS TC 67207; R. Bertini (soprano), Modo Antiquo, F. M. Sardelli (*R* 1997)
EROICA JDT 3099; (1st aria) E. Mager (soprano), Members of the Four Seasons Orchestra (*R* 2001)

RV 669 *Tra l'erbe e i zeffiri* (S, bc)
STILNOVO SN 8807; N. Anfuso (soprano), E. Baiano (harpsichord) (*R* 1991)
AGORA AG 147; R. Invernizzi (soprano), Conserto Vago (*R* 1997)
MONDO MUSICA MM 90011; C. Gasdia (soprano), Barocco Veneziano, C. Ferrarini (*R* 1997)
TACTUS TC 67208; E. Cecchi Fedi (soprano), Modo Antiquo, F. M. Sardelli (*R* 1997)

RV 670 *Alla caccia dell'alme e de' cori* (A, bc)
ETCETERA KTC 1069; D. L. Ragin (counter-tenor), V. de Hoog (cello), C. Farr (harpsichord) (*R* 1989)
STILNOVO SN 8807; N. Anfuso (soprano), E. Baiano (harpsichord) (*R* 1991)
AGORA AF 147.1; C. Calvi (contralto), Conserto Vago (*R* 1997)
BRILLIANT CLASSIC 99562/39; S. Buwalda (counter-tenor), Netherlands Bach Collegium, P. J. Leusink (*R* 2000)
OPUS 111 OP 30358; L. Polverelli (mezzo-soprano), L'Astrée (*R* 2000)
CAMERATA 602; K. Kashira (contralto), S. Sakurai (viola da gamba), Y. Ban (harpsichord) (*R* 2003)
CAPRICCIO 67042; M. E. Cencic (counter-tenor), Ornamente 99, K. E. Ose (*R* 2003)
VIRGIN CLASSICS 5 45721 2; P. Jaroussky (counter-tenor), Ensemble Artaserse (*R* 2004)
DOREMI DDR71148; G. Casiraghi (mezzo-soprano), Strings Ensemble Archimede (*R* 2005)

RV 671 *Care selve, amici prati* (A, bc)
ETCETERA KTC 1069; D. L. Ragin (counter-tenor), V. de Hoog (cello), C. Farr (harpsichord) (*R* 1989)
STILNOVO SN 8807; N. Anfuso (soprano), E. Baiano (harpsichord) (*R* 1991)
AGORA AF 147.1; C. Calvi (contralto), Conserto Vago (*R* 1997)
BRILLANT CLASSICS 99562/40; S. Buwalda (counter-tenor), Netherlands Bach Collegium, P. J. Leusink (*R* 2000)
OPUS 111/CD OP 30358; L. Polverelli (mezzo-soprano), L'Astrée (*R* 2000)

CAPRICCIO 67042; M. E. Cencic (counter-tenor), Ornamente 99, K. E. Ose (*R* 2003)

VIRGIN CLASSICS 5 45721 2; P. Jaroussky (counter-tenor), Ensemble Artaserse (*R* 2004)

RV 672 *Filli, di gioia vuoi farmi morir* (A, bc) – doubtful

CBS D 37.231 (LP); (1st aria) F. von Stade (mezzo-soprano), M. Katz (piano) (*R* 1980)

RV 673 *Ingrata Lidia, ha vinto il tuo rigor* (A, bc) – doubtful

ENSAYO ENY-CD-9708 (LP); (extract) C. Bergonzi (tenor), F. Lavilla (piano) (*R* 1973)

RV 674 *Perfidissimo cor! Iniquo fato!* (A, bc)

ARCHIV 2533.385 (LP); R. Jacobs (counter-tenor), Complesso Barocco, A. Curtis (*R* 1978)

ADDA 58.1053; G. Lesne (counter-tenor), Il Seminario Musicale (*R* 1985)

ETCETERA KTC 1069; D. L. Ragin (counter-tenor), V. de Hoog (cello), C. Farr (harpsichord) (*R* 1989)

NUOVA ERA 6859; A. Ruffini (soprano), C. Calvi (contralto), Ensemble Concerto, R. Gini (*R* 1989)

AGORA AF 147.1; C. Calvi (contralto), Conserto Vago (*R* 1997)

BRILLANT CLASSICS/CD 99562/40; S. Buwalda (counter-tenor), Netherlands Bach Collegium, P. J. Leusink (*R* 2000)

ASV Gaudeamus GAU 339; C. Humphries (counter-tenor), The Band of Instruments (*R* 2002)

VIRGIN CLASSICS 5 45721 2; P. Jaroussky (counter-tenor), Ensemble Artaserse (*R* 2004)

RV 675 *Piango, gemo, sospiro e peno* (A, bc) – spurious

CYCNUS (LP) / NONESUCH 71.088; L. Malaguti (bass), Società cameristica di Lugano, E. Loehrer (*R* 1963)

DISKY 70666 (LP); (1st aria, transcribed) T. Gobbi (baritone), D. Simpson (cello), R. Jesson (harpsichord) (*R* 1963)

DECCA SXL S629 (LP); (1st aria, transcribed D. Gamley) R. Tebaldi (soprano), New Philharmonia Orchestra, R. Bonynge (*R* 1973)

DEUTSCHE GRAMOPHON 2531 192 (LP); (1st aria, transcribed) T. Berganza (mezzo-soprano), R. Requejo (piano) (*R* 1979)

FREQUENZ VENETIA 1 DVE (LP); G. Banditelli (mezzo-soprano), Accademia Strumentale Italiana, H. L. Hirsch (*R* 1980)

ARION ARN 68046 (LP); J. Bowman (counter-tenor), J. Bernfeld (viola di gamba), S. Sempe (harpsichord) (*R* 1981)

SPIRELLA 2111 XD (LP); F. Hahne (soprano), F. Sander (organo) (*R* 1981)

NUOVA ERA 6859; A. Ruffini (soprano), C. Calvi (contralto), Ensemble Concerto, R. Gini (*R* 1989)

CLAVES 9016; (1st aria, transcribed) T. Berganza (mezzo-soprano), English Chamber Orchestra, M. Viotti (*R* 1990)

RIVE 65010; (1st aria, transcribed) P. Lorengar (mezzo-soprano), M. Zanetti (piano) (*R* 1992)
NIMBUS NI 5395; (1st aria, transcribed) S. Gehrman (= Numa Labinsky) (counter-tenor), A. Farmer (piano) (*R* 1995)
ASTREE/CD E 8 634; J.-L. Charvet (counter-tenor), Les Passions de l'Âme (*R* 1996)
AGORA /CD AF 147.1; C. Calvi (contralto), Conserto Vago (*R* 1997)

RV 676 *Pianti, sospiri e dimandar mercede* (A, bc)
ETCETERA KTC 1069; D. L. Ragin (counter-tenor), V. de Hoog (cello), C. Farr (harpsichord) (*R* 1989)
AGORA AF 147.1; C. Calvi (contralto), Conserto Vago (*R* 1997)
OPUS 111 OP 30395; S. Mingardo (contralto), Concerto Italiano, R. Alessandrini (*R* 2002)
VIRGIN CLASSICS 5 45721 2; P. Jaroussky (counter-tenor), Ensemble Artaserse (*R* 2004)

RV 677 *Qual per ignoto calle* (A, bc)
ARCHIV 2533.385 (LP); R. Jacobs (counter-tenor), Complesso Barocco, A. Curtis (*R* 1978)
ADDA 58.1053; G. Lesne (counter-tenor), Il Seminario Musicale (*R* 1985)
ETCETERA KTC 1069; D. L. Ragin (counter-tenor), V. de Hoog (cello), C. Farr (harpsichord) (*R* 1989)
AGORA AF 147.1; C. Calvi (contralto), Conserto Vago (*R* 1997)
ASV Gaudeamus GAU 211; M. White (counter-tenor), The Four Nations Ensemble (*R* 1998)
ASV Gaudeamus GAU 339; C. Humphries (counter-tenor), The Band of Instruments (*R* 2002)
CAMERATA 602; K. Kashira (contralto), S. Sakurai (viola da gamba), Y. Ban (harpsichord) (*R* 2003)
VIRGIN CLASSICS 5 45721 2; P. Jaroussky (counter-tenor), Ensemble Artaserse (*R* 2004)

RV 678 *All'ombra di sospetto* (S, fl, bc)
FREQUENZ VENEZIA 21012; T. d'Althann (soprano), Accademia Monteverdi di Venezia, H. L. Hirsch (*R* 1988)
TUDOR 735; Y. Hashimoto (soprano), K. Schickhaus (salterio) (*R* 1988)
L'OISEAU LYRE 433 198 2; C. Bott (soprano), New London Consort, P. Pickett (*R* 1989)
DORIAN DOR 30147; J. Baird (soprano), Philomel Baroque Orchestra (*R* 1991)
TACTUS TC 672204; E. Cecchi Fedi (soprano), Modo Antiquo, F. M. Sardelli (*R* 1994)
CEDILH RECORDS CDR 90000 025; P. Michaels Bedi (soprano), Chicago Baroque Ensemble (*R* 1995)
AGORA AG 147; R. Invernizzi (soprano), Conserto Vago (*R* 1997)

MONDO MUSICA MM 90031; C. Gasdia (soprano), Barocco Veneziano, C. Ferrarini (*R* 1997)
HELICON RECORDS HE 1019; R. Wong (sopranista), L. Miller (flute), P. Hale (cello), L. Burman-Hall (harpsichord) (*R* 1998)
SYRIUS SYR 14350; E. Crommen (soprano), Ensemble Baroque Le Rondeau, J.-P. Boulet (*R* 1998)
TACTUS TC 672210; N. Kennedy (soprano), Modo Antiquo, F. M. Sardelli (*R* 1999)
BRILLIANT CLASSIC 99562/39; M. Strijk (soprano), Netherlands Bach Collegium, P. J. Leusink (*R* 2000)
ASV Gaudeamus GAU 339; M. Nelson (soprano), The Band of Instruments (*R* 2002)

RV 679 *Che giova il sospirar, povero core* (S, str, bc)
MONDO MUSICA MM 90031; C. Gasdia (soprano), Barocco Veneziano, C. Ferrarini (*R* 1997)
TACTUS TC 672210; N. Kennedy (soprano), Modo Antiquo, F. M. Sardelli (*R* 1999)
BRILLANT CLASSICS/CD 99562/40; M. Strijk (soprano), Netherlands Bach Collegium, P. J. Leusink (*R* 2000)

RV 680 *Lungi dal vago volto* (S, vn, bc)
CBS 74.094 (LP); B. Hendricks (soprano), La Grande Écurie et la Chambre du Roy, J.-C. Malgoire (*R* 1979)
L'OISEAU LYRE 433 198 2; C. Bott (soprano), New London Consort, P. Pickett (*R* 1989)
NUOVA ERA 6859; A. Ruffini (soprano), Ensemble Concerto, R. Gini (*R* 1989)
CEDILH RECORDS CDR 90000 025; P. Michaels Bedi (soprano), Chicago Baroque Ensemble (*R* 1995)
MONDO MUSICA MM 90031; C. Gasdia (soprano), Barocco Veneziano, C. Ferrarini (*R* 1997)
HELICON RCORDS HE 1019; R. Wong (sopranista), E. Blumenstock (violino), P. Hale (cello), L. Burman-Hall (harpsichord) (*R* 1998)
TACTUS TC 672210; N. Kennedy (soprano), Modo Antiquo, F. M. Sardelli (*R* 1999)
OPUS 111 OP 30381; L. Polverelli (mezzo-soprano), L'Astrée (*R* 2000)
ASV Gaudeamus GAU 339; M. Nelson (soprano), The Band of Instruments (*R* 2002)
SIGNUM SIG 033; L. Perillo (soprano), Cordaria, W. Reiter (*R* 2002)
AVIE CKD 281; M. Lawson (soprano), La Serenissima, A. Chandler (*R* 2006)

RV 681 *Perché son molli* (S, str, bc)
MONDO MUSICA MM 90031; C. Gasdia (soprano), Barocco Veneziano, C. Ferrarini (*R* 1997)

TACTUS TC 672210; N. Kennedy (soprano), Modo Antiquo, F. M. Sardelli (*R* 1999)
BRILLANT CLASSICS/CD 99562/40; M. Strijk (soprano), Netherlands Bach Collegium, P. J. Leusink (*R* 2000)

RV 682 *Vengo a voi, luci adorate* (S, str, bc)
L'OISEAU LYRE 433 198 2; C. Bott (soprano), New London Consort, P. Pickett (*R* 1989)
MONDO MUSICA MM 90031; C. Gasdia (soprano), Barocco Veneziano, C. Ferrarini (*R* 1997)
TACTUS TC 672210; N. Kennedy (soprano), Modo Antiquo, F. M. Sardelli (*R* 1999)
OPUS 111 OP 30381; L. Polverelli (mezzo-soprano), L'Astrée (*R* 2000)

RV 683 *Amor, hai vinto, hai vinto: ecco il mio seno* (A, str, bc)
ARCHIV 2533.385 (LP); R. Jacobs (counter-tenor), Complesso Barocco, A. Curtis (*R* 1978)
ADDA 58.1053 (LP); G. Lesne (counter-tenor), Il Seminario Musicale (*R* 1985)
NUOVA ERA 6877.; C. Calvi (contralto), Ensemble Concerto, R. Gini (*R* 1989)
OPUS 111 OPS 30 181 ; S. Mingardo (mezzo-soprano), Concerto Italiano, R. Alessandrini (*R* 1996)
DYNAMIC CDS 222 ; M. Lazzara (counter-tenor), Orchestra da Camera di Genova, A. Plotino (*R* 1998)
BRILLANT CLASSICS/CD 99562/38; S. Buwalda (counter-tenor), Netherlands Bach Collegium, P. J. Leusink (*R* 2000)
OPUS 111 OP 30381; L. Polverelli (mezzo-soprano), L'Astrée (*R* 2000)
ARION ARN 68635; R. Expert (counter-tenor), Ensemble Ariana (*R* 2001)
CAPRICCIO 67042; M. E. Cencic (counter-tenor), Ornamente 99, K. E. Ose (*R* 2003)

RV 684 *Cessate, omai cessate* (A, str, bc)
RCA (Radio e Televisione Italiana) A 12 R – 0098 (LP); (trascrizione) L. Ribacchi (mezzo-soprano), Società Corelli (*R* 1953)
CYCNUS (LP) / NONESUCH 71.088; L. Malaguti (bass), Società cameristica di Lugano, E. Loehrer (*R* 1963)
ANGELICUM (LP) / ARS NOVA VST 61.124; M. Rochow-Costa (contralto), Orchestra dell'Angelicum, B. Martinotti (*R* 1965)
ARCHIV PRODUKTION 2533.385 (LP); R. Jacobs (counter-tenor), Complesso Barocco, A. Curtis (*R* 1978)
CBS 74.094 (LP); P. Esswood (counter-tenor), La Grande Écurie et la Chambre du Roy, J.-C. Malgoire (*R* 1979)
HUNGAROTON SXLP 12087 (LP); C. Takács (contralto), Ferenc Liszt Chamber Orchestra, F. Szekeres (*R* 1980)
ARION ARN 238.032 (LP); N. Anfuso (soprano), Insieme da Camera Fiorentino, E. Sciarra (*R* 1981)

ADDA 58.1053 (LP); G. Lesne (counter-tenor), Il Seminario Musicale (*R* 1985)

NUOVA ERA 6877; C. Calvi (contralto), Ensemble Concerto, R. Gini (*R* 1989)

PIERRE VERANY PV 73043; (1. Aria) J. Nirouët (counter-tenor), Orchestre de Chambre Paul Kuentz, P. Kuentz (*R* 1994)

HARMONIA MUNDI HMC 901571; A. Scholl (counter-tenor), Ensemble 415, C. Banchini (*R* 1995)

VIRGIN Veritas 5452 632.; D. L. Ragin (counter-tenor), Teatro Lirico, S. Stubbs (*R* 1995)

OPUS 111 OPS 30 181; S. Mingardo (mezzo-soprano), Concerto Italiano, R. Alessandrini (*R* 1996)

ARCHIV PRODUKTION 457 617 2; A. S. von Otter (contralto), Musica Antiqua Köln, R. Goebel (*R* 1997)

DYNAMIC CDS 222; M. Lazzara (counter-tenor), Orchestra da Camera di Genova, A. Plotino (*R* 1998)

ARION ARN 68635; R. Expert (counter-tenor), Ensemble Ariana (*R* 2001)

CAPRICCIO 67042; M. E. Cencic (counter-tenor), Ornamente 99, K. E. Ose (*R* 2003)

RV 684a *Cessate, omai cessate* (A, str, bc)

ARION ARN 238.032 (LP); (2nd movement, Andante molto) N. Anfuso (soprano), Insieme da Camera Fiorentino, E. Sciarra (*R* 1981)

RV 685 *O mie porpore più belle* (A, str, bc)

ARCHIV 2533.385 (LP); R. Jacobs (counter-tenor), Complesso Barocco, A. Curtis (*R* 1978)

DYNAMIC CDS 222 ; M. Lazzara (counter-tenor), Orchestra da Camera di Genova, A. Plotino (*R* 1998)

CAPRICCIO 67042; M. E. Cencic (counter-tenor), Ornamente 99, K. E. Ose (*R* 2003)

RV 686 *Qual in pioggia dorata i dolci rai (*A, 2 horns, str, bc)

PERIOD RENAISSANCE RN X58 (LP); G. Borelli (contralto), Orchestra della Scuola Veneziana, A. Ephrikian (*R* 1952)

DYNAMIC CDS 222 ; M. Lazzara (counter-tenor), Orchestra da Camera di Genova, A. Plotino (*R* 1998)

RV 796 *Usignoletto bello* (S, bc)

AGORA AG 147 ; R. Invernizzi (soprano), Conserto Vago (*R* 1997)

MONDO MUSICA MM 90011; C. Gasdia (soprano), Barocco Veneziano, C. Ferrarini (*R* 1997)

TACTUS TC 672209; N. Kennedy (soprano), Modo Antiquo, F. M. Sardelli (*R* 1998)

RV 799 *Tremori al braccio e lagrime sul ciglio* (S, bc)

TACTUS TC 672210; N. Kennedy (soprano), Modo Antiquo, F. M. Sardelli (*R* 1999)

AVIE CKD 281; M. Lawson (soprano), La Serenissima, A. Chandler (*R* 2006)

Domenico Zipoli (1688–1726)

Dell'offese a vendicarmi (S, str, bc)
　　K617 K 617 037; A. Fernandez (soprano), Ensemble Elyma, G. Garrido (*R* 1993)
　　TACTUS TC 682603; E. Cecchi Fedi (soprano), B. Hoffmann (cello), A. Fedi (harpsichord) (*R* 2003)
Mia bella Irene (S/B, str, bc)
　　K617 K 617 037; V. Torres (baritone), Ensemble Elyma, G. Garrido (*R* 1993)
　　TACTUS TC 682603; E. Cecchi Fedi (soprano), B. Hoffmann, (cello) A. Fedi (harpsichord) (*R* 2003)
O Daliso (S, str, bc)
　　TACTUS TC 682603; E. Cecchi Fedi (soprano), B. Hoffmann (cello), A. Fedi (harpsichord) (*R* 2003)

Bibliography

This Bibliography lists comprehensively the books, articles, essays and dissertations cited in the course of the present volume, together with selected modern editions of music, which appear under the names of their respective editors.

Alexandre, Ivan A., *Guide de la musique ancienne et baroque*. Paris: Laffont, 1993.

——, 'Le printemps des Anciens'. In Ivan A. Alexandre (ed.), *Guide de la musique ancienne et baroque*, Paris: Laffont, 1993, pp. v–xlviii.

Allen, David, 'The "Lost" Stradella Manuscripts and their Relationship to the Estense Holdings of his Music in Modena'. In Carolyn Gianturco (ed.), *Alessandro Stradella e Modena: Atti del Convegno internazionale di studi (Modena, 15–17 dicembre 1983)*, Modena: Teatro Comunale di Modena, 1985, pp. 125–35.

Amato, Mauro, 'Le antologie di arie e di arie e cantate tardo-seicentesche alla Biblioteca del Conservatorio "S. Pietro a Majella" di Napoli'. Doctoral dissertation, Cremona, Scuola di Paleografia Musicale, 1998, 2 vols.

Anon., 'Hullah's New Music Hall', *The Musical Times and Singing Class Circular*, vol. 2 no. 39 (1 August 1847): 113–14.

Anon., 'St Martin's Hall', *The Musical Times and Singing Class Circular*, vol. 2 no. 39 (1 August 1847): 292–3.

Anon., 'Salvator Rosa as a Musician', *The Harmonicon*, 2 (1824): 62–4 and 83–7.

Anon., *Le pompe funebri celebrate da' signori Accademici infecondi di Roma per la morte dell'illustrissima Signora Elena Lucrezia Cornara Piscopia*. Padua, 1686.

Anthony, James R., *French Baroque Music from Beaujoyeulx to Rameau*, rev. 3rd edn. Portland: Amadeus Press, 1997.

Antolini, Bianca Maria, Gialdroni, Teresa M. and Pugliese, Annunziato (eds), *'Et facciam dolçi canti'. Studi in onore di Agostino Ziino in occasione del suo 65° compleanno.* Lucca: Libraria Musicale Italiana, 2003.

Aristotle, *Poetics*, ed. and trans. Stephen Halliwell. Chapel Hill: University of North Carolina Press, 1987. Later edn, Cambridge, MA: Harvard University Press, 1999.

Artiano, Fulvio and Cantillo, Clementina (eds), *Forme del linguaggio musicale tra contemporaneità e tradizione*. Potenza: Conservatorio di Musica 'Gesualdo da Venosa', 2009.

Avison, Charles, *An Essay on Musical Expression*. London: Davis, 1752; repr. from 1753 edn, New York: Broude, 1967.

Barthélemy, Maurice, *André Campra (1660–1744): étude biographique et musicologique*. [Arles]: Actes Sud, 1995.

——, 'Les cantates de Jean-Baptiste Stuck', *Recherches sur la musique française classique*, 2 (1961–62): 125–37.

Bartlett, Clifford (ed.), *Giovanni Legrenzi, Idee armoniche estese per due e tre voci, Venice, 1678*, facsimile edition. London: n.d.

Basso, Alberto, 'Le nuove frontiere del barocco musicale: i repertori ricuperati ai confini dell'Europa e nelle Americhe'. In Francesco Fanna and Michael Talbot (eds), *Cinquant'anni di produzioni e consumi della musica dell'età di Vivaldi, 1947–1997*, Florence: Olschki, 1998, pp. 401–408.

—— (ed.), *Storia dell'opera*, 6 vols. Turin: UTET, 1977.

Becherini, Bianca, 'Dal "barocco" all'oratorio di Giovanni Bononcini'. In Adelmo Damerini and Gino Roncaglia (eds), *Musicisti della scuola emiliana*, Siena: Ticci, 1956, pp. 97–110.

Bembo, Pietro, *Prose di M. Pietro Bembo nelle quali si ragiona della volgar lingua*. Venice: Tacuino, 1525.

Bennett, Lawrence, 'A Little-known Collection of Early-Eighteenth-Century Vocal Music at Schloss Elisabethenburg, Meiningen', *Fontes artis musicae*, 48 (2001): 250–302.

——, 'The Italian Cantata in Vienna, 1700–1711: An Overview of Stylistic Traits'. In Brian W. Pritchard (ed.), *Antonio Caldara: Essays on His Life and Times*, Aldershot: Ashgate, 1987, pp. 183–211.

——, 'The Italian Cantata in Vienna, c. 1700–c. 1711', PhD dissertation, New York University, 1980; published Ann Arbor: UMI Research Press, 1980.

Benoit, Marcelle, *Musiques de cour: Chapelle, Chambre, Écurie*. Paris: Picard, 1971.

Bianconi, Lorenzo and Bossa, Renato (eds), *Musica e cultura a Napoli dal XV al XIX secolo*. Florence: Olschki, 1983.

Bianconi, Lorenzo and Morelli, Giovanni (eds), *Antonio Vivaldi. Teatro musicale, cultura e società*. Florence: Olschki, 1982.

Bianconi, Lorenzo and Walker, Thomas, 'Production, Consumption and Political Function of Seventeenth-Century Italian Opera', *Early Music History*, 4 (1984): 209–296.

Bini, Annalisa, *Il fondo Mario nella biblioteca musicale di Santa Cecilia di Roma: Catalogo dei manoscritti*. Rome: Torre d'Orfeo, 1995.

Bizzarini, Marco, *Benedetto Marcello*. Palermo: L'Epos, 2006.

——, *Benedetto Marcello. Le cantate profane: i testi poetici*. Venice: Fondazione Levi, 2003.

Blume, Friedrich (ed.), *Die Musik in Geschichte und Gegenwart*, [1st edn], 14 vols. Kassel: Bärenreiter, 1948–68.

Boileau, Nicolas (trans.). *Le traité du sublime ou du merveilleux dans le discours*. Paris: Thierry, 1674.

Bonta, Stephen, 'The Church Sonatas of Giovanni Legrenzi'. Unpublished PhD dissertation, Harvard University, 1964.

Boyd, Malcolm, 'Cantata: §1, 6. Alessandro Scarlatti'. In Stanley Sadie and John Tyrrell (eds), *The New Grove Dictionary of Music and Musicians*, 2nd edn, London: Macmillan, 2001, vol. 3, pp. 698–9.

——, 'The Cantata since 1800'. In Stanley Sadie and John Tyrrell (eds), *The New Grove Dictionary of Music and Musicians*, 2nd edn, London: Macmillan, 2001, vol. 5, pp. 40–41.

—— (ed.), *Cantatas by Alessandro Scarlatti (1660–1725)*. New York: Garland, 1986.

——, 'Form and Style in Scarlatti's Chamber Cantatas', *Music Review*, 25 (1964): 17–26.

Braun, Werner, 'Arten des Komponistenporträts'. In Ludwig Finscher and Christoph-Hellmut Mahling (eds), *Festschrift für Walter Wiora zum 30. Dezember 1966*, Kassel etc.: Bärenreiter, 1967, pp. 86–94.

Brenet, Michel, *Les concerts en France sous l'ancien régime*. Paris: Fischbacher, 1900.

Brossard, Sébastien de, 'Dissertation sur cette espèce de concert qu'on nomme cantate', F-Pn, ms. fr. n.a. 5269.

——, *Dictionaire de musique*. Paris, 1703; facsimile repr. Amsterdam: Antiqua, 1964.

Brossard, Yolande de (ed.), *La collection Sébastien de Brossard, 1655–1730: Catalogue (Département de la Musique, Rés. Vm 8 20)*. Paris: Bibliothèque Nationale de France, 1994.

Brossard, Yolande de and Kocevar, Érik, 'États de la France (1644–1789). La Musique: les institutions et les hommes', *Recherches sur la musique française classique*, 30 (1999–2000): 323–35.

Brown, Howard Mayer (ed.), *Giovanni Bononcini, Il trionfo di Camilla, regina de' Volsci*. New York and London: Garland, 1978.

——, (ed.), *Giovanni Legrenzi/Matteo Noris, Totila*. New York and London: Garland, 1978.

Brown, Jennifer Williams, 'Con nuove arie aggiunte. Aria Borrowing in the Venetian Opera Repertory, 1672–1685'. PhD dissertation, Cornell University, 1992.

Bucciarelli, Melania and Joncus, Berta (eds), *Music as Social and Cultural Practice: Essays in Honour of Reinhard Strohm*. Woodbridge: Boydell Press, 2007.

Buelow, George J., *A History of Baroque Music*. Bloomington: Indiana University Press, 2004.

—— (ed.), *Man & Music: The Late Baroque Era from the 1680s to 1740*. London: Macmillan, 1993.

Burke, Edmund, *A Philosophical Enquiry into the Origins of our Ideas of the Sublime and Beautiful*. London: 1757.

Burney, Charles, *A General History of Music, from the Earliest Ages to the Present Period* (1789), 4 vols. London: Becket and others, 1776–89; also in 2 vols, ed. Frank Mercer. London: Foulis, 1935; facsimile repr. New York: Dover, 1957.

——, *The Present State of Music in France and Italy*. London: Becket, 1771.
Burrows, David and Bonta, Stephen (eds), *Cantatas by Antonio Cesti (1623–1669) and Giovanni Legrenzi (1626–1690)*. New York: Garland, 1986.
Cabrini, Michele, 'Expressive Polarity: The Aesthetics of *tempête* and *sommeil* in the French Baroque Cantata'. PhD dissertation, Princeton University, 2005.
Caldwell, John, Olleson, Edward and Wollenberg, Susan (eds), *The Well Enchanting Skill: Music, Poetry, and Drama in the Culture of the Renaissance: Essays in Honour of F. W. Sternfeld*. Oxford: Clarendon Press, 1990.
Candiani, Rosy, 'Originalità e serialità nella scrittura del Metastasio: l'esempio delle cantate'. In Marta Columbro and Paologiovanni Maione (eds), *Pietro Metastasio: il testo e il contesto*, Naples: Altrastampa, [2000], pp. 111–24.
Caraci, Maria, 'Le cantate romane di Alessandro Scarlatti nel fondo Noseda'. In Nino Pirrotta and Agostino Ziino (eds), *Händel e gli Scarlatti a Roma. Atti del Convegno Internazionale di Studi, Roma 1985*, Florence: Olschki, 1987, pp. 93–112.
Carboni, Fabio, Gialdroni, Teresa M. and Ziino, Agostino, 'Cantate ed arie romane del tardo Seicento nel Fondo Caetani della Biblioteca Corsiniana: Repertorio, forme e strutture', *Studi musicali*, 18 (1989): 49–192.
Carreras, Juan José, 'Tra la Sicilia e la Penisola iberica: il barone d'Astorga alla corte di Filippo V di Spagna', *Avidi LUMI Research Press*, 5 (14 February 2002): 59–67.
——, 'Amores difíciles: la ópera de corte en la España del siglo XVIII'. In Emilio Casares Rodicio and Álvaro Torrente (eds), *La ópera en España e Hispanoamérica. Actas del Congreso Internacional (Madrid, 29.XI/3.XII de 1999)*, Madrid: ICCMU, 2001, pp. 205–230.
——, 'Hijos de Pedrell. La historiografía musical española y sus orígenes nacionalistas (1780–1980)', *Il Saggiatore Musicale*, 8 (2001): 123–73.
Casares Rodicio, Emilio and Torrente, Álvaro (eds), *La ópera en España e Hispanoamérica. Actas del Congreso Internacional (Madrid, 29.XI/3.XII de 1999)*. Madrid: ICCMU, 2001.
Cessac, Catherine, 'La duchesse du Maine et la musique'. In Catherine Cessac, Manuel Couvreur and Fabrice Prévat (eds), *La duchesse du Maine (1676–1753). Une mécène à la croisée des arts et des siècles*, Brussels: Université de Bruxelles, 2003, pp. 97–107.
——, *Nicolas Clérambault*. Paris: Fayard, 1998.
——, *Élisabeth Jacquet de La Guerre: une femme compositeur sous le règne de Louis XIV*. [Arles]: Actes Sud, 1995.
Cessac, Catherine, Couvreur, Manuel and Prévat, Fabrice (eds), *La duchesse du Maine (1676–1753). Une mécène à la croisée des arts et des siècles*. Brussels: Université de Bruxelles, 2003.
Chiarelli, Alessandra, *I codici di musica della Raccolta Estense: Ricostruzione dall'inventario settecentesco*. Florence: Olschki, 1987.
Chirico, Teresa, 'L'inedita serenata alla regina Maria Casimira di Polonia: Pietro Ottoboni committente di cantate e serenate (1689–1708)'. In Nicolò Maccavino

(ed.), *La serenata tra Seicento e Settecento*, Reggio Calabria: Laruffa, 2007, pp. 397–449.

——, 'Il fondo dei Campello di Spoleto: autografi Ottoboniani e altri testi per musica', *Analecta musicologica*, 37 (Studien zur italienischen Musikgeschichte, 16), ed. Markus Engelhardt (Laaber, 2005), pp. 85–178.

Churchill, William Algernon, *Watermarks in Paper in Holland, England, France, etc. In the XVII and XVIII Centuries and their Interconnection*. Amsterdam: Menno Herzberger, 1935.

Colas, Damien, and Di Profio, Alessandro (eds), *D'une scène à l'autre l'opéra italien en Europe*, vol. 1: *Les pérégrinations d'un genre*. Paris: Mardaga Editions, 2009.

Collins, Michael, 'L'orchestra nelle opere di Vivaldi'. In Antonio Fanna and Giovanni Morelli (eds), *Nuovi studi vivaldiani. Edizione e cronología critica delle opere*, Florence: Olschki, 1988, pp. 285–312.

Columbro, Marta and Maione, Paologiovanni (eds), *Pietro Metastasio: il testo e il contesto*. Naples: Altrastampa, [2000].

Colzani, Alberto, Dubowy, Norbert, Luppi, Andrea and Padoan, Maurizio (eds), *Il teatro musicale italiano nel Sacro Romano Impero nei secoli XVII e XVIII. Atti del VII Convegno internazionale sulla musica italiana nei secoli XVII–XVIII, Loveno di Menaggio (Como), 15–17 luglio 1997*. Como: AMIS, 1999.

Colzani, Alberto, Dubowy, Norbert, Luppi, Andrea and Padoan, Maurizio (eds), *Relazioni musicali tra Italia e Germania nell'età barocca. Atti del VI convegno internazionale sulla musica italiana nei secoli XVII–XVIII, Loveno di Menaggio (Como), 11–13 luglio 1995*. Como: AMIS, 1997.

Colzani, Alberto, Luppi, Andrea and Padoan, Maurizio (eds), *Seicento inesplorato. L'evento musicale tra prassi e stile: un modello di interdipendenza. Atti del III Convegno internazionale sulla musica in area lombardo-padana del secolo XVII*. Como: AMIS, 1993.

Crescimbeni, Giovan Mario, *Comentarj intorno all'istoria della volgar poesia*, 5 vols. Rome: Antonio de' Rossi, 1702–20; repr. ed. T. J. Mathias, London: Becket, 1803.

——, *Dell'istoria della volgar poesia*, 3rd edn, 6 vols. Venice: Basegio, 1730–31.

—— (ed.), *Notizie istoriche degli Arcadi morti*, 3 vols. Rome: Antonio de' Rossi, 1720–21.

——, *Le vite degli Arcadi illustri*, 4 vols. Rome, Antonio de' Rossi, 1708–27.

——, *L'Arcadia*. Rome: Antonio de' Rossi, 1708.

Cyr, Mary (ed.), *Elisabeth-Claude Jacquet de La Guerre: Three Sacred Cantatas*. New York: Broude, 2005.

——, 'Performing Rameau's Cantatas', *Early Music*, 11 (1983): 480–89.

Damerini, Adelmo and Roncaglia, Gino (eds), *Musicisti della scuola emiliana*. Siena: Ticci, 1956.

Damuth, Laura, 'Alessandro Scarlatti's Cantatas for Soprano and Continuo'. PhD dissertation, Columbia University, 1993.

Davison, Archibald T. and Apel, Willi, *Historical Anthology of Music*, II: *Baroque, Rococo and Pre-Classical Music*. Cambridge, MA: Harvard University Press, 1950.

Daw, Brian, 'Alessandro Scarlatti's Cantatas for Solo Soprano and Continuo, 1708–1717'. PhD dissertation, University of Southern California, 1984.

Dean, Winton, 'Bordoni […], Faustina'. In Stanley Sadie and John Tyrell (eds), *The New Grove Dictionary of Music and Musicians*, 2nd edn, London: Macmillan, 2001, vol. 3, pp. 894–5.

——, *Handel's Dramatic Oratorios and Masques*. London: Oxford University Press, 1959.

Degrada, Francesco, 'L'opera napoletana'. In Alberto Basso (ed.), *Storia dell'opera*, Turin: UTET, 1977, vol. 1, pp. 237–332.

——, '"Scuola napoletana" e "opera napoletana": nascita, sviluppo e prospettive di un concetto storiografico'. In Carlo Marinelli Roscioni (ed.), *Il teatro di S. Carlo: la cronologia 1737–1987*, Naples: Edizioni Scientifiche Italiane, 1987, pp. 9–20.

Della Seta, Fabrizio, 'La musica in Arcadia al tempo di Corelli'. In Sergio Durante and Pierluigi Petrobelli (eds), *Nuovissimi studi corelliani. Atti del terzo congresso internazionale (Fusignano, 4–7 settembre 1980)*, Florence: Olschki, 1982, pp. 123–50.

Dellaborra, Mariateresa and Gianturco, Carolyn, *Alessandro Stradella, 'La forza dell'amor paterno'*, Edizione Nazionale dell'Opera Omnia di Alessandro Stradella, Series II, vol. 2. Pisa: ETS, 2006.

Dent, Edward J., *Alessandro Scarlatti: His Life and Works*. London: Arnold, 1905.

Diderot, Denis and Alembert, Jean le Rond d' (eds), *Encyclopédie, ou Dictionnaire raisonné des sciences, des arts et des métiers Encyclopédie, ou Dictionnaire raisonné des sciences, des arts et des métiers*, 35 vols. Paris, 1751–80.

Dieci, Sara, 'Due "Clori" di Giovanni Bononcini ritrovate', *Rivista italiana di musicologia*, 38 (2002): 249–64.

Dolmetsch, Arnold, *The Interpretation of the Music of the Seventeenth and Eighteenth Centuries Revealed by Contemporary Evidence*. London: Novello, [1915].

Dorival, Jérôme, *La cantate française au XVIIIe siècle*. Paris: Presses Universitaires de France, 1999.

——, 'André Campra et la cantate française'. In Jean Lionnet (ed.), *Le concert des Muses*, Versailles: Centre de Musique Baroque de Versailles, 1997, pp. 319–31.

Dratwicki, Benoît, 'François Colin de Blamont à la cour de Sceaux: le jeu des influences et des rencontres'. In Catherine Cessac, Manuel Couvreur and Fabrice Prévat (eds), *La duchesse du Maine (1676–1753). Une mécène à la croisée des arts et des siècles*, Brussels: Université de Bruxelles, 2003, pp. 109–15.

Dubowy, Norbert, 'Bemerkungen zu einigen Ulisse-Opern'. In Silke Leopold and Joachim Steinheuer (eds), *Claudio Monteverdi und die Folgen*, Kassel: Bärenreiter, 1998, pp. 215–43.

——, 'Ernst August, Giannettini und die Serenata in Venedig (1685/86)', *Analecta musicologica*, 30 (= Studien zur italienischen Musikgeschichte, 15), ed. F. Lippmann (Laaber, 1998), pp. 167–235.

——, 'Pollarolo e Ziani a Verona. Annotazioni in margine a tre partiture ritrovate'. In Alberto Colzani, Andrea Luppi and Maurizio Padoan (eds), *Seicento inesplorato. L'evento musicale tra prassi e stile: un modello di interdipendenza. Atti del III Convegno internazionale sulla musica in area lombardo-padana del secolo XVII.*, Como: AMIS, 1993, pp. 509–535.

——, '"Una nuova foggia di componimenti": sulla formazione dei caratteri del testo della cantata italiana', *I Quaderni della Civica Scuola di Musica*, 19–20 (1990): 9–18.

Dunning, Albert (ed.), *Intorno a Locatelli. Studi in occasione del tricentenario della nascita di Pietro Antonio Locatelli (1695–1764)*. Lucca: Libreria Musicale Italiana, 1995.

Durante, Sergio and Petrobelli, Pierluigi (eds), *Nuovissimi studi corelliani. Atti del terzo congresso internazionale (Fusignano, 4–7 settembre 1980)*. Florence: Olschki, 1982.

Duron, Jean, 'Aspects de la présence italienne dans la musique française de la fin du XVIIe siècle'. In Jean Lionnet (ed.), *Le concert des Muses*, Versailles: Centre de Musique Baroque de Versailles, 1997, pp. 97–115.

Écorcheville, Jules, 'La Schola Cantorum et le style de Bach', *Mercure musical*, April 1907: 399–406.

Emans, Reinmar, 'Giovanni Legrenzis Oper *Eteocle e Polinice* in der Bearbeitung Antonio Gianettinis. Ein Beitrag zur musikästhetischen Entwicklung der Arie'. In Alberto Colzani, Andrea Luppi and Maurizio Padoan (eds), *Seicento inesplorato. L'evento musicale tra prassi e stile: un modello di interdipendenza. Atti del III Convegno internazionale sulla musica in area lombardo-padana del secolo XVII.*, Como: AMIS, 1993, pp. 559–90.

——, *Die einstimmigen Kantaten, Canzonetten und Serenaden Giovanni Legrenzis*. Bonn: Rheinische Friedrich-Wilhelms-Universität, 1984.

Eximeno, Antonio, *Dell'origine e delle regole della musica, colla storia del suo progresso, decadenza e rinnovazione*. Rome, Barbiellini, 1774; facsimile repr. Hildesheim–Zürich–New York: Olms, 1983.

Fabbri, Paolo, 'Riflessioni teoriche sul teatro per musica nel Seicento: "La poetica toscana all'uso" di Giuseppe Gaetano Salvadori'. In Gianfranco Folena, Maria Teresa Muraro and Giovanni Morelli (eds), *Opera & Libretto. I*, Florence: Olschki, 1990, pp. 1–32.

Fabris, Dinko, '"Adesso se no conosce il merito, e vivente si lacerava": la fama europea di Leonardo Vinci', in Damien Colas and Alessandro Di Profio (eds), *D'une scène à l'autre l'opéra italien en Europe*, vol. 1: *Les pérégrinations d'un genre*. Paris: Mardaga Editions, 2009, pp. 85–117.

——, *Music in Seventeenth-Century Naples: Francesco Provenzale (1624–1704)*. Aldershot: Ashgate, 2007.

Fabris, Dinko and Maione, Paologiovanni (eds), *Domenico Scarlatti: musica e storia*. Naples: Turchini, 2009.

Fabris, Dinko and Veneziano, Giulia, 'Le cantate giovanili di Domenico Scarlatti'. In Dinko Fabris and Paologiovanni Maione (eds), *Domenico Scarlatti: musica e storia*. Naples: Turchini, 2009, forthcoming.

Fabris, Dinko and Veneziano, Giulia, 'Le cantate da camera di Domenico Scarlatti'. In Teresa M. Gialdroni (ed.), *La cantata da camera intorno agli anni 'italiani' di Händel: problemi e prospettive de ricerca. Atti del convegno internazionale di studi, Roma, 12–14 ottobre 2007*. Rome: Accademia Nazionale di S. Cecilia, 2009 pp. 169–95.

Fabris, Dinko and Veneziano, Giulia, 'Mito e realtà della cosiddetta "scuola napoletana"'. In Fulvio Artiano and Clementina Cantillo (eds), *Forme del linguaggio musicale tra contemporaneità e tradizione*. Potenza: Conservatorio di Musica 'Gesualdo da Venosa', 2009, pp. 33–48.

Fader, Don, 'Philippe II d'Orléans's "chanteurs italiens", the Italian cantata and the *goûts-réunis* under Louis XIV', *Early Music*, 35 (2007): 237–49.

——, 'Musical Thought and Patronage of the Italian Style at the Court of Philippe II, duc d'Orléans (1674–1723)'. PhD dissertation, Stanford University, 2000.

Fanna, Antonio and Morelli, Giovanni (eds), *Nuovi studi vivaldiani. Edizione e cronología critica delle opere*. Florence: Olschki, 1988.

Fanna, Francesco and Talbot, Michael (eds), *Cinquant'anni di produzioni e consumi della musica dell'età di Vivaldi, 1947–1997*. Florence: Olschki, 1998.

Fenlon, Iain and Carter, Tim (eds), *'Con che soavità': Studies in Italian Opera, Song, and Dance, 1500–1740*. Oxford: Clarendon Press, 1995.

Ferand, Ernst T., *Improvisation in Nine Centuries of Western Music* (Anthology of Music, 12). Cologne: Volk, 1956.

Finscher, Ludwig (ed.), *Die Musik in Geschichte und Gegenwart*, 2nd rev. edn, 21 vols. Kassel etc.: Bärenreiter, 1994–2007.

Finscher, Ludwig and Mahling, Christoph-Hellmut (eds), *Festschrift für Walter Wiora zum 30. Dezember 1966*. Kassel etc.: Bärenreiter, 1967.

Folena, Gianfranco, Muraro, Maria Teresa and Morelli, Giovanni (eds), *Opera & Libretto. I*. Florence: Olschki, 1990.

[Fontana, Francesco Luigi and Sacchi, Giovenale], *Vita di Benedetto Marcello patrizio veneto*. Venice: Zatta, 1788.

Foster, Donald (ed.), *Louis-Nicolas Clérambault: Two Cantatas for Soprano and Chamber Ensemble*. Madison: A-R Editions, 1979.

Fourés, Olivier and Talbot, Michael, 'A New Vivaldi Cantata in Vienna', *Informazioni e studi vivaldiani*, 21 (2000): 99–108.

Fragalà Data, Isabella and Colturato, Annarita, *Biblioteca Nazionale Università di Torino, I: Raccolta Mauro Foà, Raccolta Renzo Giordano*. Rome: Torre d'Orfeo, 1987.

Freitas, Roger, *Atto Melani: Complete Cantatas*. Madison: A-R Editions, 2006.

Freund, Cecilia Kathrin van de Kamp, 'A. Scarlatti's Duet Cantatas and Solo Cantatas with Obbligato Instruments'. PhD dissertation, Northwestern University, 1979.

Fux, Johann Joseph, *Gradus ad Parnassum*. Vienna: van Ghelen, 1725; German translation as *Gradus ad Parnassum oder Anführung zur regelmäßigen musikalischen Composition*, Leipzig: Mizler, 1742.

Garden, Greer, 'Réflexions sur les cantates scéniques d'André Campra et sur les cas de *Pomone* de Charles-Hubert Gervais', *XVIIe siècle*, 198 (1998): 29–36.

——, '*Les amours de Vénus* (1712) et le *Second livre de cantates* (1714) de Campra', *Revue de musicologie*, 77 (1991): 96–107.

Gasparini, Francesco, *L'armonico pratico al cembalo*. Venice: Bortoli, 1708; trans. Frank S. Stillings as *The Practical Harmonist at the Harpsichord*, New Haven, CT: Yale School of Music, [1963].

Gasperini, Guido and Gallo, Franca, *Catalogo delle opere musicali teoriche e pratiche di autori vissuti sino ai primi decenni del secolo XIX, esistenti nelle biblioteche e negli archivi pubblici e privati d'Italia. Città di Napoli, Biblioteca del R. Conservatorio di Musica di S. Pietro a Majella*, serie X. Parma: Fresching, 1934.

Gentili, Alberto, 'La raccolta di antiche musiche "Renzo Giordano" alla Biblioteca Nazionale di Torino', *Accademie e biblioteche d'Italia*, 4 (1930–31): 117–25.

——, 'La raccolta di rarità musicali "Mauro Foà" alla Biblioteca Nazionale di Torino', *Accademie e biblioteche d'Italia*, 1 (1927–28): 36–50.

Gentili Verona, Gabriella, 'Le collezioni Foà e Giordano della Biblioteca Nazionale di Torino', *Accademie e biblioteche d'Italia*, 32 (1964): 405–430.

Gerber, Ernst Ludwig, *Neues historisch-biographisches Lexikon der Tonkünstler*, 4 vols [1812–14], ed. Othmar Wessely. Graz: Akademischer Druck- und Verlagsanstalt, 1966.

Gerini, Emanuele, *Memorie storiche di illustri scrittori e di uomini dell'antica e moderna Lunigiana*. Massa: Frediani, 1839.

Gialdroni, Teresa M. (ed.), *La cantata da camera intorno agli anni 'italiani' di Händel: problemi e prospettive di ricerca. Atti del convegno internazionale di studi, Roma, 12–14 ottobre 2007*. Rome: Accademia Nazionale di S. Cecilia, 2009.

——, 'Silvio Stampiglia autore di testi di cantata'. In Gaetano Pitarresi (ed.), *Intorno a Silvio Stampiglia*. Librettisti, Compositori e interpreti nell'età premetastasiana. Atti del Convegno internazionale di Studi (Reggio Calabria, 5–6 ottobre 2007) (forthcoming).

——, 'Leonardo Vinci e la cantata spirituale a Napoli nella prima metà del Settecento'. In Agostino Ziino (ed.), *Musica senza aggettivi: studi per Fedele d'Amico*, Florence: Olschki, 1991, pp. 123–43.

——, 'Bibliografia della cantata da camera italiana (1620–1740 ca.)', *Le fonti musicali in Italia. Studi e ricerche*, 4 (1990): 31–131.

——, 'Vinci "operista" autore di cantate'. In Francesco Luisi (ed.), *Studi in onore di Giulio Cattin*, Rome: Torre, d'Orfeo, 1990, pp. 307–29.

——, 'Vivaldi, la cantata e gli altri: ancora sul manoscritto di Meiningen Ed. 82c', *Studi musicali*, 37, 2009: 359–86.

Gialdroni, Teresa M. and Ziino, Agostino, 'Un'altra fonte per *Povero giglio, oh Dio!* e il problema della datazione di alcune cantate "napoletane" di Hasse'. In Michael Jahn and Angela Pachovsky (eds), *Figaro là, Figaro qua. Gedenkschrift Leopold M. Kantner (1932–2004)*, Vienna: Der Apfel, 2006, pp. 253–77.

Giannini, Tula, 'The Music Library of Jean-Baptiste Christophe Ballard, Sole Music Printer to the King of France, 1750 Inventory of his Grand Collection Brought to Light'. *E-Documentation in the Humanities*, Series 1, Spring 2003.

Gianturco, Carolyn, *Stradella, 'uomo di gran grido'*. Pisa: ETS, 2007.

—— (ed.), *Alessandro Stradella: Moro per amore*, Edizione Nazionale dell'Opera Omnia di Alessandro Stradella, serie II, vol. 1. Pisa: ETS, 2003.

——, 'Stradella, Alessandro'. In Stanley Sadie and John Tyrrell (eds), *The New Grove Dictionary of Music and Musicians*, 2nd edn, London: Macmillan, 2001, vol. 24, pp. 451–2.

——, *Alessandro Stradella (1639–1682): His Life and Music*. Oxford: Oxford University Press, 1994.

——, 'Naples: A City of Entertainment'. In George J. Buelow (ed.), *Man & Music: The Late Baroque Era from the 1680s to 1740*, London: Macmillan, 1993, pp. 94–127.

——, 'The Italian Seventeenth-Century Cantata: A Textual Approach'. In John Caldwell, Edward Olleson and Susan Wollenberg (eds), *The Well Enchanting Skill: Music, Poetry, and Drama in the Culture of the Renaissance: Essays in Honour of F. W. Sternfeld*, Oxford: Clarendon Press, 1990, pp. 41–51.

—— (ed.), *Alessandro Stradella e Modena: Atti del Convegno internazionale di studi (Modena, 15–17 dicembre 1983)*. Modena: Teatro Comunale di Modena, 1985.

Gianturco, Carolyn and McCrickard, Eleanor, *Alessandro Stradella (1639–1682): A Thematic Catalogue of His Compositions*. Stuyvesant, NY: Pendragon Press, 1991.

Gianturco, Carolyn and Rostirolla, Giancarlo (eds), *Atti del convegno 'Alessandro Stradella e il suo tempo' (8–12 settembre 1982)*, 2 vols [= *Chigiana*, 39, nuova serie, 19 (1982)].

Gildon, Charles, *The Life of Mr Thomas Betterton, the Late Eminent Tragedian*. London: Gosling, 1710); facsimile repr. in *Eighteenth Century Shakespeare*, 4, London: Cass, 1970.

Grout, Donald Jay, *Alessandro Scarlatti: An Introduction to his Operas*. Berkeley, Los Angeles and London: University of California Press, 1979.

Guaita, Carlo, 'Le cantate-lamento della seconda metà del diciasettesimo secolo', *I Quaderni della Civica Scuola di Musica*, 19–20 (1990): 40–57.

Gustafson, Bruce (ed.), *Recueil de pièces choisies pour de clavessin, 1702* (GB-Lbl, Add. 39,569). Facsimile edn in *17th Century Keyboard Music: Sources*

Central to the Keyboard Art of the Baroque, vol. 19, New York: Garland, 1987.

——, 'The Legacy in Instrumental Music of Charles Babel, Prolific Transcriber of Lully's Music'. In Jérôme de La Gorce and Herbert Schneider (eds), *Jean-Baptiste Lully: Saint-Germain-en-Laye and Heidelberg 1987*, Laaber: Laaber-Verlag, 1990, pp. 495–516.

Hanley, Edwin, 'Alessandro Scarlatti's Cantate da camera: A Bibliographical Study'. PhD dissertation, Yale University, 1963; published Ann Arbor: UMI Research Press, 1973.

——, 'Scarlatti, Alessandro'. In Friedrich Blume (ed.), *Die Musik in Geschichte und Gegenwart*, Kassel: Bärenreiter, 1948–68, vol. 11, coll. 1501–1503.

Harris, Ellen T., '"Cantate, que me veux-tu" or: Do Handel's Cantatas matter?'. In Melania Bucciarelli and Berta Joncus (eds), *Music as Social and Cultural Practice: Essays in Honour of Reinhard Strohm*, Woodbridge: Boydell Press, 2007, pp. 159–84.

——, *Handel as Orpheus: Voice and Desire in the Chamber Cantatas*. Cambridge, MA: Harvard University Press, 2001.

Hawkins, John, *A General History of the Science and Practice of Music* [1776]; 2nd edn, London: Novello, 1853; facsimile repr. New York: Dover, 1963.

Heawood, Edward, *Watermarks mainly of the 17th and 18th Centuries*. Hilversum, Paper Publications Society, 1950.

Heinichen, Johann David, *Der Generalbass in der Composition*. Dresden: author, 1728; English edn by George J. Buelow, *Thorough-Bass Accompaniment according to Johann David Heinichen*. Berkeley: University of California Press, 1966.

Highfill, Philip H., Jr., Burnim, Kalman A. and Langhans, Edward A., *A Biographical Dictionary of Actors, Actresses, Musicians, Dancers, Managers & Other Stage Personnel in London: 1660–1800*, 16 vols. Carbondale: Southern Illinois University Press, 1973–93.

Hill, John Walter, *The Life and Works of Francesco Maria Veracini*. Ann Arbor: UMI Research Press, 1979.

Holman, Peter, 'An Orchestral Suite by François Couperin?', *Early Music*, 15 (1986): 71–6.

Hucke, Helmut, rev. Cafiero, Rosa, 'Leo, Leonardo'. In Stanley Sadie and John Tyrrell (eds), *The New Grove Dictionary of Music and Musicians*, 2nd edn, London: Macmillan, 2001, vol. 14, pp. 553–6.

Hughes-Hughes, Augustus, *Catalogue of Manuscript Music in the British Museum*, II: *Secular Vocal Music*. London: British Museum, 1908; photolithographic repr. 1966.

Hutchings, Arthur, *The Baroque Concerto*. London: Faber and Faber, 1961.

Insom, Giovanni and others, *Il fondo musicale dell'Archivio di Montecassino*, 2 vols. Montecassino: Pubblicazioni cassinesi, 2003.

Jacobs, René, *La controverse sur le timbre du contre-ténor*. Arles: Actes Sud, 1985.

Jahn, Michael and Pachovsky, Angela (eds), *Figaro là, Figaro qua. Gedenkschrift Leopold M. Kantner (1932–2004)*. Vienna: Der Apfel, 2006.
Jakoby, Richard, *The Cantata*, trans. Robert Kolben, Anthology of Music, 32. Cologne: Volk, 1968.
Jander, Owen (compiler), *Alessandro Stradella (1644–1682)*, Wellesley Edition Cantata Index Series, 4. Wellesley, MA: Wellesley College, 1969.
Jander, Owen, with Jean Lionnet, 'Bernabei, (1) Ercole Bernabei'. In Stanley Sadie and John Tyrrell (eds), *The New Grove Dictionary of Music and Musicians*, 2nd edn, London: Macmillan, 2001, vol. 3, p. 423.
Knighton, Tess and Torrente, Álvaro (eds), *Devotional Music in the Iberian World: The Villancico and Related Genres*. Aldershot: Ashgate, 2007.
Kümmerling, Harald, *Katalog der Sammlung Bokemeyer*. Kassel: Bärenreiter, 1970.
La Gorce, Jérôme de, 'L'orchestra de l'Opéra et son évolution de Campra à Rameau', *Revue de musicologie*, 76 (1990): 23–43.
La Gorce, Jérôme de and Schneider, Herbert (eds), *Jean-Baptiste Lully: Saint-Germain-en-Laye and Heidelberg 1987*. Laaber: Laaber-Verlag, 1990.
Landowska, Wanda, *Musique ancienne. Style-Interprétation/Instruments-Artistes*. Paris: 1909; repr. 1996; trans. William Aspenwall Bradley as *Music of the Past*, London: Bles, [1926].
Larsson, Roger Barnett, 'Charles Avison's "Stiles in Musical Expression"', *Music & Letters*, 63 (1982): 242–61.
Lausberg, Heinrich, *Elemente der literarischen Rhetorik*. Munich: Hueber, 1967.
Le Cerf de la Viéville, Jean-Laurent, *Comparaison [...] françoise: Index*, compiled and annotated by Carl B. Schmidt. Geneva: Minkoff, 1993.
———, *Comparaison de la musique italienne, et de la musique françoise*. Brussels: Foppens, 1704–06; facsimile repr. Geneva: Minkoff, 1972.
Leopold, Silke, *Die Oper im 17. Jahrhundert*. Laaber: Laaber-Verlag, 2004.
Leopold, Silke and Steinheuer, Joachim (eds), *Claudio Monteverdi und die Folgen*. Kassel: Bärenreiter, 1998.
Lesure, François (ed.), *Recueils imprimés, XVIIIe siècle*, International Inventory of Musical Sources (RISM), B II. Munich-Duisburg: Henle, 1964.
Lesure, François and Sartori, Claudio, *Il nuovo Vogel: Bibliografia della musica italiana vocale profana pubblicata dal 1500 al 1700*. Pomezia: Staderini-Minkoff, 1977.
Liess, Andreas, 'Materialen zur römischen Musikgeschichte des Seicento: Musikerlisten des Oratorio San Marcello, 1664–1728', *Acta musicologica*, 24 (1957): 137–71.
Lindgren, Lowell, 'J. S. Cousser, Copyist of the Cantata Manuscript in the Truman Presidential Library, and Other Cantata Copyists of 1697–1707, who Prepared the Way for Italian Opera in London'. In Bianca Maria Antolini, Teresa M. Gialdroni and Annunziato Pugliese (eds), *'Et facciam dolçi canti'. Studi in onore di Agostino Ziino in occasione del suo 65° compleanno*, Lucca: Libraria Musicale Italiana, 2003, pp. 737–82.

——, 'Giovanni, Antonio Maria, Giovanni Maria (ii) Bononcini'. In Stanley Sadie and John Tyrrell (eds), *The New Grove Dictionary of Music and Musicians*, 2nd edn (London: Macmillan, 2001), vol. 3, pp. 872–9.

——, 'Vienna, the "natural centro" for Giovanni Bononcini'. In Alberto Colzani, Norbert Dubowy, Andrea Luppi and Maurizio Padoan (eds), *Il teatro musicale italiano nel Sacro Romano Impero nei secoli XVII e XVIII. Atti del VII Convegno internazionale sulla musica italiana nei secoli XVII–XVIII, Loveno di Menaggio (Como), 15–17 luglio 1997*, Como: AMIS, 1999, pp. 365–420.

——, 'Musicians and Librettists in the Correspondence of Gio. Giacomo Zamboni (Oxford: Bodleian Library, MSS Rawlinson Letters 116–138)', *R. M. A. Research Chronicle*, 24 (1991): 1–194.

——, 'The Accomplishments of the Learned and Ingenious Nicola Francesco Haym (1678–1729)', *Studi musicali*, 16 (1987): 247–380.

—— (ed.), *Cantatas by Giovanni Bononcini (1640–1747)*. New York: Garland, 1985.

——, '*Camilla* and *The Beggar's Opera*', *Philological Quarterly*, 59 (1980): 44–61.

——, 'I trionfi di Camilla', *Studi musicali*, 6 (1977): 89–159.

——, 'A Bibliographic Scrutiny of Dramatic Works Set by Giovanni and His Brother Antonio Maria Bononcini'. PhD dissertation, Harvard University, 1972; published Ann Arbor: UMI Research Press, 1974.

Lionnet, Jean, 'Les copies de musique italienne et leur diffusion'. In Jean Lionnet (ed.), *Le concert des Muses. Promenade musicale dans le baroque français*, Versailles: Centre de Musique Baroque de Versailles, 1997, pp. 81–95.

—— (ed.), *Le concert des Muses. Promenade musicale dans le baroque français*. Versailles: Centre de Musique Baroque de Versailles, 1997.

——, 'Innocenzo Fede et la musique à la cour des Jacobites à Saint-Germain-en-Laye', *Revue de la BN*, no. 46 (Winter, 1992): 14–18.

Litta, Pompeo and others, *Famiglie celebri italiane*, 13 vols. Milan, 1819–74.

Lodi, Pio, *Catalogo delle opere musicali: Città di Modena, R. Biblioteca Estense*. Parma: Fresching, 1923; facsimile repr. Bologna: Forni, 1967.

Lucchi, Marta, 'Stradella e i duchi D'Este: Note in margine a documenti d'archivio e agli inventari estensi'. In Carolyn Gianturco (ed.), *Alessandro Stradella e Modena: Atti del Convegno internazionale di studi (Modena, 15–17 dicembre 1983)*. Modena: Teatro Comunale di Modena, 1985, pp. 107–15.

Luin, Elizabeth J., 'Repertorio dei libri musicali di S. A. S. Francesco II D'Este nell'Archivio di Stato di Modena', *La bibliofilia: Rivista di storia del libro*, 38 (1936): 418–45.

——, 'Antonio Giannettini e la musica a Modena alla fine del secolo XVII', *Atti e memorie della R. Deputazione di storia patria per le provincie modenesi*, ser. 7, vol. 7 (1931): 145–230.

Luisi, Francesco, *Studi in onore di Giulio Cattin*. Rome: Torre, d'Orfeo, 1990.

—— (ed.), *Cantatas by Luigi Rossi (c.1597–1653)*. New York: Garland, 1986.

Lütolf, Max (ed.), *André Campra: Les festes venitiennes*. Paris: Heugel, 1972.

Maccavino, Nicolò (ed.), *La serenata tra Seicento e Settecento: Musica, Poesia, Scenotecnica: Atti del convegno internazionale di studi (Reggio Calabria, 16–17 maggio 2003)*. Reggio Calabria: Laruffa, 2007.

——, *Catalogo delle cantate del Fondo Pisani del Conservatorio 'V. Bellini' di Palermo*. Palermo: Regione Siciliana, 1990.

Maccavino, Nicolò and Tonino Battista, '*Il ritratto dell'eroe* (Venezia, 1726): una serenata di Giovanni Porta dedicata al Cardinale Ottoboni falsamente attribuita a Leonardo Vinci'. In Gaetano Pitarresi (ed.), *Leonardo Vinci e il suo tempo. Atti dei convegni internazionali di studi (Reggio Calabria, 10–12 giugno 2002; 4–5 giugno 2006)*. Reggio Calabria: iiriti, 2004, pp. 339–96.

[Macnutt, Richard], *Catalogue 114: A Small Selection from our Stock of Printed, Manuscript and Autograph Music, Dance & Theatre*. Withyham, Sussex, 1987.

Madricardo, Claudio and Rossi, Franco (eds), *Benedetto Marcello: la sua opera e il suo tempo*. Florence: Olschki, 1988.

Maier, Bruno, *Rimatori d'Arcadia. Giambattista Felice Zappi, Faustina Maratti Zappi, Eustachio Manfredi, Carlo Innocenzo Frugoni*. Udine: Del Bianco, 1971.

Mancini, Giambattista, *Riflessioni pratiche sul Canto figurato* Milan: Galeazzi, 1777; facsimile repr. Bologna: Forni, 1970.

Mancurti, Francesco Maria, 'Vita del Poeta Gio. Battista Zappi'. In Giovan Mario Crescimbeni (ed.), *Le vite degli Arcadi illustri*, Rome, Antonio de' Rossi, 1708–27, vol. 4, p. 68.

Marín, Miguel Ángel, *Music on the Margin: Urban Musical Life in Eighteenth-century Jaca (Spain)*. Kassel: Bärenreiter, 2002.

Marinelli Roscioni, Carlo (ed.), *Il teatro di S. Carlo: la cronologia 1737–1987*. Naples: Edizioni Scientifiche Italiane, 1987.

Markstrom, Kurt, *The Operas of Leonardo Vinci, Napoletano*. Hillsdale: Pendragon Press, 2007.

Marpurg, Friedrich Wilhelm (ed.), *Historisch-kritische Beyträge zur Aufnahme der Musik*, 8 vols. Berlin: Lange, 1754–78.

Martini, Giambattista, 'Scrittori e professori di musica modenesi', in Gaetano Gaspari (ed.), 'Miscellanea musicale' (I-Bc, UU 12).

Marx, Hans Joachim, 'Die "Giustificazioni della casa Pamphilj" als musikgeschichtliche Quelle', *Studi musicali*, 12 (1983): 121–87.

——, 'Die Musik am Hofe Pietro Kardinal Ottobonis unter Arcangelo Corelli', *Analecta musicologica*, 5 (1968): 104–177.

Marx, Hans Joachim and Voss, Steffen, 'Unbekannte Kantaten von Händel, A. Scarlatti, Fago und Grillo in einer neapolitanischen Handschrift von 1710'. In Bianca Maria Antolini, Teresa M. Gialdroni and Annunziato Pugliese (eds), '"*Et facciam dolçi canti*". Studi in onore di Agostino Ziino in occasione del suo 65° compleanno*, Lucca: Libraria Musicale Italiana, 2003, pp. 797–806.

Massenkeil, Günther (ed.), *Cantatas by Giacomo Carissimi (1605–74)*. New York: Garland, 1986.

Massip, Catherine, 'La collection musicale Toulouse-Philidor à la Bibliothèque nationale', *Fontes Artis Musicae*, 30 (1983): 181–207.
Maylender, Michele, *Storia delle Accademie d'Italia*, 5 vols. Bologna: Cappelli, 1926–30.
Mayrhofer, Marina, 'Sei cantate napoletane di Alessandro Scarlatti anteriori al 1694'. In Nino Pirrotta and Agostino Ziino (eds), *Händel e gli Scarlatti a Roma. Atti del Convegno Internazionale di Studi, Roma 1985*, Florence: Olschki, 1987, pp. 155–63.
McCleave, Sarah (ed.), *Dance & Music in French Baroque Theatre: Sources & Interpretations*. London: Institute of Advanced Musical Studies, 1998.
McCrickard, Eleanor F. (ed.), *Alessandro Stradella: Cantate sacre*, Edizione Nazionale dell'Opera Omnia di Alessandro Stradella, serie I, vol. 20. Pisa: ETS, 2004.
—— (ed.), *Alessandro Stradella. Esule dalle sfere: A Cantata for the Souls of Purgatory*. Chapel Hill: University of North Carolina Press, 1983.
Metastasio, Pietro, *Tutte le opere*, ed. Bruno Brunelli, 5 vols. Milan: Mondadori, 1951–65.
Mioli, Pietro, *A voce sola. Studio sulla cantata italiana del XVII secolo*. Florence: SPES, 1988.
—— (ed.), *Domenico Gabrielli, Cantate a voce sola, Bologna 1691*, facsimile repr. Florence: SPES, 1980.
—— (ed.), *Giovanni Legrenzi, Echi di riverenza di cantate e canzoni, Bologna 1678*, facsimile repr. Florence: SPES, 1980.
Mischiati, Oscar, *Indici, cataloghi e avvisi degli editori e librai musicali italiani dal 1591 al 1798*. Florence: Olschki, 1984.
Montagnier, Jean-Paul C., *Charles-Hubert Gervais: un musicien au service du Régent et de Louis XV*. Paris: CNRS, 2001.
Morelli, Arnaldo, 'Mecenatismo musicale nella Roma barocca. Il caso di Cristina di Svezia', *Quaderni storici*, 95, n. 2 (1997): 387–408.
Morelli, Giorgio and Cardinale, Flavia, Sebastiano Baldini (1615–1685): Le poesie per musica nei codici della Biblioteca Apostolica Vaticana. Rome: IBIMUS, 2000.
Morris, Robert B., 'A Study of the Italian Solo Cantata before 1750'. DME dissertation, Indiana University, 1955; published Ann Arbor: University Microfilms, 1978.
Müller, Walther, *Johann Adolf Hasse als Kirchenkomponist*. Leipzig: Breitkopf & Härtel, 1911.
Münster, Robert, 'Peli, Francesco'. In Stanley Sadie and John Tyrrell (eds), *The New Grove Dictionary of Music and Musicians*, 2nd edn, London: Macmillan, 2001, vol. 19, p. 295.
Nemeitz, Joachim Christoph, *Séjour de Paris*. Leiden: Abcoude, 1727.
Nettl, Paul, *Forgotten Musicians*. New York: Philosophical Library, 1951.
Newman, William S., *The Sonata in the Baroque Era*. Chapel Hill: University of North Carolina, 1959.

Nuti, Giulia, *The Performance of Italian Basso Continuo: Style in Keyboard Accompaniment in the Seventeenth and Eighteenth Centuries*. Aldershot: Ashgate, 2007.

Pagano, Roberto, *Alessandro and Domenico Scarlatti: Two Lives in One*, trans. Frederick Hammond. Hillsdale: Pendragon Press, 2006.

Pagano, Roberto and Bianchi, Lino, *Alessandro Scarlatti*. Turin: ERI, 1972.

Passadore, Francesco and Rossi, Franco, *La sottigliezza dell'intendimento. Catalogo tematico di Giovanni Legrenzi*. Venice: Fondazione Levi, 2002.

Pastore, Giuseppe A., *Don Leonardo. Vita e opere di Leonardo Leo*. Cuneo: Bertola & Locatelli, 1994.

Penna, Lorenzo, *Li primi albori musicali*. Bologna: Monti, 1684; facsimile repr. Bologna: Forni, 1996.

Pierre, Constant, *Histoire du Concert Spirituel, 1725–1790*. Paris: Société Française de Musicologie, 1975.

Pintacuda, Salvatore, *Catalogo del fondo antico, Genova, Biblioteca dell'Istituto Musicale 'Nicolò Paganini'*, Bibliotheca Musicae, 4 (Milan: Istituto Editoriale Italiano, 1966).

Piperno, Franco, '"Su le sponde del Tebro': eventi, mecenati e istituzioni musicali a Roma negli anni di Locatelli. Saggio di cronologia'. In Albert Dunning (ed.), *Intorno a Locatelli. Studi in occasione del tricentenario della nascita di Pietro Antonio Locatelli (1695–1764)*, Lucca: Libreria Musicale Italiana, 1995, pp. 793–877.

Pirrotta, Nino and Ziino, Agostino (eds), *Händel e gli Scarlatti a Roma. Atti del convegno internazionale di studi (Roma, 12–14 giugno 1985)*. Florence: Olschki, 1987.

Pitarresi, Gaetano (ed.), *Intorno a Silvio Stampiglia. Librettisti, Compositori e interpreti nell'età premetastasiana. Atti del Convegno internazionale di Studi (Reggio Calabria, 5–6 ottobre 2007)* (forthcoming).

—— (ed.), *Leonardo Vinci e il suo tempo. Atti dei convegni internazionali di studi (Reggio Calabria, 10–12 giugno 2002; 4–5 giugno 2006)*. Reggio Calabria: iiriti, 2004.

Platt, Richard (ed.), *Corelli: Concerti grossi*. London: Eulenburg, 1997.

Pritchard, Brian W., *Antonio Caldara: Essays on His Life and Times*. Aldershot: Ashgate, 1987.

Quadrio, Francesco Saverio, *Della storia e della ragione d'ogni poesia*, 5 vols. Bologna and Milan: Pisarri and Agnelli, 1739–52.

Quargnolo, Daniela, 'Le cantate di Leonardo Leo (1694–1744)'. *Tesi di laurea*, Università degli Studi di Milano, 1993/94.

Radicchi, Patrizia and Burden, Michael (eds), *Florilegium musicae: Studi in onore di Carolyn Gianturco*. Pisa: ETS, 2004.

Raguenet, François, *A Comparison between the* French *and* Italian *Musick and Opera's. Translated* [anonymously] *from the* French *with Some Remarks* [by Nicola Francesco Haym]. London: Lewis, 1709; facsimile repr. with an introduction by Charles Cudworth, Farnborough: Gregg, 1968.

———, *Défense du parallèle*. Paris: Bertin, 1705.

———, *Paralele des italiens et des françois, en ce qui regarde la musique et les opéra*. Paris: Moreau, 1702; facsimile repr. Geneva: Minkoff, 1976.

Rainbow, Bernarr, 'John Hullah'. In Stanley Sadie and John Tyrrell (eds), *The New Grove Dictionary of Music and Musicians*, 2nd edn, London: Macmillan, 2001, vol. 11, p. 815.

[Riccati, Giordano], 'Lettere del co[nte] Giordano Riccati al dottissimo padre D. Giovenale Sacchi, professore d'eloquenza nel Collegio Imperiale di Milano', *Nuovo giornale de' letterati d'Italia*, 36 (1787): 172–200.

Riemann, Hugo (ed.), *Auserwählte Kammer-Kantaten der Zeit um 1700*. Leipzig: Breitkopf & Härtel, 1911.

Rinaldi, Mario, *Arcangelo Corelli*. Milan: Curci, 1953.

Robinson, Michael F., *Naples and Neapolitan Opera*. Oxford: Clarendon Press, 1972; Italian edn as *Opera napoletana: storia e geografia di un'idea musicale settecentesca*, trans. Giovanni Morelli and Luca Zoppelli, Venice: Marsilio, 1984.

Rosand, Ellen, 'The Descending Tetrachord: An Emblem of Lament', *Musical Quarterly*, 65 (1979): 346–59.

Rosow, Lois, 'Paris Opéra Orchestration, 1686–1713: Deciphering the Code in the Orchestral Parts'. In Sarah McCleave (ed.), *Dance & Music in French Baroque Theatre: Sources & Interpretations*, London: Institute of Advanced Musical Studies, 1998, pp. 33–53.

Rostirolla, Giancarlo, 'La musica nelle istituzioni religiose romane al tempo di Stradella dal Diario n. 93 (1675) della Cappella Pontificia e dalle "Memorie dell'Anno Santo" di R. Caetano, con alcune precisazioni storiche sulla "stagione" di oratori a S. Giovanni dei Fiorentini'. In Carolyn Gianturco and Giancarlo Rostirolla (eds), *Atti del convegno 'Alessandro Stradella e il suo tempo' (8–12 settembre 1982)*, 2 vols [= *Chigiana*, 39, nuova serie, 19 (1982)], vol. 2, pp. 575–831, at p. 796.

———, 'Catalogo generale delle Opere di Alessandro Scarlatti'. In Roberto Pagano and Lino Bianchi, *Alessandro Scarlatti*, Turin: ERI, 1972, pp. 317–595: cantate da camera, pp. 377–494.

Rousseau, Jean-Jacques, *Dictionnaire de musique*. Amsterdam: Rey, 1768.

Sacchi, Giovenale, *Vita del Cavaliere Don Carlo Broschi detto il Farinello*. Venice: Coleti, 1784; modern edn, Naples: Flavio Pagano, 1994.

Sadie, Julie Anne, *The Bass Viol in French Baroque Chamber Music*. Ann Arbor: UMI Research Press, 1980.

Sadie, Stanley (ed.), *The New Grove Dictionary of Music and Musicians*, [1st edn], 20 vols. London: Macmillan, 1980.

Sadie, Stanley and Bashford, Christina (eds), *The New Grove Dictionary of Opera*, 4 vols. London: Macmillan, 1992.

Sadie, Stanley and Tyrrell, John (eds), *The New Grove Dictionary of Music and Musicians*, 2nd edn, 29 vols. London: Macmillan, 2001.

Sadler, Graham, 'Rameau's Singers and Players: a Little-known Inventory of 1738', *Early Music*, 11 (1983): 453–67.

——, 'Rameau and the Orchestra', *Proceedings of the Royal Musical Association*, 108 (1981–82): 47–68.

Salvadori, Giuseppe Gaetano, *La poetica toscana all'uso*. Naples: Gramignani, 1691.

Sartori, Claudio, *I libretti italiani a stampa dalle origini al 1800*, 7 vols. Cuneo: Bertola & Locatelli, 1990–94.

——, *Bibliografia della musica strumentale italiana stampata in Italia fino al 1700*. Florence: Olschki, 1952.

Sawkins, Lionel, *A Thematic Catalogue of the Works of Michel-Richard de Lalande (1657–1726)*. Oxford: Oxford University Press, 2005.

Scheibe, Johann Adolph, *Critischer Musikus. Neue, vermehrte und verbesserte Auflage*. Leipzig: Breitkopf, 1745.

Schlager, Karl-Heinz (ed.), *Einzeldrucke vor 1800*, International Inventory of Musical Sources (RISM), series A, 15 vols. Kassel: Bärenreiter, 1971–2003.

Schmitz, Eugen, *Geschichte der weltlichen Solokantate*. Leipzig: Breitkopf & Härtel, 1914; facsimile repr. Hildesheim: Olms, 1966; second edn, Leipzig: VEB Breitkopf & Härtel, 1955.

Schulze, Hendrik, *Odysseus in Venedig. Sujetwahl und Rollenkonzeption in der venezianischen Oper des 17. Jahrhunderts*. Frankfurt am Main: Lang, 2004.

Seay, Albert (ed.), *Giovanni Legrenzi, Cantatas and Canzonets for Solo Voice*. Madison: A-R Editions, 1972.

Seifert, Herbert, *Die Oper am Wiener Kaiserhof im 17. Jahrhundert*. Tutzing: Schneider, 1985.

Selfridge-Field, Eleanor, *The Music of Benedetto and Alessandro Marcello. A Thematic Catalogue*. Oxford: Oxford University Press, 1990.

Semmens, Richard, *The 'Bals publics' at the Paris Opera in the Eighteenth Century*. Hillsdale: Pendragon Press, 2004.

Setton, Kenneth M., *Venice, Austria, and the Turks in the Seventeenth Century*. Philadelphia, PA: American Philosophical Society, 1991.

Simi Bonini, Eleonora, 'Giovanni Battista Vulpio: cantore pontificio, compositore e collezionista'. In Patrizia Radicchi and Michael Burden (eds), *Florilegium musicae: Studi in onore di Carolyn Gianturco*, Pisa: ETS, 2004, pp. 927–66.

Sites, Caroline, 'More on Marcello's Satire', *Journal of the American Musicological Society*, 11 (1958): 141–8.

Smith, Peter (adapted from), 'Bassani, Giovanni Battista'. In Ludwig Finscher (ed.), *Die Musik in Geschichte und Gegenwart, Personenteil*, Kassel etc.: Bärenreiter, 1994–2007, vol. 2, pp. 447–51.

Snyder, Kerala J. and Webber, Geoffrey, 'Österreich, Georg'. In Stanley Sadie and John Tyrrell (eds), *The New Grove Dictionary of Music and Musicians*, 2nd edn, London: Macmillan, 2001, vol. 18, pp. 778–80.

[Sotheby's], *Catalogue of a Selected Portion of the Valuable Library at Hornby Castle, Bedale, Yorkshire, the Property of His Grace the Duke of Leeds* (London, 2–3 June 1930).

Steblin, Rita, 'Did Handel meet Bononcini in Rome?', *Music Review*, 45 (1984): 179–93.

Strohm, Reinhard, 'Apostolo Zeno's *Teuzzone* and its French Models'. In Reinhard Strohm, *Dramma per musica: Italian Opera Seria of the Eighteenth Century*. New Haven, CT and London: Yale University Press, 1997.

——, 'The Neapolitans in Venice'. In Iain Fenlon and Tim Carter (eds), '*Con che soavità': Studies in Italian Opera, Song, and Dance, 1500–1740*, Oxford: Clarendon Press, 1995, pp. 249–74.

——, 'Scarlattiana at Yale'. In Nino Pirrotta and Agostino Ziino (eds), *Händel e gli Scarlatti a Roma. Atti del convegno internazionale di studi (Roma, 12–14 giugno 1985)*, Florence: Olschki, 1987, pp. 113–52.

Strunk, Oliver, *Source Readings in Music History*. New York: Norton, 1950.

Talbot, Michael, '"Loving without Falling in Love": Pietro Paolo Bencini's Serenata *Li due volubili*'. In Nicolò Maccavino (ed.), *La serenata tra Seicento e Settecento*, Reggio Calabria: Laruffa, 2007, pp. 373–95.

——, *The Chamber Cantatas of Antonio Vivaldi*. Woodbridge: Boydell Press, 2006.

——, 'How Recitatives End and Arias Begin in the Solo Cantatas of Antonio Vivaldi', *Journal of the Royal Musical Association*, 126 (2001): 169–92.

——, 'Serenata'. In Stanley Sadie and John Tyrrell (eds), *The New Grove Dictionary of Music and Musicians*, 2nd edn, London: Macmillan, 2001, vol. 23, pp. 113–15.

——, *Benedetto Vinaccesi: A Musician in Brescia and Venice in the Age of Corelli*. Oxford: Oxford University Press, 1994.

——, *Vivaldi*, rev. edn. London: Dent, 1993.

——, *Tomaso Albinoni. The Venetian Composer and His World*. Oxford: Oxford University Press, 1990.

——, 'The Effects of Music: Benedetto Marcello's Cantata *Il Timoteo*'. In Claudio Madricardo and Franco Rossi (eds), *Benedetto Marcello: la sua opera e il suo tempo*, Florence: Olschki, 1988, pp. 103–125.

——, 'Modal shifts in the Sonatas of Domenico Scarlatti', *Chigiana*, n. s. 20 (1985): 25–43.

——, 'The Serenata in Eighteenth–Century Venice', *R. M. A. Research Chronicle*, 18 (1982): 1–50.

—— (ed.), *Tomaso Albinoni. Twelve Cantatas, Opus 4*. Madison: A-R Editions, 1979.

Talbot, Michael and Timms, Colin, 'Music and the Poetry of Antonio Ottoboni (1646–1720)'. In Nino Pirrotta and Agostino Ziino, *Händel e gli Scarlatti a Roma*, Florence: Olschki, 1987, pp. 367–437.

Tedesco, Anna, 'La serenata a Palermo alla fine del Seicento e il duca di Uceda'. In Nicolò Maccavino (ed.), *La serenata tra Seicento e Settecento*, Reggio Calabria: Laruffa, 2007, pp. 547–98.

Timms, Colin, 'A New Cantata by Domenico Scarlatti (Words by Antonio Ottoboni)'. In Patrizia Radicchi and Michael Burden (eds), *Florilegium Musicae. Studi in onore di Carolyn Gianturco*, Pisa: ETS, 2004, pp. 967–79.

——, 'Cavata'. In Stanley Sadie and John Tyrrell (eds), *The New Grove Dictionary of Music and Musicians*, 2nd edn, London: Macmillan, 2001, vol. 5, p. 315.

——, 'The Dissemination of Steffani's Operas'. In Alberto Colzani, Norbert Dubowy, Andrea Luppi and Maurizio Padoan (eds), *Relazioni musicali tra Italia e Germania nell'età barocca, Atti del VI convegno internazionale sulla musica italiana nei secoli XVII–XVIII, Loveno di Menaggio (Como), 11–13 luglio 1995*, Como: AMIS, 1999, pp. 323–49.

——, 'The Italian Cantata since 1945: Progress and Prospects'. In Francesco Fanna and Michael Talbot (eds), *Cinquant'anni di produzioni e consumi della musica dell'età di Vivaldi, 1947–1997*, Florence: Olschki, 1998, pp. 75–94.

——, 'The *Cassandra* Cantata of Conti and Marcello'. In Claudio Madricardo and Franco Rossi (eds), *Benedetto Marcello: la sua opera e il suo tempo*, Florence: Olschki, 1988, pp. 127–59.

——, '"Prendea con man di latte": A Vivaldi spuriosity?', *Informazioni e studi vivaldiani*, 6 (1985): 64–72.

——, 'The Dramatic in Vivaldi's Cantatas'. In Lorenzo Bianconi and Giovanni Morelli (eds), *Antonio Vivaldi. Teatro musicale, cultura e società*, Florence: Olschki, 1982, pp. 97–129.

Timms, Colin and Catherine Wyatt (eds), *Alessandro Stradella: Tre Cantate profane con accompagnamento strumentale*, Edizione Nazionale dell'Opera Omnia di Alessandro Stradella, serie I, vol. 13. Pisa: ETS, 2007.

Tintori, Giampiero (ed.), *A. Scarlatti. 4 cantate inedite*. Milan: Ricordi, 1958.

Torrente, Álvaro, 'The Sacred Villancico in Early Eighteenth-Century Spain: The Repertory of Salamanca Cathedral'. PhD dissertation, Cambridge, 1997.

Tosi, Pier Francesco, *Opinioni de' cantori antichi e moderni*. Bologna: Lelio dalla Volpe, 1723.

Travers, Roger-Claude, '1947–1997: Vivaldi, les baroques et la critique'. In Francesco Fanna and Michael Talbot (eds), *Cinquant'anni di produzioni e consumi della musica dell'età di Vivaldi, 1947–1997*, Florence: Olschki, 1998, pp. 53–74.

Tunley, David, 'Cantata, §III. The French cantata to 1800'. In Stanley Sadie and John Tyrrell (eds), *The New Grove Dictionary of Music and Musicians*, 2nd edn, London: Macmillan, 2001, vol. 5, p. 33.

——, *The Eighteenth-Century French Cantata*. London: Dobson, 1974; 2nd edn, Oxford: Clarendon Press, 1997.

—— (ed.), *The Eighteenth-Century French Cantata: A Seventeen-Volume Facsimile Set of the Most Widely Cultivated and Performed Music in Early Eighteenth-Century France*. New York: Garland, 1990.

Turellier, François, 'Des cantates anonymes attribuables à Jean-Baptiste Morin (1677–1745) dans le manuscrit F-Pc. Rés 1451: "Cantates de Mancin[i]"', *Ostinato rigore: Revue internationale d'études musicales*, 8/9, 1997: 329–39.

[various authors], *Dictionnaire de Trévoux* (= *Dictionnaire universelle françois et latin*), 7 vols (Paris: Delaulne and others, 1743–52).

Veneziano, Giulia, 'Un Corpus de cantatas Napolitanas del siglo XVIII en Zaragoza: Problemas de difusión del repertorio italiano en España', *Artigrama. Revista del Departamento de Historia del Arte de la Universidad de Zaragoza*, 12 (1996–97): 277–91.

Viollier, Renée, 'La musique à la cour de la Duchesse du Maine, de Châtenay aux grandes nuits de Sceaux, 1700–1715', *La revue musicale*, 20 (1939): 96–105 and 133–8.

Vitali, Carlo, Roberto Pagano and Francesca Boris, *La solitudine amica. Lettere al conte Sicino Pepoli*. Palermo: Sellerio, 2000.

Vogel, Emil, *Bibliothek der gedruckten weltlichen Vokalmusik Italiens aus den Jahren 1500–1700*, 2 vols. Berlin: Haack, 1892.

Vollen, Gene E., *The French Cantata: A Survey and Thematic Catalog*. Ann Arbor: UMI Research Press, 1982.

Walker, Frank, 'Salvator Rosa and Music', *Monthly Musical Record*, 79 (1949): 199–205.

Wilson, John (ed.), *Roger North on Music*. London: Novello, 1959.

Wolff, Barbara Mahrenholz, *Music Manuscripts at Harvard: A Catalogue of Music Manuscripts from the 14th to the 20th centuries in the Houghton Library and the Eda Kuhn Loeb Music Library*. Cambridge, MA: Harvard University Library, 1992.

Wolff, Hellmuth Christian, 'Das Märchen von der neapolitanischen Oper und Metastasio', *Analecta musicologica*, 9 (1970), 94–111.

——, 'Bononcini oder die Relativität historischer Urteile', *Revue belge de musicologie*, 11 (1957): 3–16.

Wood, Caroline, *Music and Drama in the* tragédie en musique, *1673–1715*. New York: Garland, 1996.

——, 'Orchestra and Spectacle in the *tragédie en musique* 1673–1715: oracle, *sommeil* and *tempête*', *Proceedings of the Royal Musical Association*, 108 (1981–82): 25–46.

Wright, Josephine, 'The Secular Cantatas of Francesco Mancini (1672–1736)'. PhD dissertation, New York University, 1975; published Ann Arbor: UMI Research Press, 1976.

Zeno, Apostolo, *Lettere di Apostolo Zeno cittadino veneziano*, 3 vols. Venice: Valvasense, 1752.

Ziino, Agostino (ed.), *Musica senza aggettivi: studi per Fedele d'Amico*. Florence: Olschki, 1991.

Index of Vocal Works

This index lists, in alphabetical order of incipit and/or title, all the individual vocal works mentioned in this book. Alphabetization follows the word-by-word system (note that the letters 'D' and 'L' are here treated as full words when followed by an apostrophe). First come cantatas, including dramatic cantatas (serenatas), sacred cantatas and chamber duets; next come operas and oratorios; finally, I list titled vocal works of any other kind. Collections and non-vocal works are listed under the names of their composers in the General Index. Where works are identified in the text both by an independent title and by an incipit, the first is treated as a rejected heading and cross-referenced (via 'see') to the second. Unless otherwise indicated, 'Bach' is Johann Sebastian Bach, 'Bononcini' is Giovanni Bononcini, 'Gasparini' is Francesco Gasparini, 'Marcello' is Benedetto Marcello and 'Scarlatti' is Alessandro Scarlatti.

1. Index of cantatas

A battaglia vi sfida Cupido (Cesti), 7
A bella donna crudele (Bononcini), see *Già fugavan le stelle*
A piè d'un fonte (Legrenzi), 68–9, 74
A piè della sua Clori (A. or G. Bononcini), 169
A povero amator (Legrenzi), 63–7, 69–71, 74
A ricalcare in Tebro (Melani), 345
A Tirsi che pena e tace (Bononcini), see *Peno e l'alma fedele*
A voi che l'accendeste (Bononcini), 163n
A voi che l'accendeste (Lulier), 163n
A voi che l'accendeste (Mangiarotti), 163n
A voi che l'accendeste (Perti), 163n
A voi che l'accendeste (Scarlatti), 121, 163n
Acceso da bei lumi (Bononcini), 169
Ad altro amante in seno (Legrenzi), 58–61
Ad onta del timore (Bononcini), 174
Ad onta del timore (Porpora), 347
Adónde fugitivo (Vinci), 359

Agrippina condotta a morire (Handel), see *Dunque sarà pur vero*
Ah che pur troppo è vero (Handel), 328
Ah! crudel, nel pianto mio (Handel), 328
Ah no, che non si more (Scarlatti or Bononcini), 135n, 142n
Ah, non havesse, no, permesso il fato (Bononcini), 163, 312, 322
Ah, troppo è ver! (Hasse), 341
Ai begli occhi del mio bene (Bononcini), 174
Al fin m'ucciderete, o miei pensieri (Scarlatti), xxiv, 115–16, 131–4
Al fragor di lieta tromba (Scarlatti), 113n
Al soave spirar d'aure serene (Rossi), 7
All'arco tuo fatale (Bononcini), 135n, 163
All'armi, pensieri (Se d'un volto mi struggo all'ardore) (Melani), 345
All'hor ch'il dio di Delo (Mancini), 128
All'hor ch'il dio di Delo (Scarlatti), 128
All'ombra d'un bel faggio (Vivaldi), 359
All'ombra di sospetto (Vivaldi), 274, 365–6

Alla (Della) beltà d'un volto (Bononcini), 163
Alla caccia (Handel), 328–9
Alla caccia dell'alme e de' cori (Vivaldi), 316, 363
Alle sue pene intorno (Bononcini), 163
Allor ch'io dissi Addio (Handel), 329
Allor che il cieco nume (Bononcini), 163
Allor che in dolce oblio (Fago or Bononcini), 135n
Allor che in mille petti (Bononcini?), 169, 173n
Allor che lo sguardo (Vivaldi), 359
Alpestre monte (Handel), 329
Alphée et Aréthuse (Clérambault), 239
Amai ed amo ancora (Bononcini), 163
Amai, no'l niego, una gentil sembianza (Marcello), 344
Amante recidivo (Caldara), 324
Amanti curiosi (Grossi), 87n
Amarissime pene (Albinoni, Ariosti or Bononcini), 135n
Amato tesoro che dolce ristoro (Bononcini), 169
Amenissimi prati, fiorite piagge (D. Scarlatti), 353
Ammore, brutto figlio de pottana (Scarlatti), 120, 349
Amo e l'ardor ch'io sento (Bononcini), 163
Amo e ridir no'l posso (Bononcini), 163, 166
Amo ma poco io spero (Bononcini), 163
Amo, peno, gioisco (Bononcini), 150–51, 154n, 157–8, 160, 163
Amo sì, ma non so dire (Bononcini), 163
Amor, Amor vincesti: ho già perduto il core (d'Astorga or Bononcini), 135n
Amor, che far deggio (d'Astorga or Bononcini), 135n
Amor gioje mi porge (Handel), 148n
Amor, hai vinto, hai vinto: ecco il mio seno, RV 651 (Vivaldi), 359–60
Amor, hai vinto, hai vinto: ecco il mio seno, RV 683 (Vivaldi), 367
Amor, io son contento (Stradella), 15
Amor, non ho più core (Bononcini), 163
Amor privo di libertà (Bononcini), see *Soave libertade, nasci, è vero*
Amor, re de' tiranni (Bernabei), 34–5, 45, 48–50
Amor sfortunato (Bononcini), see *Non ho pace nel mio core*
Amor, Sorte, Destino! (Albinoni), 318
Amor, tiranno Amor, fanciullo traditor (Bononcini), 163
Amore, e come mai d'un sguardo (Bononcini or Rignatti), 144, 163
Amore è quel tiranno (Bononcini), 163
Amore traditore (Bach), 302, 320–21
Amore uccellatore (Handel), see *Venne voglia ad Amore*
Anche i tronchi, anche le rupi (Bononcini), 163
Andate, o miei sospiri (Gasparini), 281–5, 327
Andate, o miei sospiri (Sarro), 348
Andate, o miei sospiri (Scarlatti), 281–2, 349
Andromède et Persée (Mouret), 238
Anima del cor mio, volami o cara in sen (Bononcini), 169
Antonio e Cleopatra (Hasse), 217n
Antri romiti e solitarie selve (Bononcini), 169
Api che raccogliete dell'alba il dolce amor (Bononcini), 169
Applauso musicale (Lulier), 121
Appresso a i molli argenti (Strozzi), 81
Apre l'uomo infelice all'or che nasce (Stradella), 14
Arde il mio petto amante (Bononcini), 144, 163
Ardo, sospiro e piango (Stradella), 357
Arianna abbandonata da Teseo (Marcello), see *Dove, misera, dove lungi da me*
Armida abbandonata (Handel), see *Dietro l'orme fugaci*
Astri di quel bel viso (Caldara), 324
Augellin vago e canoro (Scarlatti), 349
Aure che sussurranti (Bononcini), 163
Aure soavi e lieti (Handel), 329
Aure, voi che mormorando (Bononcini), 163
Aure, voi che sì liete (Bononcini), 163
Aure, voi più non siete (Vivaldi), 360
Bachus (Morin), 231, 234

Barbara gelosia (Sarro), 313n
Barbara ninfa ingrata (Bononcini), 174
Basta cosi, vi ho inteso (Strozzi), 280
Bei crini d'oro (Bononcini), 150–51, 155, 159, 160, 161, 163
Bella dama di nome Santa (Scarlatti), see *Tu sei quella che al nome*
Bella Donna costante (Bononcini), see *Ch'io ti manchi di fede, idolo mio?*
Bella madre dei fiori (Scarlatti), 349
Bella, mi parto, a Dio (Hasse), 341
Bella rosa adorata, cara pompa di Flora (D. Scarlatti), 354
Belle labra porporine (Bononcini), 174
Bionde crini, chiome vaghe (Bononcini), 169
Brama d'esser amante (d'Astorga or Bononcini), 135n, 172n
Cantata notturna (Scarlatti), 118
Cantata sopra arcicalascione (Porsile), 248
Cara, l'avverso fato (anon.), 213
Carco sempre di gloria (Handel), 301, 329
Care fonti, erbette e fiori (Bononcini?), 169, 173n
Care luci del mio bene (Bononcini), 174, 322
Care selve, amati orrori (Provenzale), 313n
Care selve, amici prati (Vivaldi), 316, 363–4
Care selve, aure grate (Handel), 329
Carissima figlia (Marcello), 224, 344
Cassandra (Marcello), 179, 180
Celinda, anima mia (Bononcini), 163
Cento pastori e cento (Bononcini), 174
Céphale et Procris (Stuck), 238
Cessate, omai cessate (Vivaldi), 300, 306, 367–8
Ch'io ami, o questo no (Stradella), 13
Ch'io canti mi dicesti (Bononcini), 163
Ch'io ti manchi di fede, idolo mio? (Bononcini), 150–51, 154–5, 158, 159–60, 161–2, 163
Che dite, o miei pensieri (Caldara), 324
Che Dori è la mia vita (Bononcini), 169
Che fiero costume (Legrenzi), 342

Che giova il sospirar, povero core (Vivaldi), 366
Che pretendi, o tiranna (D. Scarlatti), 354
Che si peni in amore (D. Scarlatti), 354
Che tirannia di stelle (Bononcini), 163, 312, 322
Che vidi, o ciel (D. Scarlatti), 354
Chi batte al mio core (Grossi), 87
Chi d'Amor tra le catene (Bononcini), 149
Chi disce che Amore (Bononcini?), 169, 171n
Chi non ode e chi non vede (Pergolesi), 345
Chi non prova amor in petto (Bononcini), 163
Chi non prova star lontano (Cesti), 7
Chi non sa che sia tormento (Bononcini), 163
Chi non sa quanto inhumano (Albinoni), 318
Chi rapì la pace al core (Handel), 329
Chi resiste al dio bendato (Stradella), 34–5, 42
Chi sa dove è la speranza (Lignani), 343
Chi vide mai, ch'intese (Bononcini), 141n, 169
Chiuse in placida quiete (Marcello), 344
Cieco Nume, tiranno spietato (Bononcini), 150–51, 160, 161, 163, 312, 323
Clori a Lisa compagne (Scarlatti), 118
Clori, bell'idol mio, fido amator (Bononcini), 174
Clori, bell'idol mio, or che dura (Bononcini), 169
Clori, Clori, mia vita (Hasse), 341
Clori, dal colle al prato (Bononcini), 135n, 174
Clori, degli occhi miei (Handel), 329
Clori, dunque mi lasci (Bononcini), 163
Clori, mi sento al core (Bononcini), 163
Clori, mia bella Clori (Caldara), 324
Clori, mia bella Clori (Handel), 329
Clori mia, Clori bella, ah non più (Scarlatti), 349
Clori, mio ben, mia vita (Bononcini), 138n, 163
Clori, perché mi fuggi (Bononcini), 169

Clori, saper vorrei, qual sia maggiore in te (Bononcini), 163
Clori sdegnosa (Caldara), 324
Clori, sei tutta bella (Conti), 313n, 326
Clori, svenar mi sento (Bononcini), 168
Clori vezzosa e bella (Scarlatti), 301, 349
Clorinda, mio core, con sommo dolore (Bononcini), 169
Col arco d'un ciglio (Bononcini), 163
Colà dove rimbomba (Melani), 345
Combattuta alma mia (Bononcini), 174
Come, ahi come cadeo (Carissimi), 7
Come siete importuni, amorosi pensieri (Bononcini), 163
Componimento a quattro voci (de Luca), 121n
Con che fasto in sen di Flora (Bononcini), 169
Con dolce mormorio (Pistocchi), 346
Con lusinghiero inganno, mascherate (Bononcini), 169
Con non inteso affanno (A. M. Bononcini), 141n
Con occhi belli e fieri (Rossi), 7
Con più lucidi candori (Conti), 326
Con qual cor mi chiede pace (D. Scarlatti), 354
Con trasparente velo (Bononcini), 169
Contrasto di pensieri amorosi (Bononcini), see *Già tutti i miei pensieri*
Contro l'empio Fileno (A. Marcello), 343
Cor di Bruto, e che risolvi? (Scarlatti), 349
Corre dal monte al prato (Bononcini), 174
Correa dietro a spocori affannato Filen (Bononcini), 137n, 174
Correa nel seno amato (Scarlatti), 349–50
Così del vostro suono (Leo), 342
Costanza, mio core (Stradella), 15
Costanza non gradita (Bononcini), see *Lumi, vezzosi lumi*
Crudel tiranno Amor (Handel), 329–30
Crudo mar di fiamme orribili (D. Scarlatti), 354
Cuando, infeliz destino (Vinci), 359
Cuopre tal volta il cielo (Handel), 330
D'Acheronte errini horribili (Albergati), 89–91, 107–8
D'Amor la bella pace (Porpora), 347

D'Amore il primo dardo (Porpora), 280, 311, 347
D'improviso Amor ferisce (Caldara), 313n, 324
D'ogni puro candore (Bononcini), 163
D'un mirto all'ombra (Bononcini), 137n, 163
Da che Tirsi mirai un occulto piacere (Bononcini), 163
Da che vidde il duo sembiante (Magini), 313n, 343
Da cuspide ferrate (Stradella), 37
Da grave incendio (Possenti), 80
Da l'arco d'un bel ciglio (Albinoni), 318
Da quel dì che per voi, amorosa saetta (Bononcini), 169
Da quel dì, da quel ora (Bononcini), 174
Da quel giorno fatale (Handel), 330
Da sventura a sventura (Scarlatti), 279n
Da te che pasci ogn'ora (Bononcini), 174
Da' tuoi lumi (Caldara), 324
Dal dì ch'il ciel severo (Bononcini), 163, 166
Dal dì ch'io non vi veggio (Bononcini), 163
Dal fatale momento (Handel), 330
Dal geminio splendor di due pupille (Bononcini), 163
Dal giorno fortunato ch'io vidi il vostro lume (Bononcini), 163
Dal stral d'Amore (Gasparini), 313, 328
Dal Zodiaco stellato (Porfirii), 100
Dalisa, oh Dio, Dalisa, che novità, che bizzarie (Bononcini), 169
Daliso, m'intendi, non voglio ti prendi (Bononcini?), 169, 173n
Dall'incurvato ferro (Bononcini), 163
Dalla guerra amorosa (Handel), 330–31
Dalle ingiuste querelle (Pietragrua or Bononcini), 135n. 171n
Dalsigre, ahi mia Dalsigre (Pergolesi), 346
Dario (Caldara), 324
Deh che fate, o mie pupille (D. Scarlatti), 354
Deh lasciatemi un momento (Marcello), 344
Deh torna, amico sonno (Scarlatti), 350

Index of Vocal Works

Deh, tu m'insegni, Amore, come fugar poss'io (Bononcini), 169
Del chiaro rio (Albinoni), 318
Del famoso oriente (Cesti), 7
Del suo fedel e taciturno ardore (Bononcini), 138n, 163
Del suo natio rigore (Vivaldi), 360
Del Tebro antico in su la verde sponda (Bononcini), 163, 170n
Del Tebro in su la riva (Bononcini), 163
Dell'offese a vendicarmi (Zipoli), 314n, 369
Della beltà (Bononcini), see *Alla beltà*
Dentro bagno fumante (Stradella?), 357
Di cipresso funesto (Scarlatti), 123n
Di Fille vendicarmi vorrei (D. Scarlatti), 354
Di sì bel faggio all'ombra (Pescetti), 281
Di smringa la bella un dì s'accese (Bononcini), 169
Di sovrana bellezza (Bononcini), 169
Di Venere dolente insanguinata prole (Bononcini), 163
Di virtude s'è armata ragione (Bononcini), 174
Diana cacciatrice (Handel), see *Alla caccia*
Diana e Apollo (Bononcini), see *Già la ridente aurora*
Diane et Endymion (Colin de Blamont), 239
Didon (Colin de Blamont), 238, 239, 251
Dietro l'orme fugaci (Handel), 299, 331
Dir vorrei, ah m'arrossisco (D. Scarlatti), 354
Dite, vedeste forse (Vinci), 213, 224–5
Ditemi che cos'è (Gaffi), 313n, 327
Ditemi, o care selve (Bononcini), 163
Doglianze d'Irene (Bononcini), see *Mercé d'amico raggio*
Dolc'è pur d'amor l'affanno (Handel), 331–2
Dolce mio ben, s'io taccio (Handel), 331
Dolente e mesta vo sospirando (Bononcini), 174
Dolorosa partenza (Pistocchi), 346
Dom Quichotte (Courbois), 232, 233, 240
Donna di maestà (Strozzi), 81

Dopo lunga tempesta (Bononcini), 163
Dopo lungo servire (D. Scarlatti), 354
Doppo lunga stagione (Vulpio), 34–5, 45, 50–54
Doppo tante, e sì strane (Gasparini), 313, 328
Dorindo, dormir ancor? (Porpora), 347
Dove alfin mi traeste? (Scarlatti), 350
Dove bambino rivo (Bononcini), 163
Dove con ampio giro (Bononcini), 174
Dove fuggisti, o dio (Marcello), xxiv, 181–202 *passim*
Dove le pianto giro (Bononcini), 164
Dove, misera, dove lungi da me (Marcello), 344
Dove sei, dove t'ascondi (Gasparini), 279
Dove sei, mia bella Irene (Bononcini), 169
Dunque sarà pur vero (Handel), 299, 332
Dunque, o vaga mia Diva (Scarlatti?), 125–7
È bella Irene e vanta un indole modesta (Bononcini), 164
E già tre volte sorse (Porsile), 348
È la rosa regina dei fiori (Bononcini), 164
E partirai, mia vita? (Handel), 332
E pur odo e non moro (Hasse), 341
È pure un gran portento (Vinci), 212, 215, 220
E ti par poco che t'ho dato il cor (de Luca), 150n
È un martirio della costanza (Caldara or Bononcini), 135n, 167n
Ebra d'amor fuggia (Scarlatti), 350
Ecco da me partita l'alma mia (Bononcini), 164
Ecco, Dorinda, il giorno (Bononcini), 174, 323
Ecco il sole ceppi di gelo (Pistocchi), 170n
Ecco l'infausto lido (Porpora), 222
Ecco quel tronco (Ferrandini), 327
Ed ecco in fine, oh Dio (Gasparini), 278–9
Egeria, Dorinda e Amarilli (Bononcini), 136n
Elitropio d'amor (Scarlatti), 132n, 350
Elvira, anima mia (Vivaldi), 360
Enée et Didon (Campra), 236
Enone (Morin), 231, 232, 234
Entro d'ombrosa valle (Bononcini), 169

Era la notte quando i suoi splendori (Vivaldi), 360
Erano ancora immote (A. M. Bononcini), 135n
Ero e Leandro (Handel), see *Qual ti riveggio, oh Dio*
Ero e Leandro (Scarlatti), see *Leandro, anima mia*
Esci, mio gregge florido (Gasparini), 313, 328
Esule dalle sfere (Stradella), 29
Eurilla dolente in un giardino (Bononcini), see *Tra l'amene delitie*
Fallacia del pensiero [...] nella presente guerra (Albergati), 89
Farfalla che s'aggira (Scarlatti), 122
Ferma, Borea, che tenti? (Bononcini), 174
Ferma, ferma il corso (Stradella), 13, 357
Ferma l'ardita prora? (Bononcini), 164
Ferma omai, fugace e bella (Scarlatti), 350
Figli del mesto cor (Handel), 332
Figlio d'alte speranze (Handel), 332
Filen, mio caro bene (Scarlatti), 350
Fileno, idolo mio (Steffani), 357
Fille, a freggiar di tue bellezze il velo (de Cupertinis), 222
Fille dolce, mio bene (Hasse), 341
Fille, già più non parlo (D. Scarlatti), 354–5
Fille, oh Dio (Porpora), 347
Filli che esprime la sua fede a Fileno (Scarlatti), see *Filen, mio caro bene*
Filli, chiedi al mio cor (Albinoni), 318
Filli, del tuo partire (Bononcini), 164
Filli, di gioia vuoi farmi morir (attr. Vivaldi), 364
Filli, già che la sorte (Gasparini), 164n
Filli mia, mio bel tesoro (Bononcini), 169
Filli mio ben, mia speme (Bononcini), 169
Filli pentita (Caldara), 324
Filli, tu sai s'io t'amo (Scarlatti), 350
Filli vezzosa, oh dèi (Bononcini), 164
Fillide mia, se t'amo (Bononcini), 164
Fissai, caro mio bene (Bononcini), 174
Fonti del pianto (Vivaldi), 289–90, 291, 360–61
Fonti, voi che al mio pianto crescete (Marcello), 344

Forsennato pensier, che far poss'io (Stradella), 16–17
Fra mille semplicetti augei canori (Scarlatti), 120
Fra pensieri quel pensiero (Handel), 332–3
Frena, o Filli, il fiero orgoglio (Stradella), 358
Fugge del bosco al prato (Platti), 347
Fuor della stigia sponda (Stradella), 358
Gelosia (Bononcini), see *O d'affetto gentil, figlia crudele*
Gelosia, so che t'affanna (Bononcini), 164
Geme l'onda che parte dal fonte (Vivaldi), 361
Genio che amar volea (Ariosti or Bononcini), 135n
Genio, che amar volea (Bononcini), 164
Genuflesso a tue piante (Stradella), 15
Già di trionfi onusto (Scarlatti), 118, 119
Già fra l'onde il sol t'asconde (unknown composer), 173n
Già fugavan le stelle (Bononcini), 164
Già l'auriga splendente (Grossi), 87
Già la ridente aurora (Bononcini), 174
Già la stagion d'Amore (Bononcini), 174, 323
Già languiva la notte (Stradella), 9, 11–12, 17
Già lusingato appieno (Scarlatti), 119–20, 350
Già tornava l'aurora (Albinoni or Bononcini), 135n, 140n
Già tra l'onde il sol t'asconde (Bononcini), 169, 173n
Già tutti i miei pensieri (also *Tutti li miei pensieri*) (Bononcini), 169
Giacea di verde mirto all'ombra in giorno (Bononcini), 138n, 164
Godea dolce sapore Tirsi sopra l'arene (Bononcini), 169
Guardati a core (Steffani), 357
Ha più foco un sen ferito (Bassani), 97, 98, 106
Hai finto di lusingarmi (Steffani), 357
Havete il torto a fé (Legrenzi), xxvin, 71–2, 73
Hendel, non può mia musa (Handel), 333
Heraclite et Démocrite (Stuck), 238

Ho fuggito Amore anch'io (Handel), 333
Idolatrata e cinta (Porpora), 311, 347
Il barcheggio (Stradella), 29, 44
Il ciel seren, le fresche aurette (Scarlatti), 126
Il consiglio (Handel), see *Tra le fiamme*
Il Coriolano (Scarlatti), see *La fortuna di Roma*
Il Damone (Stradella), 23, 29
Il delirio amoroso (Handel), see *Da quel giorno fatale*
Il duello (Stradella), 4, 29
Il gelsomino (Caldara), 324
Il gelsomino (Handel), see *Son gelsomino*
Il genio di Mitilde (Scarlatti), 350
Il Germanico (Scarlatti), see *Già di trionfi onusto*
Il lamento d'Olimpia (Bononcini), see *Le tenui ruggiade*
Il mio cor fu sempre mio (Bononcini), 164
Il naufragio (Ariosti), 320
Il Nerone (Bononcini), see *Tra mille fiamme ardenti*
Il Nerone (Scarlatti), 287–8
Il nome glorioso in terra, santificato in cielo (Albinoni), 258
Il nume d'Amore (Bononcini), 149
Il partir del caro bene (Bononcini), 174
Il pastore disperato (Bononcini), see *Dove bambino rivo*
Il pensiero che rapido vola (Amadei), 319
Il più felice e sfortunato amante (Steffani), 357
Il povero mio cor (Vivaldi), 361
Il rosignolo se scioglie il volo (Scarlatti), 350
Il rosignuolo (Scarlatti), see *Qui dove alfin m'assido*
Il silentio (Caldara), 324
Il sonno (Scarlatti), see *Deh torna, amico sonno*
Il Timoteo (Marcello), 180
Il trionfo degli dèi (Bononcini), 136n
Il trionfo della Gloria (Leo), see *Così del vostro suono*
Il trionfo delle stagioni (Scarlatti), 121n
Immagini d'orrore (Scarlatti), 350

Impara a non dar fede (Bononcini), 150–53, 157n, 160–61, 164, 175n
In due luci vezzosette (Bononcini), 164
In morte d'un rosignuolo (Bononcini), see *Per un colpo di sorte maligna*
In quel sol che in grembo al Tago (Stradella), 15
In siepe odorosa (Bononcini), 164
In tante pene e in così acerbo duolo (Bononcini), 169
In una valle amena (Bononcini), 164
Incominciate a piangere (Bononcini), 164
Incredule Amarilli (Bononcini), 169
Indarno cerca la tortorella (Vivaldi), 361
Infelice quel cor che vi crede (Bononcini), 164
Ingrata Lidia,[h]a vinto il tuo rigor (Bononcini?), 169, 173n
Ingrata Lidia, ha vinto il tuo rigor (attr. Vivaldi), 300n, 364
Io che a Filli lontano (Bononcini), 164
Io lo vedo (Rossi), 154n
Io mi parto, o cara (Steffani), 120n
Io morirei contento (Scarlatti), 131, 132n, 351
Io non vuò più star così (Stradella), 12
Io parto, e con qual core (Vinci), 220n
Io son lungi alla mia vita (Bononcini), 164
Io vi chiedo, o selve amene (Bononcini), 169
Irene, idolo mio (Handel), 333
Irene, idolo mio, in questo a me fatale (Bononcini), 169
Irene, idolo mio, Irene, addio (Bononcini), 164
Irene mia che tanto bella (Bononcini), 169
Irene orgogliosa (Caldara), 324
Irene sdegnata (A. Marcello), see *Contro l'empio Fileno*
Jonas (La Guerre), 251
L'accademia d'amore (Stradella), 29
L'amante impazzito (Coya), 313n, 327
L'amore onesto (Ariosti), 320
L'Amour et Bacchus (Clérambault), 239
L'Amour vainqueur (Bernier), 233
L'anniversario amoroso (Caldara), 325
L'Arianna (Scarlatti), see *Dove alfin mi traeste?*

L'Arianna (Scarlatti), see *Ebra d'amor fuggia*
L'Arianna (Stradella), see *Ferma, ferma il corso*
L'armi crudeli e fiere (Scarlatti), 351
L'armonica (Hasse), 341
L'aure grate, il fresco rio (Handel), 333
L'avete fatta a me (Stradella), 9
L'Été (Le Maire), 251
L'Hymen (Bernier), 239
L'infedeltà (Scarlatti), 118
L'infelice Fileno assiso (Bononcini), 169
L'infelice tortorella (A. or G. Bononcini), 174
L'Isle de Délos (Pipereau), 253
L'olmo (Ariosti), 320
L'usignolo che il suo duolo (Marcello), 274, 290–91
La Circe (Apolloni), 4
La Cleopatra crudele (Caldara), 325
La colère d'Achille (Campra), 251, 253
La costanza non gradita nel doppio amore d'Aminta (Bononcini), 147n
La dispute de l'Amour et de l'Hymen (Campra), 237
Là dove a Mergellina (Scarlatti), 351
La fama (Caldara), 325
La farfalletta s'aggira al lume (Vivaldi), 361
La fedeltà consolata dalla speranza (Giannettini), 129
La forriera del giorno (Caldara), 325
La fortuna di Roma (Scarlatti), 118
La forza delle stelle (Stradella), 4, 23–4
La gelosia (Ariosti), 320
La gelosia (Hasse), 341
La guerre (Campra), 232
La libertà di Roma (Melani), see *Pompeo in Lesbo*
La Lucretia Romana (Scarlatti), see *Lasciato haveva l'adultero superbo*
La Lucrezia (Handel), see *Oh numi eterni*
La Lucrezia (Marcello), see *Lasciato avea l'adultero*
La lyre d'Anacréon (Bourgeois), 240, 253
La mia speme è vanità (Provenzale), 313n
La Muse de l'Opéra (Clérambault), 232, 235, 242–5, 253

La musette (Clérambault), 238, 239
La nemica d'Amore fatta amante (Bononcini), 147n, 159n
La notte, il giorno ed il merito (de Luca), 121
La nymphe de la Seine (Colin de Blamont), 239, 240, 253
La paix (Dutartre), 238, 239
La Pazzia (Scarlatti), 122
La primavera (Bononcini), see *Nella stagion che di viole e rose*
La rosa (Ariosti), 320
La rosa (Caldara), 325
La rosa regina dei fiori (Bononcini), see *Non sarei de' fior reina*
La scusa (Hasse), 341
La solitudine (Handel), see *L'aure grate, il fresco rio*
La Stravaganza (Scarlatti), see *La Pazzia*
La toilette de Vénus (Colin de Blamont), 238, 239
La tromba (Melani), see *Quai bellici accenti ascolti, mio core?*
La viola gialla (Bononcini) see *Ferma, Borea, che tenti?*
La violetta (Bononcini), see *Presso allo stuol pomposo*
Lagrime dolorose (Steffani), 357
Lagrime mie a che vi trattenete (Strozzi), 81
Langue accesa d'amore (Bononcini), 164
Languia di bocca lusinghiera (Handel), 333
Lascamenti al mio duolo speranze adultrici (Fedeli), 313n, 327
Lascia di tormentarmi, tiranna gelosia (Bononcini), 164
Lascia più di tormentarmi, rimembranza (Scarlatti), 351
Lasciami un sol momento (Bononcini), 174, 323
Lasciate ch'io respiri, ombre gradite (Stradella), 34–5
Lasciato avea l'adultero (Marcello), 344
Lasciato haveva l'adultero superbo (Scarlatti), 118, 119
Le berger fidèle (Rameau), 238

Le charme de la voix (Colin de Blamont), 239
Le jaloux (Campra), 233
Le jaloux (Clérambault), 251
Le Parnasse lyrique (Colin de Blamont), 233n, 239, 251, 253
Le retour de la Paix (Montéclair), 240
Le soleil, vainqueur des nuages (Clérambault), 232, 234–6, 238, 239, 246n, 251–2
Le sommeil d'Ulisse (La Guerre), 251
Le temple rebasti (La Guerre), 249–50
Le tenui ruggiade (Bononcini), 174, 323
Le triomphe de la Paix (Clérambault), 236
Le vicende d'amore (Bononcini), see *Alla beltà d'un volto*
Léandre et Héro (Clérambault), 232, 238, 239, 251
Leandro, anima mia (Scarlatti), 351
Les bains de Toméry (Stuck), 238
Les festes bolonnoises (Stuck), 232, 234, 240
Les heureux époux (Campra), 236
Les nymphes de Diane (Bernier), 239
Lettera del Sig.r Carlo Ant.o Benati (Marcello), see *Carissima figlia*
Li due volubili (Bencini), 126n
Libertà acquistata in amore (Ariosti), 320
Lidia, bell'idolo mio (Bononcini), 169
Lidia, tu sai ch'io t'amo (Bononcini), 164
Lidio, schernito amante di Lucilla (Bononcini), 164
Lisa, del foco mio (Scarlatti), 126
Lo sapete, occhi lucenti (Bononcini), 174
Lo schiavo liberato (Stradella), 4, 29
Lo sfortunato (Scarlatti), see *Per un momento solo*
Lontan da la sua Clori (Scarlatti), 351
Lontan da te, mia vita (Albinoni), 259–62, 266
Lontan dal tuo bel viso (Bononcini), 144, 164
Lontananza (Bononcini), see *Io son lungi alla mia vita* and *Viver lungi dal suo bene è un tormento*
Lontananza crudel, mi squarci il core (Albinoni), 318

Lontananza crudel, se tu pretendi (Bononcini), 164, 166
Lontananza dell'amato (Conti), 326
Lontananza e gelosia (Marcello), 344
Luce degli occhi miei (Pergolesi), 346
Luci barbare, spietate (Bononcini), 149n
Luci belle, pupille adorate (Bononcini), 169
Luci, siete pur quelle (Bononcini), 150–51, 154n, 159, 164
Lumi, vezzosi lumi (Bononcini), 150–51, 159, 160, 161, 164
Lunge dal sole amato (Melani), 345
Lunghi da te, mio bene (Bononcini), 164
Lunghi dalla mia Filli (Bononcini), 164
Lungi da me, pensier tiranno (Handel), 333
Lungi da voi, che siete poli (Handel), 333–4
Lungi dal ben ch'adoro (Gaffi), 139n
Lungi dal mio bel nume (Handel), 334
Lungi dal vago volto (Vivaldi), 274, 366
Lungi dall'idol mio (Caldara), 325
Mai non s'udì cred'io (Bononcini), 174
Mai non vidi il sol più adorno (Bononcini), 169
Manca pur quanto sai (Handel), 334
Marte, ammore, guerra e pace (Faggioli), 313n, 327
Me sento 'na cosa (Provenzale), 348
Medea in Corinto (Caldara), 313n, 325
Mentre il tutto è in furore (Handel), 334
Mentre l'ascoso ardor (Bononcini), 164
Menzognere speranze (Handel), 334
Mercé d'amico raggio (Bononcini), 174
Mesta, oh Dio, fra queste selve (Vinci), 212, 214–15, 216–18
Mi costa tante lacrime (Vinci), 213, 220, 222
Mi dà pena quando spira (Albinoni), 318
Mi palpita il cor (Handel), 305–6, 334–5
Mi tormenta il pensiero (A. Scarlatti), 170n
Mi tormenta il pensiero (D. Scarlatti), 355
Mia bella Irene (Zipoli), 314n, 369
Mia vita, mio bene (Alveri), 107, 313n, 319
Misero amante (Stradella), 19–21
Misero e che far deggio (Bononcini), 174
Misero pastorello ardo di sete (Bononcini), 174, 323

Moderazione d'amore (Bononcini), see
    Poiché speme non v'è
Morirei disperato (Scarlatti), 121–2
Musico raffreddato (Albergati), see
    D'Acheronte errini horribili
Nacqui a' sospiri e al pianto (Scarlatti),
    351
Nel chiuso centro (Pergolesi), 346
Nel dolce dell'oblio (Handel), 299, 335–6
Nel dolce tempo (Handel), 336
Nel partir da te, mio caro (Vivaldi), 361–2
Nel partire per restituirsi alla Sua Donna
    (Bononcini), see *O foriera del
    giorno*
Nel petto ho sol un core (Gaffi), 139n
Nel silentio comune (Scarlatti), 351
Nell'africane selve (Handel), 336
Nell'orror più profondo (Bononcini), 164
Nella stagion che di viole e rose
    (Bononcini), 164
Nella stagion che di viole e rose (Handel),
    336
Nelle scuole erudite (Bononcini), 169,
    170n
Neptune (Stuck), 239
Nice, che fa? che pensa? (Handel), 336
Nice, mia cara Nice (Bononcini), 174
Ninfe, pastori, ahimé (Bononcini), 169
No, non fuggire, o Nice (D. Scarlatti), 355
No, più non vi crede, no (Bononcini), 164
Noiosi pensieri, fuggite dal seno
    (Stradella), 12, 15–16
Non ardisce di scoprirsi amante
    (Bononcini), see *Se per soverchio
    duolo*
Non ardisco pregarti, anima bella
    (Bononcini), 168
Non avea il sole ancora (Stradella), 358
Non ho che lagnarmi (Legrenzi), 67–8
Non ho pace nel mio core (Bononcini), 164
Non per anche disciolta (A. or G.
    Bononcini), 169
Non sa che sia dolore (Bach), 302, 321–2
Non sa dir che pena sia (Bononcini), 167n,
    169–70
Non sarei de' fior reina (Bononcini), 164
Non so qual più m'ingombra (*Cantata
    pastorale*) (Scarlatti), 351

Non sospirar, non piangere (Handel), 336
Non v'aprite ai rai del sole (Gasparini),
    313, 328
Non v'è pena (Caldara), 325
Notte ch'in carro d'ombre (Scarlatti), 129
Notte placida e cheta (Handel), 336
O ch'io son pur sfortunato (Porfirii),
    100–104
O che lacci io sento al core (Bononcini),
    148n
O come in un'istante (F. Scarlatti), 356
O d'affetto gentil, figlia crudele
    (Bononcini), 164
O Daliso (Zipoli), 369
O Fileno, Filen (*O Irene, Iren*) *crudele,
    ingrato sì* (Bononcini), 164
O Fille, amata Fille (Bononcini), 174
O foriera del giorno (Bononcini), 164
O frondoso arboscello (Bononcini), 135n,
    174
O Irene, Iren (Bononcini), see *O Fileno,
    Filen*
O mesta tortorella (Bononcini), 174
O mie porpore più belle (Vivaldi), 368
O pace del mio cor (Scarlatti), 351
O penosa lontananza (Scarlatti), 149n
O qual meco Nice cangiata (D. Scarlatti),
    355
O quanto omai diverso (Fago or
    Bononcini), 135n
O spettacolo pur troppo funesto
    (Ferrandini), 327
O tu che sì fastosa (Bononcini), 164
Occhi miei, che faceste? (Handel), 337
Œnone (Destouches), 232, 235, 238, 246
Oh di Betlemme altera povertà (*Cantata
    pastorale per la nascita di Nostro
    Signore*) (Scarlatti), 351
Oh! Dio! che non è vero (Porpora), 313n,
    347
Oh numi eterni (Handel), 336–7
Ohimè chi mi risveglia (Bononcini), 164–5
Olà, pensieri, olà (Carissimi), 7
Ombre, fuggite e voi, notturni orrori
    (Rossi), 7
Ombre tacite e sole (Scarlatti), 352
Ombre, voi che celate (Stradella), 358
Onda d'amaro pianto (Marcello), 344

Onde della mia Nera (D. Scarlatti), 355
Or [Hor] che di Febo ascosi (Scarlatti), 352
Or che d'orrido verno (Porpora), 347
Or che una nube ingrata (Porpora), 311, 347
Or nel bosco ed or nel prato (Bononcini), 168
Oratio Coclite (Melani), see *A ricalcare in Tebro*
Orfeo (Pergolesi), see *Nel chiuso centro*
Orphée (Clérambault), 232n, 238, 239
Ove rivolgo il piede (Albinoni), 318–19
Palesar vorria gl'ardori (Gasparini), 313, 328
Par che tardo oltre il costume (Vivaldi), 362
Partenza (Caldara), 325
Partenza che parti in pezzi il mio core (Bononcini), 165
Partenza di G. B. (Handel), see *Stelle, perfide stelle*
Partì, l'idolo mio (Handel), 337
Parti, mi lasci (Albinoni), 319
Partirò ma con qual core (Bononcini), 170
Partite dal mio sen (Cesti), 7
Parto, ma con qual core (Vinci), 218–20
Parto, sì parto, mio bene (Bononcini), 165
Passan i giorni e l'ore (Bononcini), 169n, 170
Pastor, come diverso (Bononcini), 174
Pastor d'Arcadia, è morta Clori (Bononcini), 135n, 170
Pastorella vagha, bella (Handel?), 340
Pecorelle che pascete (Marcello), 344
Pende dal sen di Fille (Bononcini), 165
Peno e l'alma fedele (Bononcini), 150-51, 155-6, 157, 160, 161, 165, 167n
Pensier che ti nutrisci (Bononcini), 170
Pensieri notturni di Filli (Handel), see *Nel dolce dell'oblio*
Per combater (anon.), 320
Per due vaghe pupille (Fregiotti), 173n
Per palestri appieno (Hasse), 341
Per sollevar quest'alma (Bononcini), 165
Per un colpo di sorte maligna (Bononcini), 165
Per un momento solo (Scarlatti), 352

Perché dar non ti posso (Caldara), 135n
Perché mai, nume adorato (Gabrielli), 140n
Perché non dirmi un sì del cor tiranna (Bononcini), 170
Perché son molli (Vivaldi), 366-7
Perché tacete, regolati concenti? (Scarlatti), 352
Perfidissimo cor! Iniquo fato! (Vivaldi), 316, 364
Però che scende in petto (Brusa), 269–71
Piangete, occhi dolenti (D. Scarlatti), 355
Piango in van dall'idol mio (Bononcini), 165, 168n
Piango, gemo, sospiro e peno (attr. Vivaldi), 302, 308–9, 364–5
Piango, sospiro e peno (Scarlatti), 352
Pianti, sospiri e dimandar mercede (Vivaldi), 365
Pietosa l'aurora in cielo (Vinci), 211, 213, 220, 224
Pietoso nume arcier (Bononcini), 149n
Più dell'Alpi gelato (Bononcini), 165
Poi ché riseppe Orfeo (Scarlatti), 352
Poiché al vago seren di due pupille (Albinoni), 319
Poiché Fille superba (Bononcini), 174
Poiché la bella Clori (Scarlatti), 129
Poiché lo Sdegno intese (Carissimi), 7
Poiché speme non v'è (Bononcini), 174
Pomone (Gervais), 235
Pompeo in Lesbo (Melani), 345
Posa sopra d'un faggio (anon.), 320
Povero afflitto cor, come à tanto dolor (Scarlatti), 142n
Prendea con man di latte (attr. Vivaldi), 171n
Presso allo stuol pomposo (Bononcini), 165, 173n
Presso allo stuol pomposo (unknown composer), 173n
Prigionier d'un bel sembiante (Bononcini), 148n
Prigionier di bionde chiome (Bononcini), 170
Prima d'esservi infedele (Scarlatti), 119
Proserpine (Stuck), 239
Pur al fin gentil (Ariosti), 320

Pur deggio partire (Hasse), 341
Pur dicesti, o bocca bella (Lotti), 343
Pur nel sonno almen tal'ora (D. Scarlatti), 355
Pur vi riveggio ancora (Bononcini), 165
Quai bellici accenti ascolti, mio core? (Melani), 345
Qual in pioggia dorata i dolci rai (Vivaldi), 300–301, 368
Qual mormorio giocondo (Melani), 345
Qual nuovo sole è questo (Hasse), 341
Qual oggetto (Gaffi), 139n
Qual pensier, quale ardire ti guida? (D. Scarlatti), 355
Qual per ignoto calle (Vivaldi), 316, 365
Qual più cercando ai bella tiranna mia (Bononcini), 170
Qual ti riveggio, oh Dio (Handel), 337
Quando la finirai di tormentarmi (Bononcini), 165
Quando m'innalza Amore (Bononcini), 165
Quando mai, Cupido ingrato (Bononcini), 165
Quando mai, vermigli labri (Bononcini), 165
Quando mai vi stancherete (Stradella), 358
Quando miro il vostro foco (D. Scarlatti), 355
Quando, o bella, io ti viddi (Bononcini), 165
Quando parli e quando ridi (Bononcini), 144, 165, 166n
Quando sarai senz'onde (Polani), 280–81
Quando sperasti, o core (Handel), 337
Quando voi, amiche stelle (Bononcini), 149n
Quanto dolce è quell'ardore (Mancini), 343
Quanto peno e quanto piango (Bononcini), 165
Quanto piace agl'occhi miei (Bononcini), 174
Quanto sarei felice (Bononcini), 165
Quel fior che all'alba ride (Handel), 338
Quel vago seno, O Fille (Hasse), 341–2
Quella pace gradita (Scarlatti), 352
Quella speranza, o Dio (Bononcini), 170

Questa dunque è la selva (Porpora), 311, 347
Queste che miri, o Nice (Porpora), 313, 347
Queste voci dolenti (Gasparini), 328
Questo è il piano (Pergolesi), 346
Qui dove alfin m'assido (Scarlatti), 122, 301, 352
Rendimi un sguardo solo (Brevi), 93
Ride il prato e fra l'erbe (Conti), 326
Riedi a me, luce gradita (Albinoni), 319
Rimirai la rosa un dì (D. Scarlatti), 355
Rompi l'arco, rompi i lacci (Bononcini), 168
Rondinella vaga e bella (Mangini?), 140n
S'io piango e tu non m'odi (Bononcini), 174
Santa Maria Maddalena in viaggio alla solitudine (Bononcini), 166n
Sappia e pianga ogni core (Bononcini), 170
Sarei troppo felice (Scarlatti), 117–18, 119, 131
Scherza di fronda in fronda (Vivaldi), 362
Scherza meco il destino (Bononcini), 165
Sciogliete in dolci nodi (Stradella), 44
Sciolto in placidi umori (Bononcini), 170
Sconsigliato consiglio (Bononcini), 165
Scritte con falso inganno (D. Scarlatti), 356
Sdegno, campion audace (Tricarico), 358
Se bella son io (Bononcini), 148n
Se ben vivono senz'alma (Vivaldi), 362
Se dal indiche arene (Bononcini), 165
Se del pianeta ardente (Stradella), 21–23, 44
Se di Tantalo si dice (Bononcini), 165
Se fedele tu m'adori (D. Scarlatti), 356
Se ferirmi sapesti (Gasparini or Bononcini), 135n
Se il cantor trace, oh Dio (Hasse), 342
Se Nerone lo vuole (Stradella), 17–19
Se pari è la tua fé (Handel), 338
Se parti io morirò, dolce mia vita (Bononcini?), 170, 173n
Se per soverchio duolo (Bononcini), 165
Se sai qual sia la pena (D. Scarlatti), 355
Se ti dicesse un core (D. Scarlatti), 355

Se v'è chi amante peni (Bononcini), 174
Seguir fera che fugge (Gasparini), 313, 328
Sei nata a farmi piangere (Bononcini), 174
Sémelé (Destouches), 232, 238, 239
Sempre mi torna in mente (Caldara), 325
Sempre piango e dir non so (Bononcini), 148n
Senti, Filli (Caldara), 325
Sentite, o tronchi (Sarro or Scarlatti), 173n
Sentite, o tronchi, o sassi (Marcello), 344
Sento dentro del petto (Bononcini), 168
Sento già che nel mezzo al mio core (Marcello), 344
Sento là che ristretto (Handel), 338
Senza gran pena non si giunge al fine (Marcello), 344
Senza il core del mio bene (Albinoni), 273n
Si apra al riso ogni labbro (Stradella), 21–2
Sì, ch'io temo (Stradella), 13
Si levi dal pensier (Vivaldi), 362
Si salvi chi può (Stradella), 358
Sì, sì, luci adorate (Vivaldi), 362
Sì, t'intendo, tu vuoi ch'io non pensi (Bononcini?), 170, 173n
Siamo in contesa, la bellezza ed io (Scarlatti), 119
Siedi, Amarilli mia (Bononcini), 174, 323
Siete rose ruggiadose (Handel), 338
Siete unite a tormentarmi (Scarlatti), 352
Silène (Campra), 236
So d'essermi d'Amor (Bononcini), 174
Soave libertade, nasci, è vero (Bononcini), 169n, 174
Soffri, mio caro Alcino (Caldara), 313n, 325
Solitudini amene, apriche collinette (Scarlatti), 352
Solitudini campestre (Hasse), 342
Solitudini care, amata libertà (Handel), 338
Son ferrito d'un labbro di giglio (Aldrovandini), 319
Son gelsomino (Handel), 338
Son' io barbara donna, infida Clori (Bononcini), 174
Son qual Tantalo novello (Albinoni), 319

Son tradita e pur non moro (Bononcini), 170
Sono amante e due tormenti (Bononcini?), 170, 173n
Sono in dubbio d'amar (Stradella), 10–12
Sono liete, fortunate (Handel), 148n
Sopra candido foglio (Stradella), 358
Sopra l'orme d'Irene (A. Bononcini), 141n
Sopra l'orme d'Irene (G. Bononcini), 141n, 170
Sopra le verdi sponde che la Brenta superba (Scarlatti), 123n
Sopra un'eccelsa torre (Stradella), 14
Sorge l'alba e torna il dì (Bononcini), 165
Sorge Lidia la notte (Leo), 342
Sorge vermiglia in ciel la bella Aurora (Vivaldi), 362–3
Sospendi, o man, per poco (D. Scarlatti), 355
Sospirato ben mio, dolcezza del mio core (Bononcini), 165
Sotto l'ombra d'un pino (Rossi), 7
Sotto quest'empie mura (Simonelli), 34, 39, 44–8
Sovente amore mi chiama (Scarlatti), 352
Sovra il famoso fiume (Bononcini), 165
Sovra un bel poggio assisa (Bononcini), 165
Spande ancor a mio dispetto (Handel), 338
Speranze del mio cor (Porpora), 347
Speranze mie, addio (Scarlatti), 132n, 352
Spezza, amor (Steffani), 357
Splenda l'alba in oriente (Handel), 301, 338
Splende più dell'usato (Leo), 343
Splendeano in bel sembiante (Scarlatti), 353
Sprezzata mi credi, ma non tradita (Stradella), 17n
Squarciato appena havea (Provenzale), 348
Stanca di più penar Clori la bella (Bononcini), 165
Stanco del tuo gran duolo (Bononcini), 165
Stella ria (Caldara), 325
Stelle, perfide stelle (Handel), 339
Sto poglietta presuntuso (Faggioli), 327

Stravaganze d'amore: Cantata enarmonica (Marcello), see *Senza gran pena non si giunge al fine*
Su la riva del mar tutto dolente (Pistocchi), 262–6
Su la sponda del mare per un ingrato (Scarlatti), 129
Su le fiorite sponde (Sarro), 222
Su le sponde del Tebro (Scarlatti), 300, 353
Su tapeto odoroso d'erbe (Bononcini?), 170, 173n
Sui palchi delle stelle (Provenzale), 313n
Sulla sponda d'un rio afflitta e mesta (Bononcini), 165, 166n
Sulla sponda del mar stava Fileno (Bononcini), 174
Sulla sponda odorosa (A. or G. Bononcini), 170
Sulle ripe dell'Ebro (Bononcini), 165
Sventurato Fileno siedeva un dì (Bononcini), 138n, 165
Sventurato Mirtillo, e che farai? (Bononcini), 165
Sventurato pastor (Bononcini), 174
T'intendo sì, mio cor (Vivaldi), 363
Talor per suo diletto (Scarlatti), 123
Ti ricorda, o bella Irene (D. Scarlatti), 356
Ti sento, o Dio Bendato (Lotti), 343
Tinte a note di sangue (D. Scarlatti), 356
Titolo di costante non merta quel amante (Bononcini), 165
Tormento del mio seno (Bononcini), 165
Torna il giorno fatale (G. M. Bononcini II, called Angelo), 135n
Torna, torna alla capanna (Bononcini), 174
Torno a voi, piante amorose (Bononcini), 174, 323
Tortorella al monte, al piano (Marcello or Bononcini), 135n
Tortorella che priva (Bononcini), 170
Tra catene haver il piede (Bononcini), 165
Tra dubbiosi pensieri (Bononcini), 165
Tra i raggi d'un bel volto (Bononcini or Gasparini), 165
Tra i smeraldi di prato gentile (Bononcini?), 170, 173n
Tra l'amene delitie (Bononcini), 165
Tra l'erbe e i zeffiri (Vivaldi), 363

Tra le fiamme (Handel), 339
Tra mille fiamme ardenti (Bononcini), 165
Tremori al braccio e lagrime sul ciglio (Vivaldi), 266–9, 368–9
Triste, ausente, en esta selva (Vinci), 214, 217, 359
Troppo cruda, troppo fiera (Handel), 148n
Tu fedel? Tu costante? (Handel), 301, 339
Tu mi chiedi, o mio ben (D. Scarlatti), 356
Tu sei quella che al nome (Scarlatti), 118
Tu volgesti altrove i vanni (Bononcini), 170
Tutti li miei (Bononcini), see *Già tutti i miei*
Tutto cinto di ferro (Rossi), 7
Udite, amanti, un prodigio novello (Stradella), 15
Udite il mio consiglio (Handel), 339–40
Udite, o Cieli (Porta), 313n
Un'alma innamorata (Handel), 340
Un dì che nel mio core (Bononcini), 165
Un dì tre pastorelle (Bononcini), 174–5
Un sospir a chi si muore (Handel), 340
Usignol che col mio pianto (Bononcini), 175
Usignoletto bello (Vivaldi), 368
V'amo sì, care luci (Torri), 358
Va sospirando il core (Mancini), 140n
Va, credi e spera, mio cor traditor (Bononcini), 165
Vado ben spesso cangiando loco (Bononcini), 150–51, 156, 161, 165, 166n
Vaga madre di cari diletti (Hasse), 342
Vaganti pensieri (Stradella), 17n
Vaghi augelletti che d'amor (Conti), 326
Vago augelletto al patrio nido (Bononcini), 175
Vago prato, ben ristori (Bononcini?), 170, 173n
Vanne sì, ruscelletto contento (Bononcini), 175
Vantar alma di gelo (Bononcini), 165
Varie pene d'amore (Bononcini), 170
Vedendo Amor (Handel), 340
Vedrò senz'onde il mare (Caldara), 326
Veggio la bella Dori (Bononcini), 175
Veggo la selva e 'l monte (Vinci or Benati), 212, 215, 223–4

Venere, Adone et Amore (Scarlatti), 121n
Vengo a voi, luci adorate (Vivaldi), 367
Venne voglia ad Amore (Handel), 340
Verrà un dì che la mia bella (Polani), 280–81
Vi conosco, occhi bugiardi (Handel or Bononcini), 135
Vicino a un rivoletto (Caldara), 313n, 326
Vidi in cimento due vaghi Amori (Bononcini), 165, 312, 323
Viver e non amar fora delitto (Bononcini), 165
Viver lungi dal suo bene è un tormento (Bononcini), 175
Voglio senza speranza (Bononcini), 165
Voi carbonchi animate (Bononcini), 170
Voi ch'io dica che t'adoro (Bononcini?), 170, 173n
Voi che tutto dolente (Bononcini), 165
Vola, vola in altri petti (Stradella), see *Il duello*
Vorrei un zeffiretto (Scarlatti?), 125–6
Zéphyre et Flore (Clérambault), 239

2. Index of operas, oratorios and ballets

Abdolomino (Bononcini), 172n
Adriano in Siria (Vinci), 212, 223
Alceste (Gluck), 180
Alcyone (Marais), 243n
Armida al campo d'Egitto (Vivaldi), 315n
Artaserse (Vinci), 212, 221–3
Artemisia (Cavalli), 58
Astianatte (Vinci), 213, 217, 223
Bajazete (Leo), 218
Catone in Utica (Vinci), 212, 223
Dafni (Scarlatti), 121n
Didon (Campra), 236
Endimione (A. Bononcini), 172n
Endimione (G. Bononcini), 172n
Enea in Italia (Draghi), 76
Eraclea, o vero Il ratto delle Sabine (Bononcini: pasticcio), 150
Esther (Handel), 156n
Euristeo (Hasse), 221, 222
Farnace (Courcelle), 217
Farnace (Vinci), 217
Farnace (Vivaldi), 315n
Giuditta (Scarlatti), 127n
Hippolyte et Aricie (Rameau), 301n
I trionfi del fato (Steffani), 138n
Il pastor di Corinto (Scarlatti), 121n
Il prigioniero fortunato (Scarlatti), 121n
Il ritorno d'Ulisse in patria (Monteverdi), 73
Il trionfo di Camilla, regina de' Volsci (Bononcini), 141n, 150, 159n, 168n
Issipile (Hasse), 221, 222
Judas Maccabaeus (Handel), 156n
L'Eraclea (Vinci), 217
L'Europe galante (Campra), 235
L'Olimpia vendicata (Scarlatti), 129
L'Olimpiade (Vivaldi), 300n
L'ultima persecuzione di Saule contro Davidde (Peli), 172n
La caduta dei Decemviri (Vinci), 213, 223
La clemenza d'Augusto (Bononcini and others), 150
La forza dell'Allegrezza (anon.), 76
La forza dell'amor paterno (Stradella), 4–5, 29, 41
La Psiche (Scarlatti), 132n
La rinovata Camilla, regina de' Volsci (Bononcini), 141, 145, 150
La Suite d'Armide (Philippe, duc d'Orléans), 231n
Les amours de Mars et de Vénus (Campra), 236
Les amours de Protée (Gervais), 235
Les festes vénitiennes (Campra), 237, 246–9
Les folies de Cardenio (Lalande), 238n
Les noces de Vénus (Campra), 237
Medo (Vinci), 217

Moro per amore (Stradella), 29, 37, 38, 41
Orlando (Vivaldi), 301
Partenope (Sarro), 218
Partenope (Vinci), 218
Publio Cornelio Scipione (Vinci), 218
Pyrrhus and Demetrius (Scarlatti), 145, 146n

Rosmira fedele (Vinci), 218
San Giovanni Battista (Stradella), 37
Totila (Legrenzi), 56–73 *passim*
Viriate (Hasse), 221, 222

3. Index of other vocal works

Care Jesu suavissime (Stradella), 4
Dixit angelis suis iratus Deus (Stradella), 4
Exultate in Deo, fideles (Stradella), 4
Il Biante (Stradella), 29
Locutus est (Stradella), 19
O vos omnes, qui transitis (Stradella), 4

Reggetemi, non posso più (Stradella), 37n
Sistite sidera (Stradella), 19
Te Deum (Lalande), 237
Volgi, volgi, mio Dio, deh volgi un de' tuoi sguardi (Marcello, B621), xxiv, 182–202 *passim*

General Index

Alphabetization follows the word-by-word system. For libraries, I give only the principal references. Publisher's names (except those of music publishers active before 1750) are omitted. The names of cities appear as headings only where they precede the names of churches, conservatories or universities. Technical and analytical terms are generally listed only in connection with their definitions in the main text. To save space, I have not indexed the names of artists and ensembles appearing in the appendix to Chapter 12.

abate, defined, 120n
Académie Royale de Musique, of Paris, 235, 241–2
Academy of Ancient Music, 306n
Accademia degli Infecondi, of Rome, 120, 123
Accademia degli Intrecciati, of Rome, 123
Accademia degli Umoristi, of Rome, 117
Accademia degli Unisoni, of Venice, 81
Accademia filarmonica, of Bologna, 147
Accademia Musicale Chigiana, of Siena, 298n, 300n
Accademia Strumentale Italiana, 309n
Accademici disuniti, of Rome, 120, 121
Adorno (Wiesengrund-Adorno), Theodor, 299n
Akademie für Alte Musik Berlin, 306n
Alarius (Hilaire Verloge), 240
Albergati (Capacelli), P. Pirro, 89–90, 107–8
   Cantate da camera a voce sola, Op. 6, 89, 106
   Cantate et oratorii spirituali a una, due e tre voci con strumenti, Op. 10, 96
   Cantate morali a voce sola, Op. 3, 89–91
   Cantate spirituali a una, due e trè voci con strumenti, Op. 9, 94, 98, 108
   Corona de' pregi di Maria. Cantate a voce sola, Op. 13, 96
Alberi, Isabella, 2

Albinoni, Tomaso, xxv, 114n, 135n, 140, 171n, 258, 259–62, 266, 273n, 299, 314, 318–19
   Cantate a voce sola, Op. 4, 96, 311
   Trattenimenti armonici per camera, Op. 6, 98
Aldobrandini Pamphilj, Olimpia, 3
Aldrovandini, Giuseppe, 171n, 314, 319
   Cantate a voce sola, Op. 2, 96
Alembert, Jean le Rond d', 233n
Alexandre, Ivan A., 296, 299, 301–304 *passim*, 310
Alexandre, Pasquier-Alexandre, 239
Algarotti, Francesco, 180
Alghisi, Paris Francesco
   Cantate, 92
Alighieri, Dante, 5
Allen, David, 30, 31, 32, 39
Altemps, Pietro, 2, 3
Altogiri, *abate*
   Cantate a voce sola, 96, 98
Alveri, Giovanni Battista, 313n, 319
   Cantate à voce sola da camera, Op. 1, 88, 89, 106–7, 314
Alvini, Laura, 313n
Amadei, Filippo, 319
Amalia Guglielmina (Wilhelmina), princess of Braunschweig-Lüneburg, empress, 172
Amato, Mauro, 211n
Ambrosini, Agnolo

La favola d'Orfeo, 5
Ameling, Elly, 302, 304
Amodei, Cataldo
   Cantate a voce sola, Op. 2, 91, 100
Andersen, Ditte, 313n
Anfuso, Nella, 304n, 307, 312, 313
Anne, queen of England, 159n
Anthony, James R., 243n
Antolini, Bianca Maria, 113n, 139n
Anton Ulrich, duke of Saxe-Meiningen, 269, 313
Apel, Willi, 154n
Apolloni, Giovan Filippo, 4
Arcadian Academy, of Rome, 6, 120, 123–8
arioso, defined, xiii, 14–15
Ariosti, Attilio, 135n, 320
   Six Cantatas and Six Lessons for the Viola d'amore, 99, 105
Ariosto, Ludovico
   Orlando furioso, 5, 129
   Satire, 5
Aristotle, 42, 55
   Poetics, 55
Arrigoni, Carlo
   Cantate da camera, 99
Ars Antiqua Austria, ensemble, 312n
Artiano, Fulvio, 204n
Astorga, *see* d'Astorga
Astroa, Giovanna, 221
Astronio, Claudio, 312n
Atkins, T., 98, 99
Aubert, Isabella, 171
Aumont, duc d', 234
Aureli, Aurelio, 129
Avison, Charles, 201

Babel, Charles, 168
Bacci (Angelo?), 169n
Bach, Johann Sebastian, 147, 297, 299, 302, 303n, 309, 310, 311, 315, 320–21
Bachelier, J., 240
Badia, Carlo Agostino
   Tributi armonici, 95
Badoaro, Giacomo, 58, 73
Baker, Janet, 301–2
Balada, Domenico, 2

Baldini, Sebastiano, 4, 23
Ballard, Christophe, 228n, 237, 239n
Ballard, Jean-Baptiste-Christophe, 151
   Meslanges de musique latine, françoise et italienne, 151, 168
Balmonti, Mauritio, 82
Banchini, Chiara, 147n
Banditelli, Gloria, 309
Barazzoni, Beatrice, 175n
Barthélemy, Maurice, 234n, 236n
Bartleman, James, 156n
Bartlett, Clifford, 76n
Bartoli, Simone, 2
Bartoli, Vittoria, 2
Bashford, Christina, 37n
Bassani, Giovanni Battista, 79, 88, 92–3, 97–8, 106
   Affetti canori, Cantate et ariette, Op. 6, 89, 95
   Amorosi sentimenti di cantate a voce sola, Op. 14, 92
   Armoniche fantasie di cantate amorose a voce sola, Op. 15, 92, 96
   Cantate a voce sola, Op. 28, 96
   Cantate et arie amorose a voce sola con violini unissoni, Op. 31, 96
   Corona di fiori musicali – Tessuta d'ariette con varij stromenti, Op. 29, 96
   Eco armonica delle Muse, Cantate amorose à voce sola, Op. 7, 89, 92
   Il cigno canoro, Cantate amorose, Op. 3, 89, 95
   L'armonia delle Sirene, Cantate amorose musicali à voce sola, Op. 2, 86, 89, 92
   La moralità armonica, Cantate a 2 e 3 voci, Op. 4, 89, 92
   La Musa armonica, Cantate amorose musicali a voce sola, Op. 16, 92, 93
   La Sirena amorosa, Cantate a voce sola con violini, Op. 17, 92
   Languidezze amorose, Cantate a voce sola, Op. 19, 95
Basso, Alberto, 31, 209n, 314n
Battista, Tonino, 206n, 207n
Bavaria, duke of, 236n

Beaumont, Maite, 313n
Becherini, Bianca, 166n
Bedford, duke of (Wriothesley Russell), 145
Beethoven, Ludwig van
   Der glorreiche Augenblick, 46
   Symphony no. 3 (*Eroica*), 178
   Symphony no. 6 (*Pastoral*), 178
Belmonte, Amadeo, 83
Beltrano, Ottavio, 82
Bembo, Pietro, 177
   Prose della volgar lingua, 177
Benacci (erede), Vittorio, 82
Benati, Carlo, 148n, 215, 224
Benavides, Francisco de, 124
Bencini, Pietro Paolo, 126, 140n, 175n
Benedetta, duchess of Braunschweig-Lüneburg, 172n
Bennett, Lawrence, 113n, 136n, 169n, 170n, 173n, 269n, 313n
Benoit, Marcelle, 239
Beregan, Nicolò, 129
Bergalli, Luisa, 179n
Berganza, Tereza, 309
Bergiron de Briou, Nicolas-Antoine, 239
Bernabei, Ercole, xxiii, 27, 34–5, 38–9, 40, 45, 48–50
Bernardoni, Pier Antonio, 165, 169, 174
Bernier, Nicolas, 227n, 230–31, 232, 233, 234, 239, 253
Bertagnolli, Gemma, 315
Berti, Giovanni Pietro
   Cantade et arie ad una voce sola con alcune a doi, 80
Bertini, Rossana, 315
Besson, Gabriel, 240
Bianchi, Giovanni Battista
   Madrigali a due, e tre voci, Op. 1, 85
Bianchi, Lino, 112n, 115n, 116n
Bianconi, Lorenzo, 55n, 205n, 207n, 255n
binder's collection, defined, 210
Bini, Annalisa, 164n
Birmingham, University of, xxiii, 27, 32
bismolle hexachord, defined, 61n
Bizzarini, Marco, xxiv, 179n, 180n, 255n
bizzarria, taste for, 272
Blaeu, P. and I., 94
Blanchet harpsichord, 308

Blasetti, Alessandro, 161n
block sequential repetition, 256
Blume, Friedrich, 112n
Boccella, Francesco
   Primavera di vaghi fiori musicali, overo Canzonette ad una, due, e tre voci, 82
Boileau, Nicolas, 177–8
Boismortier, Joseph Bodin de, 239
Bokemeyer, Heinrich, 114n, 173n
Bologna
   Museo Internazionale e Biblioteca della Musica, 2, 114–15
   San Petronio, 84
Boncompagni, Giacomo, cardinal, 3
Boncompagni, Ugo, 2
Bonizzoni, Fabio, 316
Bononcini, Antonio (Maria), 135n, 136n, 141, 169, 170, 171n, 172n, 174
Bononcini, Francesco Maria, 166
Bononcini, Giovanni, xxiv, 135–75, 202, 227, 228, 312, 315, 322–3
   Cantate e duetti, (*Cd*), 99, 135, 149n, 162, 174, 175, 306
   Duetti da camera, Op. 8, 92, 96, 106, 142–3, 147–50
   Messe brevi a 8 voci piene, Op. 7, 147
   sonatas and concertos, Opp. 1–6, 147
Bononcini, Giovanni Maria, 106
   Cantate per camera a voce sola libro primo, Op. 10, 85
   Cantate per camera a voce sola libro secondo, Op. 13, 85
   Partitura de madrigali a cinque voci, Op. 11, 85
Bononcini, Giovanni Maria II (Angelo), 135n
Bonporti, Francesco Antonio, 273n
Bonta, Stephen, 56n, 88n
Bonynge, Richard, 308n, 309
Bordes, Charles, 297
Bordoni (Hasse), Faustina, 218–222, 224n
Borelli, Giancola, 300n
Boris, Francesca, 224n
Bortoli, Antonio, 98
Bossa, Renato, 205n
Bourgeois, Thomas-Louis, 234, 239, 240, 252, 253

Bousset, Jean-Baptiste de, 232n
Bowman, James, 305, 309
Boyd, Malcolm, 46n, 111–12, 133n, 115n, 116n, 119n, 122n, 129, 131n
Bradley, William Aspenwall, 297
Braibanzi, Francesco
  Cantate da camera a canto solo, Op. 2, 96
Bratti, Domenico, 31
Braun, Daniel, 240
Braun, Werner, 115n
Brenet, Michel, 237n, 238n
Brevi, Giovanni Battista, 93
  Cantate ed' ariette da camera à voce sola, Op. 7, 94
  I delirii d'amor Divino, Cantate morali a voce sola, Op. 5, 94, 98
  La catena d'oro, Ariette da camera a voce sola, Op. 6, 94
  Le forze d'Amore, Cantate a voce sola, Op. 1, 92
Brignole-Sale, Anton Giulio (I), 29, 30, 142
Brignole-Sale, Anton Giulio (II), 30
Britten, Benjamin, 303
Brizi, Bruno, 181n
Broschi, Carlo, 217, 223, 224n
Brossard, Sébastien de, 6, 143n, 148n, 227, 229n, 231n
Brossard, Yolande de, 148n, 240n
Brown, Howard Mayer, 56n, 141n, 168n
Brown, Jennifer Williams, 72n
Brunel, musician, 240
Brusa, Giovanni Francesco, xxv, 269–71
Bucciarelli, Melania, xxin
Buelow, George J., 111n, 116n, 207n
Bukofzer, Manfred, 205n
Burden, Michael, 41n, 216n
Burette, Bernard, 239
Burke, Edmund, 178
Burney, Charles, 111, 156, 161, 179–80, 204, 208–9, 226n, 282n
Burnim, Kalman A., 171n
Burrows, David, 56n
Busenello, Gian Francesco, 58
Busseti, Giovanni, 30n
Bylsma, Anner, 305, 306n

Cabrini, Michele, 241n, 243n
cadence forms, as system of punctuation, 255–6
Caffarelli, duke, 3
Cafiero, Rosa, 225n
Caldara, Antonio, 135n, 139, 167n, 312n, 315, 324–6
Caldwell, John, 6n, 81n, 130n
Calvi, Caterina, 309
Calzabigi, Raniero de', 180
Camagni, publisher, 86
Cambridge, Fitzwilliam Museum, 36
Cambridge, MA, Houghton Library, Harvard University, vii, 148n, 152–3
Camerata Academica Mozarteum, 300
Campra, André, 232, 234, 235, 236–7, 239, 240, 246–9, 250–51, 252, 253
Candiani, Rosy, 224n
cantata anthologies, published,
  Cantate a 1 e 2 voci con trombe e flauto (several authors), 99
  [*Cantate a voce sola*, Lucca, c.1700] (*Ad*), 137, 162–3, 165, 166
  Cantate e ariette a voce sola con violini (several authors), 99
  Cantate e ariette a voce sola senza violini (several authors), 99
  Cantate varie per musica (several authors), 96
  Canzonette amorose a una, doi, tre, voci (1656), 82
  Canzonette per camera a voce sola (1670), 84
  Melpomene coronata da Felsina, Cantate musicali à voce sola, date in luce da Signori Compositori Bolognesi (1685), 89
  Recueil d'airs serieux et a boire – livre second (1696), 94
  Recueil d'airs serieux et a boire – livre troisième (1697), 94
  Scelta delle più belle ariette, e canzoncine italiane de' più famosi autori (1691), 94
  Scelta di canzonette italiane (1679), 86
cantata, defined, 6–7
cantate françoise, xxiv, 227–54
Cantillo, Clementina, 204n

Canuti, Giovanni Antonio, 137
Cantate da camera a voce sola, 95
Cappella (della Pietà) de' Turchini, 217n, 312, 313n
Cappella Mauriziana, 312
Caproli, Carlo, 40
Caraci, Maria, 111n
Carboni, Fabio, 164n, 167n
Cardinale, Flavia, 4n
Carissimi, Giacomo, 7, 82, 142, 256, 317
Carlotta Felicità (Charlotte Felicitas), duchess of Modena, 172n
Carlson, Kent, 166n
Caroline, queen of England, 167, 281n
Carreras, Juan José, 203n, 209n
Carter, Tim, 206n
Casagrande, Luca, 93n
Casares Rodicio, Emilio, 209n
Castracani, Anna Maria, 76
Castro, War of, 2
Cattaneo, Giacomo
Trattenimenti armonici da camera [...] con due brevi cantate a soprano solo, Op. 1, 98
Cavalli (Cavallo), Francesco, 56, 58, 142
Cazzati, Maurizio, 79, 83, 84
Arie e cantate a voce sola, Op. 41, 84, 108
Cantate morali, e spirituali a voce sola, Op. 20, 82, 83, 86, 108
Canzonette per camera a voce sola, Op. 27, 84
Diporti spirituali per camera o per oratorii a uno, due, trè e quattro, Duetti per camera, Op. 66, 85
Il quarto libro delle canzonette a voce sola, Op. 43, 84
Il quinto libro delle canzonette a voce sola con violini a beneplacito, Op. 46, 84
Madrigali e canzonette per camera, a due e tre parte con violini, e parte senza con un Lamento di tre amanti per il gran caldo, Op. 26, 83
Cencic, Max Emmanuel, 316
centonization, of recitative material, 256, 259, 270
Cervi, Gino, 161n

Cessac, Catherine, 229n, 230n, 234n, 236n, 246n
Cesti, Antonio, 7, 142, 256, 317
Cetrangolo, Aníbal E., 226n
Chandos, duke of (James Brydges), 167
character speech, defined, 55n
Charles II, king of England, 76, 106
Charles of Austria, 2
Charles VI, emperor, 136n
Chelleri, Fortunato, *see* Kelleri, Fortunato
Cherici, Sebastiano
Componimenti da camera a due voci, Op. 5, 89, 95
Chiabrera, Gabriello, 5–6
Canzonette, 6
Maniere de' versi toscani, 6
Maniere, scherzi e canzonette morali, 6
Chiarelli, Alessandra, 27n, 166n
C[hiaromonte?], count of, 17
Chirico, Teresa, 119n, 163n, 165n
Christie, William, 304n
Christina, ex-queen of Sweden, 23, 38, 117
Churchill, William Algernon, 34
Churnside, Carrie, 83n
Cicero, Marcus Tullius, 177, 179n
De oratore, 179n
Orator, 177,
Rhetorica ad Herennium (attr.), 177
Cicognini, Alessandro, 161n
Cimarosa, Domenico, 277n
Ciofi, Patrizia, 315
circle of fifths, xxv, 257, 262, 266, 271
Clapton, Nicholas, 311
Clari, Giovanni Carlo Maria, 149n, 202
Clement XI, pope, 115
Clérambault, Louis-Nicolas, 232–39 *passim*, 242–5, 249, 251–2, 253, 297
Colas, Damien, 218n
Coletti, Agostino Bonaventura, 95
Armonici tributi, Op. 1, 95
Colin de Blamont, François, 232, 233, 234, 238–9, 240, 251, 253
Colista, Lelio, 40
Collins, Michael, 207n
Colonna, Filippo, 150
Colonna, Giovanni Paolo, 140, 147, 150
Colturato, Annarita, 28n, 31
Columbro, Marta, 224n

Colzani, Alberto, 100n, 136n, 138n
Comedia de santos, 205n
compact disc, advent of, 311
Concert Français, 237, 238, 239
Concert Spirituel, 237, 238
concertino, defined, 8n
concerto grosso, defined, 8n
Concerts de la Reine, 237, 238–40
Concerts des Mélophites, 234
concetto, defined, 122
consecutive fifths and octaves, tolerated in keyboard realizations, 282
Contarini family, 31
Conti, duc de, 234
Conti, Francesco Bartolomeo, 312, 313n, 314, 326
Corazza, Giacomo, 137
Corelli, Arcangelo, 32, 40, 121, 124, 128n, 143, 303
   Concerti grossi, Op. 6, 136n, 230
   Sonate a tre, Op. 1, 136n
   Sonate da camera, Op. 2, 147
   Sonate da camera, Op. 4, 143n
   Sonate a violino solo, Op. 5, 273n
Corselli (Courcelle), Francesco, 217
Cossoni, Carlo Donato, 84
   Libro primo delle canzonette amorose a voce sola, Op. 7, 84
counter-tenor voice, qualities of, 304–5
Couperin, François, 228, 246
Courbois, Philippe, 232, 233, 234, 239, 240, 252
Cousser, Johann Sigismund, 139, 167, 171
Couvreur, Manuel, 234n
Coya, Simone, 313n, 327
   L'amante impazzito con altre cantate, e serenate a solo, et a due con Violini, Op. 1, 86, 313n
Crescimbeni, Giovan Mario, 6, 40, 42, 123n, 124–8, 225n
Crivellati, Domenico
   Cantate diverse a una, due e tre voci, 80, 82
'curlicue' scribe, the, 138, 167, 168, 171
Curtis, Alan, 306n
Cuzzoni, Francesca, 221
Cyr, Mary, 229n, 233n

D'Alay, Mauro
   Cantate e suonate, 99
d'Astorga, Emanuele Rincon, 98, 135n
d'Este, Laura, 83
da capo aria, structure of, 274
da'l Pane, Domenico
   Secondo libro de' madrigali a cinque voci, 83n, 86
Dael, Lucy van, 306n
Damerini, Adelmo, 166n
Damuth, Laura, 113n, 114n, 116n, 117n, 125n, 128n
Dart, Thurston, 301
David, François, 239
Davison, Archibald T., 154n
Daw, Brian, 122n
de Avitabile, Biagio, 166
De Bonis, Novello, 91, 100
de Cupertinis, Tommaso, 221, 222
de Luca, Severo, 121, 150n, 164n
de Vittorio, Pino, 313n, 315
Dean, Winton, 156n, 218n
degli Antonii, Pietro, 106
   Cantate da camera a voce sola, Op. 6, 92
Degrada, Francesco, 205, 209n, 266n, 303
del Ricco, Antonio
   Urania armonica. Cantate a voce sola, Op. 1, 91
Della Ciaia, Azzolino Bernardino
   Cantate da camera a voce sola, Op. 2, 95
Della Seta, Fabrizio, 124n, 126n, 128n
Dellaborra, Mariateresa, 5n
Deller, Alfred, 303n, 305
Dent, Edward J., 118–19, 124n, 125
Destouches, André Cardinal, 232, 235, 238, 239, 246, 249, 297
Devise, defined, 93, 199n
di Giacomo, Salvatore, 205n
Di Profio, Alessandro, 218n
Diderot, Denis, 233n
Dieci, Sara, 109n, 135n, 169n, 172n
do Nascimento, Paulo Abel, 306
Dobozy, Borbála, 311n
Dolfino, Pietro, 81
Dolmetsch, Arnold, 296, 301
Domitilla Ceva, Maria, 83

Dorival, Jérôme, 229n, 237n, 238n
Downes, Edward O. D., 205n
Dratwicki, Benoît, 234n
Dubowy, Norbert, xxiii–xxiv, 58n, 100n, 119n, 129n, 136n, 138n
Dulcken harpsichord, 308
Duni, Antonio
   Cantate da camera, 99
Dunning, Albert, 128n
Dupré, Desmond, 301n
Durante, Francesco, 115, 276, 277n
Durante, Sergio, 124n
Durazzo, Giacomo, 28, 31
Duron, Jean, 228n
Dutartre, Jean-Baptiste, 238, 239
Dyer, Louise, 301

Early Music Movement, the, xxi, xxv, 303n, 304n, 310, 311
Écorcheville, Jules, 297–8
Edmonds, John, 302n
Ella, Péter, 305n
Emans, Reinmar, xxiii, 7n, 59, 63–4, 74n, 100n, 280n, 317n
endecasillabo, defined, 5, 197n
Engelhardt, Markus, 119n
enharmonic change, 256, 271–2
Ensemble Artaserse, 316
Ensemble Concerto, 309n
Ensemble Elyma, 314n
Ensemble 415, 147n
Ephrikian, Angelo, 300, 303
Esswood, Paul, 305, 306
Eximeno, Antonio, 201–2

Fabbri, Annibale Pio, 217n
Fabbri, Paolo, 43n
Fabris, Dinko, 203n, 205n, 218n, 223n, 224n, 225n, 312–13
Fader, Don, 142n, 144n, 154n, 228, 230n, 231n
Faggioli, Michelangelo, 313n, 327
Fago, Nicola, 135n
Falvay, Cseperke, 305n
Fanna, Antonio, 207n, 300n
Fanna, Francesco, xxiin, 204n, 311n
Farinelli, *see* Broschi, Carlo
Farnese, Isabella, 236

Farnese, Ranuccio, 106
Faustini, Giovanni, 58
Fedeli, Ruggiero, 313n, 327
Fei, Jacomo, 83n
Fenlon, Iain, 206n
Feo, Francesco, 115
Ferand, Ernst T., 148n
Ferdinand III, emperor, 106
Fernandez, Adriana, 314n
Ferrandini, Giovanni Battista, 314, 327
Ferrari, Benedetto
   Musiche e poesie varie a voce sola (Libro terzo), 80
   Musiche varie a voce sola, 80
   Musiche varie a voce sola (Libro secondo), 80
Fink, Bernarda, 312
Finscher, Ludwig, 98n, 115n
Fiorè, Stefano Andrea, 172n
Fischer-Dieskau, Dietrich, 302
Florence, Conservatorio 'Luigi Cherubini', 184, 220
Florimo, Francesco, 205n, 211
Florio, Antonio, 217n, 312, 313n
Floris, Franco, 308n
Foggia, Francesco, 40n
Folena, Gianfranco, 43n
Fondazione Giorgio Cini, of Venice, 87n
Fontana, Francesco Luigi, 179n
Fontei, Nicolo
   Bizzarrie poetiche a 1. 2. 3. voci, 80n
Fontenelle, Bernard Le Bovier de, xxi, 142n
Fortune, Nigel, xxvi
Fossà, Andrea, 151n
Foster, Donald, 235n
Foulon, Philippe, 306n
Fourés, Olivier, 266n
Fragalà Data, Isabella, 28n, 31
Francesco II D'Este, duke of Modena, 27, 29, 30–31, 106, 132n
Françœur, François, 240
Fregiotti, Dionigio, 173n
Freitas, Roger, 256
Frescobaldi, Girolamo
   Primo/Secondo libro d'arie musicali […] a una, a dua, e a tre voci, 80, 82

Freund, Cecilia Kathryn Van de Kamp, 113n, 126n
Fux, Johann Joseph, 255–6, 259n, 268n

Gabrielli, Domenico
   Cantate a voce sola, Op. 2, 92, 108, 141n
Gaffi, (Tommaso) Bernardo, 313n, 327,
   Cantate da cammera [sic] *a voce sola*, Op. 1, 81, 94, 98, 100, 138–9, 167n
Gallas, Johann Wenzel, 138n
Galliard, Johann Ernst, 146–7, 151, 159
Gallo, Franca, 210n
Gamley, Douglas, 308n, 309
Garden, Greer, 235n, 236–7
Gardiner, John Eliot, 304n
Garibaldi, Giuseppe Maria, 31–2, 39
Garri, Alejandro, 166n, 170n, 217n
Garrido, Gabriel, 314n
Gaspari, Gaetano, 148n
Gasparini, Francesco, 135n, 139, 146–7, 151, 156, 158–9, 164n, 165n, 202, 274, 275–9, 281–6, 291–2, 308, 313, 314, 327–8
   Cantate da camera a voce sola, Op. 1, 94, 95, 105, 278–9
Gasperini, Guido, 210
Geertsom, Jan van, 82
genera dicendi (or *elocutionis*), 177, 178, 179, 183, 200–201
Genoa, Biblioteca del Conservatorio 'N. Paganini', 31
Gentili, Alberto, 28n
Gentili Verona, Gabriella, 28n
genus humile, xxiv, 178, 180, 181, 182, 200
genus sublime, xxiv, 178–81, 182, 184, 200
Geoffroy-Dechaume, Antoine, 301
Georg Friedrich, margrave of Brandenburg-Ansbach, 262
George II, king of England, 167, 281n
Gerber, Ernst Ludwig, 170n, 205n
Gerber, Rudolf, 205n
Gerini, Emanuele, 1n
Gervais, Charles-Hubert, 234, 235, 239, 240
Gervais de Rouen, Laurent, 239
Geyer, Helen, 207n, 313

Gialdroni, Teresa M., xxiin, 113n, 123n, 139n, 164n, 165n, 167n, 203n, 208, 210n, 211n, 223n, 225n
Giannettini, Antonio, 129
Giannini, Tula, 228n
Gianturco, Carolyn, xxiii, 1n, 3n, 4n, 5n, 6n, 7n, 8n, 27n, 28n, 29, 30n, 31, 32, 37–8, 39, 44n, 81, 130n, 207, 317n
Gianuario, Annibale, 307, 313
Giebel, Agnes, 299–300, 302, 304
Gildon, Charles, 145n
Gini, Roberto, 309
Giron y Sandoval, Maria de, 121n
Giustiniani, Girolamo Ascanio, 183
Gluck, Christoph Willibald (von), 180
Gobbi, Tito, 302
Godbid and Playford, publishers, 86
Grandi, Alessandro, 6, 79–80
   Cantade et arie a voce sola, 79–80
Greco, Gaetano, 276
Gregori, Bartolomeo, 95, 98, 137n, 162
Gregori, Giovanni Lorenzo, 95, 105, 137
   Arie in stil francese a una e due voci, 95, 105
   Cantate a voce sola, Op. 3, 95
Gregory XIII, pope, 2
Griffin, Thomas, 121n
Grossi, Carlo, 86–8
   Il divertimento de grandi, Op. 19, 88
   L'Anfione, Musiche da camera, ò per tavola a due, e trè voci, Op. 7, 85, 86, 87–8
   La cetra d'Apollo, Op. 6, 85, 86–8
   Sacre ariose cantate a voce sola, Op. 4, 84
Grout, Donald J., 115n
Grua, *see* Pietragrua
Guaita, Carlo, 81n
Guarini, Giambattista, 5
   Il pastor fido, 5
Guido, (Giovanni) Antonio, 154n, 228, 238
Gustafson, Bruce, 168n

Haas, Robert, 205n
Hallenberg, Ann, 313n
Halliwell, Stephen, 42n, 55
Halton, Rosalind, 118n

Hammond, Frederick, 116n
Handel, George Frideric, 7–8, 118, 129, 135n, 147, 148, 149, 156n, 160n, 206n, 299, 301–2, 304, 305–6, 310, 311, 315, 316, 328–40
Handel Opera Society, 301
Hanley, Edwin, 112, 113n, 115n, 118, 120n, 128n, 132n, 141n, 150n, 170n
Harker, Dave, 299
harmonic ellipsis, 257, 266, 268, 272
Harmonices Mundi, ensemble, 312n
Harnoncourt, Nikolaus, 303n
Harris, Ellen, xxi, 129
Hasler, Jean-Michel, 306n
Hasse, Johann Adolf, xii, 206, 208, 211n, 217n, 218, 221, 222, 315, 341–2
Hawkins, John, 145n
Haydn, (Franz) Joseph, 317
Haym, Nicola Francesco, 141n, 145–7, 151, 157, 159
Heawood, Edward, 34
Heinichen, Johann David, 111
Helmholz system, of pitch differentiation, xxv
Hemsch harpsichord, 308
heroic genre, 179, 181, 201
Herreweghe, Philippe, 304n
Highfill, Philip H., jr., 171n
Hill, John Walter, 38n
Hirsch, Hans Ludwig, 309
Hogwood, Christopher, 306n
Holman, Peter, 246
Homer, 42n, 178
Horace (Quintus Horatius Flaccus), 5
Horne, Marilyn, 301
Hotteterre, Jacques-Martin, 231n
Hucke, Helmut, 205n, 225n
Hughes-Hughes, Augustus, 174n, 216n
Hullah, John, 175n
Hunold, Christian Friedrich (Menantes), 75
Hutchings, Arthur, xxii

Il Complesso Barocco, 306n
Il Seminario Musicale, ensemble, 305–6, 312n, 313n
Indy, Vincent d', 297, 301n
Innocent XI, pope, 39, 46

Insieme da Camera Fiorentino, 307n
Insom, Giovanni, 138n, 166n, 216n
intavolatura, defined, 279
intercalari, defined, 197
International Musicological Society, 204
Invernizzi, Roberta, 313n, 315
Izzarelli, Francesco Antonio, 169

Jacobs, René, 304n, 305, 306
Jahn, Michael, 208n
Jakoby, Richard, 154n
James II, ex-king of England, 119, 173n
Jander, Owen, 28–30, 31, 32n, 37, 38n, 39, 40
Jaroussky, Philippe, 316
Johann Wilhelm, Count Palatinate-Neuburg, 76
John of Garland, 178
Joncus, Berta, xxin
Joseph I, emperor, 139, 162, 172n

Kapsberger, Johannes Hieronymus, 2,
  Libro primo de madrigali a cinque voci, 2
Katschner, Wolfgang, 147n, 313
Keiser, Reinhard, 98
Kelleri, Fortunato
  Cantate e arie con stromenti, 99
Kinsky, Philipp Joseph, 137n
Kirkby, Emma, 305, 306
Knighton, Tess, 209n
Kocevar, Érik, 240n
Kohnen, Robert, 306n
Kolben, Robert, 154n
Kowalski, Jochen, 305, 306
Kuijken, Sigiswald, 305n, 306n
Kuijken, Wieland, 306n
Kümmerling, Harald, 140n, 144n, 170n, 173n

La Cerda Colonna, Lorenza de, 121n, 147n, 150
La Cerda y Aragón, Luis Francisco de, 121, 123, 150
La Gorce, Jérôme de, 168n, 241n, 242n
La Grande Écurie et la Chambre du Roy, 306n

La Guerre, Elisabeth Jacquet de, 230, 249–50, 251
La Risonanza, ensemble, 316
Lalande, Michel-Richard de, 237–8, 239n
Lamy, Rudolf, 299n
Lanciani, Flavio, 41, 121
Landini, Giovanni Battista, 80, 82
Landowska, Wanda, 296–7, 308
Langhans, Edward A., 171n
Lante, Ippolito, 2–3
Lante della Rovere, Isabella, 3
Larsson, Roger Barnett, 201n
Laurenzi, Filiberto
    Concerti et arie a una, due e tre voci con una serenata a 5, 80n
Lausberg, Heinrich, 178
Lautten Compagney, 147n, 313
Lavilla, Felix, 309
Lawrence-King, Andrew, 151n
Le Cerf de la Viéville, Jean Laurent, xxiv, 141–8 *passim*, 151, 154–7, 161, 162
Le Grand, Nicolas Ferdinand
    Cantate e ariette a voce sola (1698), Op. 1, 94
    Cantate e ariette a voce sola (1698), Op. 2, 94
Le Maire, Louis, 251
Le Noble, Christien, 239, 240
Le Roux, Charles-Henri, 240
Ledroit, Henri, 305
Legrenzi, Giovanni, xxii, xxiii, xxvin, 55–77, 79, 88, 256, 315, 342
    Acclamationi divote, Op. 10, 88, 342
    Cantate, e canzonette a voce sola, Op. 12, xxiii, 56, 59–61, 63–7, 71–2, 75–6, 85, 99–100
    Ecchi di riverenza di cantate, e canzoni, Op. 14, xxiii, 56, 67–9, 75–6, 85, 88, 100, 312, 342
    Idee armoniche estese per due e tre voci, Op. 13, 85, 88
Lemaire, Louis, 239
Leo, Leonardo, 115, 206, 208, 215, 221, 222, 225, 315, 342–3
Leonarda, Isabella, 83
Leonhardt, Gustav, 303n, 305, 306n, 309–10

Leonhardt, Marie, 303n
Leopold, Silke, 58n
Leopold I, emperor, 46, 86, 106, 140, 150, 172n
Leppard, Raymond, 301–2
Lesne, Gérard, 305–6, 312, 313n
Lesure, François, 139n, 151n
Leszczyńska, Maria, queen of France, 238
Letzbor, Gunar, 312n
lezione amorosa, defined, 269
Liess, Andreas, 39n
Lignani, composer, 343
Lindgren, Lowell, xxiv, xxvn, 136n, 139n, 141n, 145n, 147n, 159n, 162, 167n, 171n, 172n, 312
Lionnet, Jean, 38n, 173n, 228n, 237n
Lippmann, Friedrich, 129n
Liszt, Franz
    Années de pèlerinage, 161n
Litta, Pompeo, 42n
Liverpool, University of, xxvi
Lodi, Pio, 27n
Loehrer, Edwin, 302, 308, 309
Lonati, Carlo Ambrogio, 140–41n
London, British Library, 40
long-playing record, advent of, 299
Lotti, Antonio, 172n, 343
Louis XV, king of France, 235
Lovisa, Domenico, 182n
Lucchi, Marta, 31n
Luin, Elisabeth J., 28n, 132n, 172n
Luisi, Francesco, 210n
Lulier, Giovanni Lorenzo, 121, 163n
Lully, Jean-Baptiste, 297
Luppi, Andrea, 100n, 136n, 138n
Lütolf, Max, 249n

Maccavino, Nicolò, 126n, 136n, 163n, 165n, 166n, 206n, 207n
Macnutt, Richard, 32, 34
Madricardo, Claudio, 180n
madrigal, as poetic genre, 5, 6, 13, 128
Magini, Francesco, 126, 140n, 313n, 343
Magni, Bartolomeo, 80, 83, 87n
Magni, Francesco, *detto* Gardano, 80–88 *passim*
Mahling, Christoph-Hellmut, 115n
Maier, Bruno, 123n

Index 419

Maine, duchesse du (Anne-Louise-Bénédicte de Bourbon), 234
Maione, Paologiovanni, 224n
Majorano, Gaetano (Cafarelli), 217n, 221
Malaguti, Laerte, 302, 308
Malaspina, Romulo, 1
Malgoire, Jean-Claude, 306
Malipiero, Gian Francesco, 300n
Mamy, Sylvie, 312
Mancini, Francesco, 128, 129, 137, 140, 175n, 207n, 208, 343
Mancini, Giambattista, 304–5
Mancurti, Francesco Maria, 123n, 124
Manfredi, Eustachio, 121n
Mangiarotti, Antonio, 163n
Mangini, composer, 140n, 313n
Manna, Gennaro, 221
Mannelli, Carlo, 32, 40,
   Sonate a tre, Op. 2, 40n
Marais, Marin, 243n
Marcello, Alessandro, 343
   Cantate da camera a voce sola, 98
Marcello, Benedetto, xxiv, 4n, 135n, 151, 178–202, 224n, 274, 290–91, 315, 344
   Estro poetico-armonico, 181–4
Marchand, Philippe, 234, 240
Maria Anna Josepha, archduchess of Austria, 76
Maria Giovanna Battista, duchess regent of Savoy, 21
Maria of Austria, 1
Marín, Miguel Ángel, 209n
Marinelli Roscioni, Carlo, 205n
Marino, Giambattista, 5, 9, 14, 121, 148n,
   Rime, 5
Marino, Goffredo, 30n
Marino, marquis, 3
Markstrom, Kurt, 210n, 218n
Marlborough, junior duchess of (Henrietta Godolphin), 147n
Marpurg, Friedrich Wilhelm, 112n
Martini, Giambattista, 148n
Marx, Hans Joachim, 41n, 113n, 117n, 121n, 135n, 150n, 164n, 316n
Mascardi, family of printers, 81, 82, 83n, 86, 94, 95, 98, 100, 159
Masotti, Paolo, 82

Massenkeil, Günther, 7n
Massip, Catherine, 173n
Mattei, Stanislao, 276
Maylender, Michele, 120n
Mayrhofer, Marina, 118–19, 123
Mazzaferrata, Giovanni Battista, 84
   Canzonette e cantate a due voci, Op. 3, 84, 85
   Il primo libro de madrigali a due, a tre, amorosi e morali, Op. 2, 84, 85, 88
   Il primo libro delle cantate da camera a voce sola, Op. 4, 84, 85, 88
McCleave, Sarah, 232n
McCrickard, Eleanor, 4n, 27n, 28n, 29, 37n, 44n
Medici, Angelica de', 3
Medici, Giovanni Angelo, 1
Medici dynasty, 1
Medinaceli, duke of, *see* La Cerda y Aragón, Luis Francisco de
Melani, Alessandro, 345
Melani, Atto, 40n, 256n
Melkus, Eduard, 303n
Menna Foundation, of Salerno, 204n
Mercer, Frank, 156n
Metastasio, Pietro, 201, 202n, 215, 218, 223, 224n, 226n
Miatello, Cristina, 151n, 312, 315
Micheletti, Gioseffo, 88–9
Michiel, Polo, 31
Minato, Nicolò, 5, 58
Minter, Drew, 305
Mioli, Pietro, 56n, 80n, 105n
Mischiati, Oscar, 96n
modal shift, 257, 262, 266, 272
Modena, Biblioteca Estense e Universitaria, 27, 30–31
modulation chain, 257, 264, 266, 272
Moland, Brunet de, 232
Monesi, Giovanni Pietro, 81
Montagnier, Jean-Paul C., 230n
Montecassino, abbey of, 138n, 216–18
Montéclair, Michel Pignolet de, 240, 252
Monteverdi, Claudio, 73, 297, 308
Monti, Giacomo, 83, 84–6, 88, 89, 92, 99–100, 262n
Monti, Pier-Maria, 86, 92–3, 95, 100, 147
Montuoli, Giuseppe, 98, 137,

Cantate a voce sola e basso continuo,
    98
mordente, defined, 285n
Morelli, Arnaldo, 117n
Morelli, Giorgio, 4n
Morelli, Giovanni, 43n, 55n, 206n, 207n,
    255n
Morin, Jean-Baptiste, 227n, 228, 229n,
    230, 231, 234, 239n
Morini, Guido, 151n
Morris, Robert B., 139n
Mortari, Virgilio, 300
Motta, Artemio
    Cantate a voce sola, Op. 2, 96
Mouret, Jean-Joseph, 232, 234, 238, 239,
    240
mouvance baroque, 303, 305, 311n
Müller, Hertha, 313n
Müller, Walther, 205n
Münster, Robert, 172n
Muraro, Maria Teresa, 43n
Musici di Roma, 300
musique de chambre, defined, 229n
Musique de la Reine, 239
Musique du Roi, 239

Naples
    Collegio di Musica dal Convento di S.
        Sebastiano, 216n
    Conservatorio 'S. Pietro a Majella',
        210–25 *passim*
    Conservatorio dei Poveri di Gesù
        Cristo, 224
    Conservatorio della Pietà dei Turchini,
        211n
    Real Collegio, 211
Nascimbeni, Maria Francesca
    *Canzoni e madrigali morali e spirituali
        a una, due e tre voci*, 85, 86n
Natali, Pompeo
    Madrigali a tre voci pari, 82
    *Madrigali e canzoni spirituali e morali
        a due et a tre voci*, 83n
Naulleau, Gaëtan, 311n
Neapolitan School, the, 108, 203–26 *pas-
    sim*
Nelson, Judith, 305
Nemeitz, Joachim Christoph, 234n

Németh, Pál, 305n
Neri, Giovanni Battista, 89
Neri, (St) Philip, 2, 4
Néron, Louis, 239
Nestola, Barbara, 19n
Nettl, Paul, 112n, 128n
Neumeister, Erdmann, 75
Neupert harpsichord, 300, 308
New Philharmonia Orchestra, 308n, 309
Newman, William S., xxi
Newton, Isaac, 180
Noris, Matteo, 56, 57, 58, 61, 62
North, Roger, 136n
Nuti, Giulia, xxv, 87n, 276n, 279n, 282n,
    286n, 307n

Odescalchi family, 42n
Olleson, Edward, 6n, 81n, 130n
open and closed tonal structures, 51, 201,
    256–7, 272
Opéra, at Paris, orchestra of, 233n, 235–7,
    240, 241–4
Orchestra della Scuola Veneziana, 300
ornamentation, in continuo realization,
    273, 274, 279, 282, 285, 291–2
Orsi, Giovanni Giuseppe, 76
Orsini, Ferdinando, 41
Orsini, Flavio, 37–8, 40, 41–2, 120
Österreich, Georg, 173n
Ottoboni, Antonio, 120, 123, 163, 164, 170
Ottoboni, Pietro, 41, 120–21, 123, 126,
    127n, 150n, 163, 164, 165n, 166

Pachovsky, Angela, 208n
Padoan, Maurizio, 100n, 136n, 138n
Pagano, Roberto, 112n, 115n, 116n, 124n,
    224n
Paglia, Francesco Maria, 120–22, 123, 163,
    164, 165
Pamphilj (Panfili), Benedetto, 117–20,
    135n, 150n, 164, 174
Pank, Siegfried, 306n
Pannain, Giulio, 205n
parties de remplissage, 243, 245
partimento, defined, 276
partition générale, defined, 243
partition réduite, defined, xxiv, 243
Pasquini, Bernardo, 40n, 124, 125, 284n

Passadore, Francesco, 56n, 58n, 63n, 67n, 68n, 71n, 76n
Passin, Karl-Heinz, 306n
passus duriusculus, as emblem of lament, 261
pastoral genre (selected references), 5, 44, 56, 73, 74, 123, 178, 179, 201, 314
Pastore, Giuseppe A., 225n
Paulato, Andrea
  Cantate a voce sola, 88
Paumgartner, Bernhard, 300
Pegah, Rashid-Sascha, 262n
Peli, Francesco, 172n
Penna, Lorenzo, 275, 277n, 279, 280
Pepoli, Sicinio, 224n
Percimineo, Claudio, 85, 86n
Pergolesi, Giovanni Battista, 315, 345–6
  Quattro cantate da camera, 98
Perti, Giacomo Antonio, 163n, 315, 346
  Cantate morali e spirituali a una, & à due voci, con violini, e senza, Op. 1, 89
Pertorini, Rezső, 311n
Peruzzi, Anna (Maria), 217n, 223
Pescetti, Giovanni Battista, 281
Pesenti, Martino
  Arie a voce sola [...] Con una cantata nel fine, Op. 3, 80n
Petrobelli, Francesco, 83
  Cantate a una, e due voci, Op. 10, 85, 100
  Musiche da camera a due, tre, et quattro voci con violini in alcune obbligati, et in altre a beneplacito, Op. 9, 85
  Scherzi amorosi a due e tre voci con violini a beneplacito, Op. 7, 83
Petrobelli, Pierluigi, 124n
Philidor, André Danican, 140–41, 173, 237
Philip V, king of Spain, 236
Philippe (II), duke of Orléans, 144n, 154n, 228–9, 231n, 234
piano line, of verse, defined, 197n
Picht-Axenfeld, Edith, 302n
Pierre, Constant, 237n
Pietragrua ('Grua'), Carlo Luigi, 135n, 171n
Pignatelli, Maria, 175

Pini, Giovanni, 166
Pintacuda, Salvator, 166n
Pipereau, composer, 253
Piperno, Franco, 128n
Pirrotta, Nino, 112n, 113n, 150n, 163n
Pisarri, Antonio, 83, 84
Pistocchi, Francesco Antonio Mamiliano, xxv, 170n, 172n, 262–6, 346
  Cantate morali a 2 e 3 voci, Op. 1, 95
  Capricci puerili, 262n
  Duetti e terzetti, Op. 3, 262n
  Scherzi musicali [...] cantate, Op. 2, 94, 262–6
Pitarresi, Gaetano, 123n, 206n
Pius IV, pope, 1
Platt, Richard, 230n
Platti, Giovanni Benedetto, 347
Pleyel harpsichord, 308
Polani, Girolamo, 274, 280–81
Poliziano, *see* Ambrosini, Agnolo
Poppen, Irmgard, 302
Porfirii, Pietro, 100–104
  Cantate da camera a voce sola, Op. 1, 92, 100, 108
Porpora, Nicola, xii, 206, 208, 218n, 221, 222, 224n, 280, 311, 313n, 347
  nuovamente composte opre di musica vocale, 99
Porsile, Giuseppe, 348
Porta, Giovanni, 206n, 313n, 348
Possenti, Pellegrino
  Accenti pietosi d'Armillo, canzonete et arie a voce sola, 80
practice-oriented musicology, 304
Predieri, Giacomo Cesare
  Cantate morali a 2 e 3 voci, Op. 1, 95
Prescimone, Giuseppe, 136n
Presley, Elvis, 299n
Prévat, Fabrice, 234n
Pritchard, Brian W., 136n
Prota-Giurleo, Ulisse, 205n
Provenzale, Francesco, 313n, 348
Pseudo-Longinus, 177–8
  Perì hypsous, 177–8
Pugliese, Annunziato, 113n, 139n

Quadrio, Francesco Saverio, 255
Quantz, Johann Joachim, 112, 128

Quargnolo, Daniela, 225n
quinario, defined, 197n
Quintilian (Marcus Fabius Quintilianus), 177
   Institutio oratoria, 177, 178

Radicchi, Patrizia, 41n, 216n
Ragin, Derek Lee, 305, 312
Ragot de Grandval, Charles-François de, 239
Raguenet, François, xxiv, 141–7 *passim*, 151, 157, 162
Rainbow, Bernarr, 175n
Rameau, Jean-Philippe, 238, 239, 244, 297, 301n
Ravizza, Filippo Emanuele, 93n
realization on harpsichord, of a bass, 273–93
Rebel, Jean-Fery, 240
recitative, audience's alienation from, 255
Renier, Nicolas, 239
Requejo, Ricardo, 309
Ribacchi, Luisa, 300n
Riccati, Giordano, 148–50
Riemann, Hugo, 205n, 296n
Rigatti, Giovanni
   Musiche concertate, Op. 2, 87
Rignatti, composer, 144n, 163
rima chiave (key rhyme), defined, 130
rime baciate, defined, 197n
Rinaldi, Mario, 124n
Rinaldo I, duke of Modena, 172n
Rinuccini, Ottavio, 6
   Arianna, 6
   Dafne, 6
   Euridice, 6
   Narciso, 6
RISM sigla, xxv
ritornellos, in cantatas, defined, xxv
Riviera, Domenico, 124
Robinson, Michael F., 205–6
Robletti, Giovanni Battista, 80, 82
Roger, Estienne, 94, 98, 99, 262
Rome
   Cappella Giulia, 38
   Gesù, 38
   San Giacomo degli Incurabili, 117
   San Giovanni in Laterano, 38
   San Luigi dei Francesi, 38
Roncaglia, Gino, 166n
Ronco, Claudio, 313n
Rondinella, Francesco, 210, 211
Rosa, Salvator, 156
Rosand, Ellen, 261n
Rosati, Fortuniano, 94, 98
Rosow, Lois, 232n
Rossi, Franco, 56n, 58n, 63n, 67n, 68n, 71n, 76n, 180n
Rossi, Luigi, 7, 82, 118, 142, 154
Rostirolla, Giancarlo, 38n, 112n, 113n
rounding, defined, 257
Rousseau, Jean-Baptiste, 253
Rousseau, Jean-Jacques, 233, 244, 245
Roveda, Edigio, 308
Rovetta, Giovanni
   Madrigali concertati a 2, 3, [...] voci, 80
Ruggieri, Giovanni Maria
   Cantate con violini e senza, Op. 5, 80

Sabbatini, Pietro Paolo
   Il quarto di Villanelle a una, due, e tre, voci, 82
   Il terzo libro, 82
   Prima scelta di villanelle a due voci, 82
Sacchi, Giovenale, 149n, 179, 218n
Sadie, Julie Anne, 243n
Sadie, Stanley, 37n, 38n, 112n, 135n, 140n, 150n, 172n, 173n, 175n, 210n, 230n
Sadler, Graham, xxii–xxiii, xxiv, 241n
Sagredo, Niccolò, 84, 106
Sala, Francesco, 86, 88
Sala, Giuseppe, 88, 92n, 95, 96, 98, 135
Salvadori, Giuseppe Gaetano, 43n
Sances, Giovanni Felice
   Cantade [...] a voce sola, 80
Sanderson, James, 311
Sandoni, Pietro Giuseppe
   Cantate da camera e Sonate per il Cembalo, 99
Sanford, Sally, 151n
Santo Stefano, conte di, *see* Benavides, Francisco de
Sardelli, Federico Maria, 273n

Sarro (Sarri), Domenico, 173n, 218, 221, 313n, 348
Sarti, Gastone, 303n
Sartori, Claudio, 40n, 139n, 147n, 172n, 217n, 221n
Savioni, Mario
  Concerti morali e spirituali a tre voci differenti, 83n
  Madrigali morali e spirituali a cinque voci, 83n
Sawkins, Lionel, 238n
Scarlatti, Alessandro, xxiii–xxiv, 7, 111–34, 135n, 137, 140n, 141n, 142n, 145–7, 149n, 157, 163n, 170n, 171n, 173n, 178, 205, 208, 209, 216n, 274, 276, 279n, 281–2, 285n, 286n, 287–8, 300, 301, 302, 306, 314, 315, 349–53
  Cantate a 1 e 2 voci, Op. 1, 99
  keyboard toccatas, 277n
Scarlatti, Benedetto Bartolomeo, 117
Scarlatti, Domenico, 147, 225, 277n, 308, 315, 353–6
Scarlatti, Francesco, 356
Scheibe, Johann Adolph, 55, 255–6, 257
Schlager, Karl-Heinz, 148n
Schlick, Barbara, 311
Schmidt, Carl B., 154n
Schmitz, Eugen, xxii, 56, 74, 75n, 79, 106–7, 108–9, 111, 178
Schneider, Herbert, 168n
Schola Cantorum, of Paris, 297
Scholl, Andreas, 316
Scholl, Elisabeth, 287n
Schornsheim, Christine, 306n
Schulze, Hendrik, xxiii, xxviin, 61n, 73n, 74n
Schumann, Robert
  String Quartet in A minor, 271n
Sciarra, Enrico, 307n
Scimone, Claudio, 301
Seay, Albert, 56n, 70n
Seifert, Herbert, 76n
Selfridge-Field, Eleanor, 180n, 181n, 184, 224n
Selo, Nicholas, 312n
Semmens, Richard, 235n
serenata, defined, 43–5

settenario, defined, 5, 197n
Setton, Kenneth M., 39n
Sgrizzi, Luciano, 308
Shaw, Roderick, 312n
Sigismondo, Giuseppe, 211n
Sigismondo, Pietro, 174
silent 'H', treatment of, xxvin
Silvani, Giuseppe Antonio
  Cantate morali e spirituali a 1, 2 e 3 voci, Op. 5, 96
Silvani, Marino, 84, 85, 89, 92, 93n, 95–6, 140n, 262n
Simi Bonini, Eleonora, 41n
Simonelli, Giacomo, xxiii, 27, 34–5, 37, 38–9, 40, 42, 44–8
Simonelli, Matteo, 38
Sites, Caroline, 224n
Smith, Peter, 98n
Smith, William, 98, 99
Snyder, Kerala J., 173n
Società Cameristica di Lugano, 302n, 308n
Società Corelli, 300
Società Italiana di Musicologia, 207n
Solimena, Francesco, 116
Sophie Charlotte, queen of Prussia, 137
Soranzo, Jacopo, 28, 31, 41
Sperhaake harpsichord, 308
Stadler, Vilmos, 305n
Stampiglia, Silvio, 123, 147n, 150, 165, 174
Starhemberg, Ernst Rüdiger von, 45–6
Steblin, Rita, 170n
Steffani, Agostino, 120n, 138n, 149, 315, 357
Steinheuer, Joachim, 58n
Stich-Randall, Teresa, 300, 302, 304
stichomythia, 62n
stile antico, 48
stile concitato, 218
stile galante, 207–8, 209
Stillings, Frank S., 151n
stilus gravis, 177
stilus humilis, 177
stilus mediocris, 177
Strada, Anna Maria, 223
Stradella, Alessandro, xxii, xxiii, 1–25, 27–54 *passim*, 118, 256, 302–3, 357–8

Stradella, Alessio, 1–2
Stradella, Caterina, 1
Stradella, Ciro, 1
Stradella, Francesco, 27, 29, 30, 31, 32
Stradella, Fulvio, 1, 2
Stradella, Giannettino, 1
Stradella, Giovanbattista, 1, 2
Stradella, Giovanni Marco, 1
Stradella, Marc'Antonio, 2–3, 30
Stradella, Matteo (I), 1
Stradella, Matteo (II), 1, 2
Stricker, Augustin Reinhard, 98
Strohm, Reinhard, 113n, 114, 115n, 116n, 120, 150n, 167n, 179n, 206, 223n
Strozzi, Barbara, 75, 81–2, 83, 280, 317
Strunk, Oliver, 180n
Stuck, Jean-Baptiste, 154, 227n, 228, 230–1, 232, 234, 238, 239, 240, 252
sublime, category of the, xxiv, 177–82, 184, 200, 201
Sujetkantate, defined, 178
surplus of space for modulation, in recitatives, xxv, 259, 272
Szilvassy, Gyöngyver, 305n

Tagliavini, Luigi Ferdinando, 140n
Talamini, Paola, 313n
Talbot, Michael, xxiin, xxv, 30n, 43n, 44, 62n, 75n, 87n, 88n, 96, 99, 120n, 126n, 163n, 164n, 170n, 180n, 183n, 204n, 207–8, 228n, 252n, 257n, 258n, 262n, 266n, 269n, 272n, 274, 280n, 281n, 298–9, 307, 311n, 312, 317n
Taskin harpsichord, 308
Tasso, Torquato, 5
    Gerusalemme liberata, 4, 5
    L'Aminta, 5, 74
Tebaldi, Renata, 302, 308–9
Tedesco, Anna, 136n
'Telemania', 299, 300
Telemann, Georg Philipp, 299
Tesi (Tramontini), Vittoria, 217–18, 223, 224n
Ticinelli Fattori, Luciana, 303n
Timms, Colin, xxiin, xxiii, 4n, 32n, 44n, 47n, 55n, 120n, 138n, 163n, 164n, 170n, 171n, 180n, 204n, 216n, 225–6, 255n, 259, 272n, 314
Tintori, Giampiero, 131n, 132n
Tomasi, Margherita, 313n
tonal range, 257, 262, 266
Tonstudio Orchester Stuttgart, 299n
Torrente, Álvaro, 209n
Torres, Victor, 314n
Torri, Pietro, 140n, 175n, 358
Tosi, Giuseppe Felice
    Il primo libro delle cantate da camera a voce sola, Op. 2, 88, 89, 105
Tosi, Pier Francesco, 304–5
Travers, Roger-Claude, xxv, 311n
travestimento spirituale, defined, 182n
Tricarico, Giuseppe, 358
Tumat, Antje, 75n
Tunley, David, xxiin, 230, 237n
tuoni salmodici (psalm tones), 192
Turellier, François, 227n, 228n
Turin, Biblioteca Nazionale Universitaria, 28–9
Tyrrell, John, 38n, 135n, 140n, 150n, 172n, 173n, 175n, 210n, 230n

Utrecht, Treaty of, 236n

Vaccari, Patrizia, 312, 315
Vaccaro, Nicola, 116
Valsecchi, Mario, 312n
Veneziano, Giulia, xxiv, 205n, 210n, 225n, 317n
Venice, Biblioteca Nazionale Marciana, 28–9, 181–2, 184
Veracini, Francesco Maria, 38
versi sciolti, defined, 5, 6, 255
Vienna, Congress of, 46
villancico, 209
Vinaccesi, (Giovanni) Benedetto, 228
    Il consiglio degli amanti, overo Cantate da camera a voce sola, Op. 3, 88
Vincenti, Alessandro, 79, 80
Vinci, Leonardo, xxiv, 203–26, 317n, 359
violetta, name for viola, 216
Viollier, Renée, 234n
Virgil (Publius Vergilius Maro), 177, 178, 180

Aeneid, 177, 178
Bucolics, 177, 178
Georgics, 177
Vitali, Carlo, 224n
Vivaldi, Antonio, xxii, xxv, 114n, 120n, 180, 206n, 207–8, 258–9, 266–9, 272n, 273n, 274, 288–90, 291, 298n, 299, 300–301, 302, 304n, 306–311 *passim*, 315, 316, 359–69
Viviani, Giovanni Bonaventura, 88
  Cantate a voce sola, Op. 1, 89
  Veglie armoniche a una, due e tre voci con violini e senza, Op. 7, 91–2
voce mezzana, defined, 305
Vogel, Emil, 2n
Vollen, Gene E., xxiin, 235n, 238n
Voltaire (François-Marie Arouet), 180
Voss, Steffen, 113n
Vulpio, Francesco, 40, 41–2
Vulpio, Giovanni Battista, xxiii, 27, 34–42 *passim*, 45, 50–54

Walker, Frank, 156n
Walker, Thomas, 207n
Walsh, John, 243n
Watts, Helen, 301
Webber, Geoffrey, 173n
Weigel, Johann Christoph, 95

Wenzinger, August, 301
Wessely, Othmar, 170n
Wilderer, (Johann) Hugo, 171n
Wilson, John, 136n
Wissick, Brent, 151n
Wolff, Barbara Mahrenholz, 140n
Wolff, Hellmuth Christian, 145n, 166n, 205n
Wollenberg, Susan, 6n, 81n, 130n
Wollny, Peter, 166n
Wood, Caroline, 241n, 242n, 243n
word-painting, expressing keywords, 13–14, 122, 263, 271
Wotquenne, Alfred, 169n
Wright, Josephine, 140n
Wyatt, Catherine, 32n, 44n

Zanata, Domenico, 105, 108
Zappi, Giovan Battista Felice, 123–7, 130
Zaragoza, Cathedral, 209n
Zeno, Apostolo, 179
Ziino, Agostino, 112n, 113n, 150n, 163n, 164n, 167n, 208, 210n, 211n
Zingarelli, Niccolò Antonio, 317
Zipoli, Domenico, 314, 369
Zoppelli, Luca, 206n
Zuchini, Fortunato
  Cantate, 98